MW01629483

THE COLOR TEIL

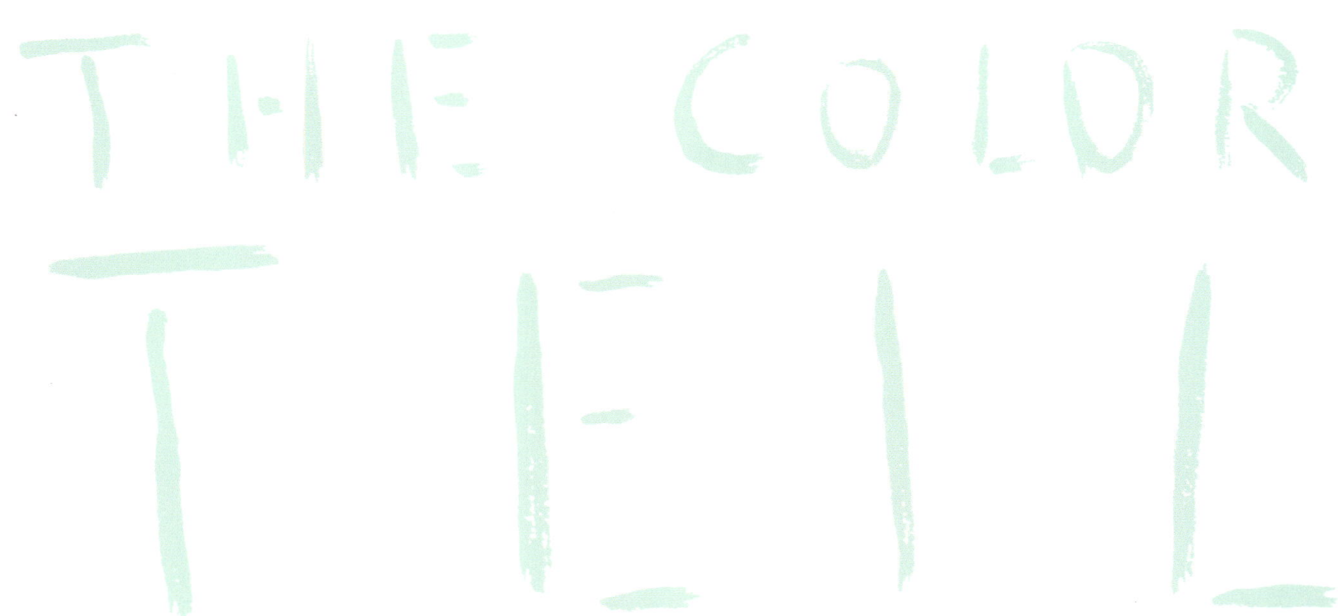

LIFE, WORK, AND INSPIRATION

Vertel Publishing
Charleston, SC

The Color Teil

Photographs courtesy of:
Gray Benko Photography
Natalie Franke Photography
Clay Austin Photography
Hailey Wist Photography
Minette Hand Photography
Olivia Rae James Photography

Text by Katie Jacobs
Book design by Danna Mathias

First Edition

Printed in the United States

ISBN-13: 978-1-64112-015-9
ISBN-10: 1-64112-015-0

TABLE OF CONTENTS

ARTISTIC

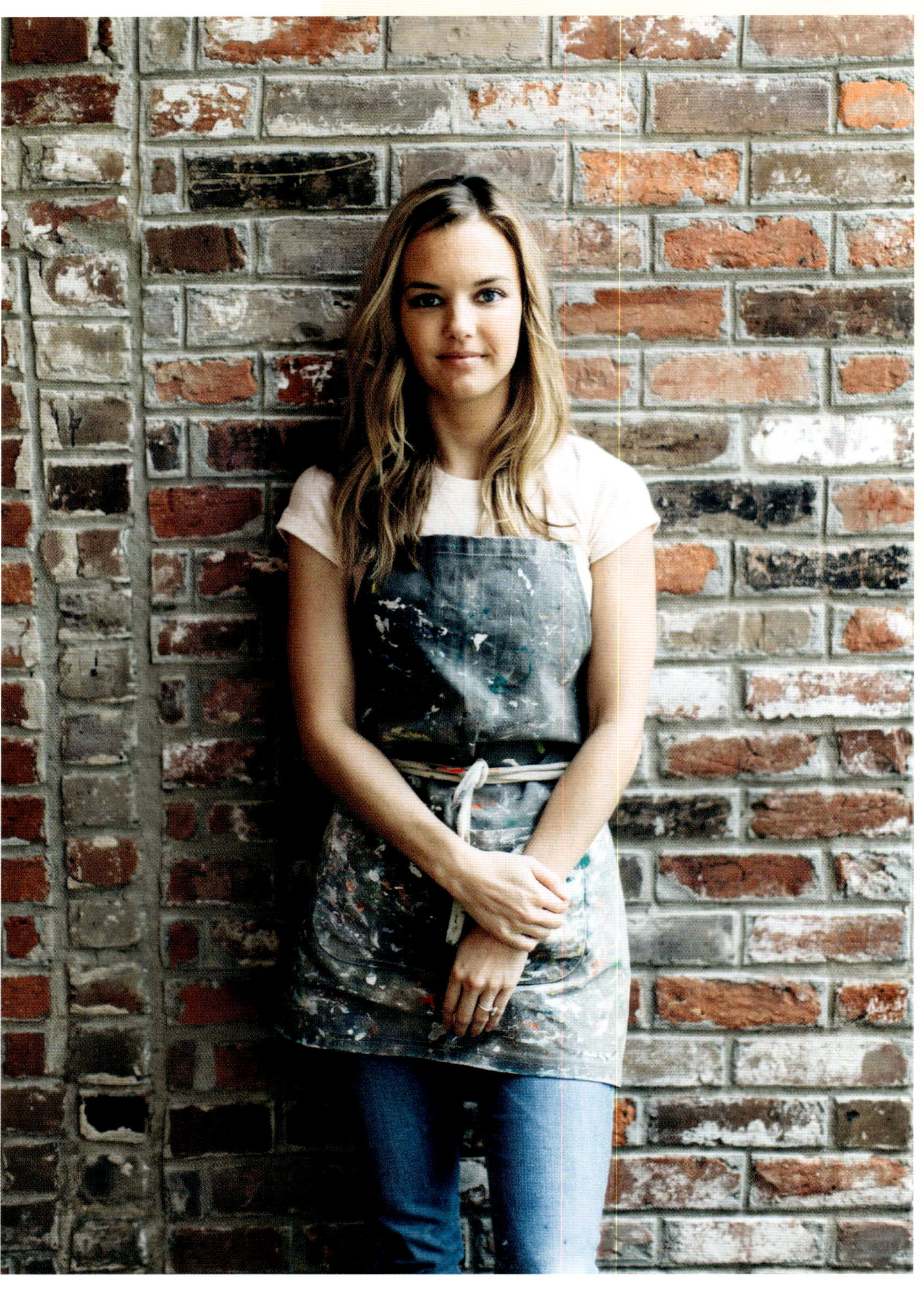

BACKGROUND

From the time she was a little girl, Teil possessed artistic curiosity that was apparent to those around her. Her mother wasted no time enrolling her in art classes in order for her to explore her creativity. While the affirmation of her family was encouraging, it was when her high school art teacher, Mr. Robert Dozier, took notice of Teil that she became more affirmed. Painting came naturally to her, and working at her craft didn't feel like work at all. She found what she loved but doubted it would ever provide a steady source of income to become a career.

Though she had many doubts about pursuing art, Teil loved it enough that she chose to enroll as an art major at Auburn University. Where the new creative education would take her in the future was unknown and brought no promise of security, but that didn't hinder her joy of making art in the meantime.

During college, Teil spent many weekends at home in Columbus, Georgia, painting in her grandmother's country home. At the end of a season of concentrated painting, her grandmother, Jane Duncan, organized an art show for all of her friends in her home. All of the artwork sold that day.

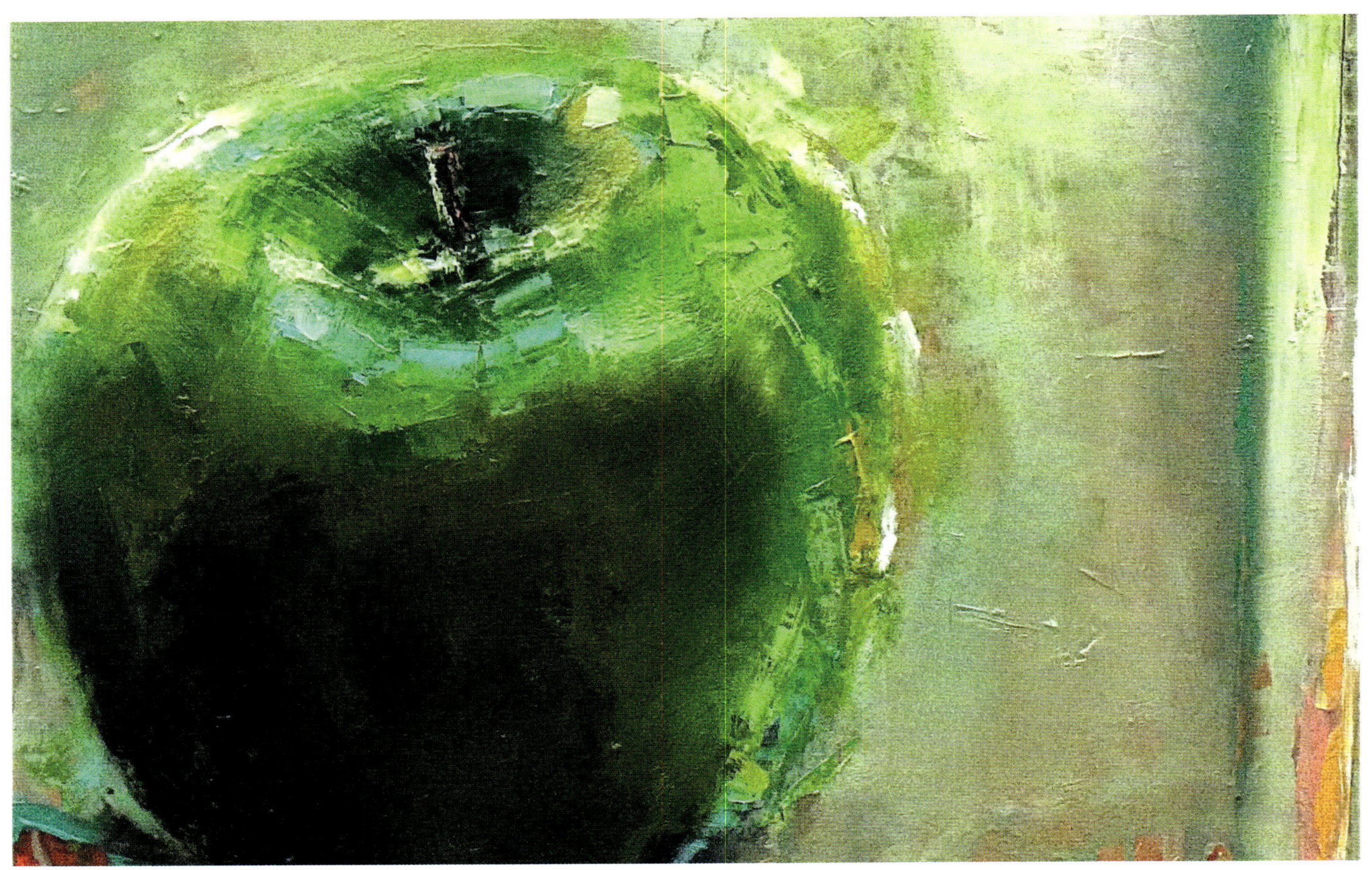

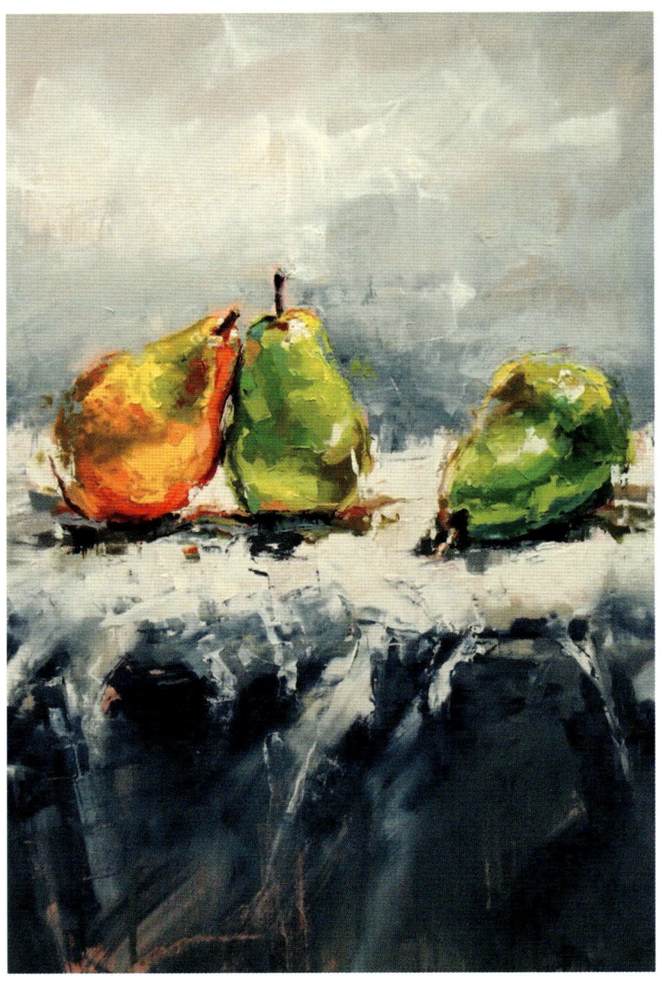

While college proved to be a time of personal artistic growth, Teil's years as an art student at Auburn University left her with an uncertain path. She loved school and learned skills and techniques that would come into play later in her career, yet she did not graduate with direction in how to turn what she loved into a business. Her option then was to find a job that incorporated some artistic aspect rather than pursue painting as a career. Teil accepted this path and took a position as an art director of a preschool in Charleston, South Carolina, while also waiting tables at a downtown restaurant.

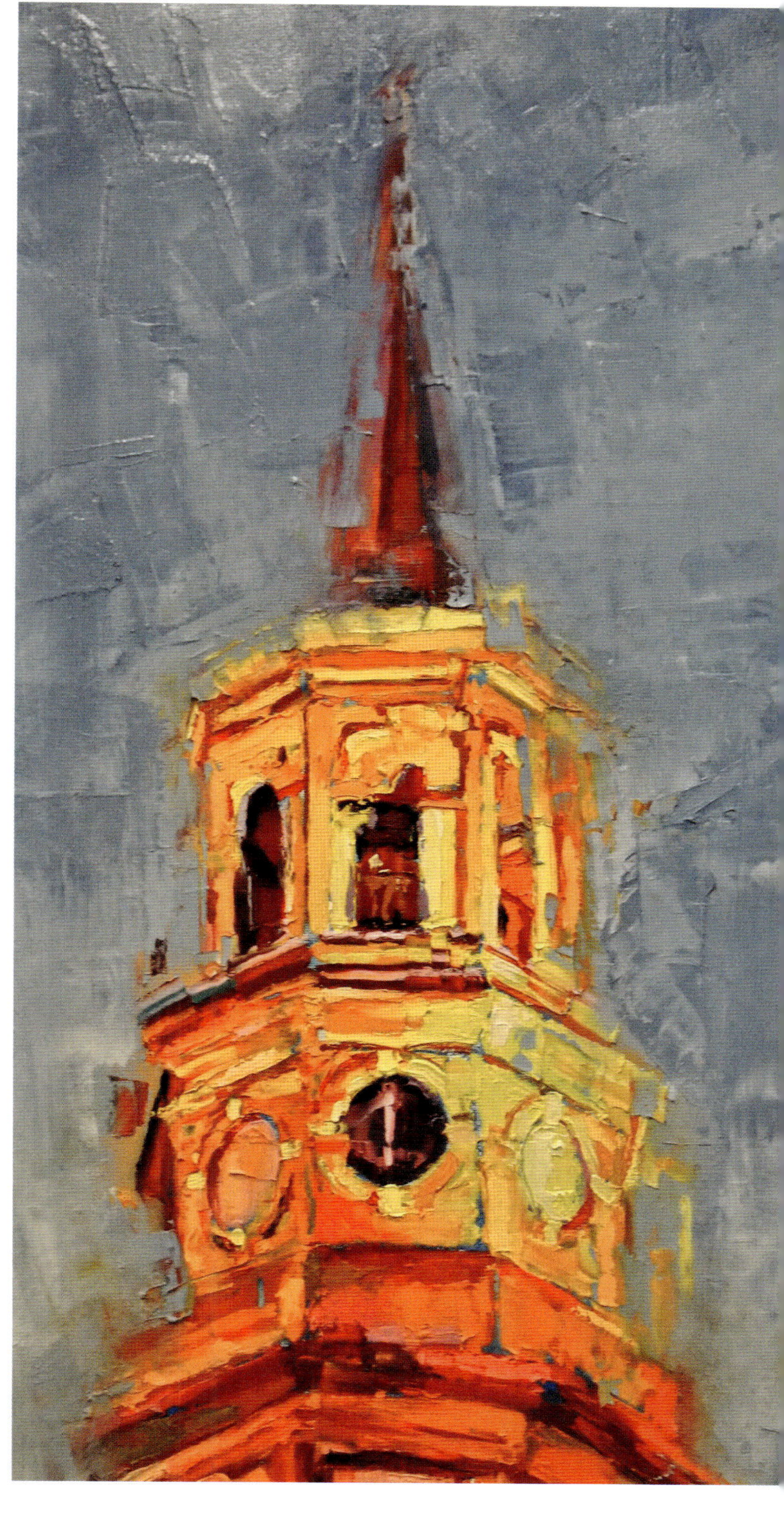

While working in the preschool position, Teil was continually painting commissions and always made time to spend in front of her easel. The Columbus Museum, familiar to her because it is situated in her hometown, held an event that showcased artists from all over the Southeast called "Let There Be Art." Teil worked hard to produce five paintings that would be displayed that evening. Just like the art showing at her grandmother's home, every one of Teil's paintings sold. The success of the night gave her a dose of confidence potent enough to decide to quit her job-juggling and pursue painting professionally.

During this time, Teil reconnected with an old friend turned successful artist, Lulie Wallace, and was introduced to a community of young, up-and-coming artists who worked out of a creative workspace called Redux. It was the first time Teil witnessed young people making a successful living as artists. The concept was so inspiring that she decided to take out a small loan and rent a space at Redux for herself.

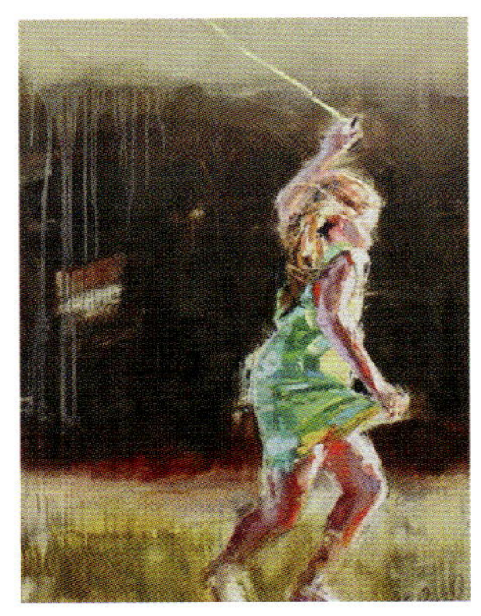

The beginning of Teil's career as an artist was a struggle, and she wrestled with the path she'd chosen many times along the way. These few years of Teil's career consisted of heavy experimentation, critical self-doubt, and severe lack of direction. The struggling artist often found herself wanting to quit and pursue something else. Each time she made up her mind to go out and find another job, she would catch a little break: a commission here, an opportunity there, or a voice of affirmation from a friend or family that kept her going.

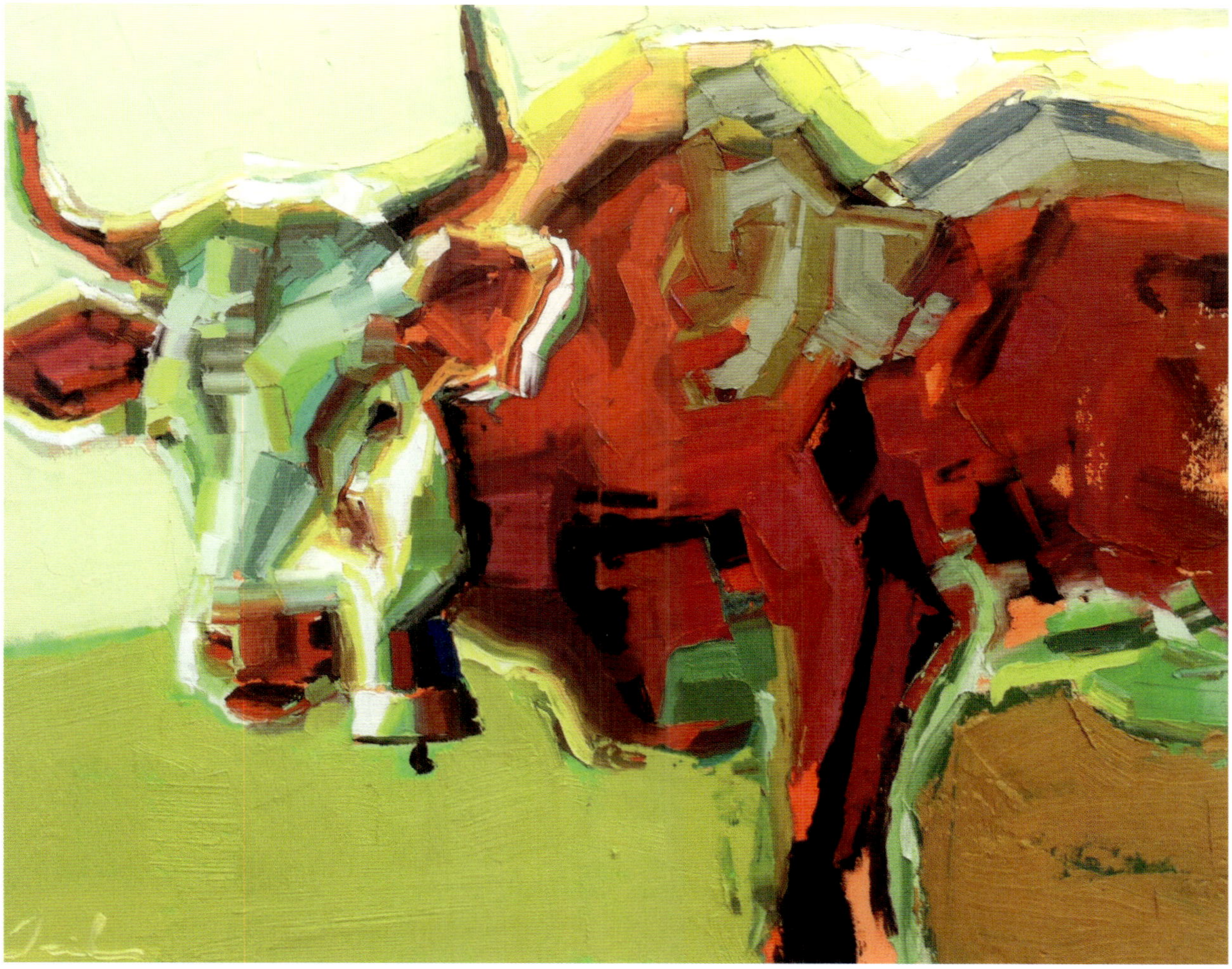

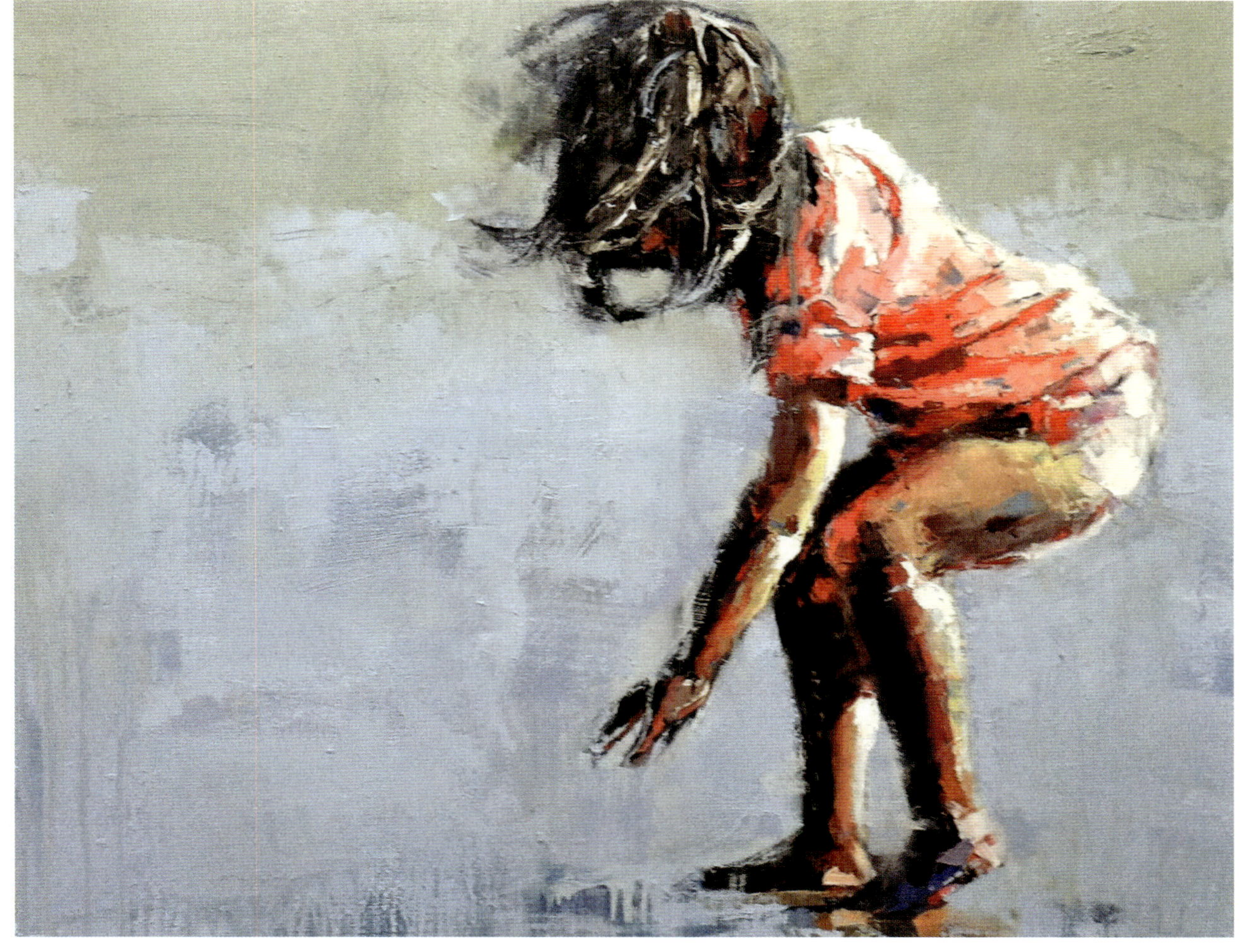

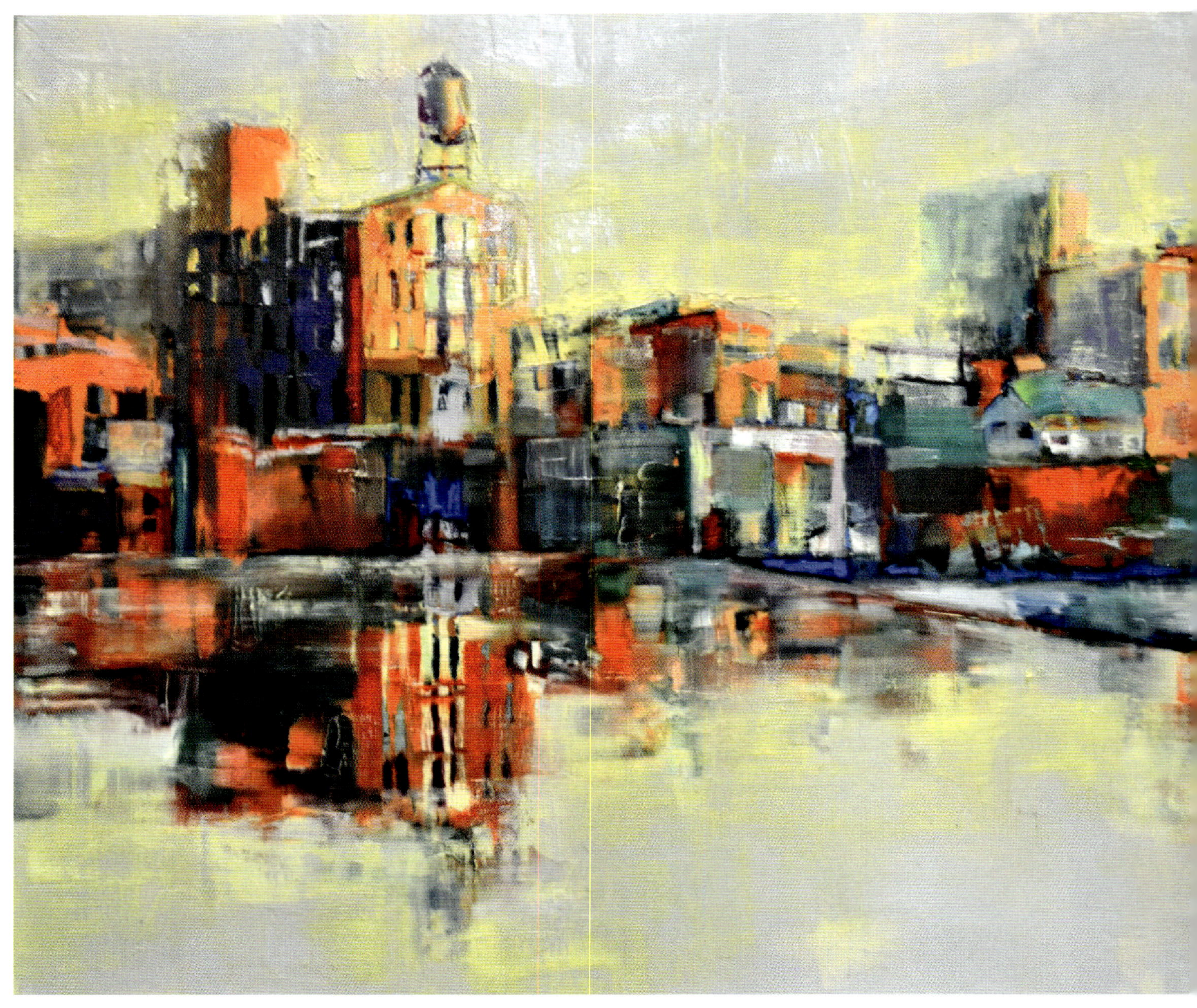

One day, exhausted, frustrated, and considering abandoning her pursuit to become an artist, Teil peeked at a figure-drawing class taking place at her Redux studio space. She loved figure painting and stopped for a few moments to observe the class. She decided to stick around afterward to ask permission to snap a few photographs to use as a painting subject. The model agreed. Teil then immediately bought a limited palette of colors, switched from oils to acrylics, and chose

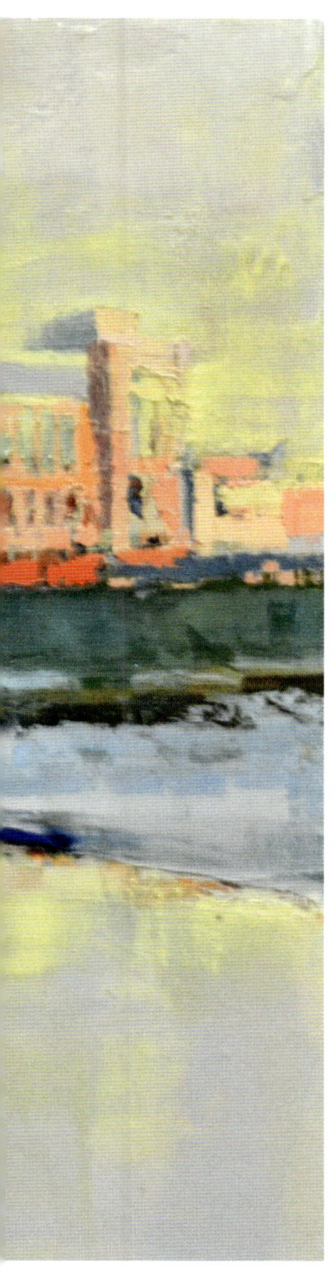

small-scale panels in order to compose a miniature figure study collection. The small panels and handful of fast-drying paint eliminated intimidation in this new pursuit. Teil painted twelve figures that day, and finally something clicked. This new approach seemed to flow effortlessly, introducing a new confidence in her final product. She photographed the new family of figures together and had a feeling she was about to enter a new chapter in her struggling career.

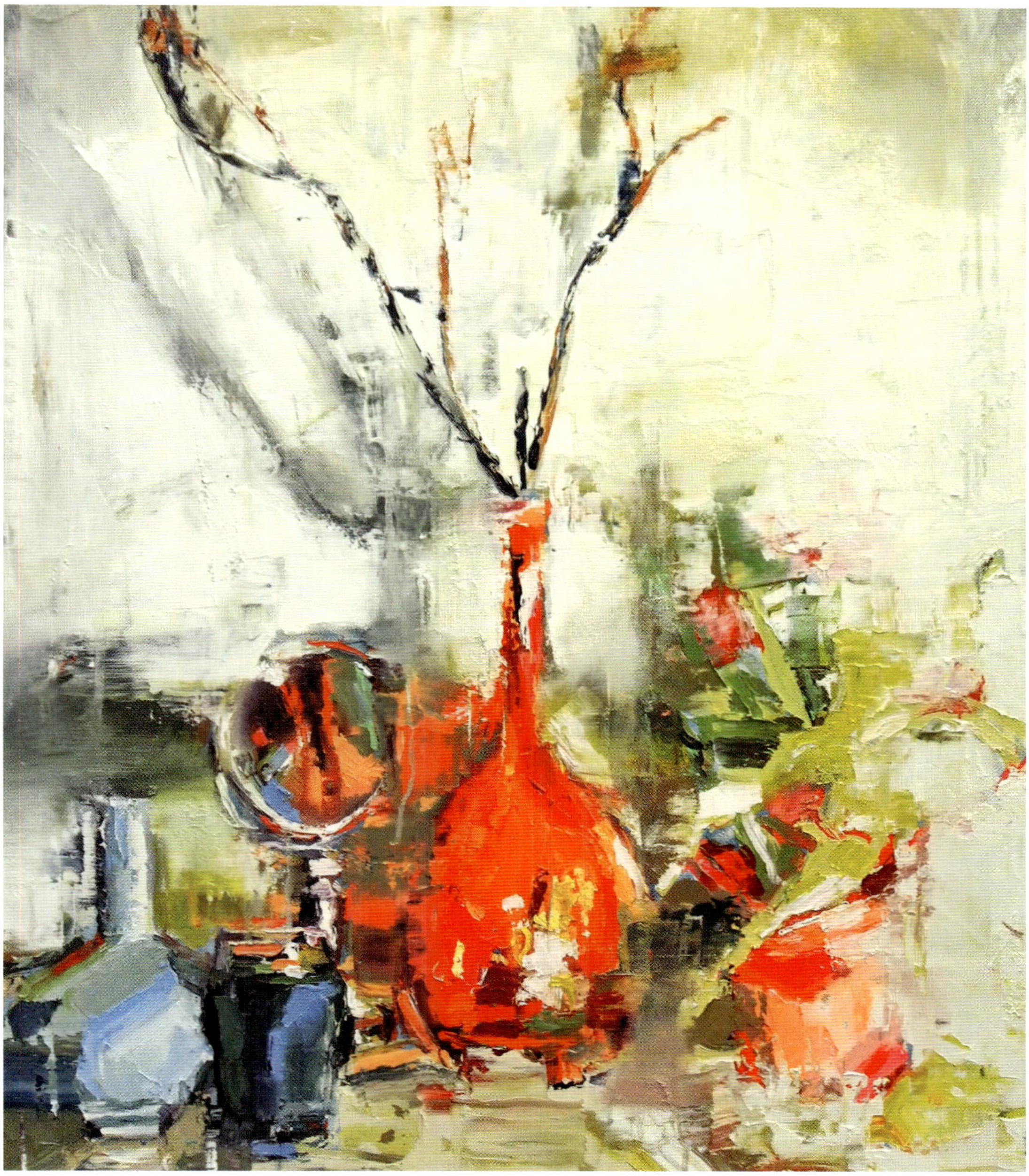

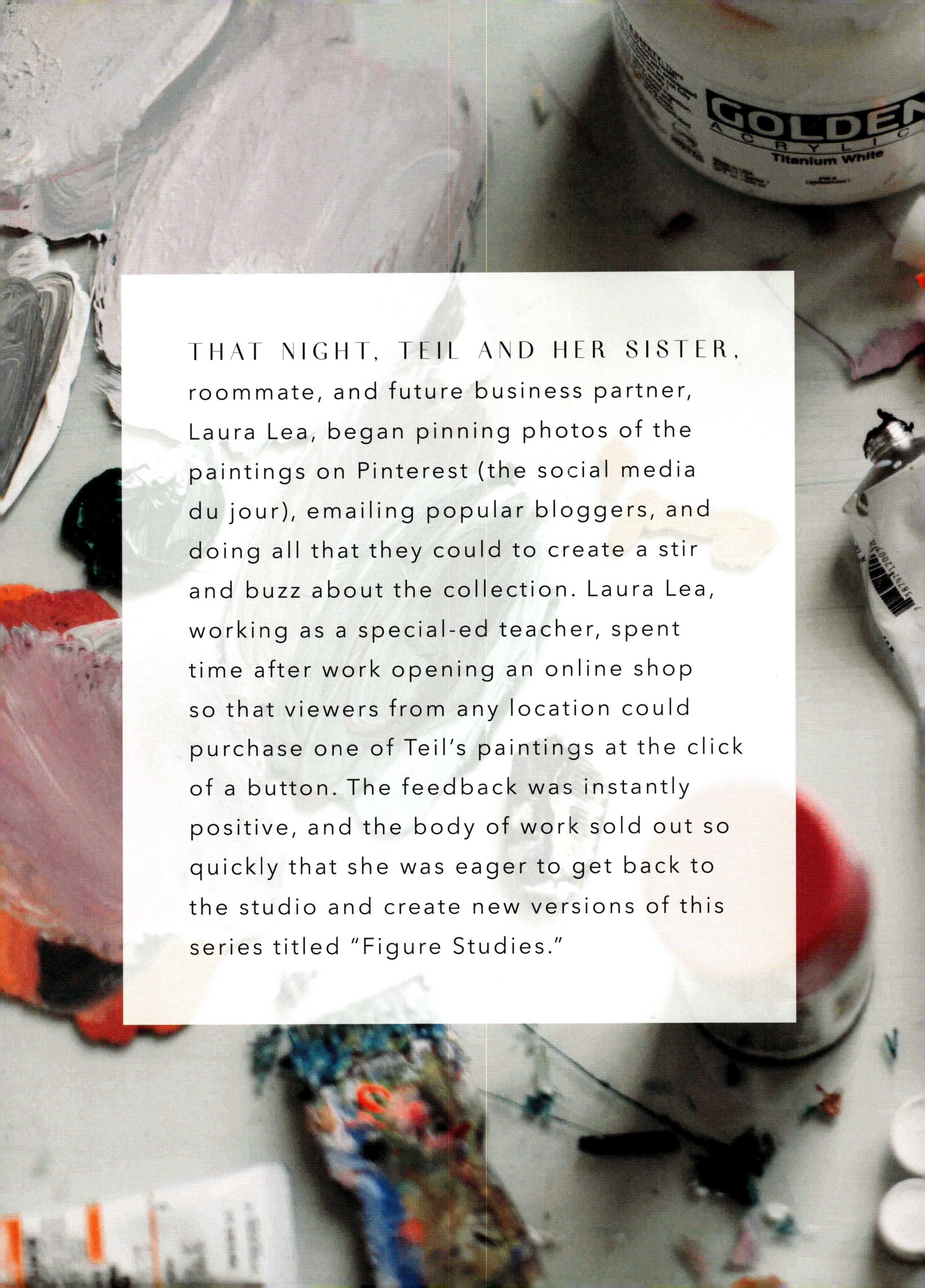

THAT NIGHT, TEIL AND HER SISTER, roommate, and future business partner, Laura Lea, began pinning photos of the paintings on Pinterest (the social media du jour), emailing popular bloggers, and doing all that they could to create a stir and buzz about the collection. Laura Lea, working as a special-ed teacher, spent time after work opening an online shop so that viewers from any location could purchase one of Teil's paintings at the click of a button. The feedback was instantly positive, and the body of work sold out so quickly that she was eager to get back to the studio and create new versions of this series titled "Figure Studies."

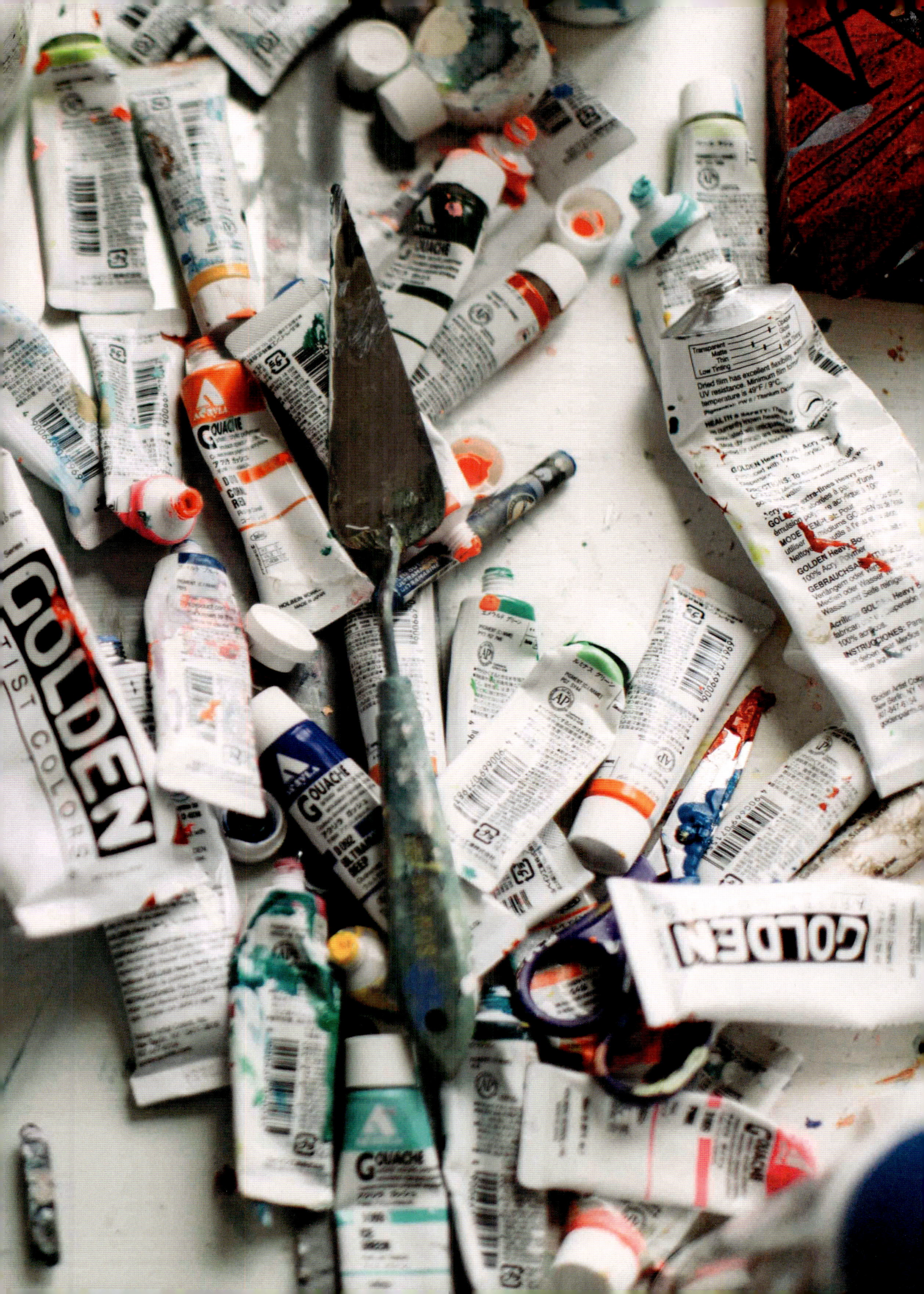
GOLDEN
GOUACHE
GOLDEN

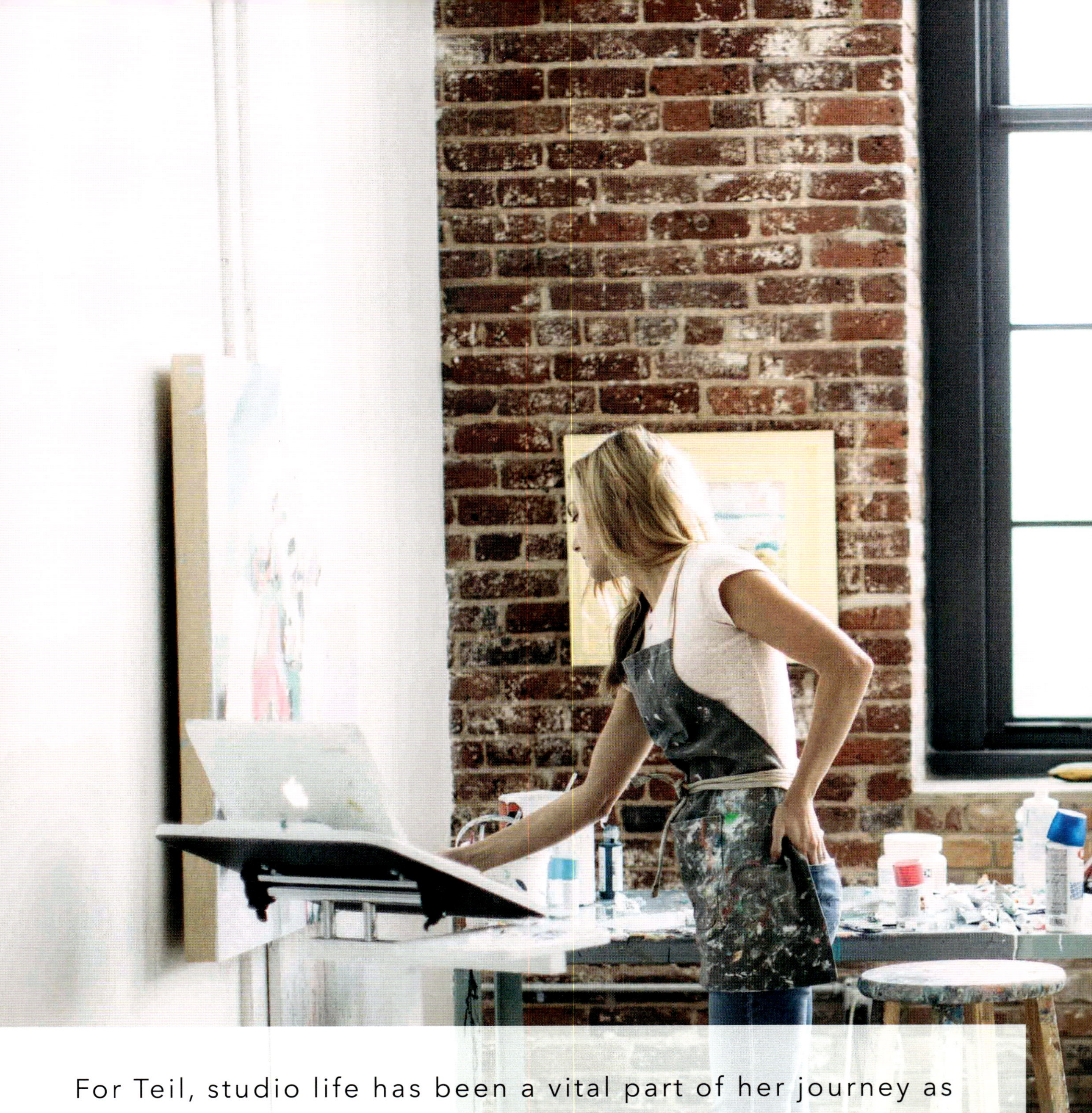

For Teil, studio life has been a vital part of her journey as an artist. Her current studio, a shared space in a stunning exposed-brick and wood-beamed refurbished historical cigar factory, is shared with a well-connected group of local creatives. Each artist brings a different flavor and source of inspiration to the studio space.

STUDIO LIFE

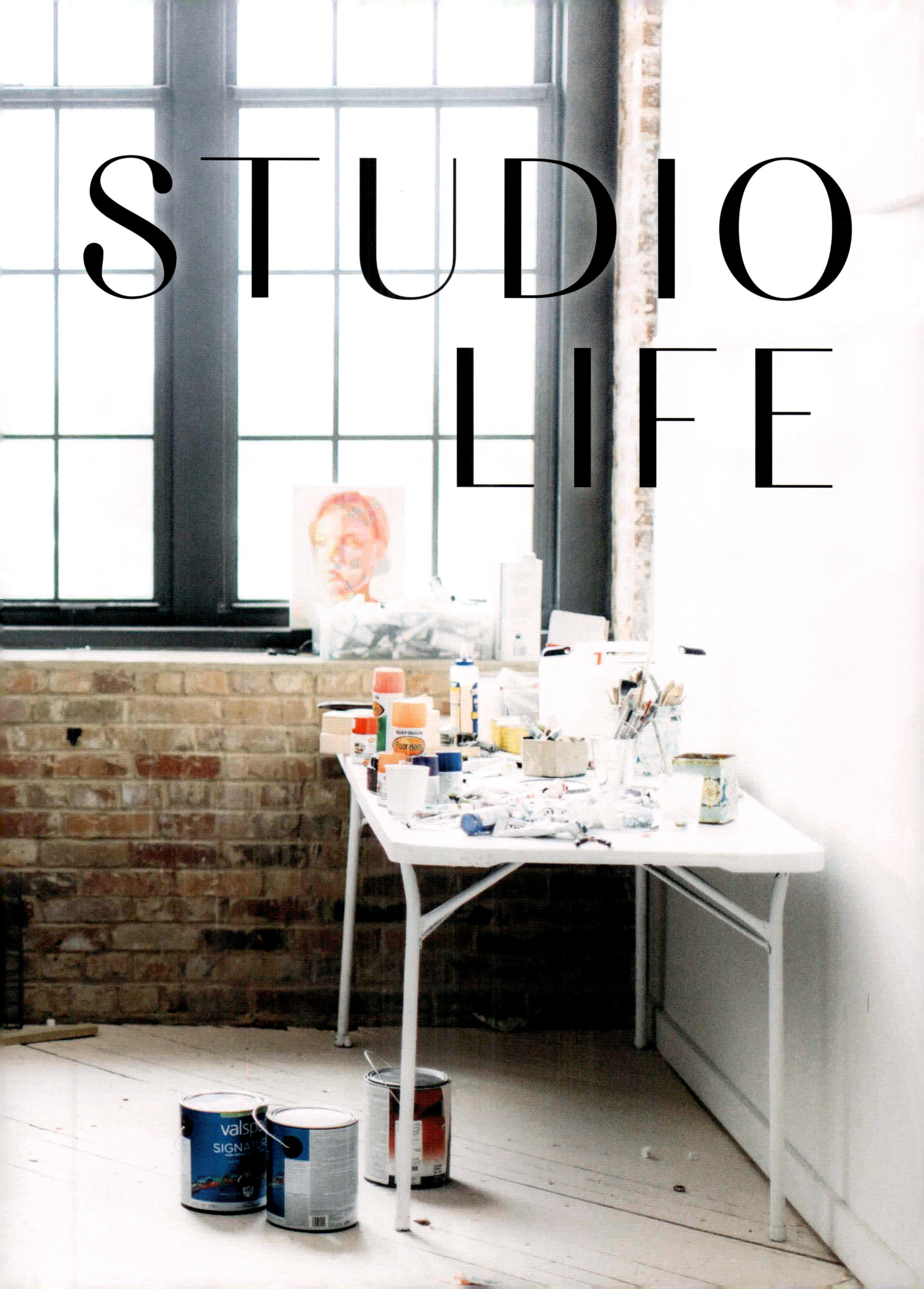

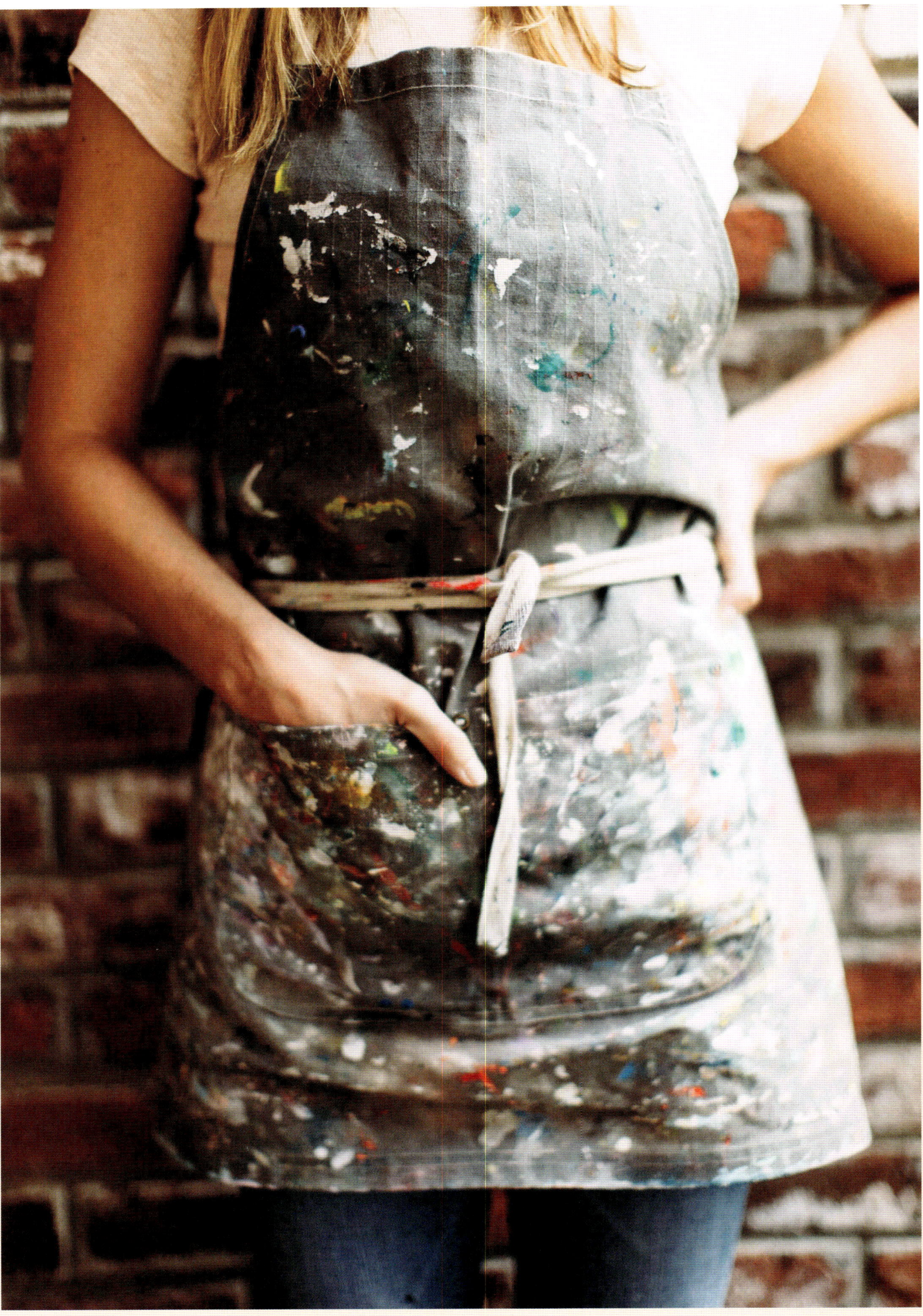

BLAKELY LITTLE IS a young artist who interned for Teil at the beginning of her career and has since blossomed into a well-known artist in her own right. Lulie Wallace, well known and loved, is the artist that in many ways mentored and guided Teil at the start of her career. Raven Roxanne, an abstract artist, is a college friend of Teil's and is described by her as the "ray of sunshine"in the studio and brings a funky, youthful presence to the mix. Together, the girls provide constant inspiration, encouragement, and motivation for one another. When one artist succeeds, the others celebrate and are inspired to push their own artistic boundaries. Teil muses that much of her success can be attributed to the contagious creativity that studio life has provided.

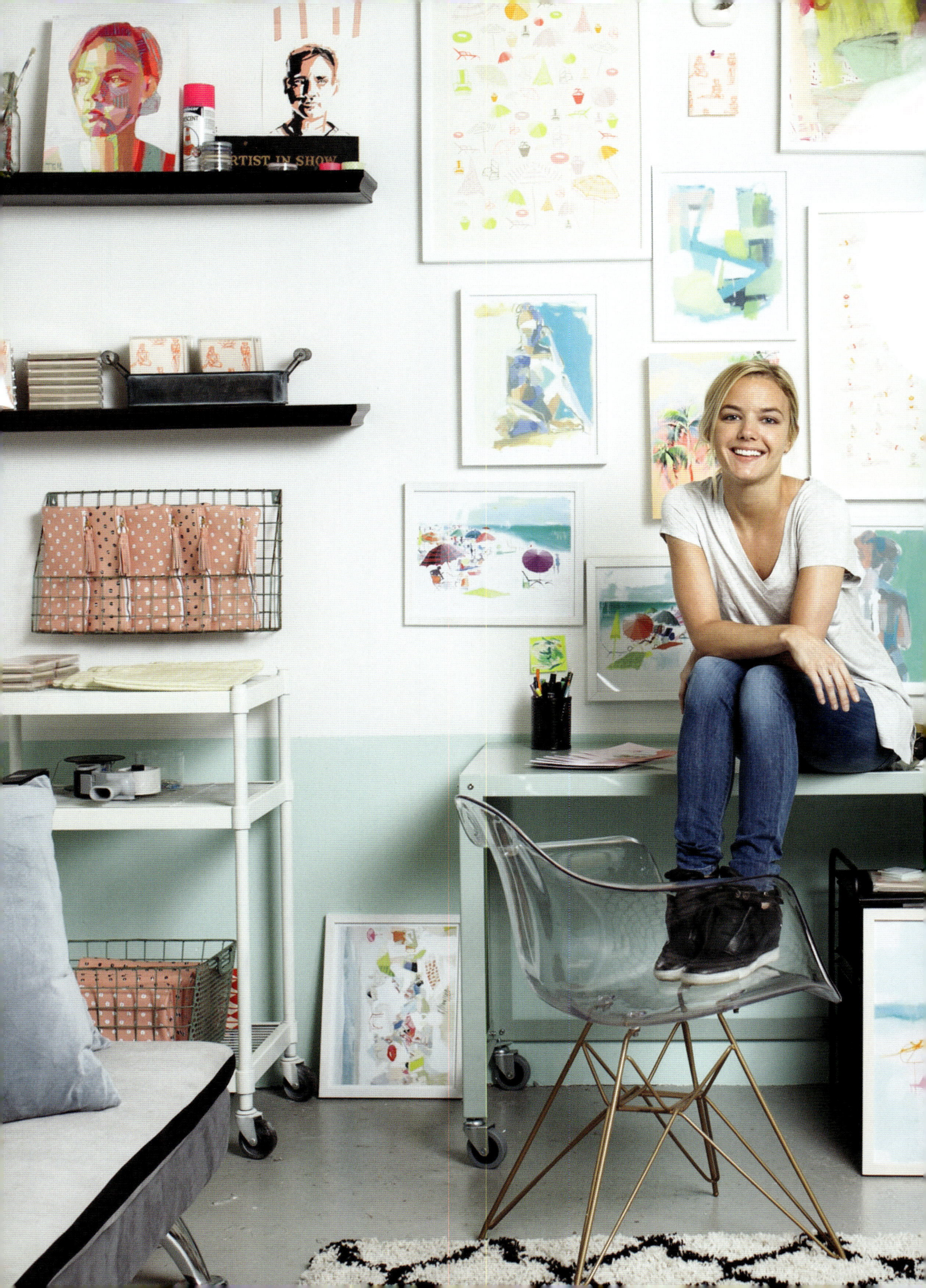

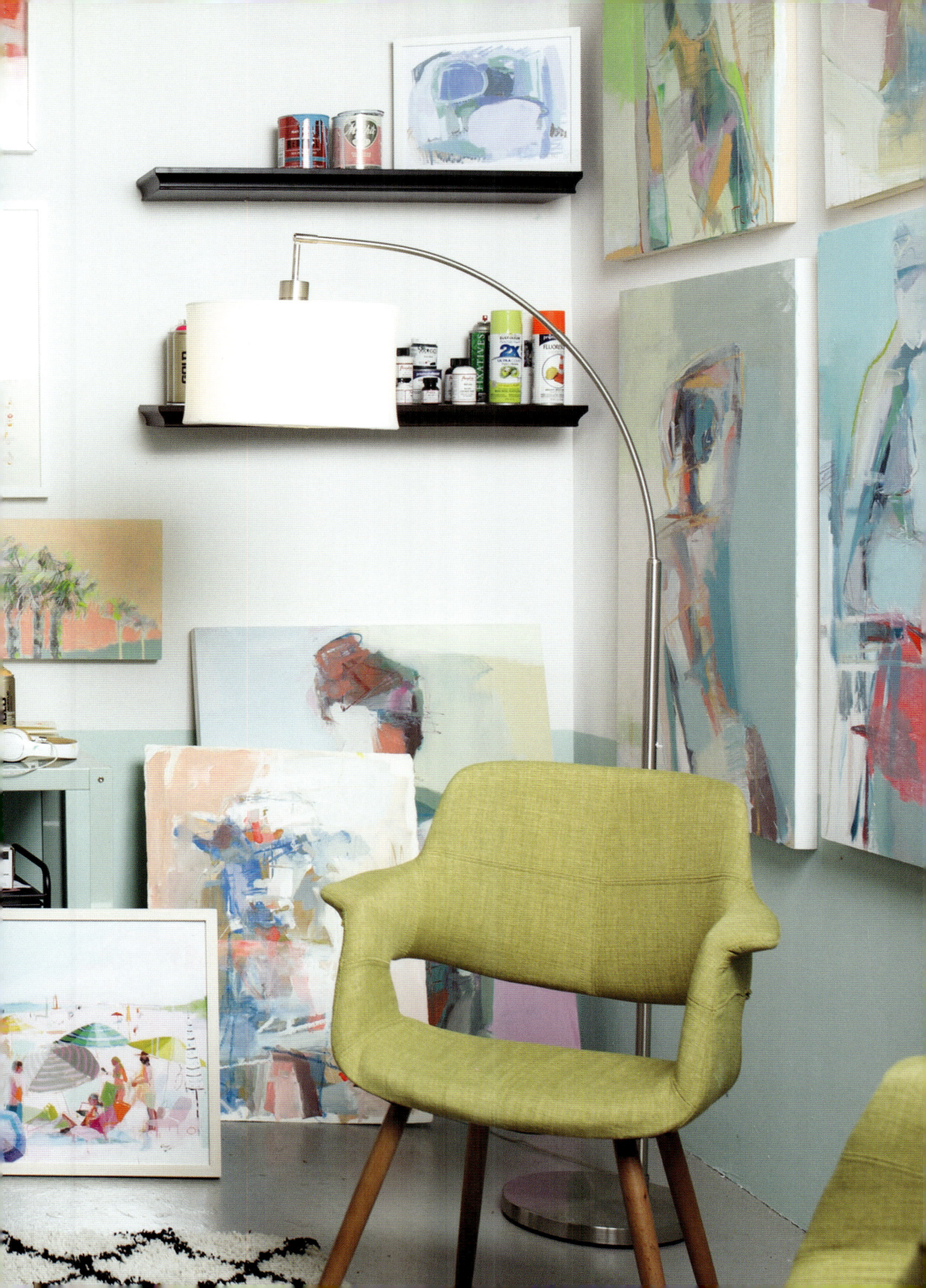
GOLD
FIXATIVES
2X

FAITH

If you were to meet Teil and ask her to tell you about herself, you would find that her faith is her most defining quality. While it is true that her walk with Jesus is Teil's first priority today, it hasn't always been the case.

Teil grew up in a genuine, loving, Christian home. She was taught biblical principles and values her whole life, and her parents took special care to make sure that she received a loving, steady diet of church, faith-based discussions in the home, and ample opportunity to welcome a personal relationship with Jesus Christ. Her mother, Sherry, exhibited a steady trust in the Lord as she raised each of her children (including two brothers, Taylor and Garrett, and younger sister Laura Lea), loving each child selflessly and equally. Beginning at an early age, she recalls memories of her dad calling the family into the den and studying the Bible, asking provoking questions about their life and salvation. Her mother considered Elisabeth Eliot her spiritual mentor, instilling in her basic Christian living in their home.

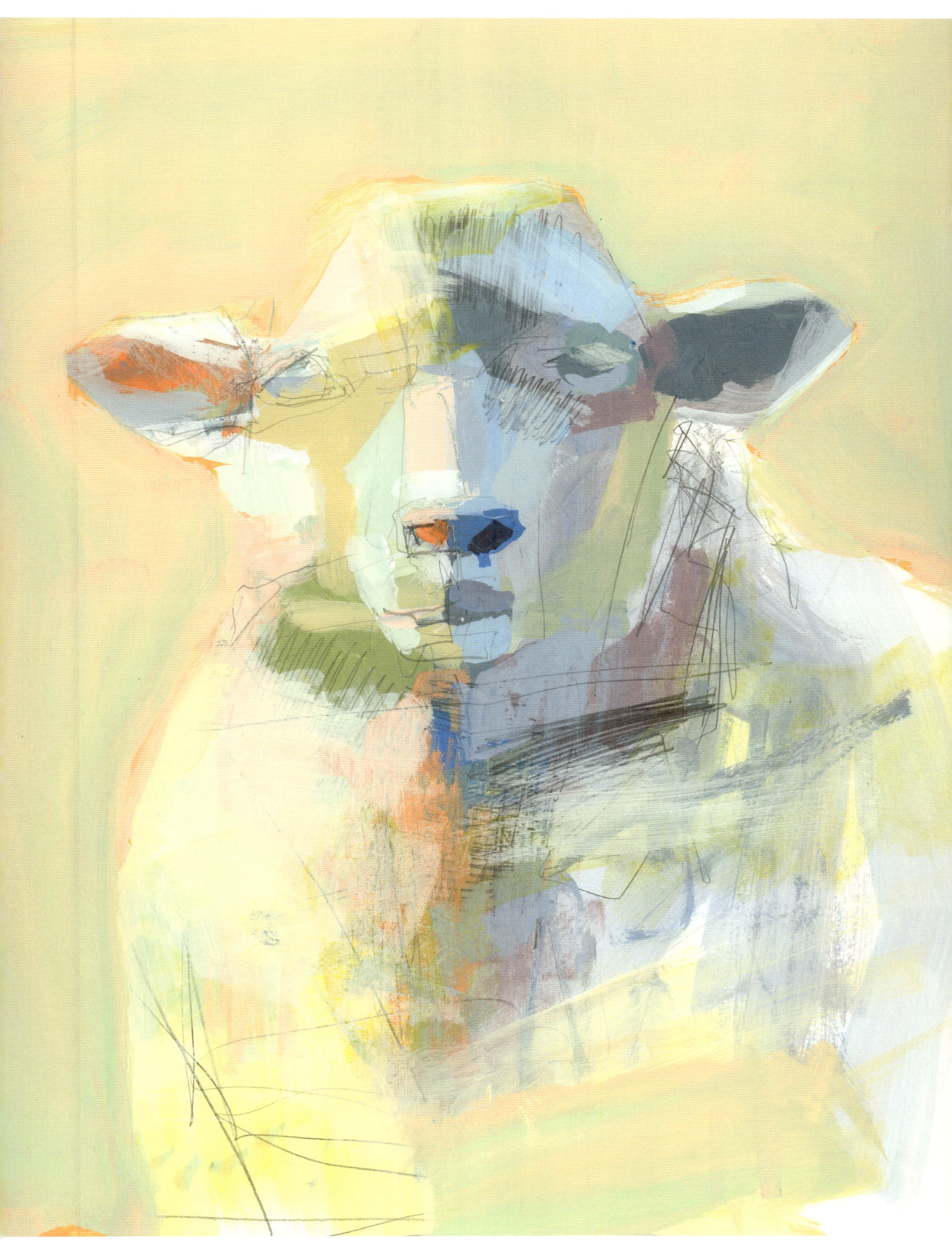

Her dad brought them regularly to the nursing home to visit the lonely and the disabled. She recalls whenever her dad dropped her and her sister off at school, he regularly reminded them to befriend those who had no friends.

They were taught the value of hard work, order and cleanliness, respect for authority, consideration of others, and gratitude. Teil accepted her upbringing without very much pushback but was eager to break out from underneath her faith-centric roots when she left home for college.

Glad to shake off all of the rules and particulars of Christian living, Teil went to Auburn and lived what she thought was the good life—one without restrictions or boundaries, and living according to her own personal ethic system. She resolved in her mind that Christianity was a social construct that imposed order according to close-minded, judgmental, self-righteous people. Anyone who followed Jesus in her eyes was a naïve person to be pitied.

Teil's views on life and God were only reinforced through the secular teaching found often at universities. This was further confirmation to confidently deny the teachings of Christianity. This realization was utterly liberating. All of her artistic friends she surrounded herself with were like-minded in their thinking patterns. Life felt free and good.

After one troublesome incident, her parents made her come home on the weekends for an entire semester in order to avoid making bad decisions. She obliged, came home each weekend, and sat through church services she used as mental check-out sessions for doodling on the bulletin and pondering her own life and goals. The weekends at home provided a time in which she grew as an artist, but her heart stayed the same.

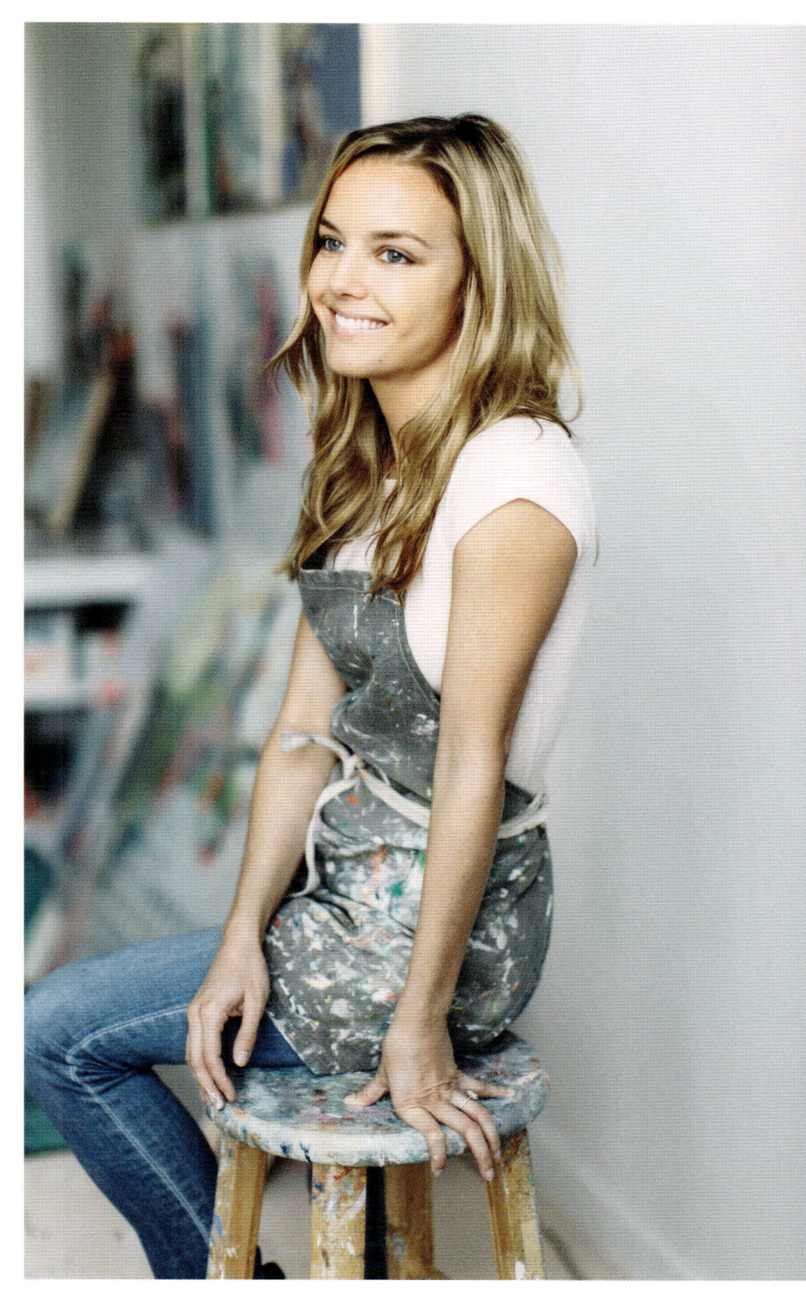

After graduation, Teil's parents finally and prayerfully gave her the space she wanted and

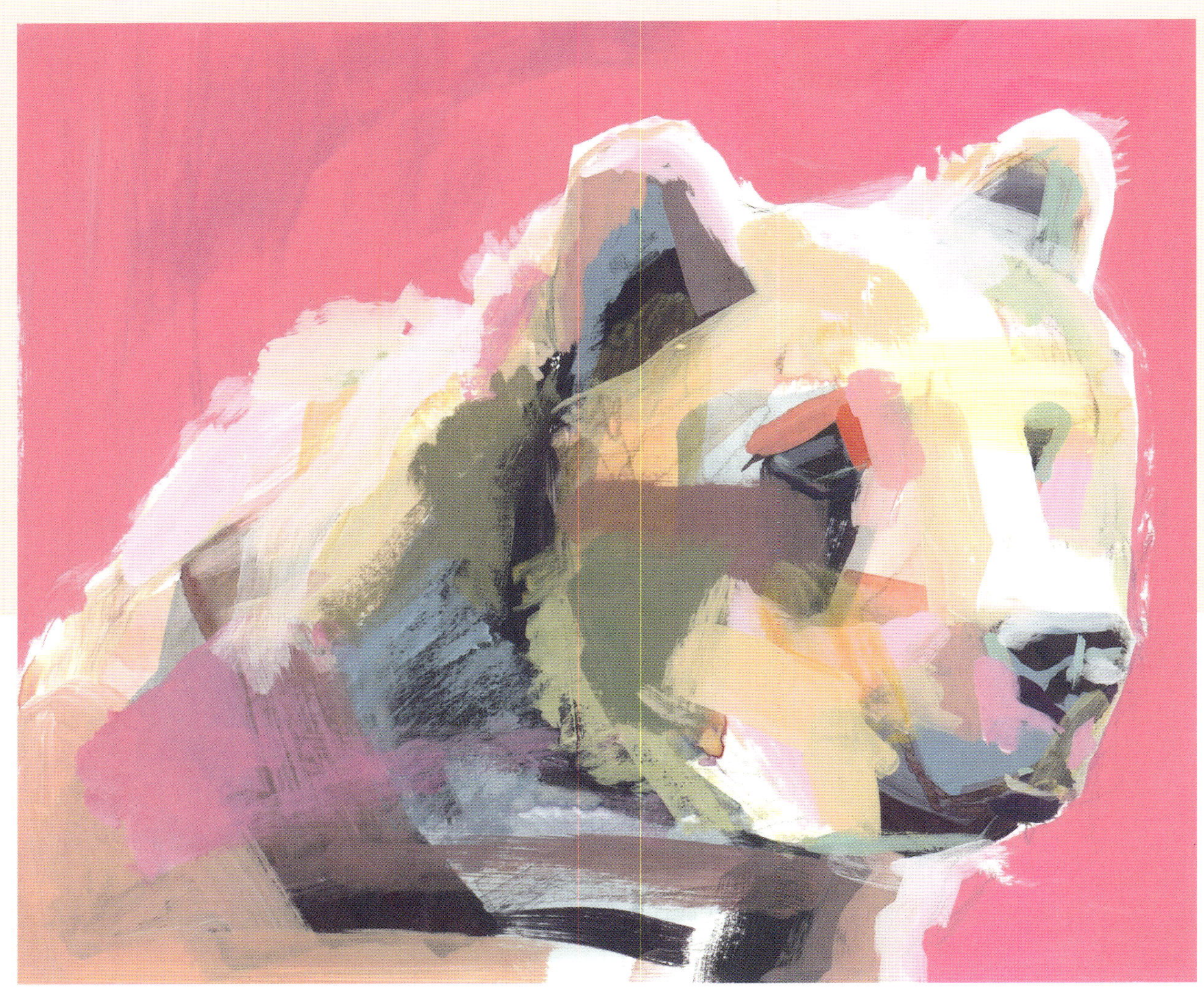

their blessing to move to Charleston, South Carolina. They tried everything to guide their daughter on a path to Christ, and they knew that it was time to let go and step into a season of prayer and fasting to allow the Lord to meet Teil where she was. Meanwhile, Teil's post-graduate plans weren't going how she thought they would. She saw her friends' lives progressing, but she felt like her wheels were spinning in place.

In April of 2011, Teil went home to visit her parents over a weekend. While she was prepared to sit through another church service that she anticipated would once again yield nothing except an hour of boredom, the pastor began talking about idols. An idol was defined by author Timothy Keller as "anything more important to you than God, anything that absorbs your heart and imagination more than God, anything you seek to give you what only God can give . . . An idol is whatever you look at and say, in your heart of hearts, 'If I have that, then I'll feel my life has meaning, then I'll know I have value, then I'll feel significant and secure.' There are many ways to describe that kind of relationship to something, but perhaps the best one is worship." This concept surprisingly caught Teil's attention, and she began to consider the "idols" she was consumed by. Her art, her appearance, social status–she jotted down a list on the bulletin that all tied for first place. She did a good job of refusing to worship God but was realizing that she had been worshipping what was counterfeit instead.

SHE LATER SHARED her thoughts with her parents. During a conversation on the back porch of a rainy evening, her dad told her she could not just deemphasize these "idols," which would only consume her, but rather she needed to replace them with Jesus Himself. Only then, the priorities in life fall into their intended order.

Over the next few months, the Lord embraced Teil in a way that caused her to finally bow to Him after years of rejecting Him. There was a moment in which Teil finally felt the Lord calling her to Him, along with the promise of peace, joy, and purpose in Jesus.

Since that day, Teil has been growing more and more in her faith in Jesus. She and her husband, Russell, are committed to their faith and are members of a church in Charleston while also remaining very close to Teil's home church in Columbus. Both Russell's and Teil's lives are marked heavily by their faith and the rich thread of salvation, woven intricately into their marriage and respective careers.

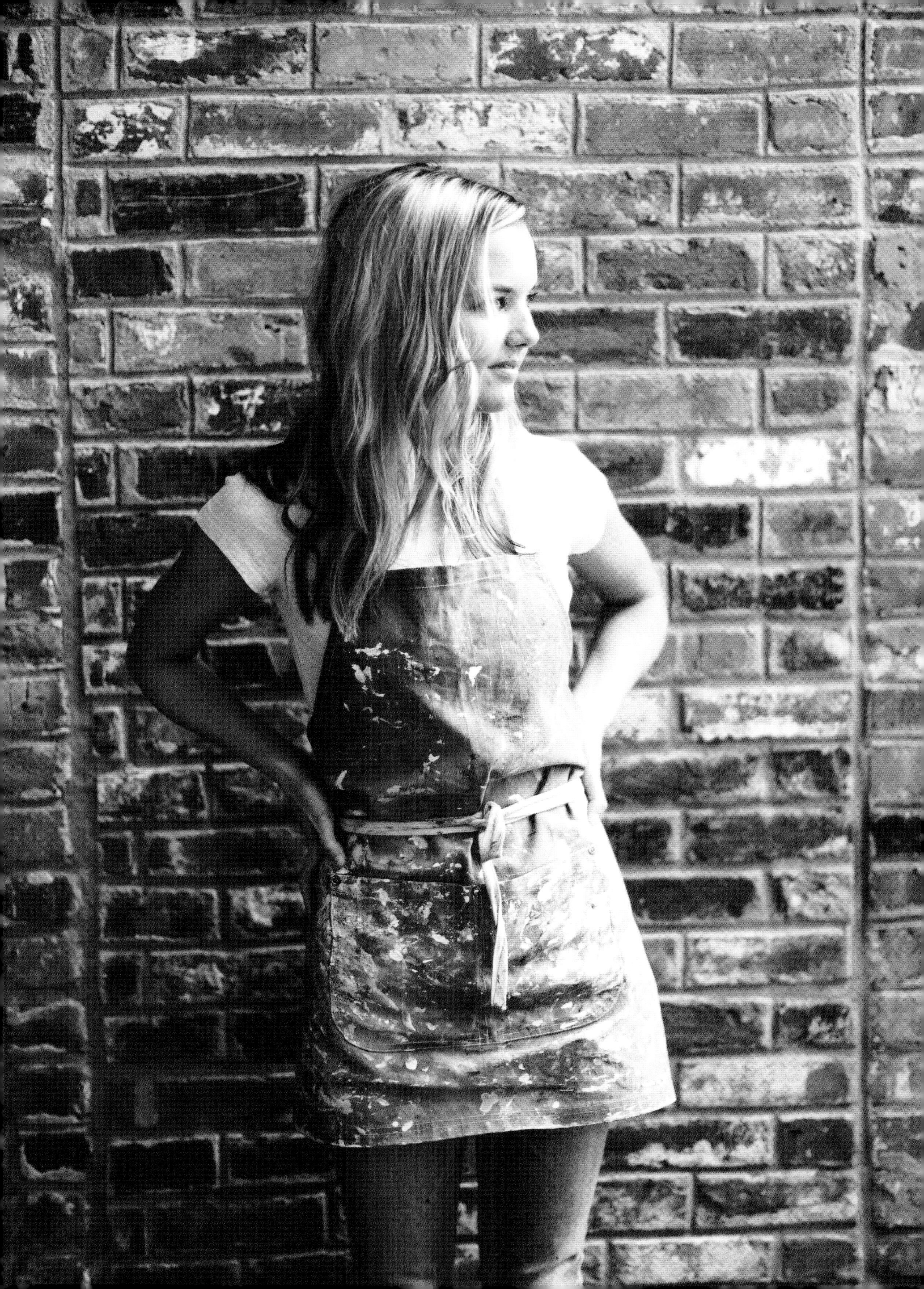

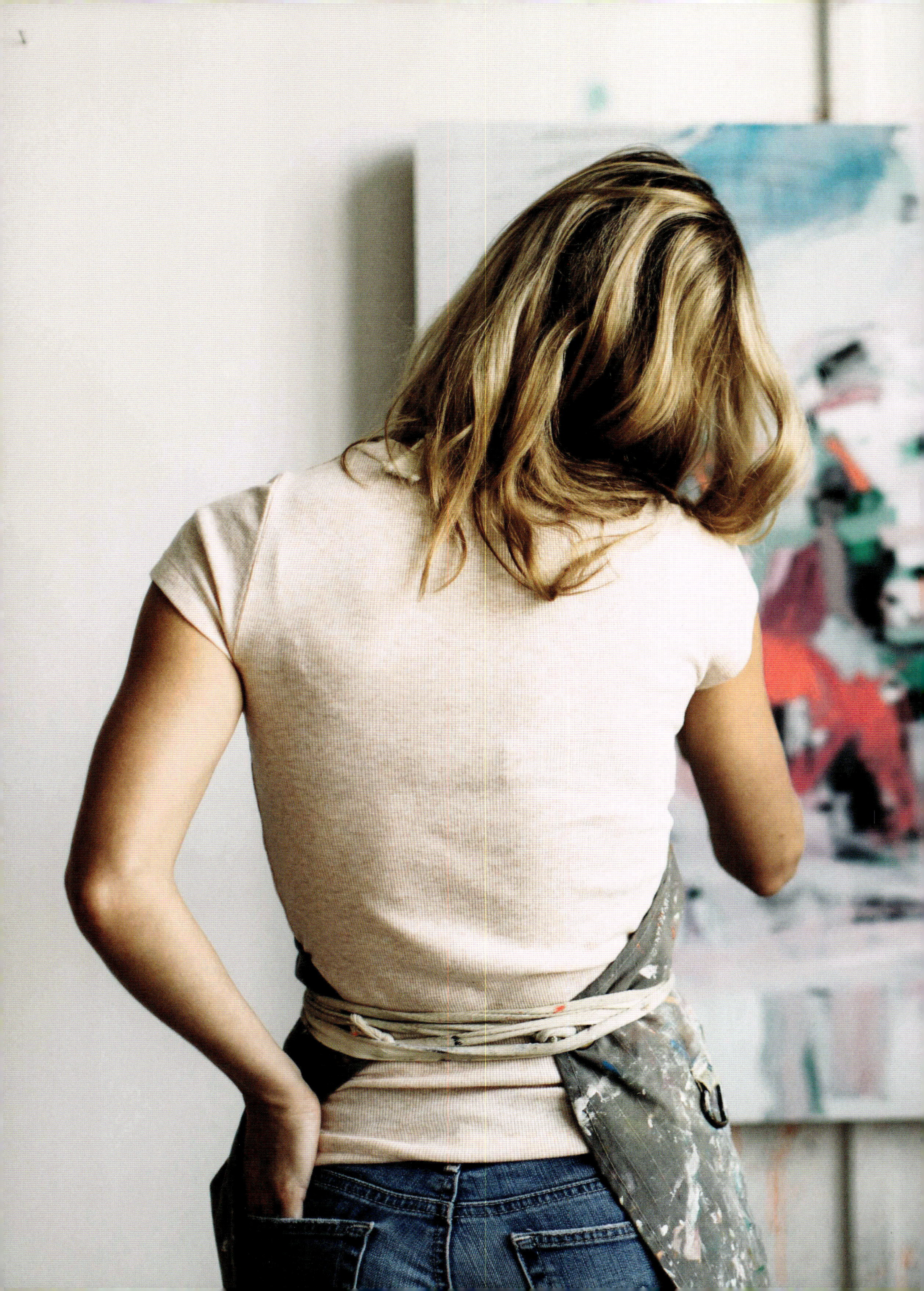

While it may seem seem like Teil's success as an artist came quickly and seamlessly, she willingly admits that this was not the case. Arriving to a distinct artistic mark took years of trial and error, fine-tuning, and starting over. To look back at the various stages of Teil's work is to witness the evolution of an artist. Even though the road to artistic success wasn't always clear and easy, it was necessary. It was a crucial time of dependency in her faith. Her hands were held open to whatever God's plan was, even if art was not the answer. If the door was shut on her artistic pursuit, she was happy to seek another avenue, which was an important attitude for her in not forcing anything.

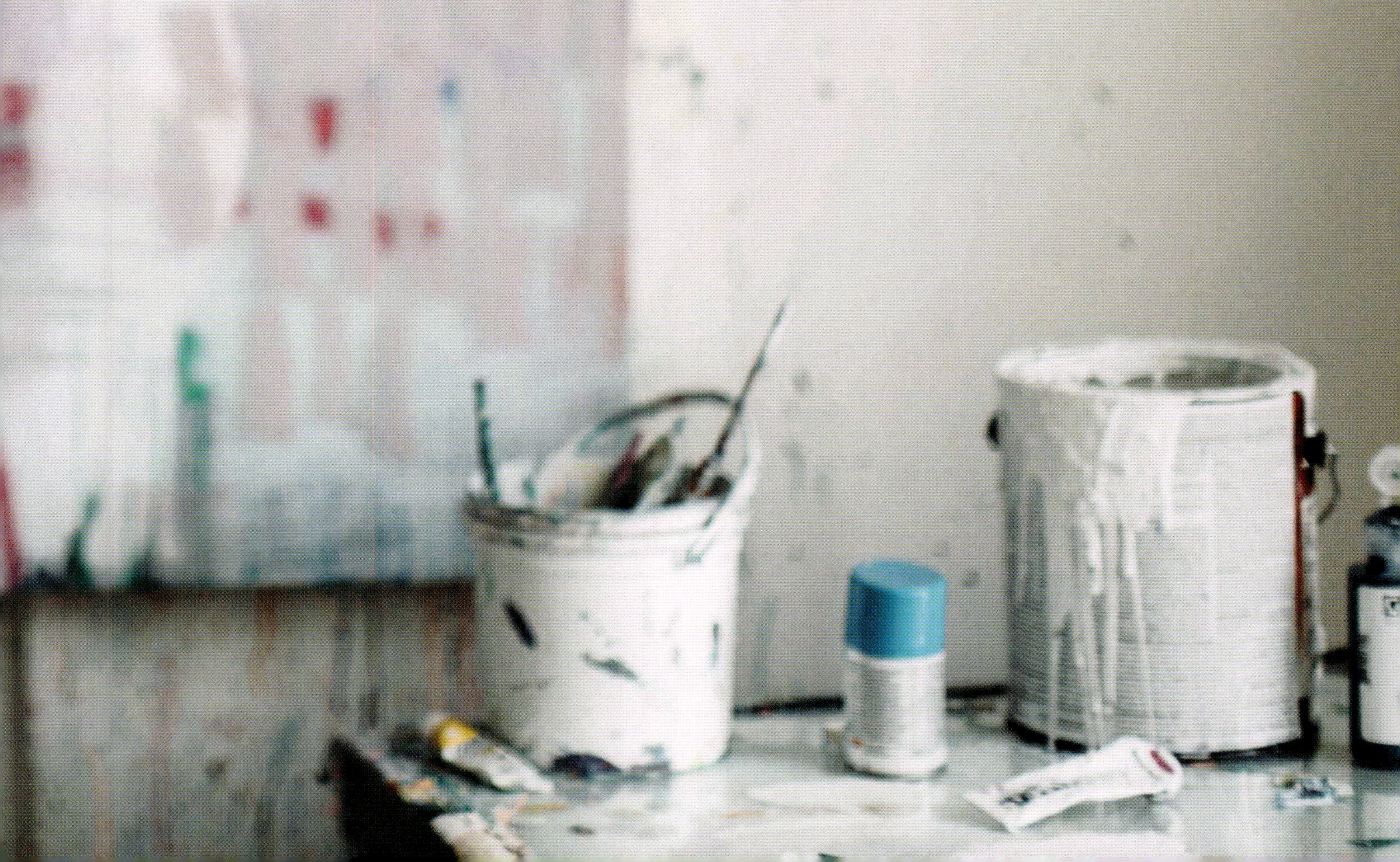

ARTISTIC INSPIRATION

Inspiration comes in all shapes and sizes to Teil. One of the greatest sources of inspiration for her is the company of other creatives—this is why she chose to rent a studio space among a few of her favorite fellow artists. Teil isn't just interested in drawing artistic inspiration from other painters; she is intensely interested in thriving, vibrant artists in almost every realm. Musicians, designers, chefs, and craftsmen have all inspired Teil in their own ways.

Getting out of town and immersing herself into new landscapes and cultures is another way that Teil likes to get her creative flow going. In her travels, she has had the opportunity to experience many visually diverse environments that have undoubtedly played a role in the distinct use of color and texture in her work.

The desire to inspire others also motivates Teil. She hopes that her aim to break boxes while creating universal appeal in her own art encourages others to live out their own creative aspirations.

TRAVEL INFLUENCES

Teil's most popular pieces of work are undoubtedly her playful, impressionistic beach scenes. In order to capture the essence of these landscapes, Teil has gone on many pilgrimages to the world's most diverse seaside spots. From Miami to coastal France and Hawaii, Teil has combed the shores of the most appealing, sunny spots. These trips have helped the artist not only convey the visually stunning elements of the shorelines, but also the mood in each of these dream-like landscapes. All of the coastal experiences can easily be felt by her audience.

Russell Henley, Teil's husband and PGA golfer, travels far and wide for his work. Teil has taken a liking to tagging along with her husband and soaking up the experiences that each new place has to offer. Traveling with Russell has given Teil the opportunity to immerse herself into cultures that she may not have otherwise encountered. Additionally, Teil has had the chance to visit art galleries and to meet international artisans during these golf expeditions—all of which have provided great enjoyment and inspiration.

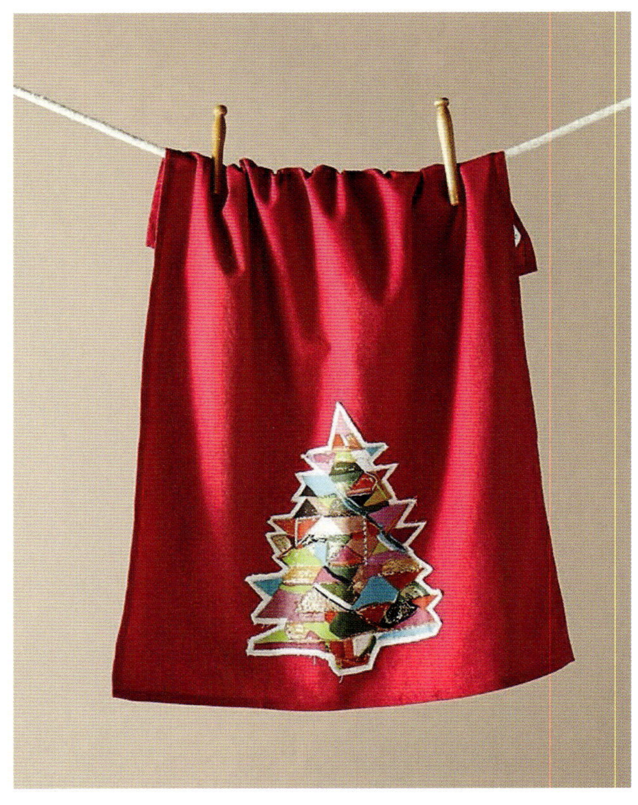

COLL

One of the greatest joys that Teil gets to experience as an artist is partnering with other companies and fellow creators.

Christian Siriano, winner of *Project Runway*, based a summer resort line on the color palette of Teil's figure paintings. The designer invited Teil to New York City, where her artwork was transformed into a backdrop for the clothing line. Experiencing how her art had been a source of inspiration for Siriano will always be one of Teil's most memorable moments as an artist.

Another fun collaboration was with the clothing store Abercrombie & Fitch—several of Teil's abstract paintings were used in the design of a collection of t-shirts. Teil's designs translate to paper and home goods as well.

ABORATIONS

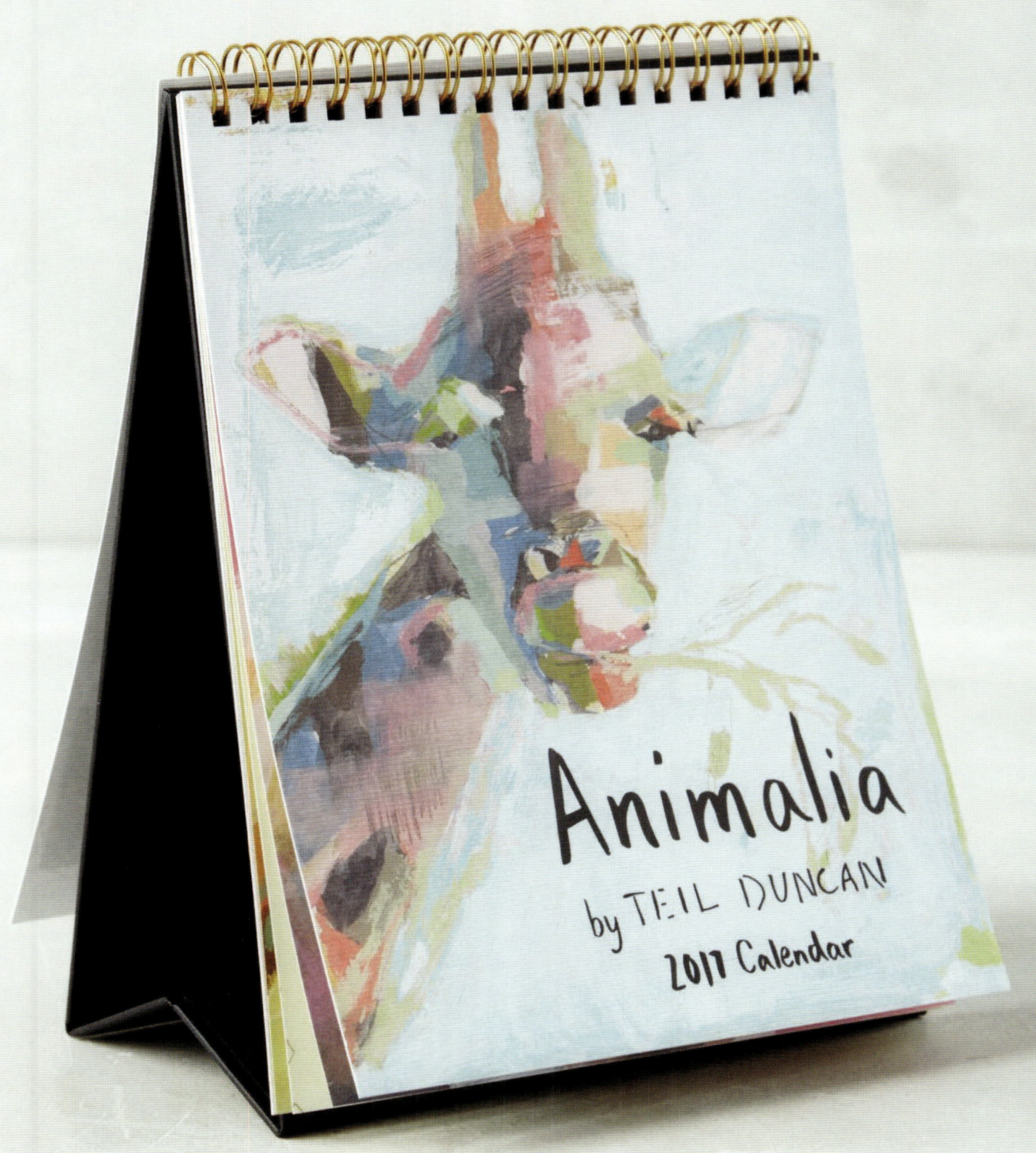

Wildsam, a publisher of niche travel books, commissioned Teil to illustrate the artwork for the Charleston addition. Home items like calendars and linens were created using Teil's art for the eclectic women's clothing and home store Anthropologie. Additionally, interior design stores like Crate & Barrel, West Elm, and One King's Lane have commissioned exclusive prints. The wide variety of collaborations that Teil has been a part of is a testament to the universal appeal of the artist's work.

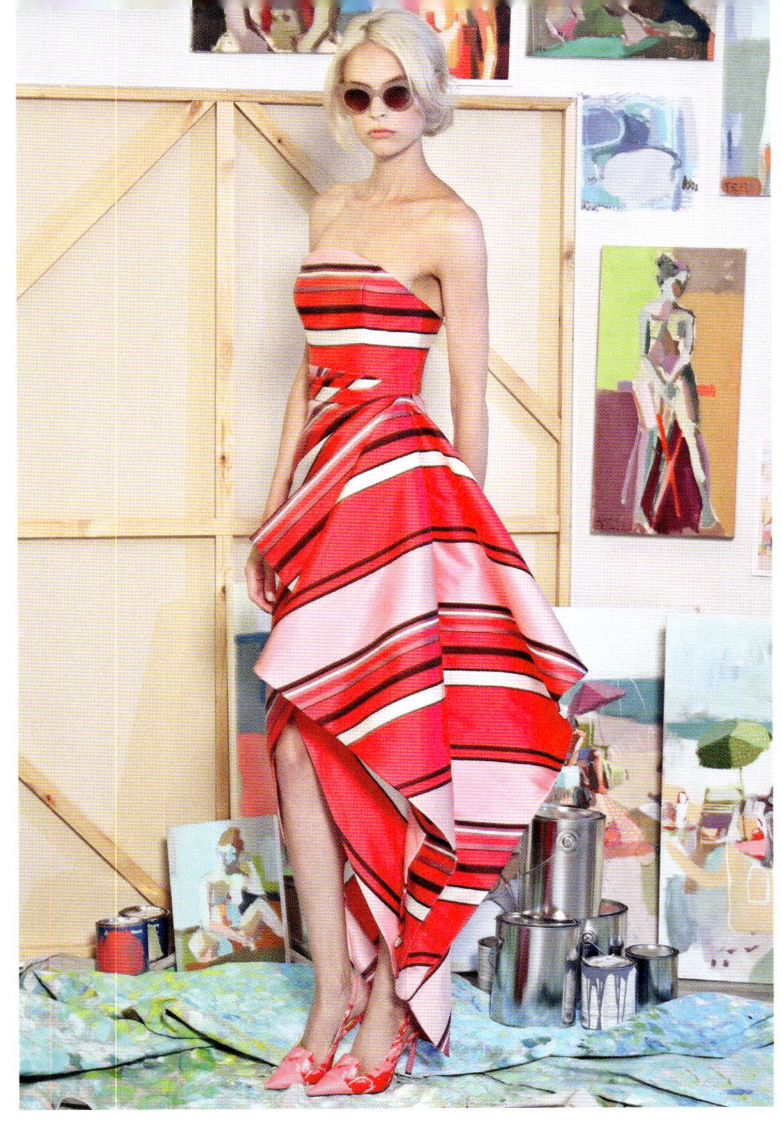

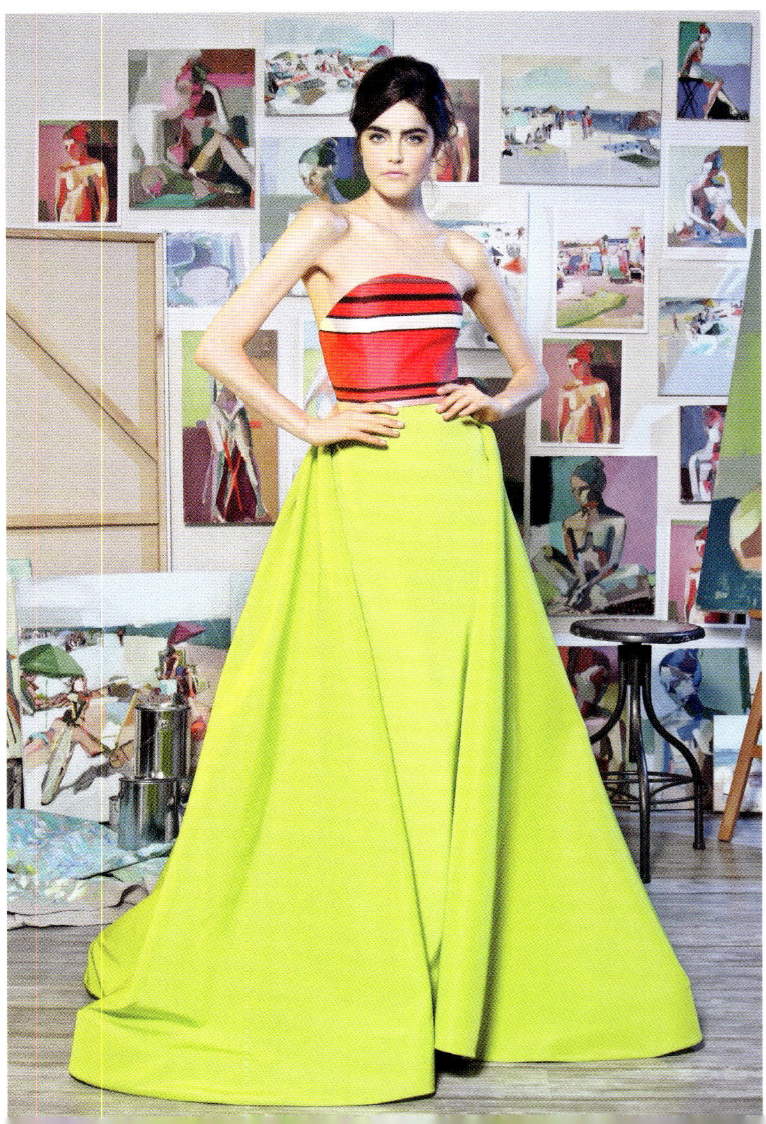

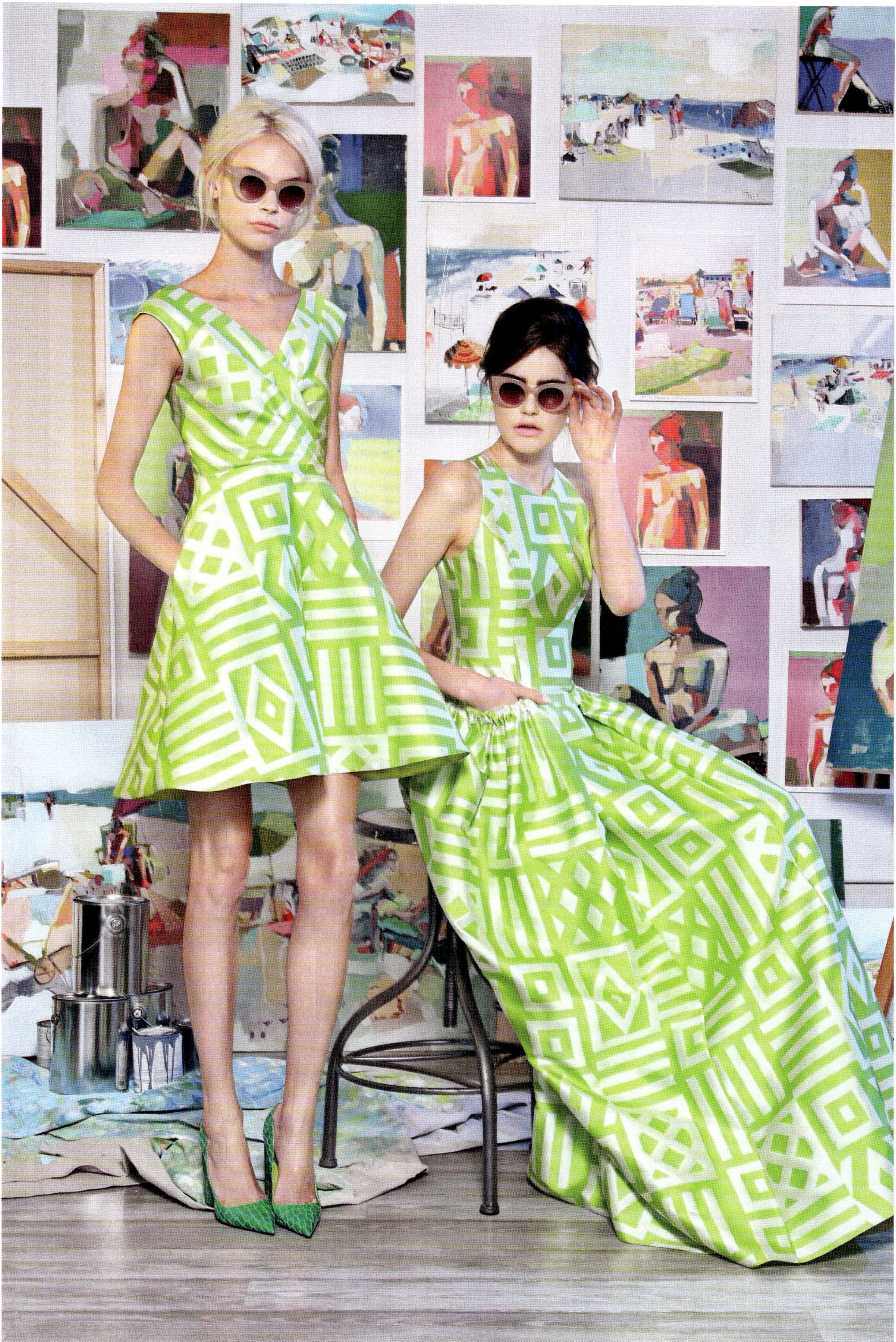

IMPACT OF SOCIAL MEDIA

There is simply no way to tell the story of Teil as an artist without commenting on the immense impact that social media has had on her business. When she was starting out in Charleston, Teil's work was sold in two downtown galleries. Sales were providing enough for a sustainable career, but she desired to have wider exposure.

At the time, online shopping was becoming increasingly common. Buying art, however, was still considered untraditional. With the help of a close friend and artist, Lulie Wallace, and Teil's sister, Laura Lea, her online presence gained headway. Web sales gave her the ability to market her work, style it, show the daily messy process, and develop a coherent brand. She could now use social media platforms to reach people from all over the world on a regular basis. Today, Instagram is Teil's main tool for connecting with her audience and building her brand as an artist. Without it, she suspects her business may not be where it is today.

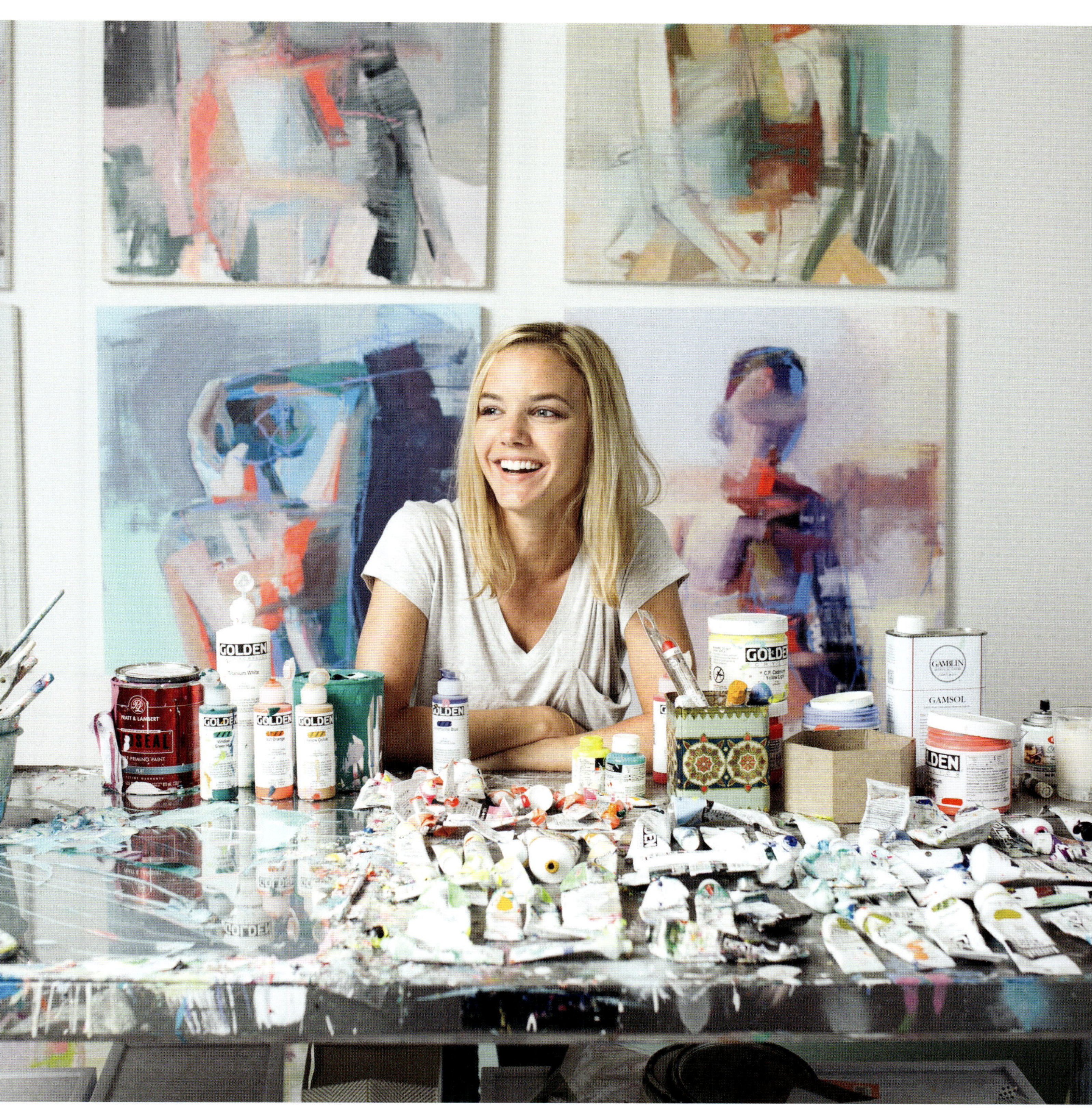
PRATT & LAMBERT
GOLDEN
GOLDEN
GAMBLIN
GAMSOL

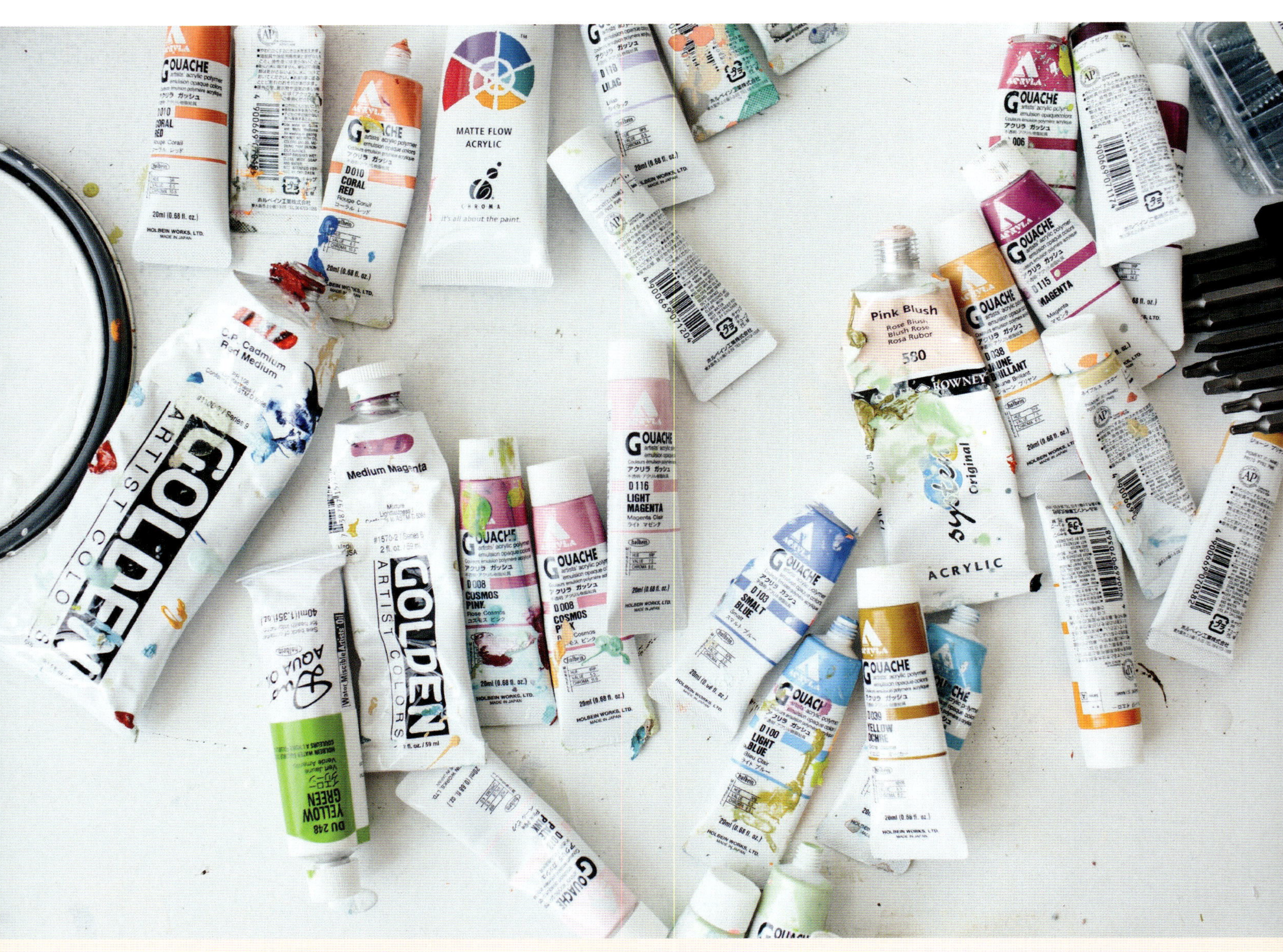
GOUACHE
D010
CORAL
RED
20ml (0.68 fl. oz.)
HOLBEIN WORKS, LTD.
MADE IN JAPAN
MATTE FLOW
ACRYLIC
It's all about the paint.
D110
LILAC
C.P. Cadmium
Red Medium
GOLDEN
ARTIST COLORS
Medium Magenta
D008
COSMOS
PINK
D116
LIGHT
MAGENTA
DU 248
YELLOW
GREEN
Pink Blush
580
ROWNEY
Original
ACRYLIC
D115
MAGENTA
D103
SMALT
BLUE
D100
LIGHT
BLUE
D039
YELLOW
OCHRE

WHILE SHE IS GRATEFUL for the opportunity to build a following on Instagram, she also admits to having a love/hate relationship with social media. While it can be used as a tool for creative inspiration for Teil and many other artists, she fears that in many ways, social media usage can be the thing that kills it. The power social media carries that allows users, particularly artists, to bring their work to audiences en masse can bring some unseemly side effects—self-absorption, vanity, and addiction to approval, just to name a few. So, while Teil loves the benefits of running her art business in the Instagram world, she remains ever vigilant to "check herself," hoping that what she puts out into the world only encourages and cultivates creative inspiration instead of adding to the ever-growing number of problems that social media causes.

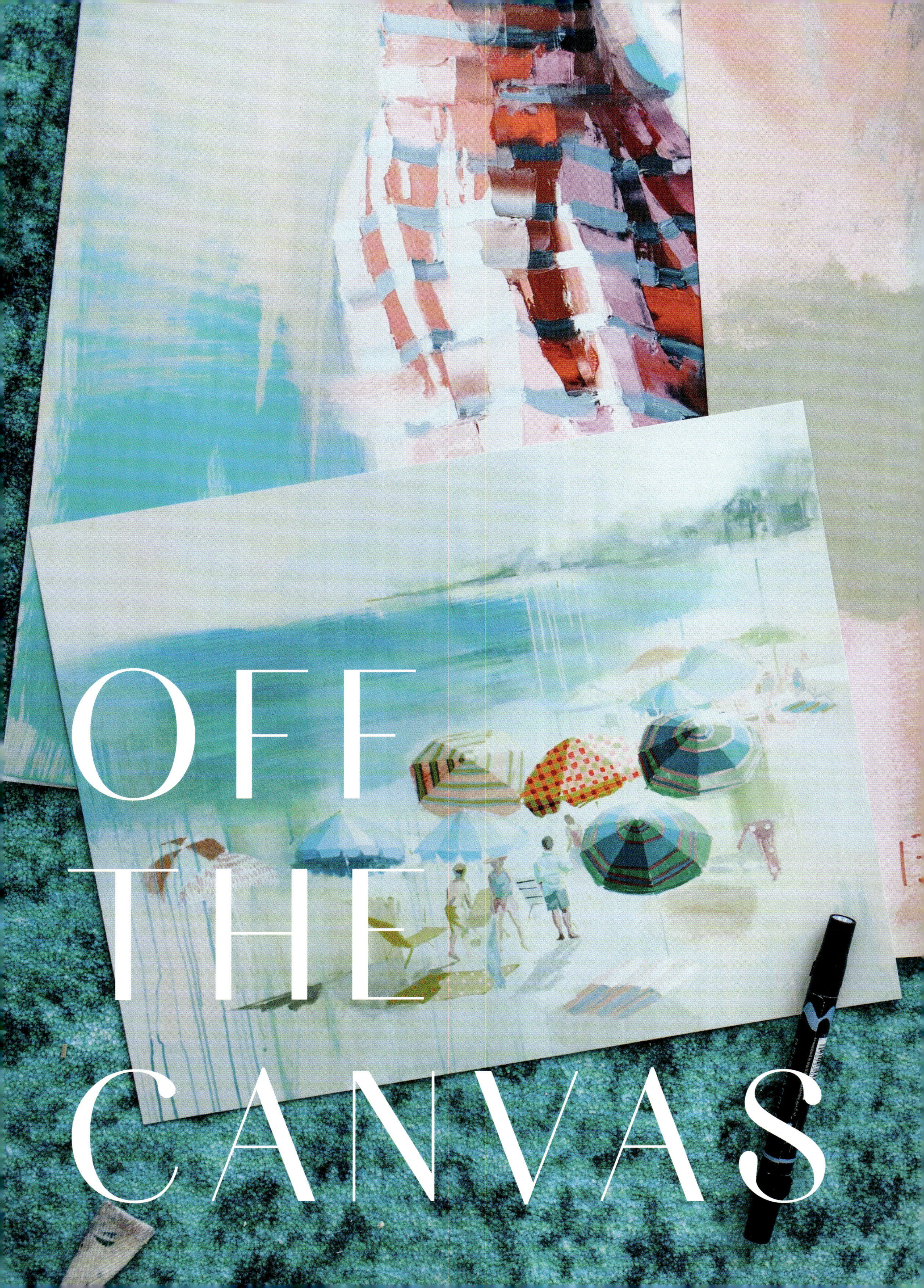

OFF THE CANVAS

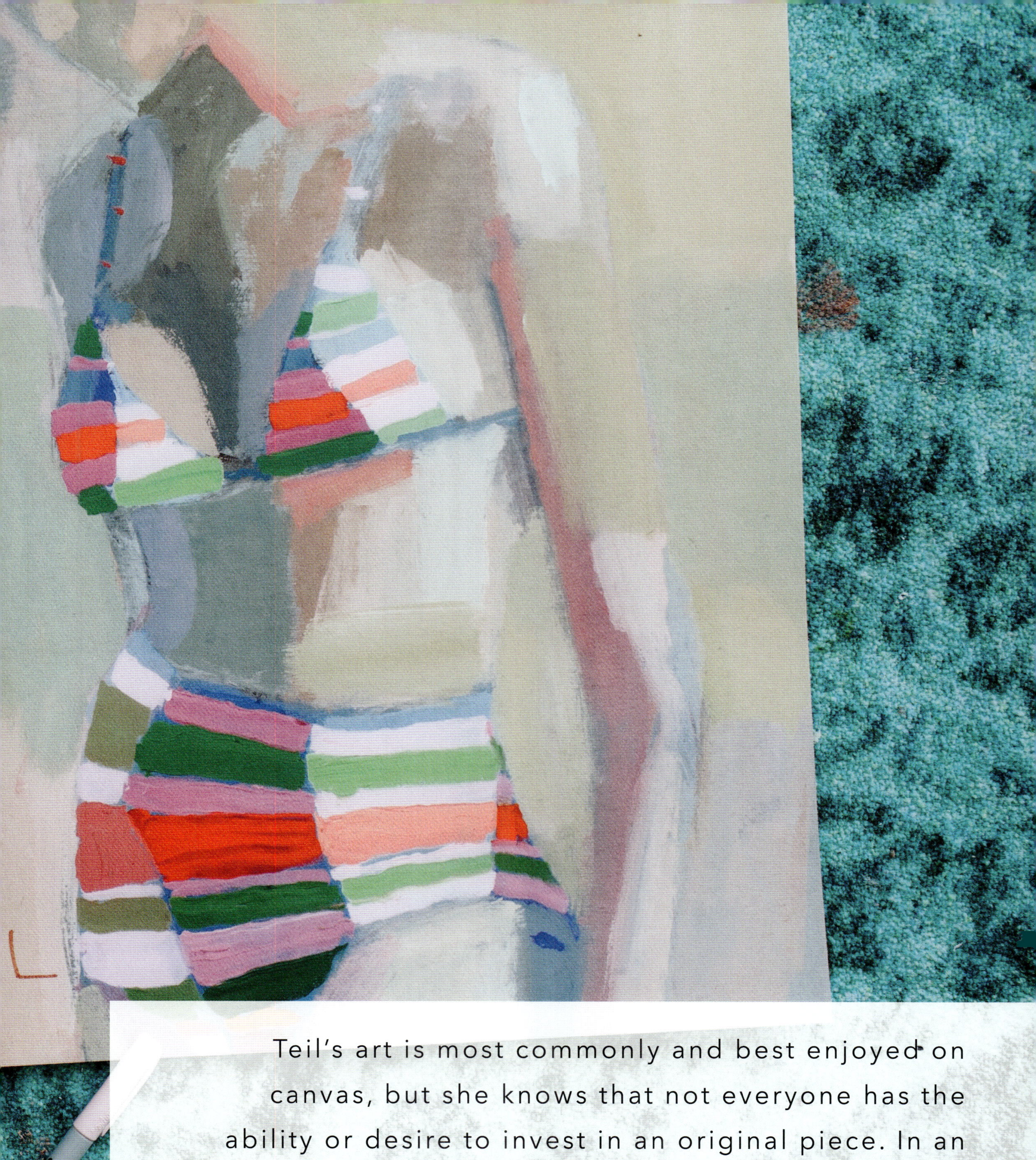

Teil's art is most commonly and best enjoyed on canvas, but she knows that not everyone has the ability or desire to invest in an original piece. In an effort to make her work available to a wider audience, Teil has worked on several projects that showcase her art in mediums other than paint on canvas.

PAINTED LEATHER CLUTCHES provided a vehicle to translate dreamy colors and textures into wearable art. One summer, Teil created a beach throw as a nod to her well-loved beach series. Additionally, Teil has designed four sets of stationery, a calendar, and journals—all popular items for gifting. For those who want one of Teil's pieces in their home, she offers a few prints with each released collection to ensure that anyone can enjoy her art.

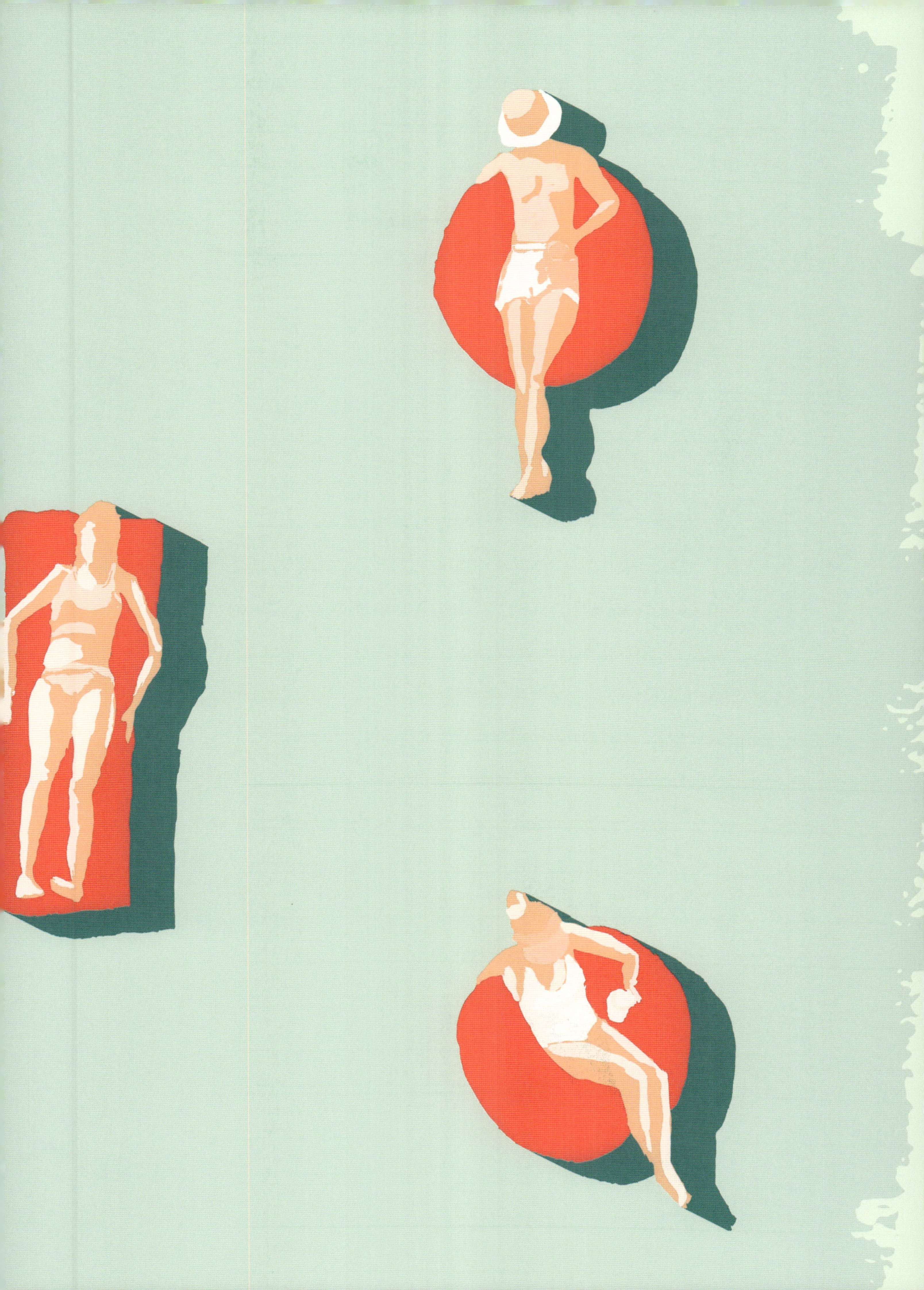

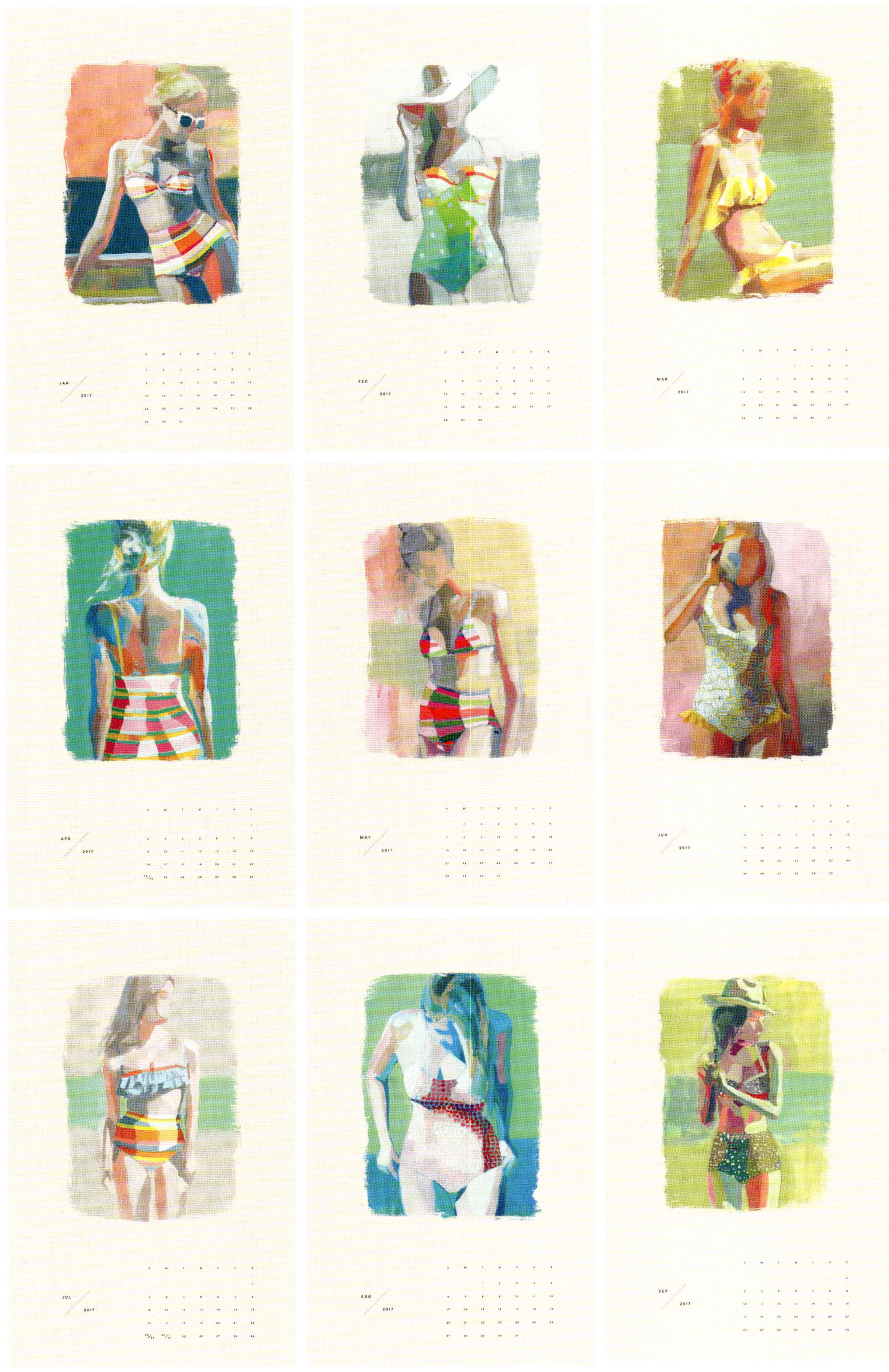
JAN
2017
FEB
2017
MAR
2017
APR
2017
MAY
2017
JUN
2017
JUL
2017
AUG
2017
SEP
2017

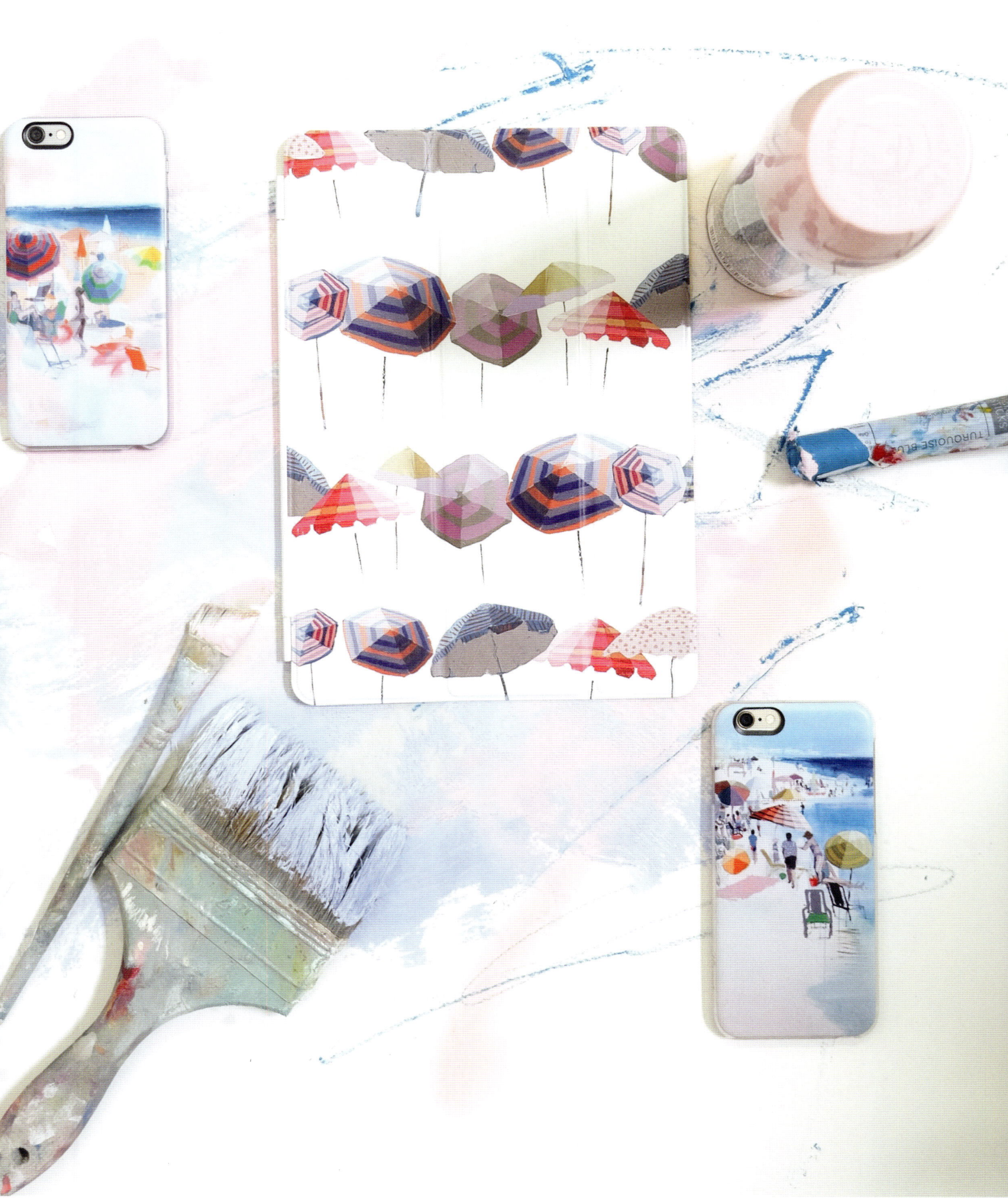

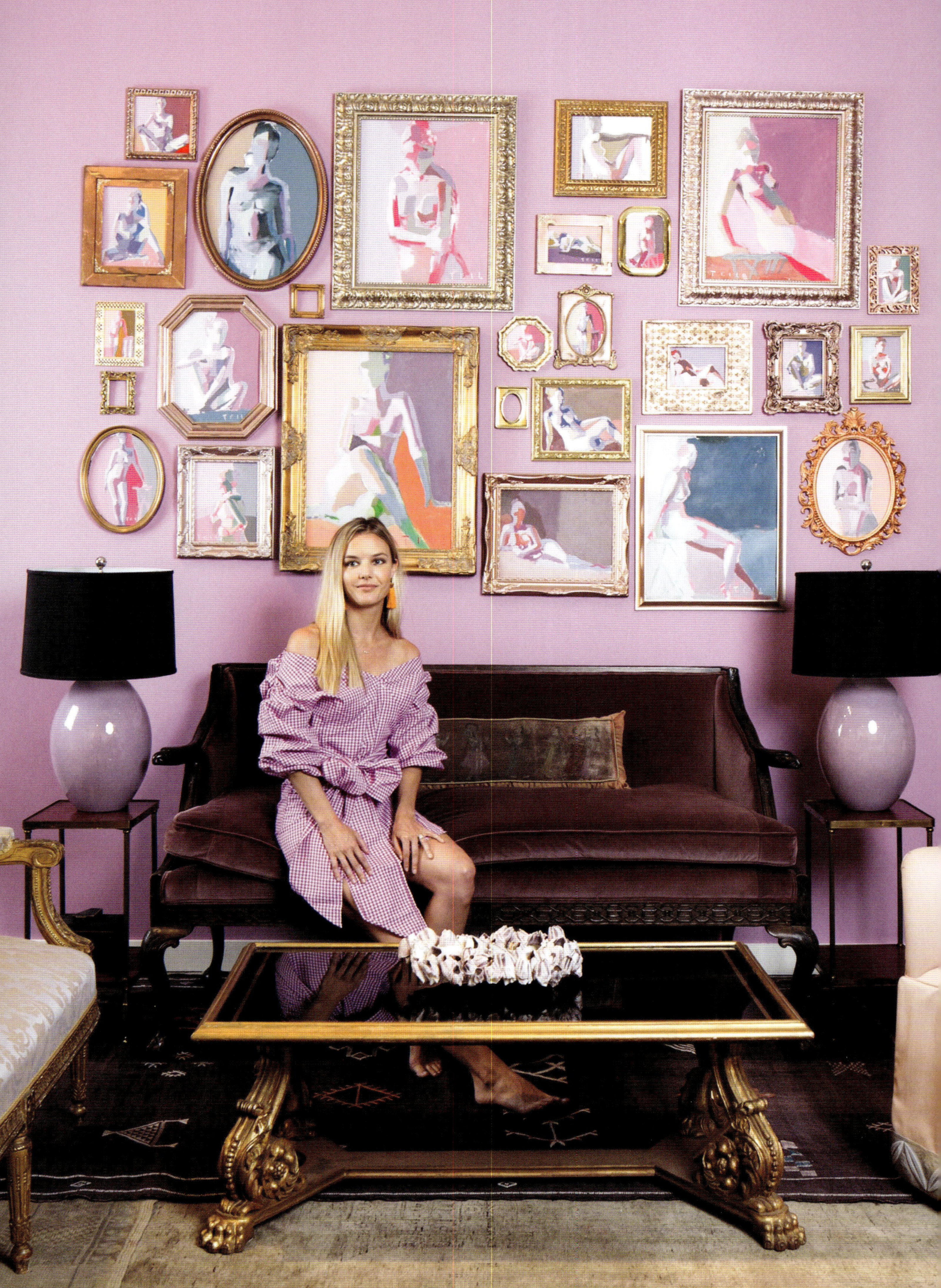

ART EVENTS

While most of her time is spent in the studio and connecting with her online audience, one of the greatest joys for Teil as an artist is when she gets to display a body of work and interact with prospective buyers at art exhibitions. Though they have grown and evolved over the years, each art show represents a special moment in Teil's career.

Her first Charleston exhibition was held in a dentist's office shortly after Teil decided to pursue art full-time. Teil arranged this show herself and was excited to display the body of work. She will never forget the elation for this art show–she was eager and curious to see whether this event would catapult her career or close the door. At the end of the night, each piece sold.

The show that introduced Teil's beach collection, her most sought-after series, took place at Stems, a local Charleston floral boutique. Teil remembers this art show, titled "Bask," as her most refined event due to the cohesive, polished body of work. This exhibition was the first time Teil showcased her beach scenes, and the feedback received was overwhelmingly positive.

The next exhibition took place in an event space at Redux Contemporary Art Center. There she displayed a beach collection based on local Charleston coastal scenes. Landmarks of Folly Beach, Sullivan's Island, and Isle of Palms made their debut within the work and resonated with the local beach-goers. The excitement over the series seemed to continually grow, and was shared over live music and a celebratory atmosphere.

The show at the American Theatre in Spring of 2017 in downtown Charleston was Teil's largest and most stirring show to date. Pieces from each collection were displayed throughout the historic theater. In celebration of Teil's seven series of works, the room was filled with local admirers along with cross-country travelers to view her art they had grown to love on social media. This show was a high point for Teil, and she planned for it to be a final "hoorah," as her priorities would soon begin to shift to the idea of a growing family.

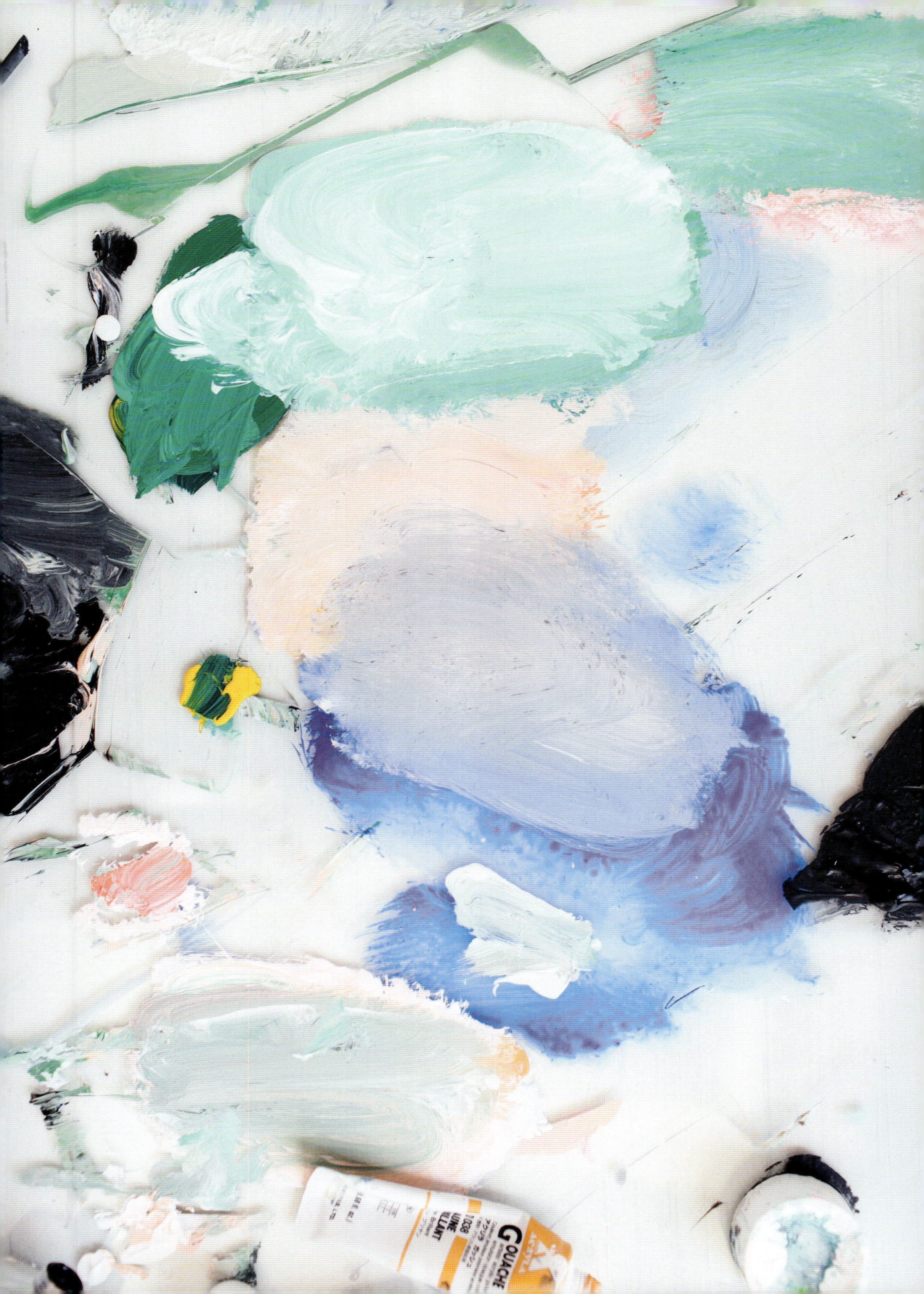
GOUACHE
1038

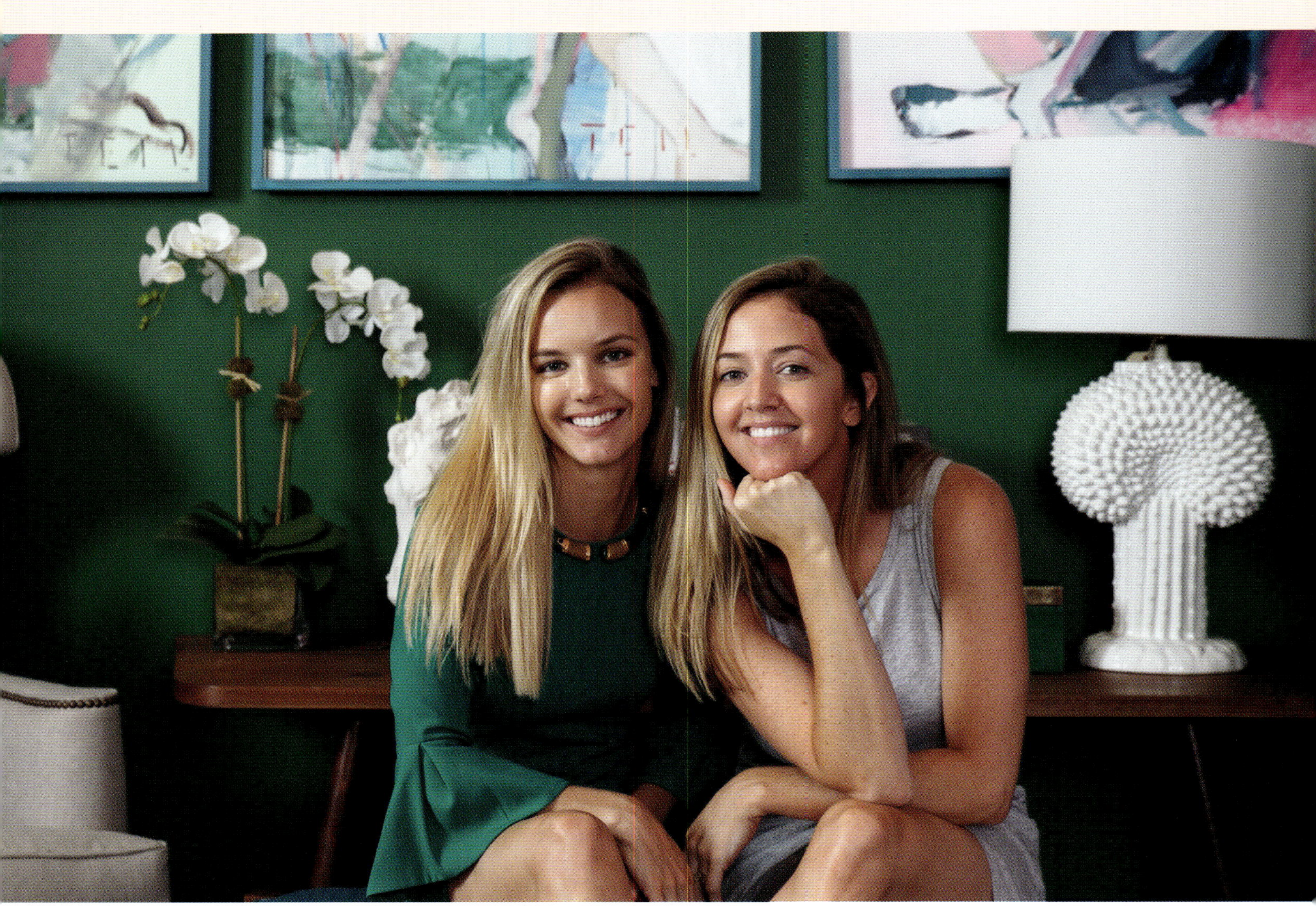

THE TEAM

Teil readily attributes credit to her younger sister, Laura Lea, for much of her success. As Teil creates the artwork, Laura Lea does the rest. From the beginning, Laura Lea has aggressively seized every opportunity to market Teil's work, accommodate customers, manage packaging and shipping, and arise to the occasion of any need that emerges. Most importantly, Laura Lea offers honest feedback about her work. The sisters keep each other grounded in their faith, which they agree is the thing that bonds them the most. Teil and Laura Lea have almost perfectly complementary talents: Teil is the creative, while Laura Lea provides energy, organization, and a business mind to the operation. All in all, the sisters share a sweet relationship that has translated beautifully into a business, which allows them to work together doing what they love.

CHAPTER ONE

FIGURES

LOOKING BACK

at my art education at Auburn University, one of my favorite courses was figure drawing. My interest extended several years later when my shared studio space offered the same class. I limited my color palette to two colors per canvas and created about twelve "figure studies" in the fall of 2013. Since then, I have continued to paint the female form using harmonious yet bold color blocks to represent light, shadow, and space.

"Dainty Waiting" 2017

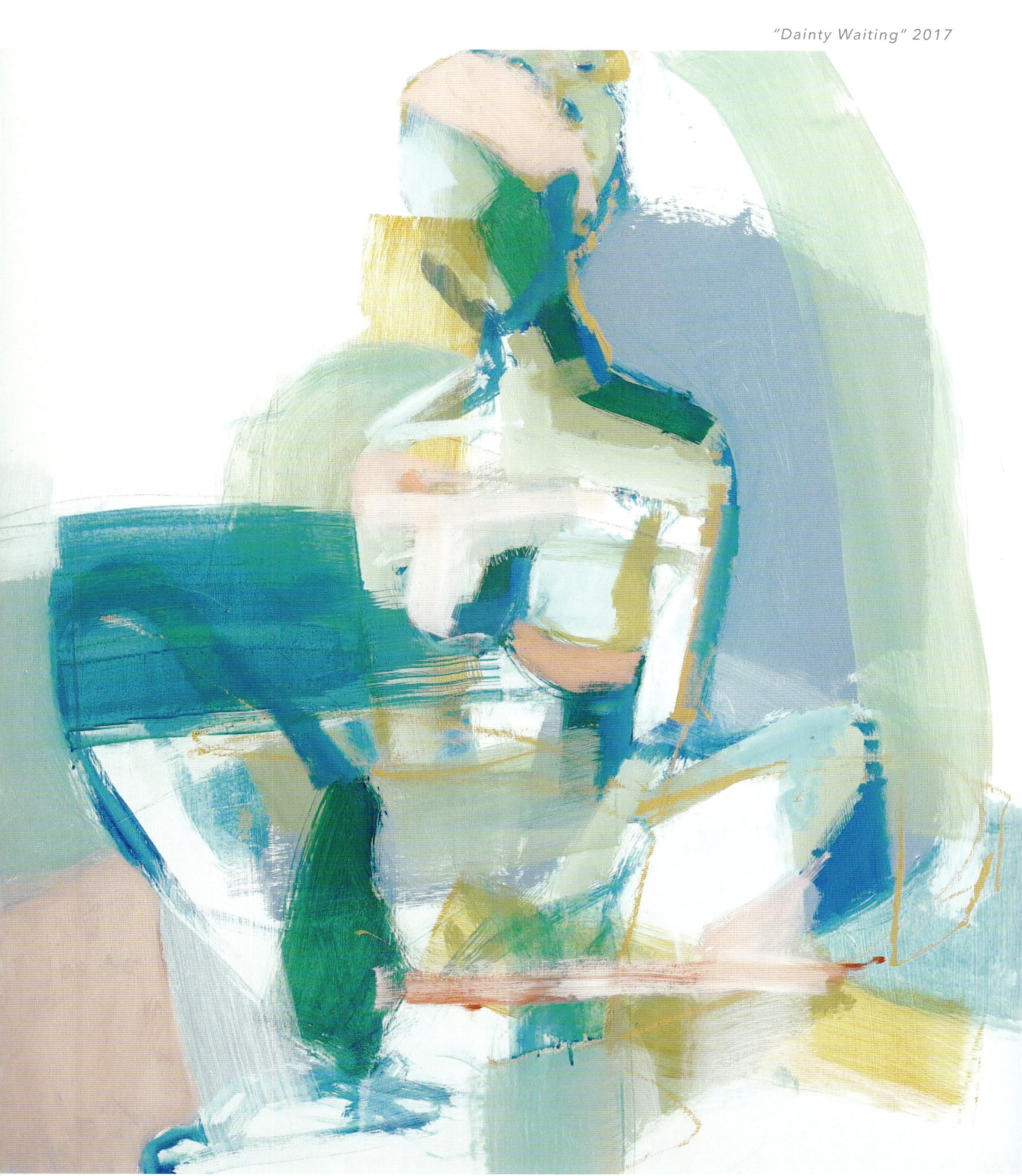

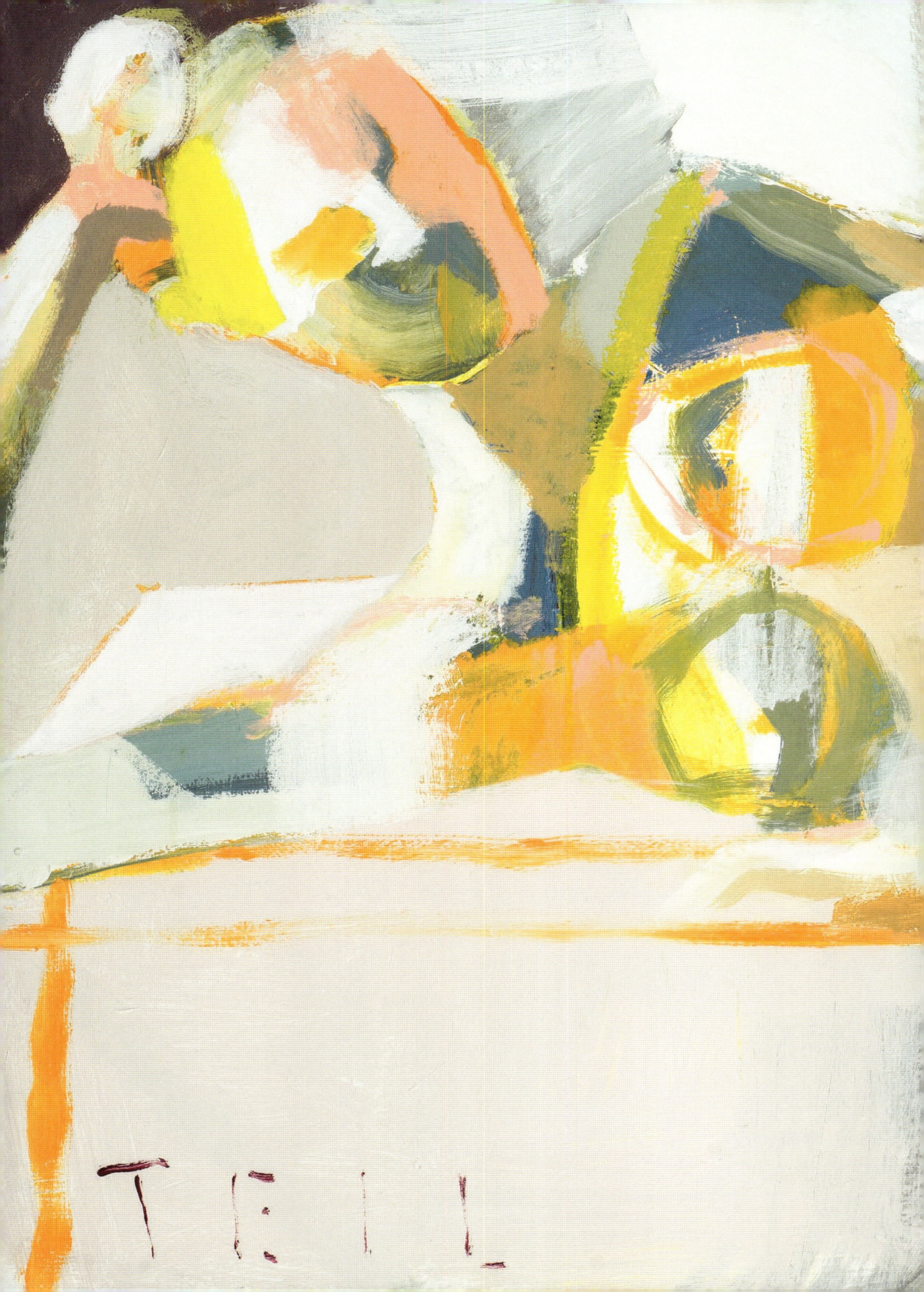
TELL

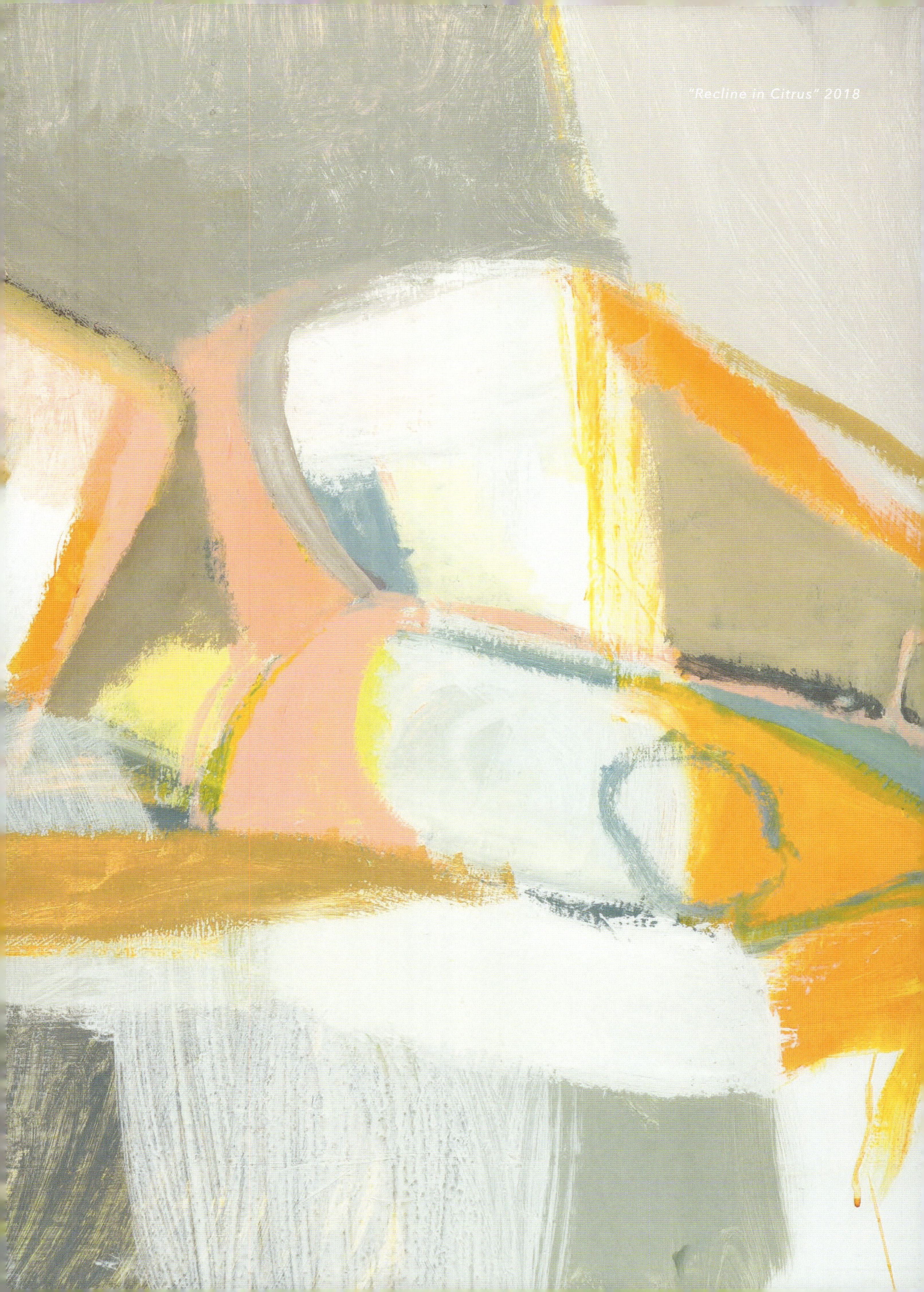
"Recline in Citrus" 2018

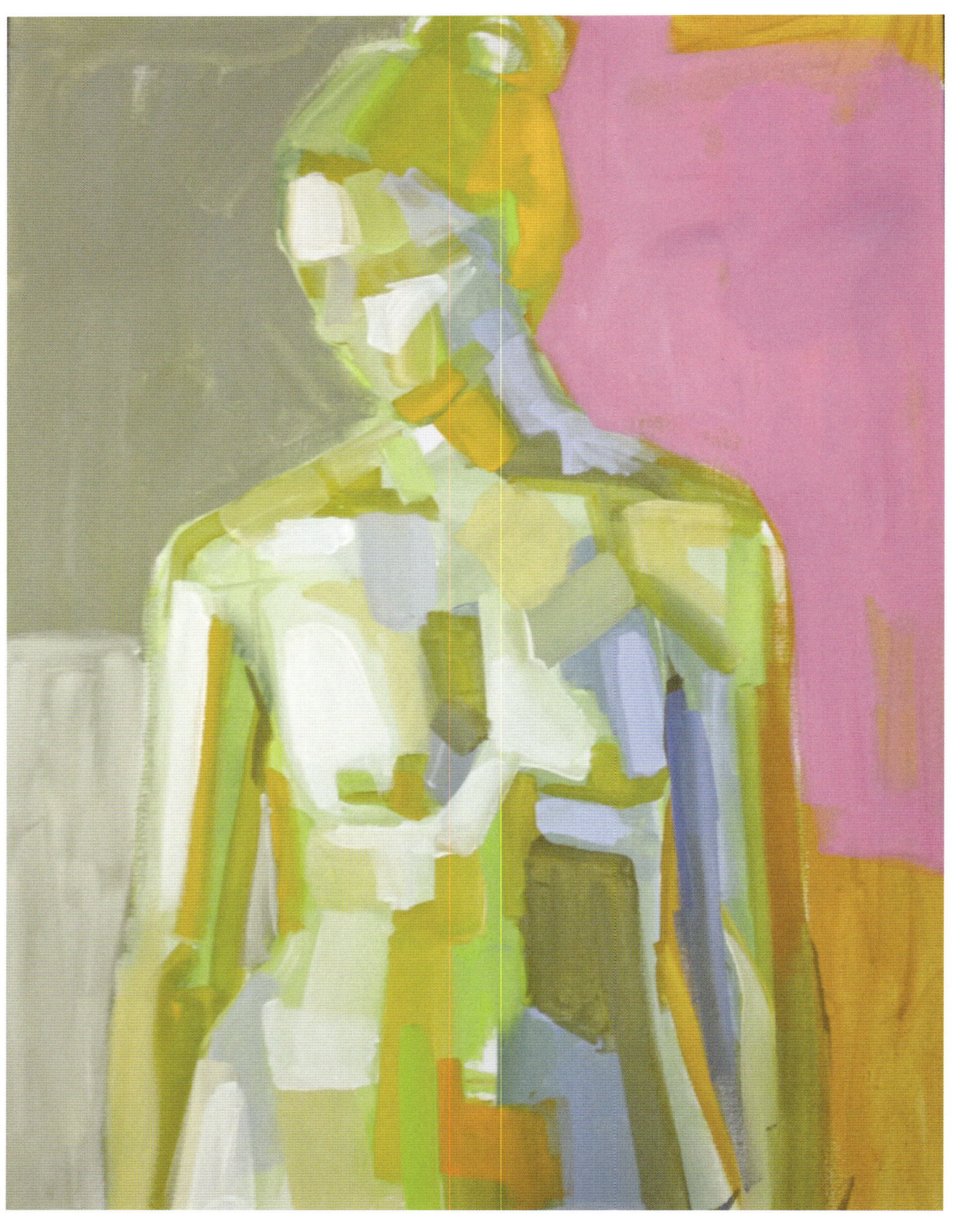

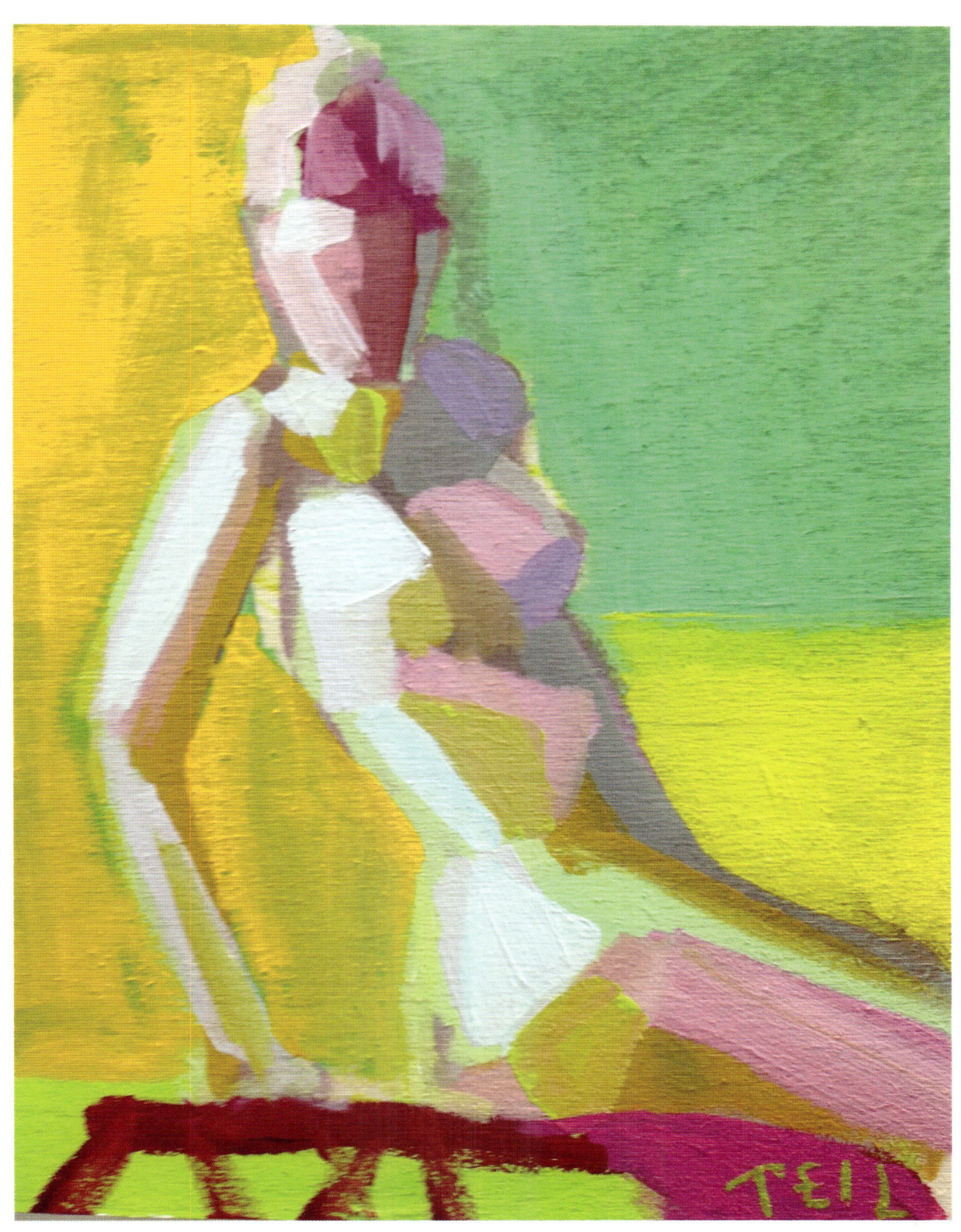
TEIL

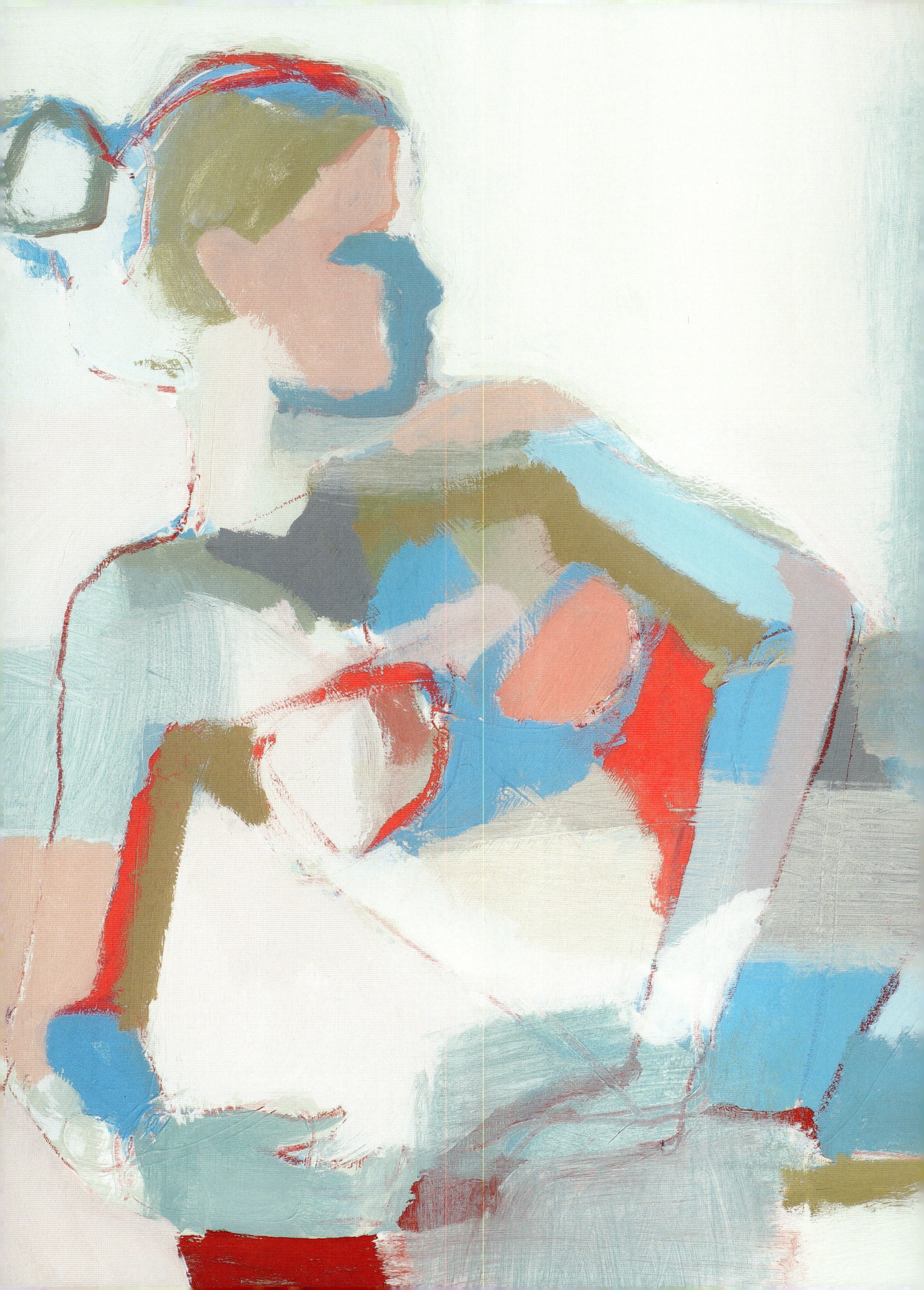

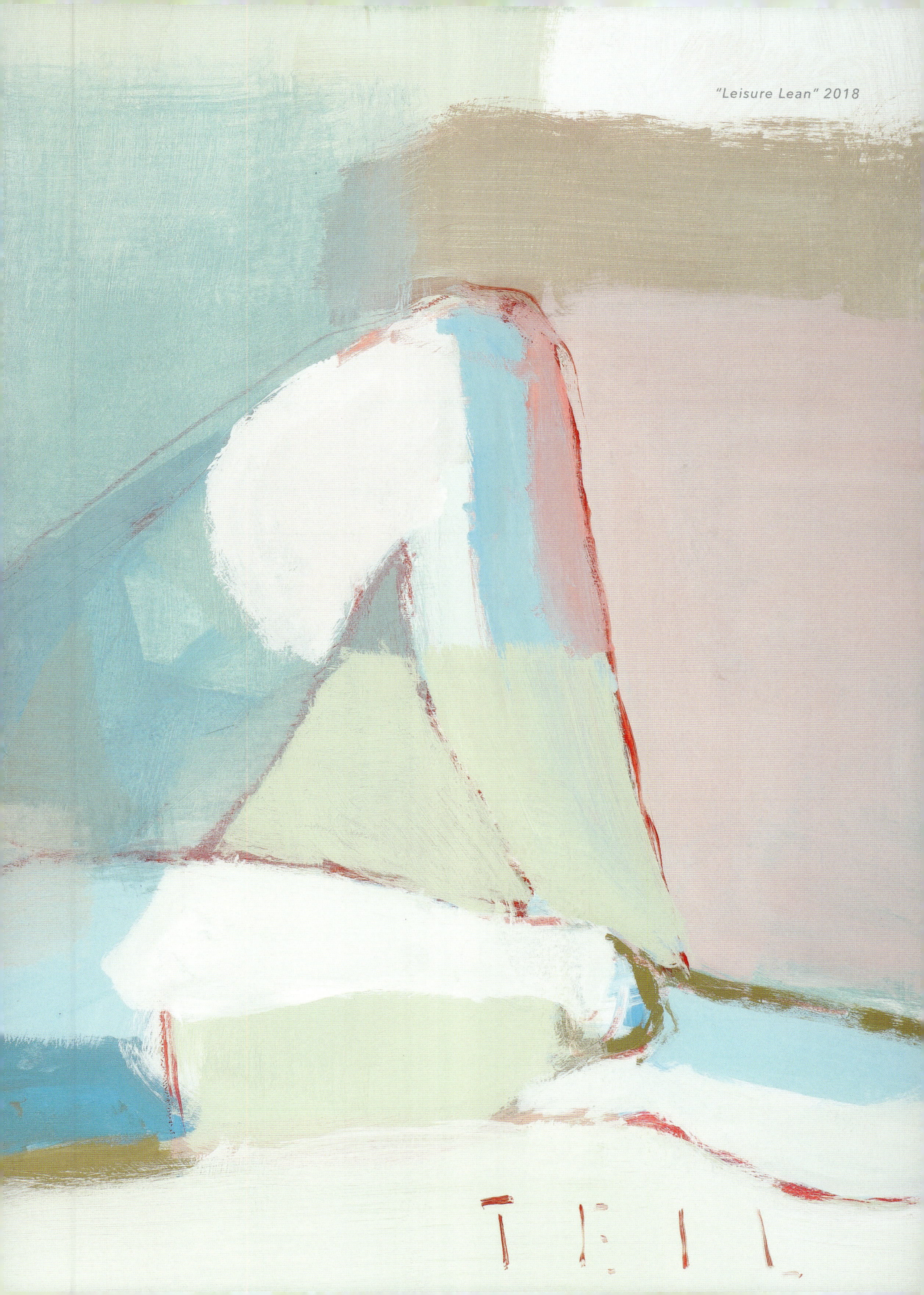
"Leisure Lean" 2018
TEIL

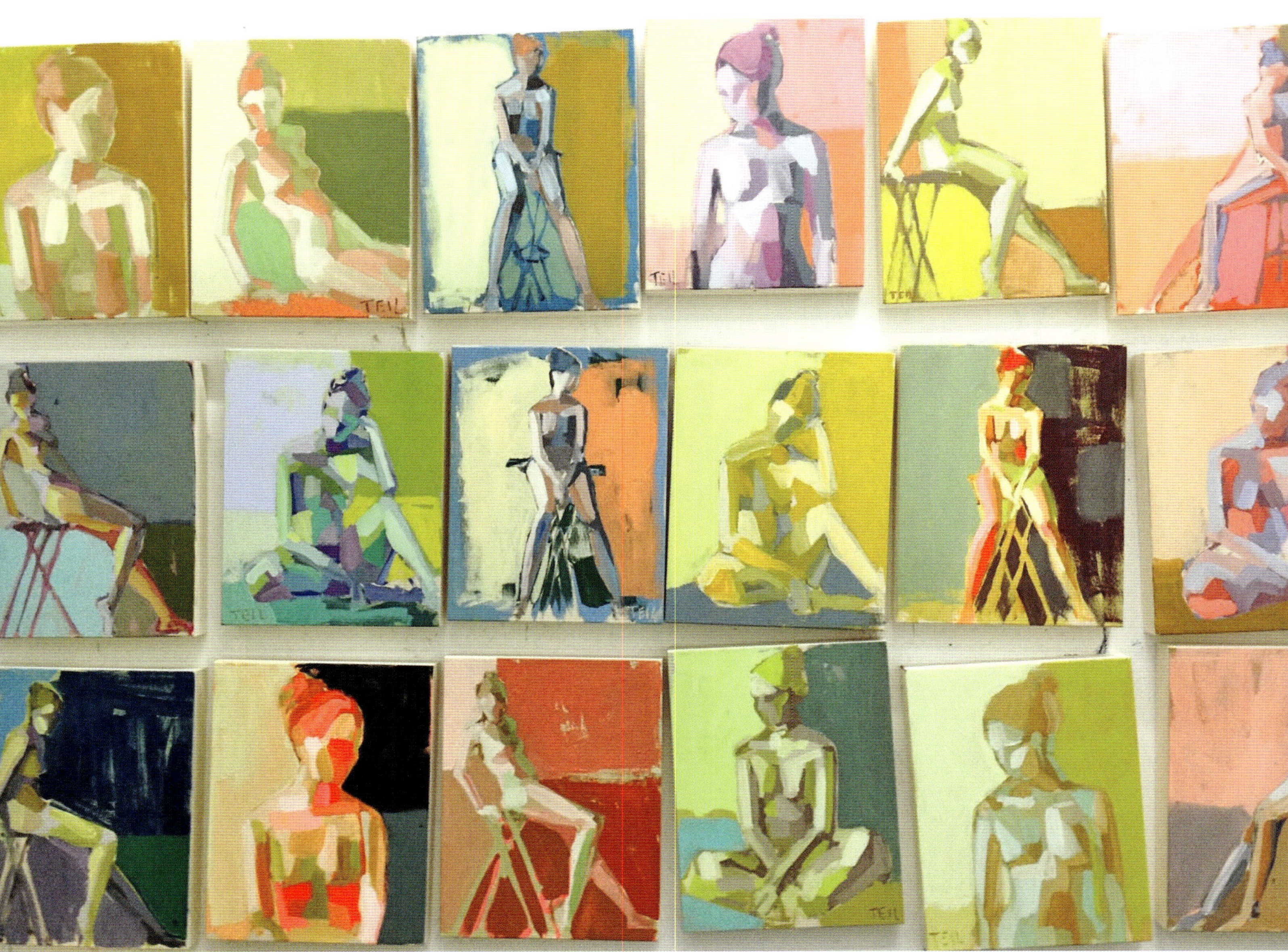

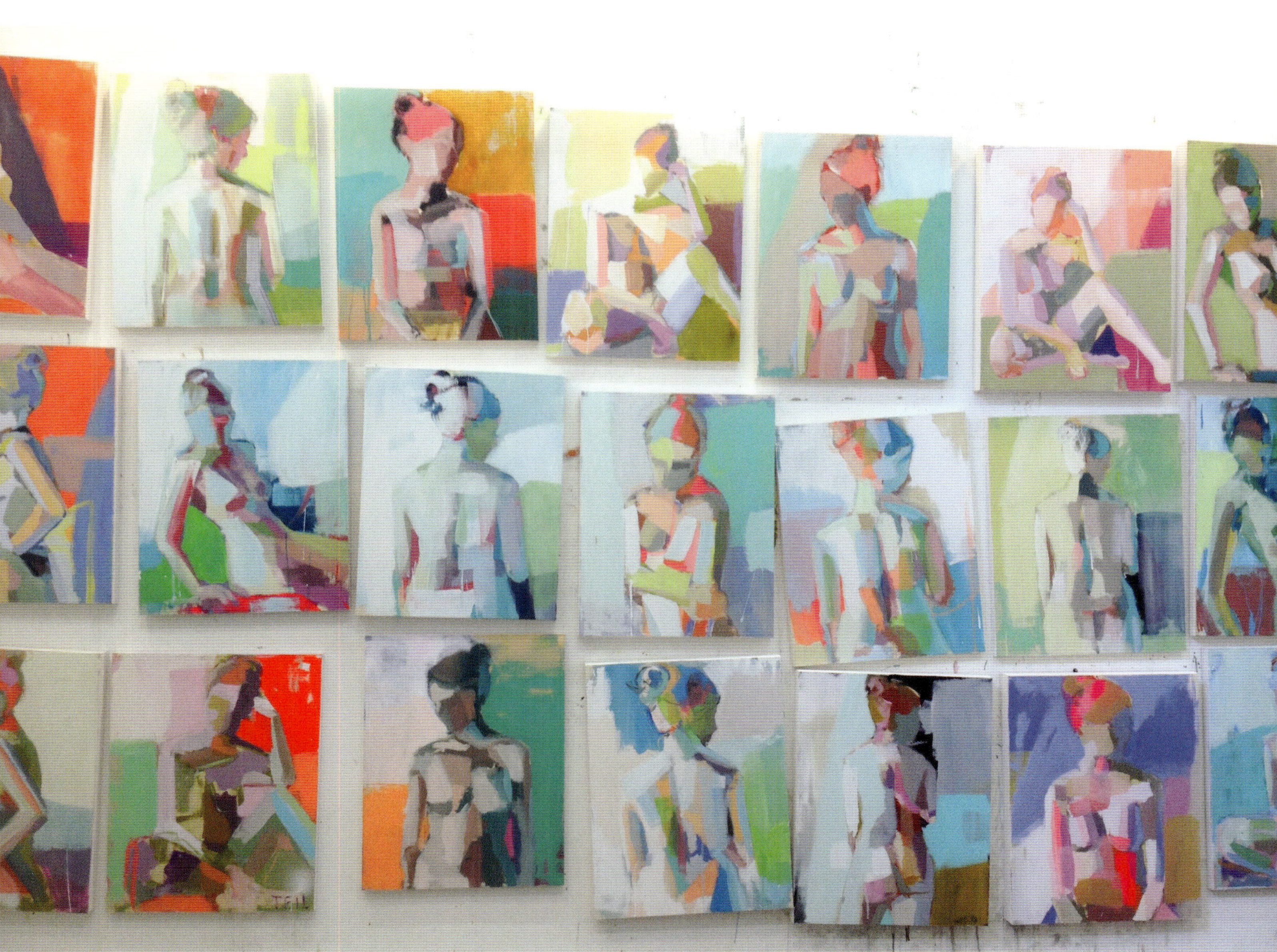

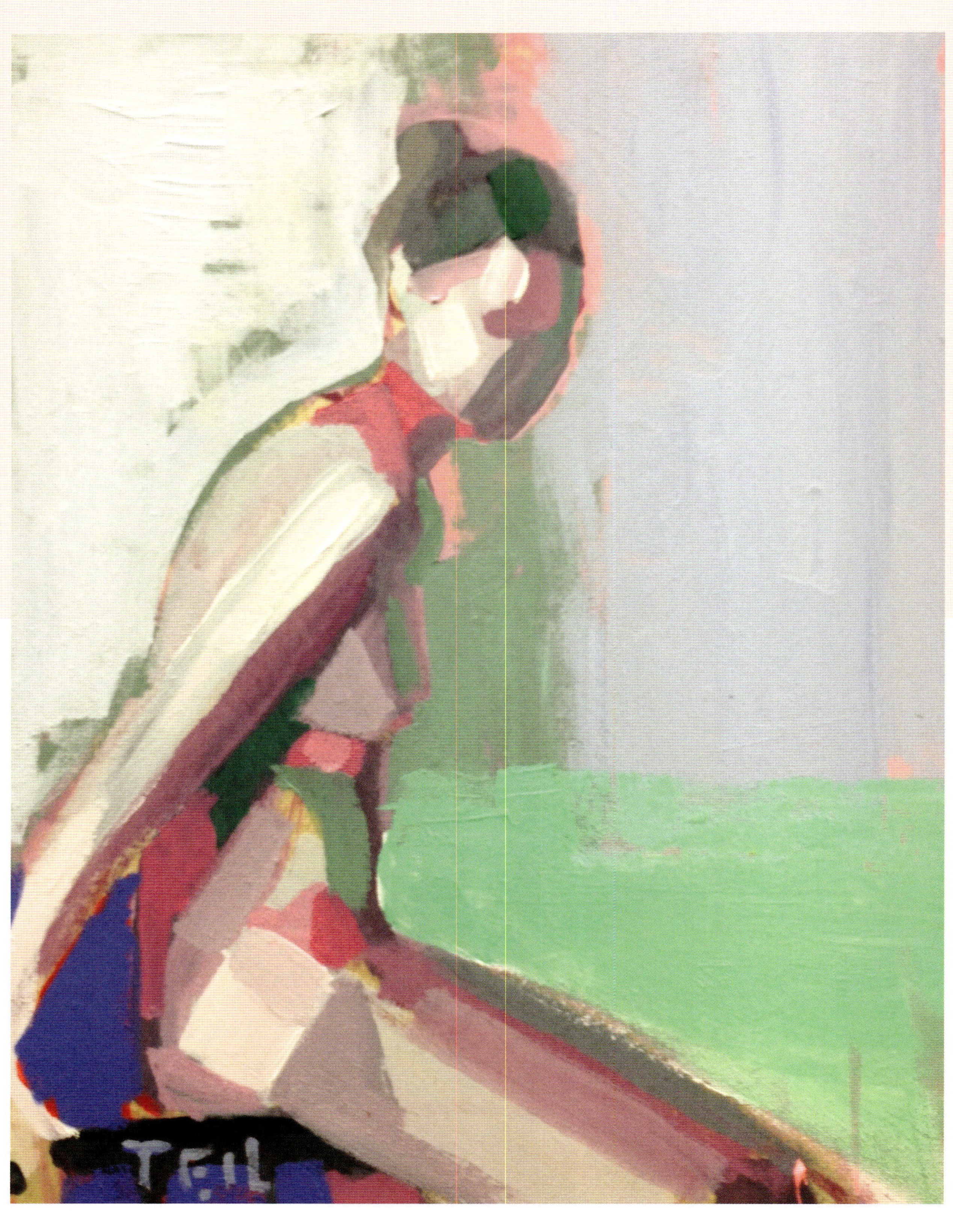
TEIL

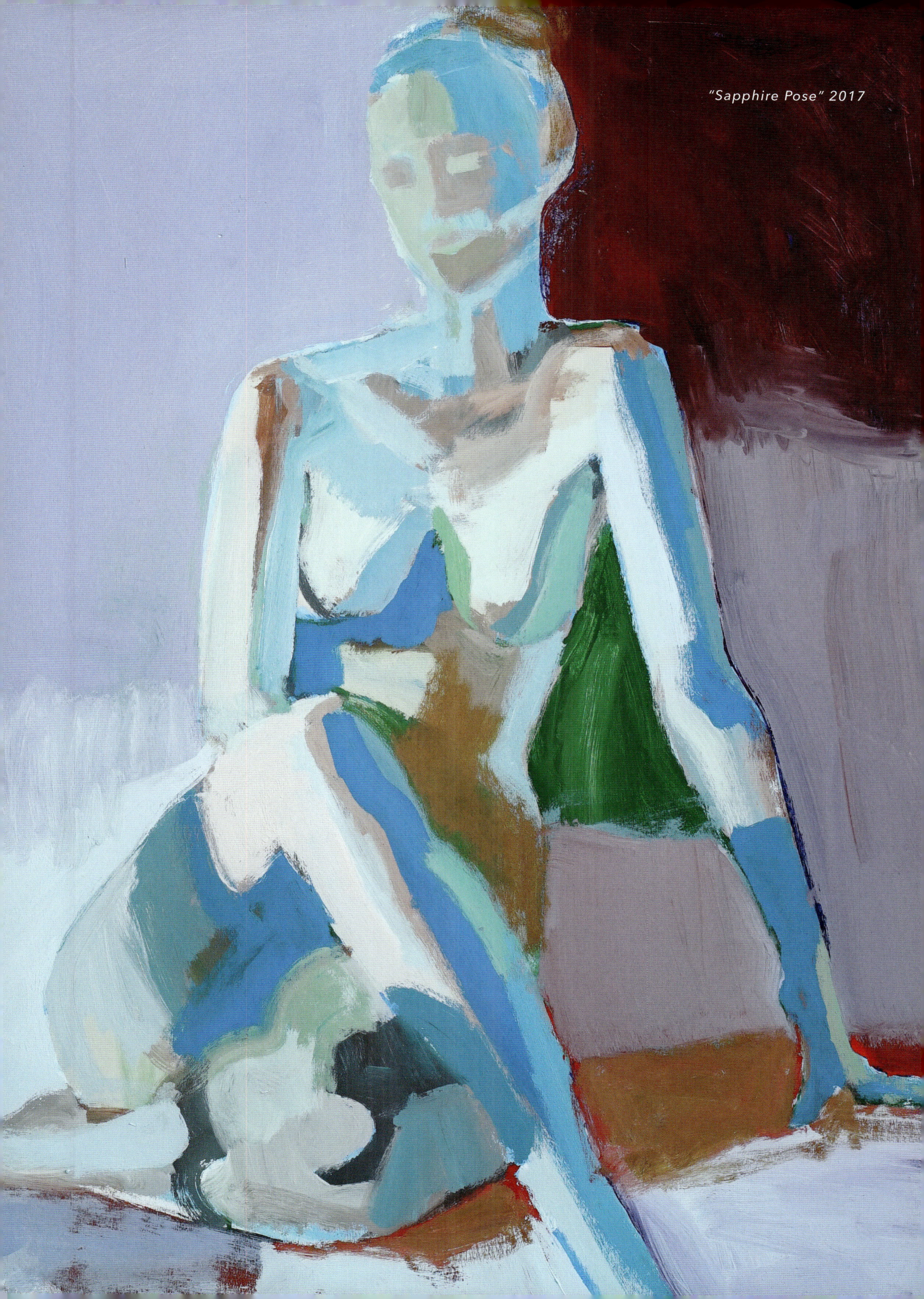

"Sapphire Pose" 2017

"Summer Figure Study No. 25" 2017

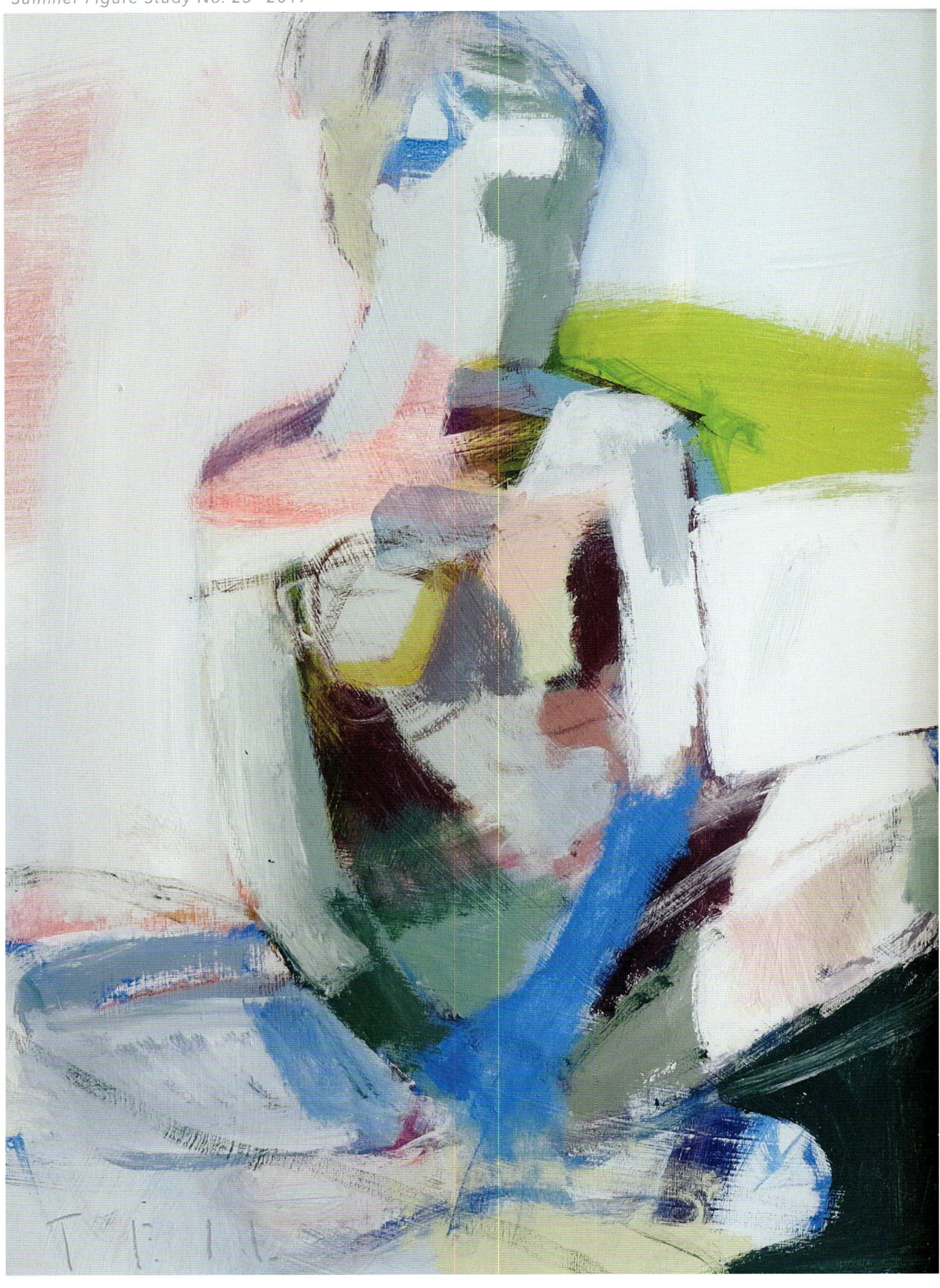

"Summer Figure Study No. 16" 2017

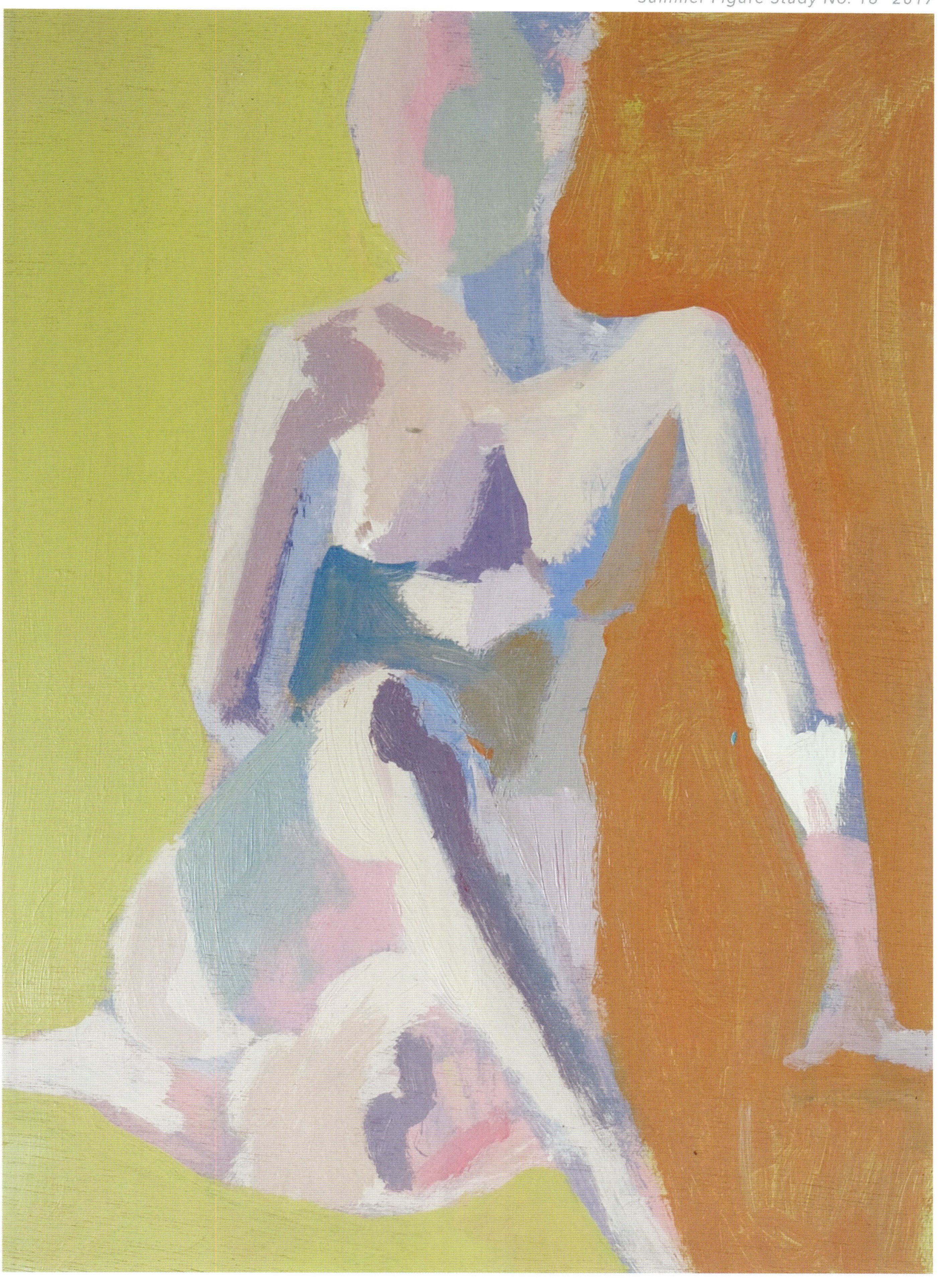

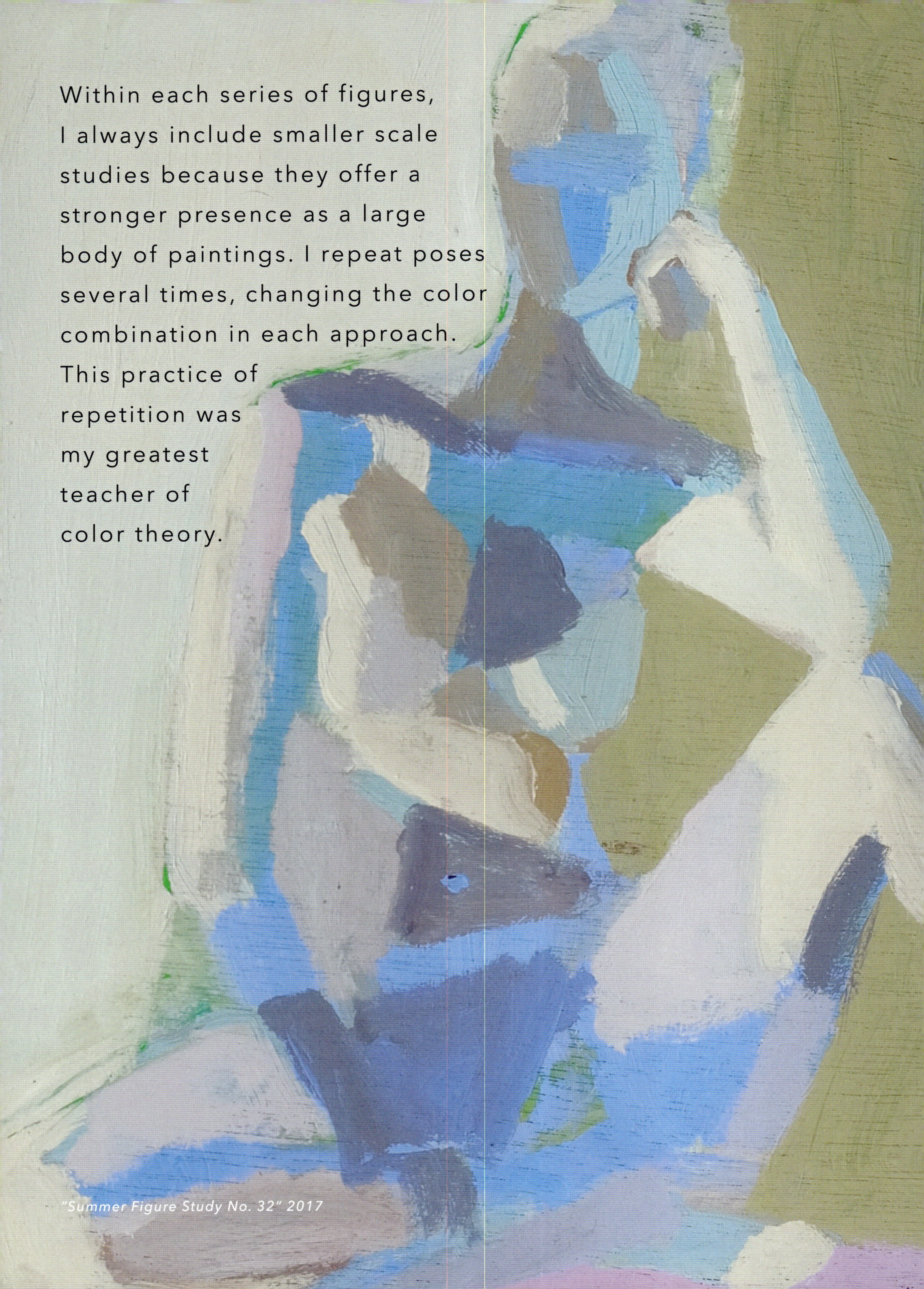

Within each series of figures, I always include smaller scale studies because they offer a stronger presence as a large body of paintings. I repeat poses several times, changing the color combination in each approach. This practice of repetition was my greatest teacher of color theory.

"Summer Figure Study No. 32" 2017

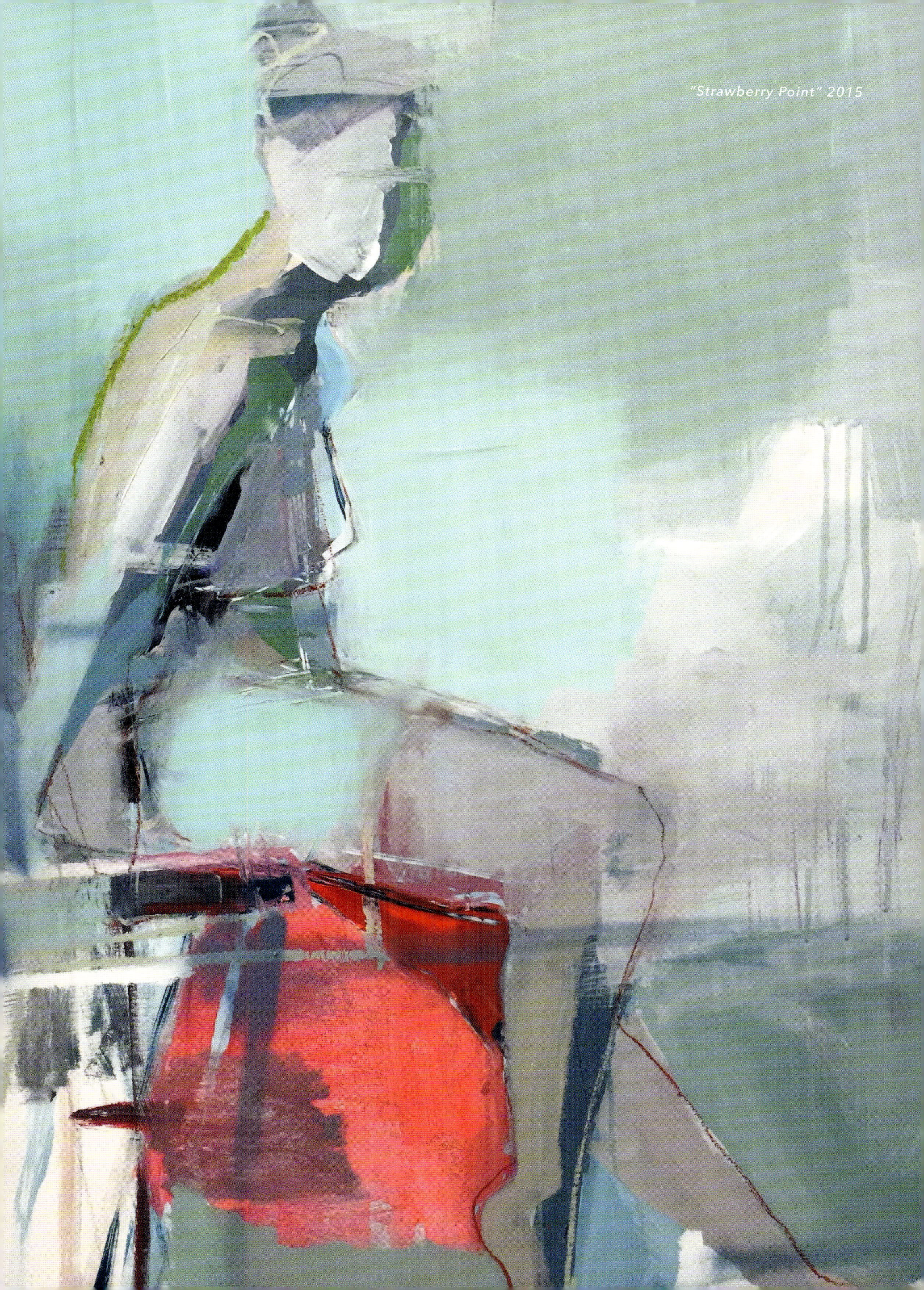

"Strawberry Point" 2015

"Summer Figure Study No. 19" 2017

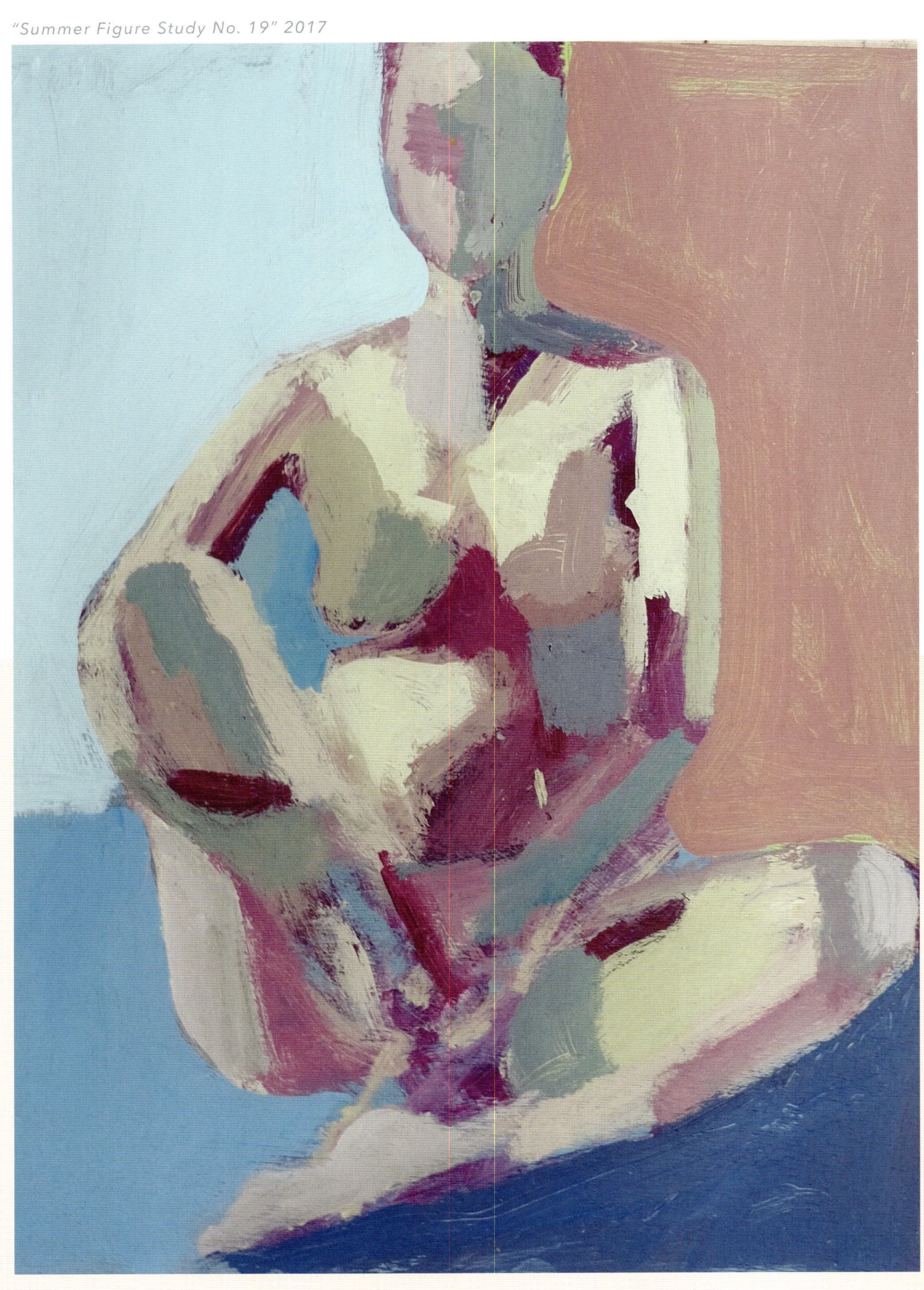

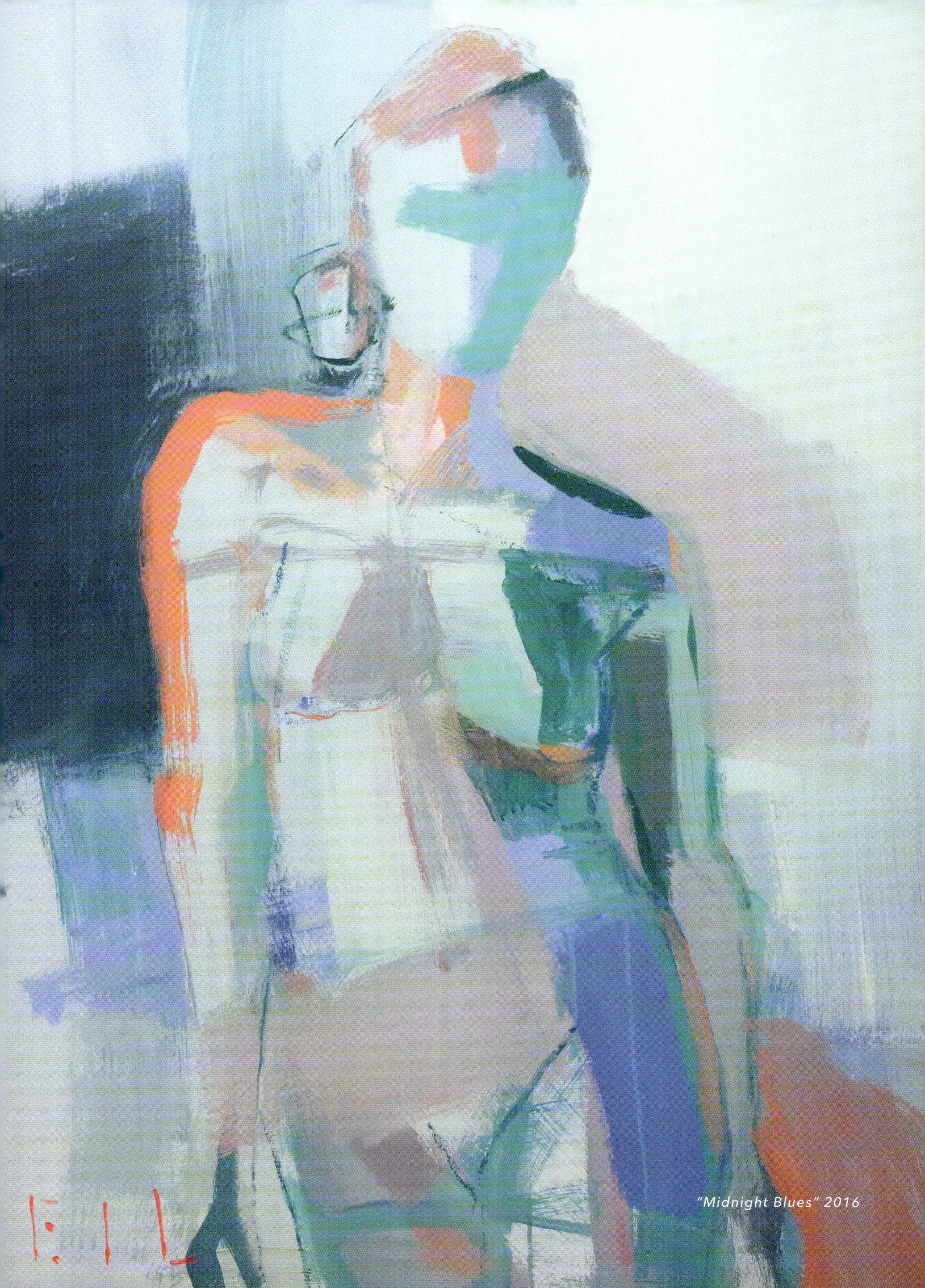

"Midnight Blues" 2016

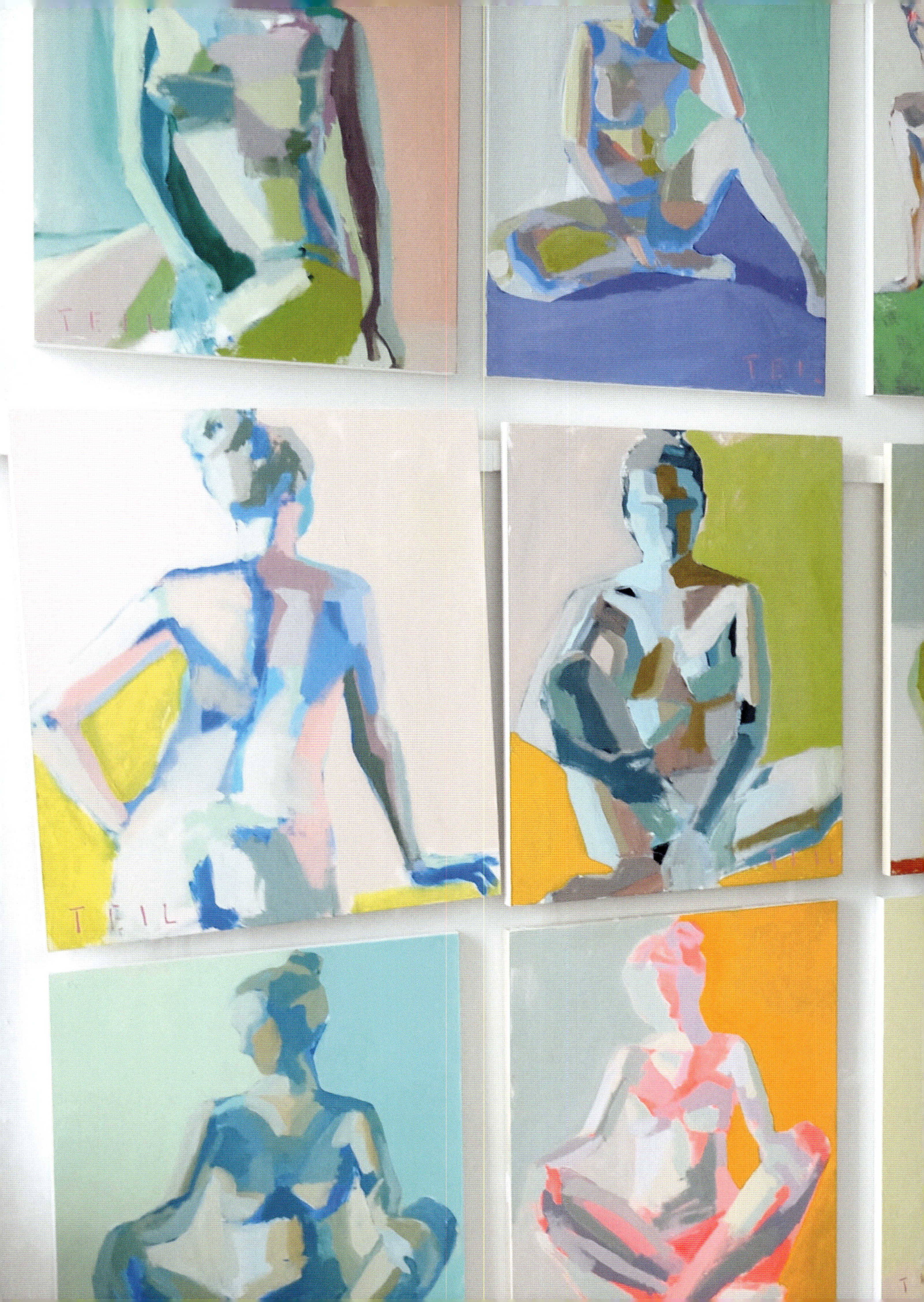
TEIL
TEIL

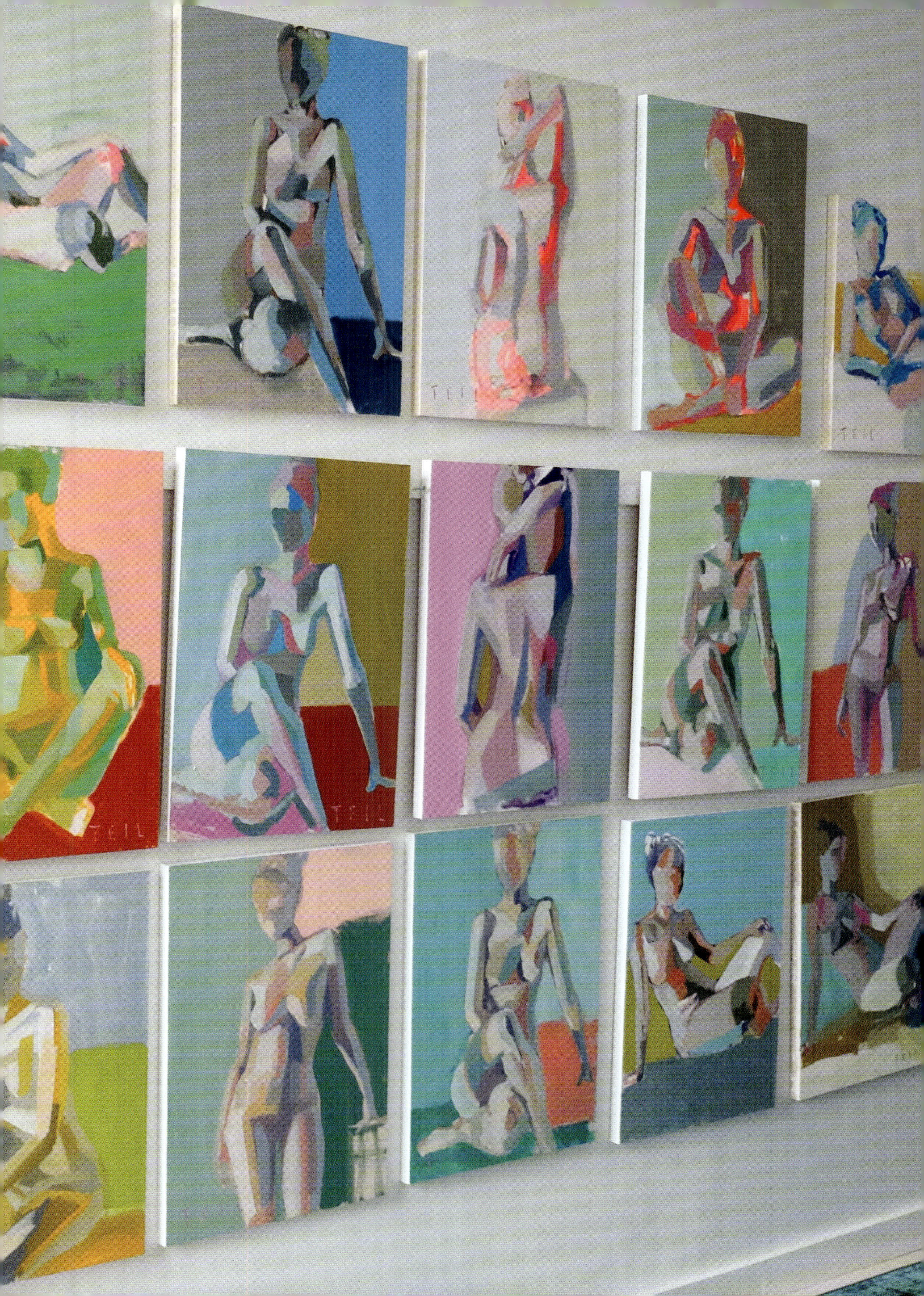
TEIL
TEIL
TEIL
TEIL
TEIL

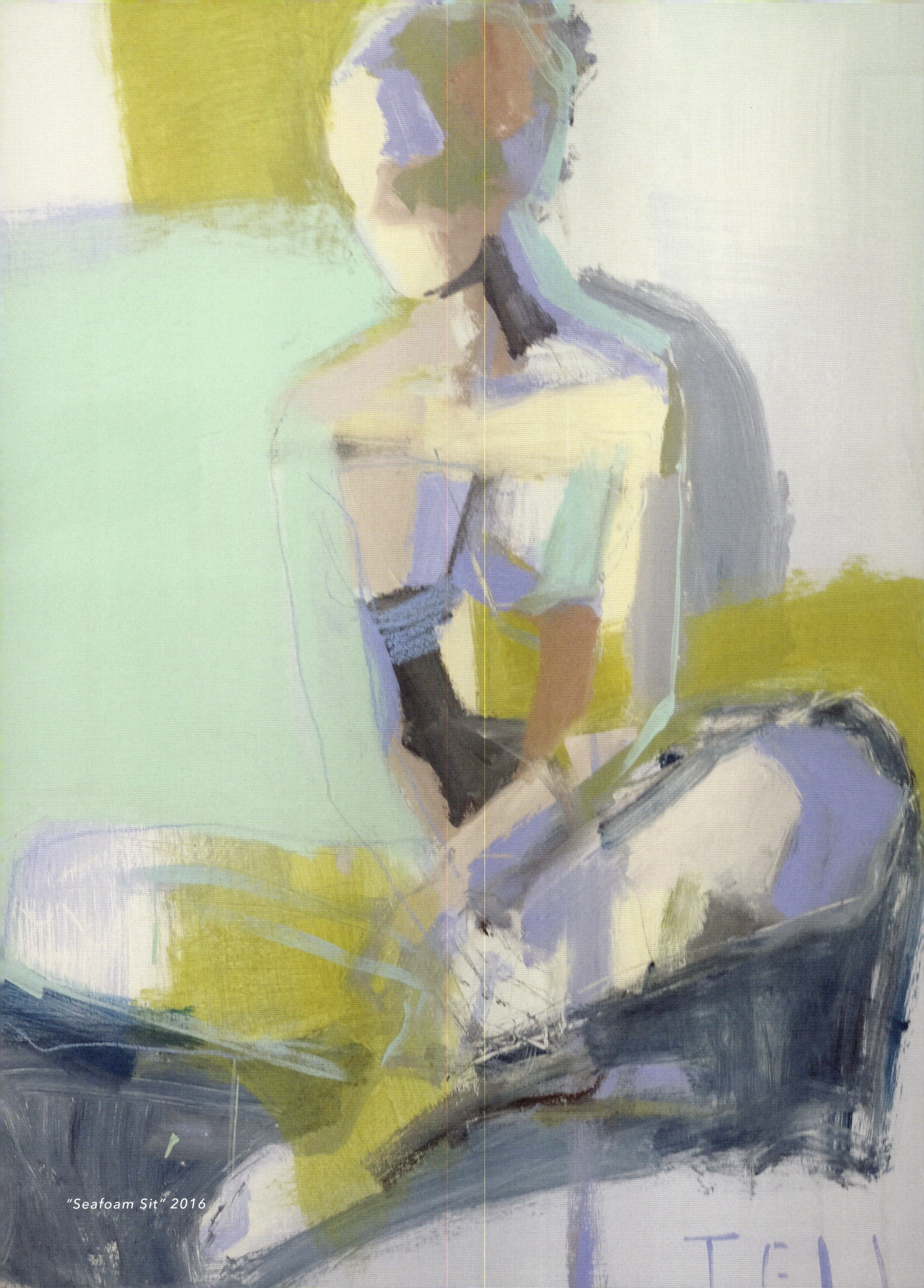

"Seafoam Sit" 2016

"Mauve Air" 2016

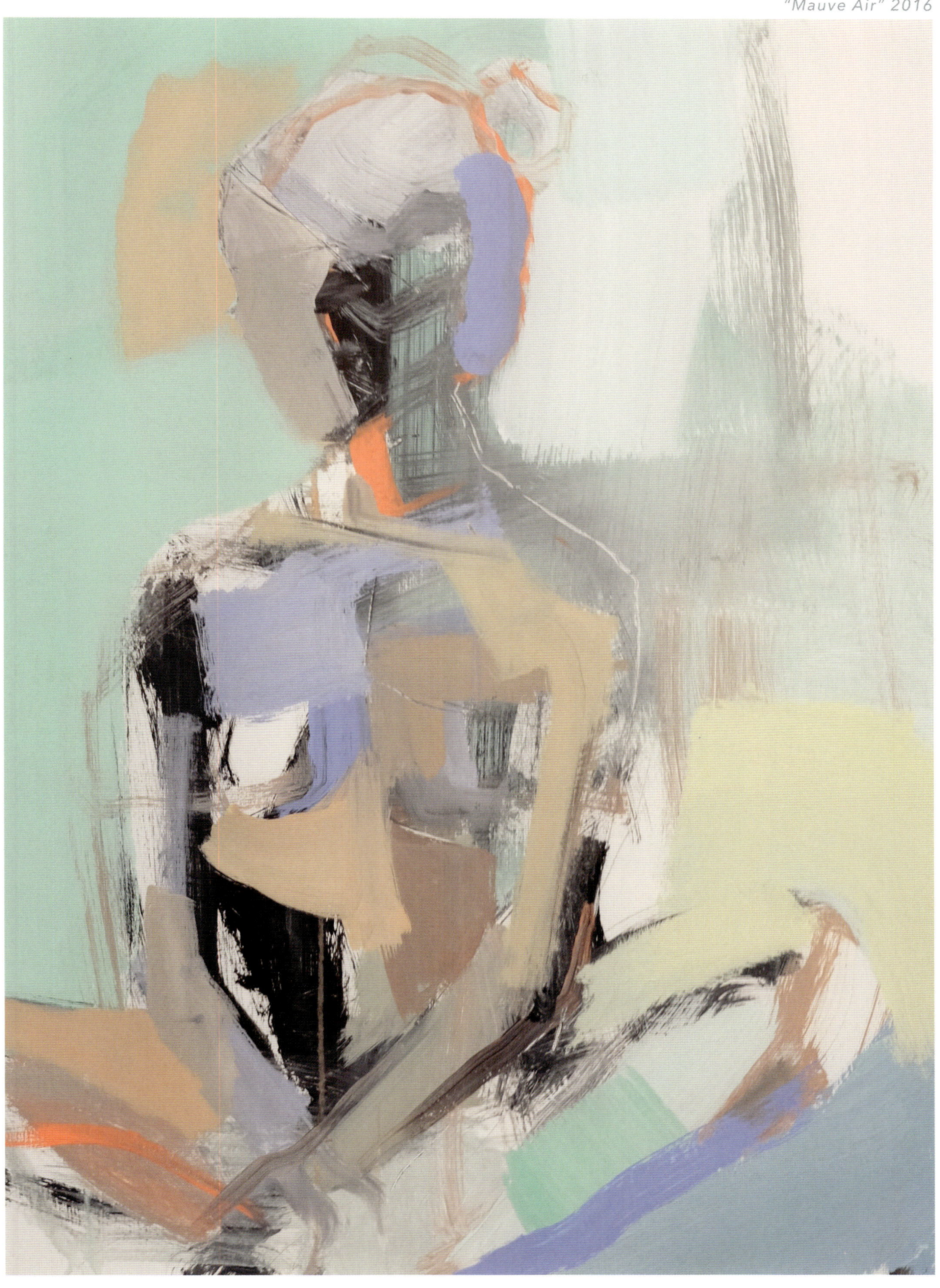

"Hunch I" 2013

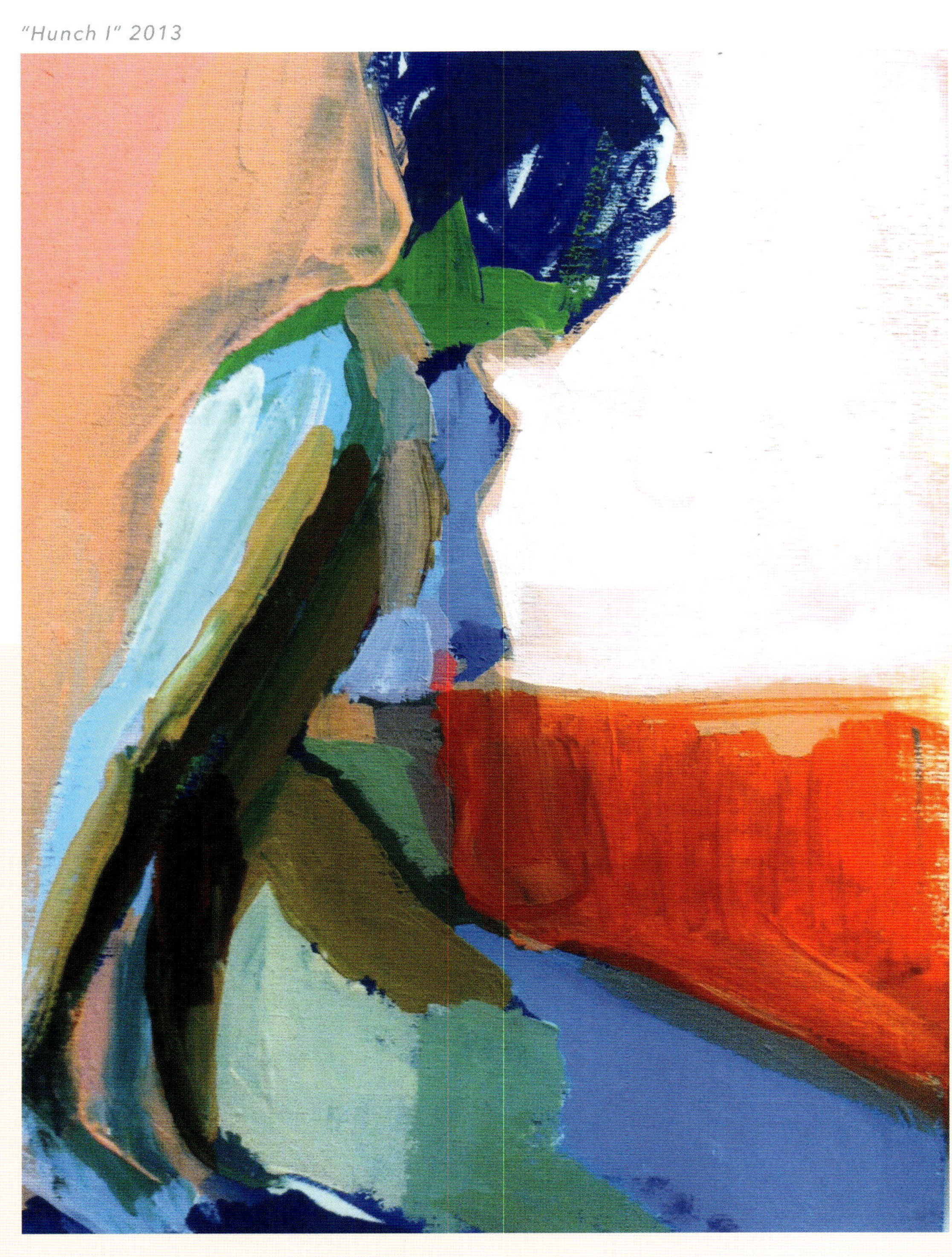

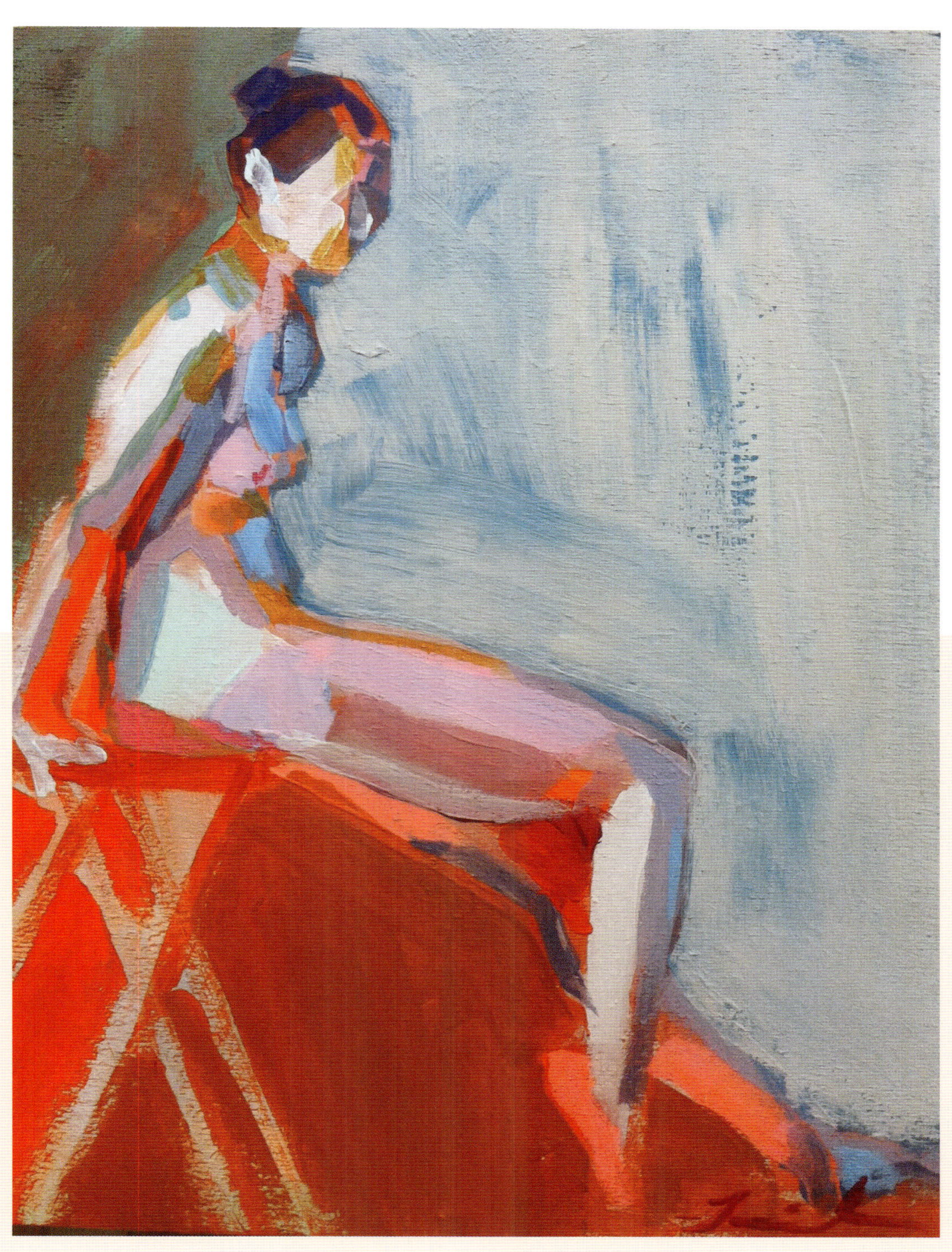

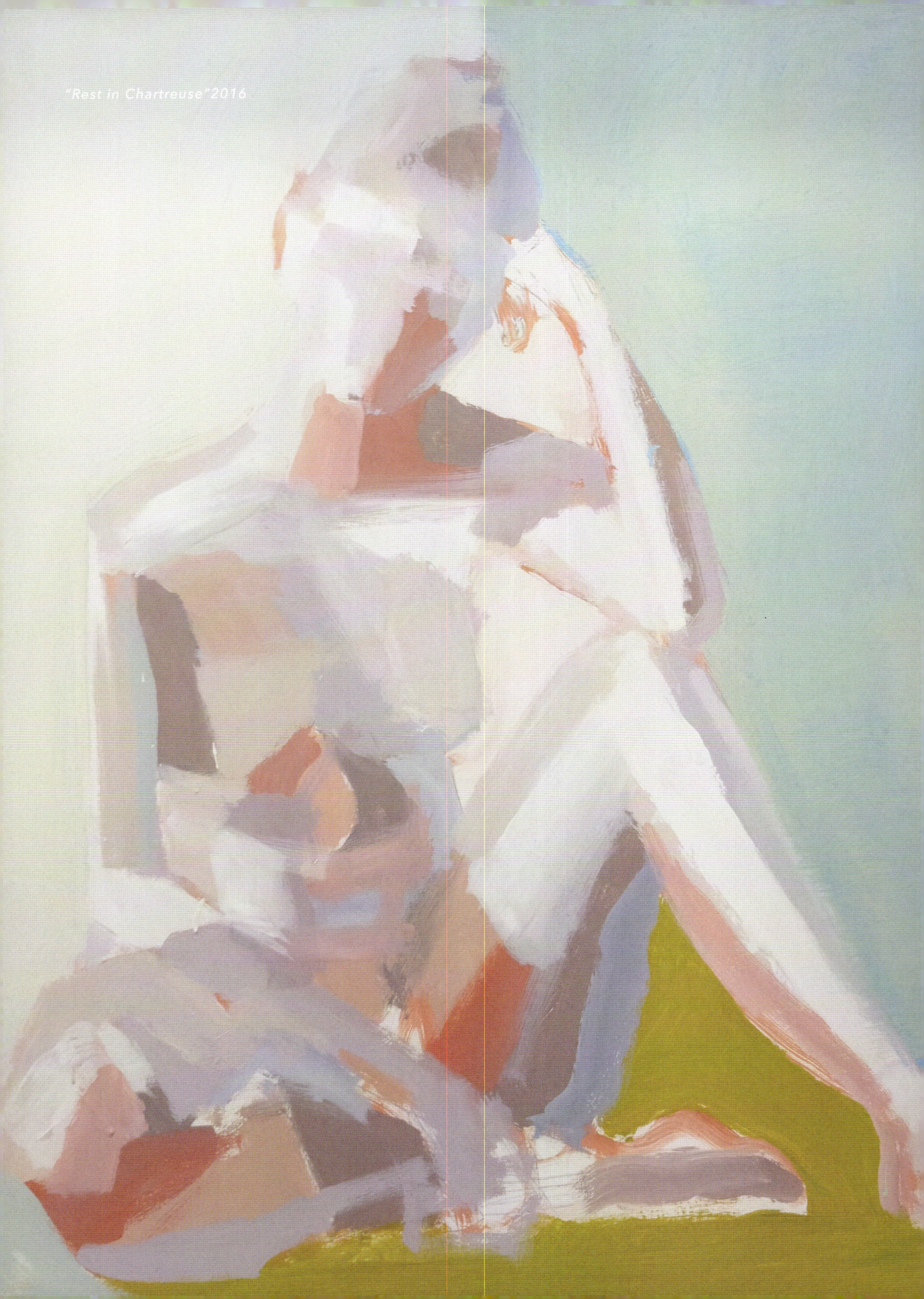

"Rest in Chartreuse" 2016

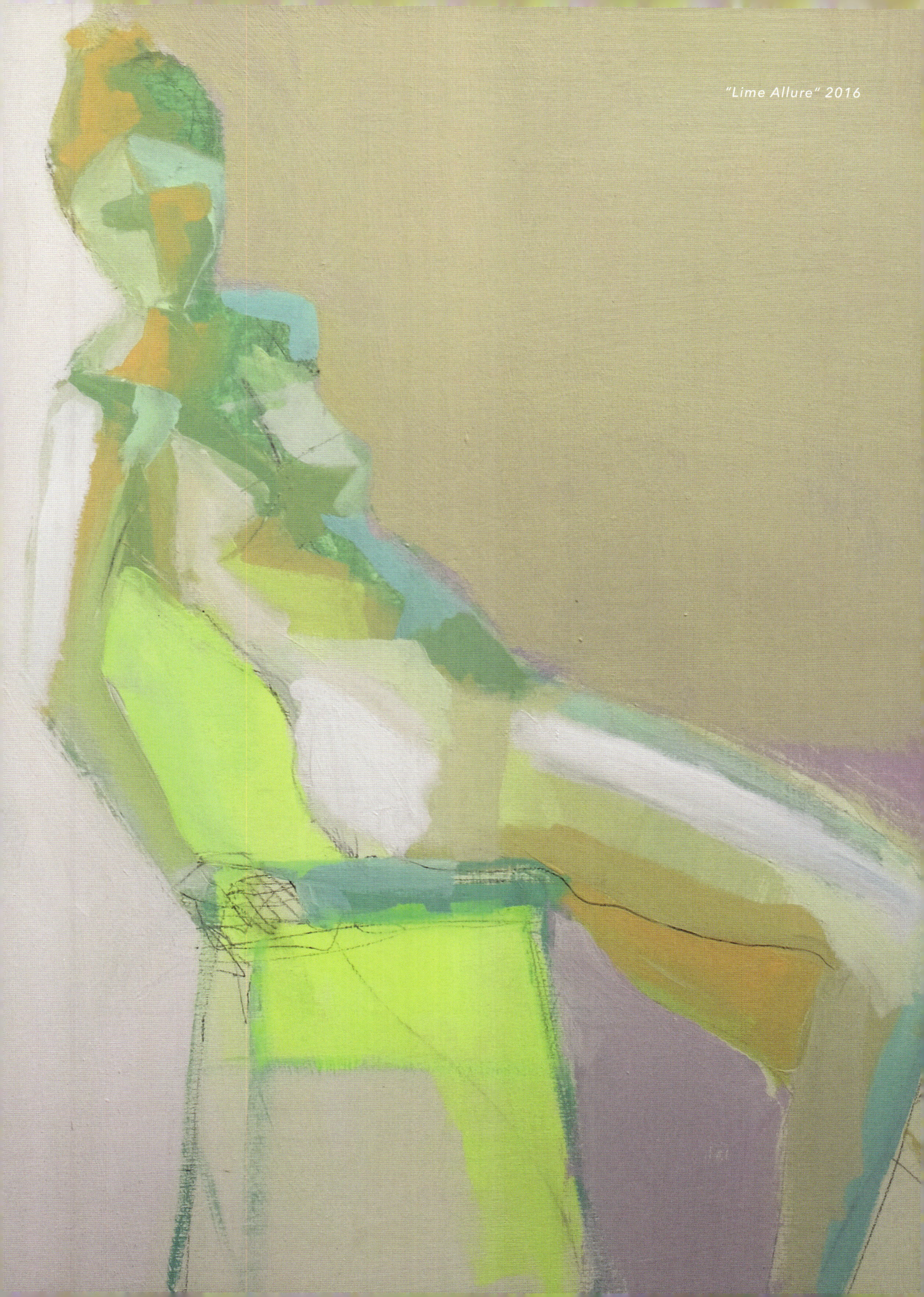

"Lime Allure" 2016

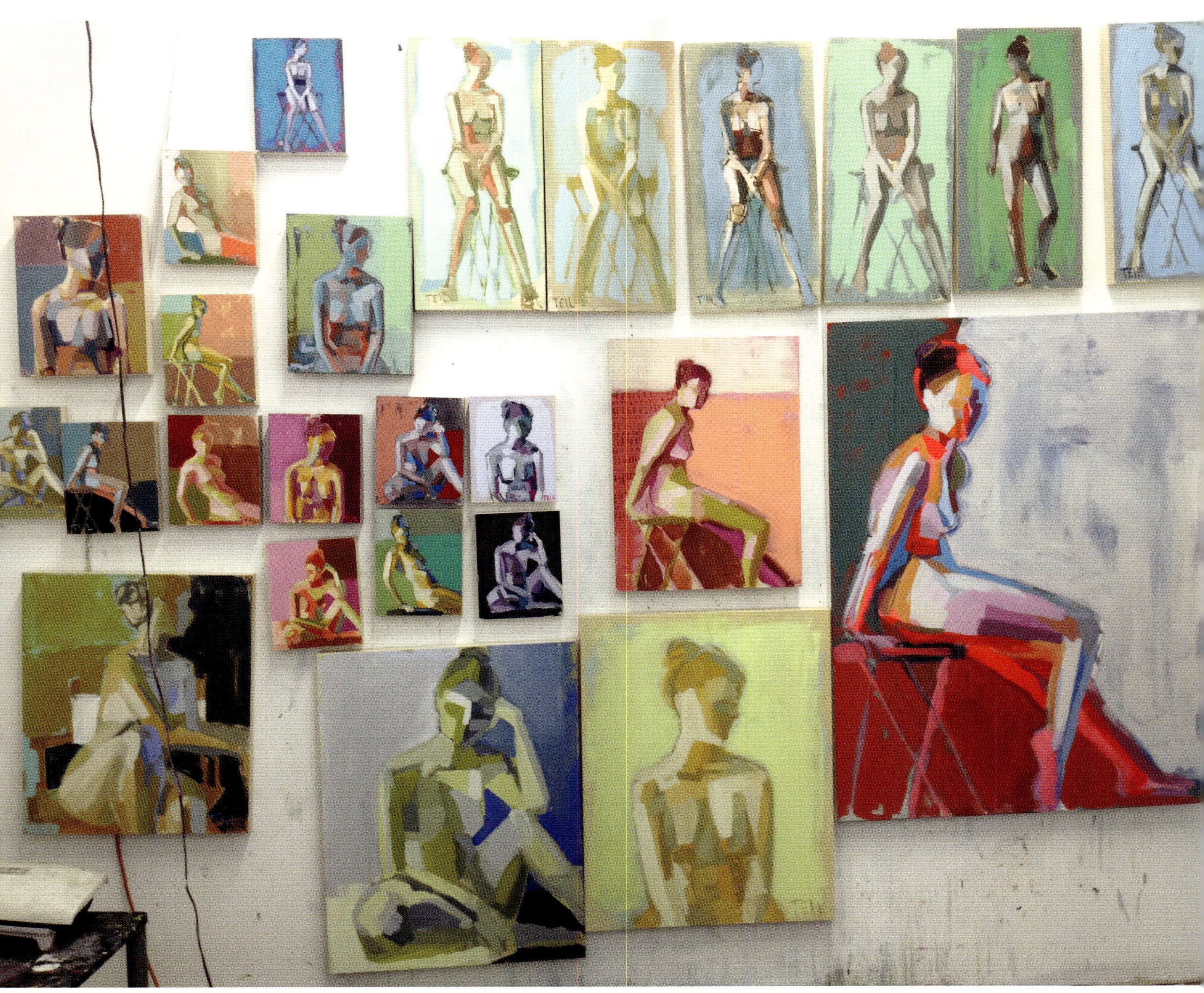

"Cobalt Teal Stare" 2016

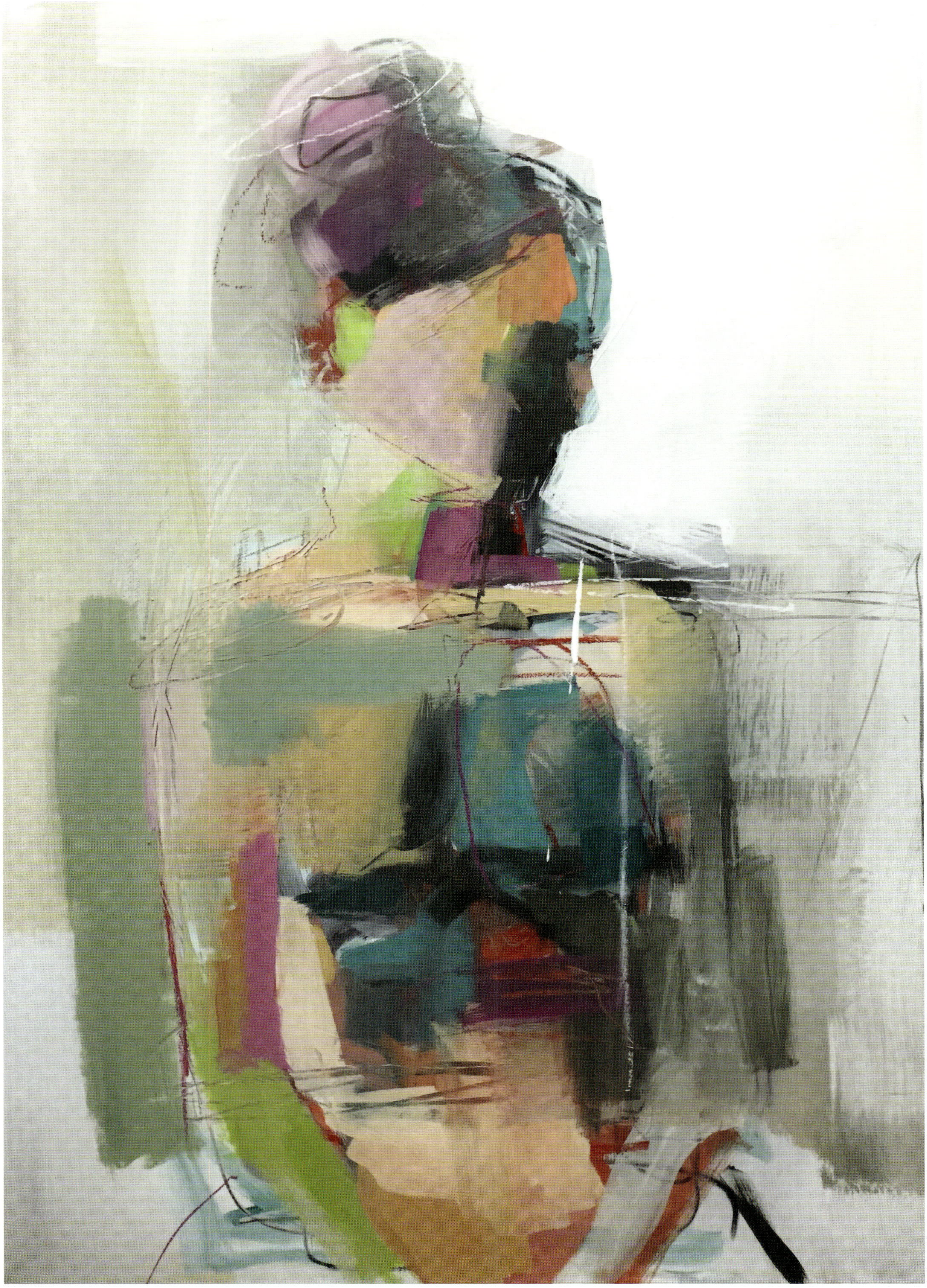

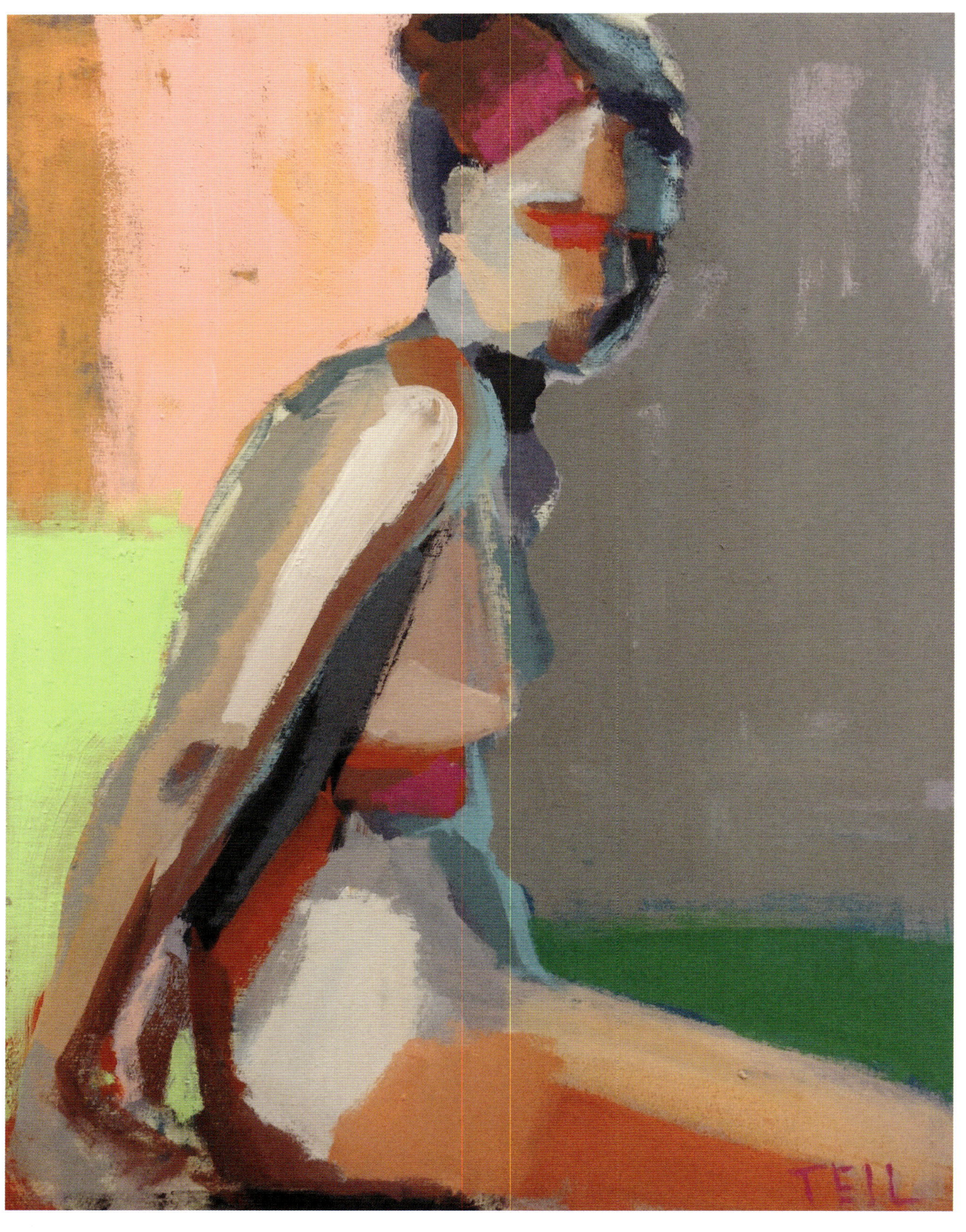
TEIL

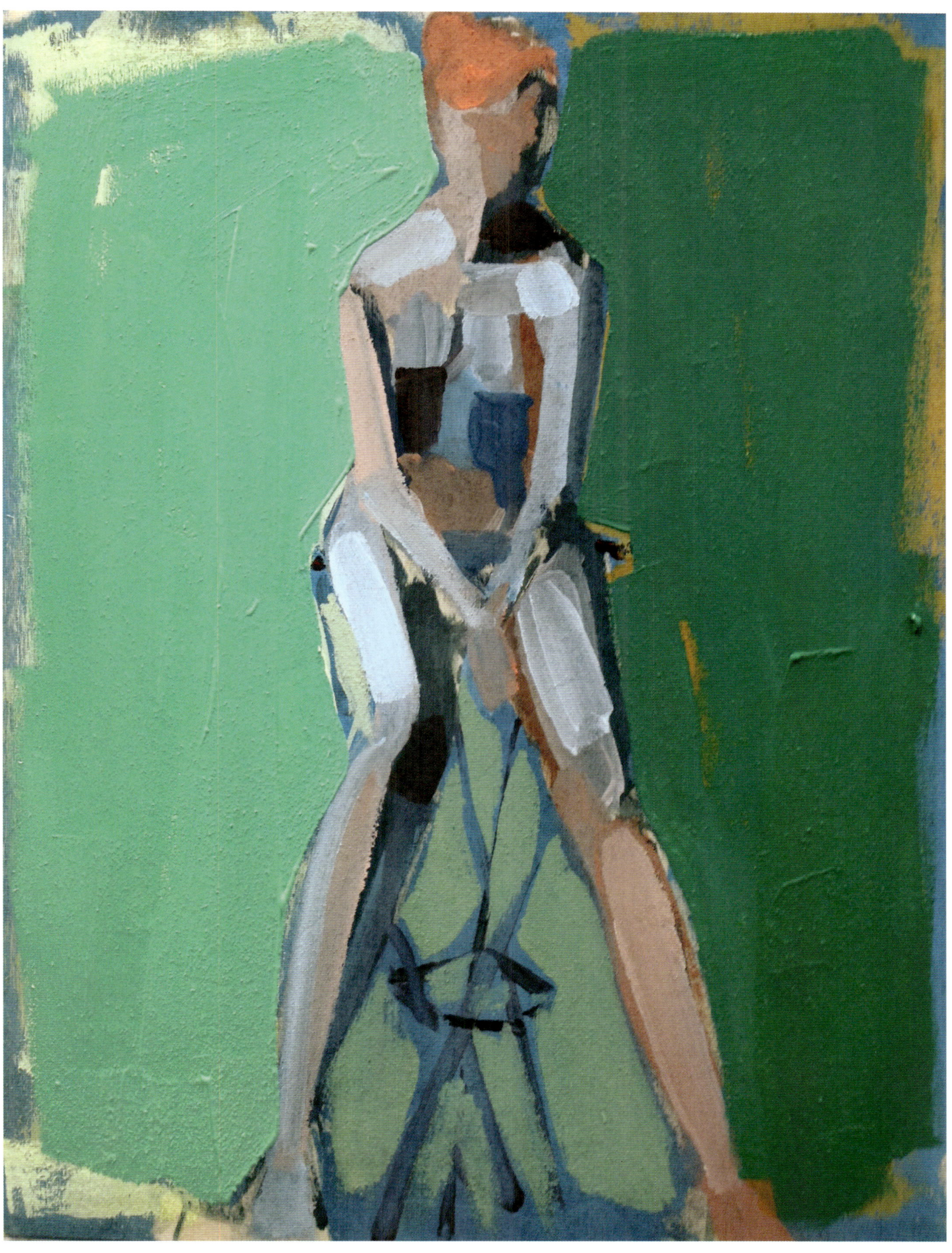

"Cheerful Waiting" 2015

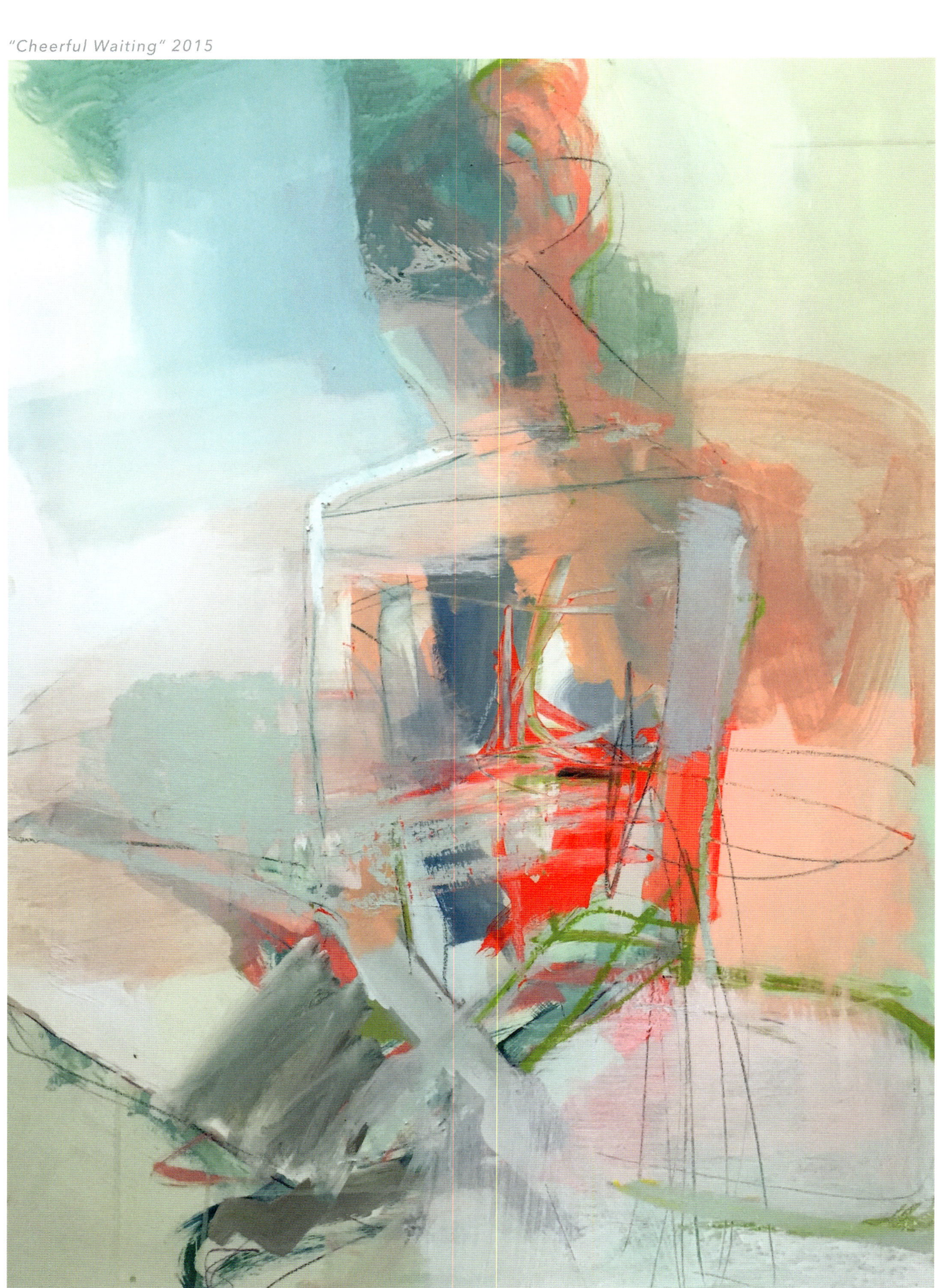

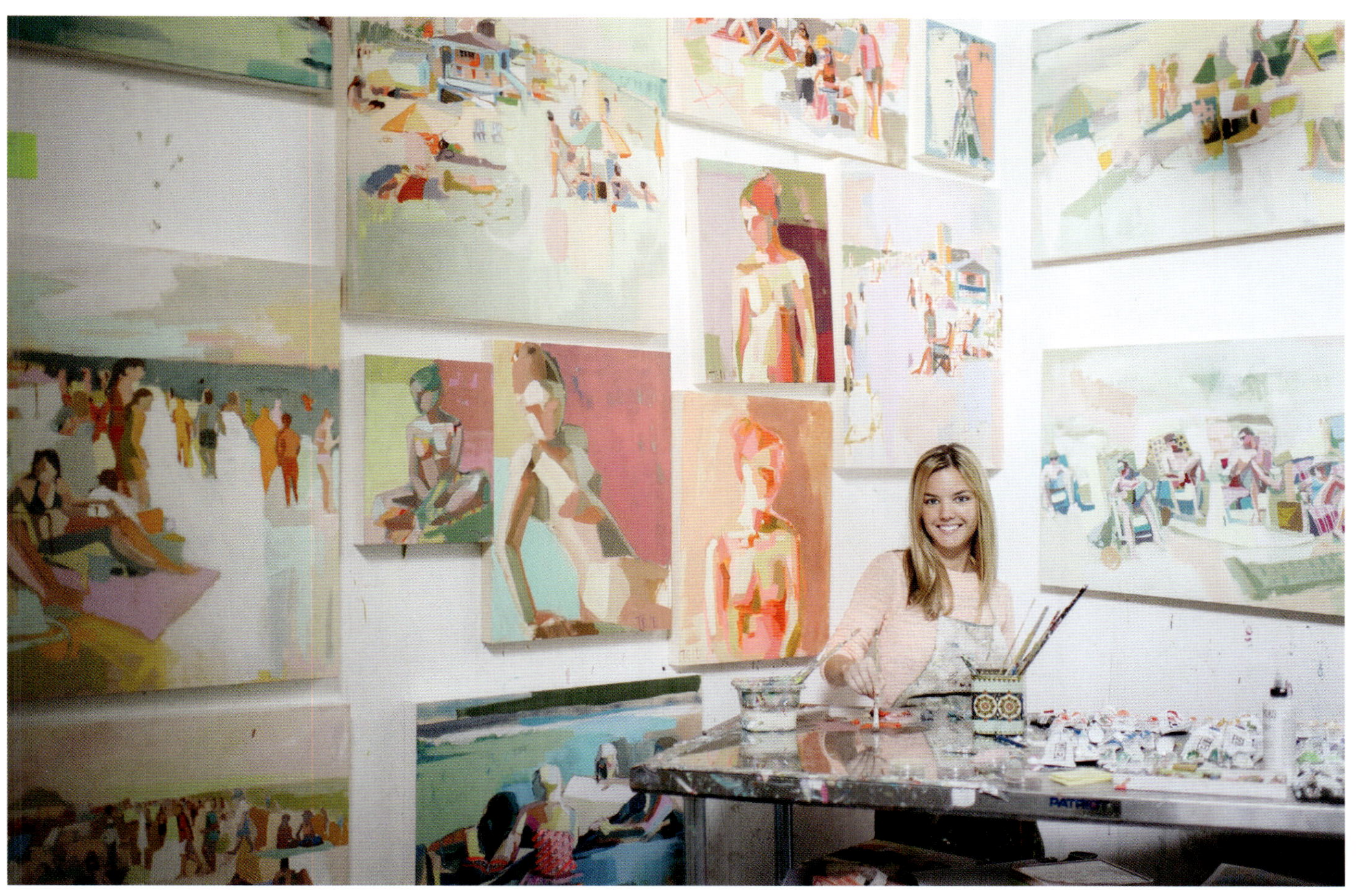

THIS SERIES REFERENCES the classical aspect of the traditional nude subject but is presented in a contemporary palette and can add a bold accent to any room. My goal with each figure is to provide just enough information to communicate the proportions, pose, and light source while simultaneously telling an exciting color story.

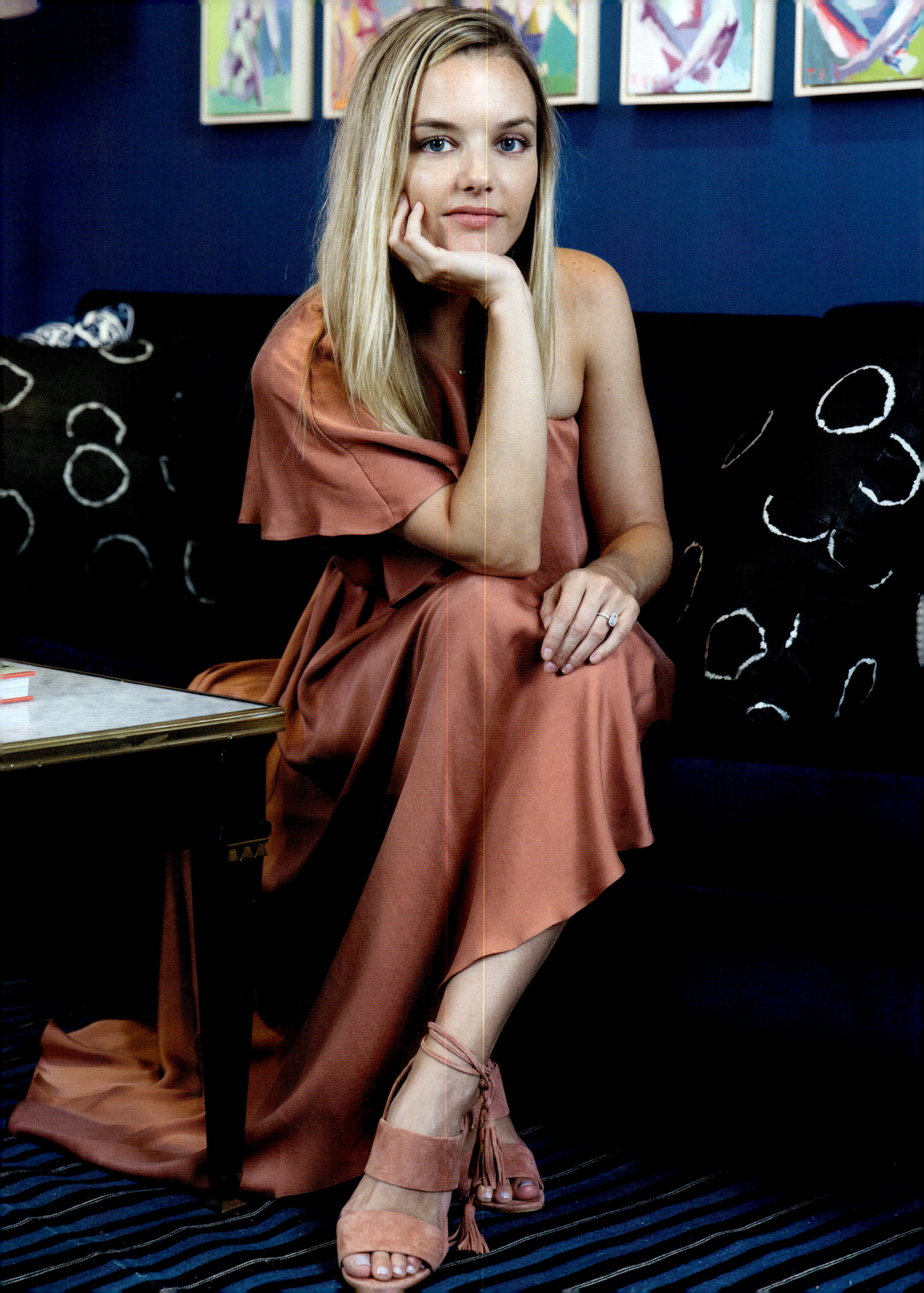

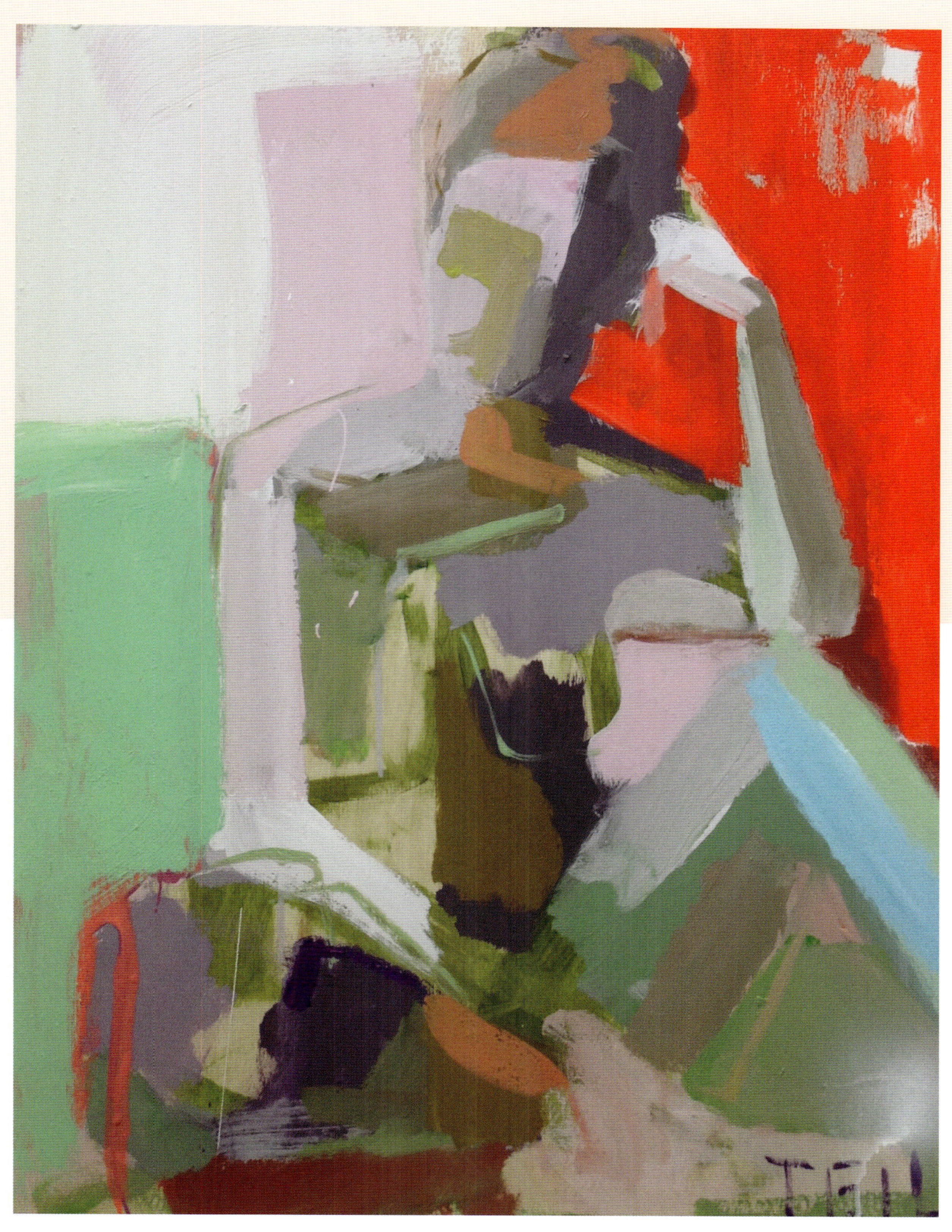

"Point and Flex" 2014

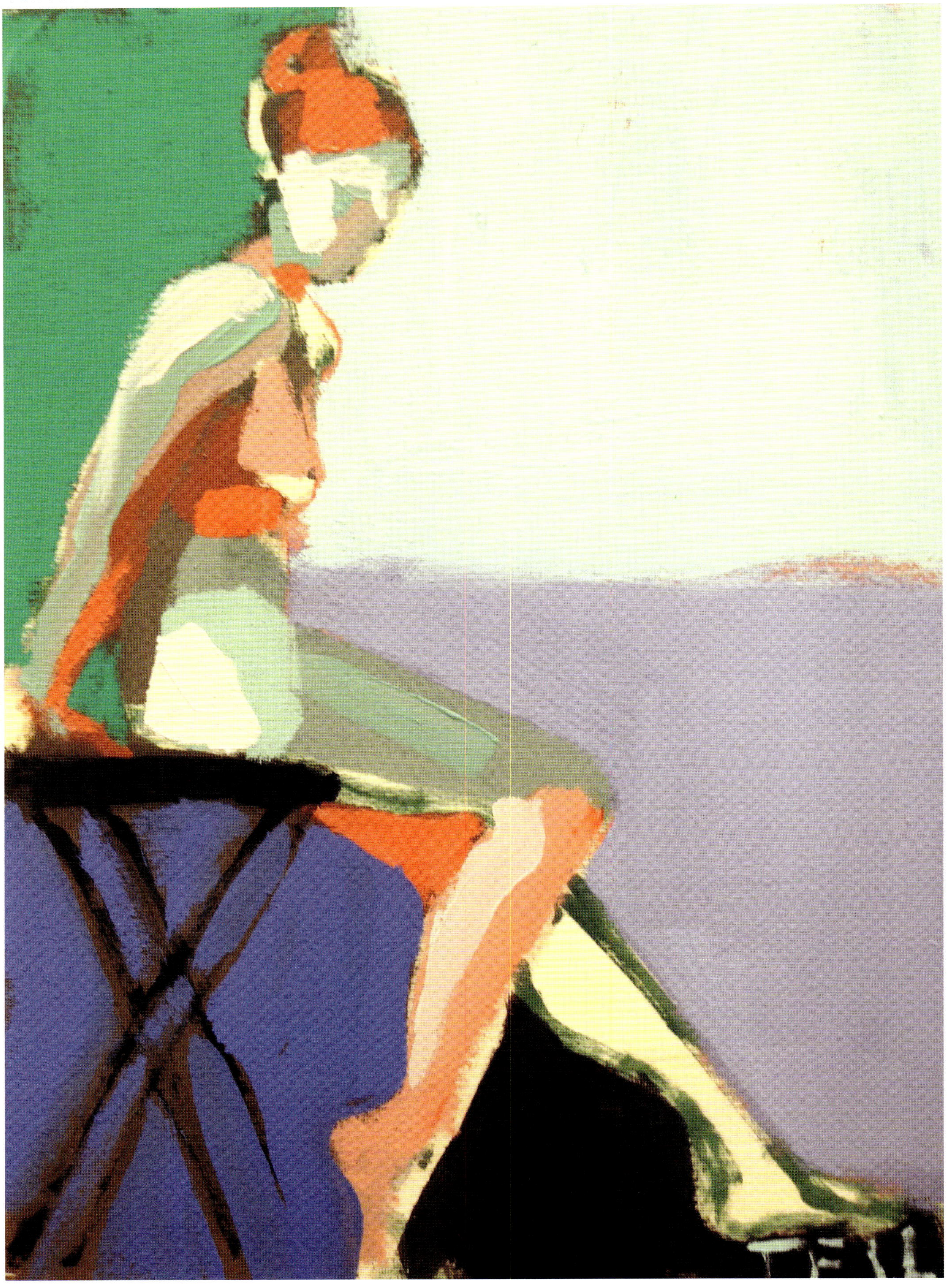

"In Waiting" 2015

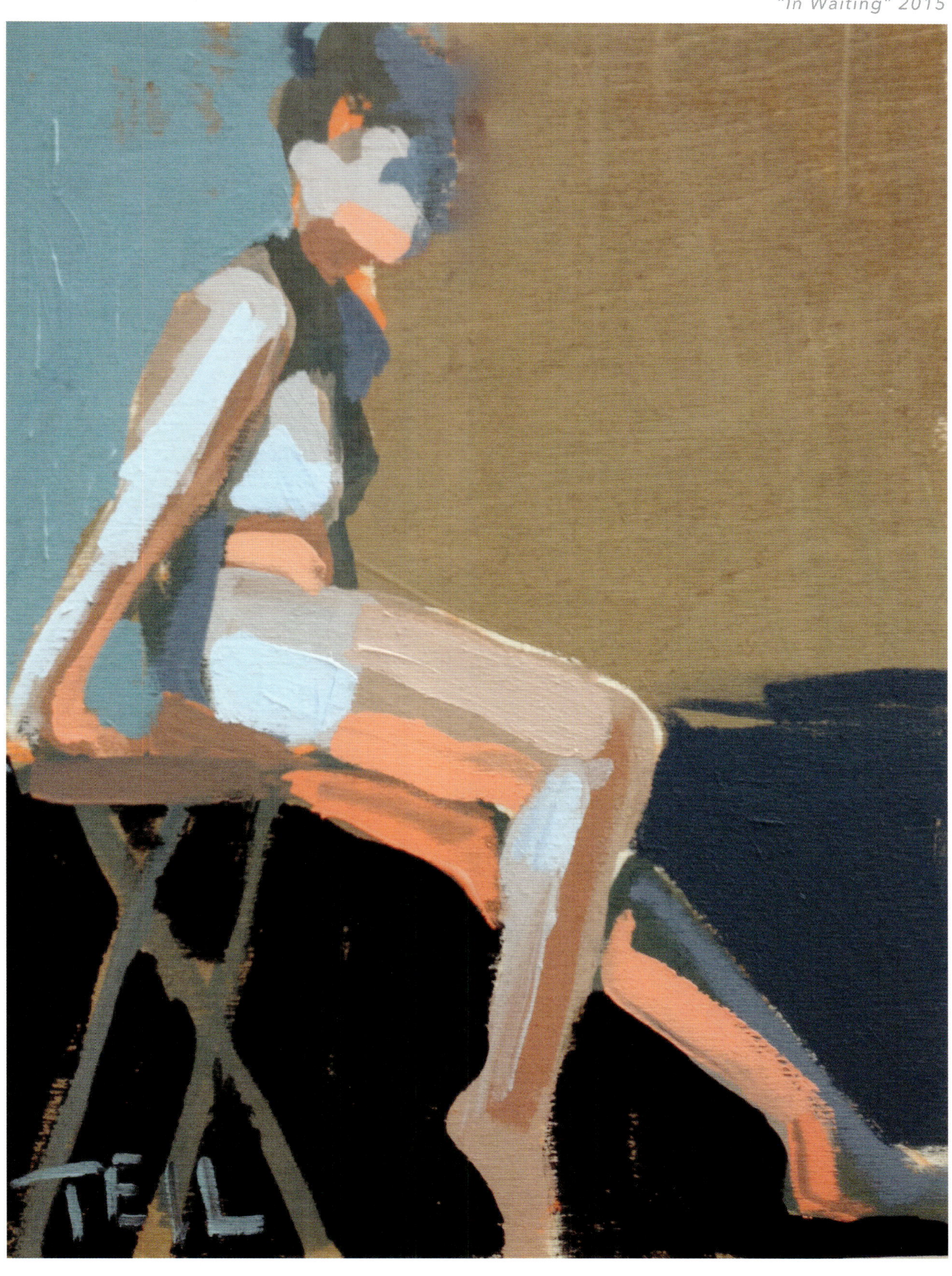

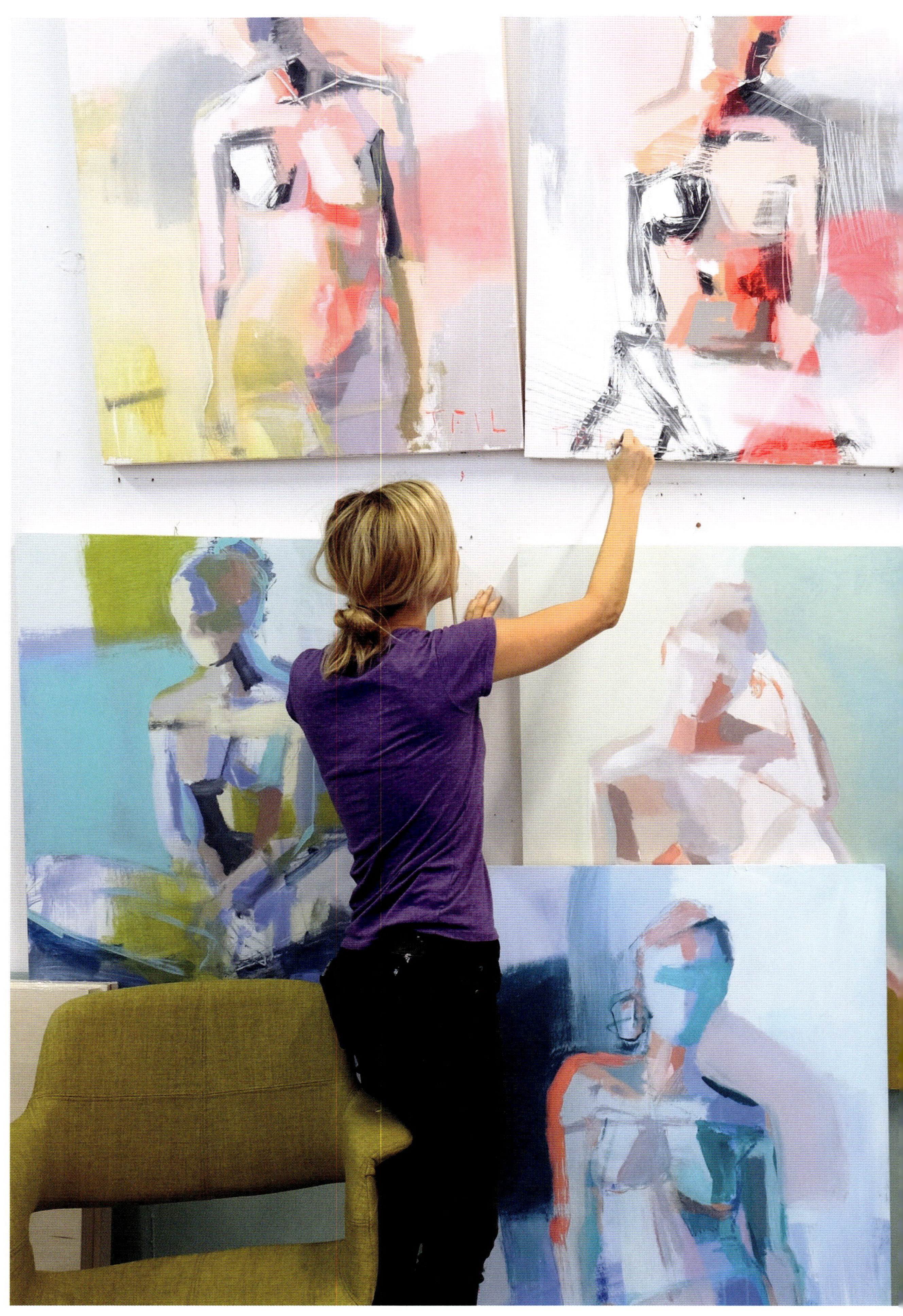

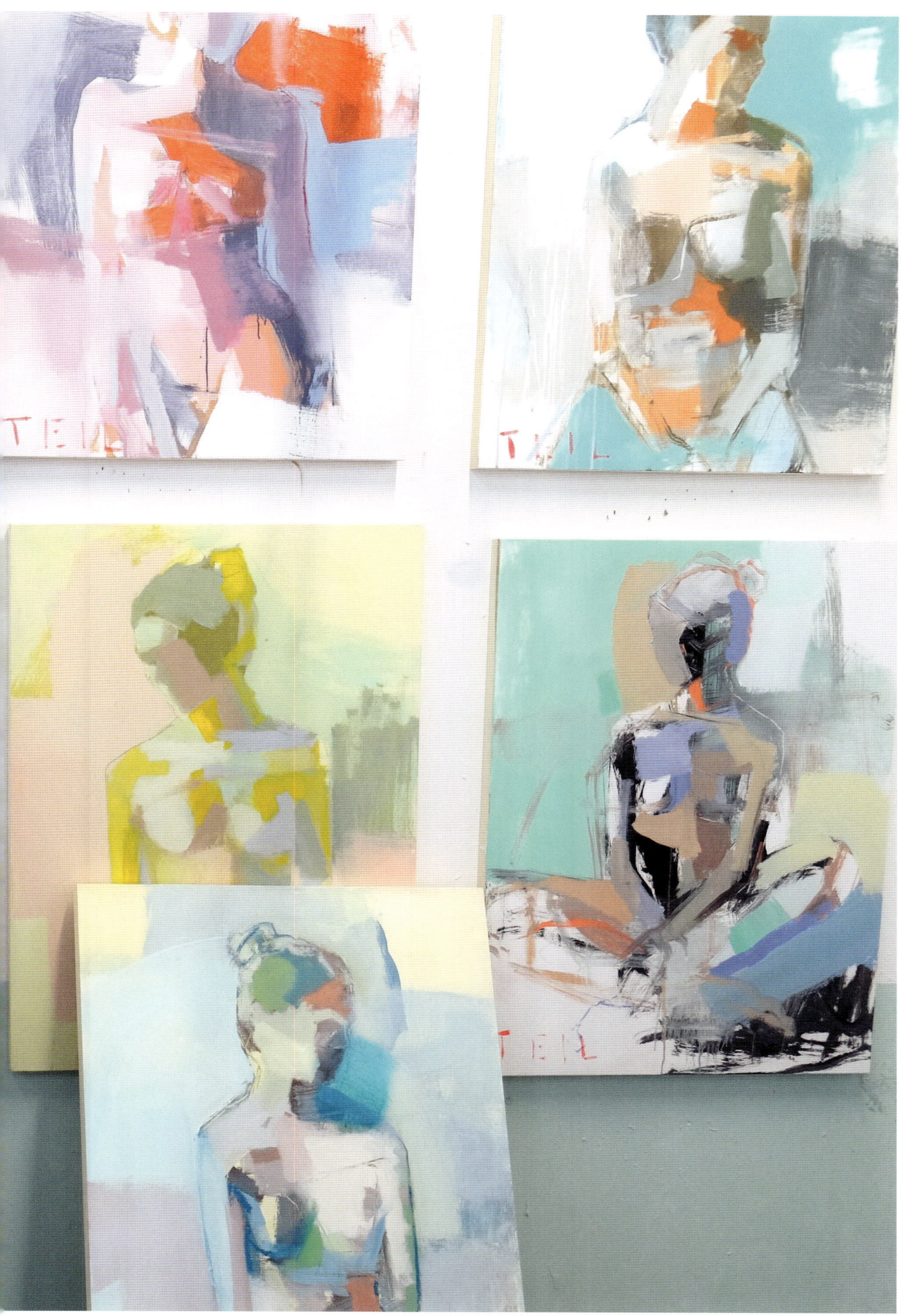

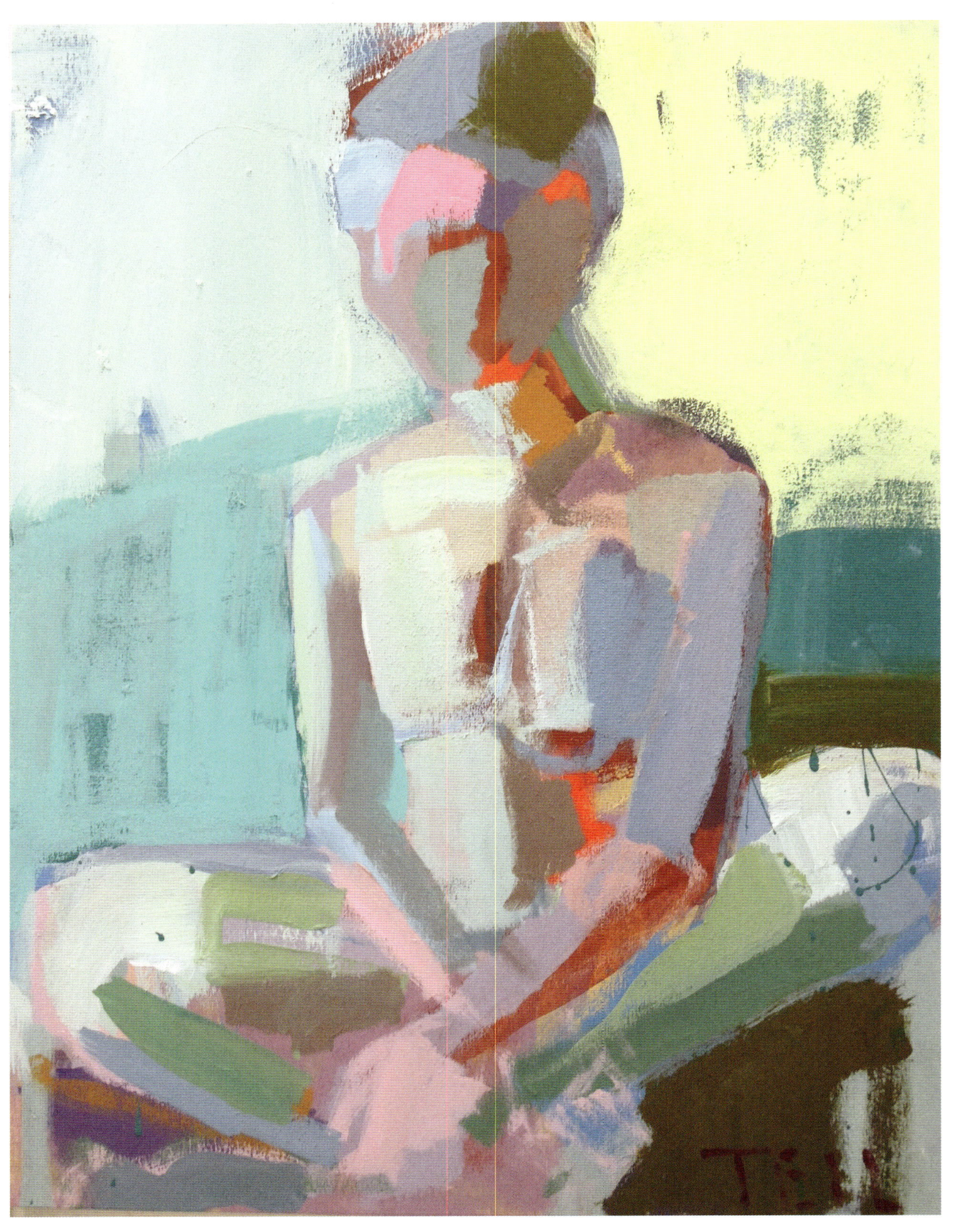

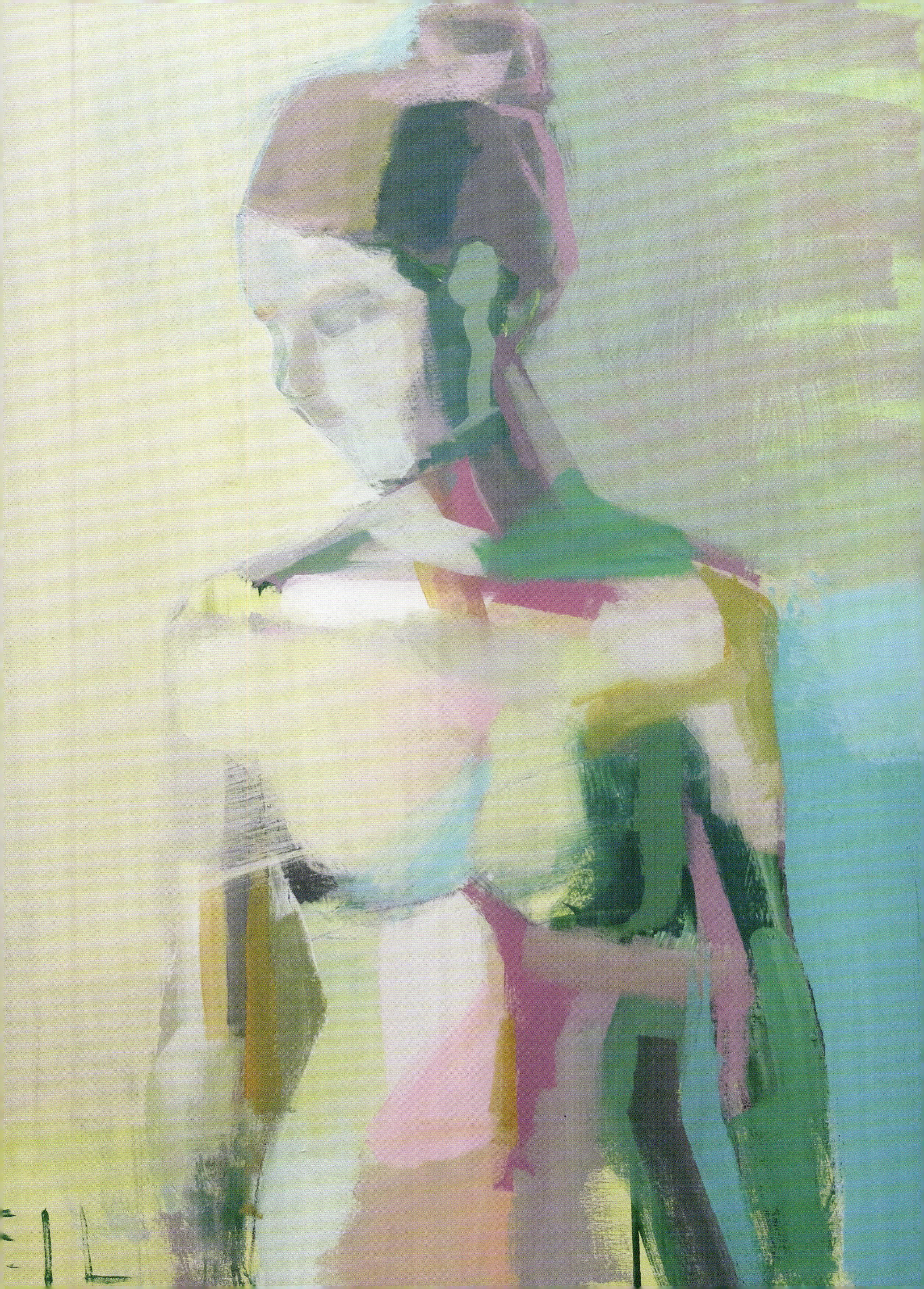

"Navy and Neutral" 2016

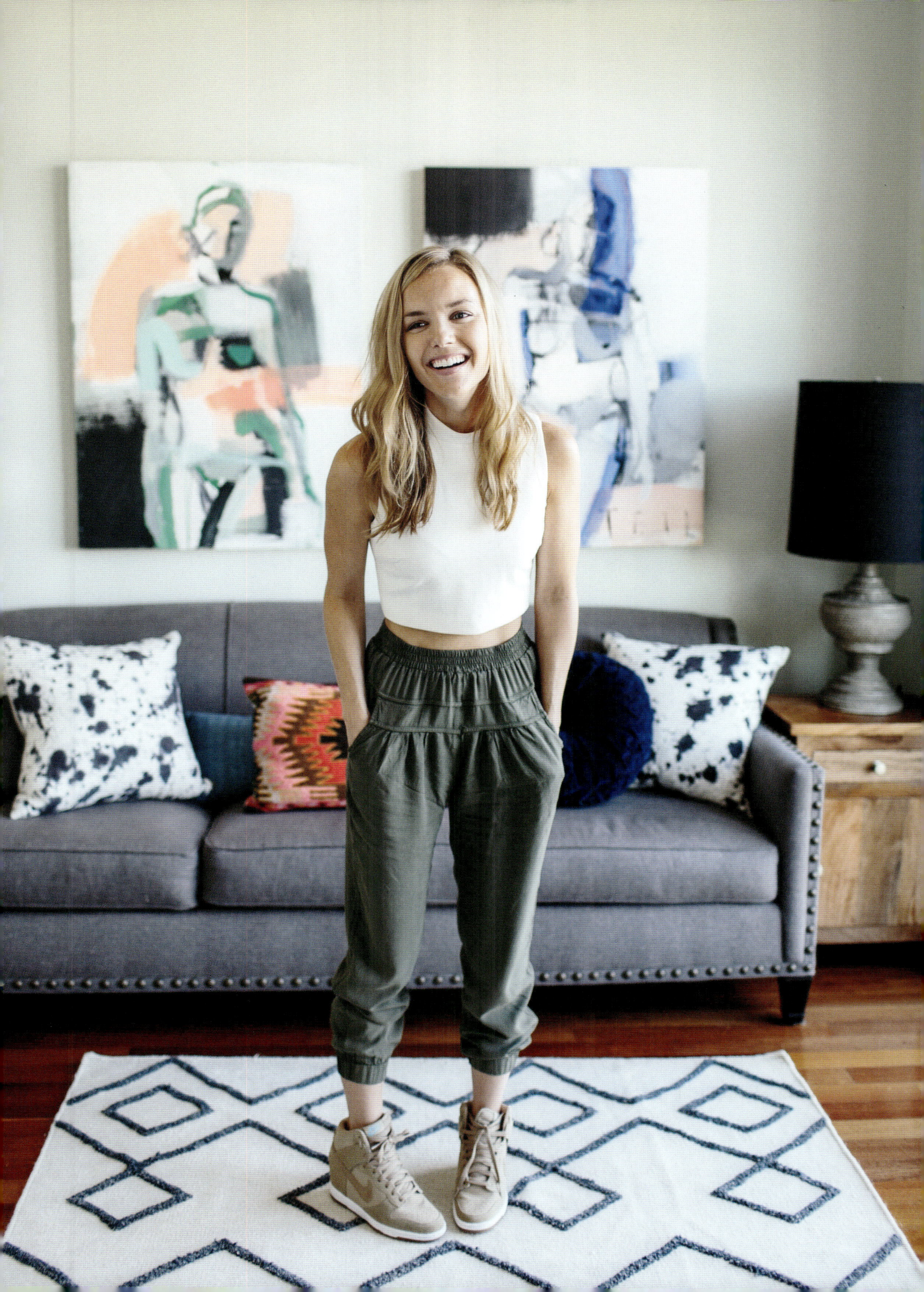

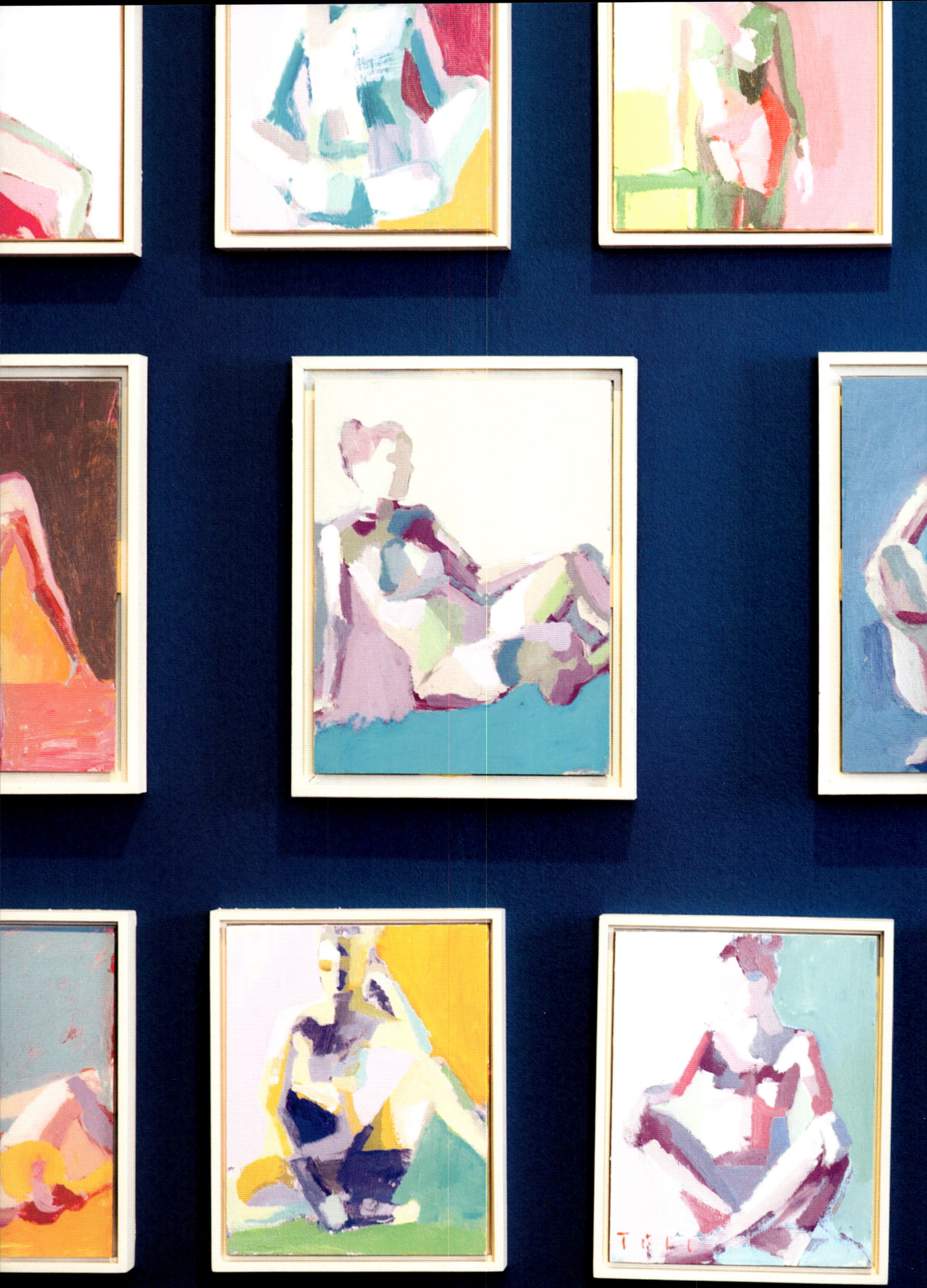

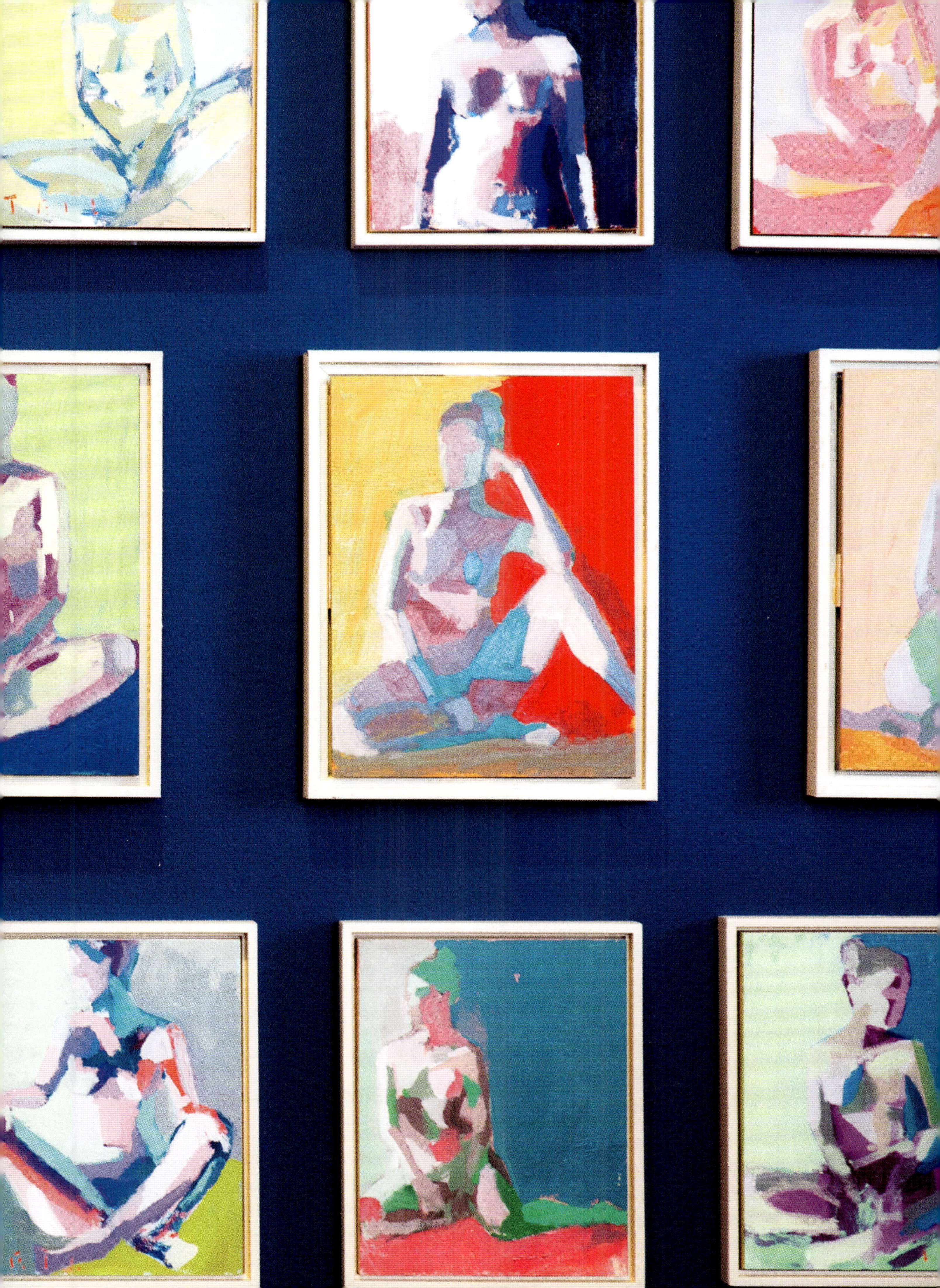

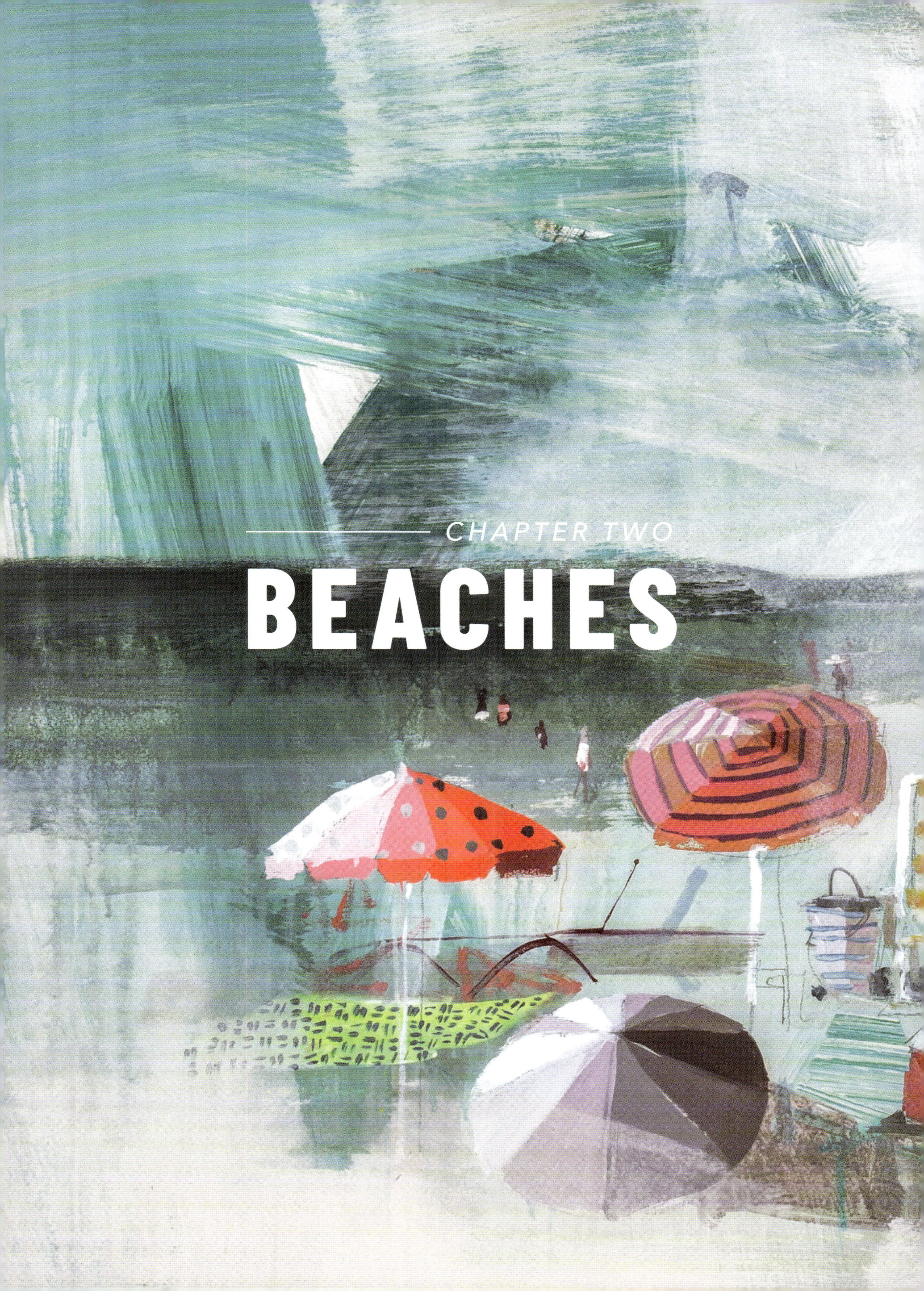

CHAPTER TWO

BEACHES

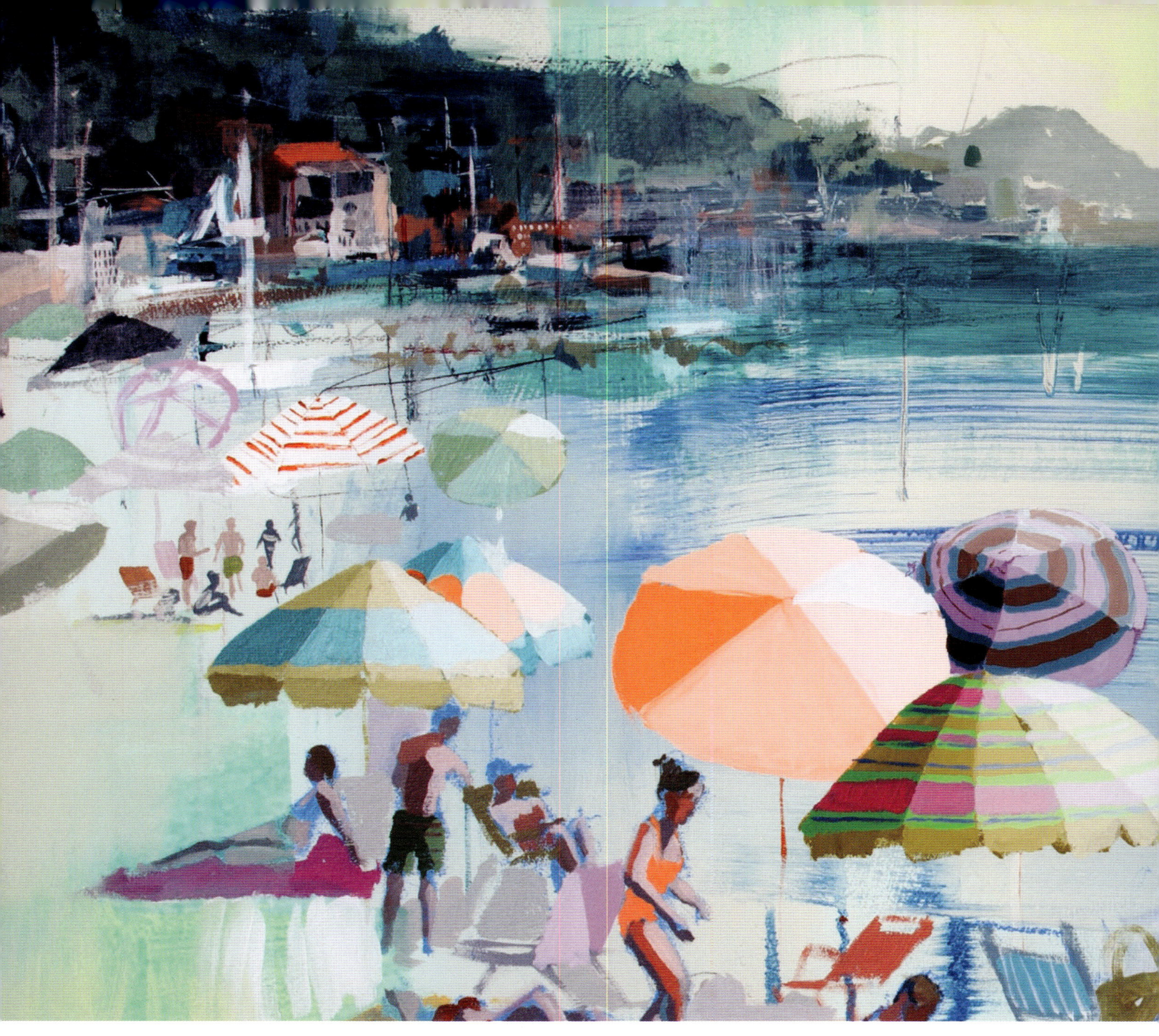

MY BEACH SCENES

are a product of my surroundings in Charleston, South Carolina. Several lively coastal towns surround the peninsula of historic Charleston, making a quick fifteen-minute drive to the beach easy and accessible.

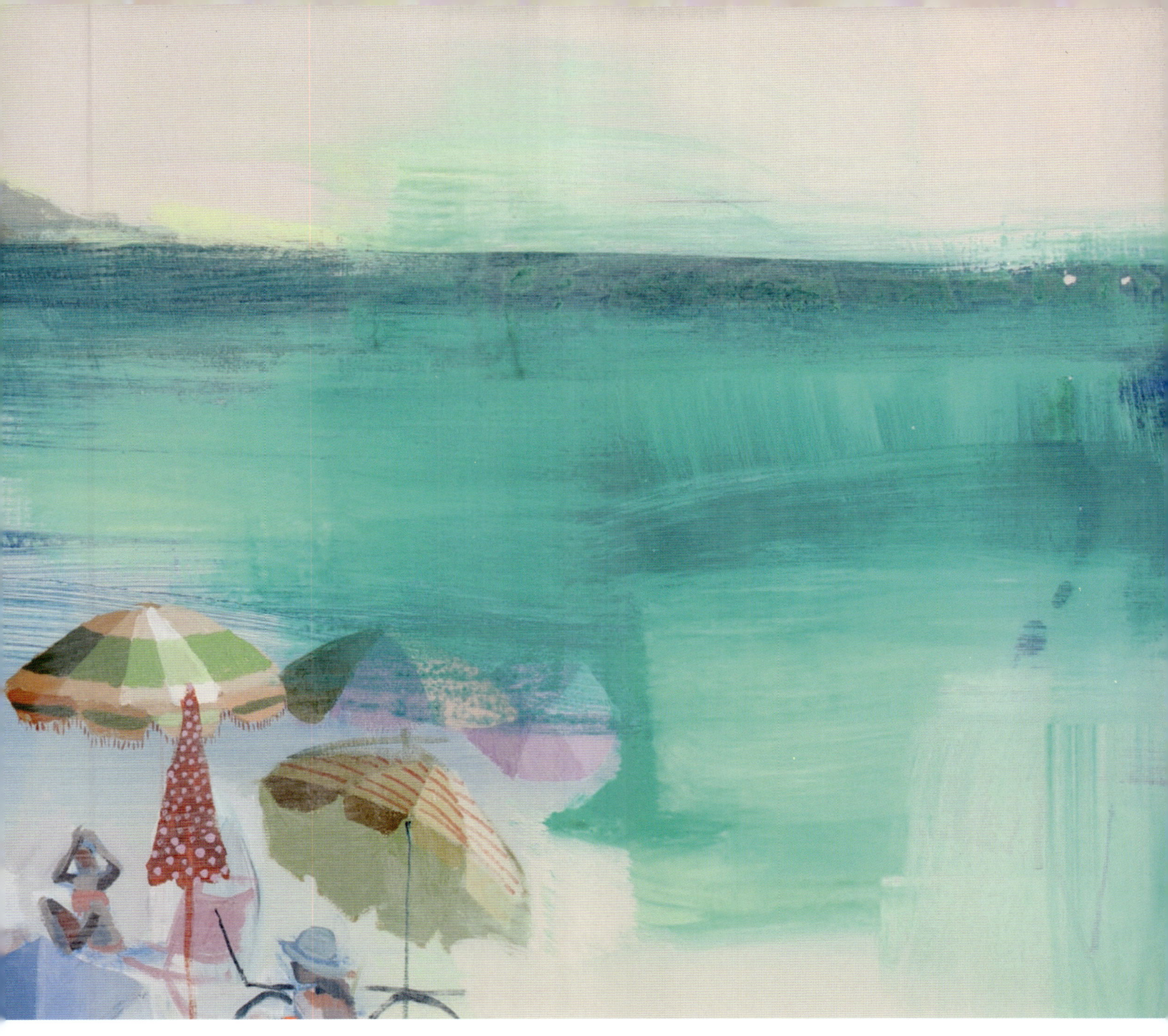

While sitting on my towel soaking in the sun on a weekend afternoon, I found myself snapping photos of the beach-goers. I had no idea at the time why I was drawn to this subject; nonetheless, I continued to snap shots of the sunny day.

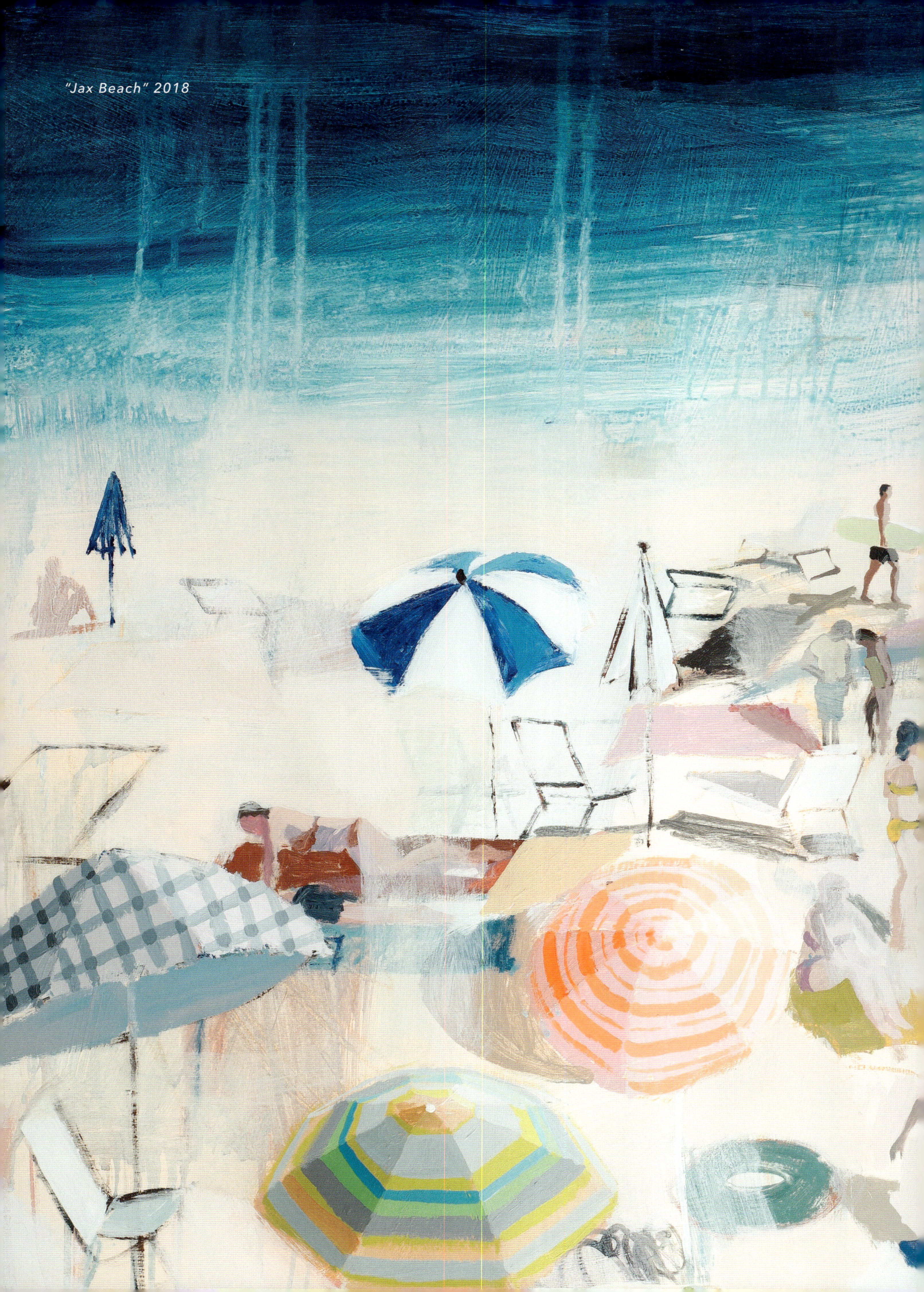
"Jax Beach" 2018

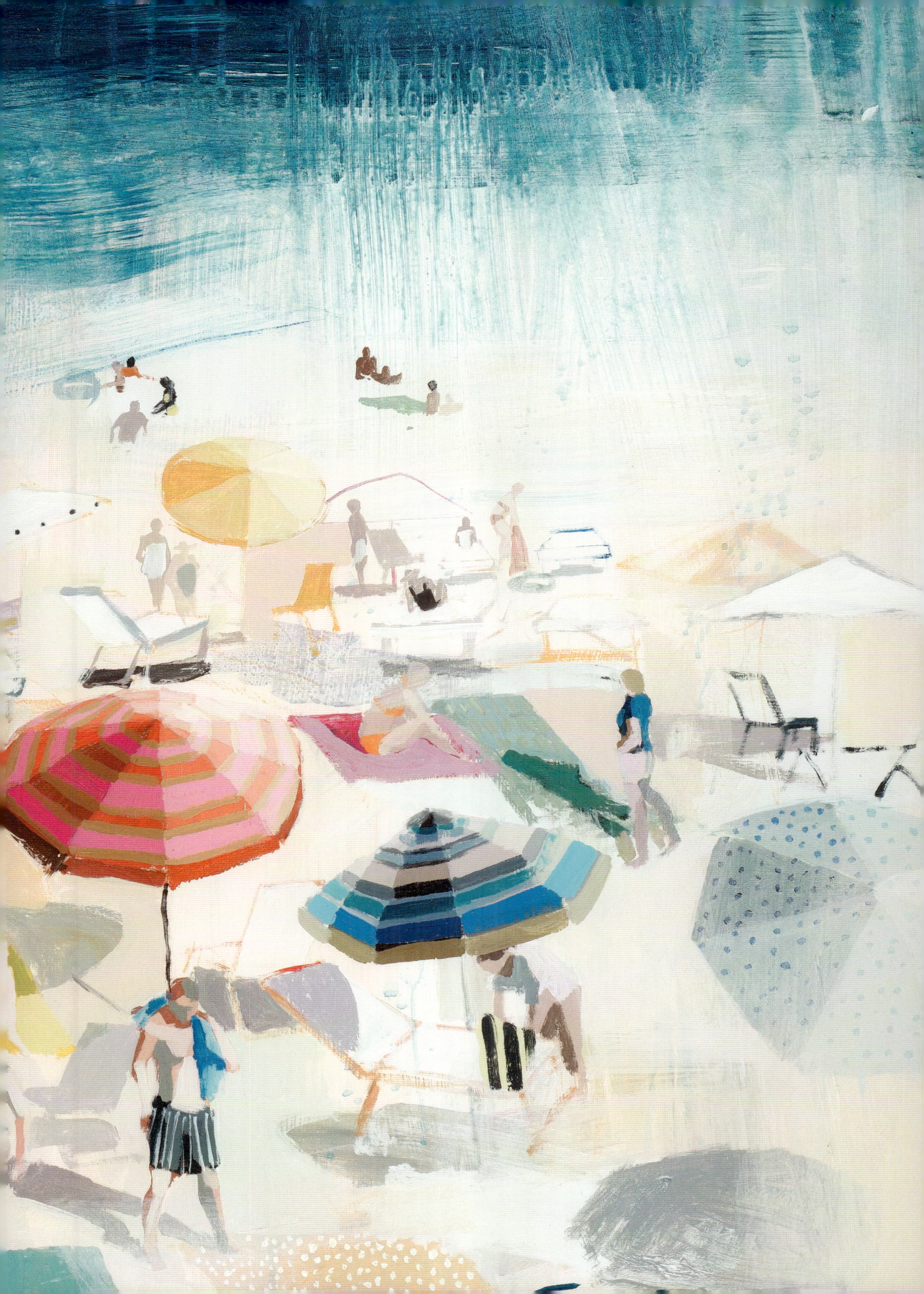

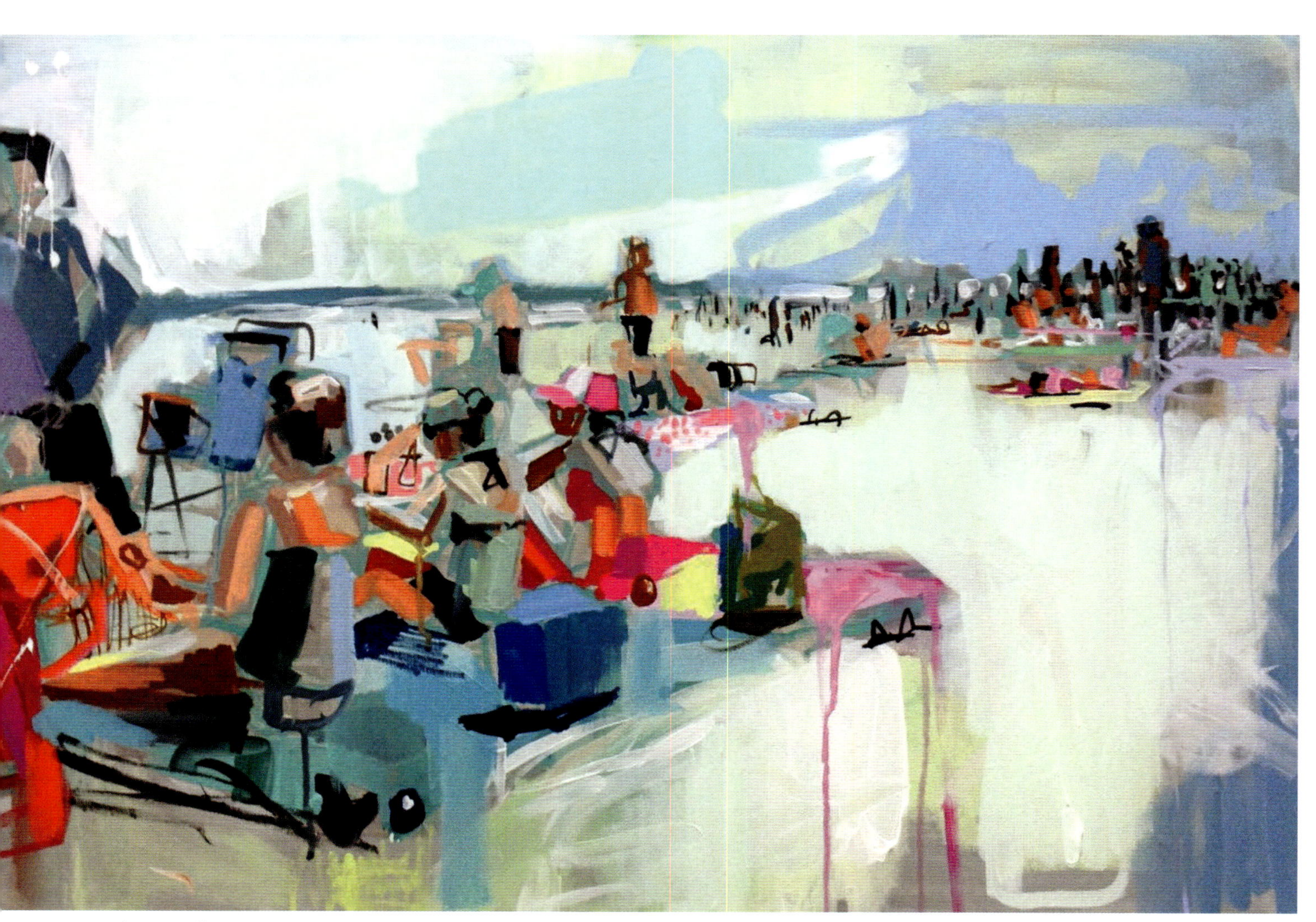

"4th at Folly" 2013

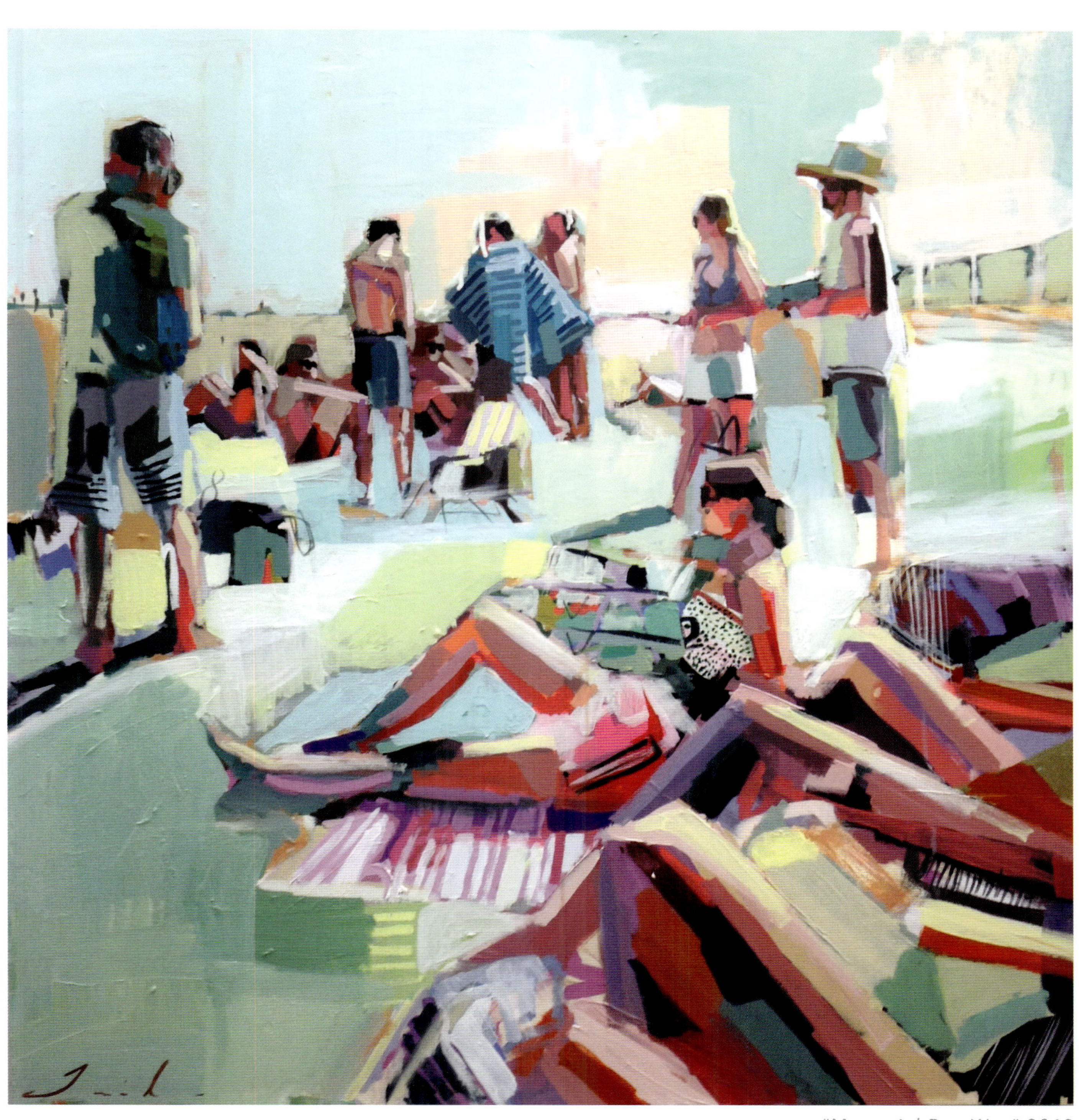

"Memorial Day Way" 2013

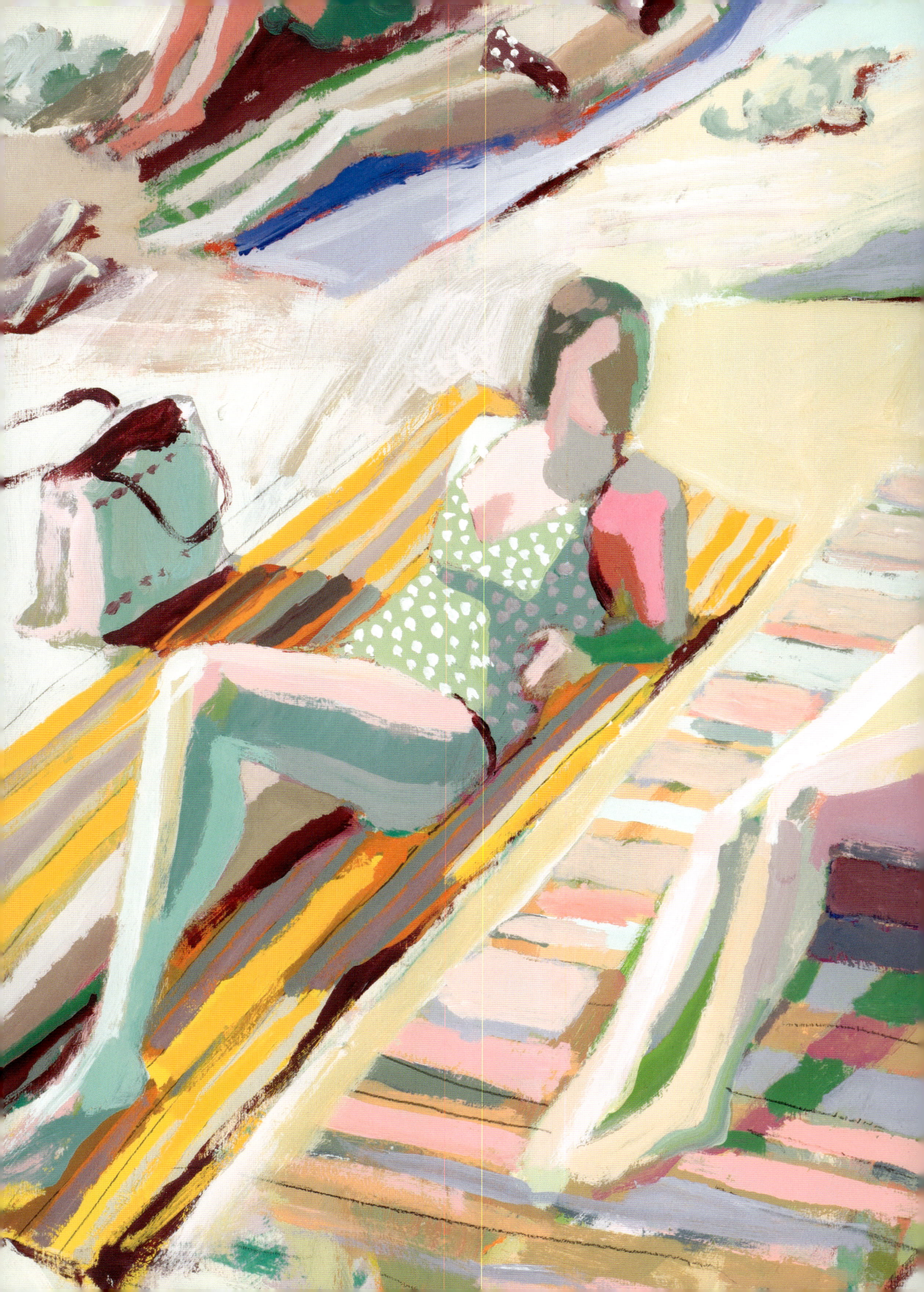

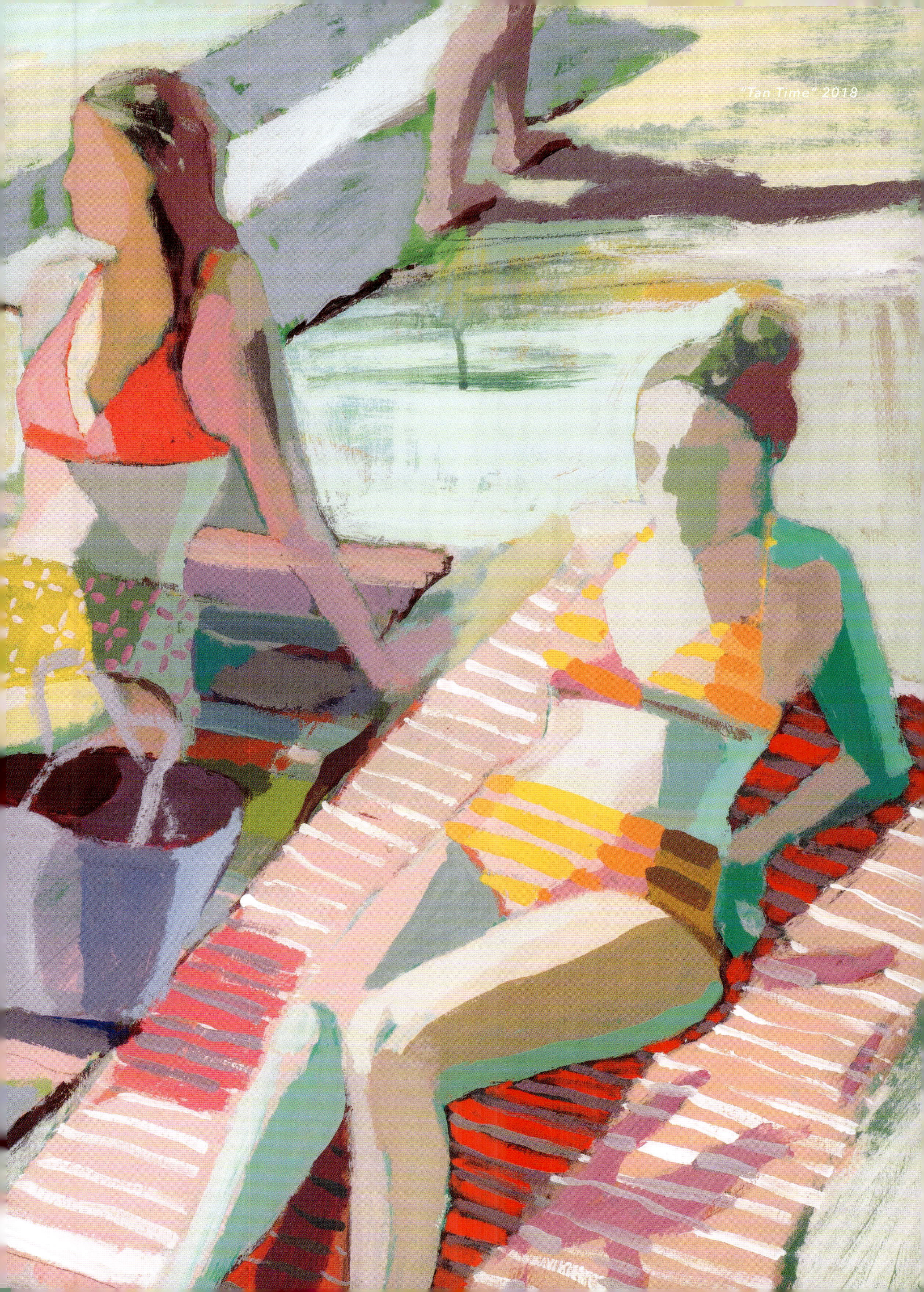

"Tan Time" 2018

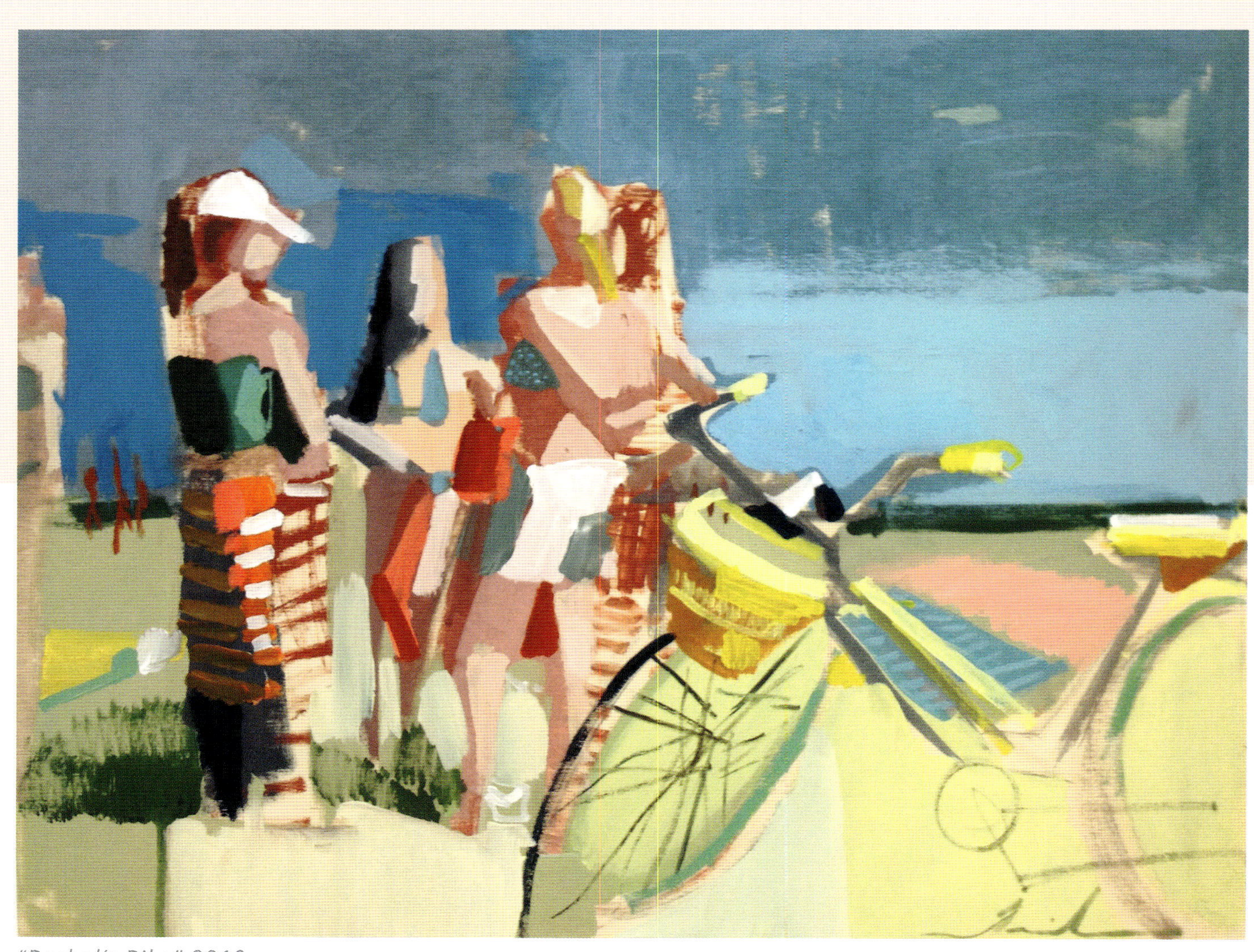

"Rachel's Bike" 2013

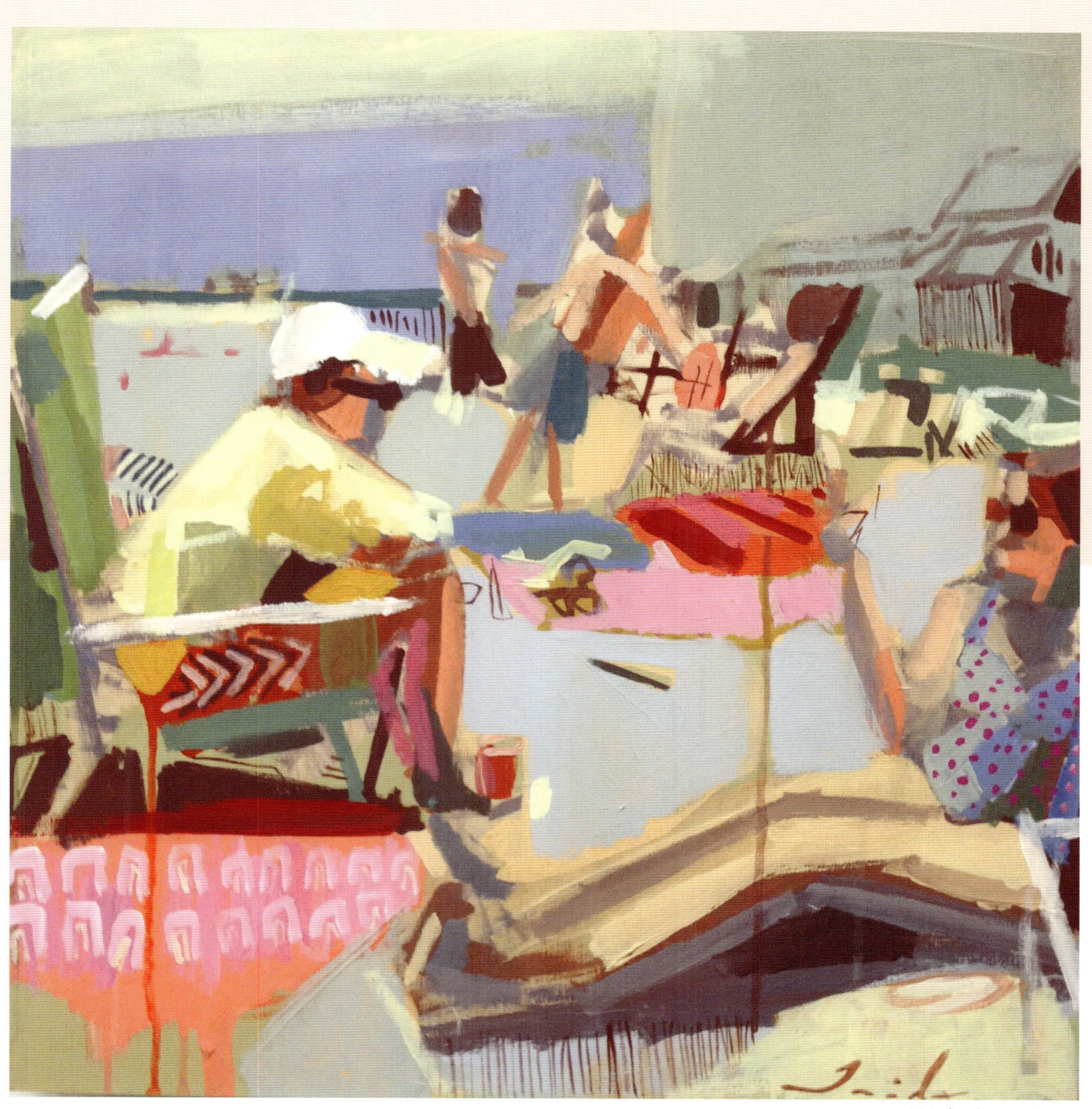

"Pink Float" 2013

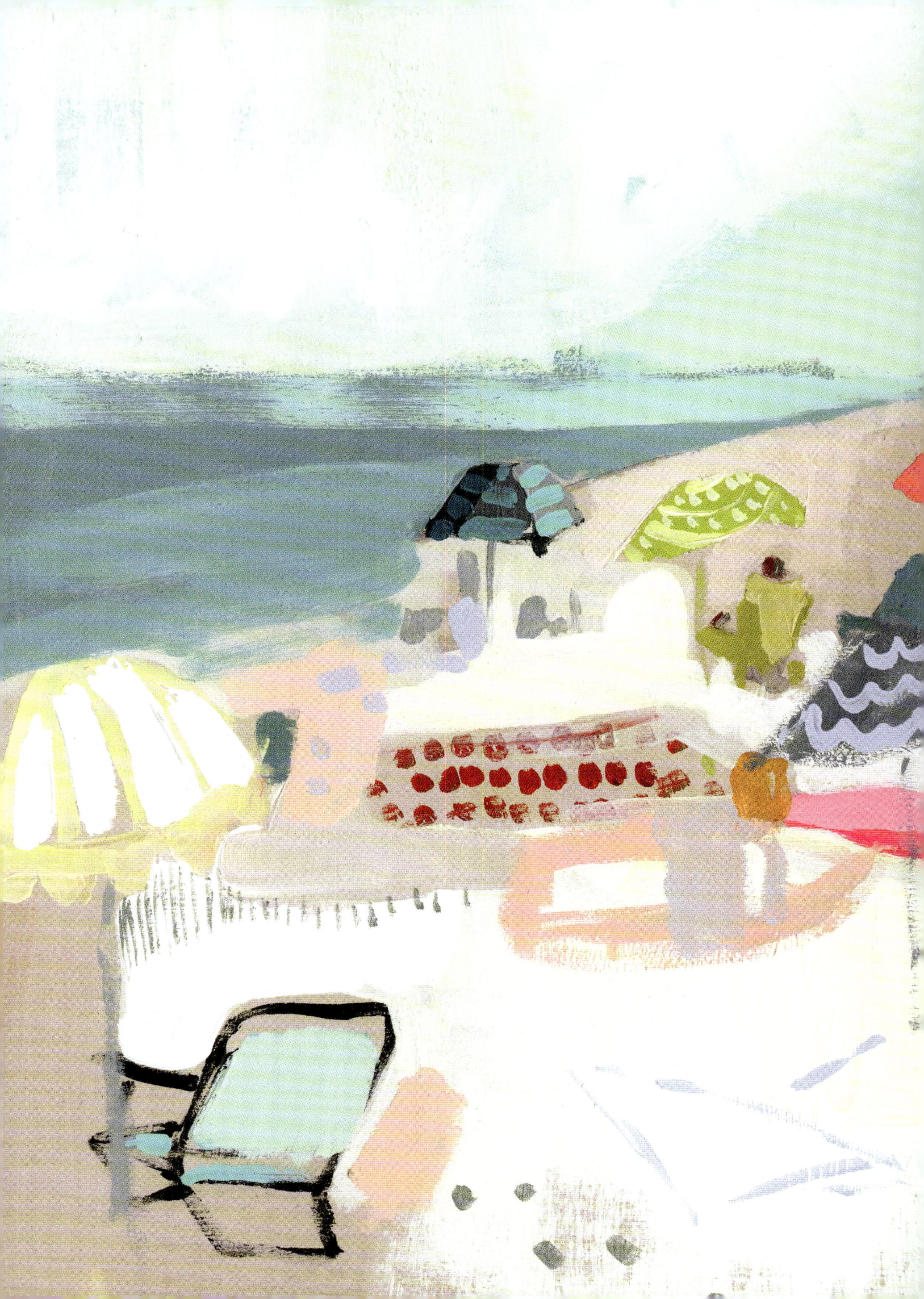

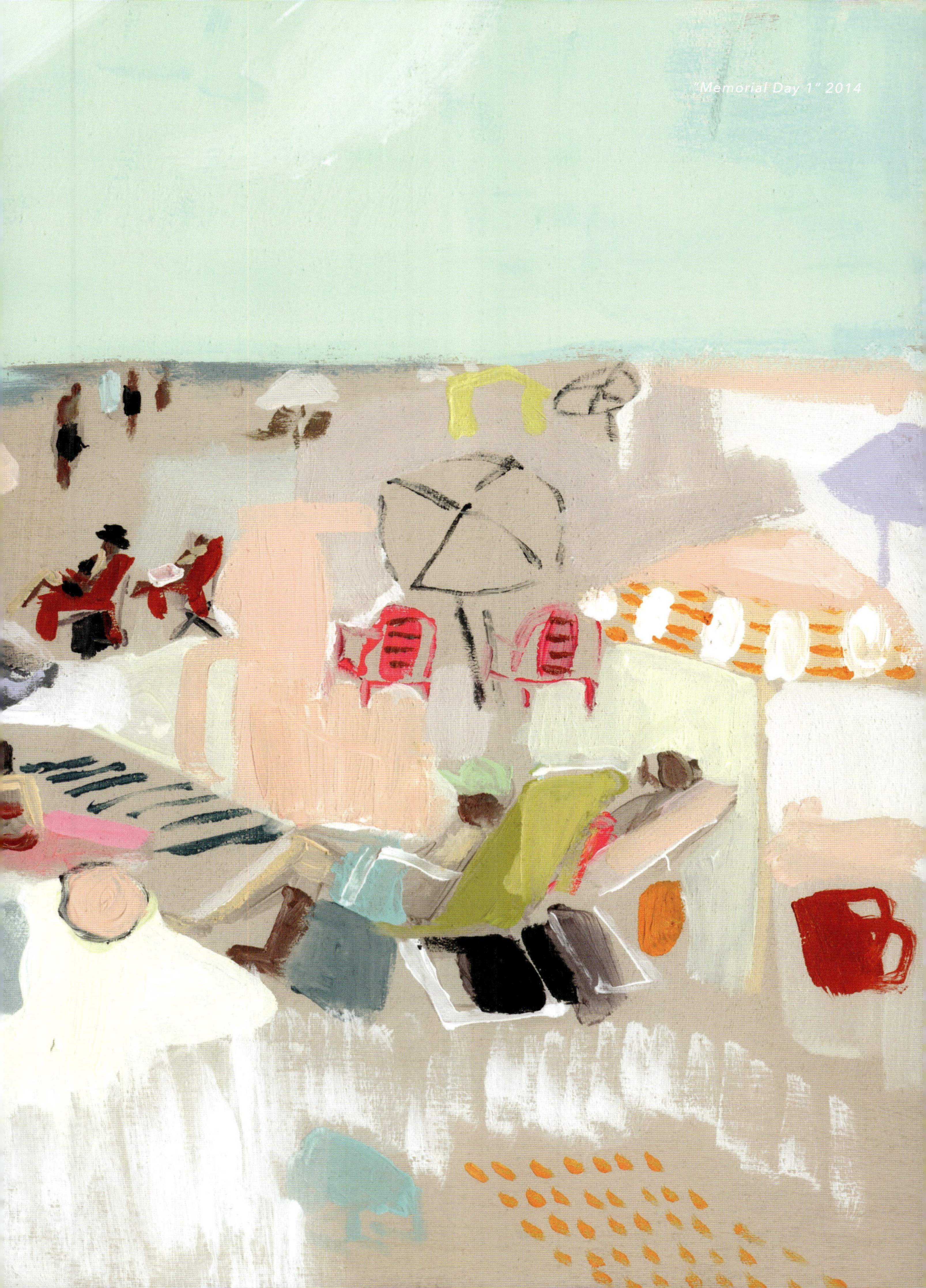

"Memorial Day 1" 2014

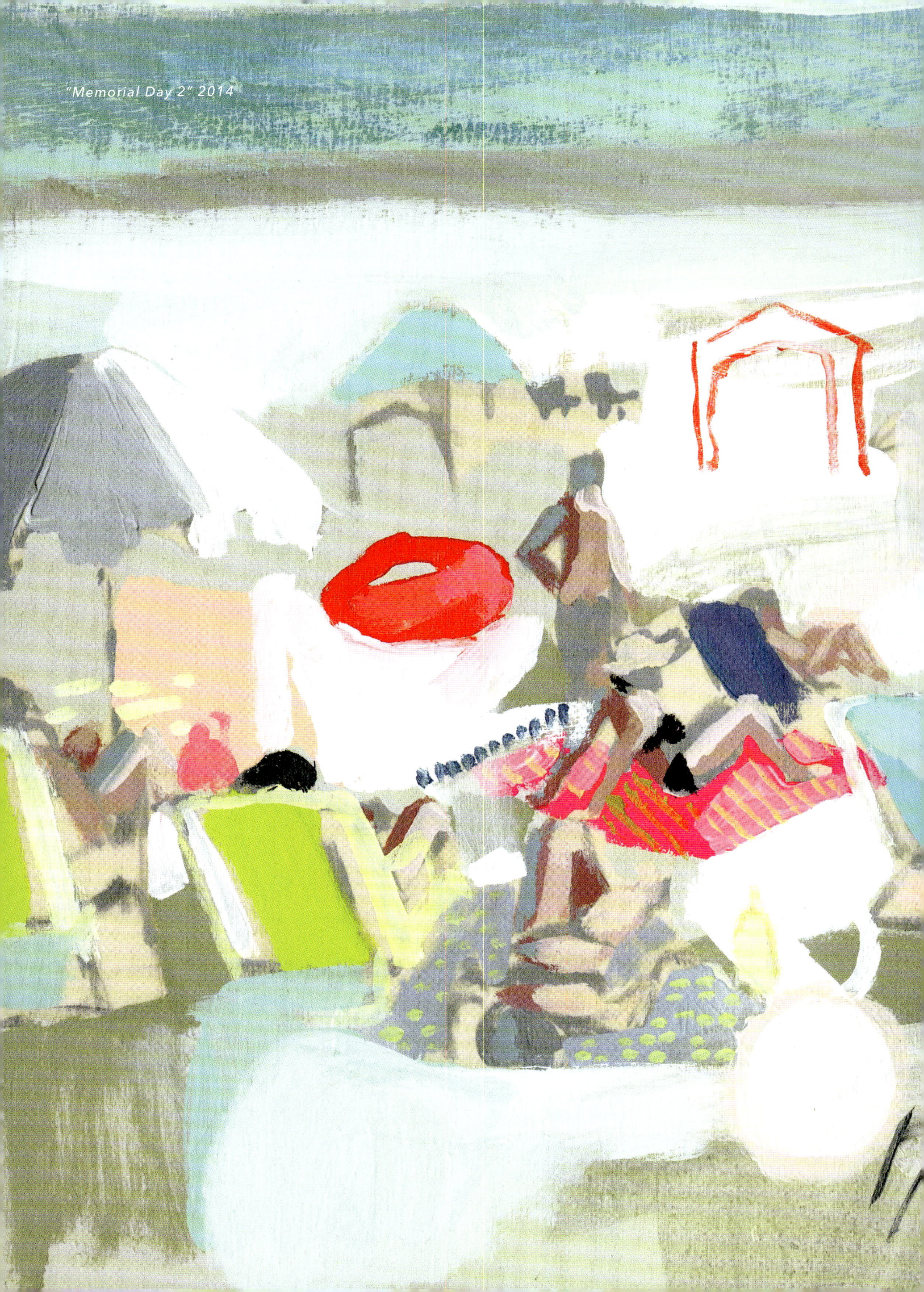

"Memorial Day 2" 2014

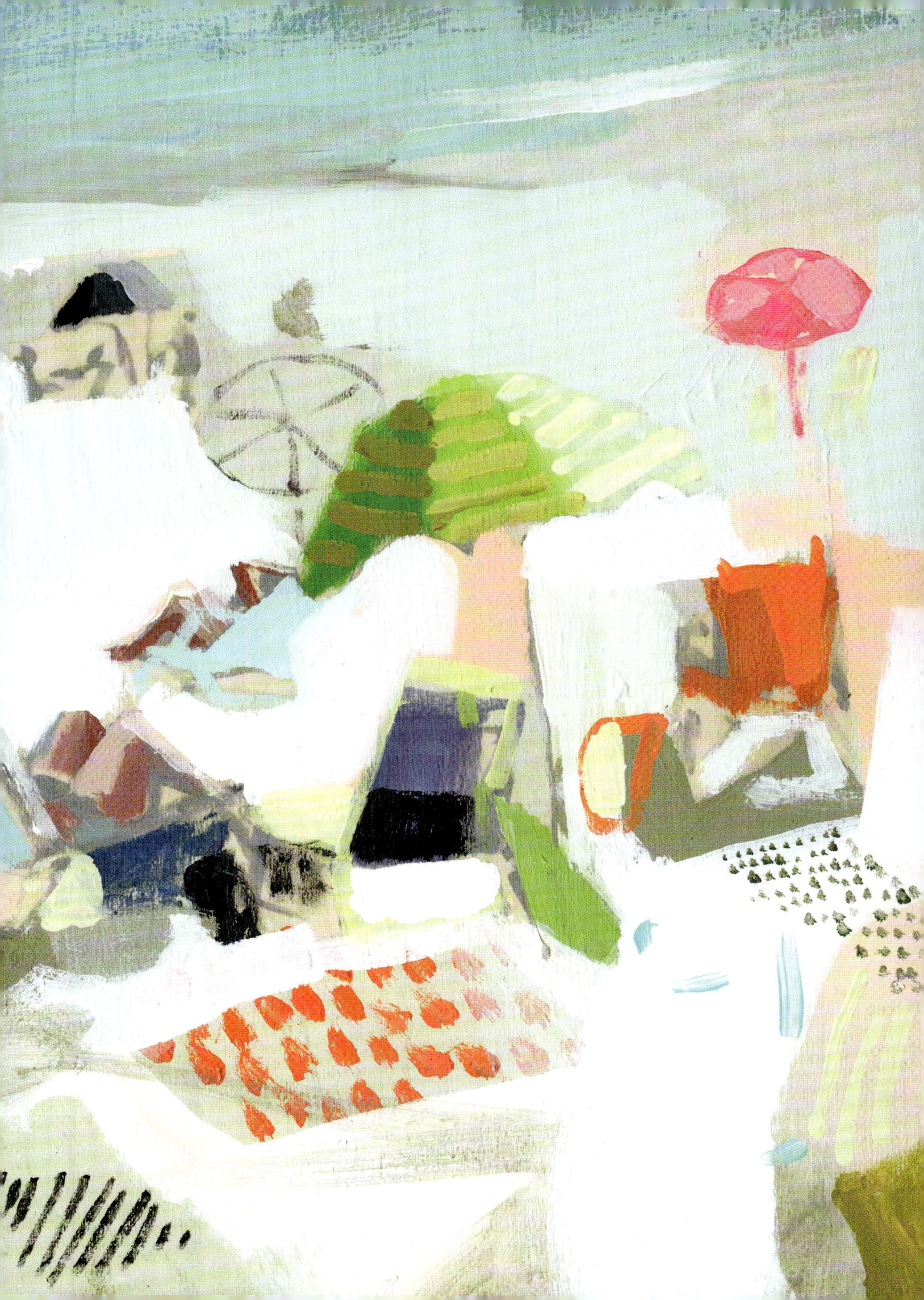

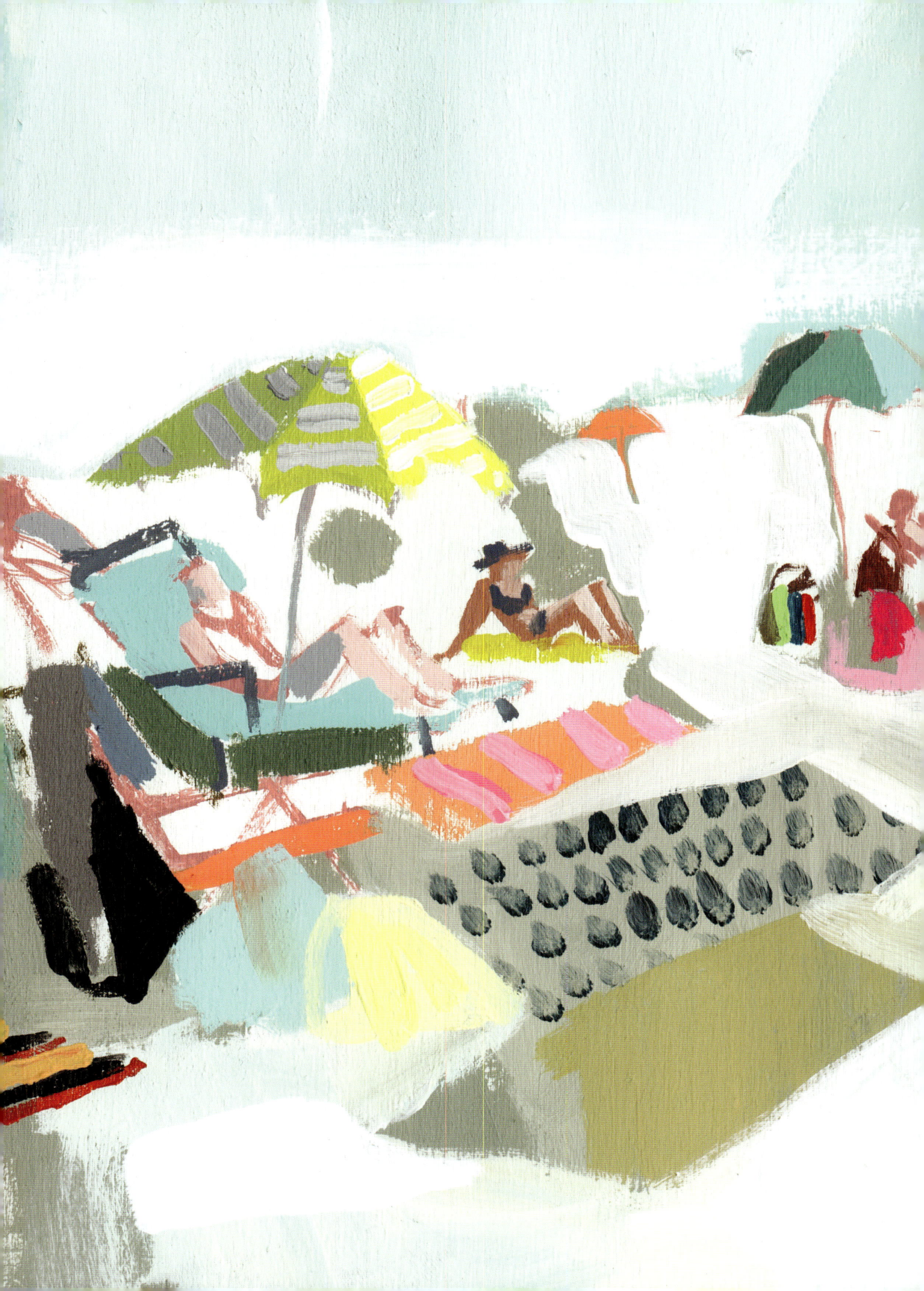

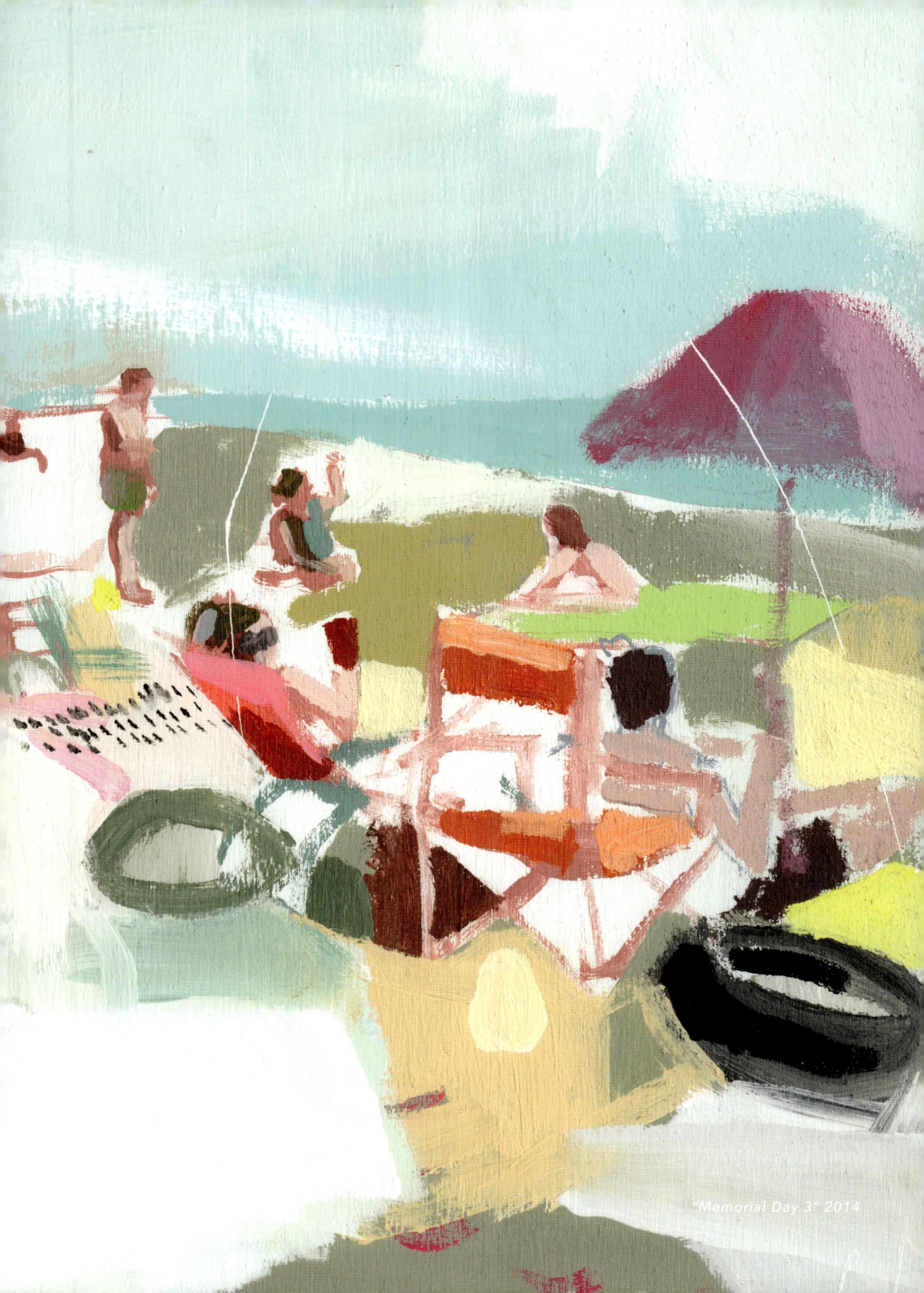
"Memorial Day 3" 2014

AS I WAS WRAPPING UP a collection of figure studies, I pondered what would be my next painting subject. Without much thought, I referred back to my stack of beach photos. I dove right in, my acrylic and gauche paint in hand, and took a stab at this coastal subject.

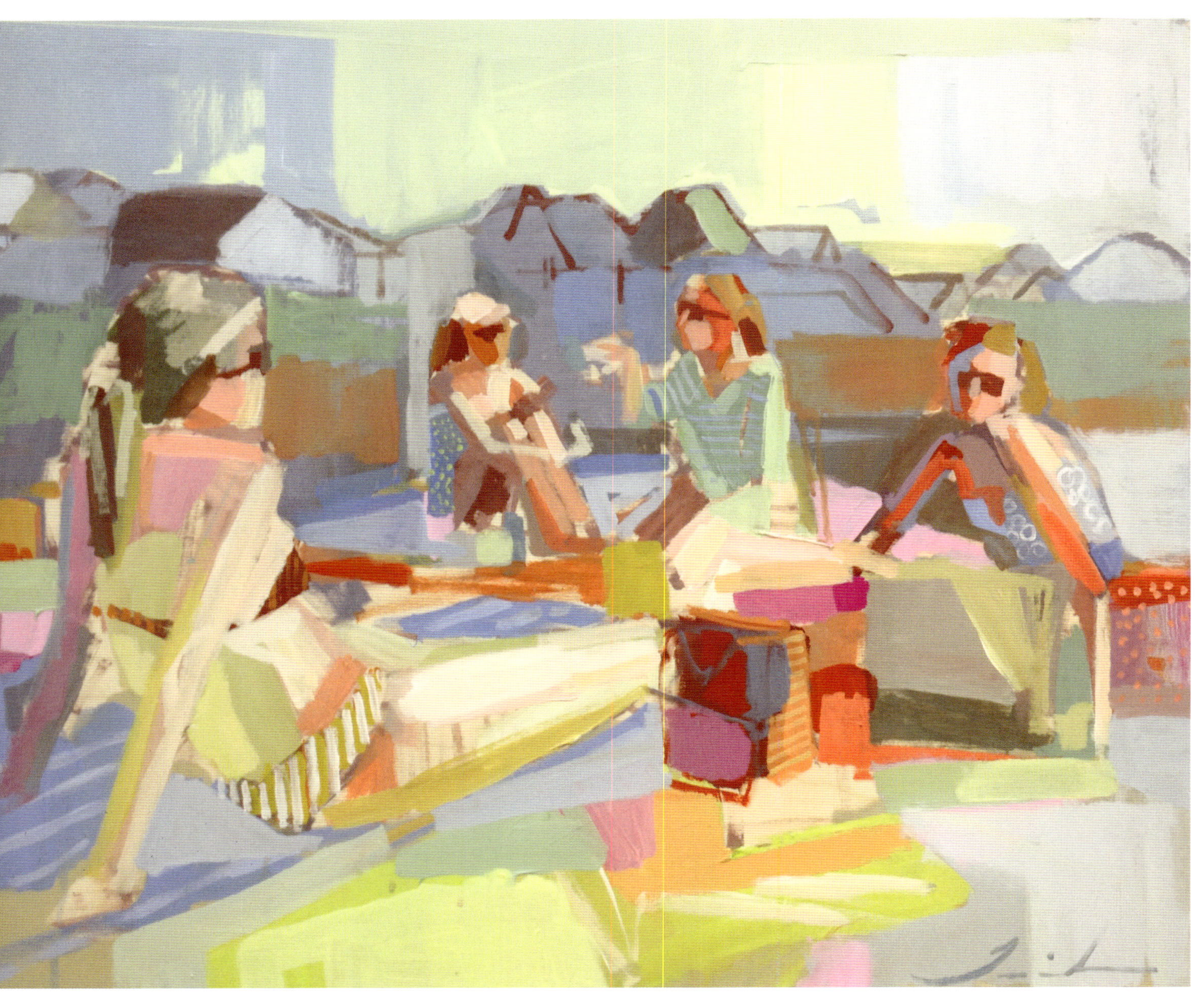

"Maggie's in Town" 2014

It was only after I completed a group of beach paintings that I realized why I was drawn to these sunbathers: it was an entire field of figure studies! It was the perfect segue into the series. While the figure studies focused on one relaxed human form featuring a distinct light source, the beaches were stocked with lounging bodies lying in beautiful light, making it so appealing for me to emulate onto the canvas.

"Beach Candy" 2014

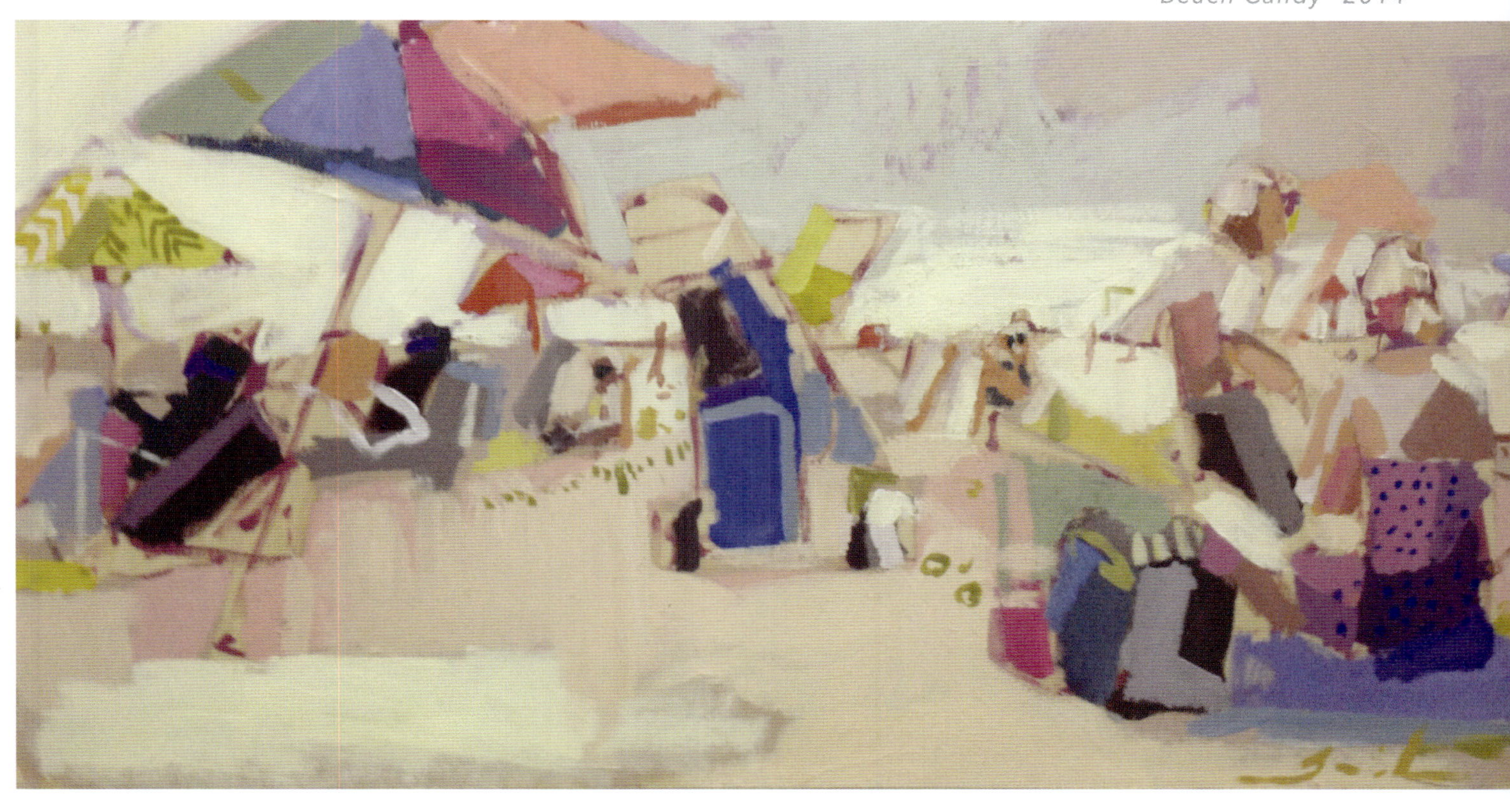

"Sand Chatter" 2014

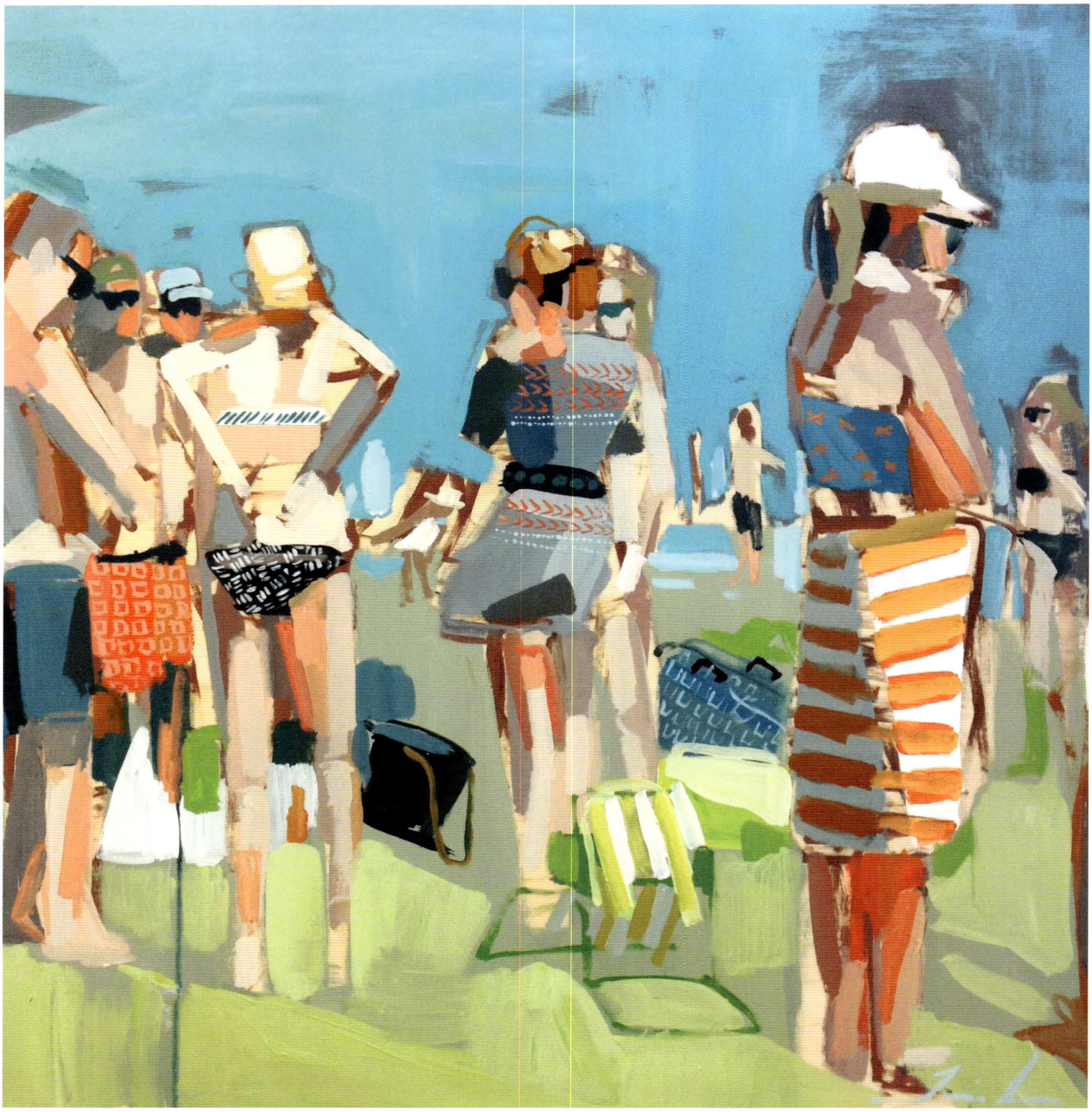

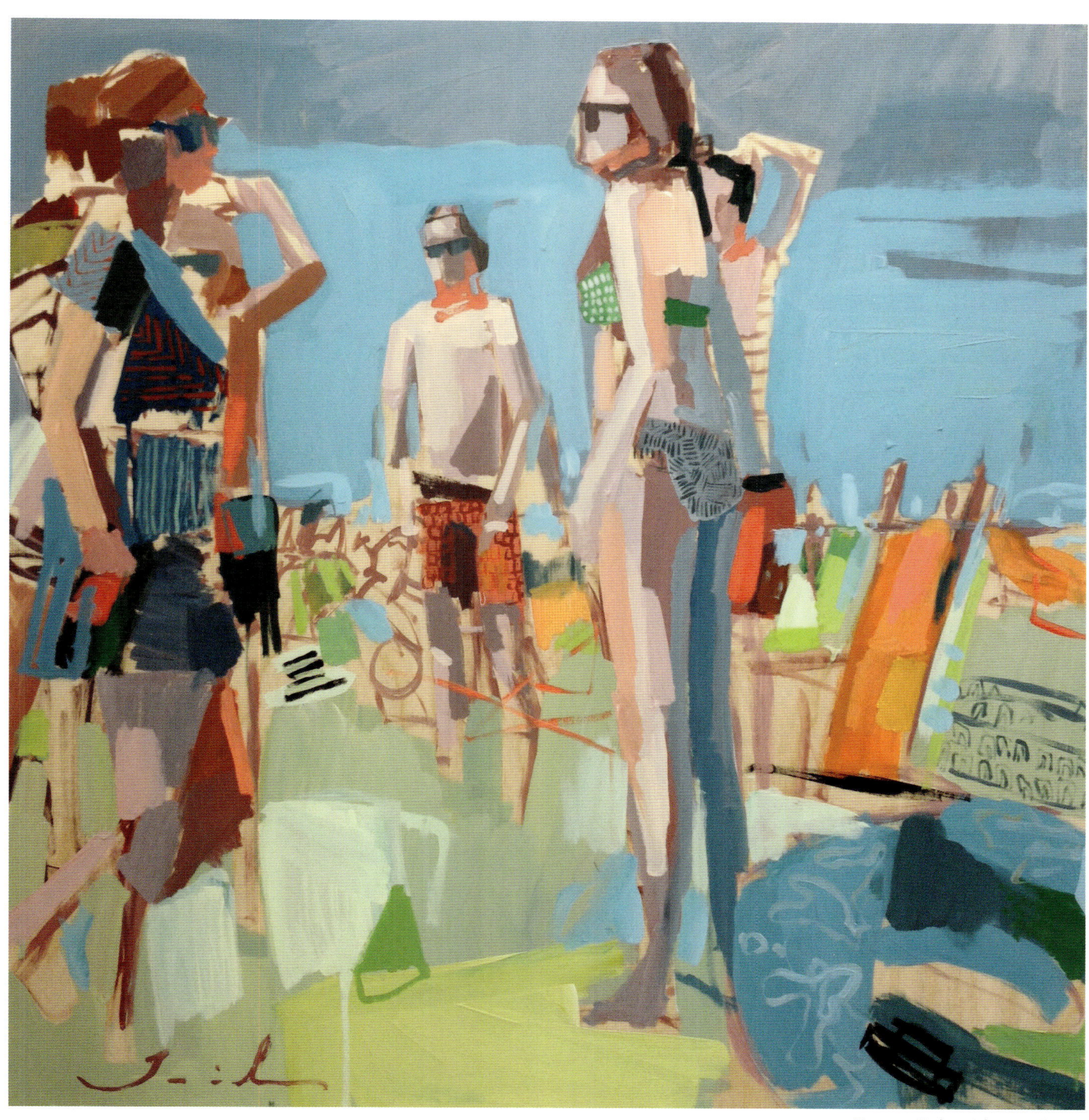

"Inner Tube Blues" 2014

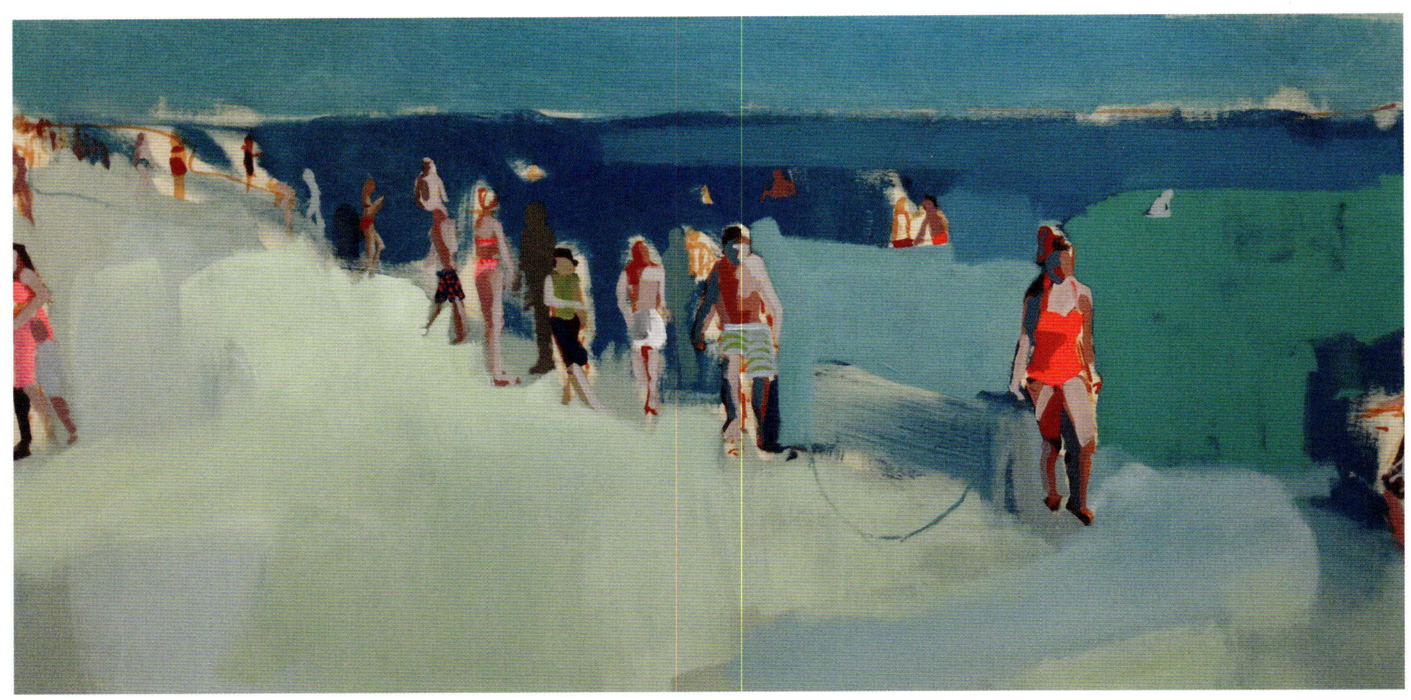

"Pink Suit" 2014

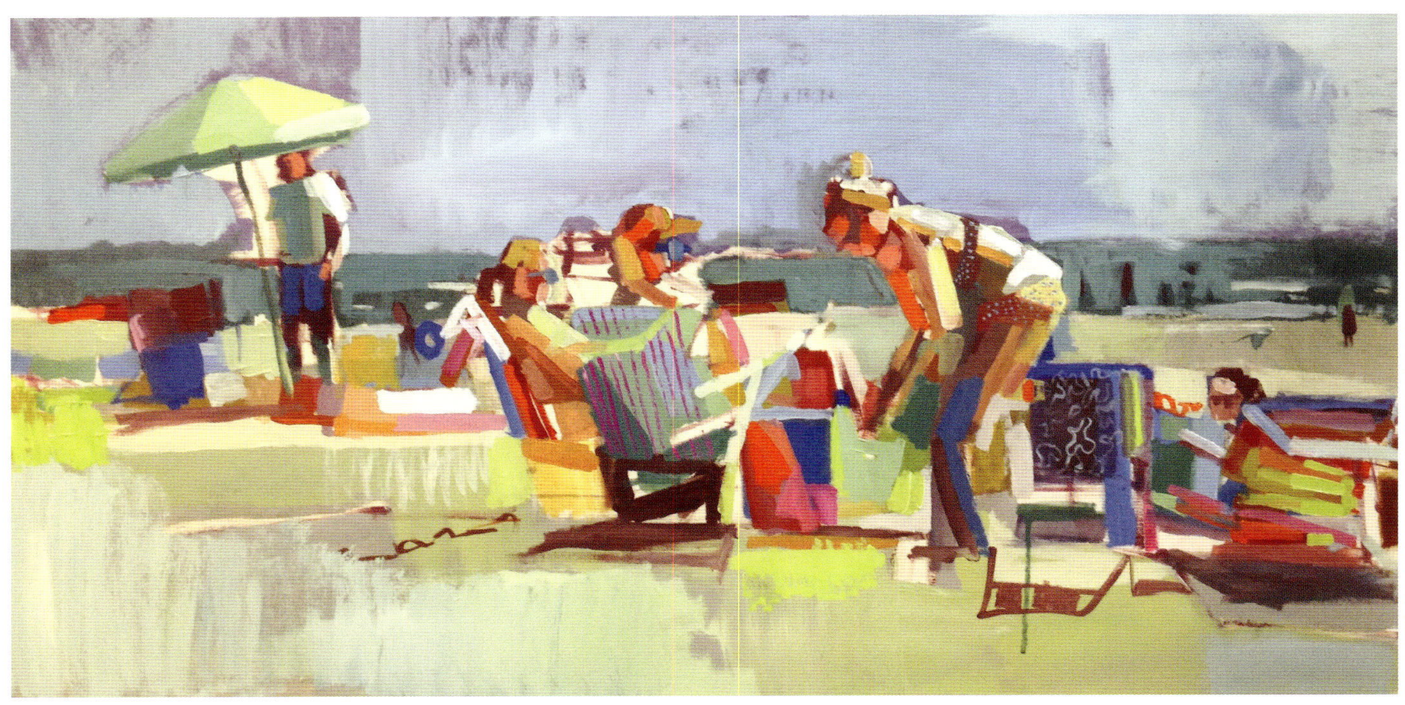

"A Cold One" 2014

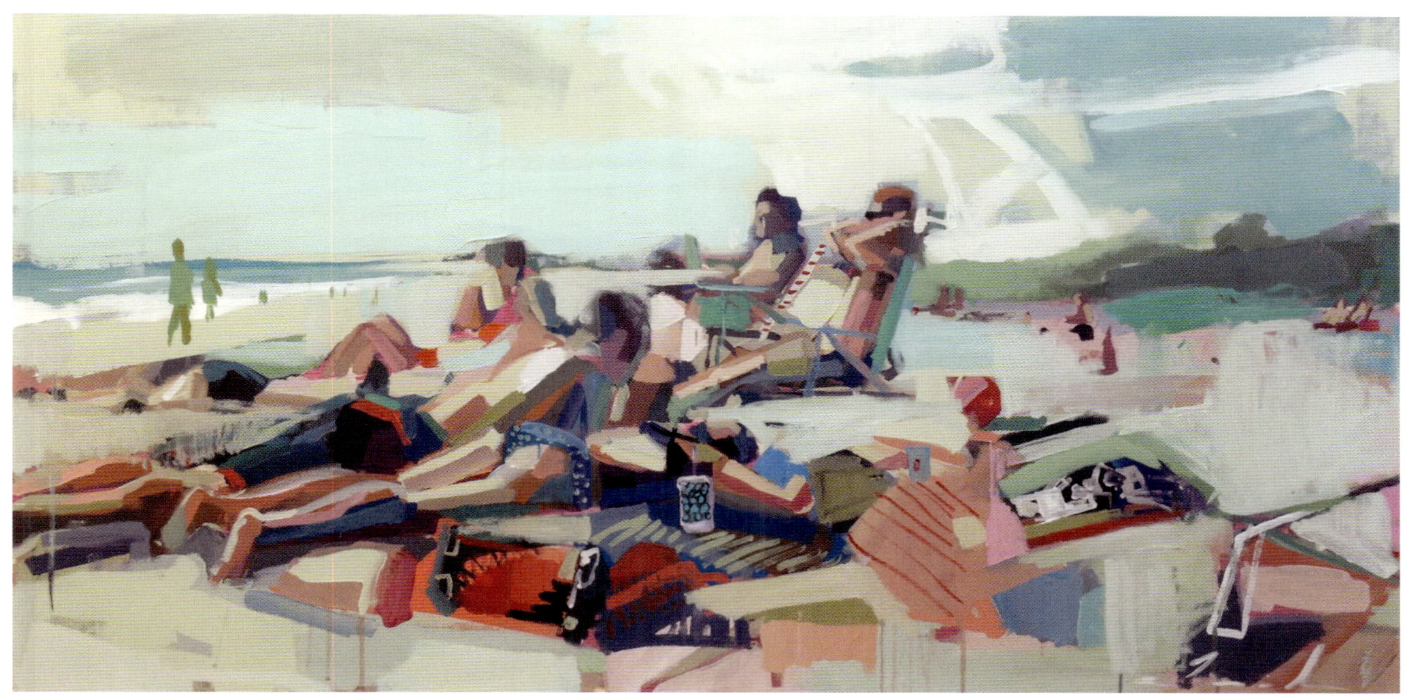

"Breathe It In" 2014

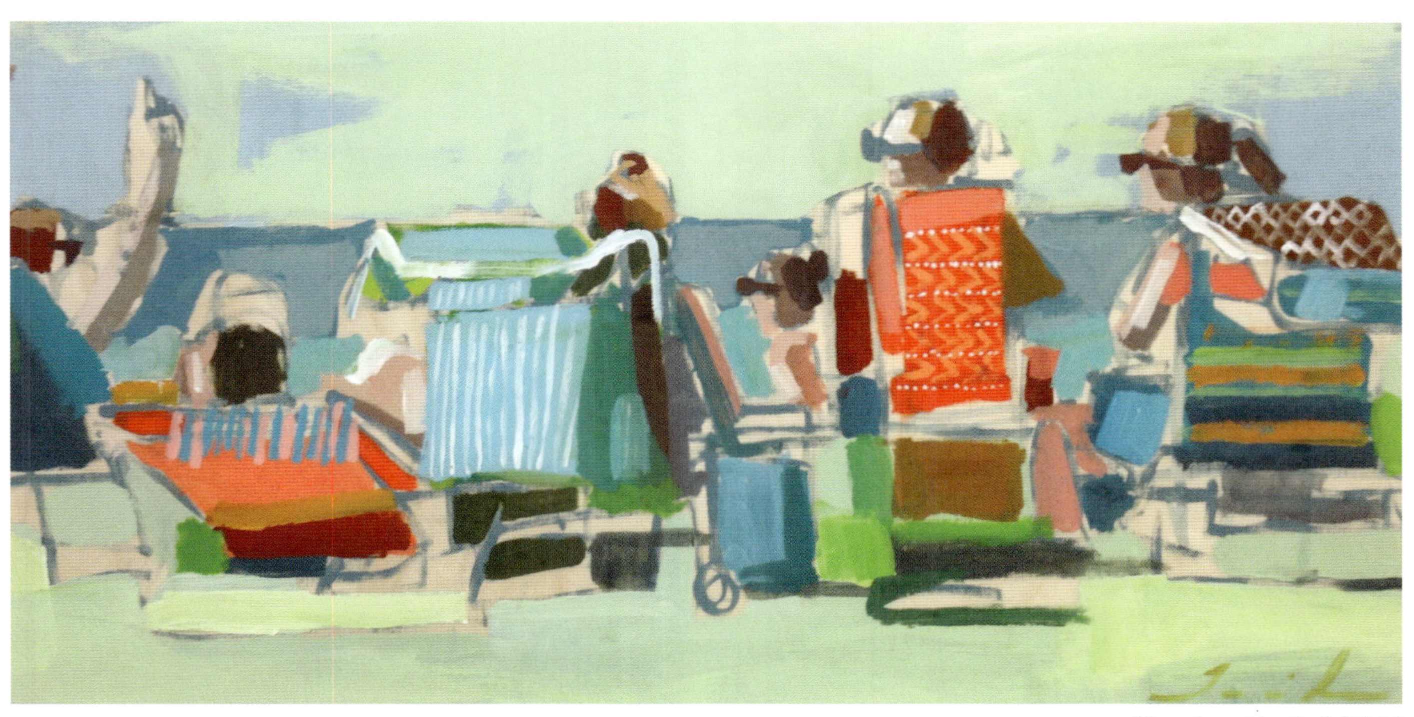

"Passing Me By" 2014

"Coastal Color" 2013

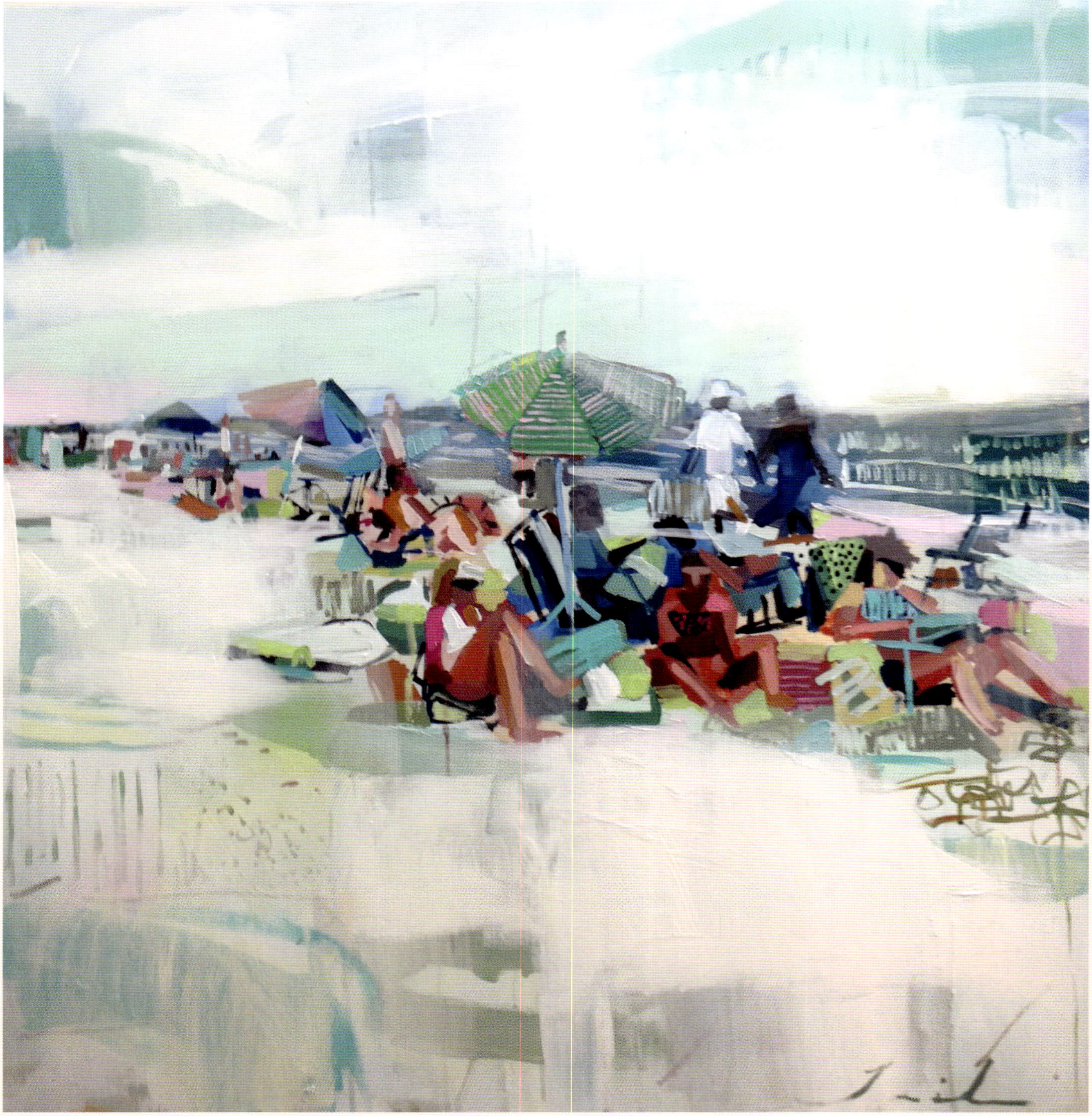

"Beyond the Pale" 2013

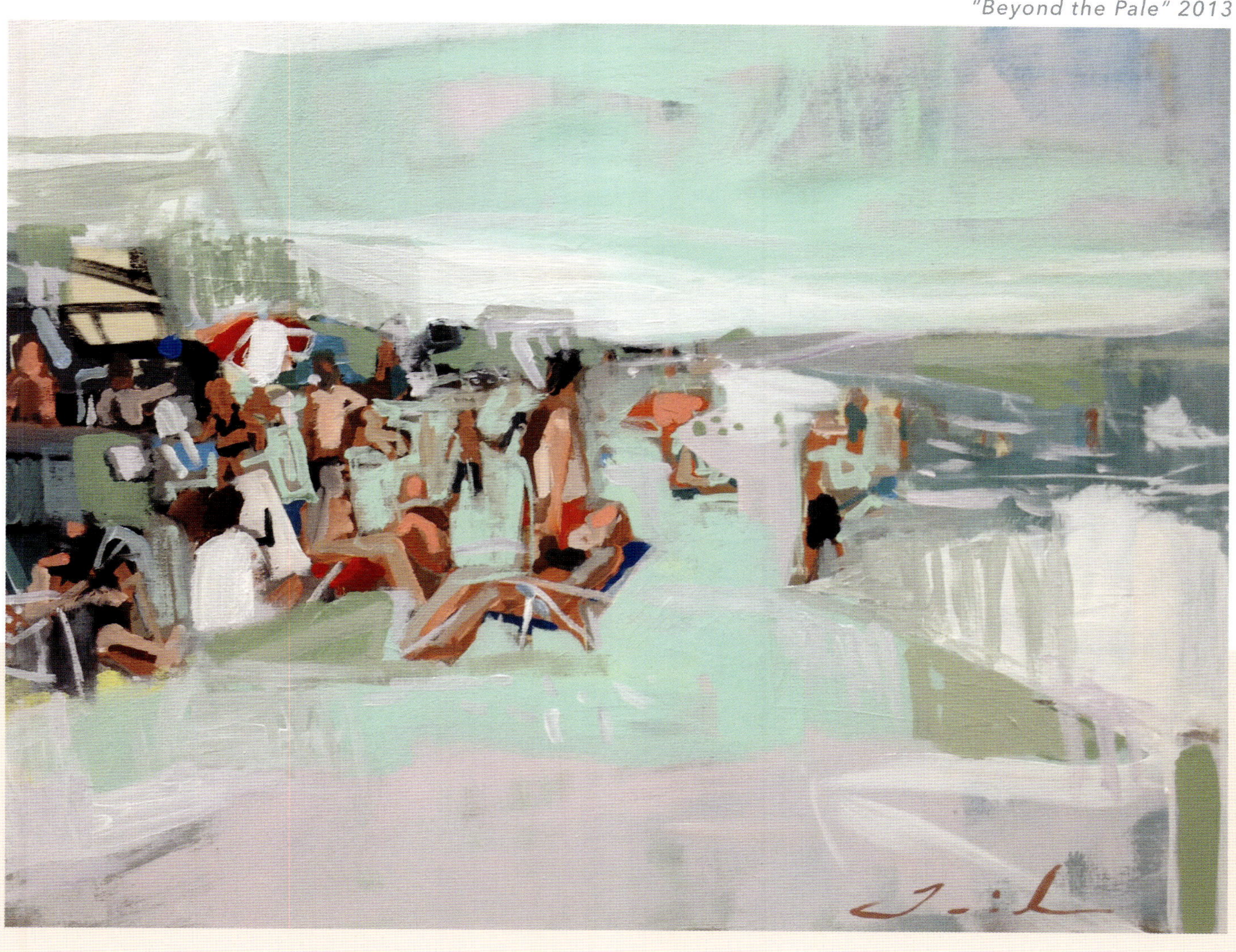

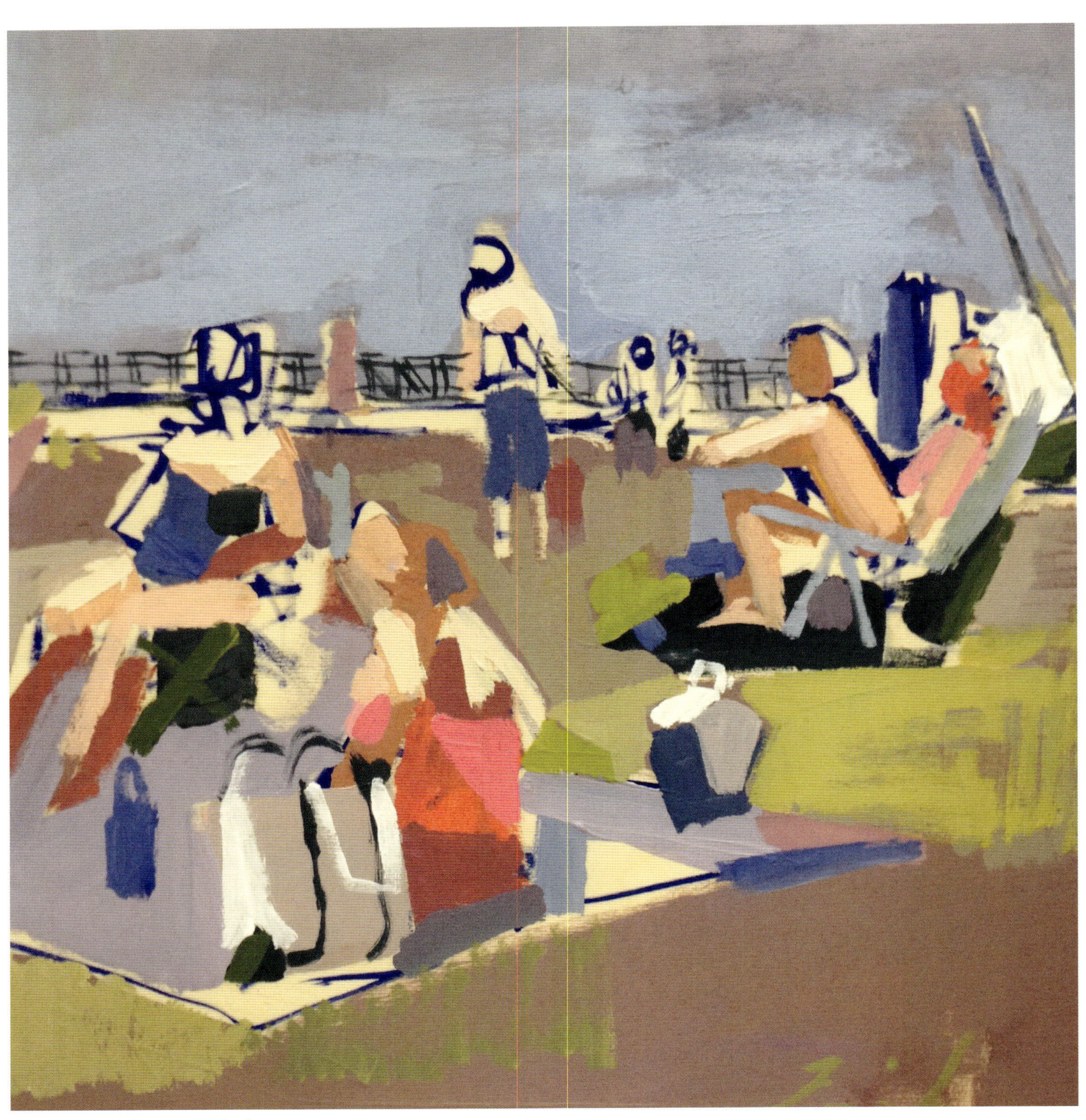

"Afternoon Shower" 2013

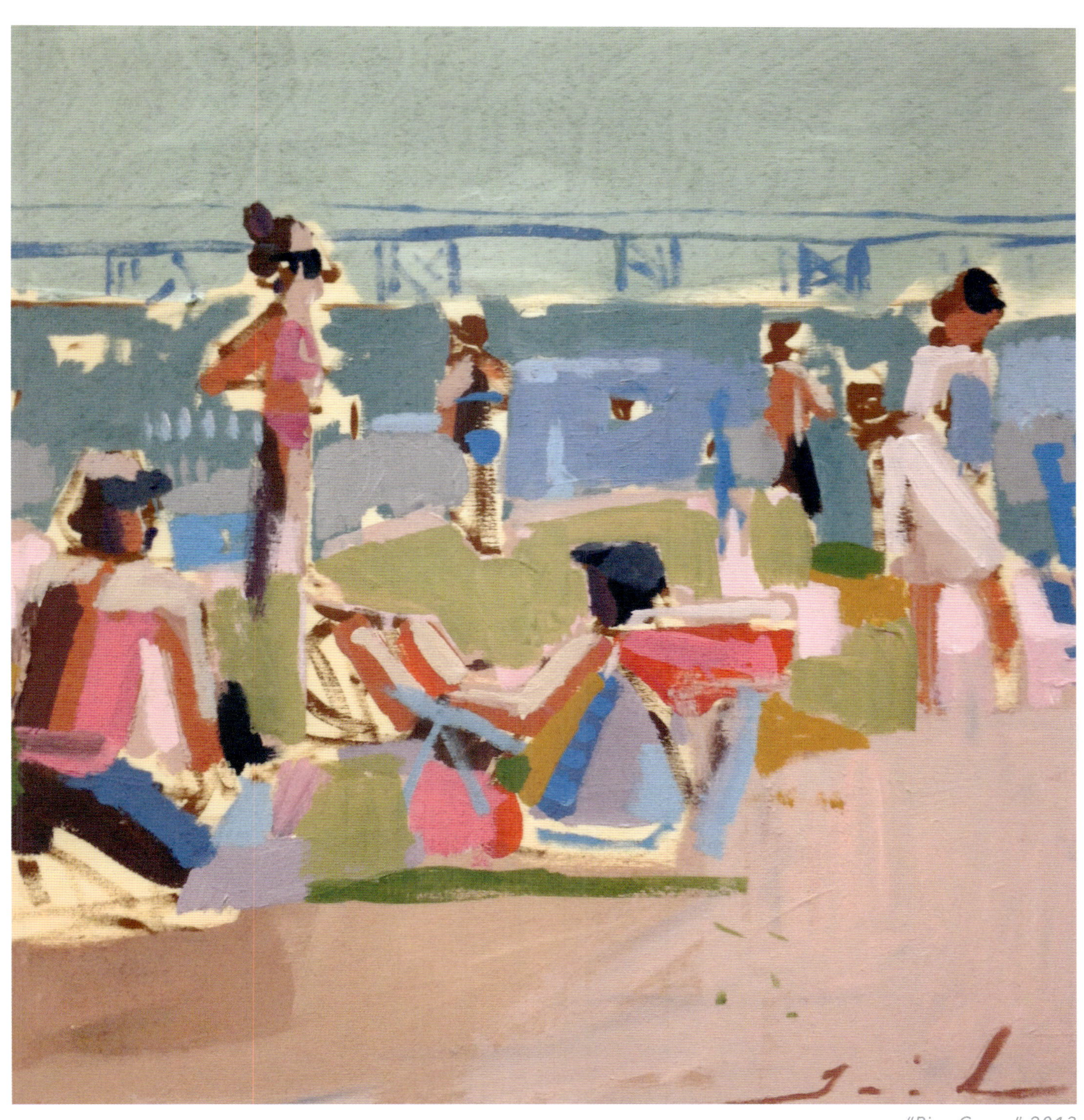

"Pier Camp" 2013

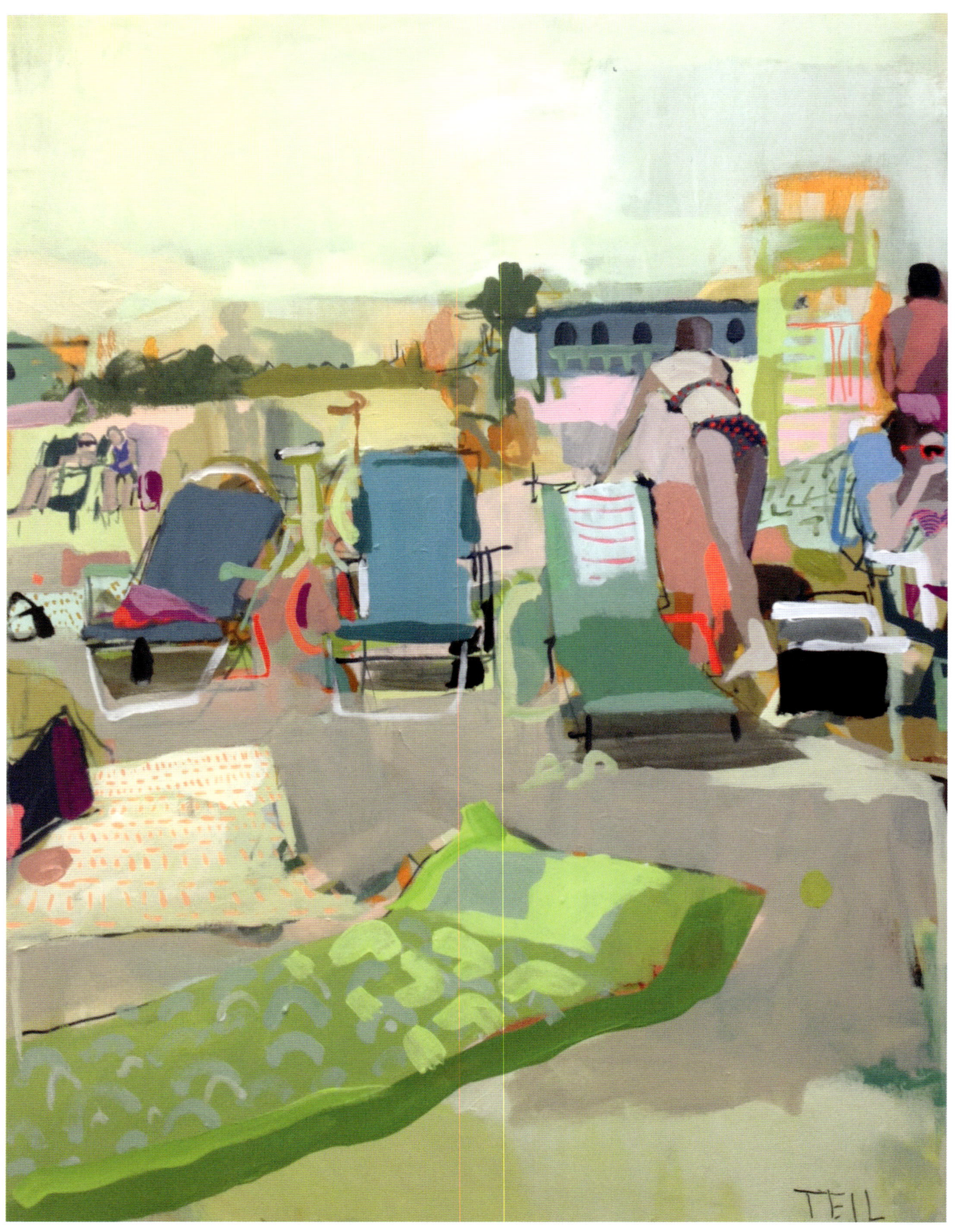
TEIL

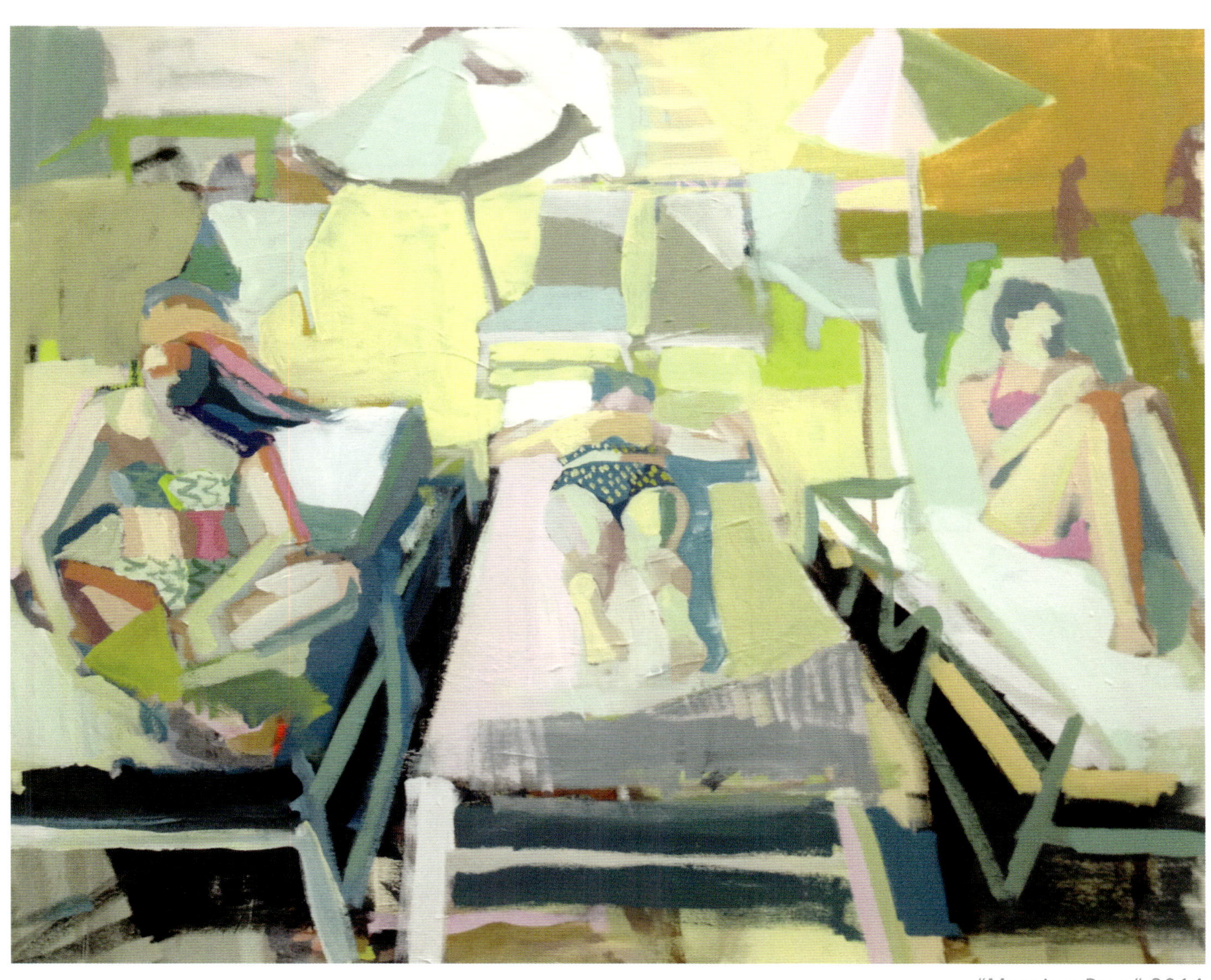

"Morning Rays" 2014

For a period of time, I put immense pressure on myself to choose the right subject and develop an underlying statement before I even picked up the paintbrush. I remember coming across a quote in the Charleston newspaper that I will never forget that freed me of this burden. Local artist Nathan Durfee stated that artists should "paint what they want to paint first, then figure out why [they're] painting it." That's exactly what happened with my beach series. I later realized a plethora of attractive elements within this subject that was wooing me the whole time: the patterns in the swimsuit, the vast open sky juxtaposed with the tightly positioned crowd, the dancing umbrellas reflecting light and dimension, and the translucent sea gradating from dark to light values.

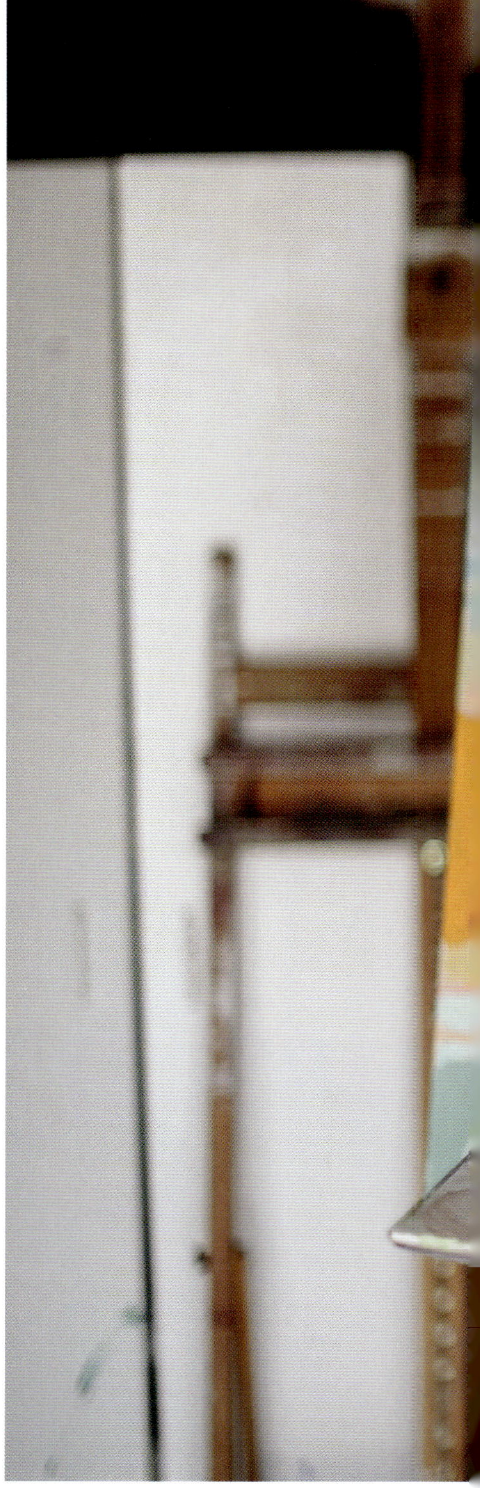

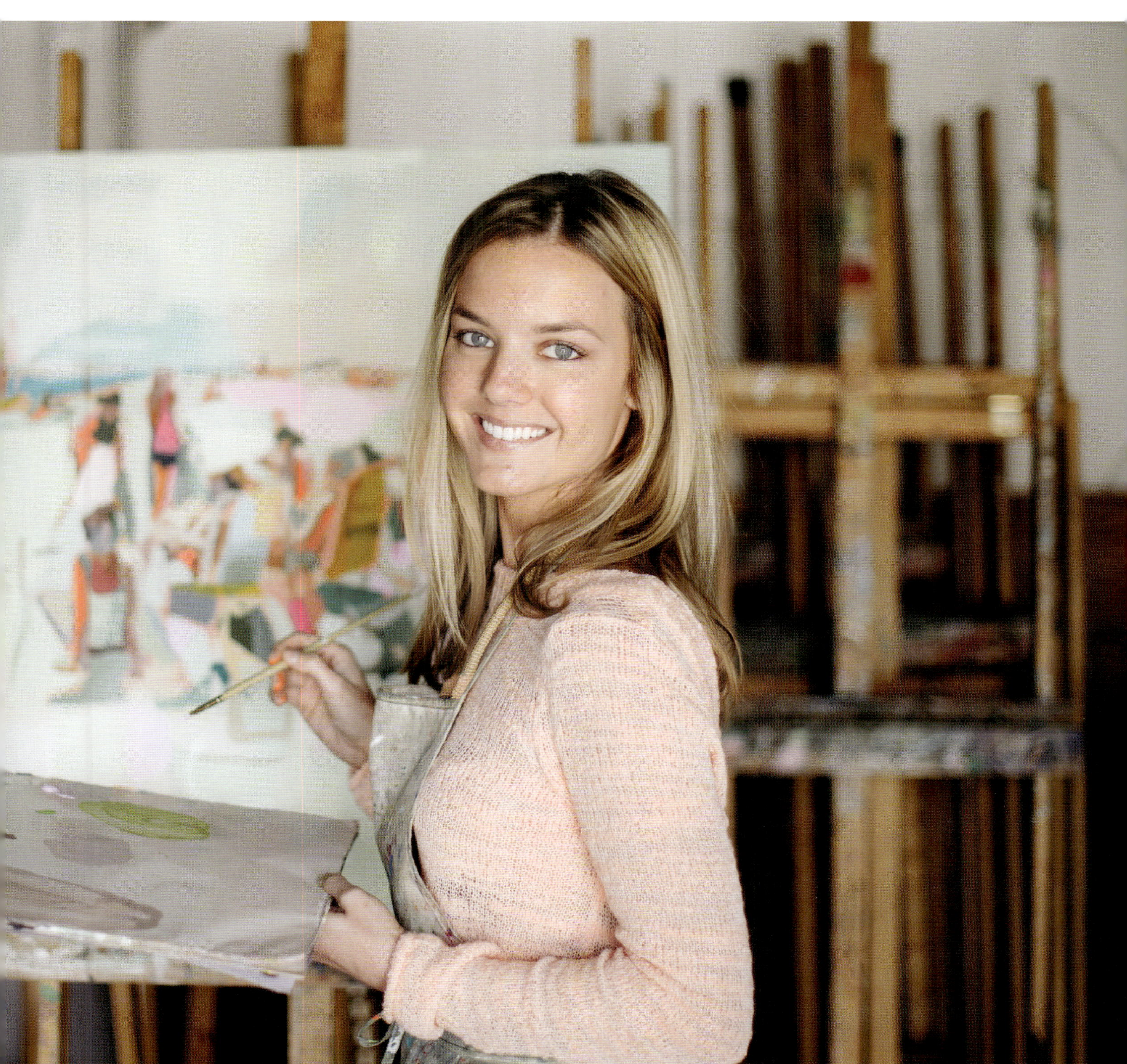

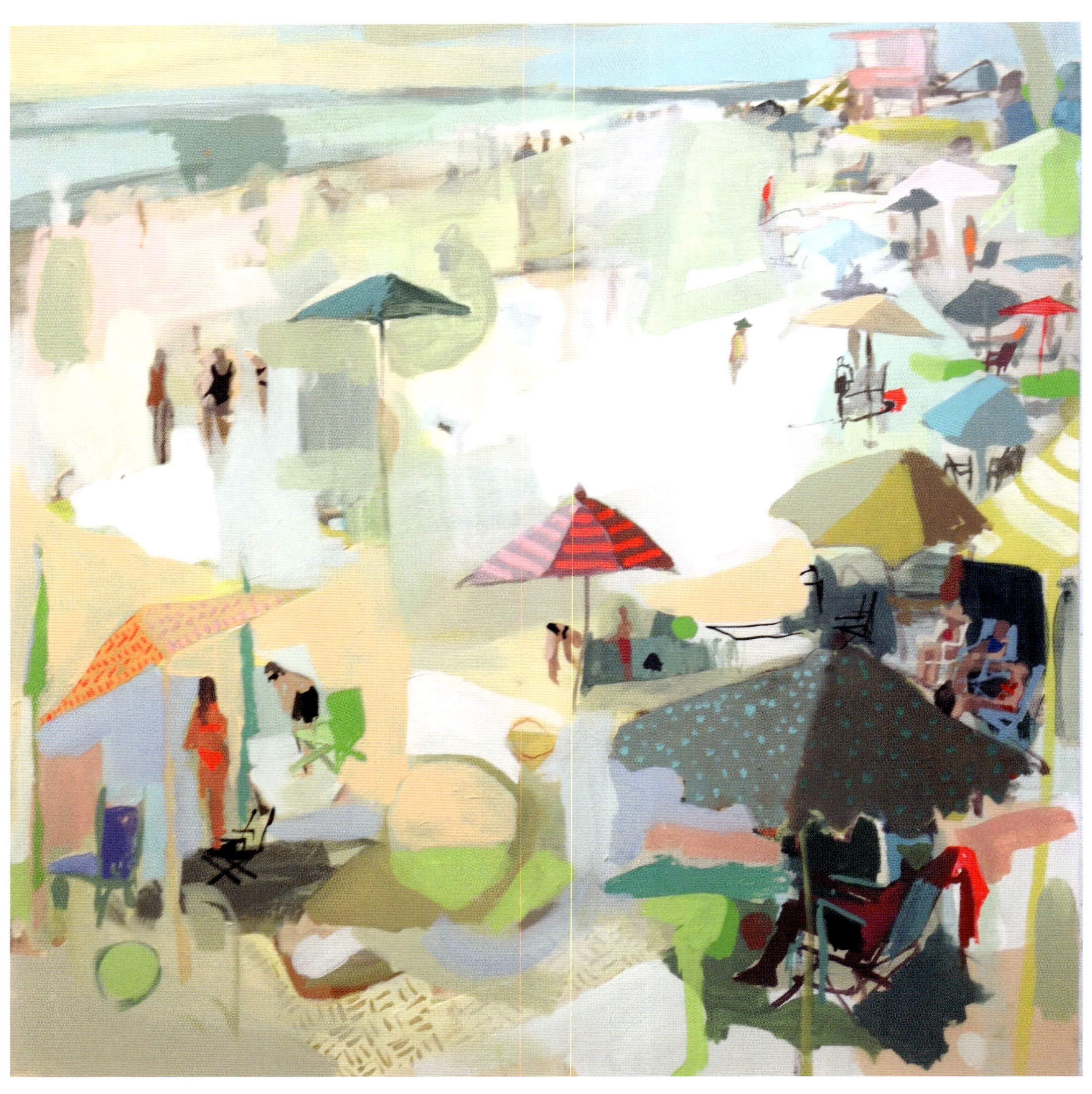

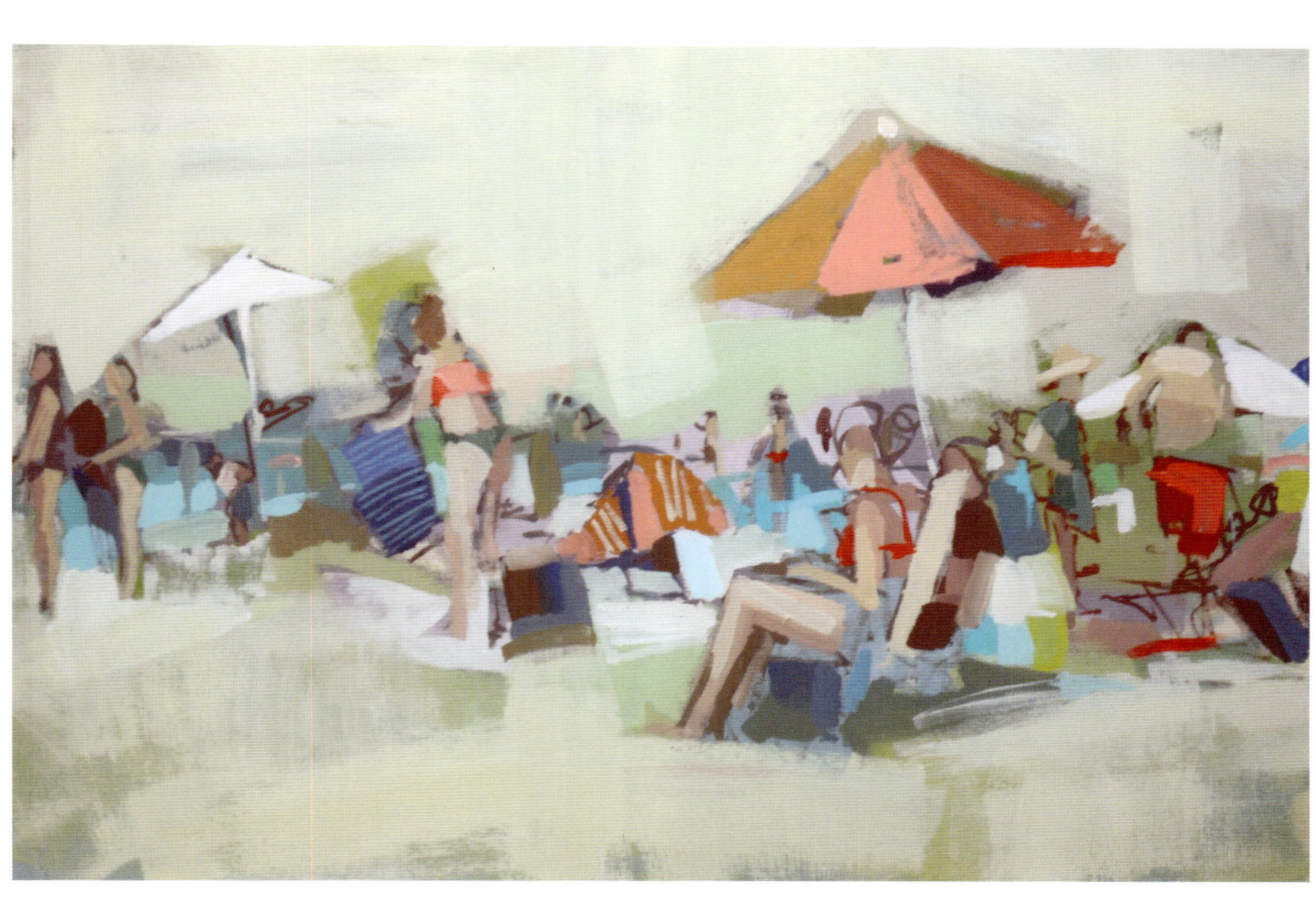

"10th at Folly" 2013

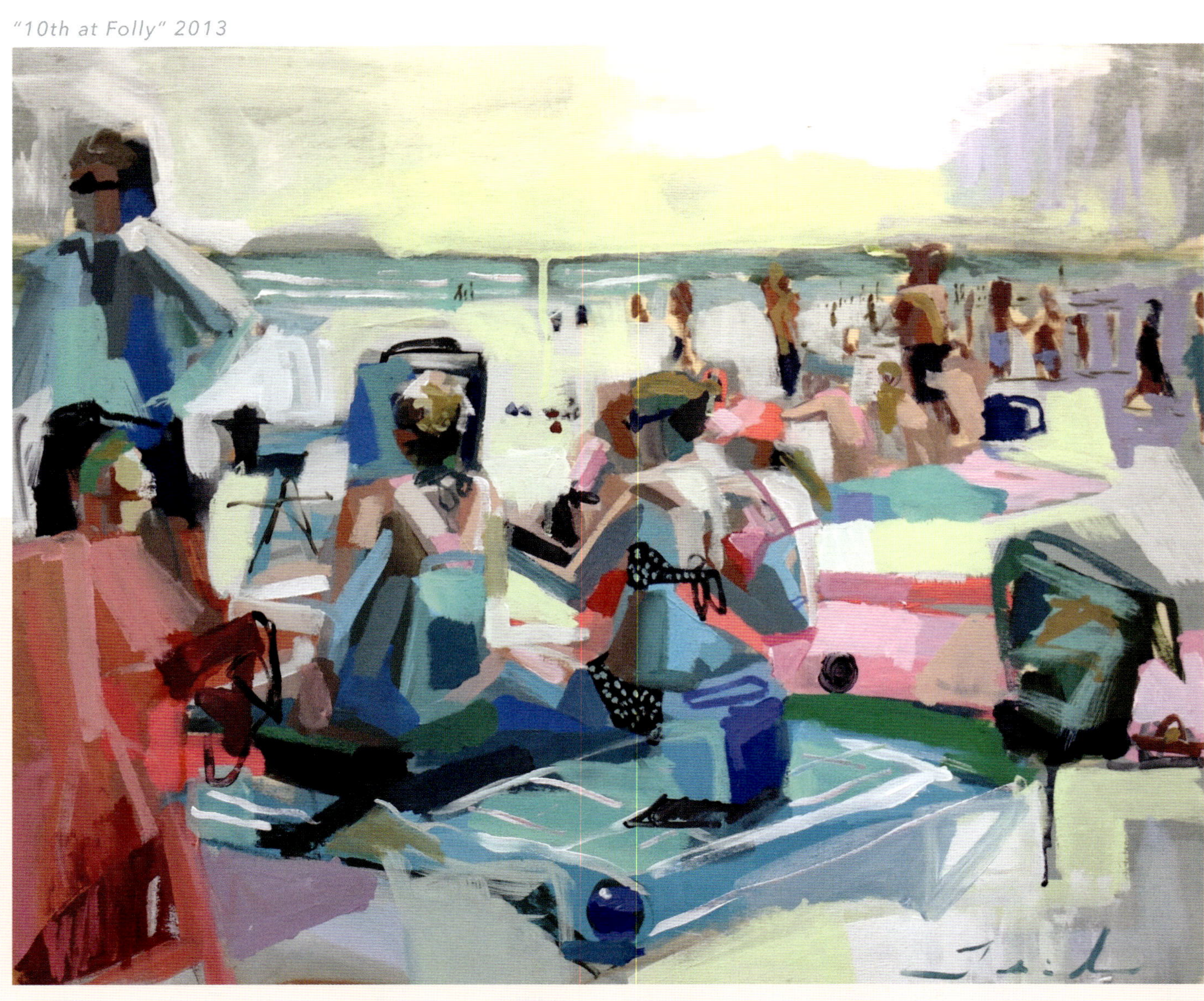

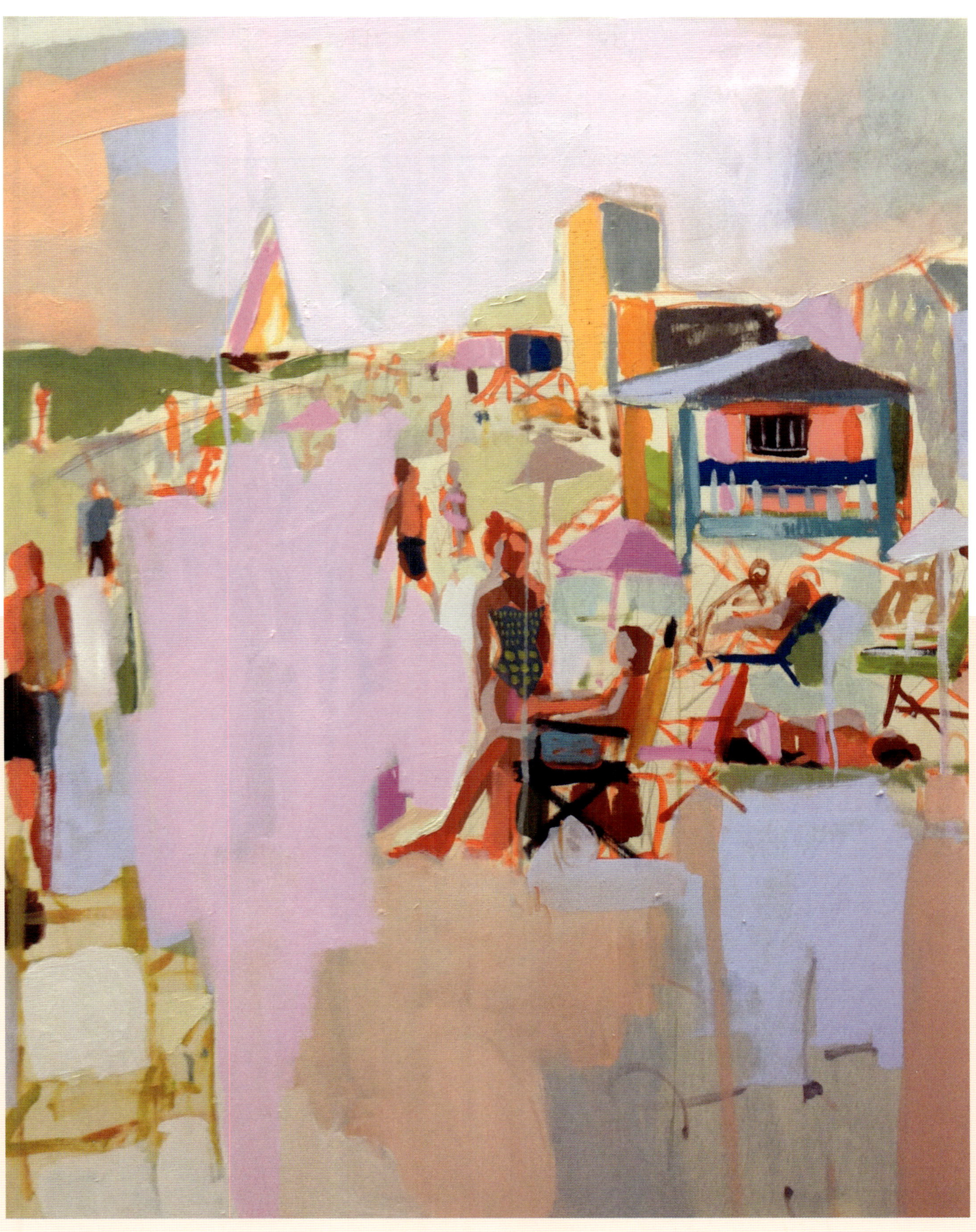

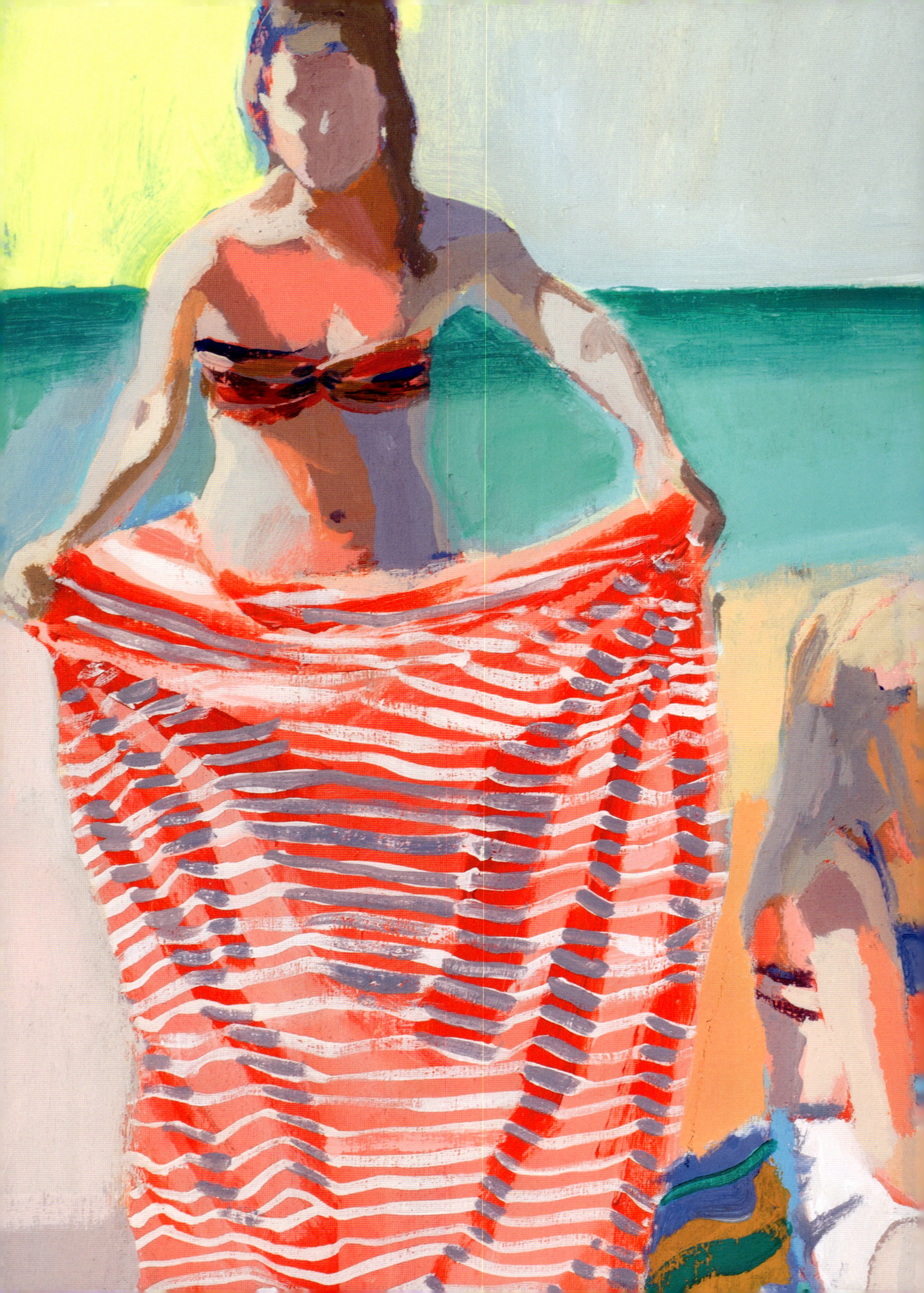

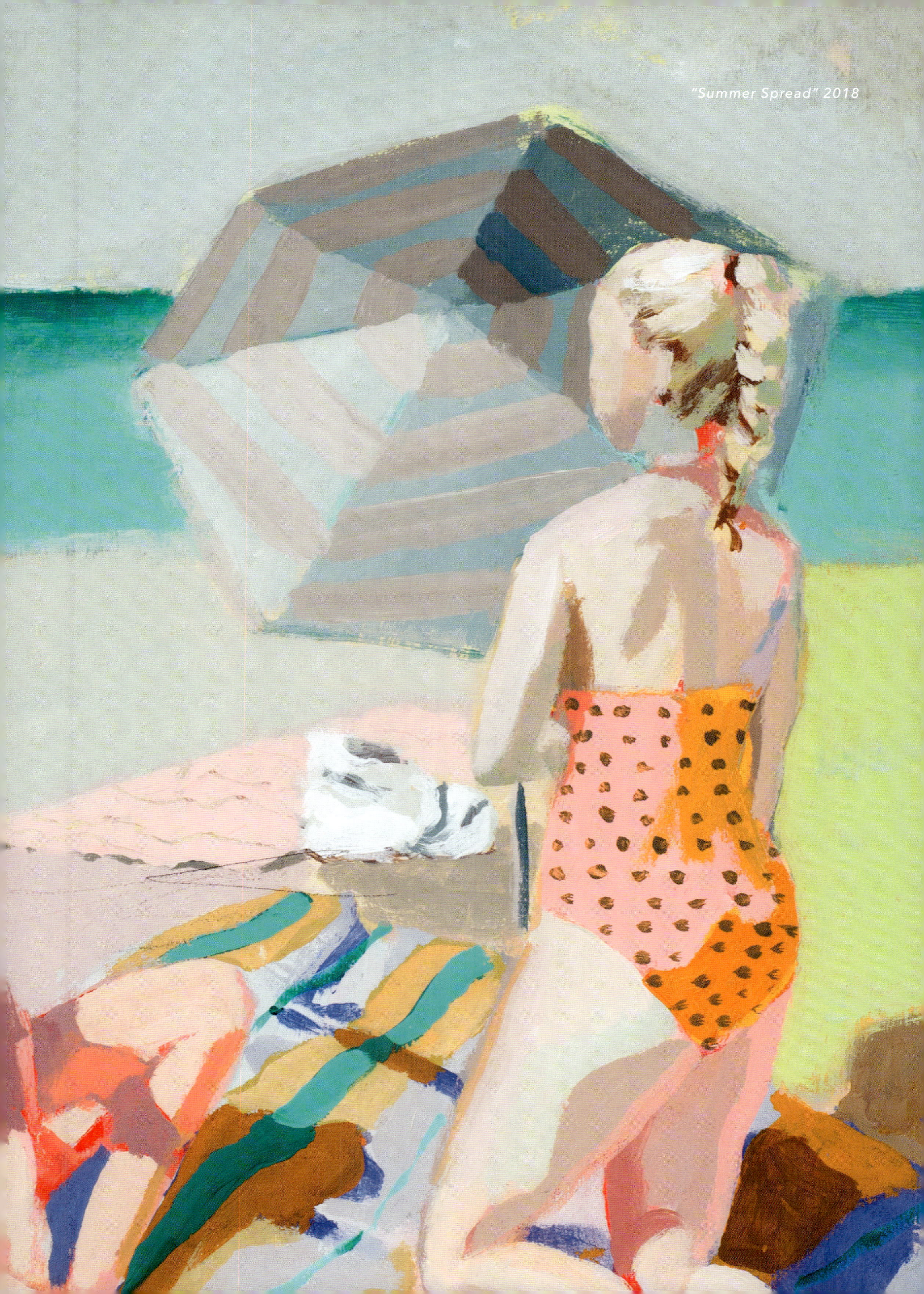

"Summer Spread" 2018

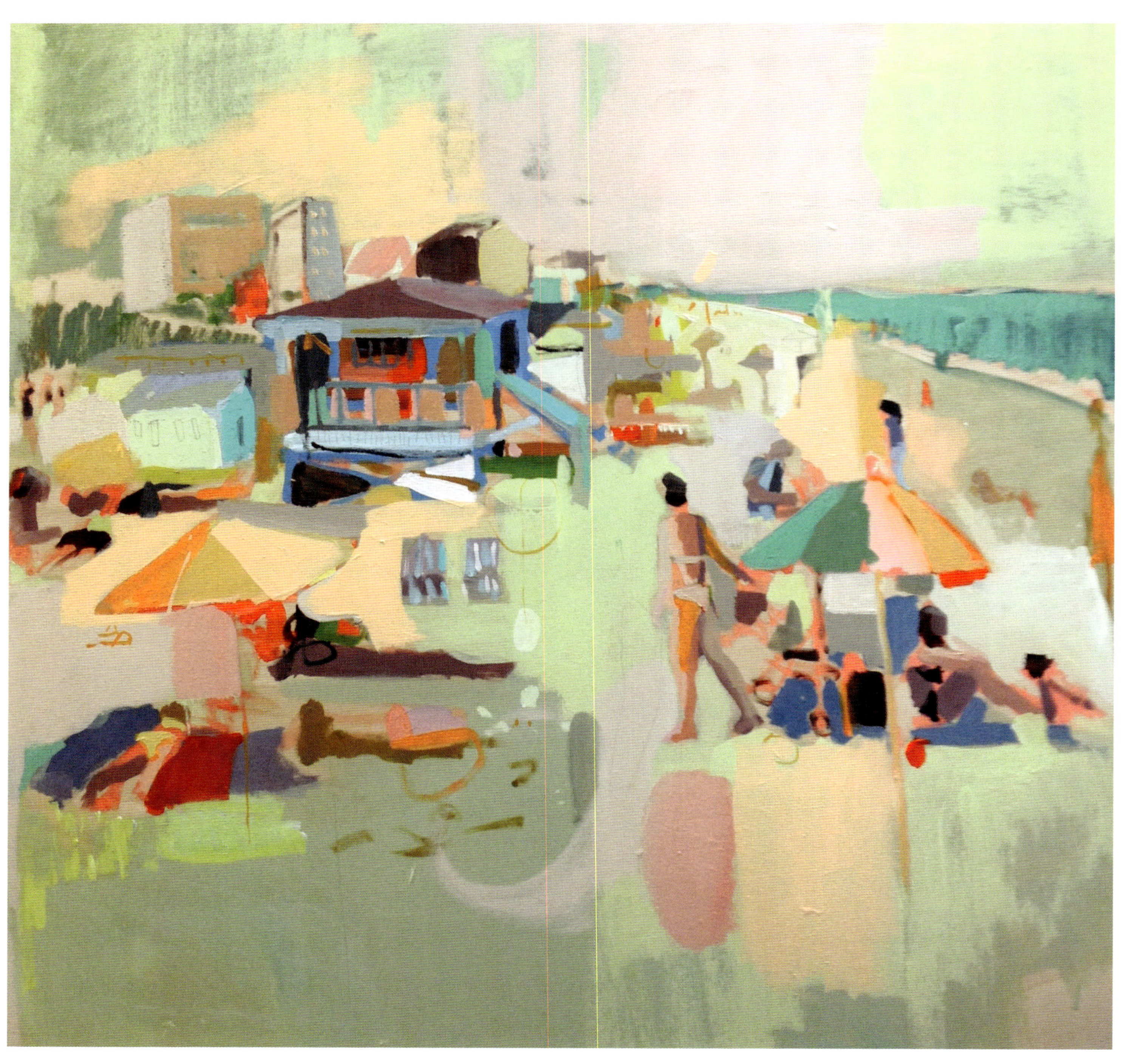

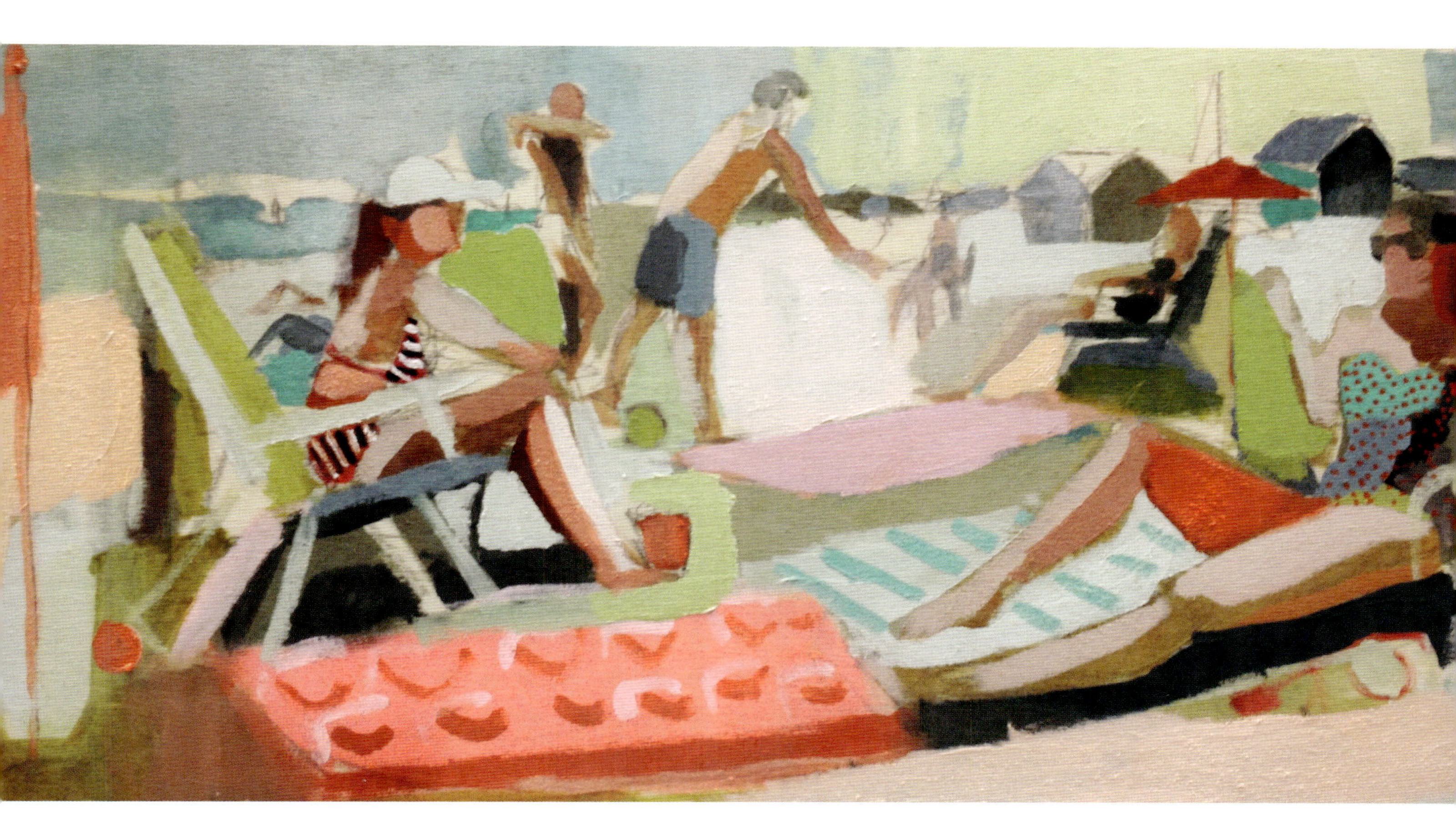

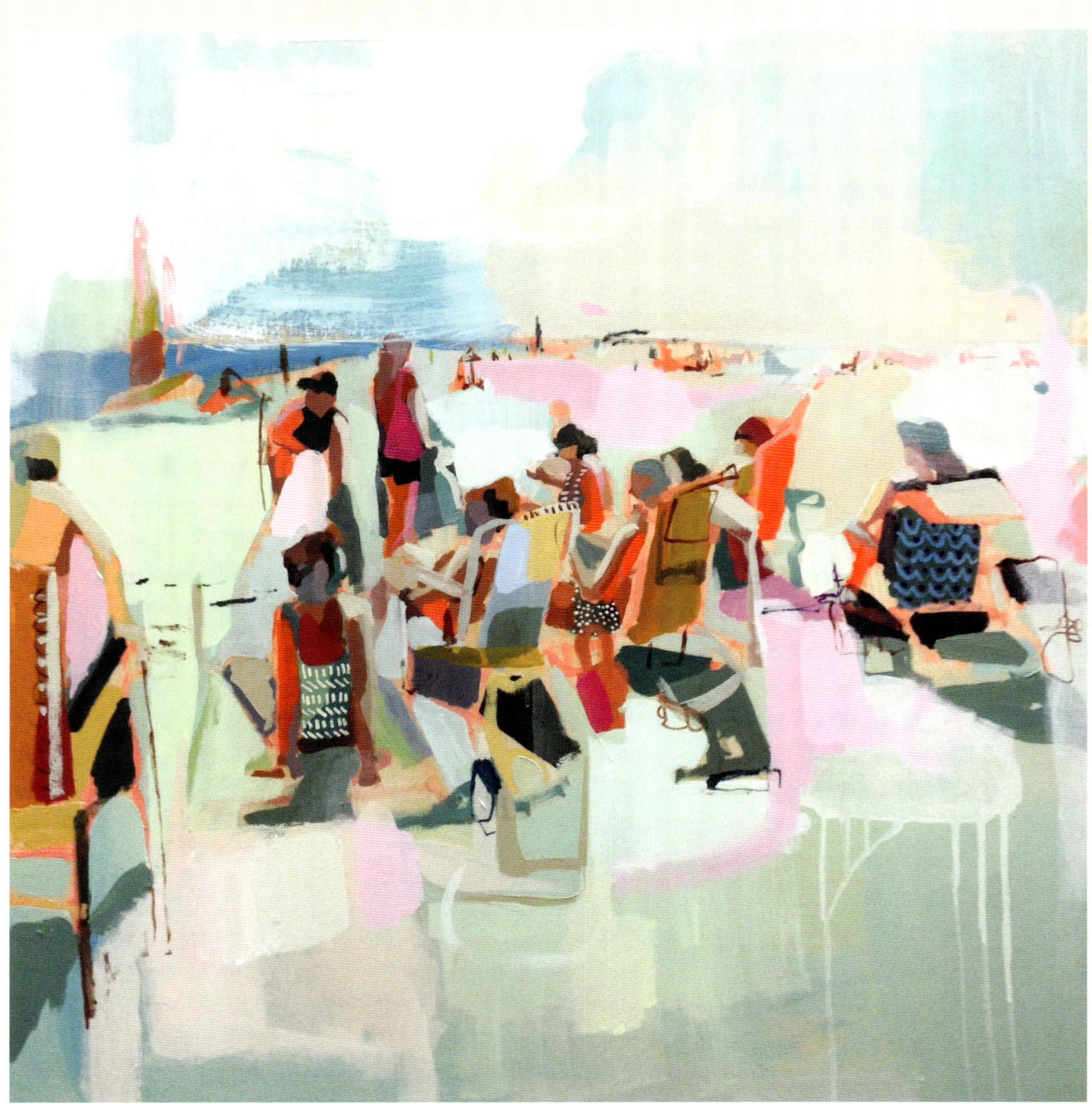

"Bask" 2014

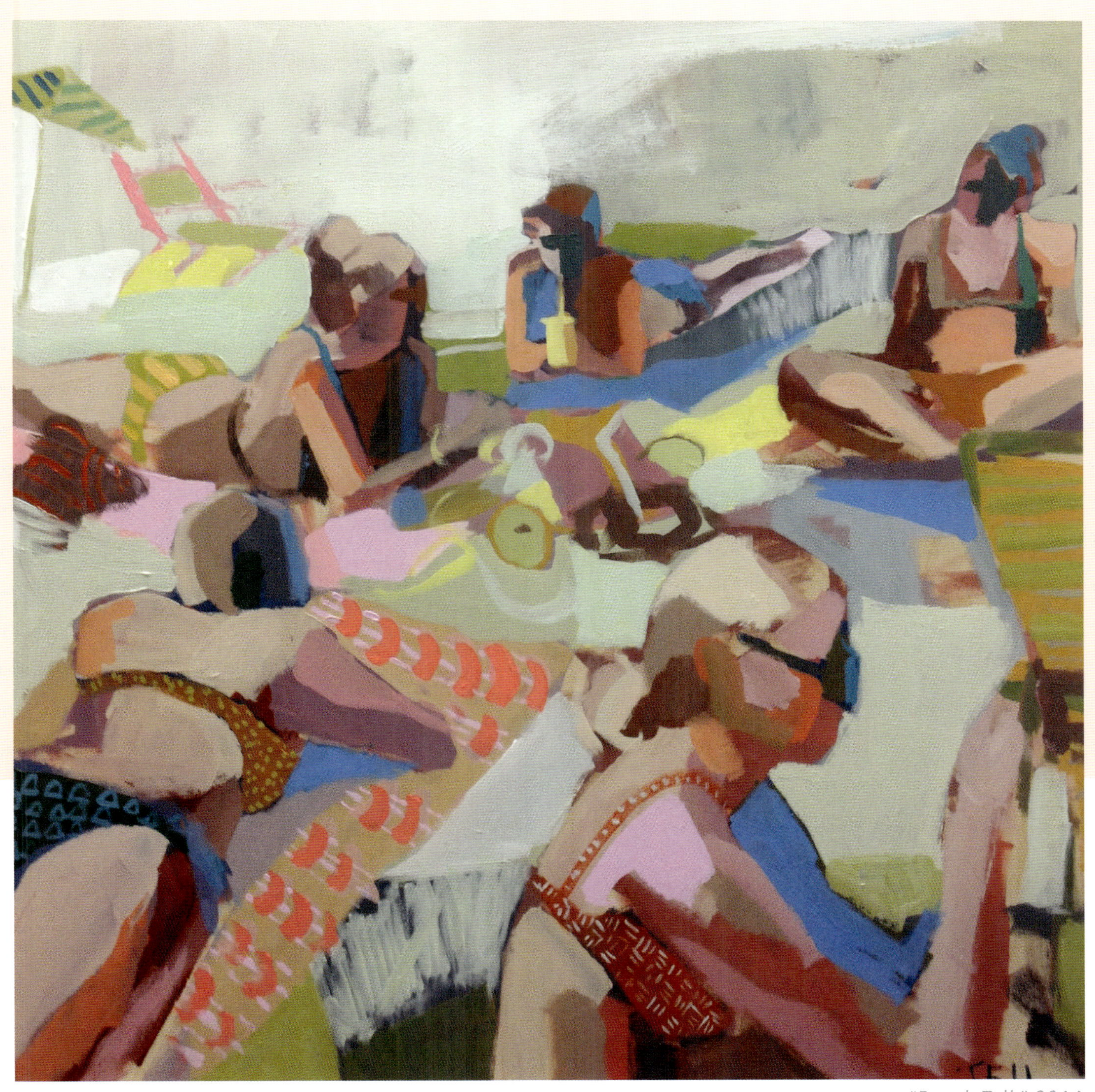

"Beach Talk" 2014

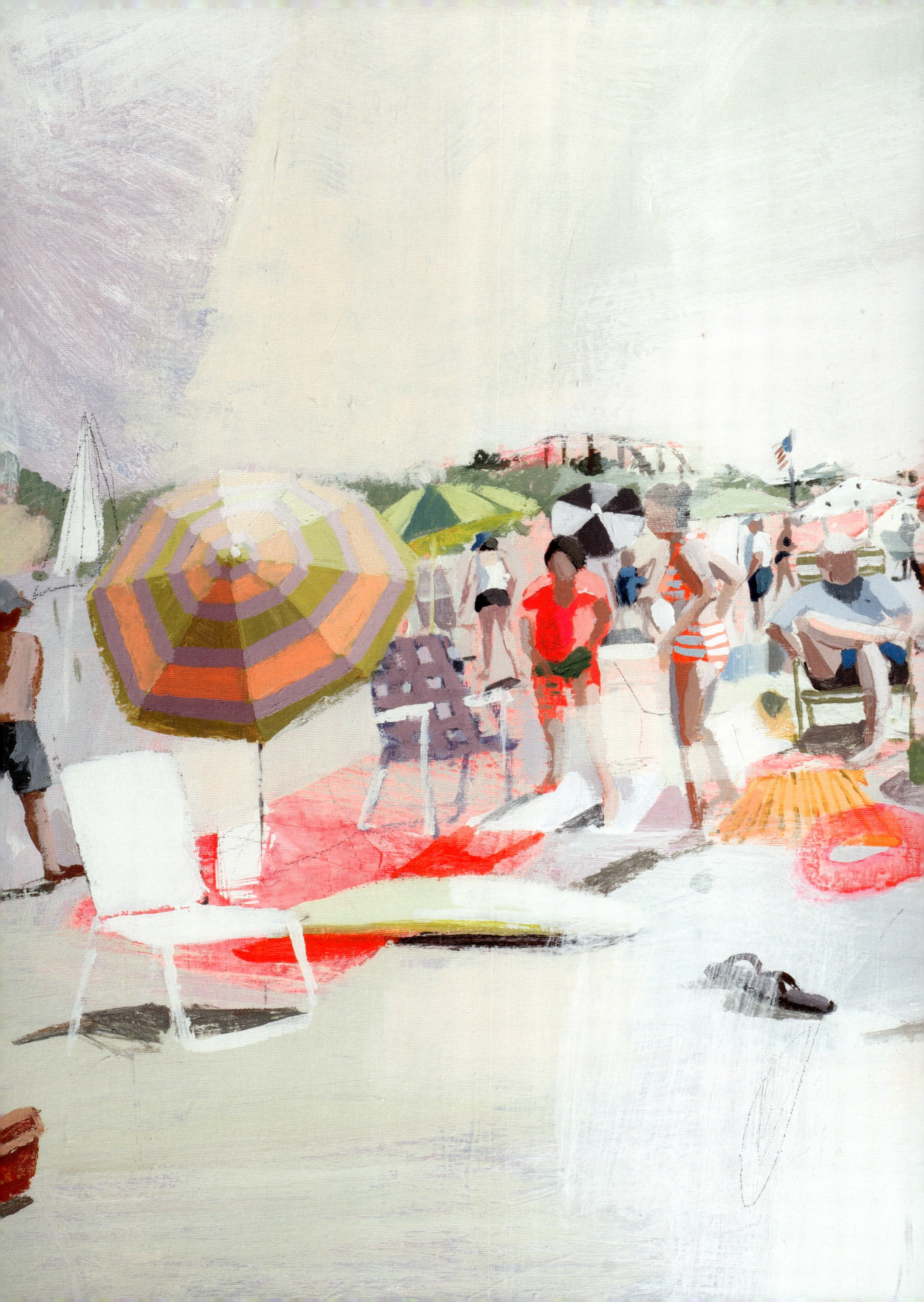

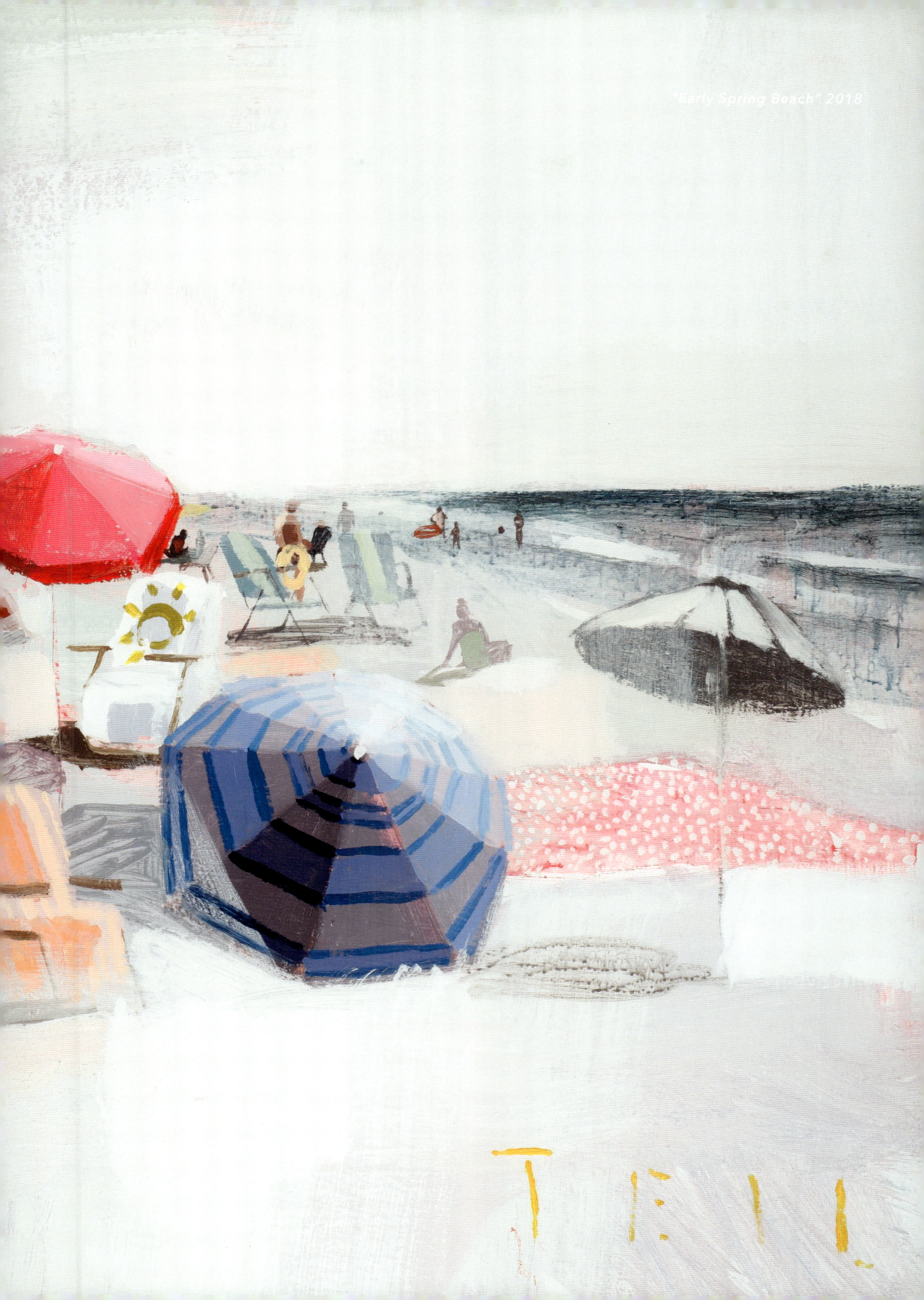

"Early Spring Beach" 2018

"Macy's Beach" 2014

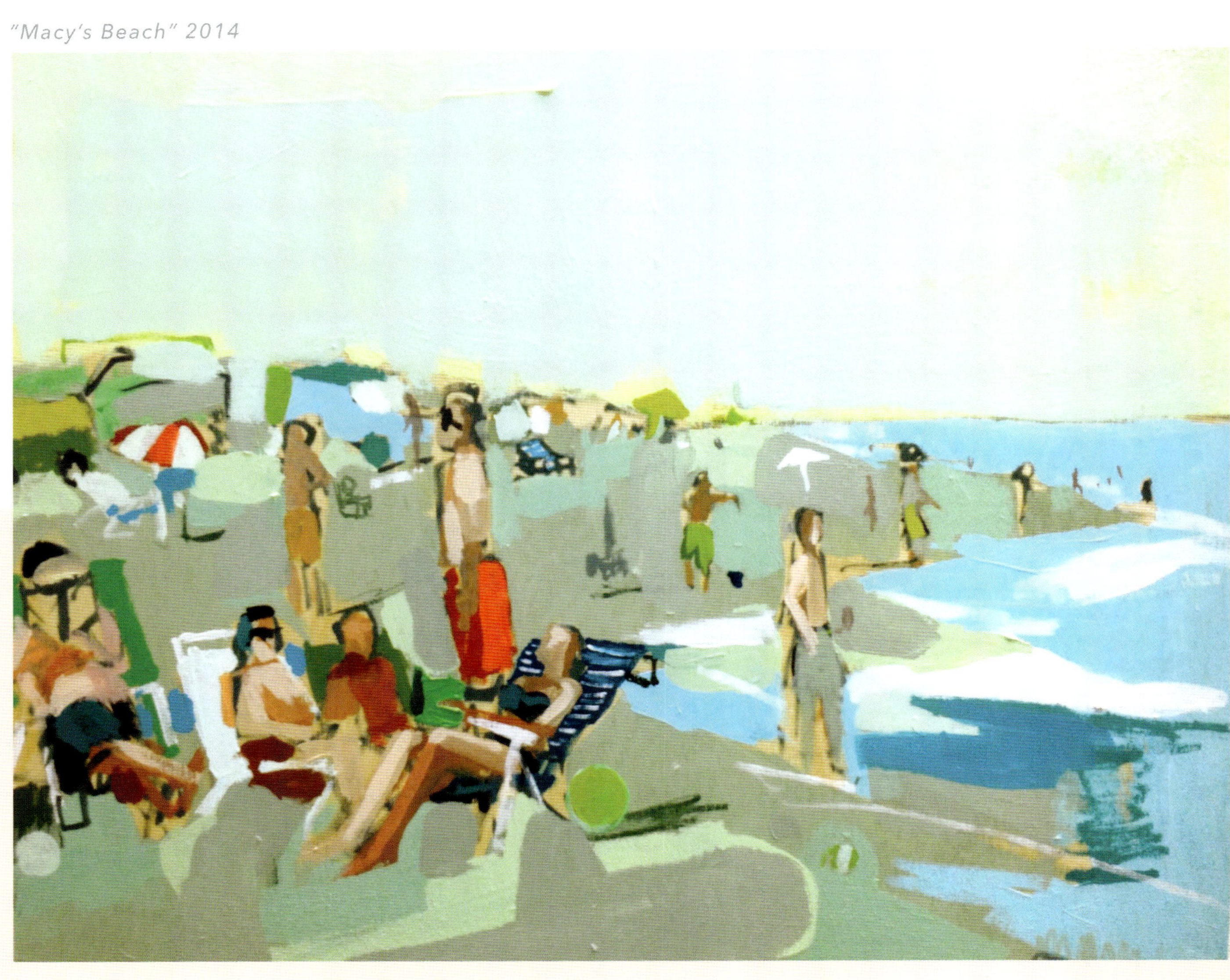

"Seeking the Spot" 2013

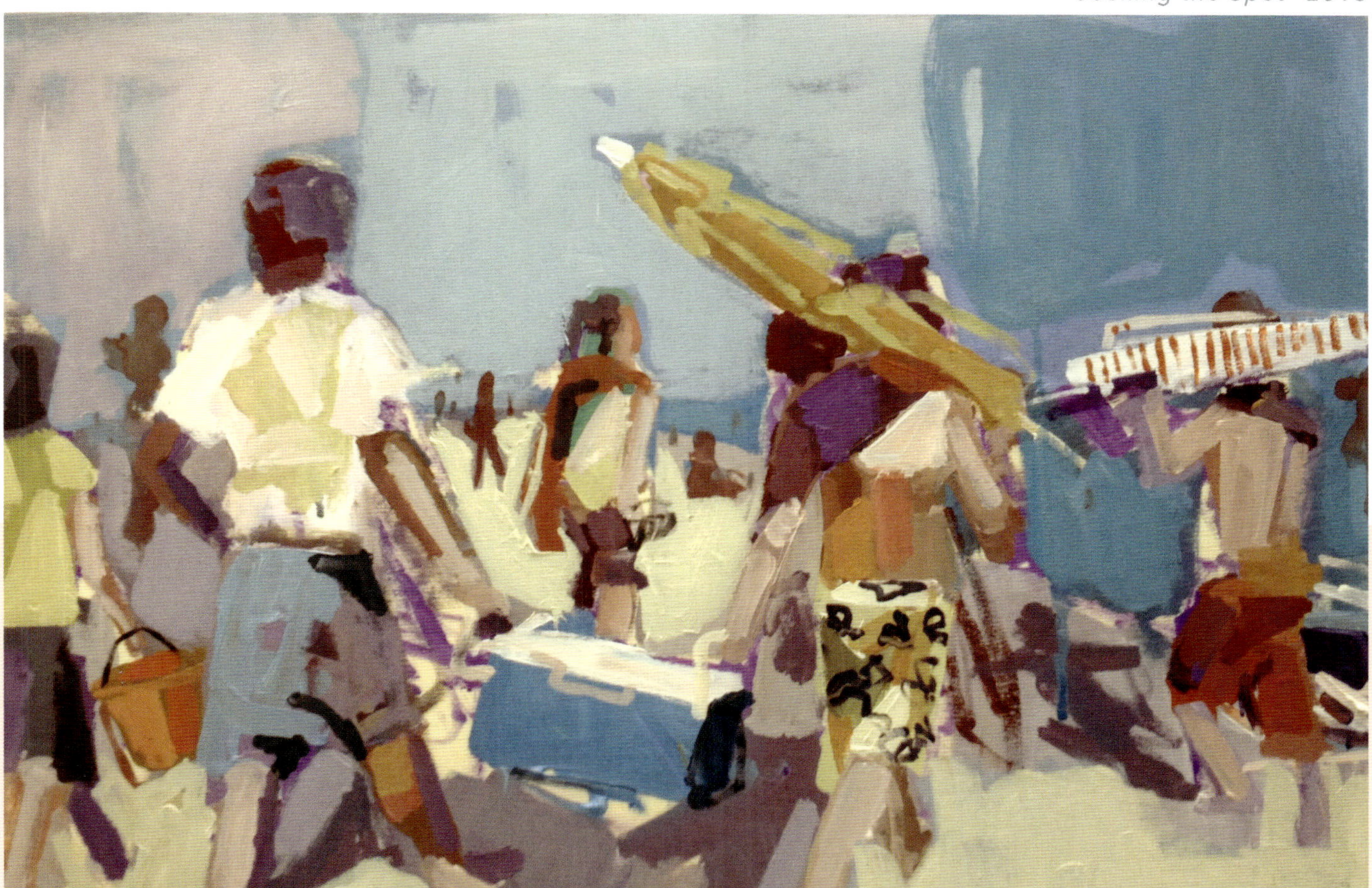

"Peaches and Cream" 2014

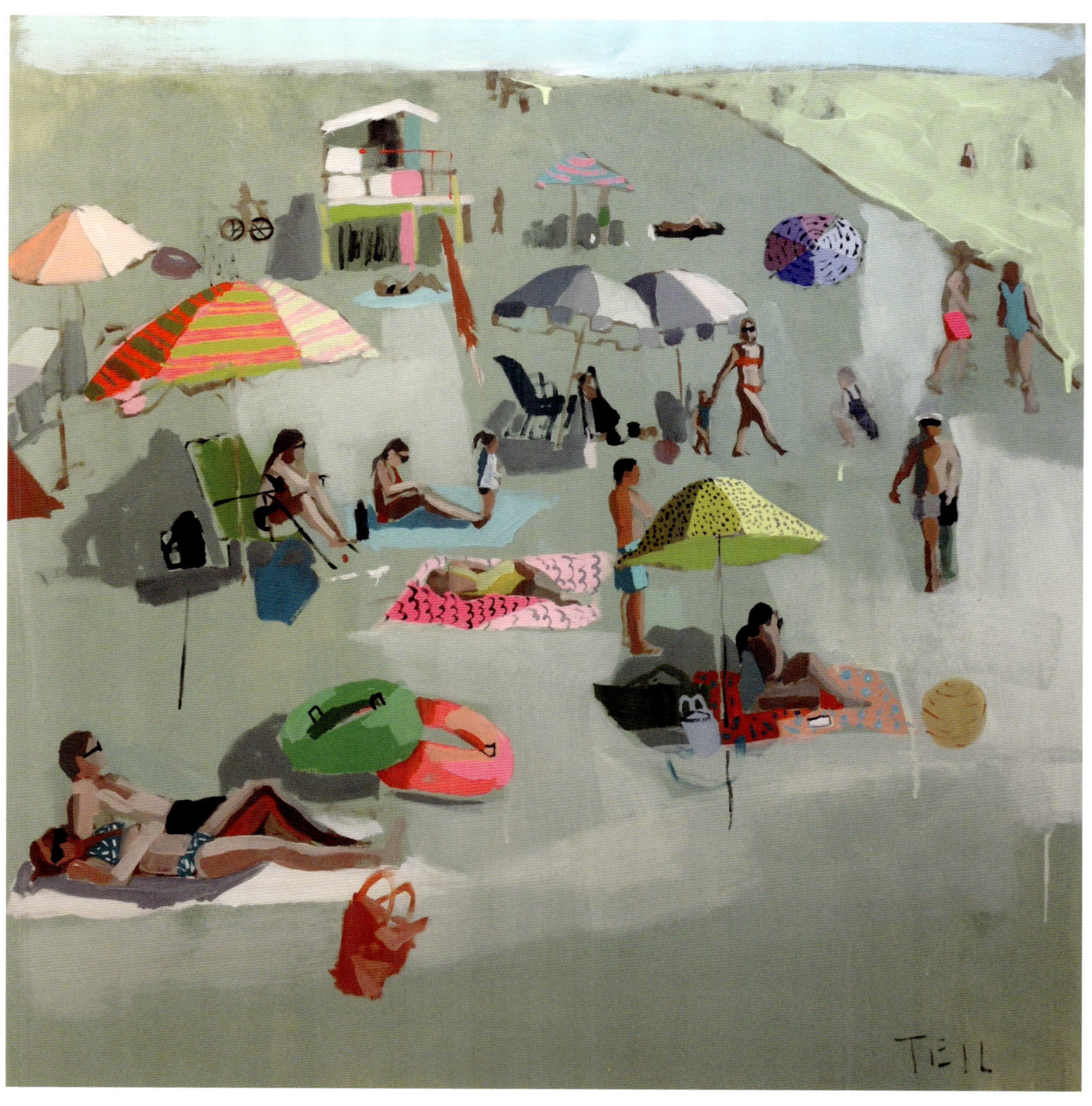
TEIL

"Weekend Tradition" 2014

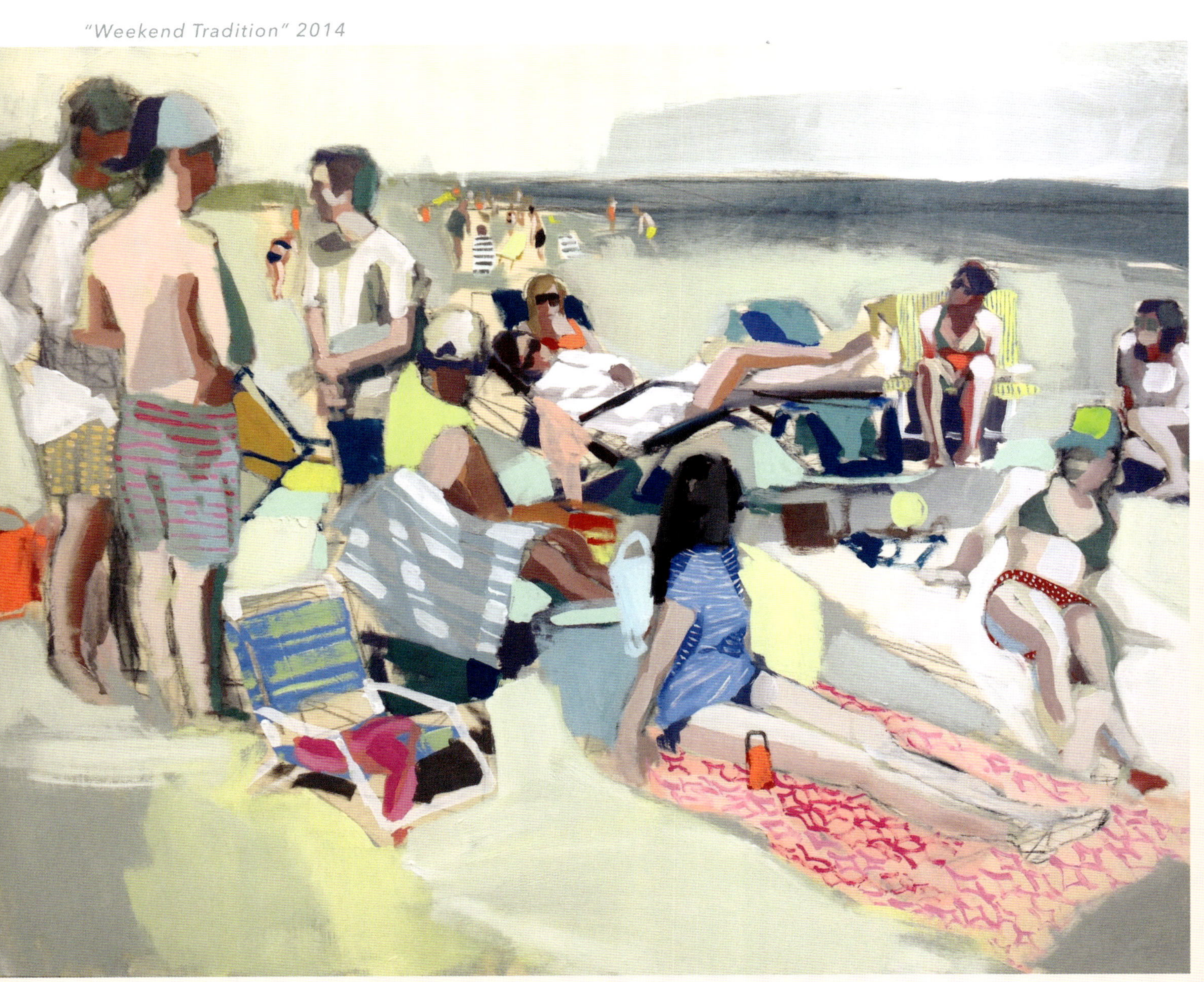

"Hipster Bathers" 2014

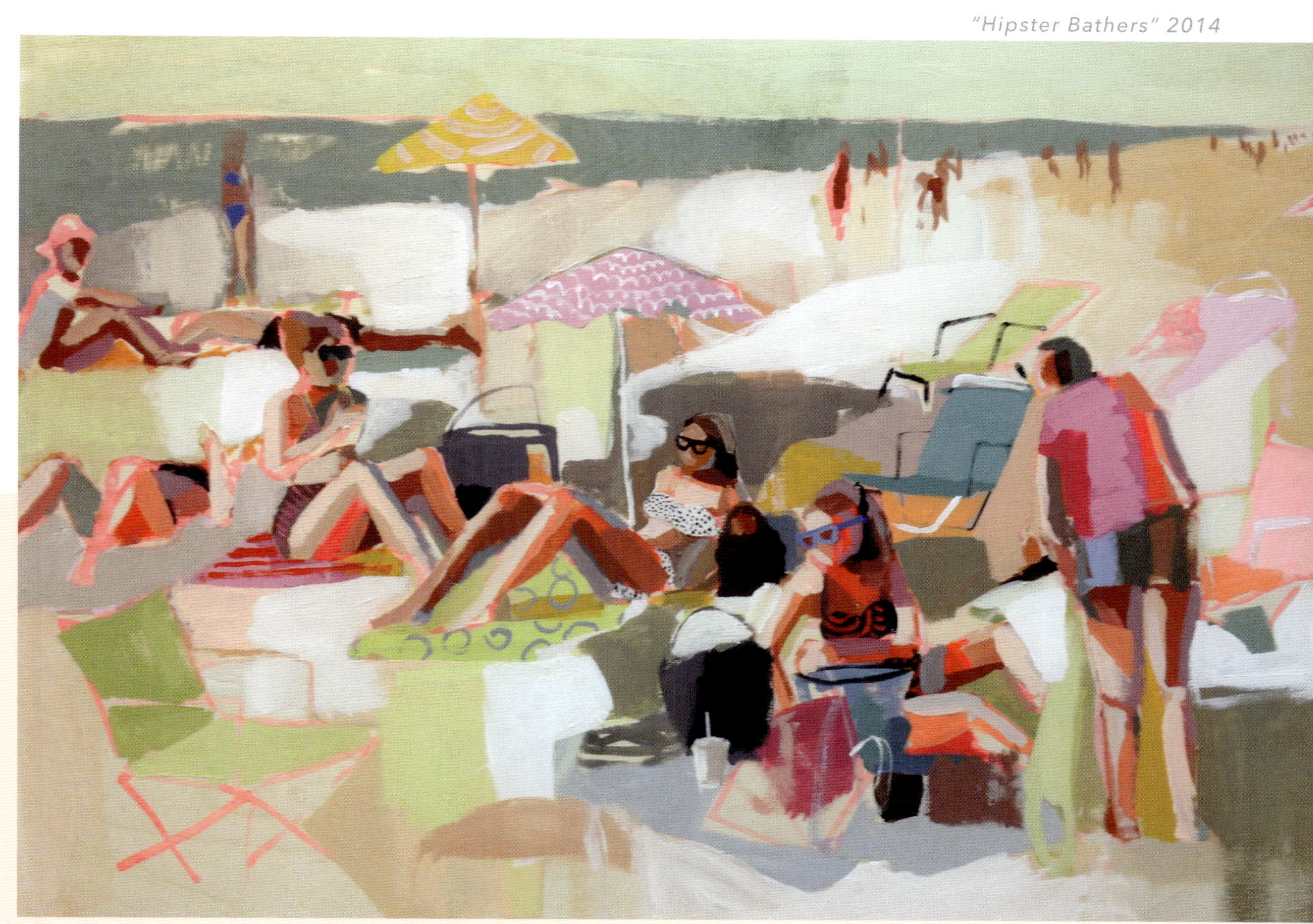

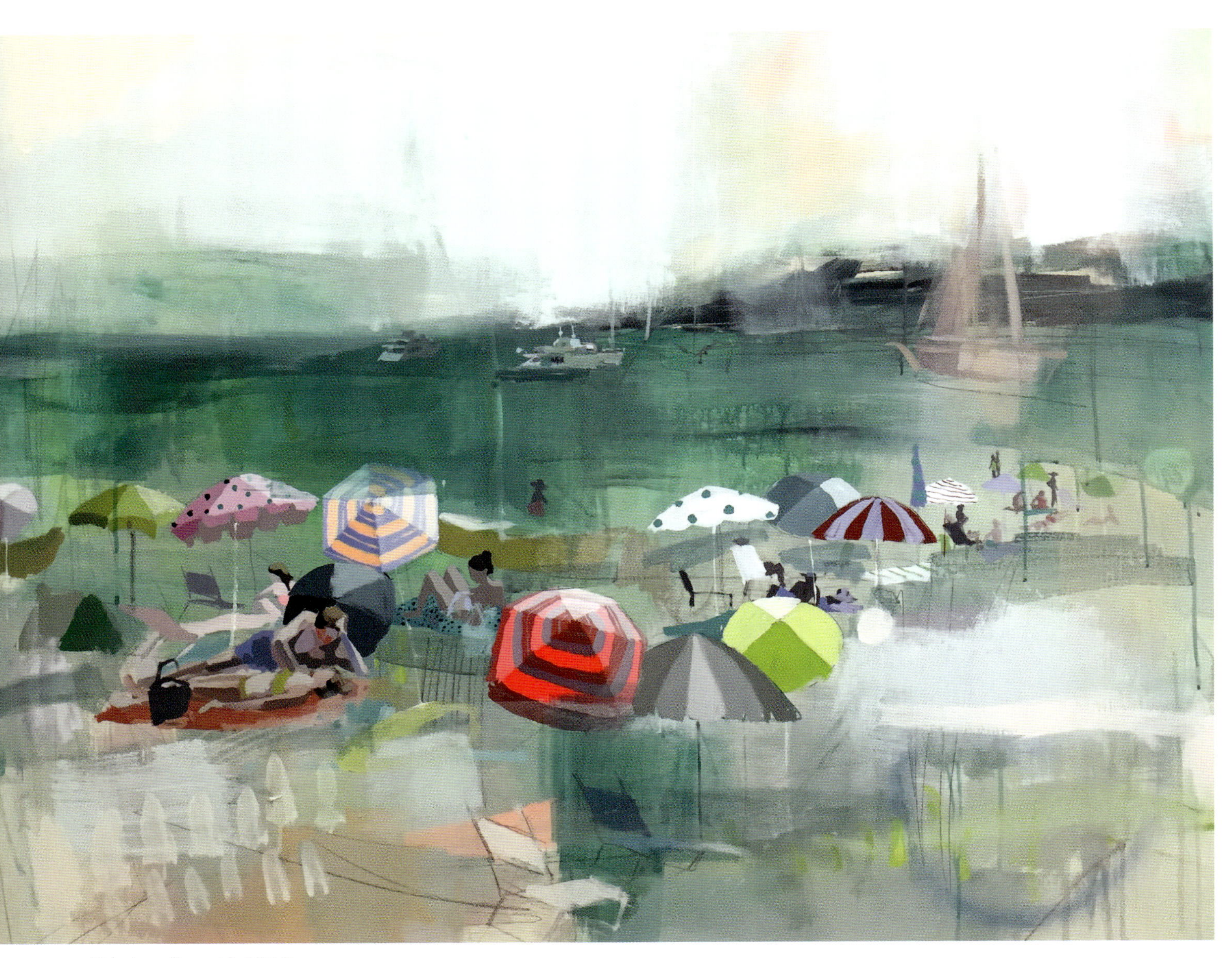

"Melon Coast" 2015

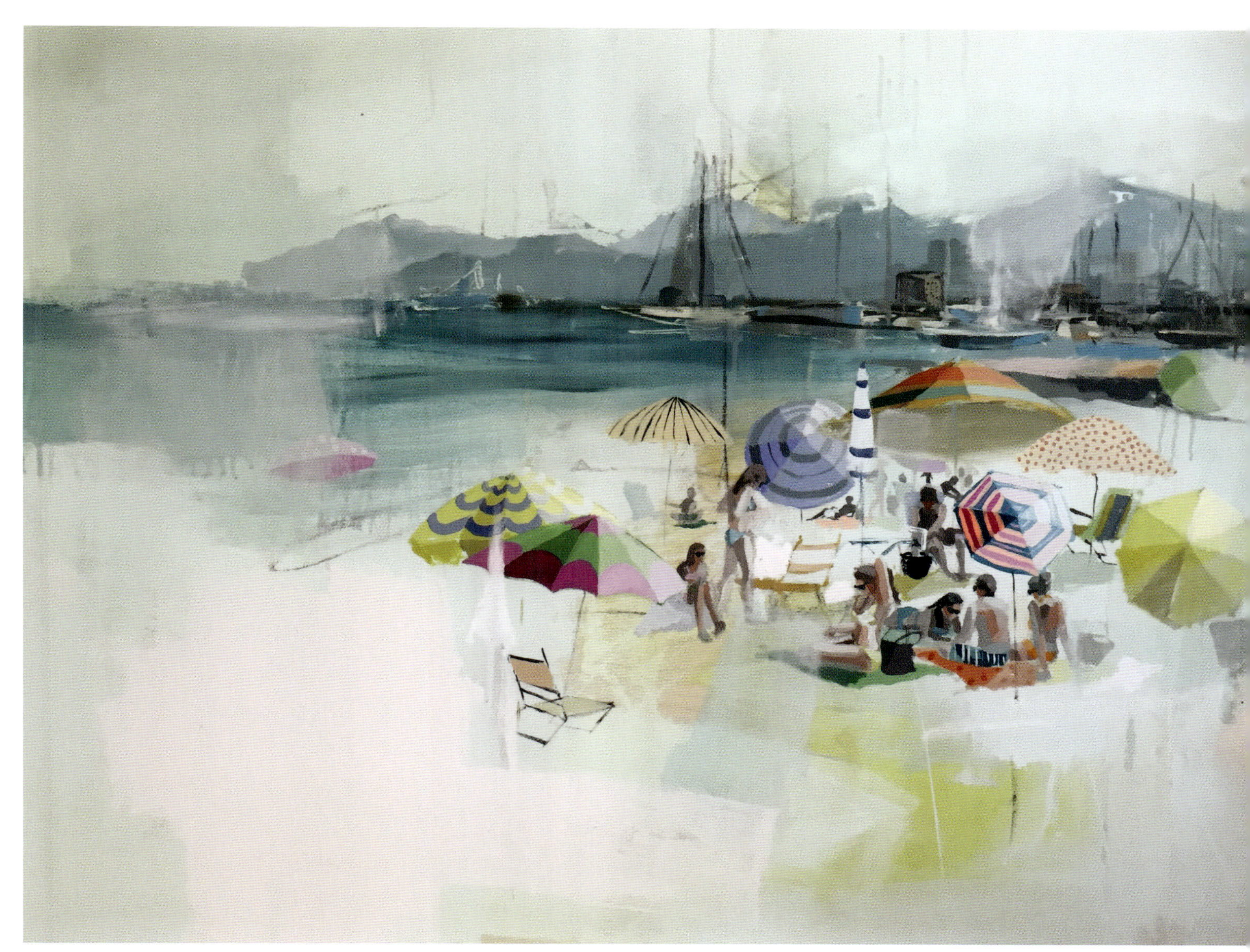

"Cannes Getaway" 2015

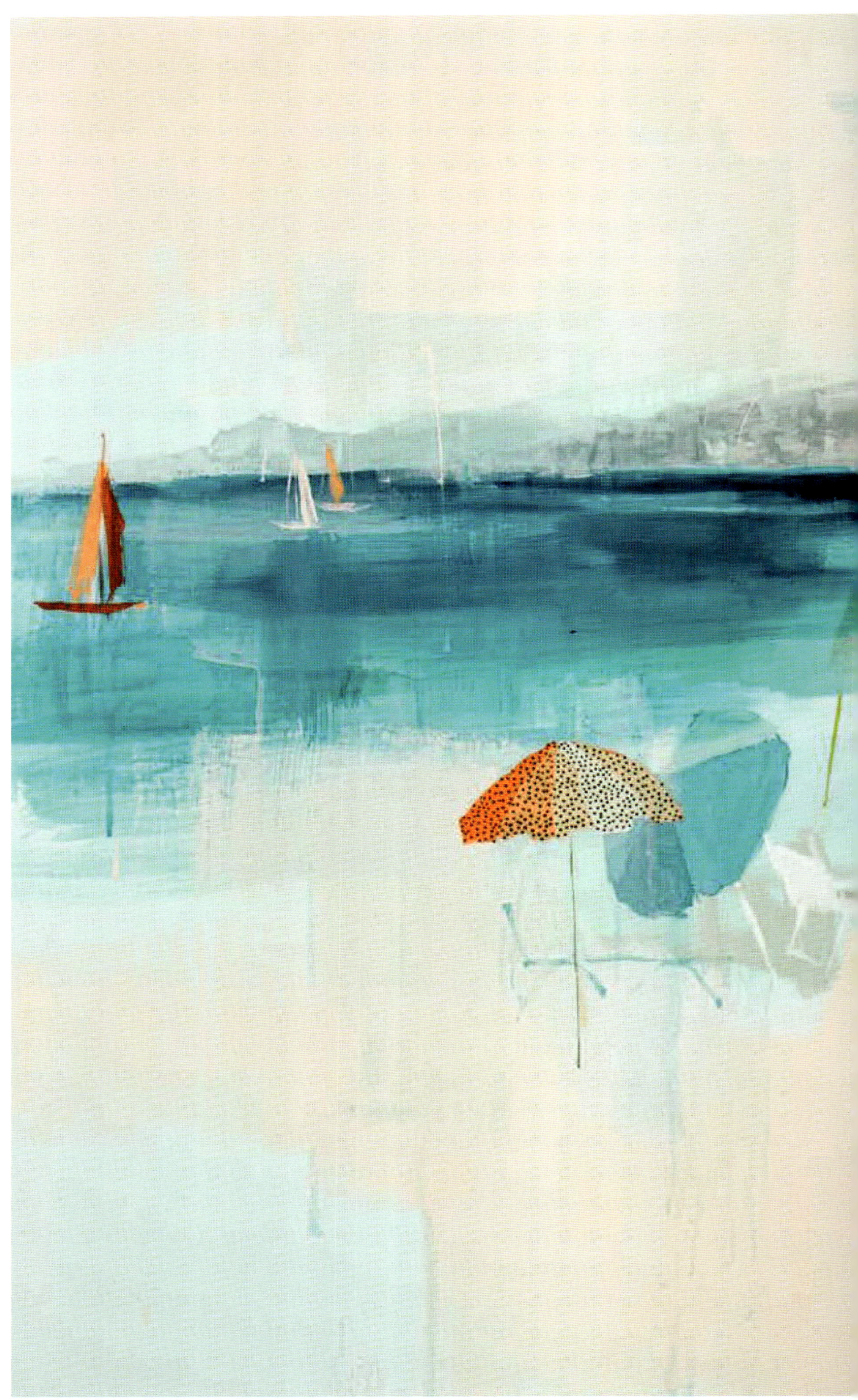

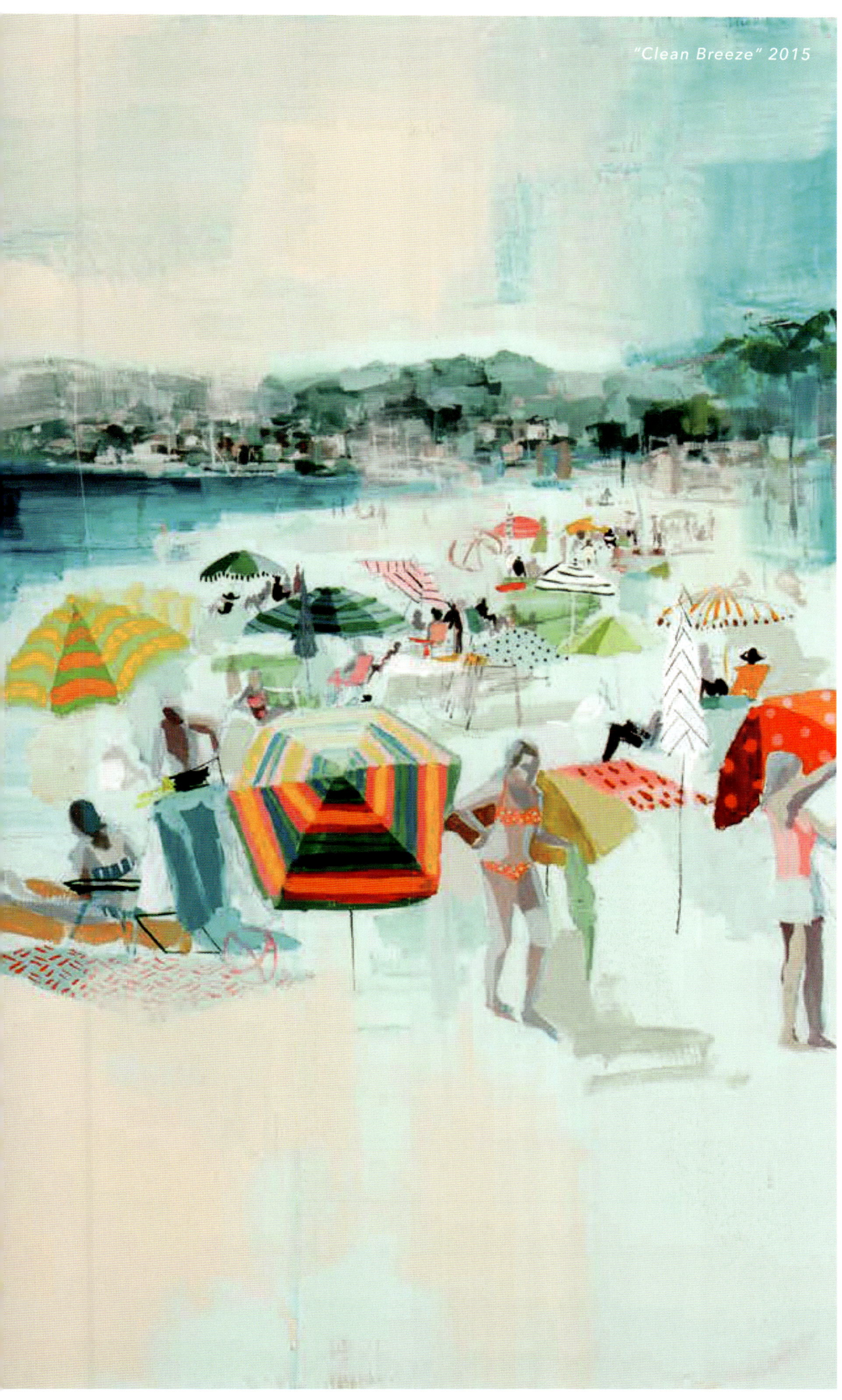
"Clean Breeze" 2015

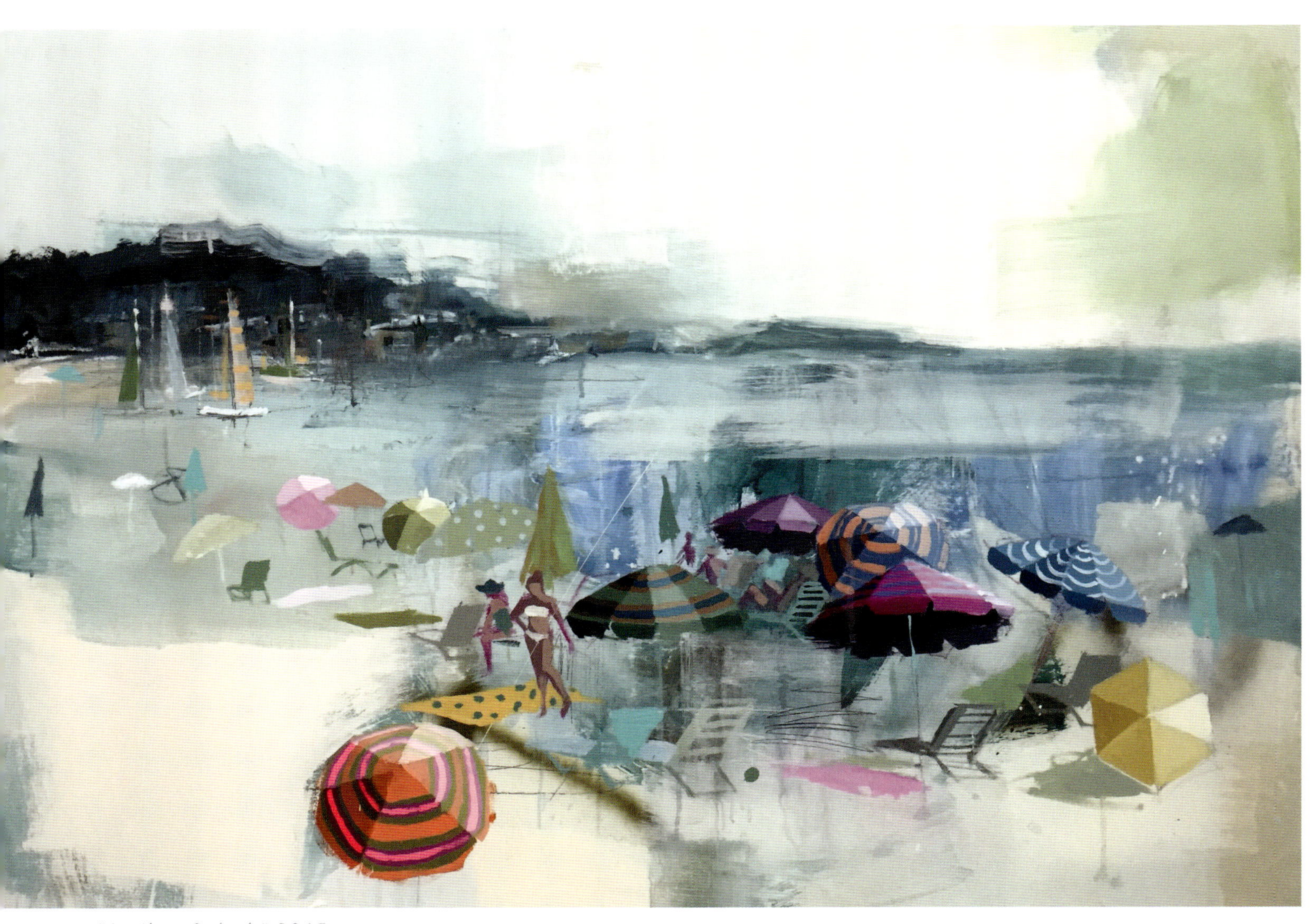

"Antibes Splash" 2015

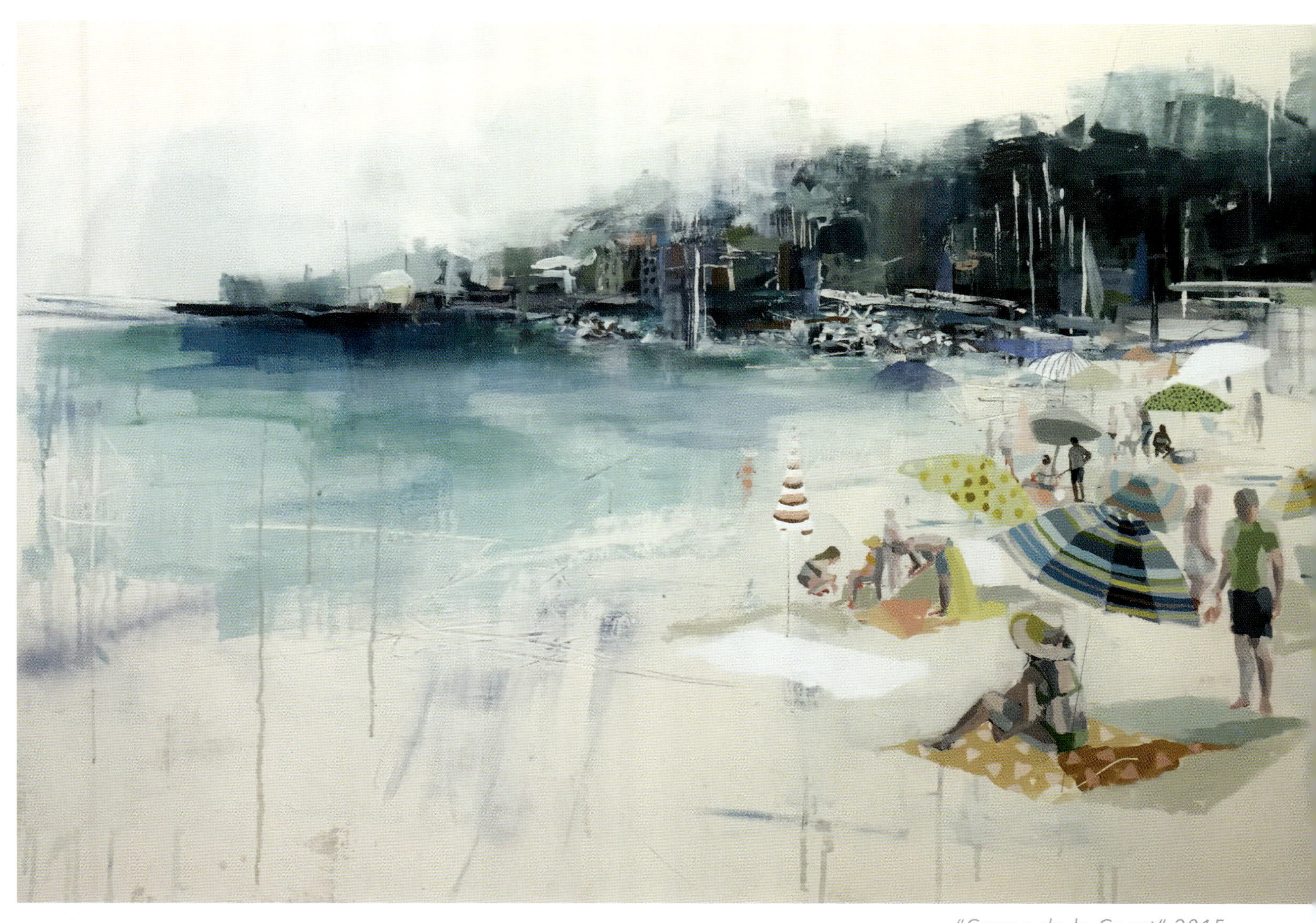

"Creme de la Coast" 2015

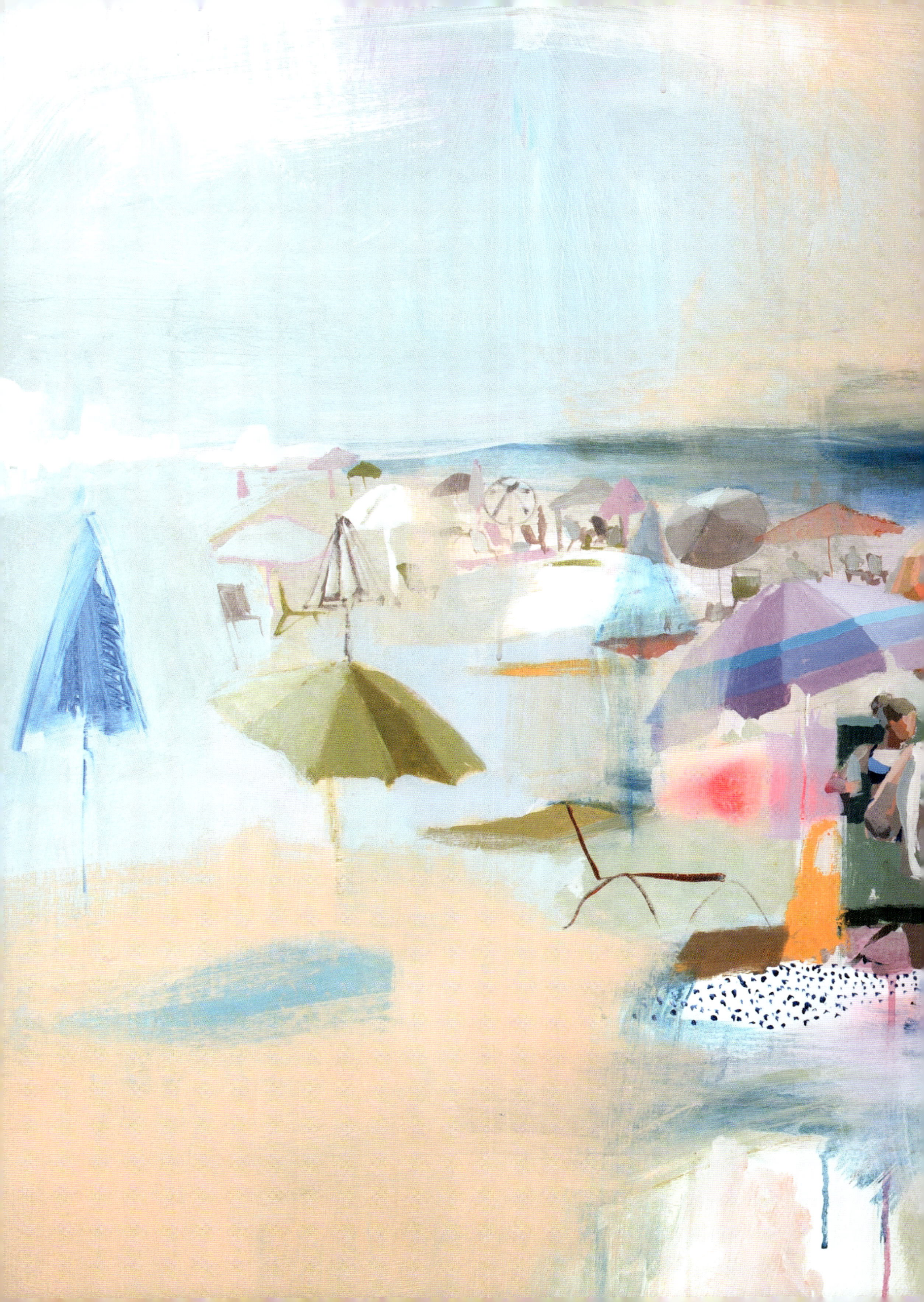

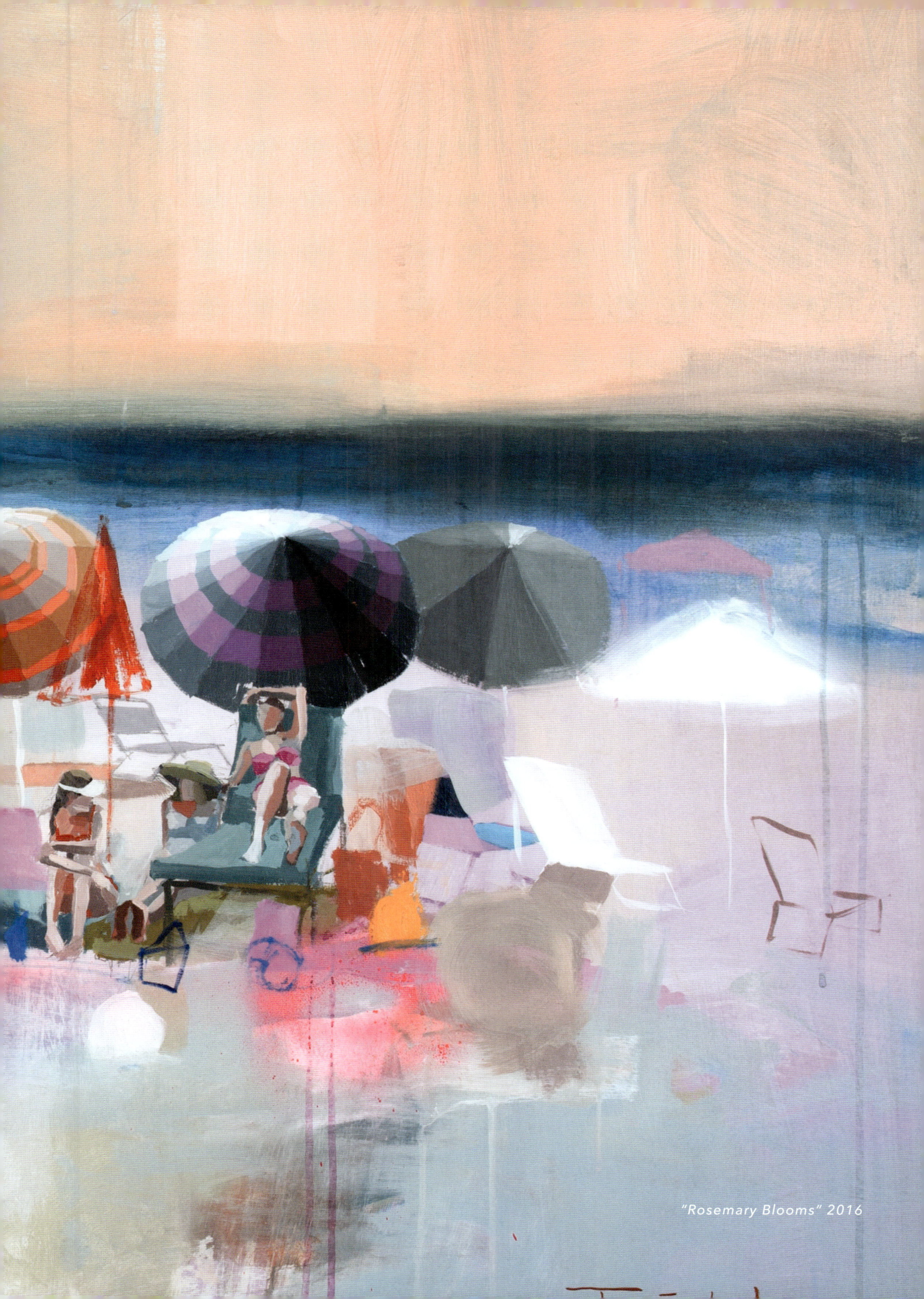

"Rosemary Blooms" 2016

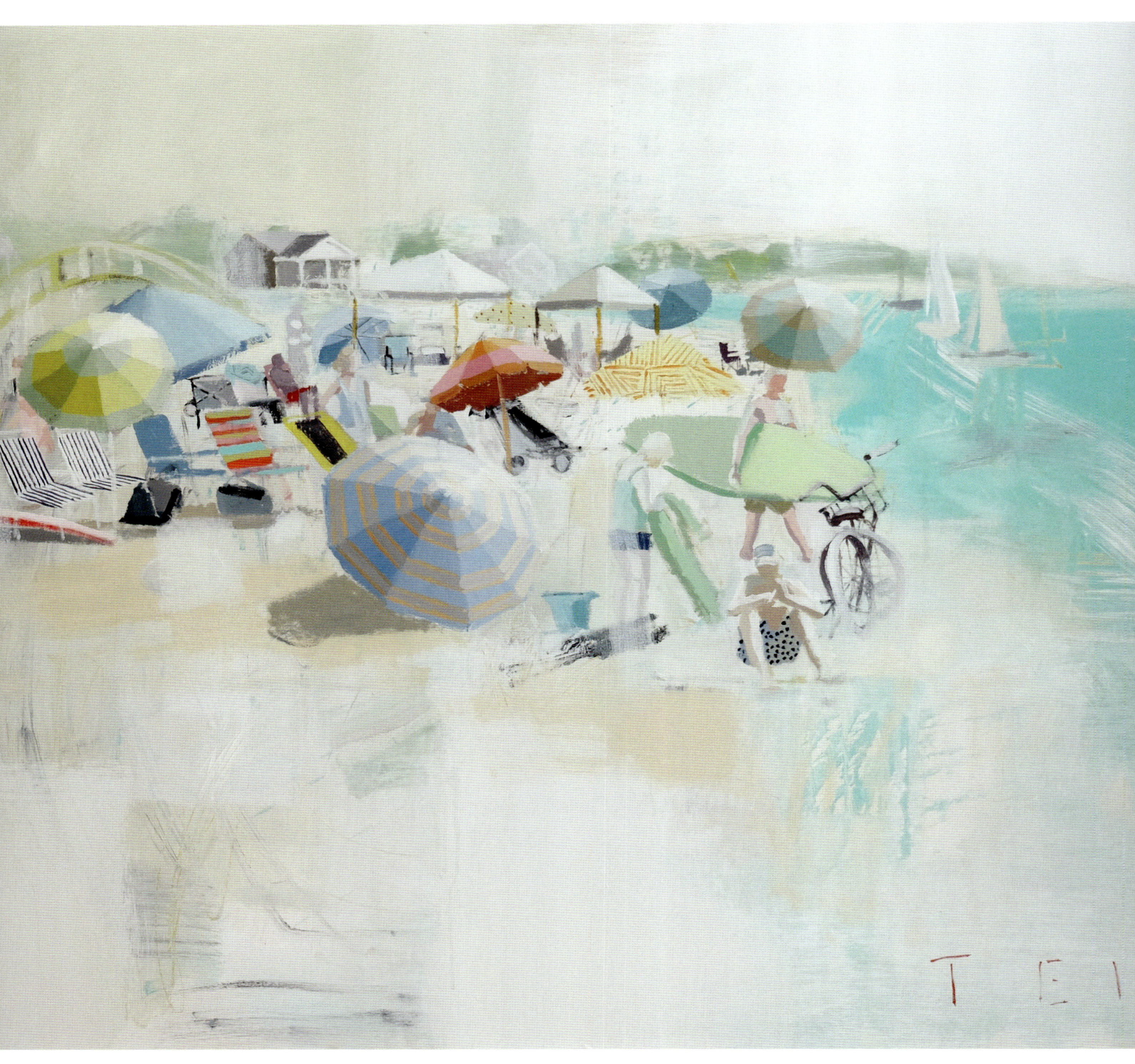

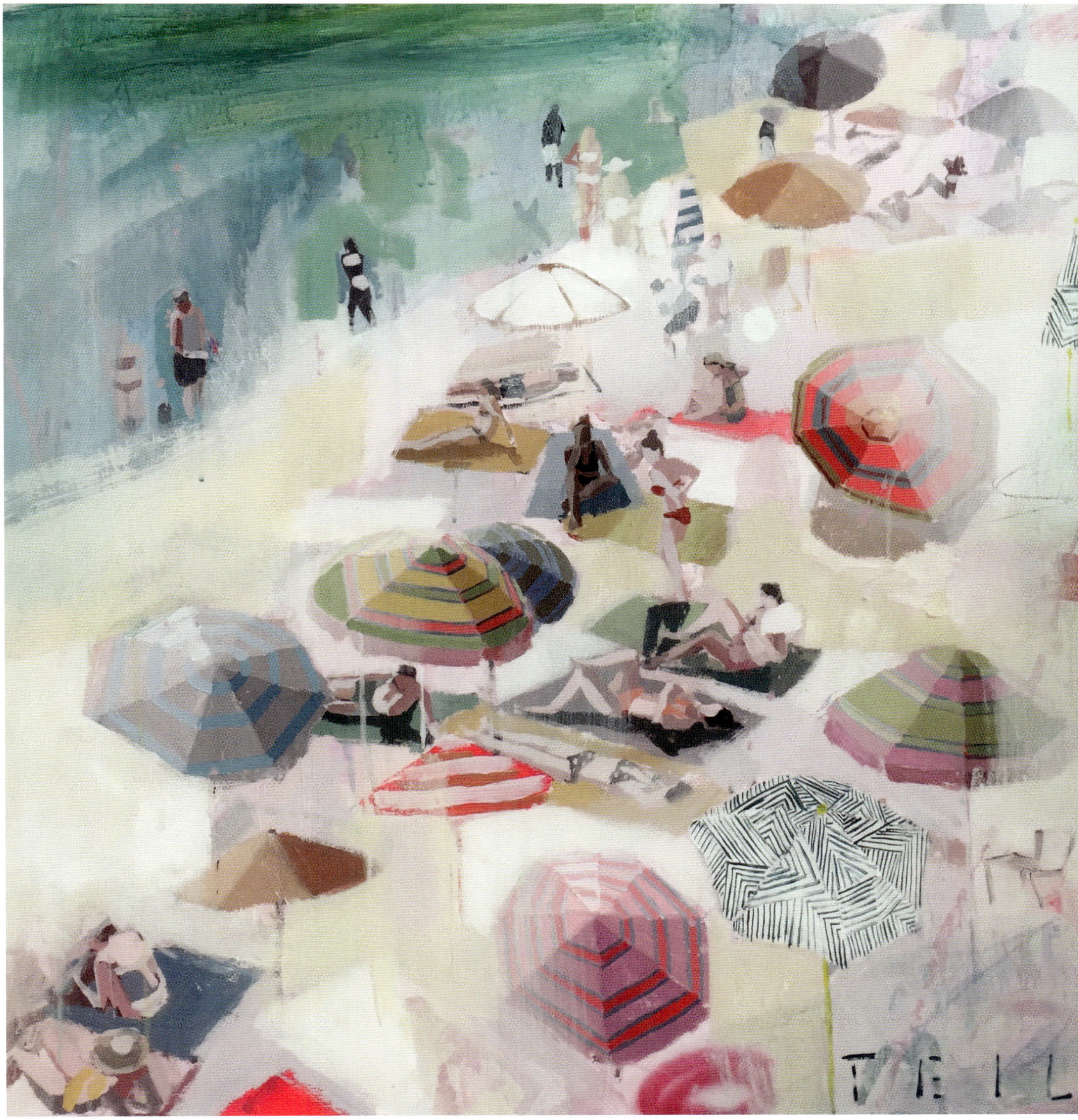

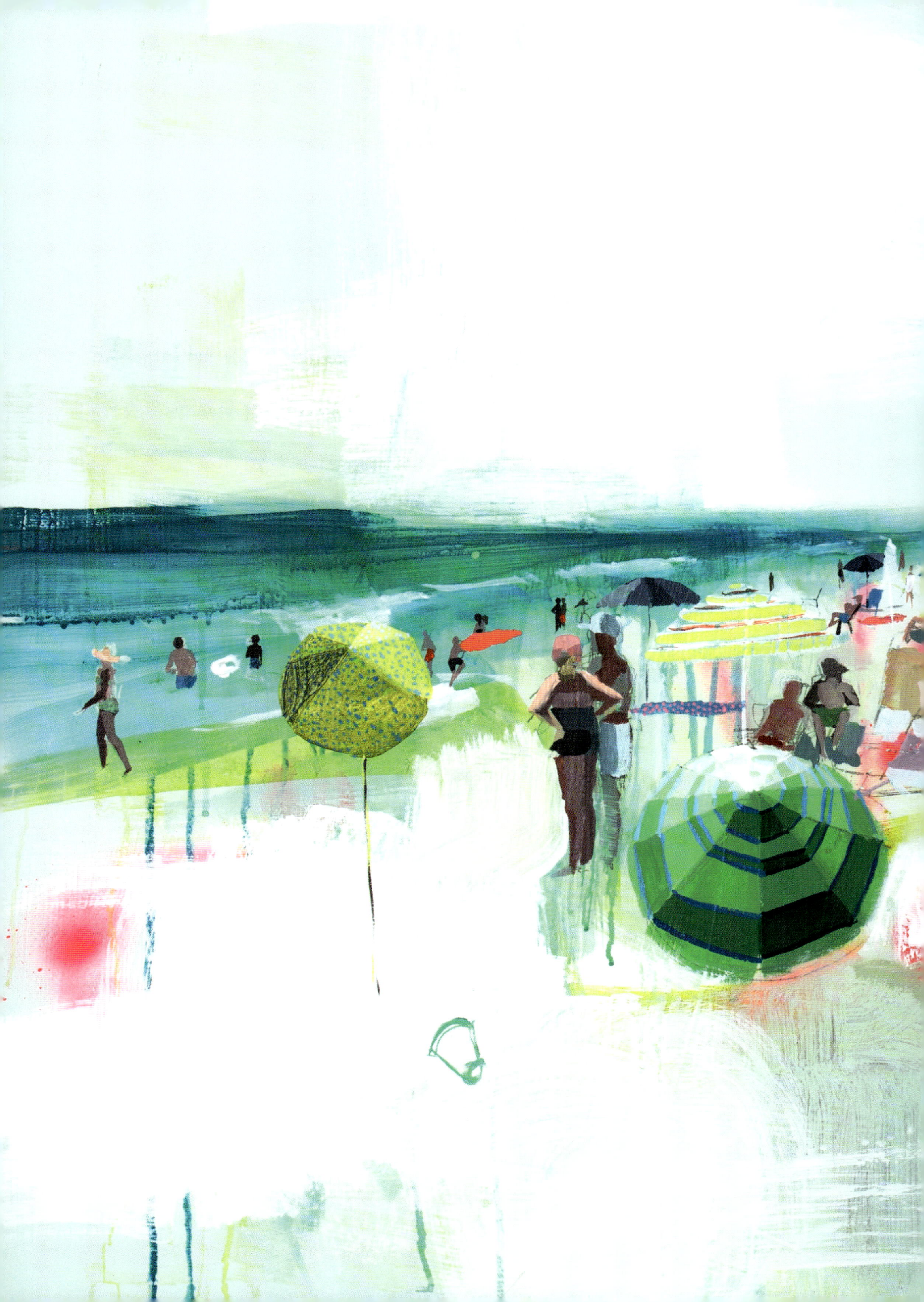

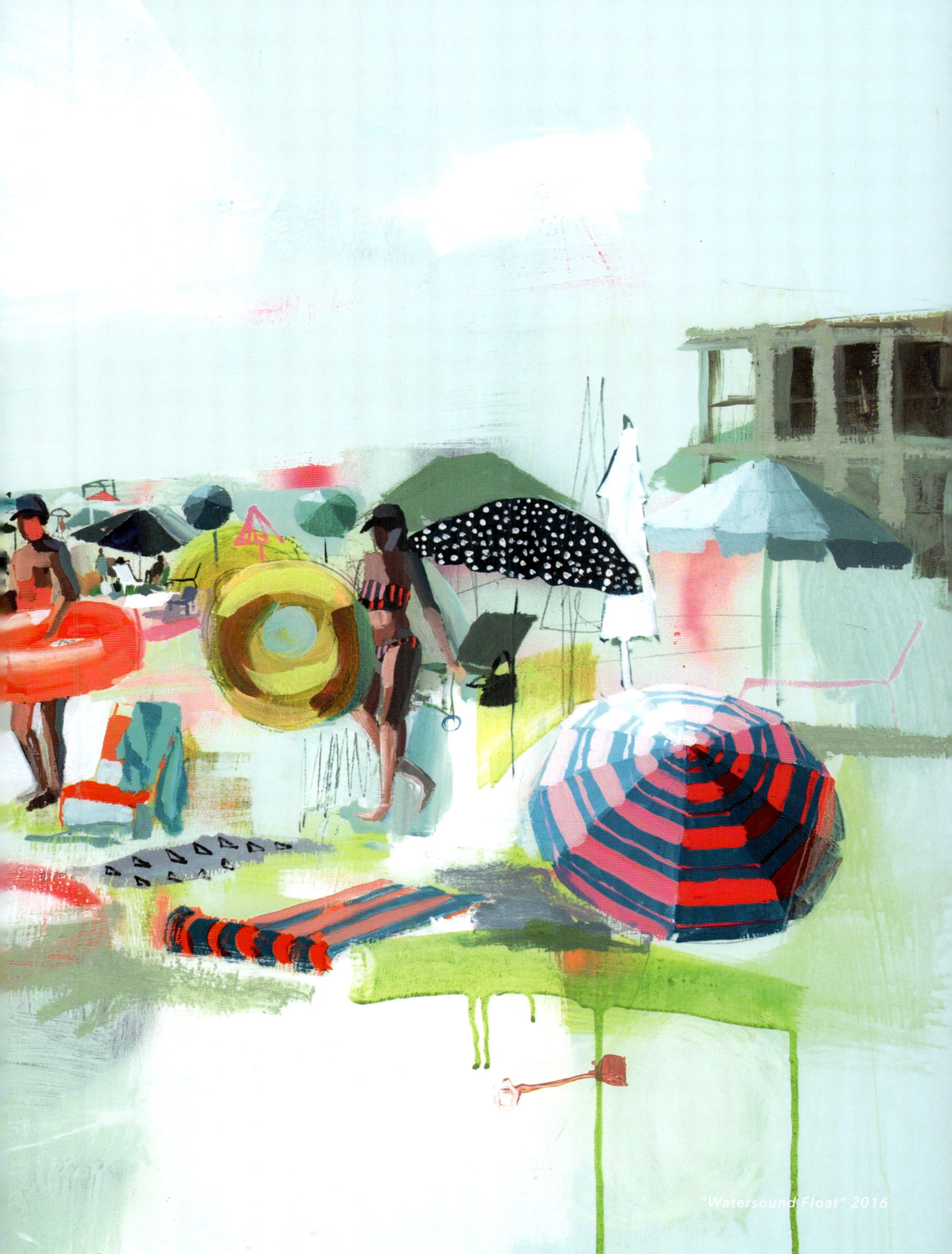

"Watersound Float" 2016

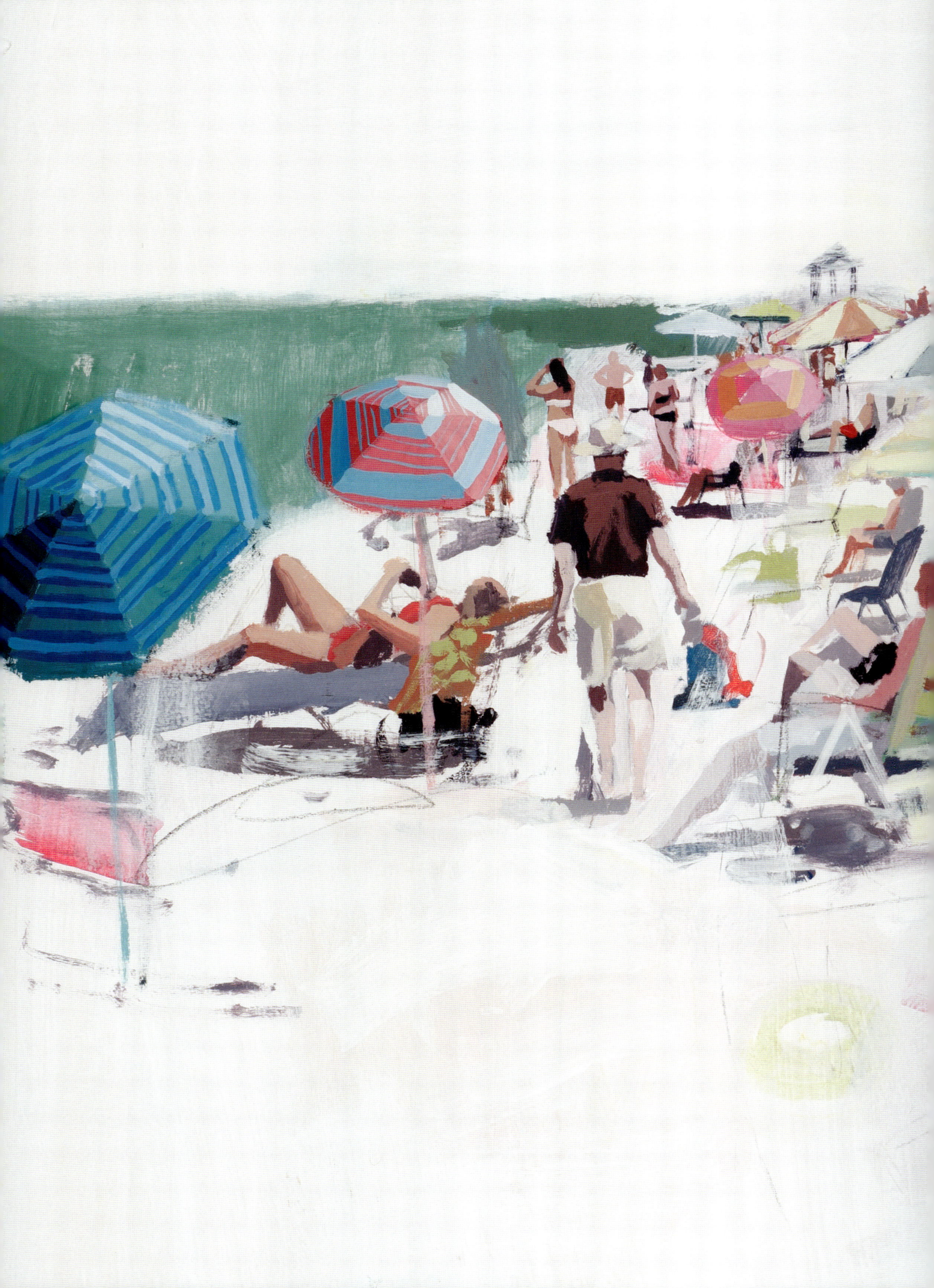

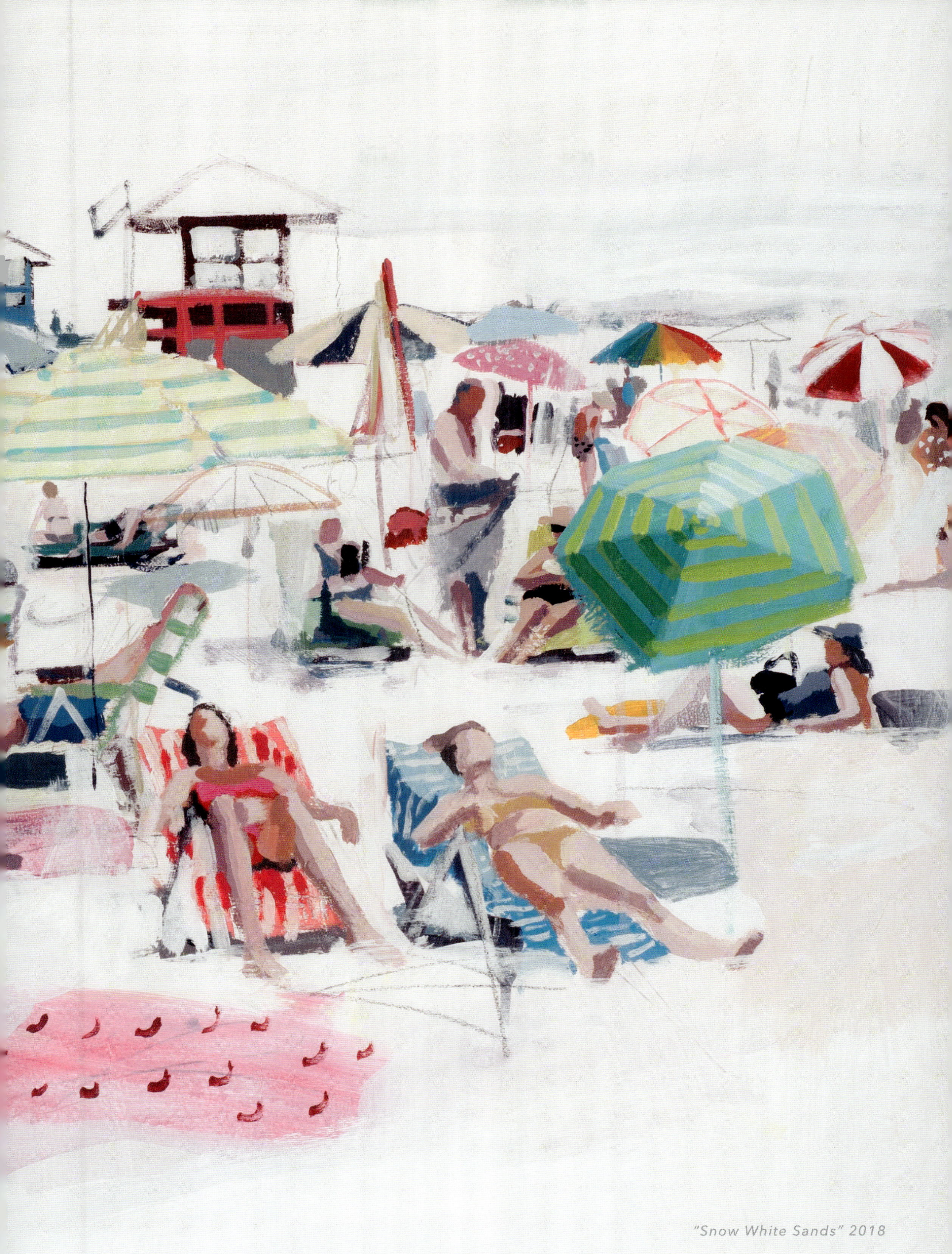

"Snow White Sands" 2018

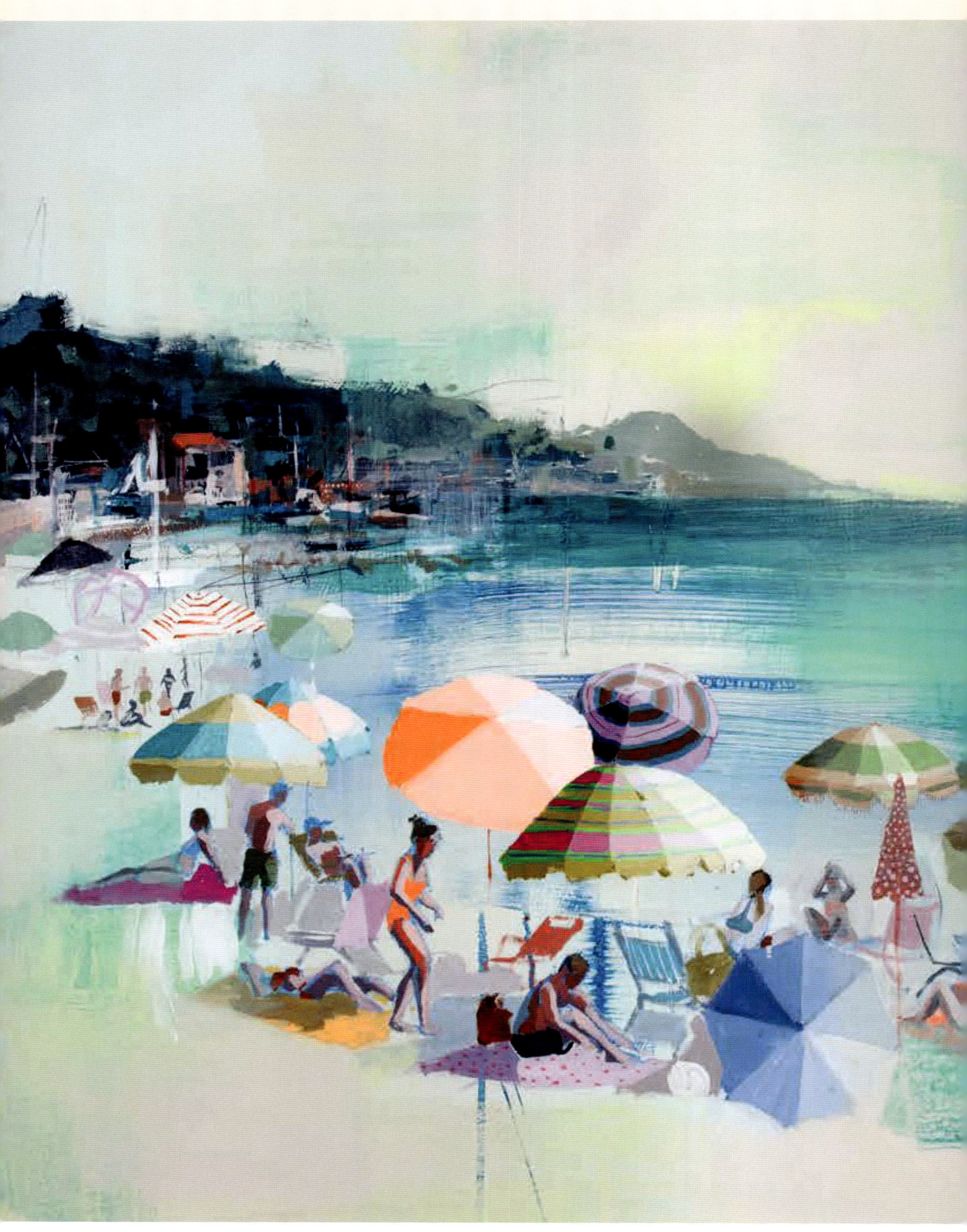

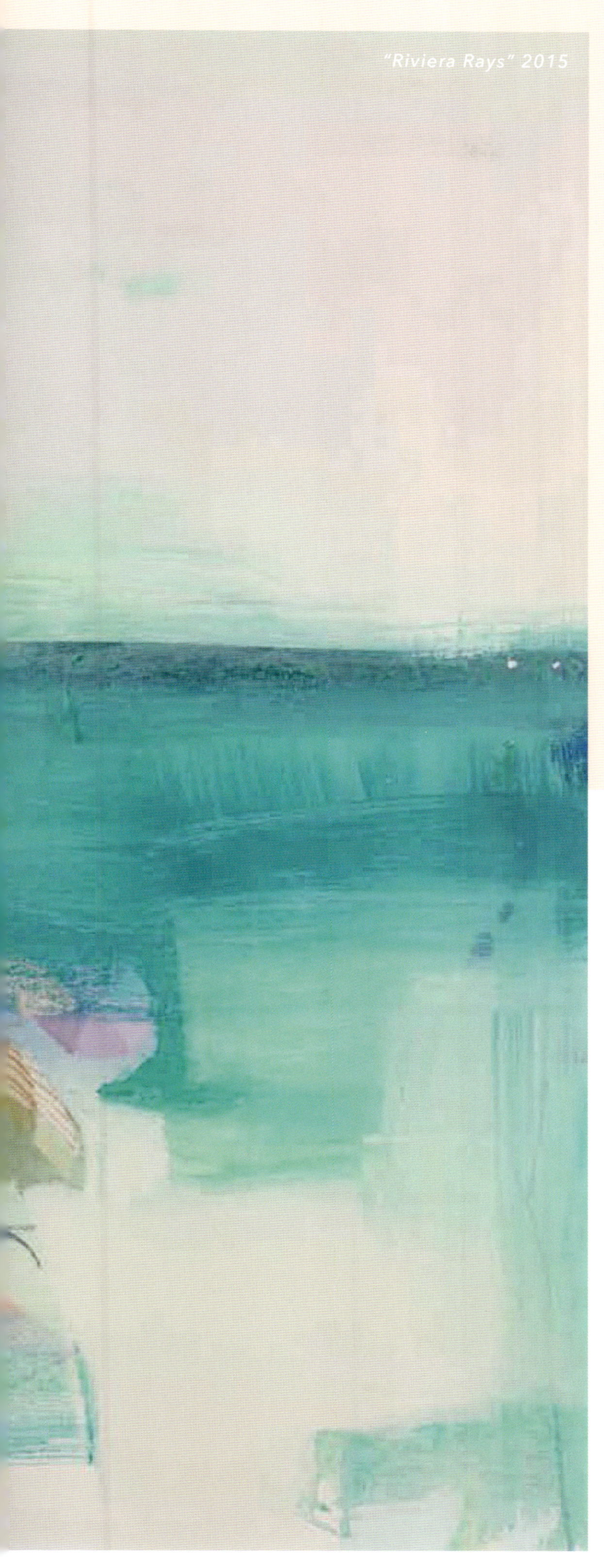
"Riviera Rays" 2015

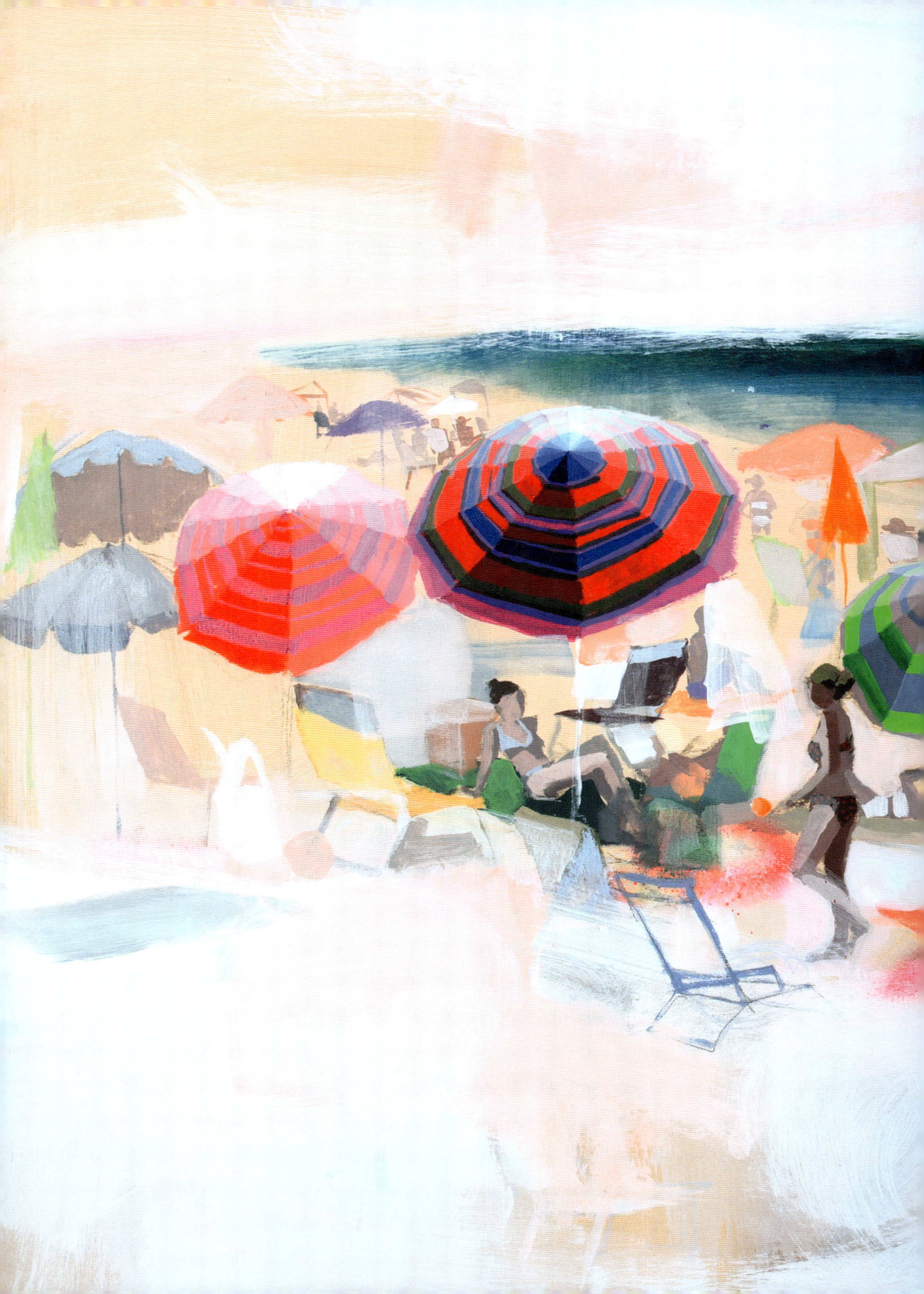

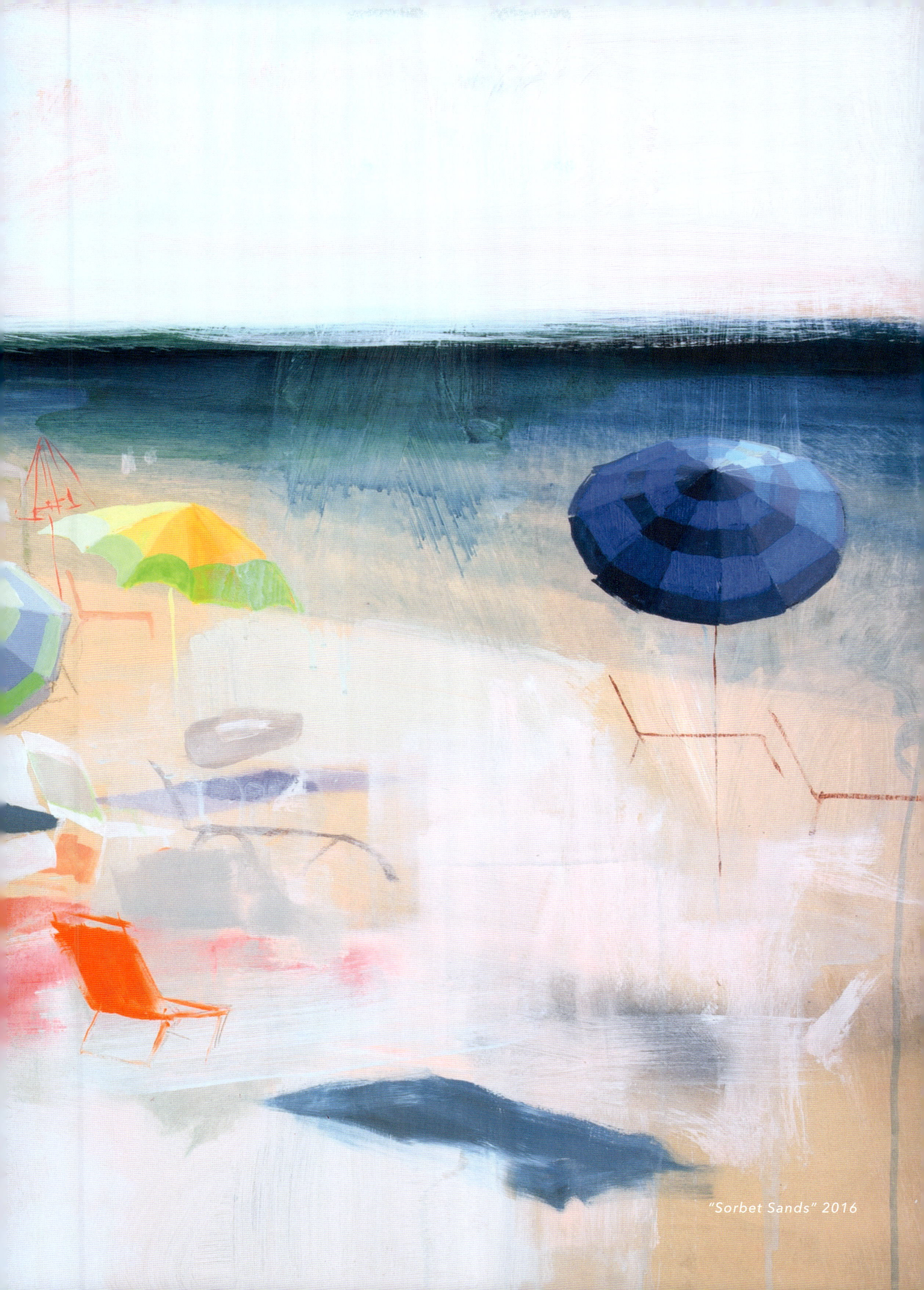

"Sorbet Sands" 2016

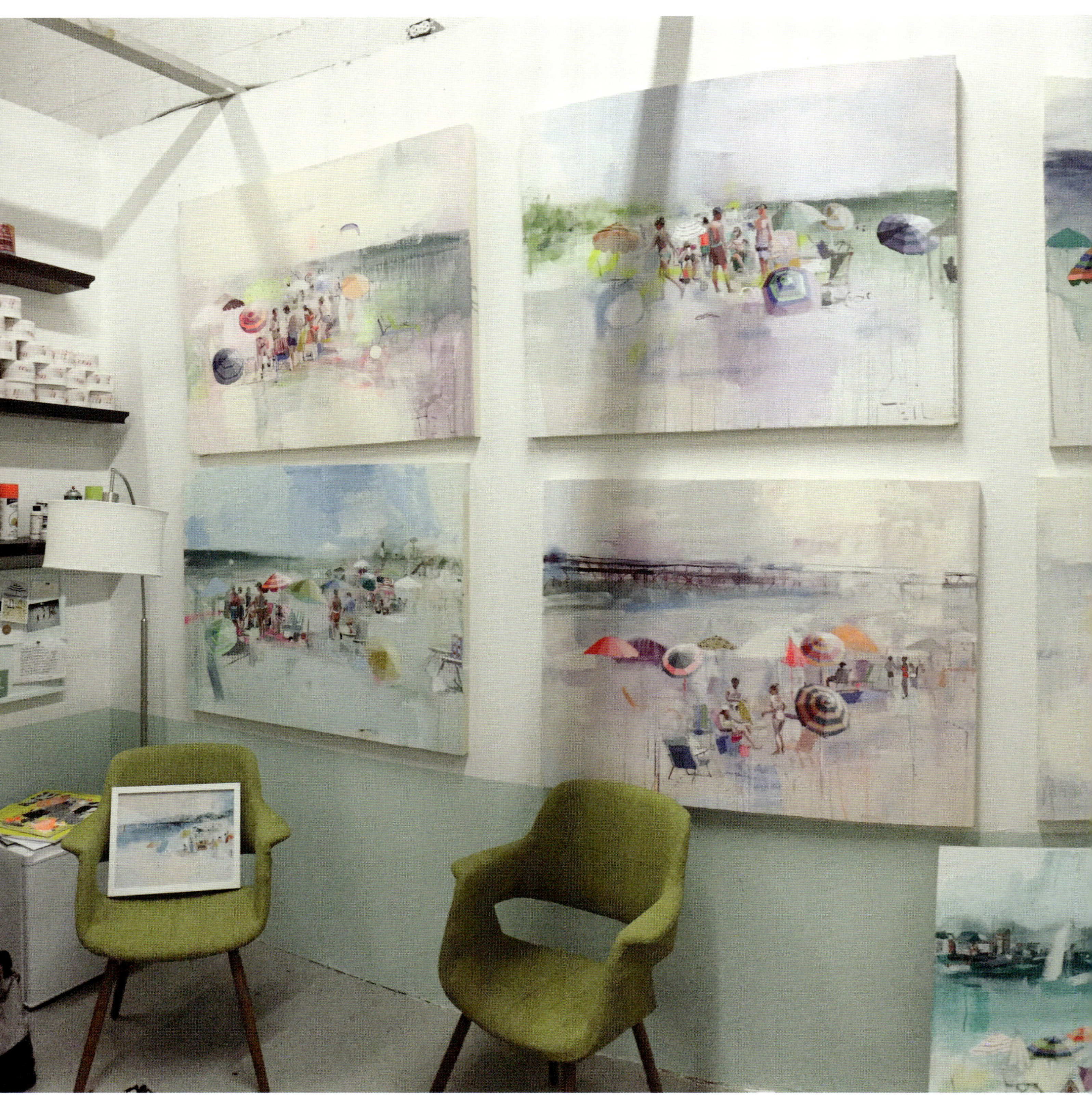

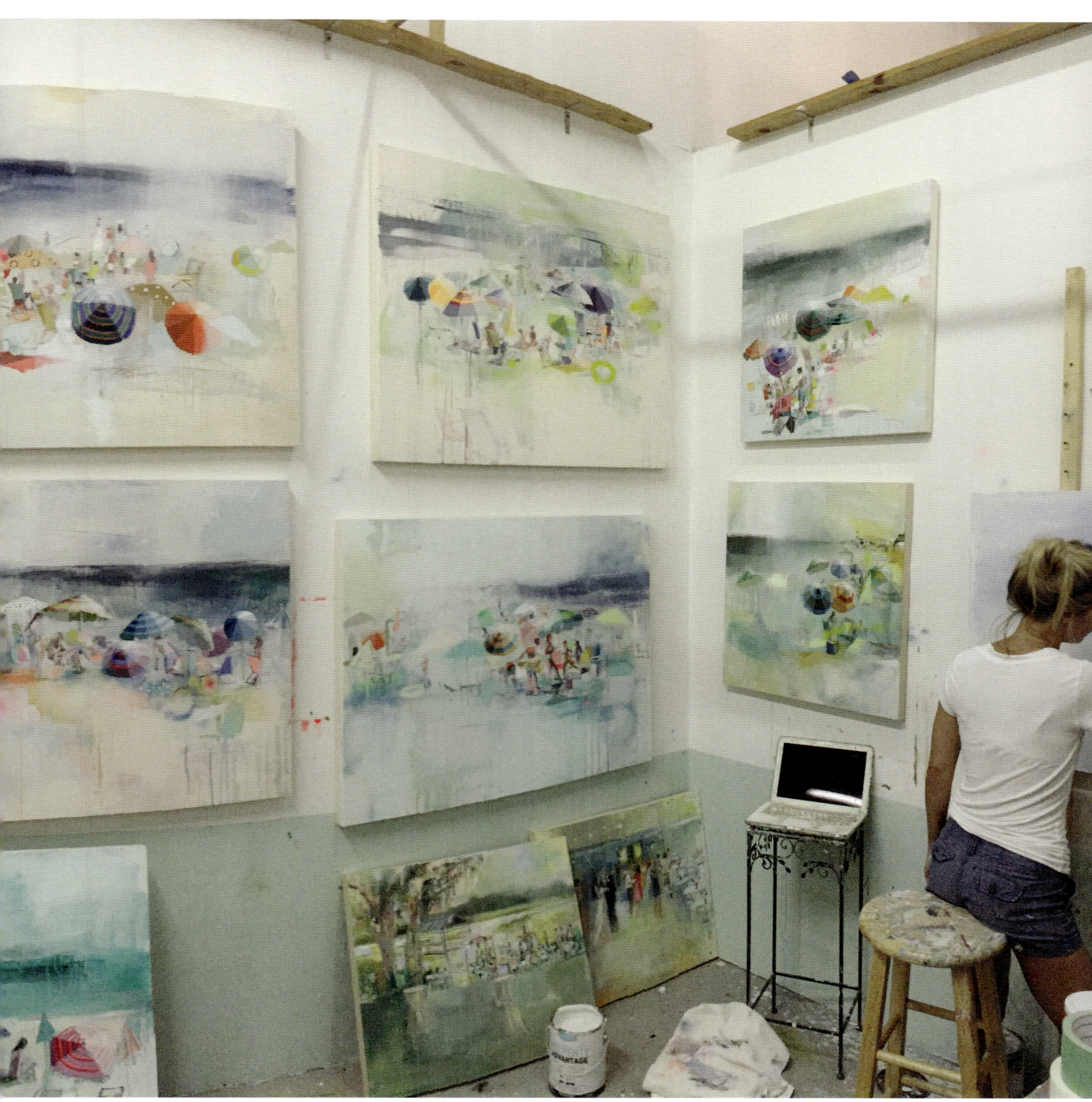

"Alys Sails" 2016

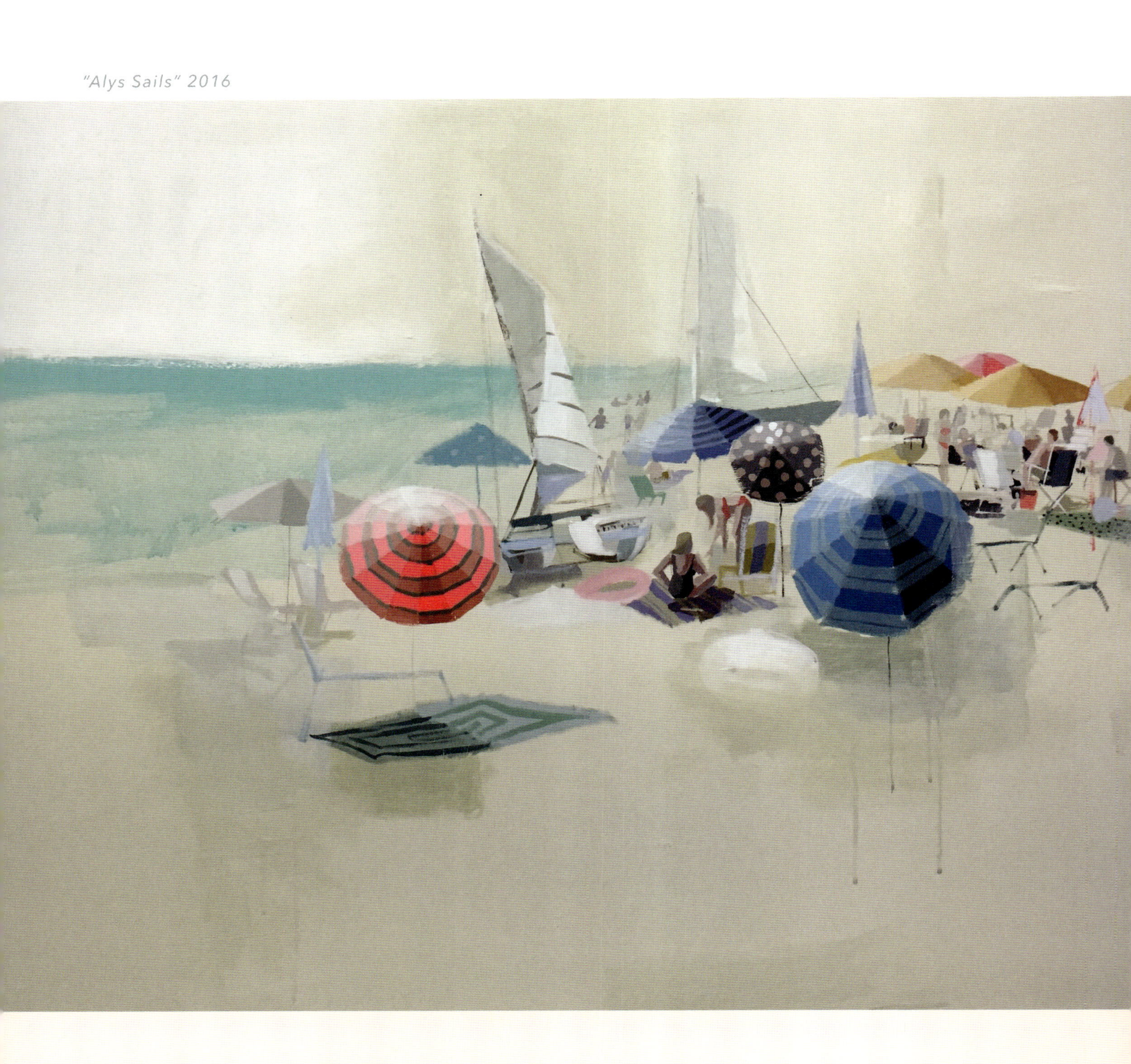

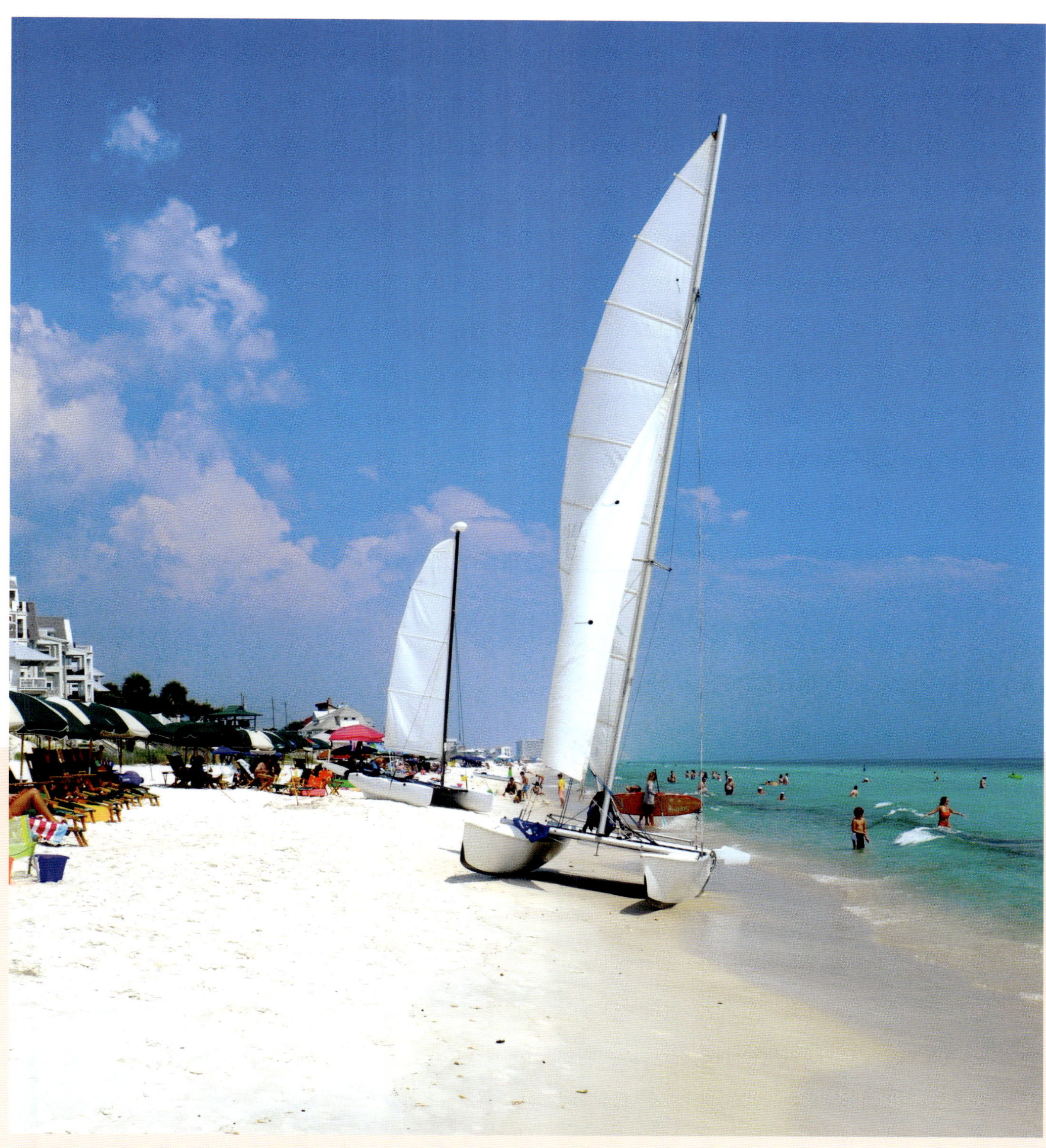

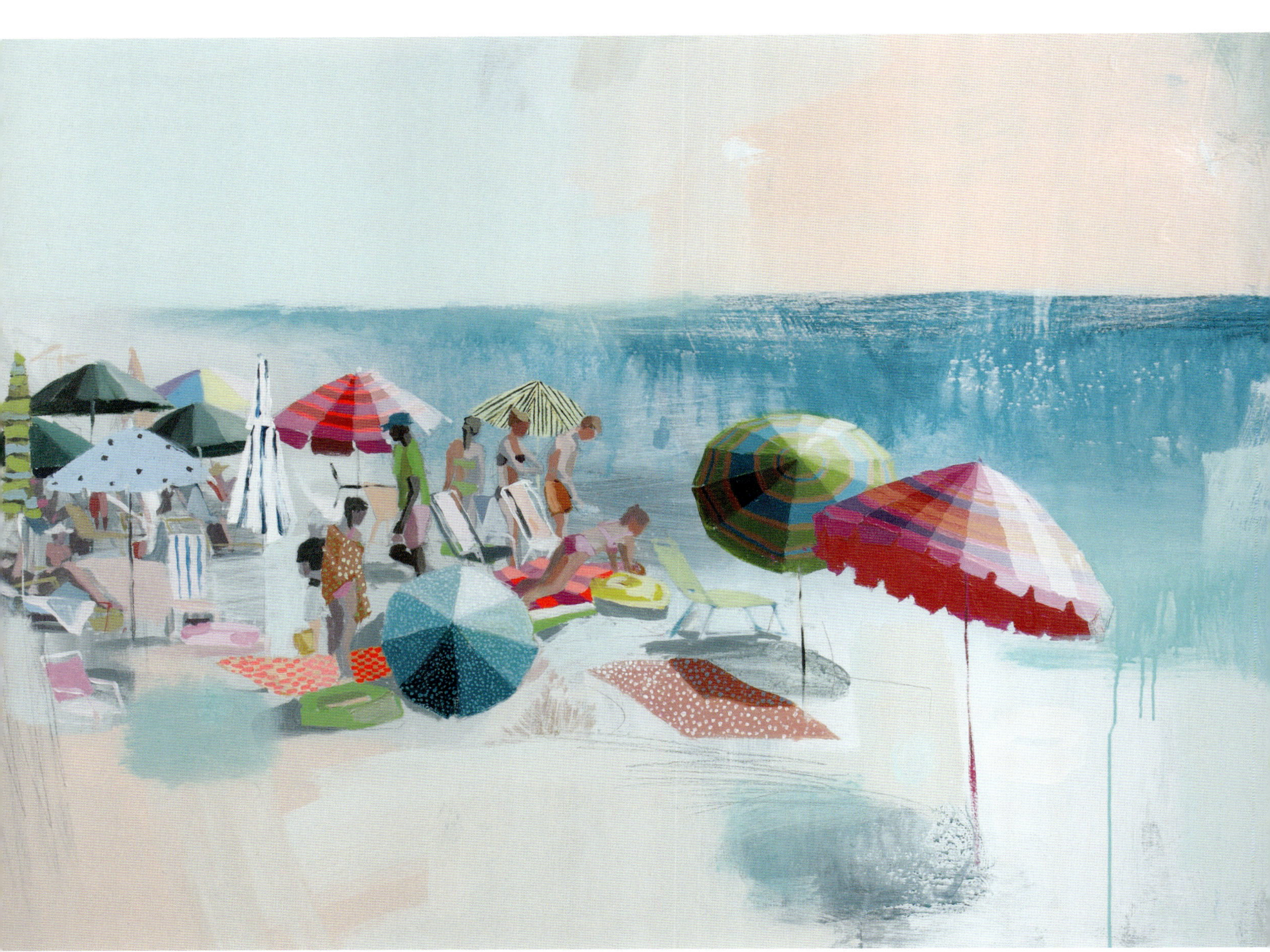

"May Getaway" 2016

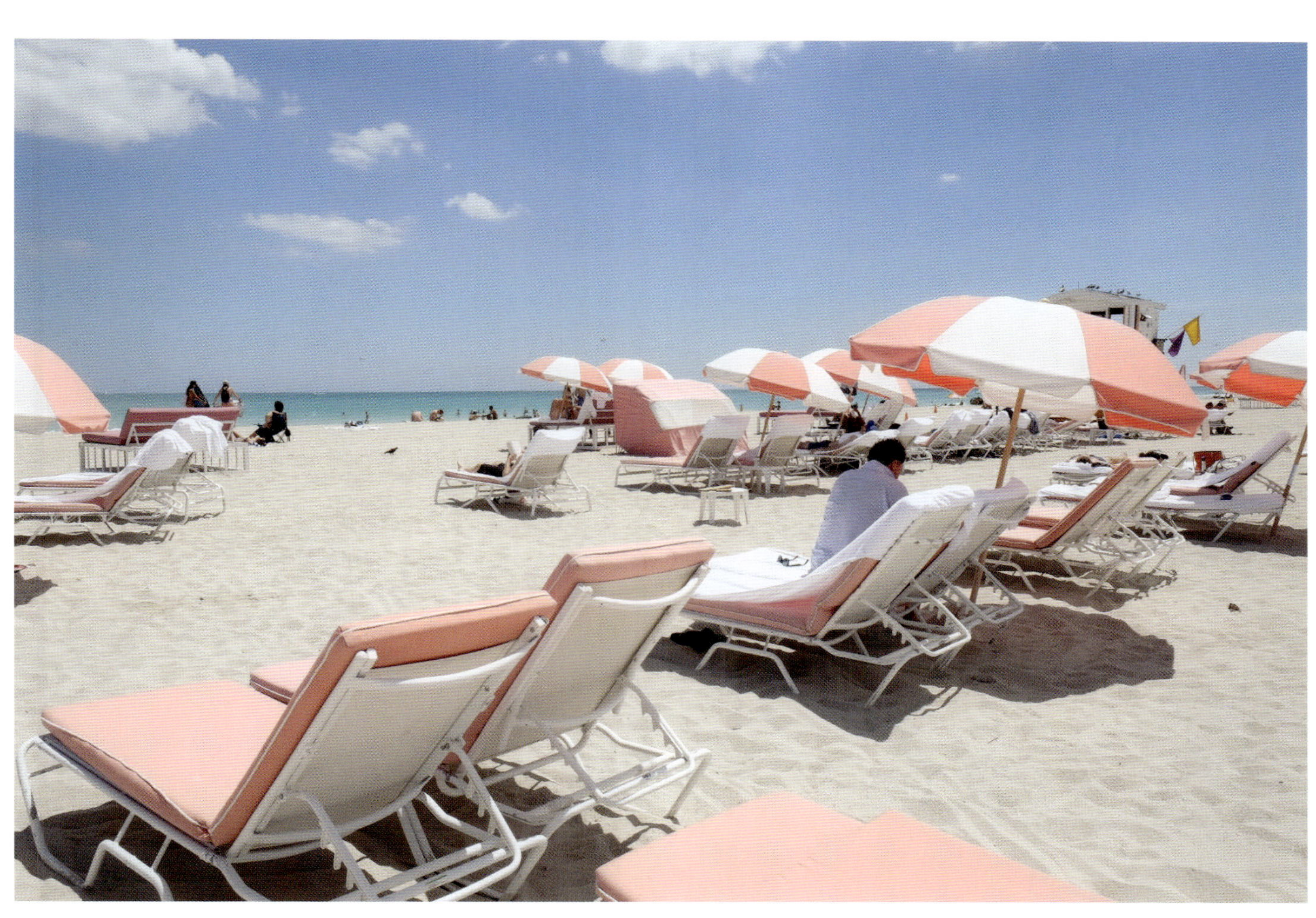

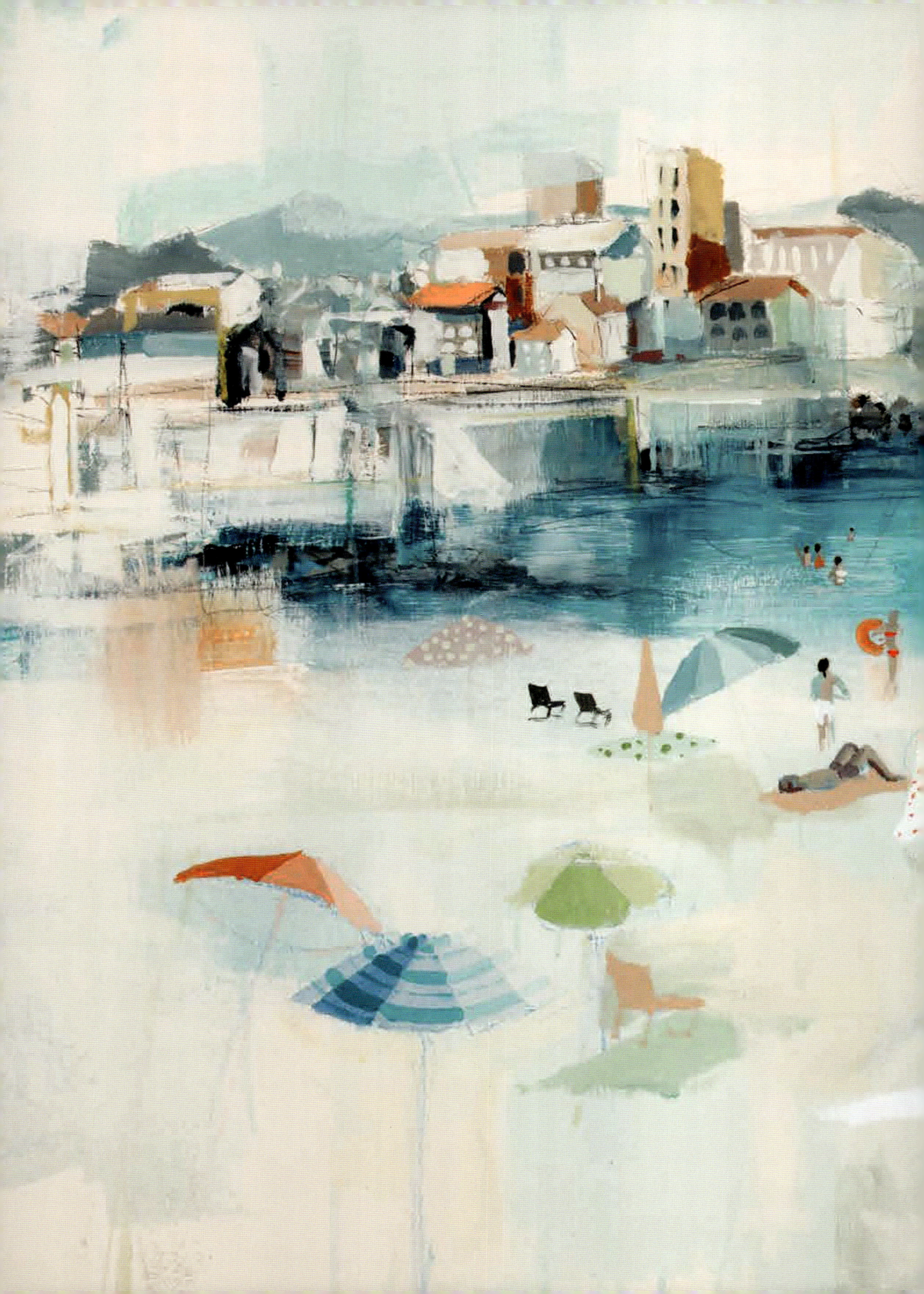

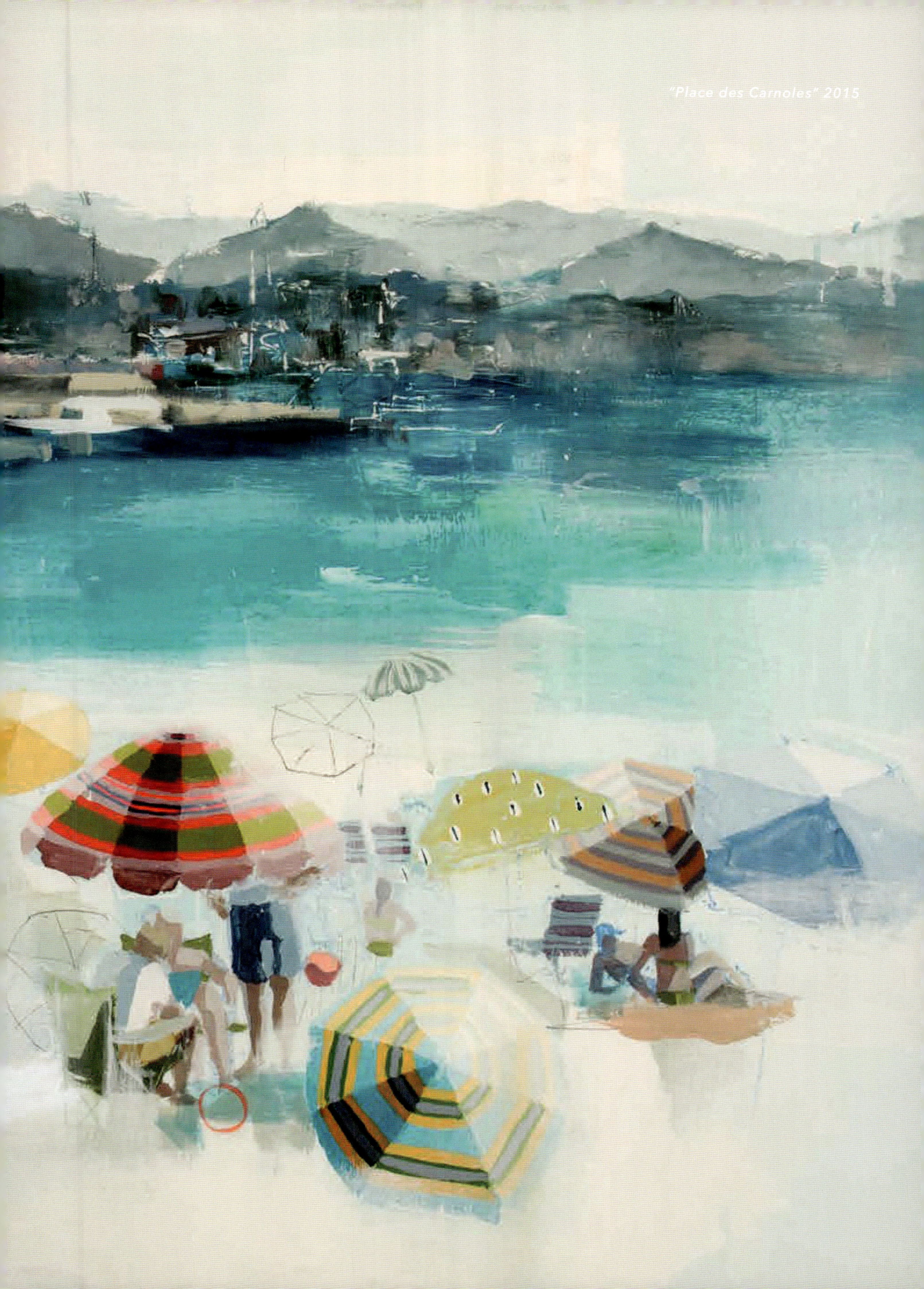

"Place des Carnoles" 2015

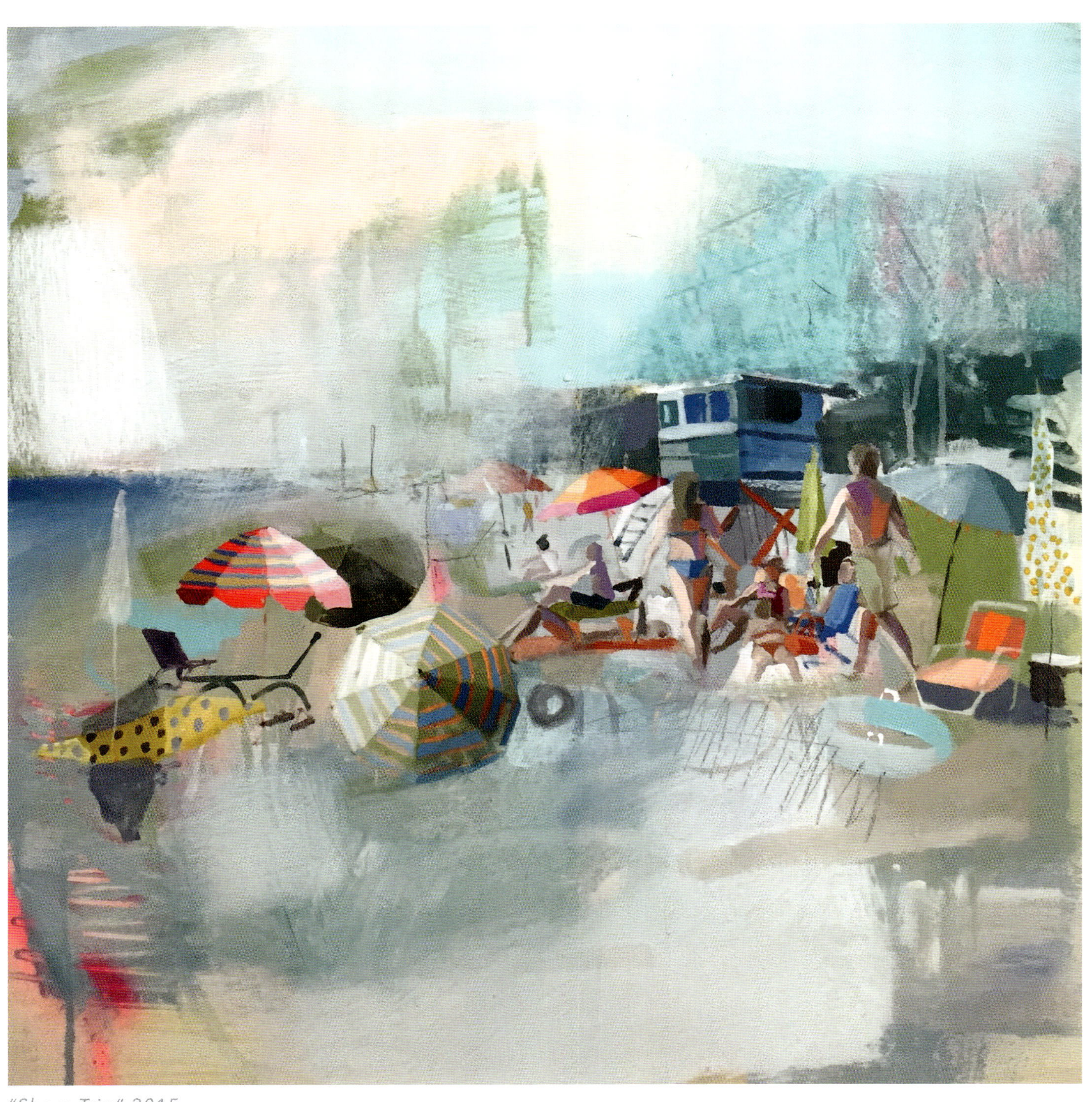

"Shore Trip" 2015

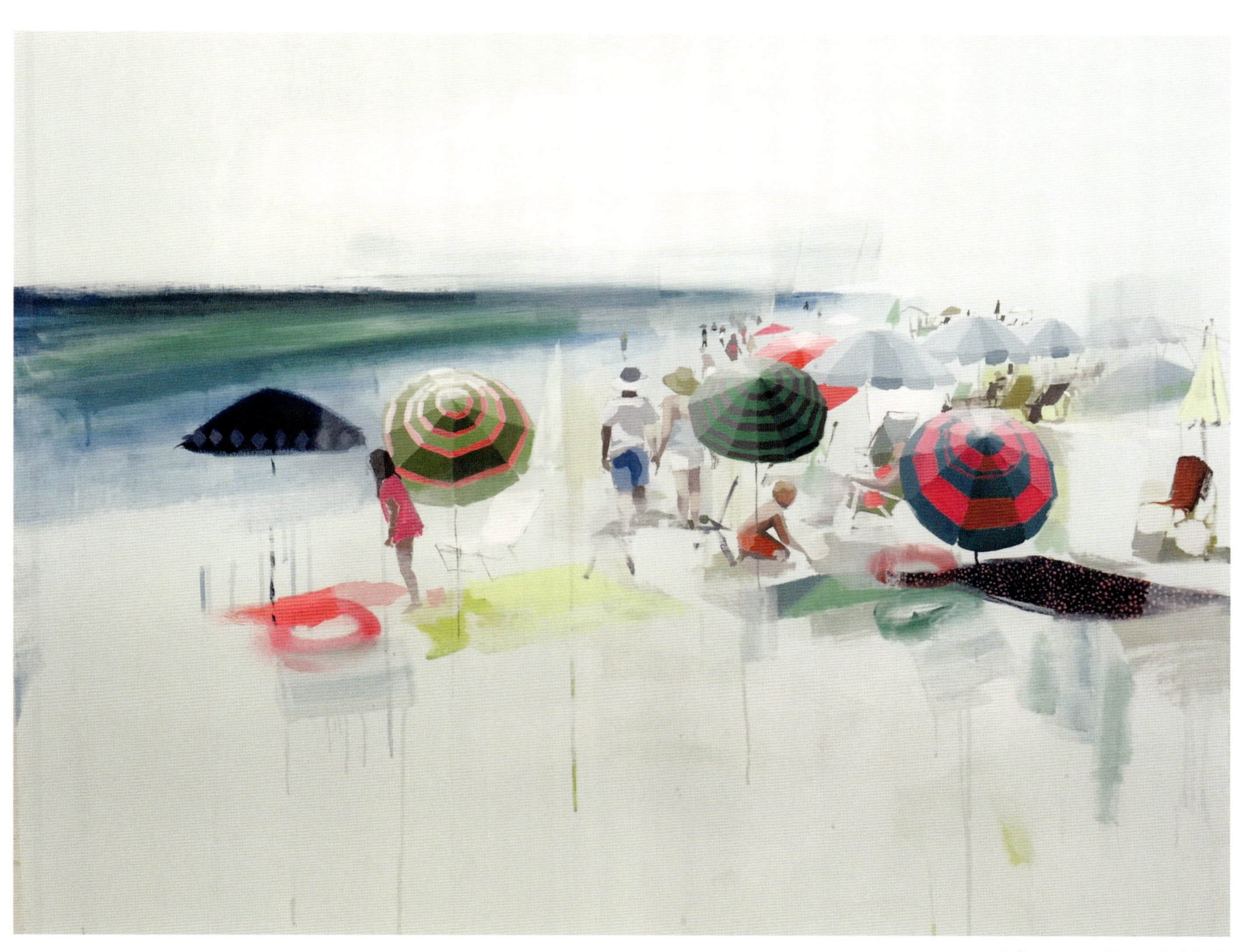

"Grayton Hues" 2015

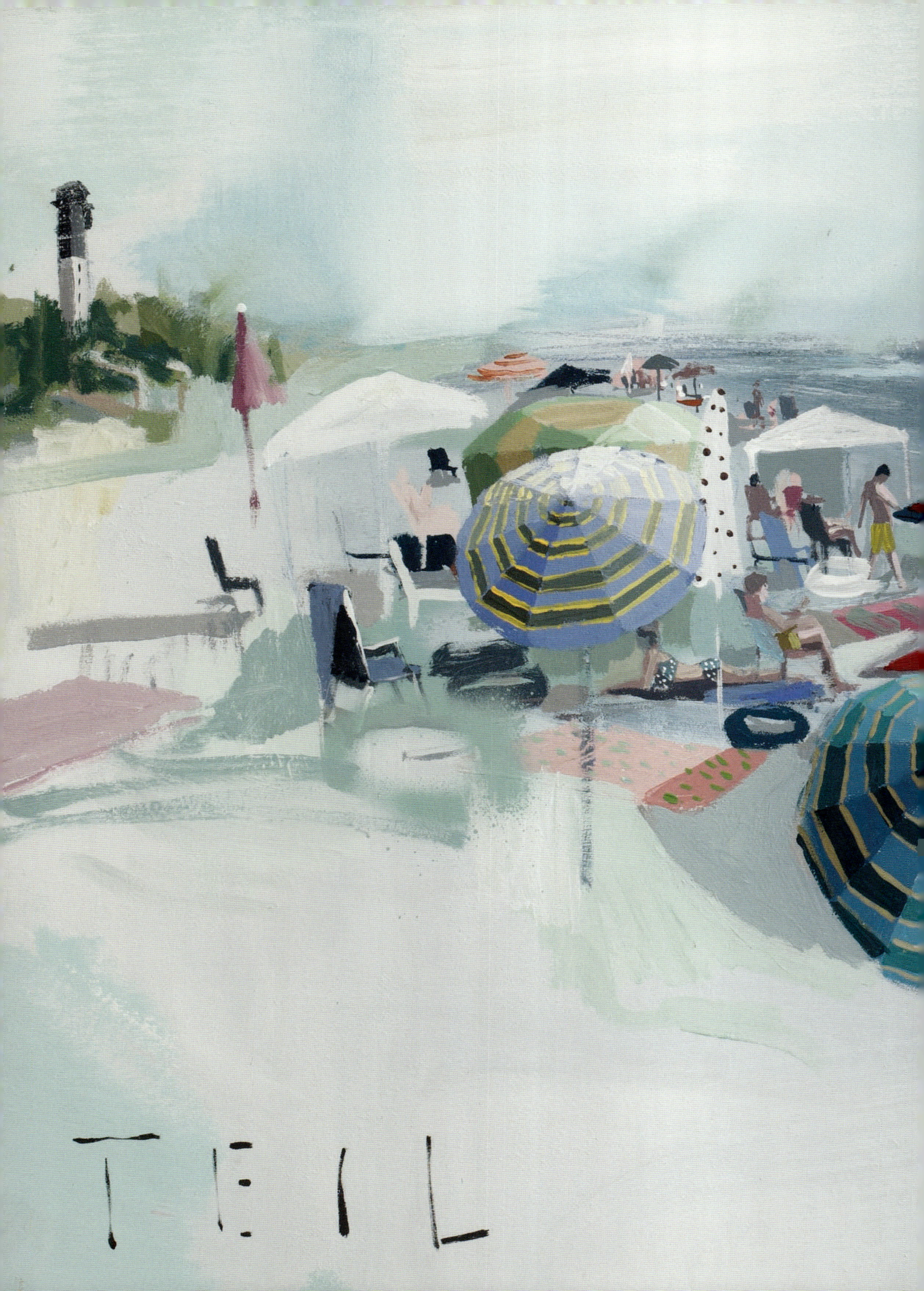

This collection has undoubtedly evolved since the beginning of the series in 2013. Initially, they began as more abstract depictions of lounging people basking in the sun. Earlier beach work is focused on a closer view of the bathing figures, featuring bold strokes that represent light and shadow, with occasional painterly sketch marks intentionally exposed in the final product. Over time, I have pushed and pulled the series by bringing the view even closer in composition and pushing it back at a smaller scale and distant perspective. The figures and umbrellas got more tightly rendered, and the negative space more abstracted and layered. This subject has provided endless technical possibilities and has also allowed various subjects to emerge: the beach babes, beach close-ups, pool scenes, and monochromatic beach scenes.

"Sullivan's Lighthouse" 2017

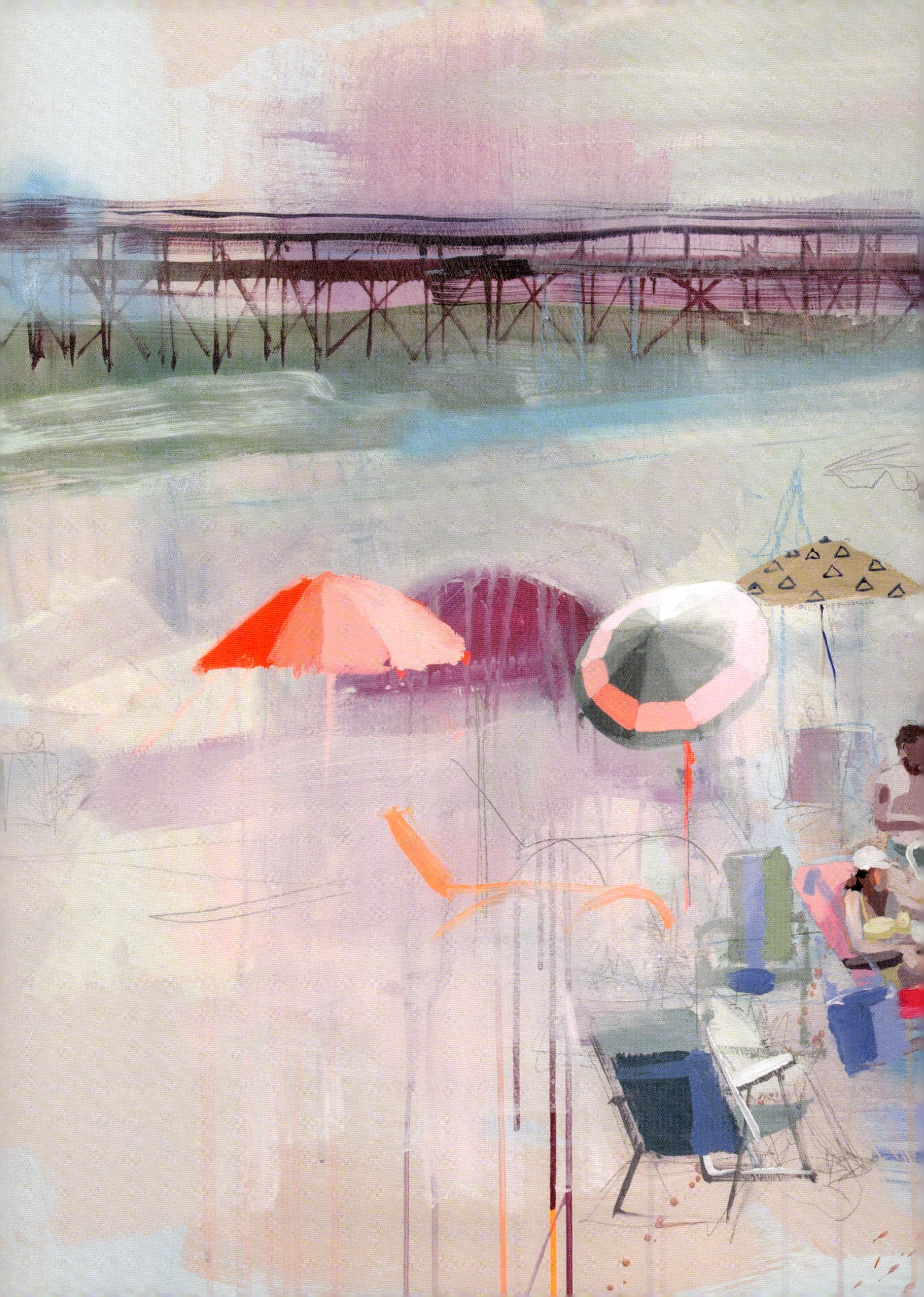

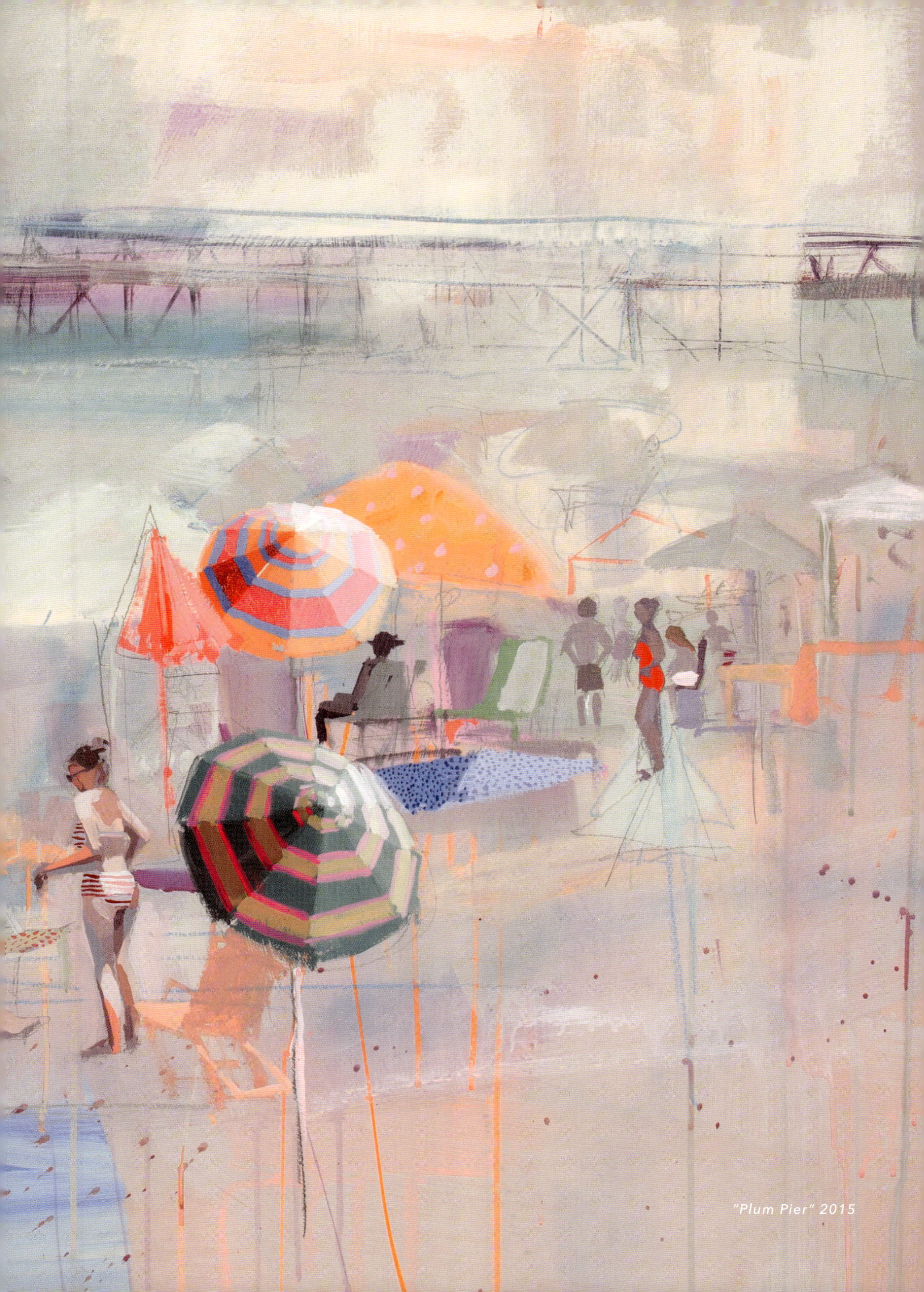

"Plum Pier" 2015

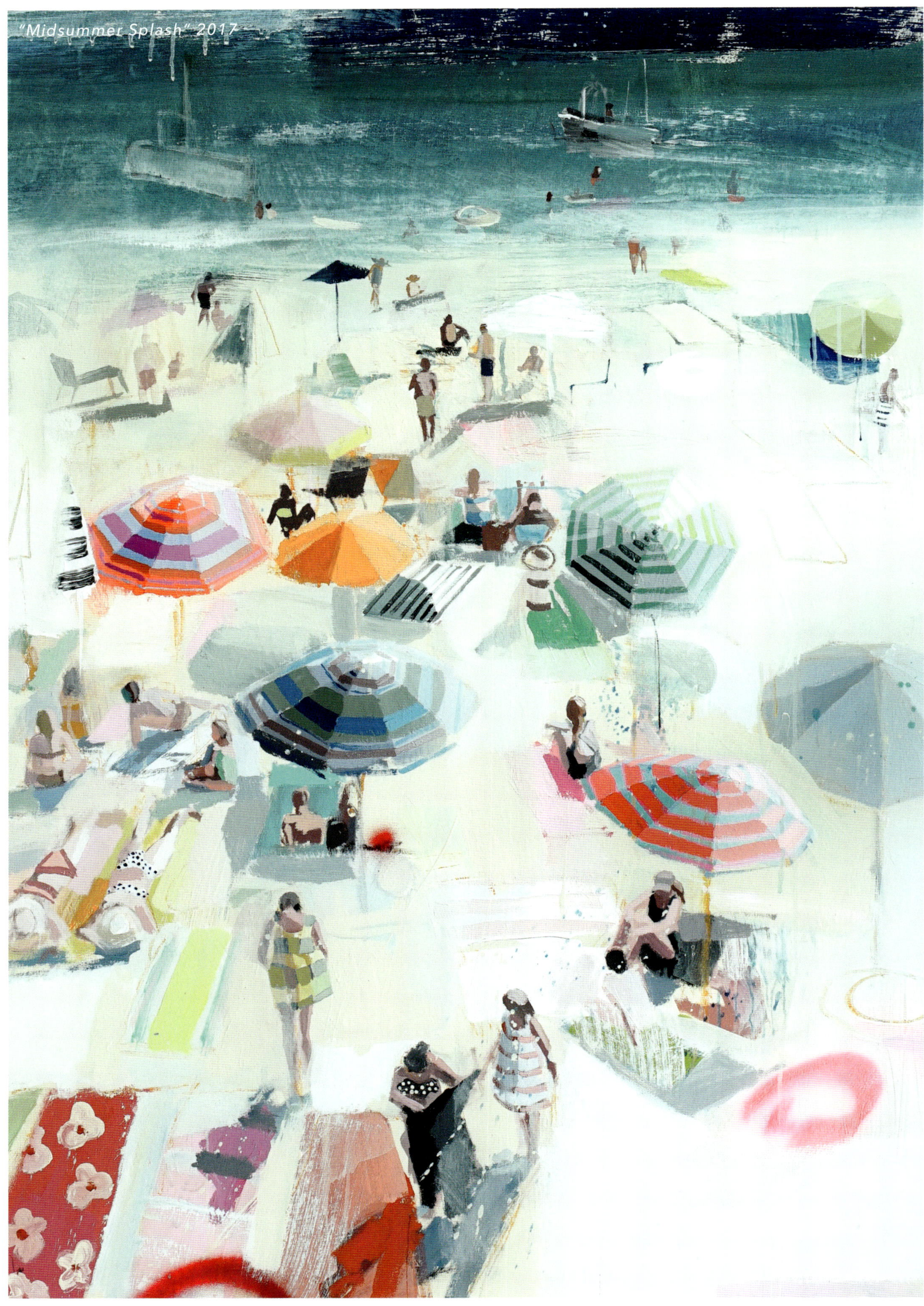

"Midsummer Splash" 2017

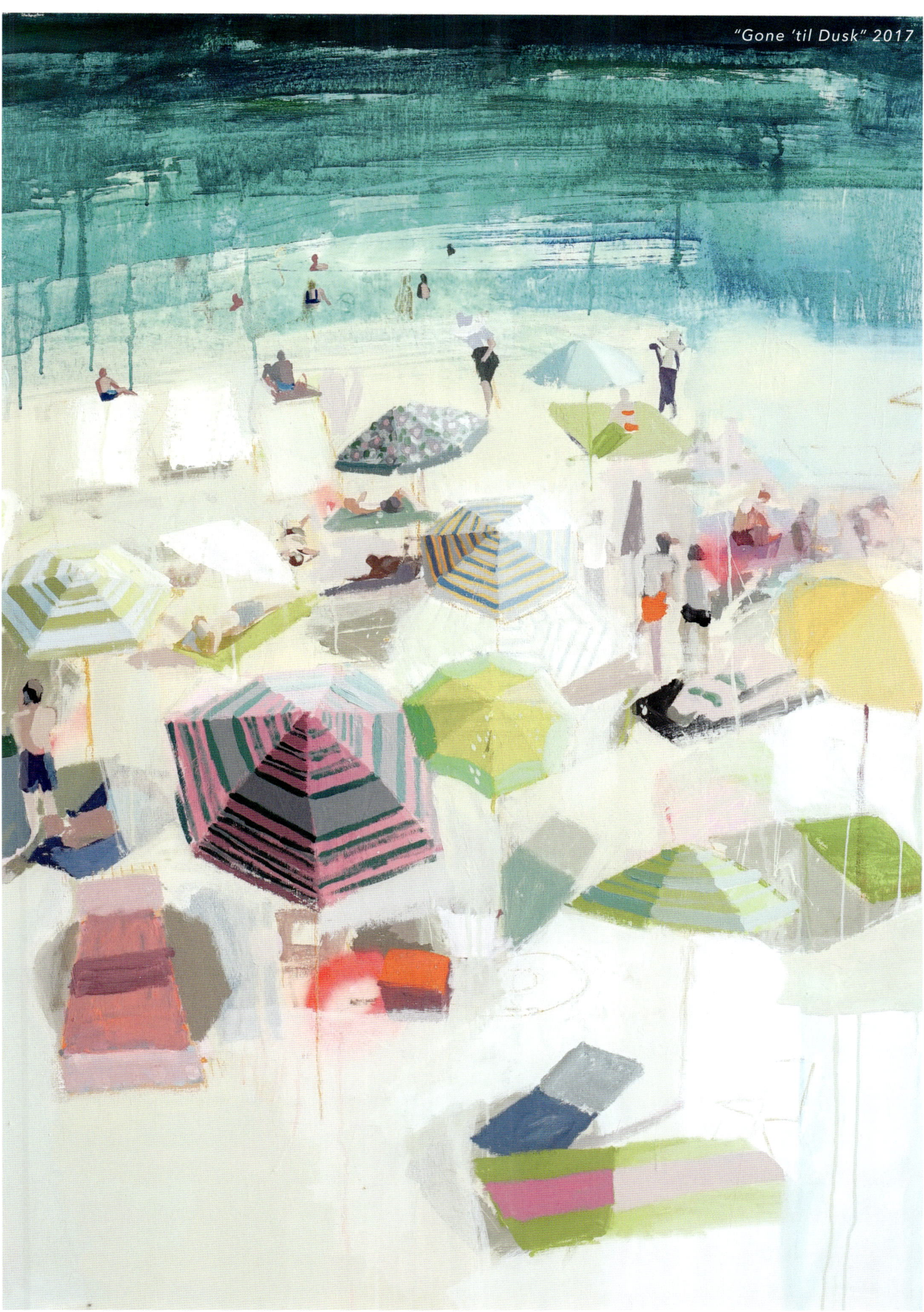

"Gone 'til Dusk" 2017

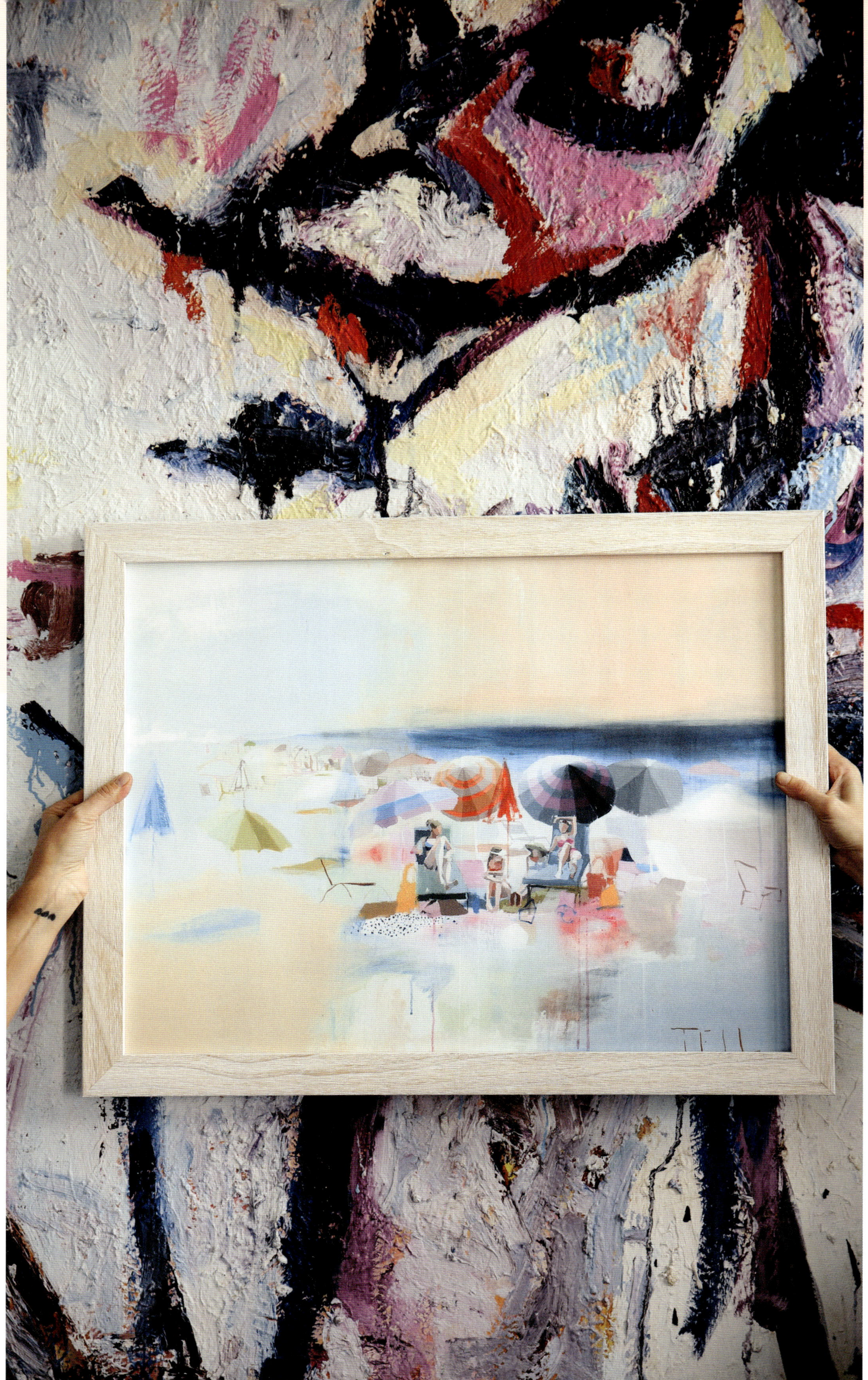

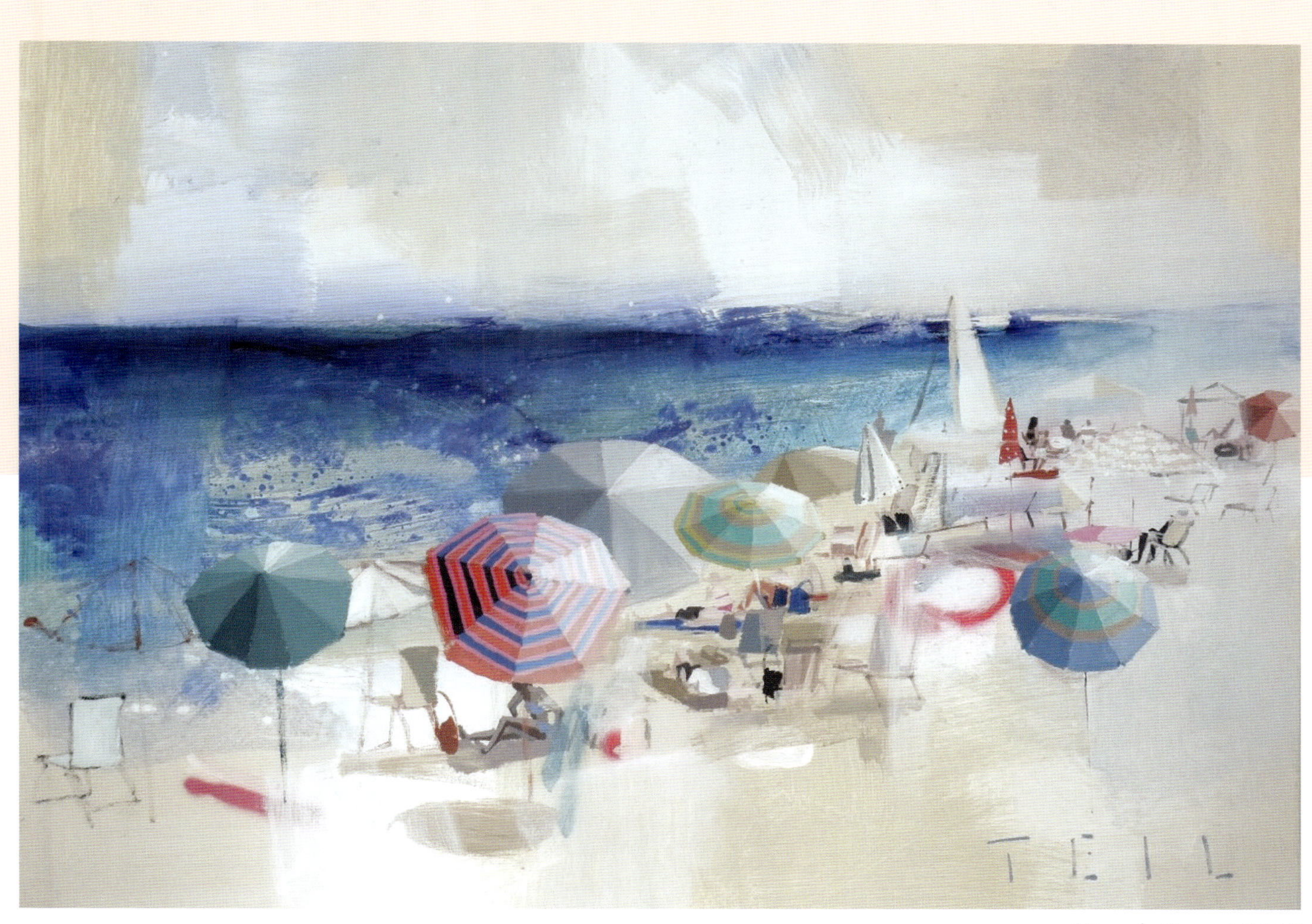

"Beach Gems" 2017

"Fruits of the Week" 2014

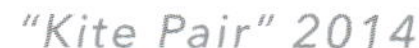

"Kite Pair" 2014

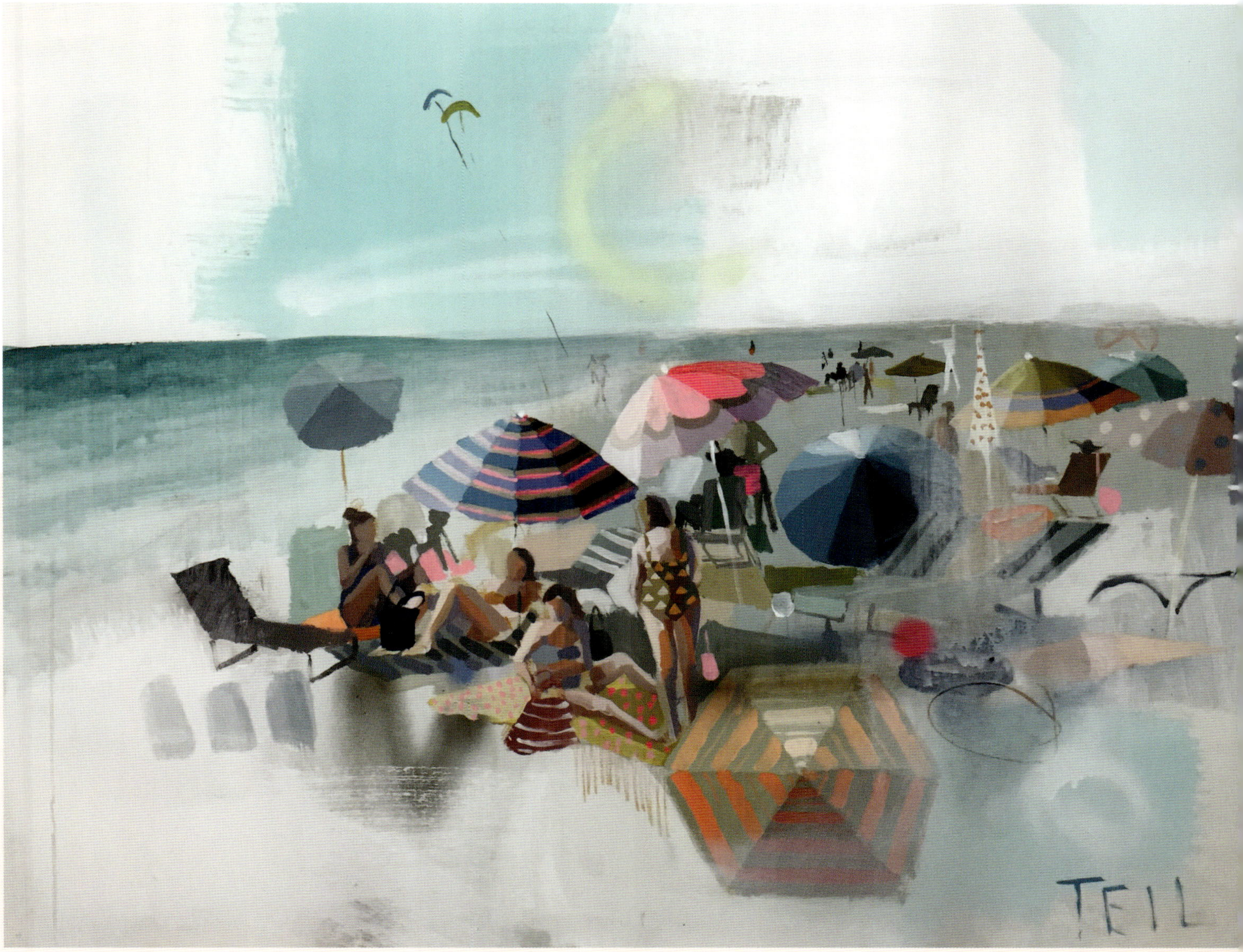

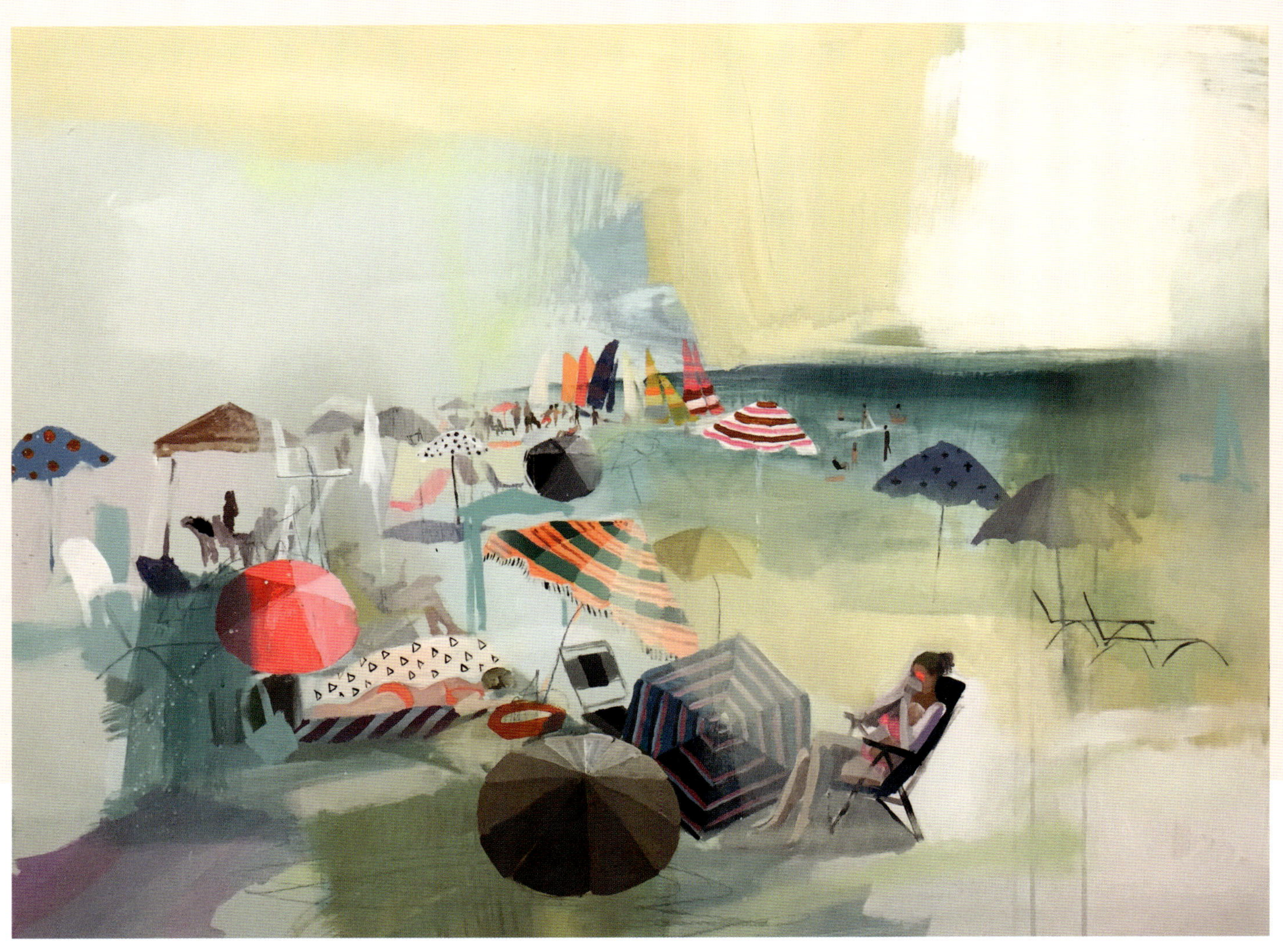

"Banana Split Break" 2014

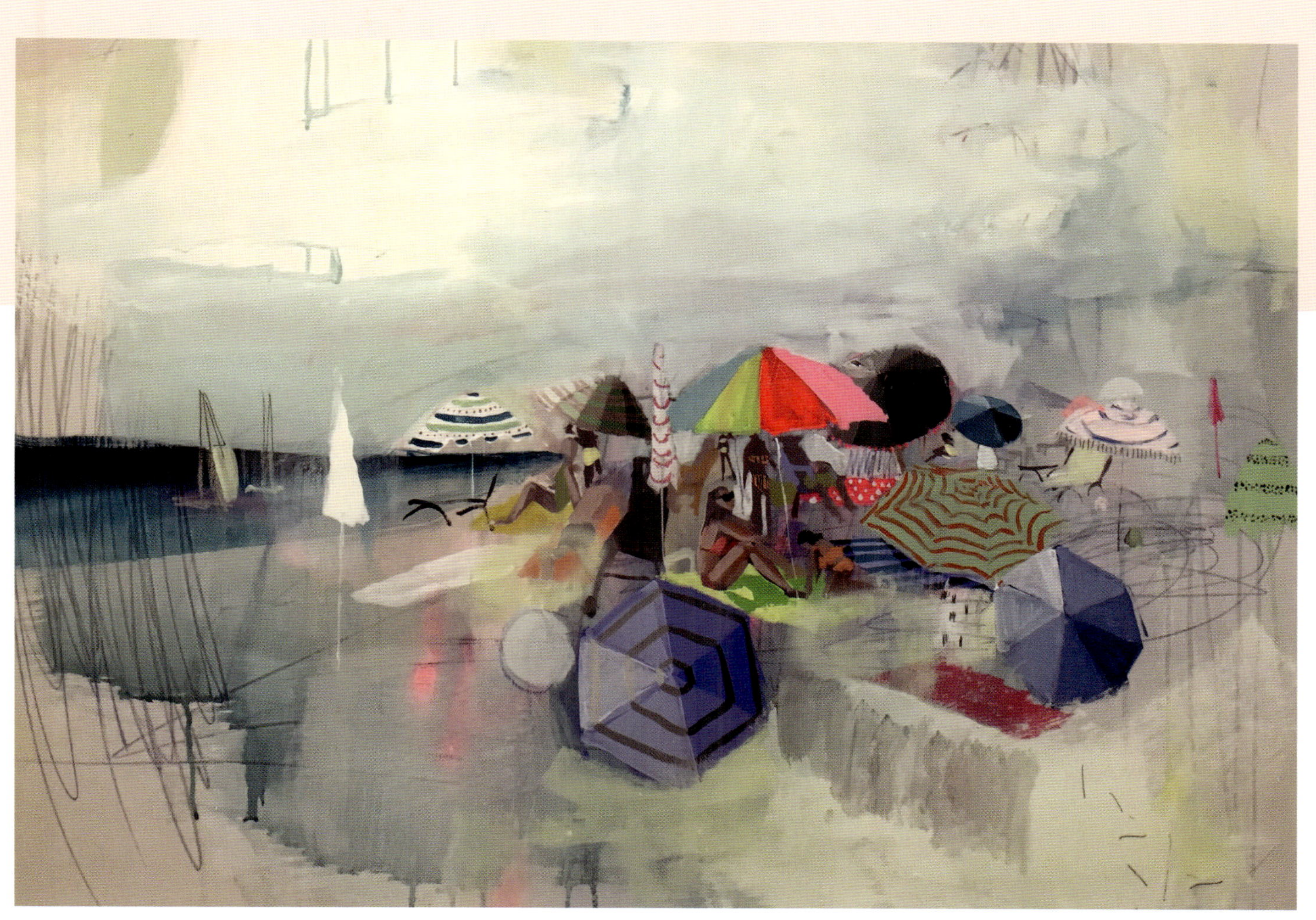

"Dusk Sail" 2014

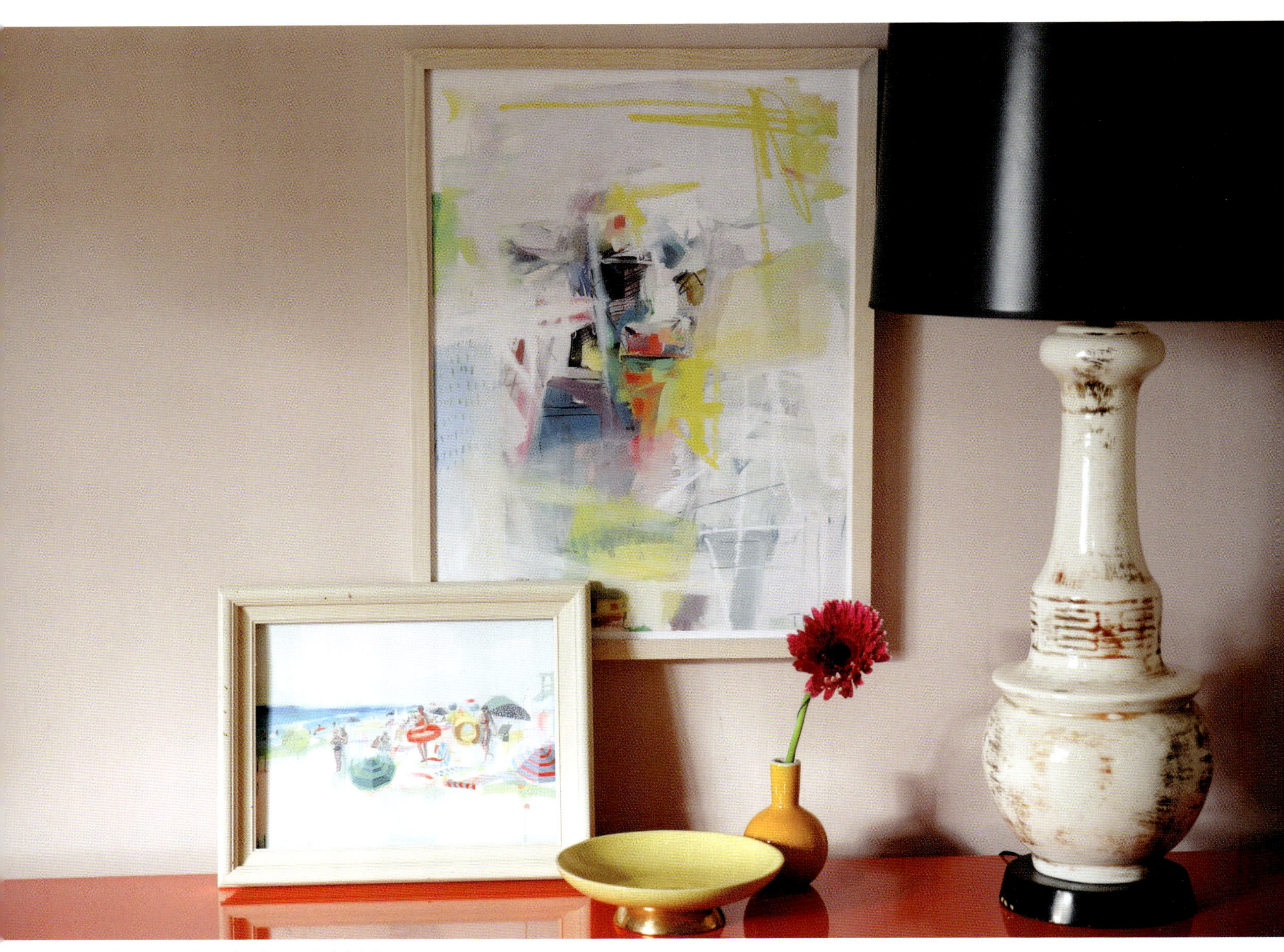

"Cotton Candy Coast" 2014

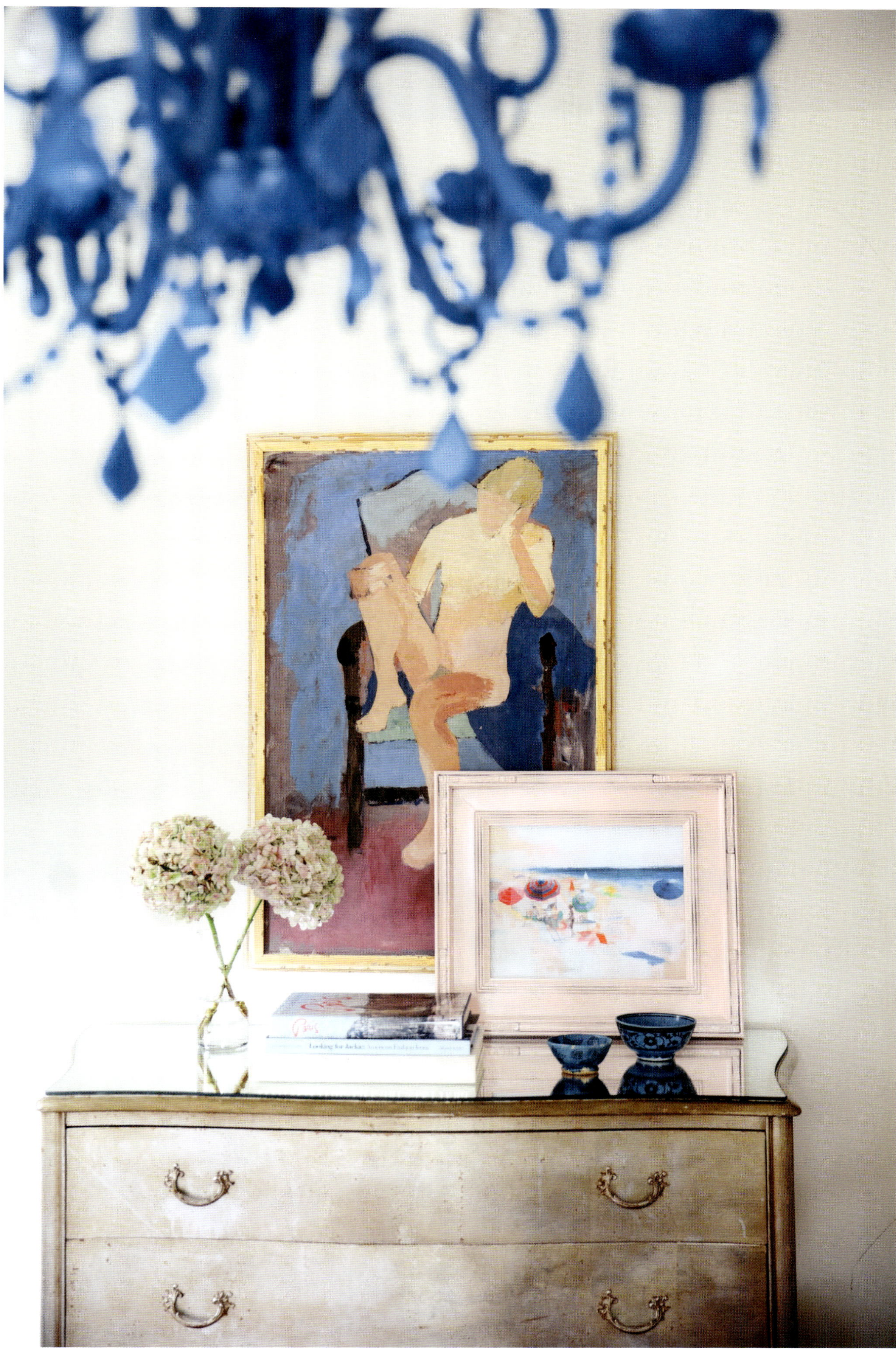
Paris
Looking for Jackie

"Cotton Candy Coast" 2014

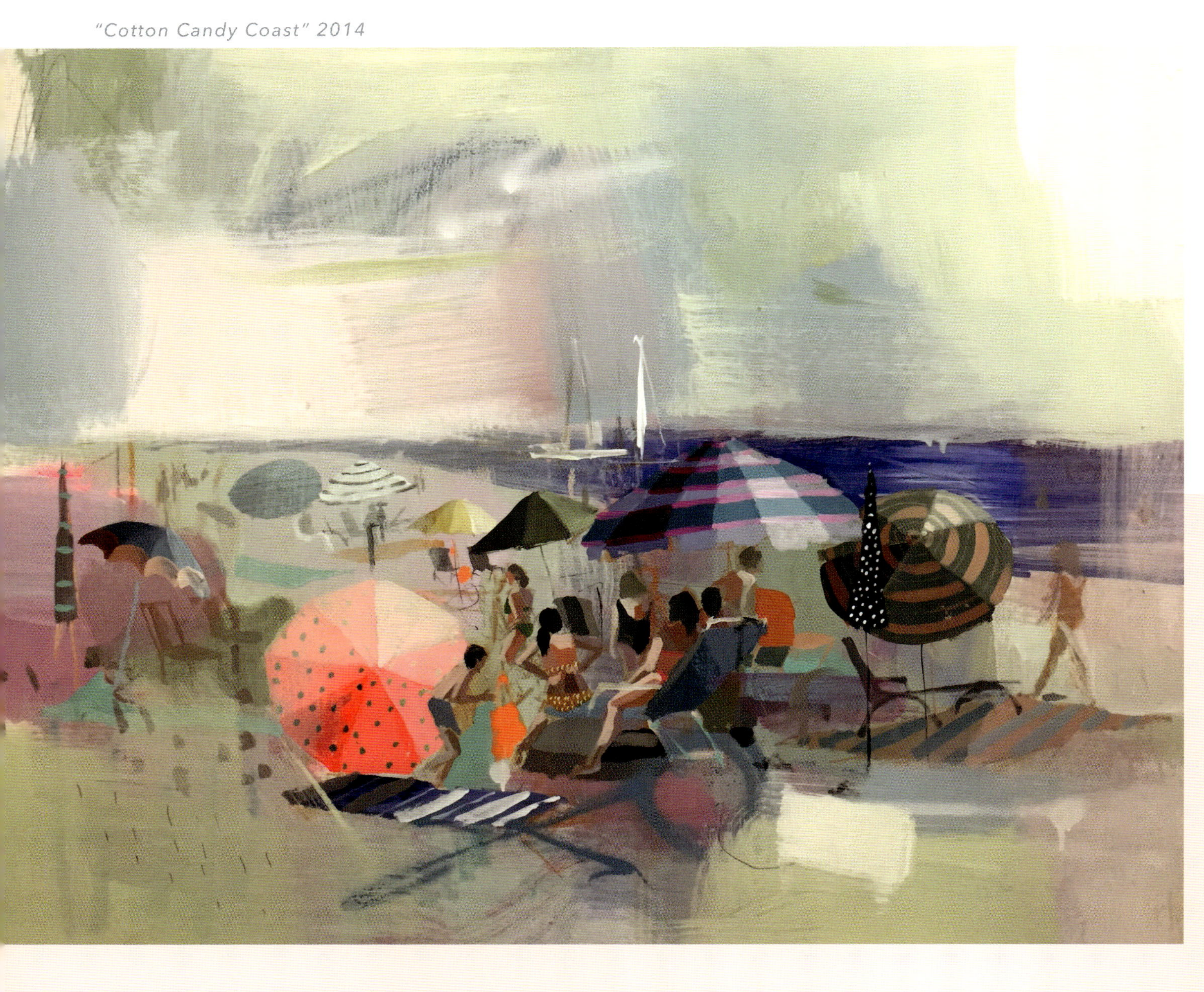

"Tangy Day" 2014

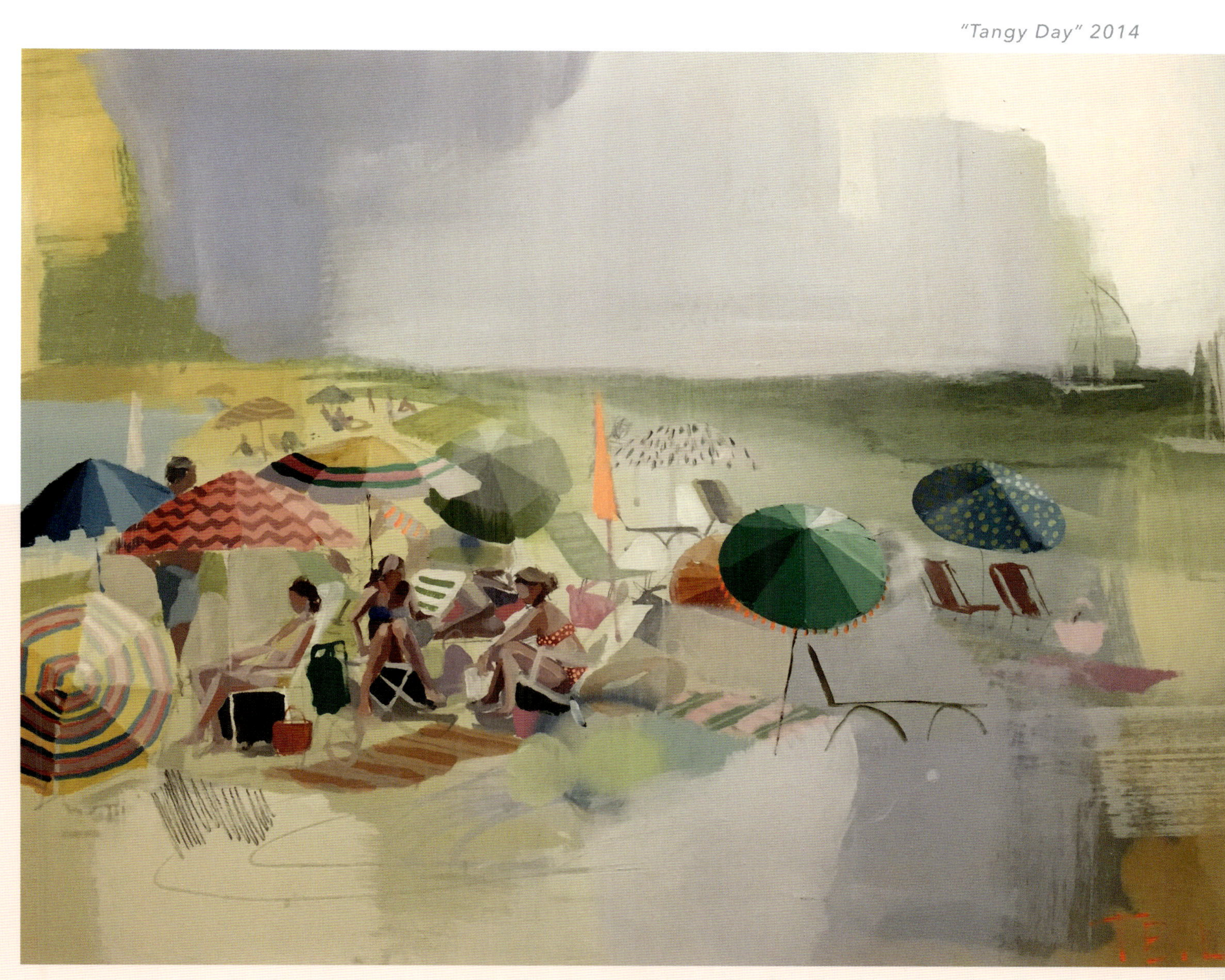

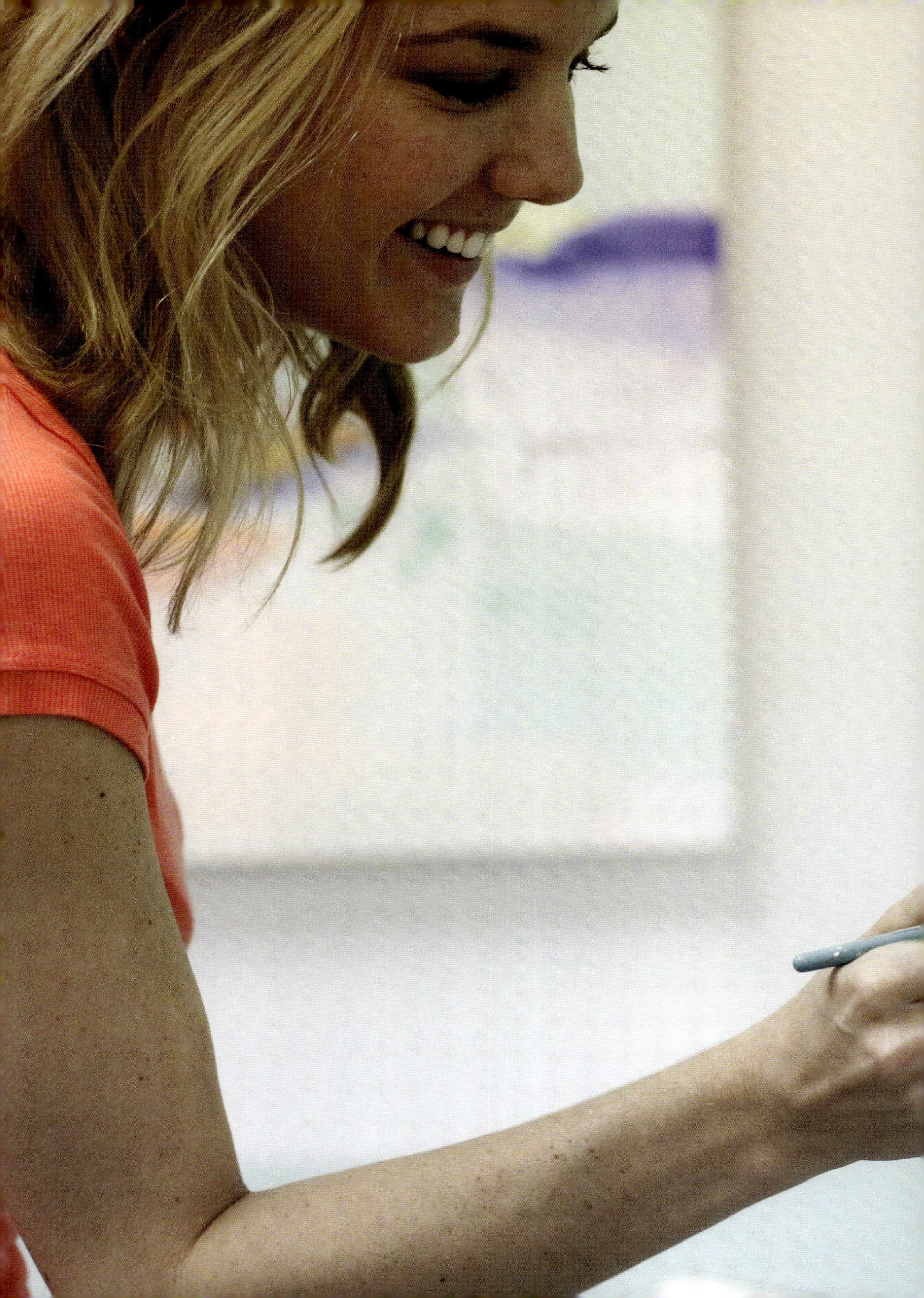

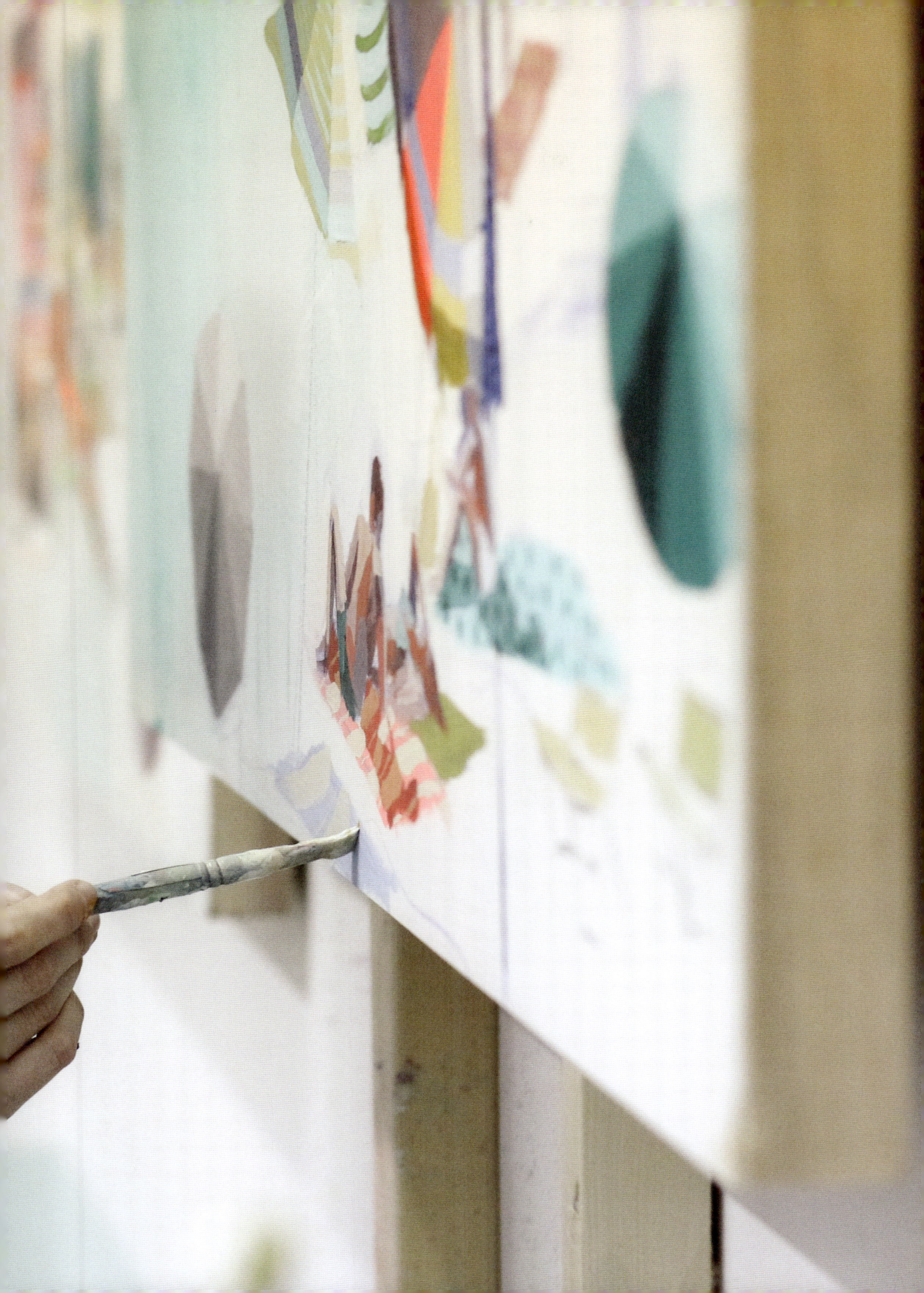

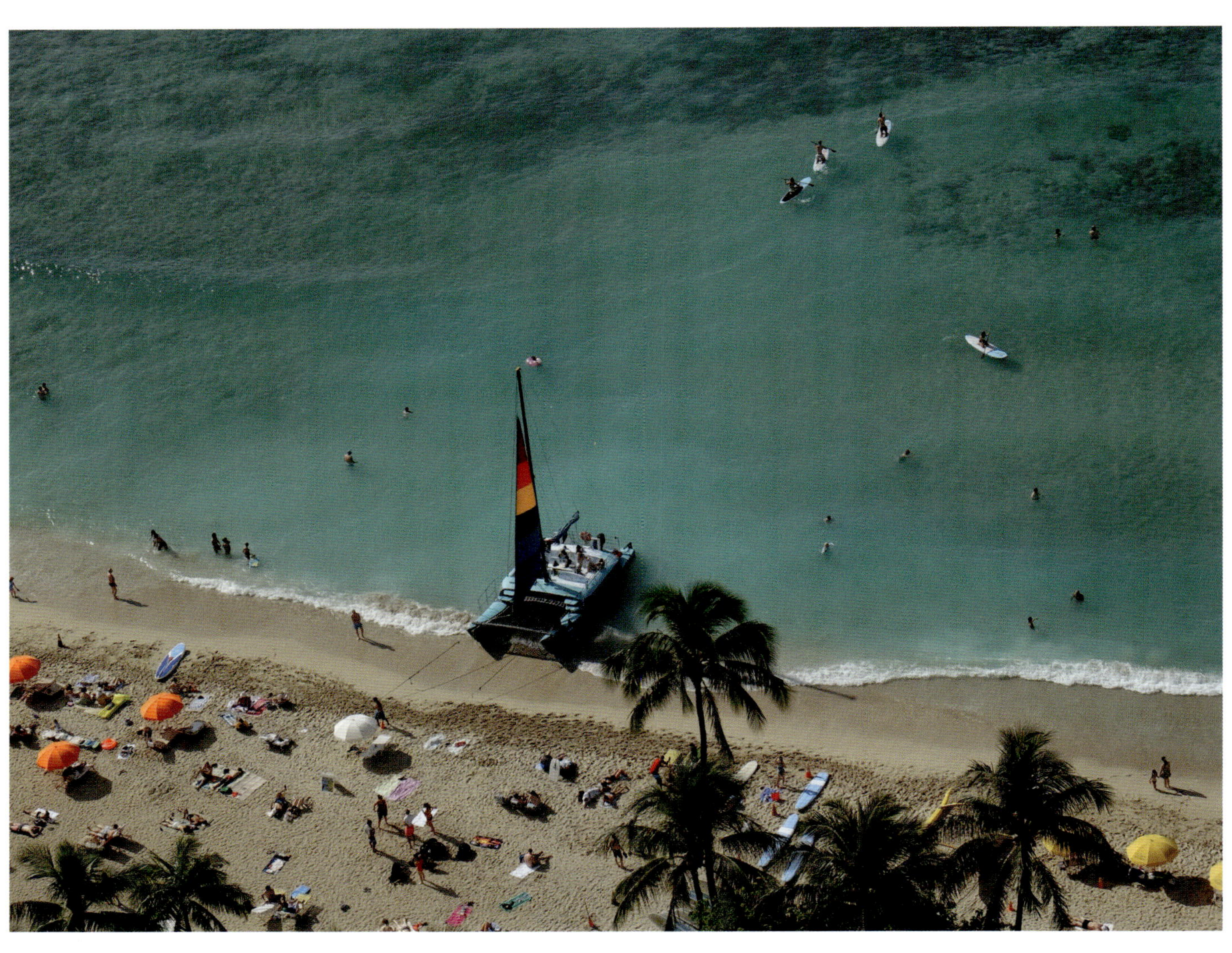

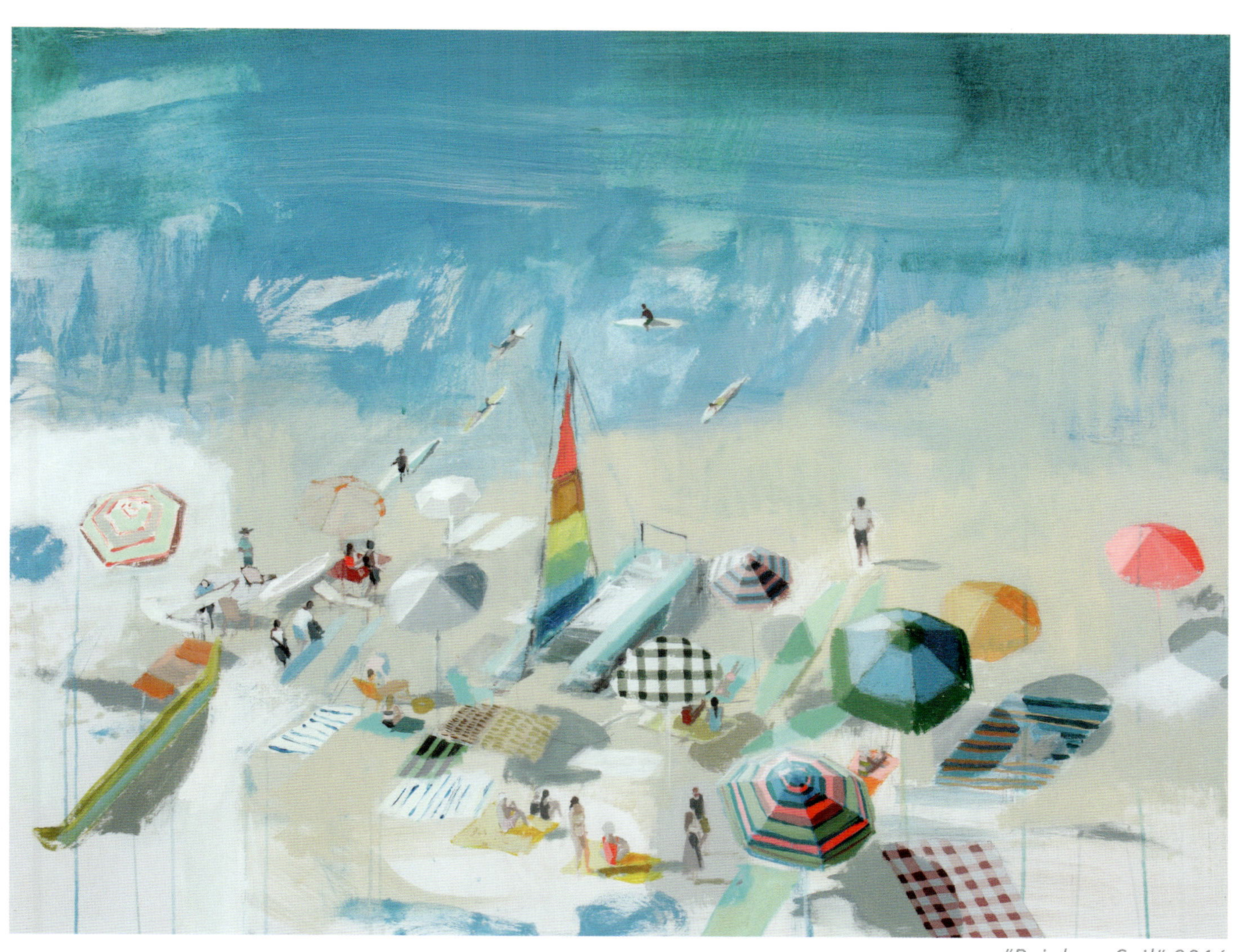

"Rainbow Sail" 2016

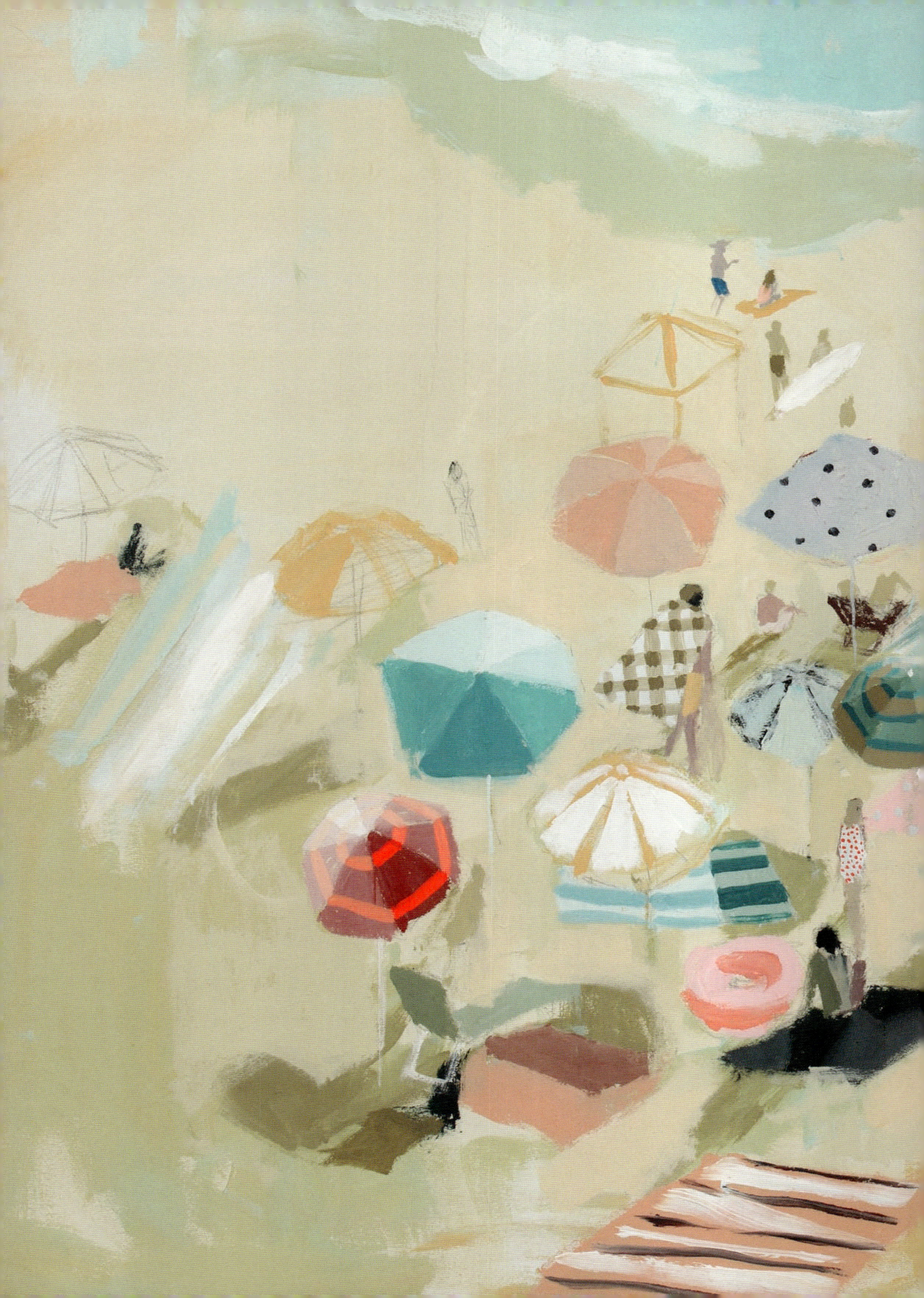

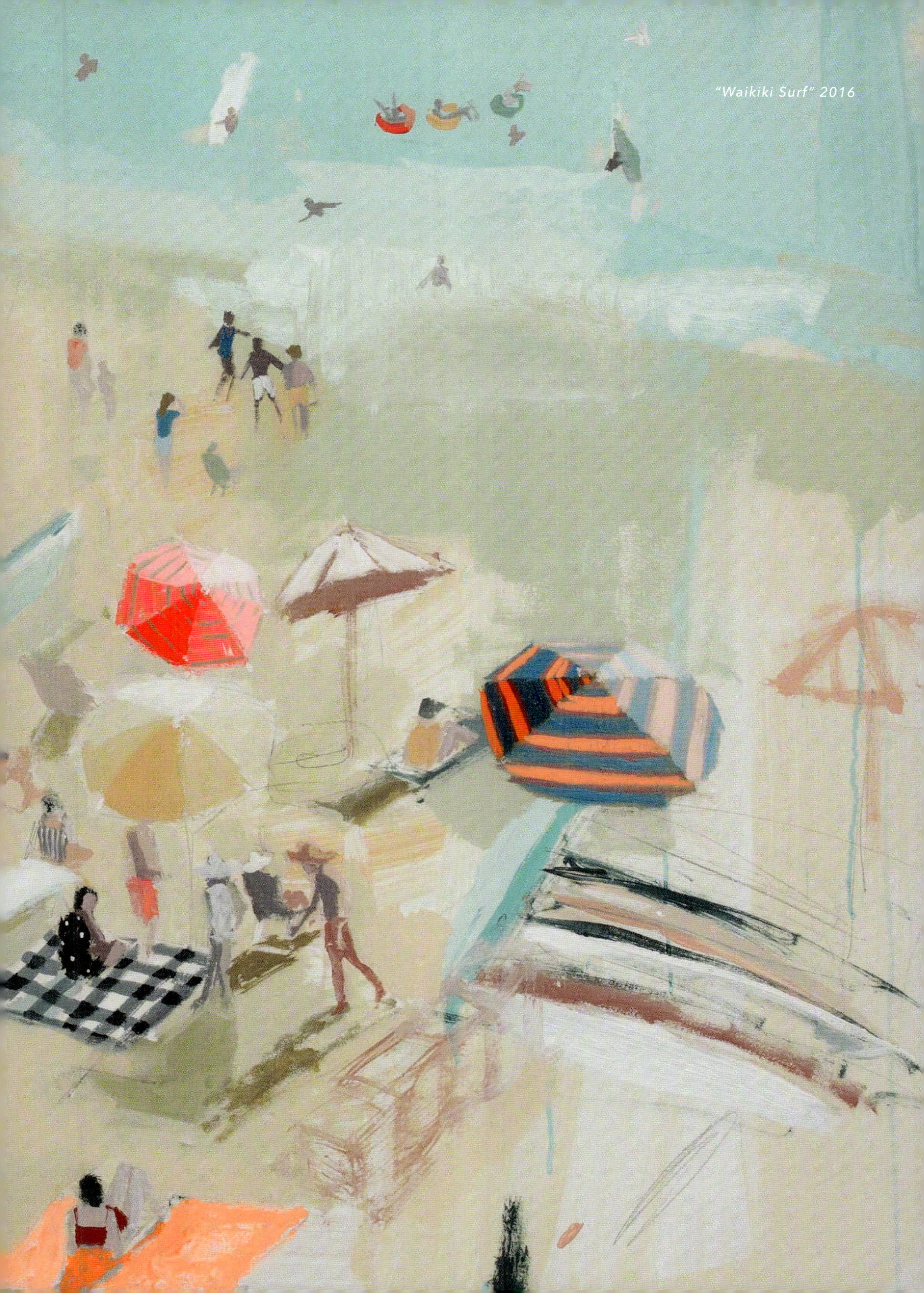

"Waikiki Surf" 2016

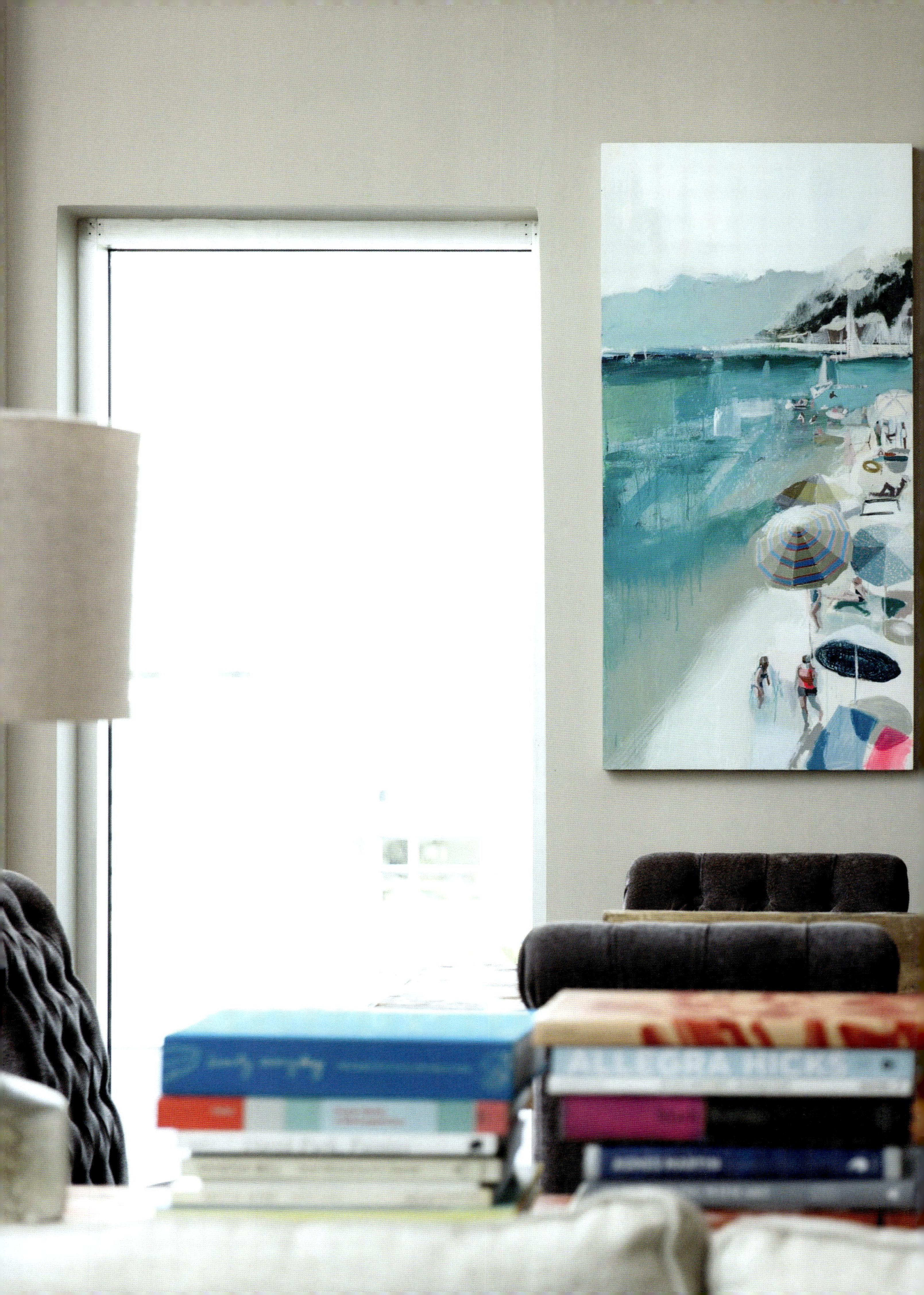
ALLEGRA HICKS

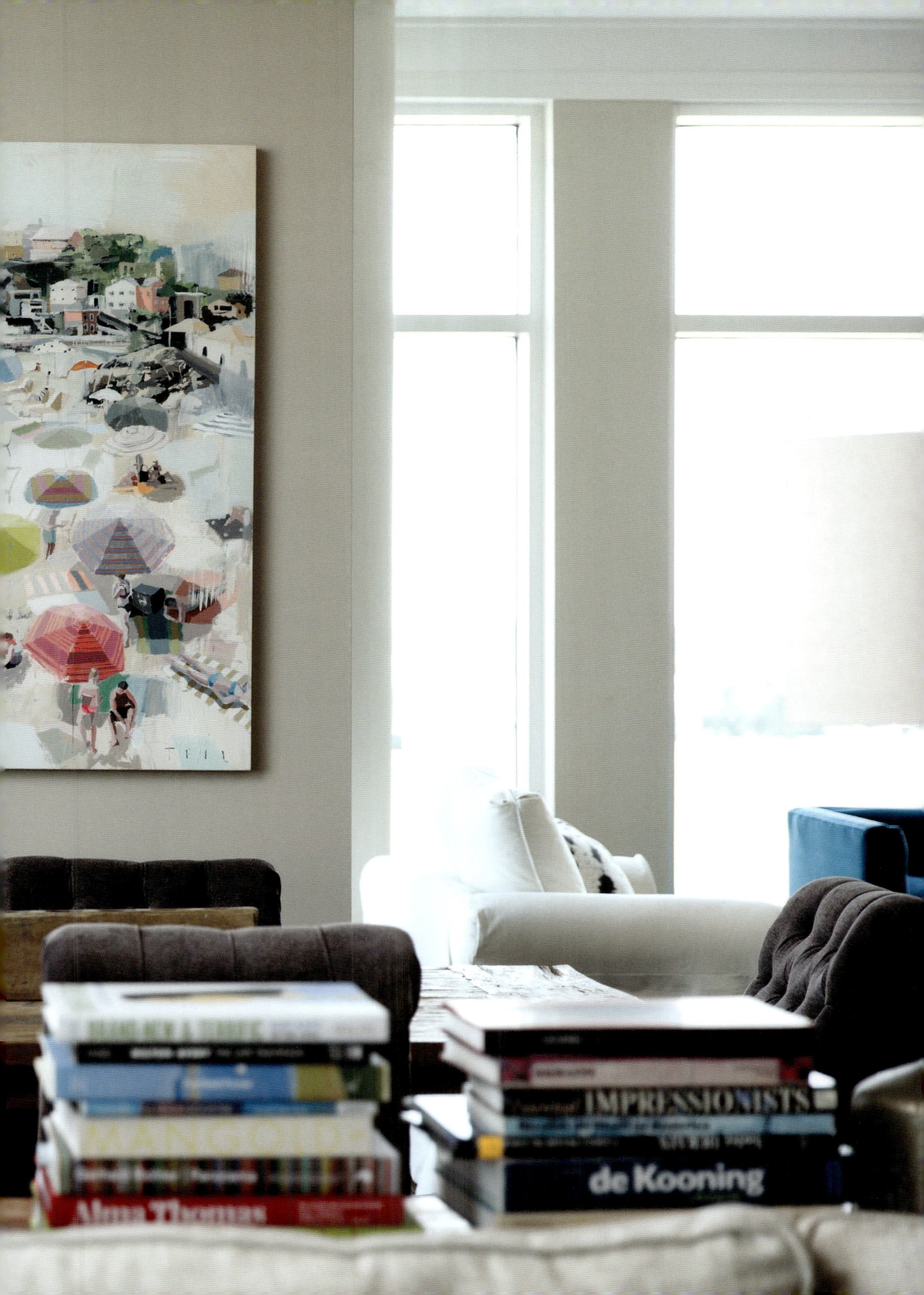
IMPRESSIONISTS
de Kooning
Alma Thomas

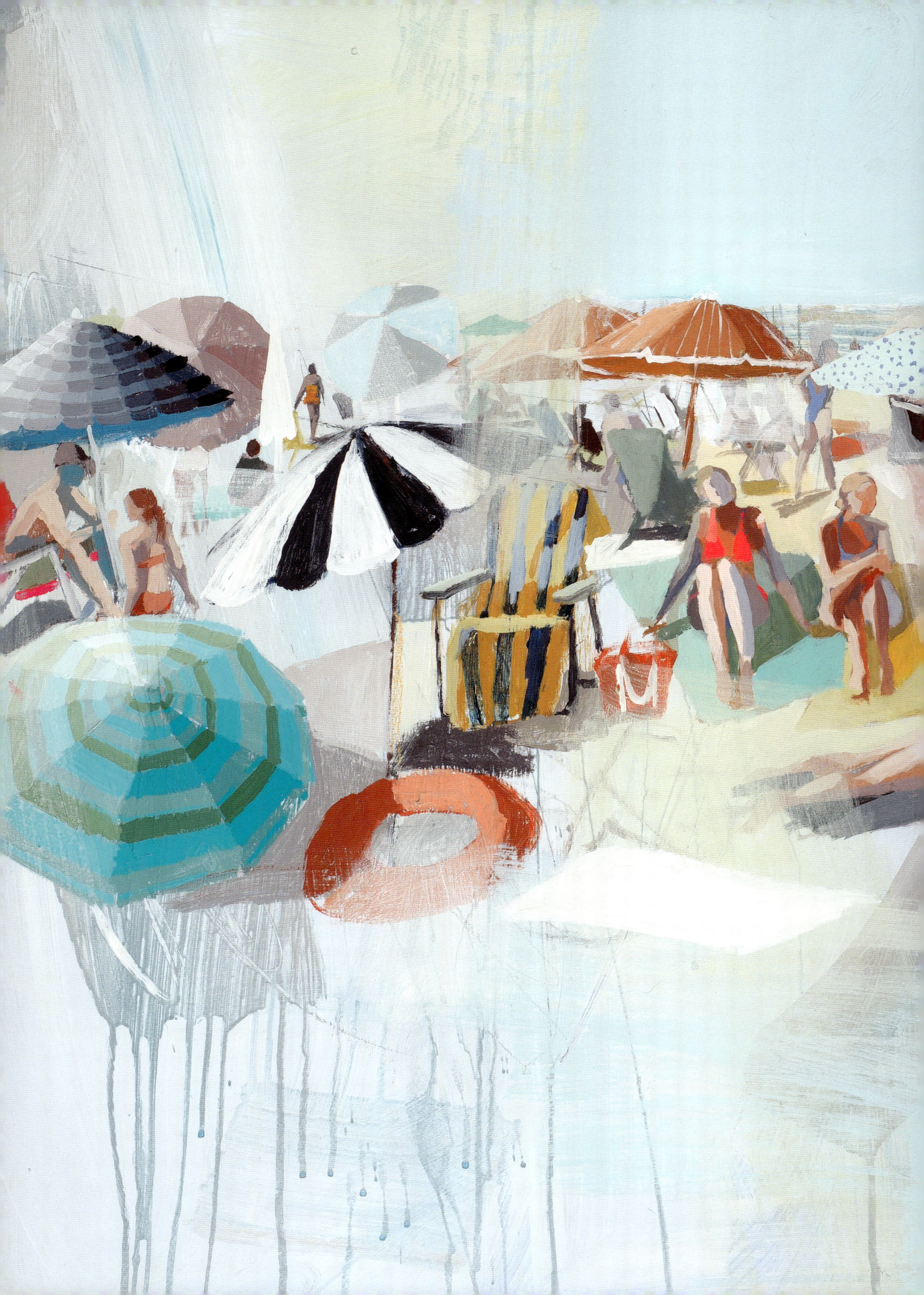

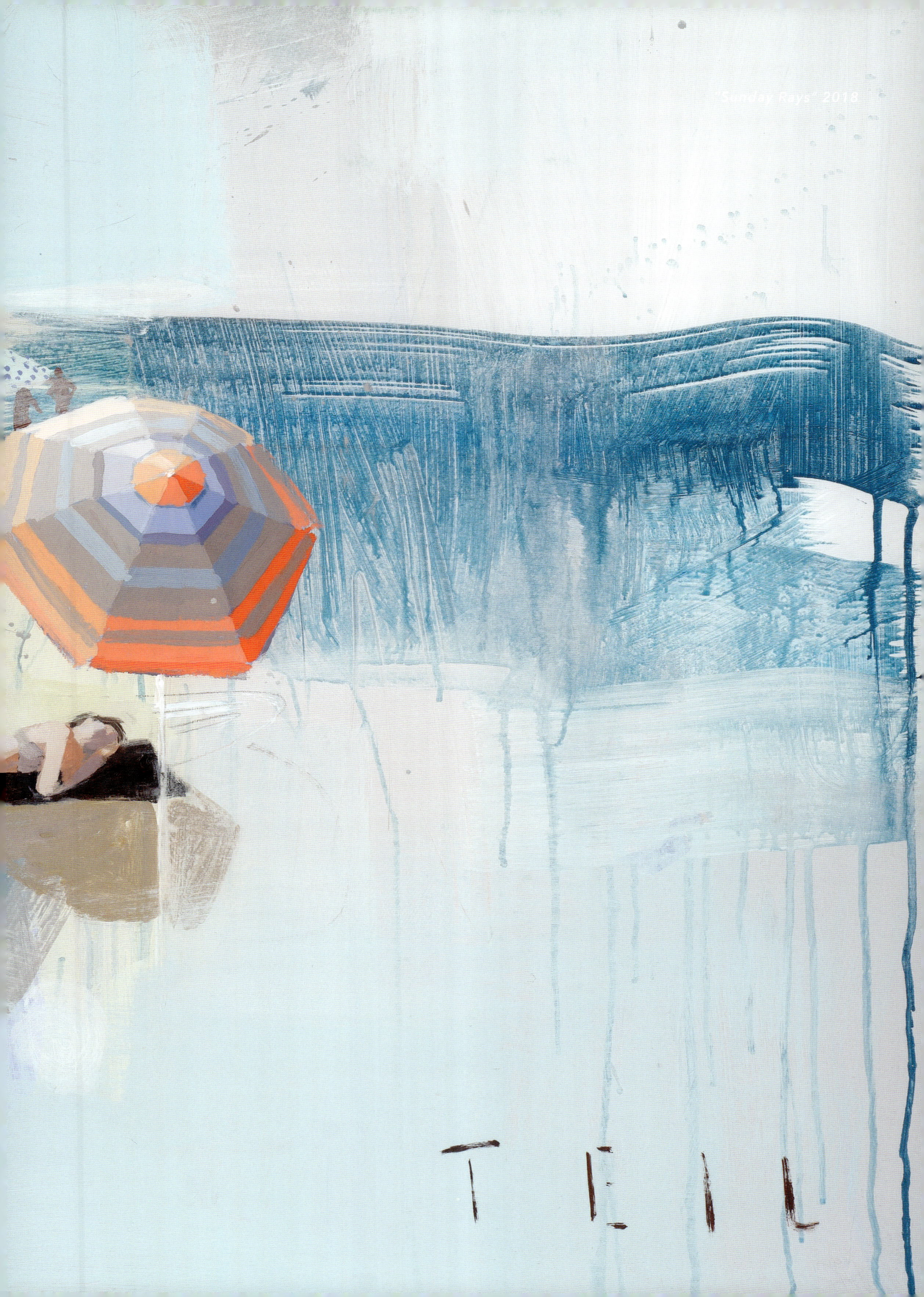

"Sunday Rays" 2018

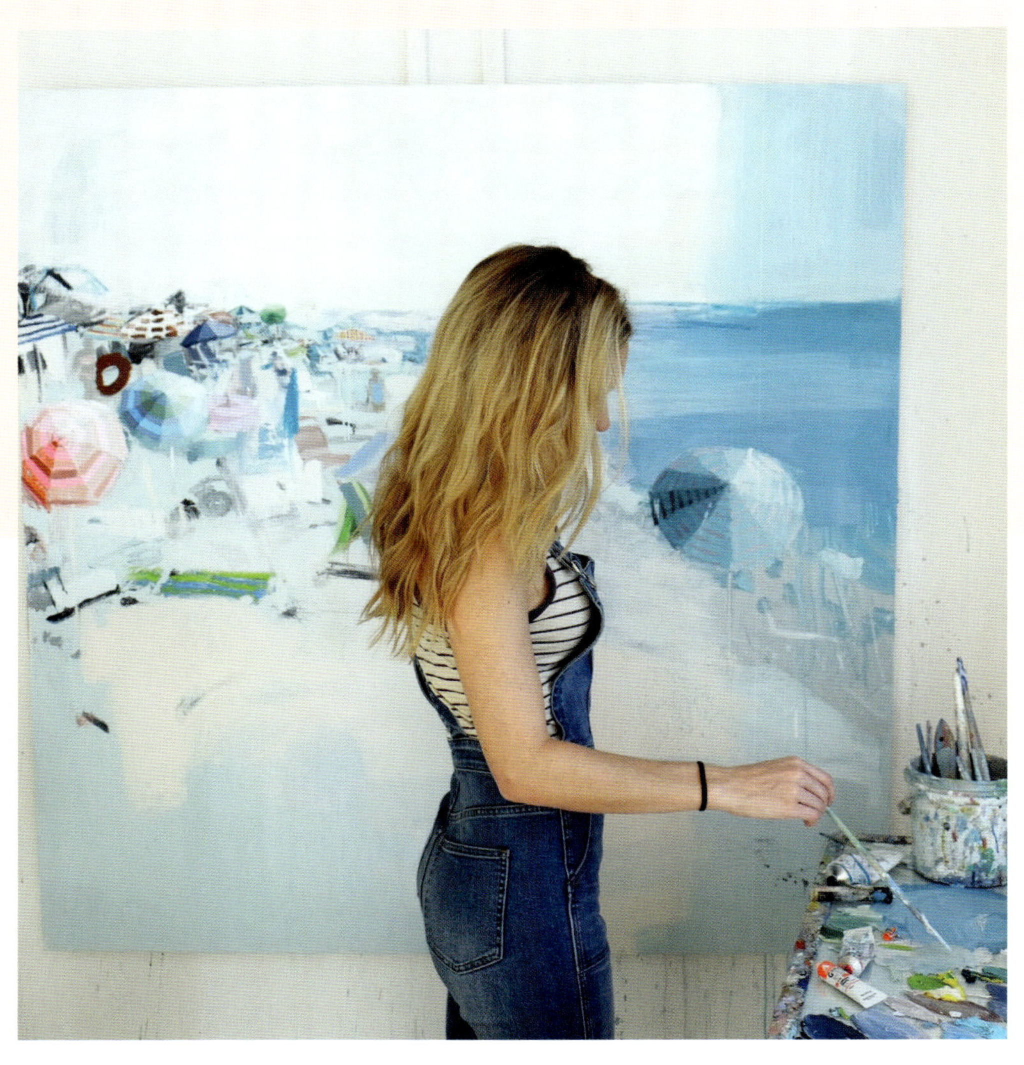

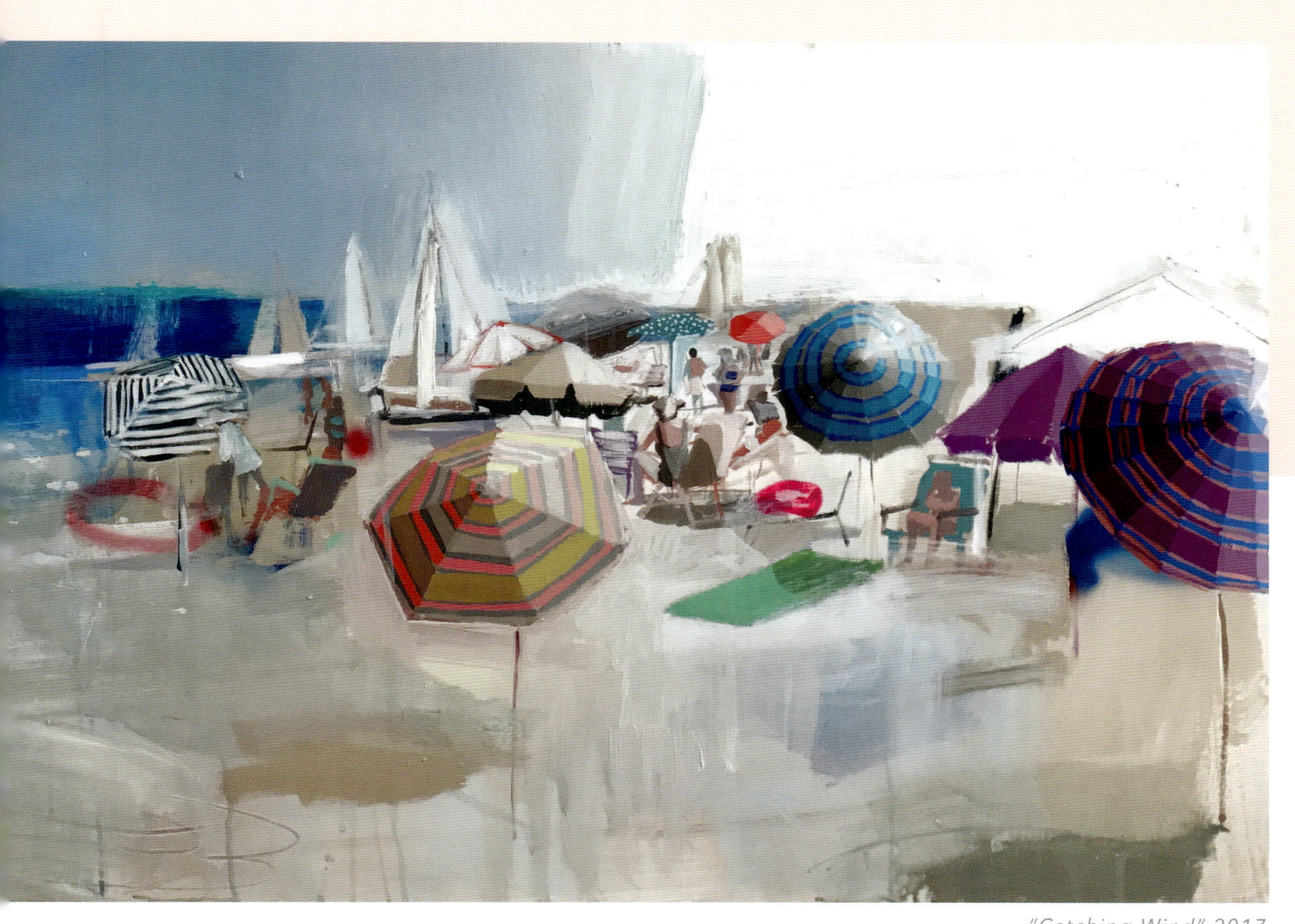

"Catching Wind" 2017

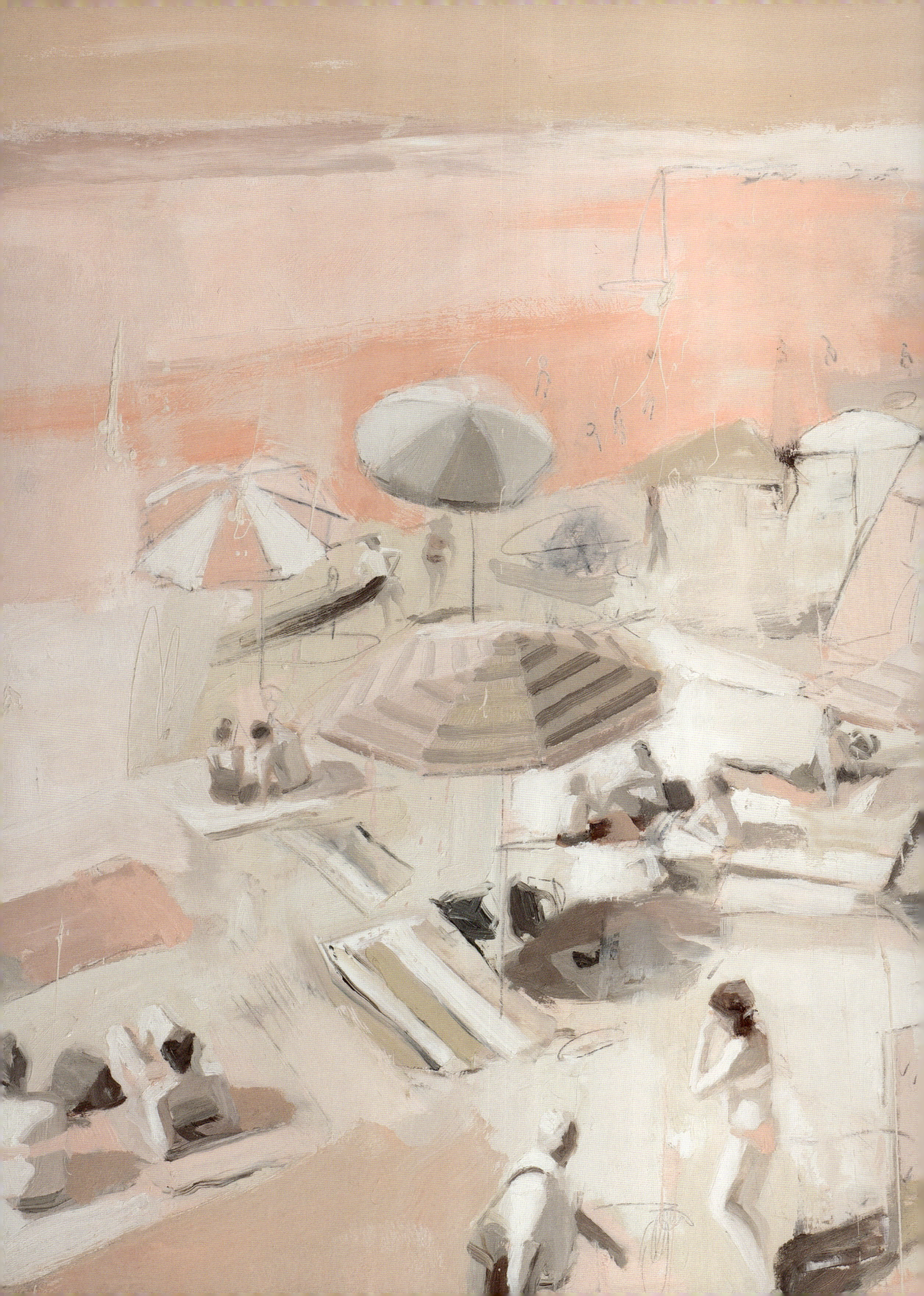

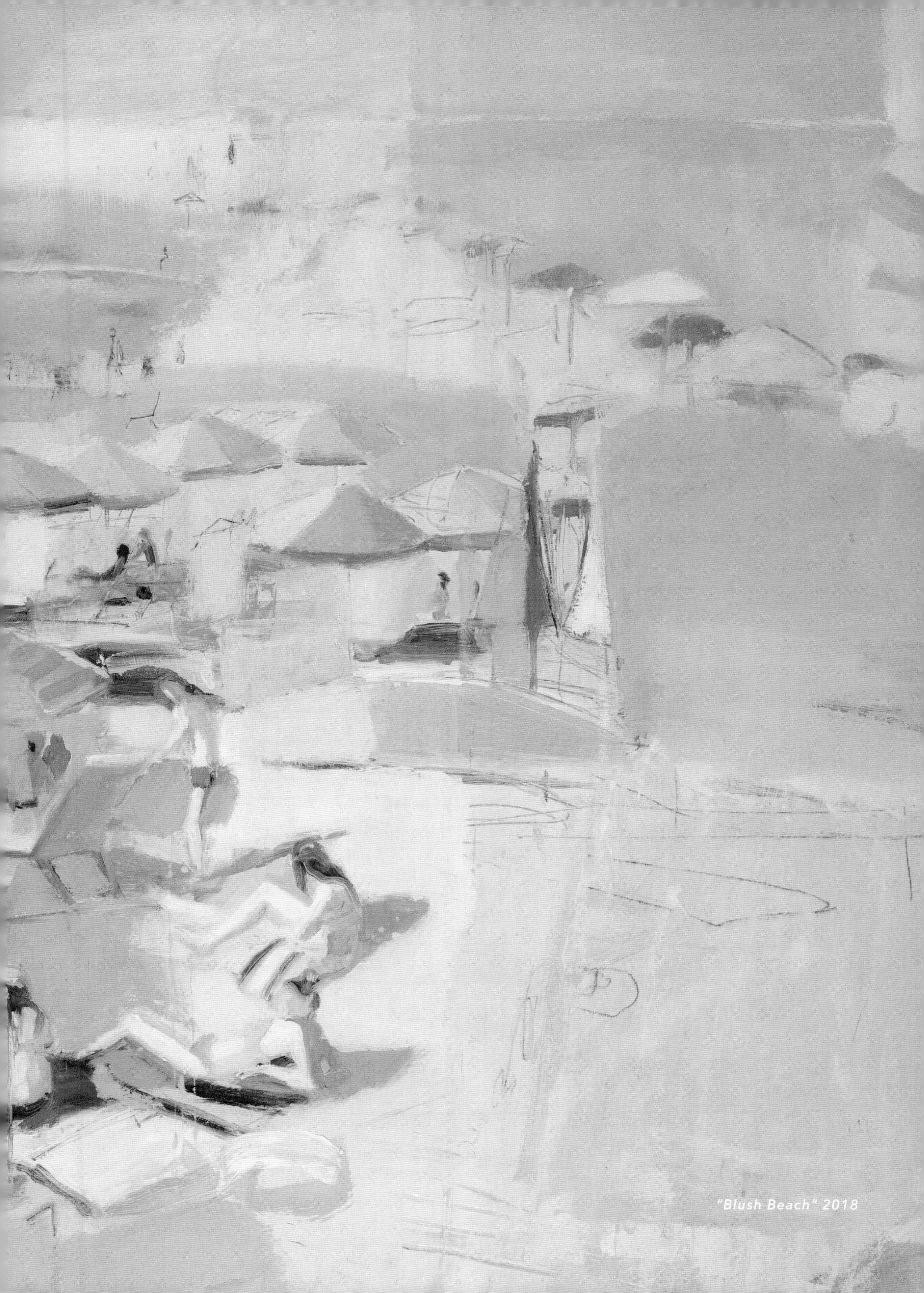

"Blush Beach" 2018

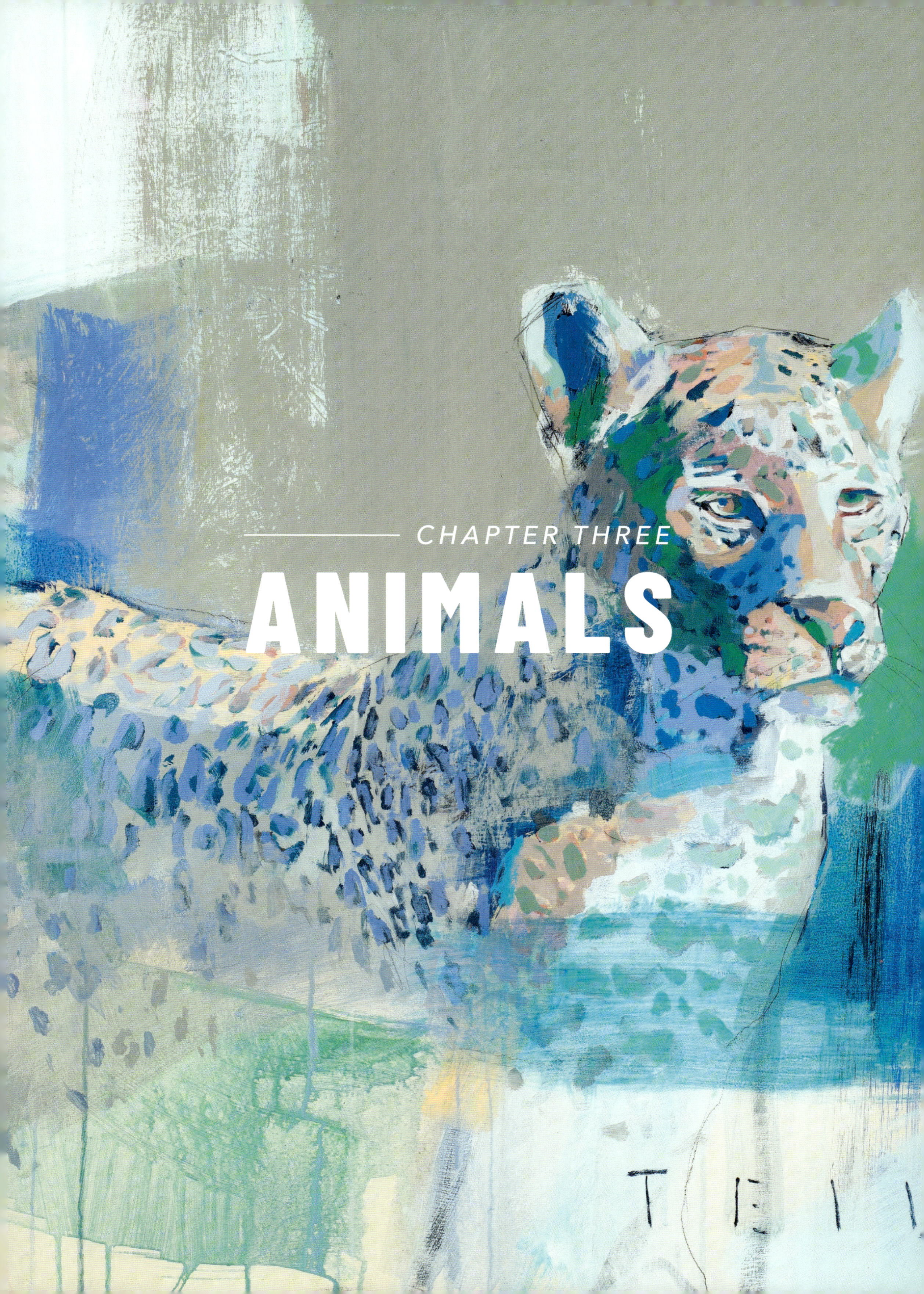

CHAPTER THREE

ANIMALS

"Curiosity in Color" 2018

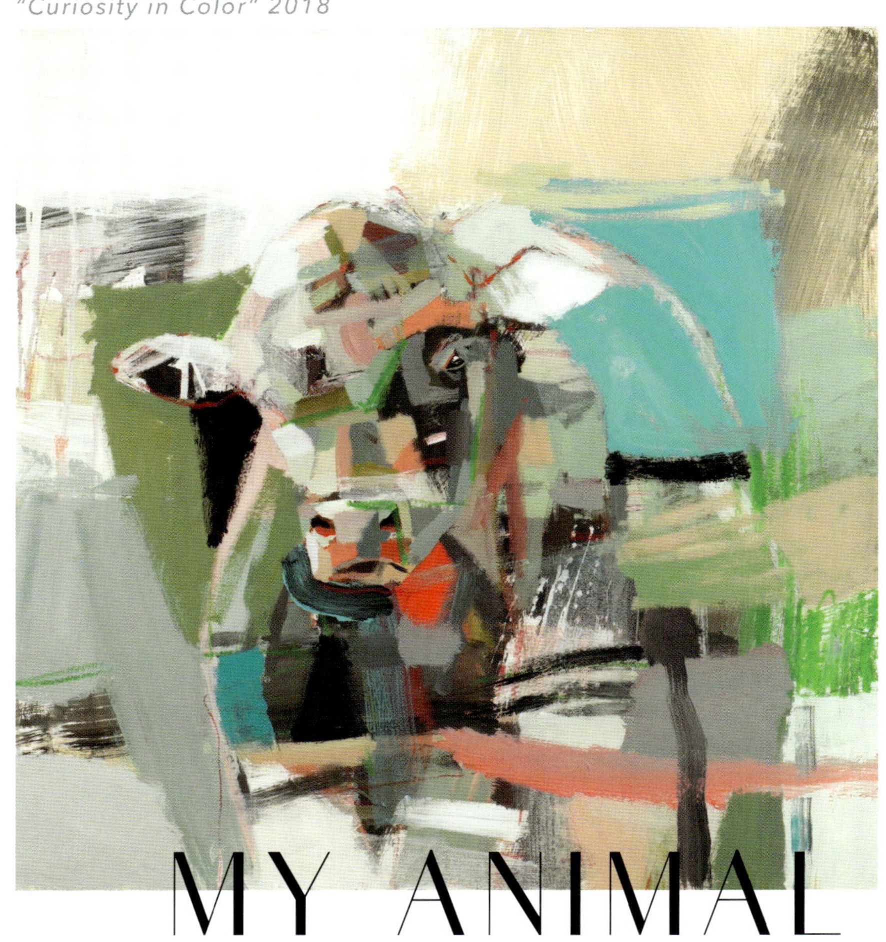

MY ANIMAL SERIES

exhibits a single animal, usually containing a fixed gaze into the viewer's eye. This body of work was a great opportunity to explore various textures and focus in on the facial expression. A common theme that exists within this collection, as it does with most of my work, is the combination of realism and abstraction. Within the approach to the animal series, I strived to tighten the facial features and various coat textures while pushing and pulling the subject into abstraction. The goal in each animal piece was to establish a balance of bold versus playful, combining a stern expression of the creature mixed with loose, playful elements within an otherworldly palette.

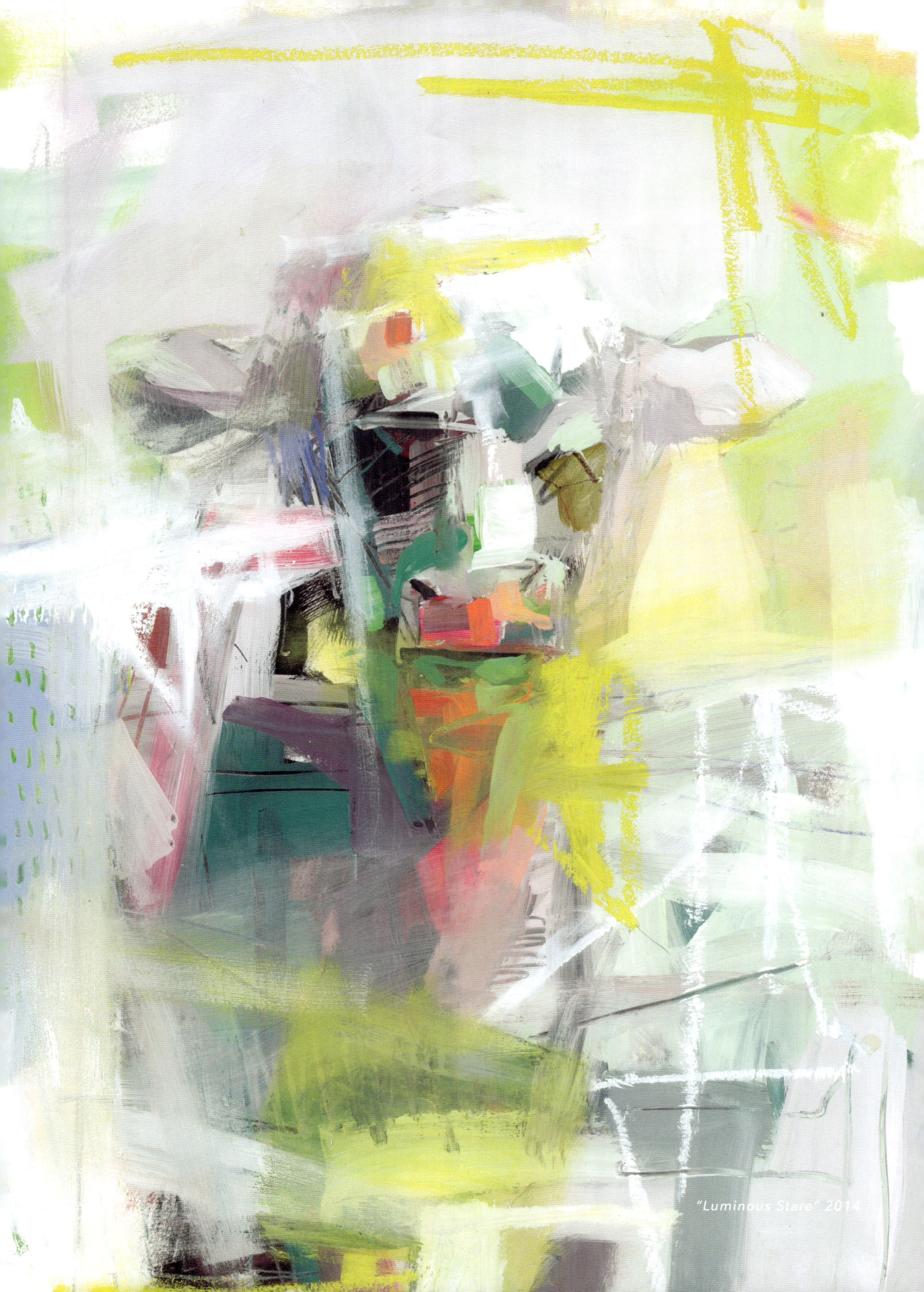

"Luminous Stare" 2014

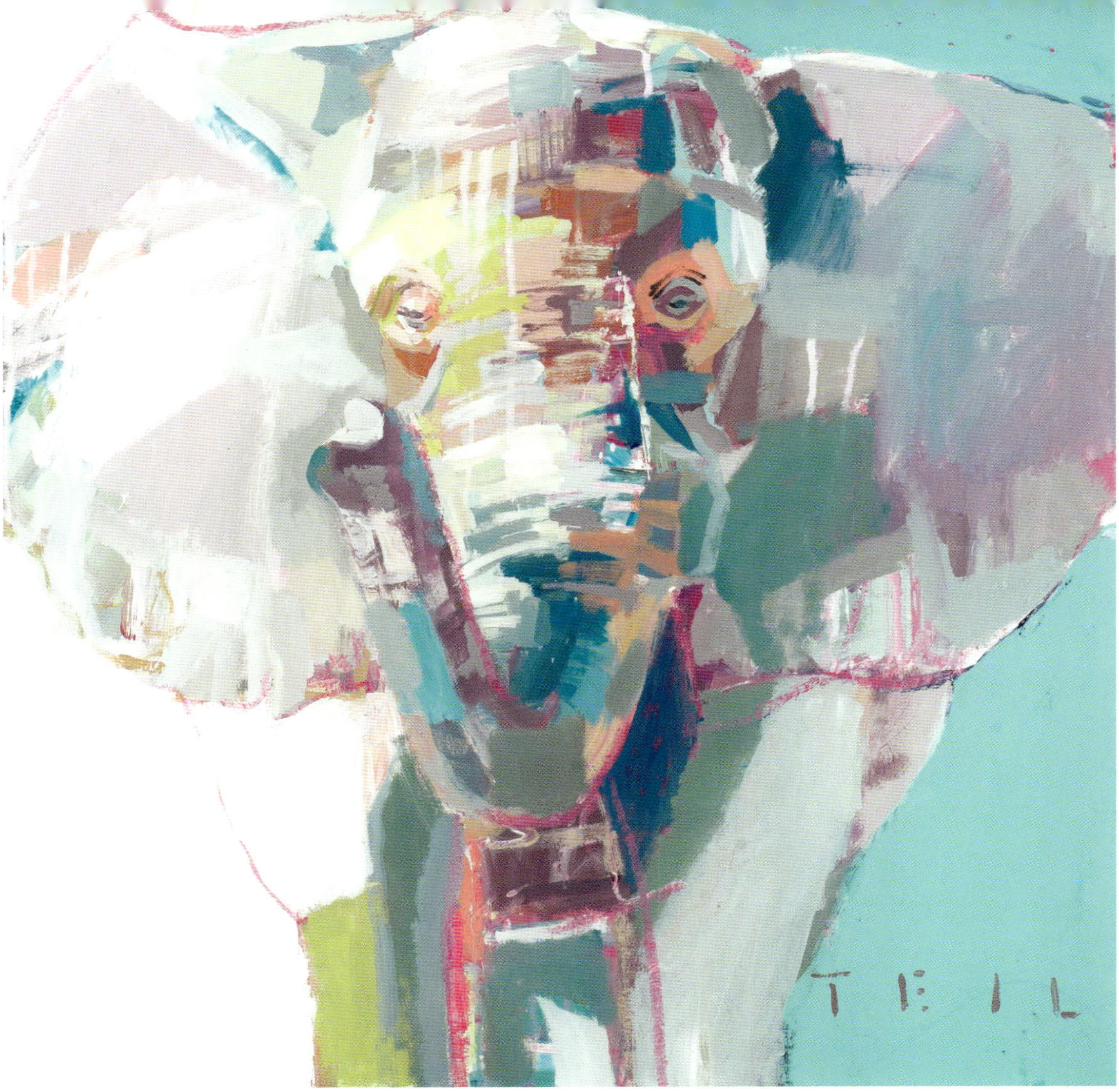

TEIL

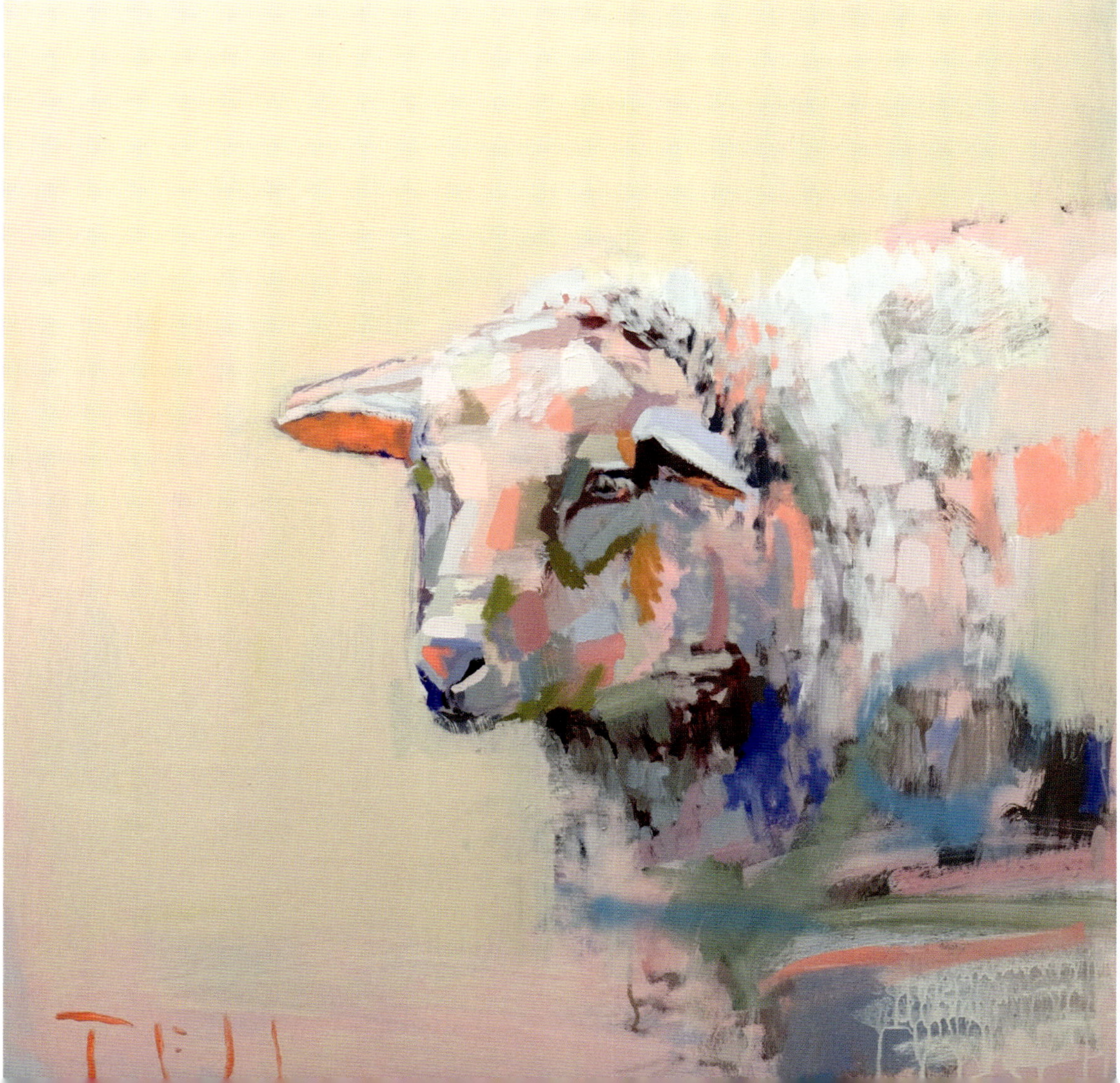

TEIL

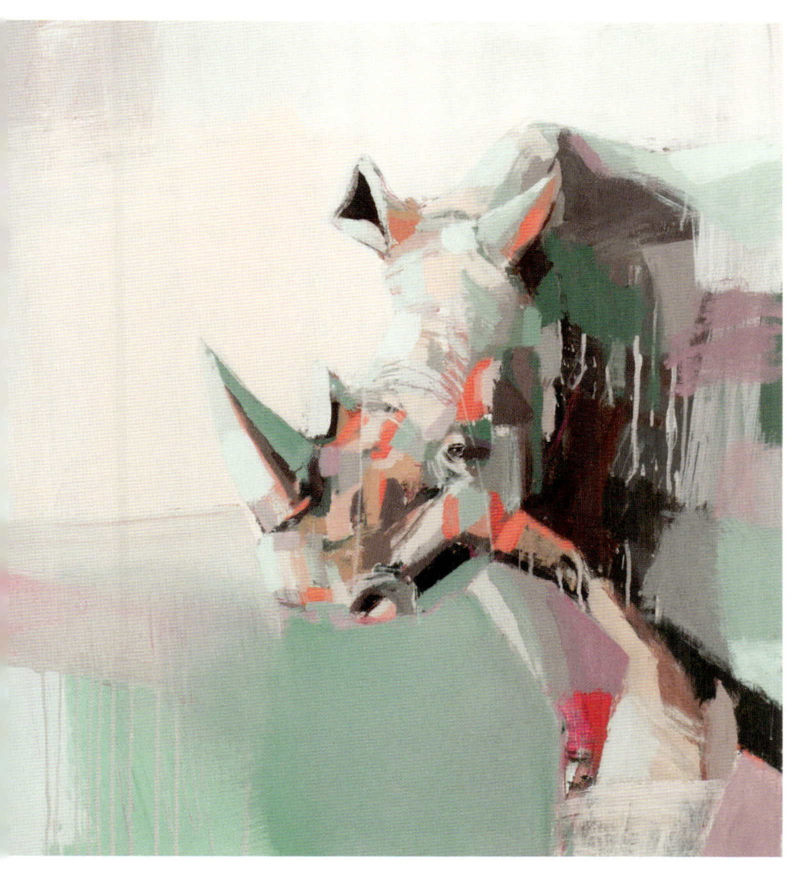

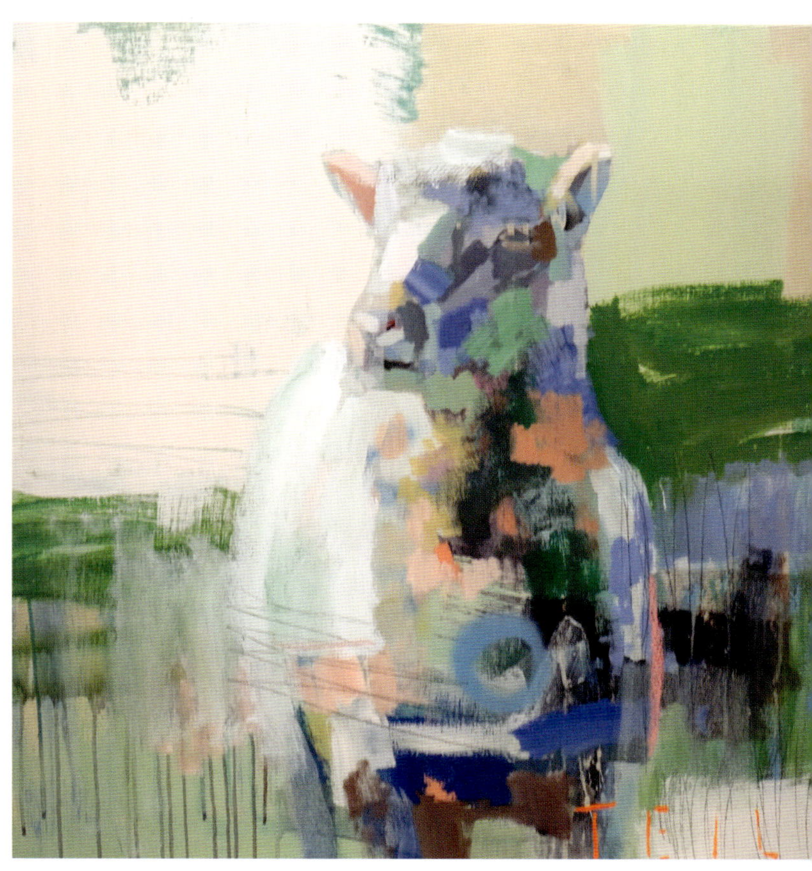

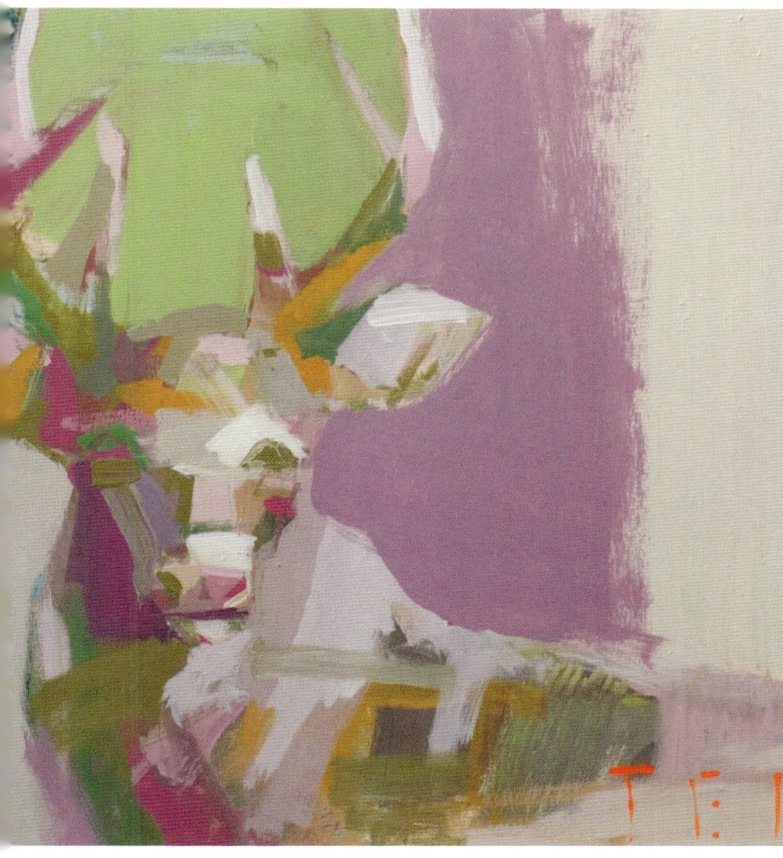

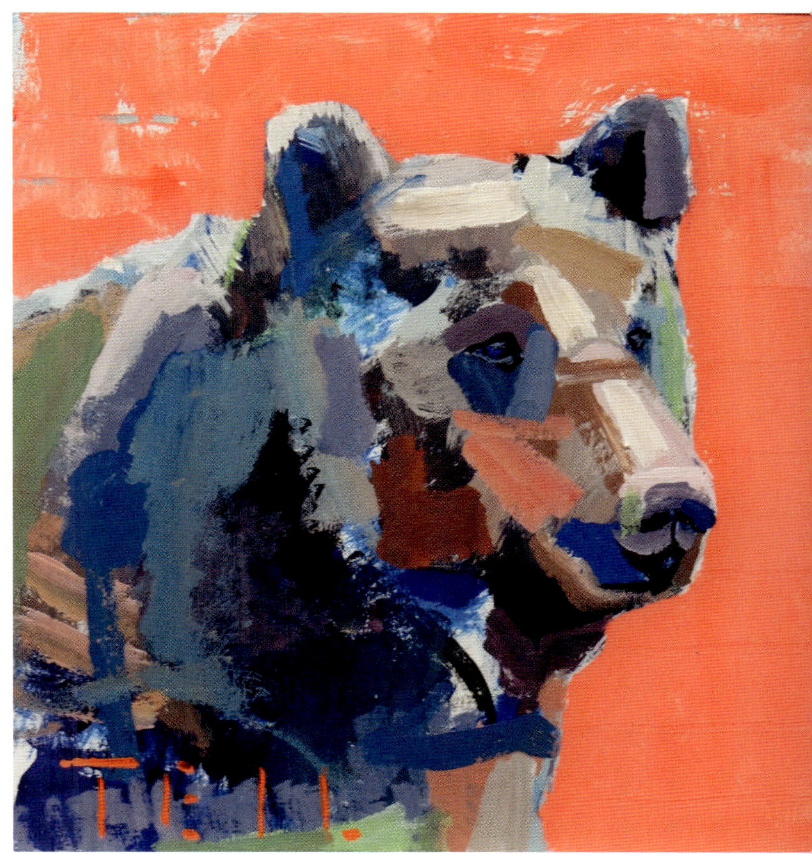

"Soft in Sun" 2018

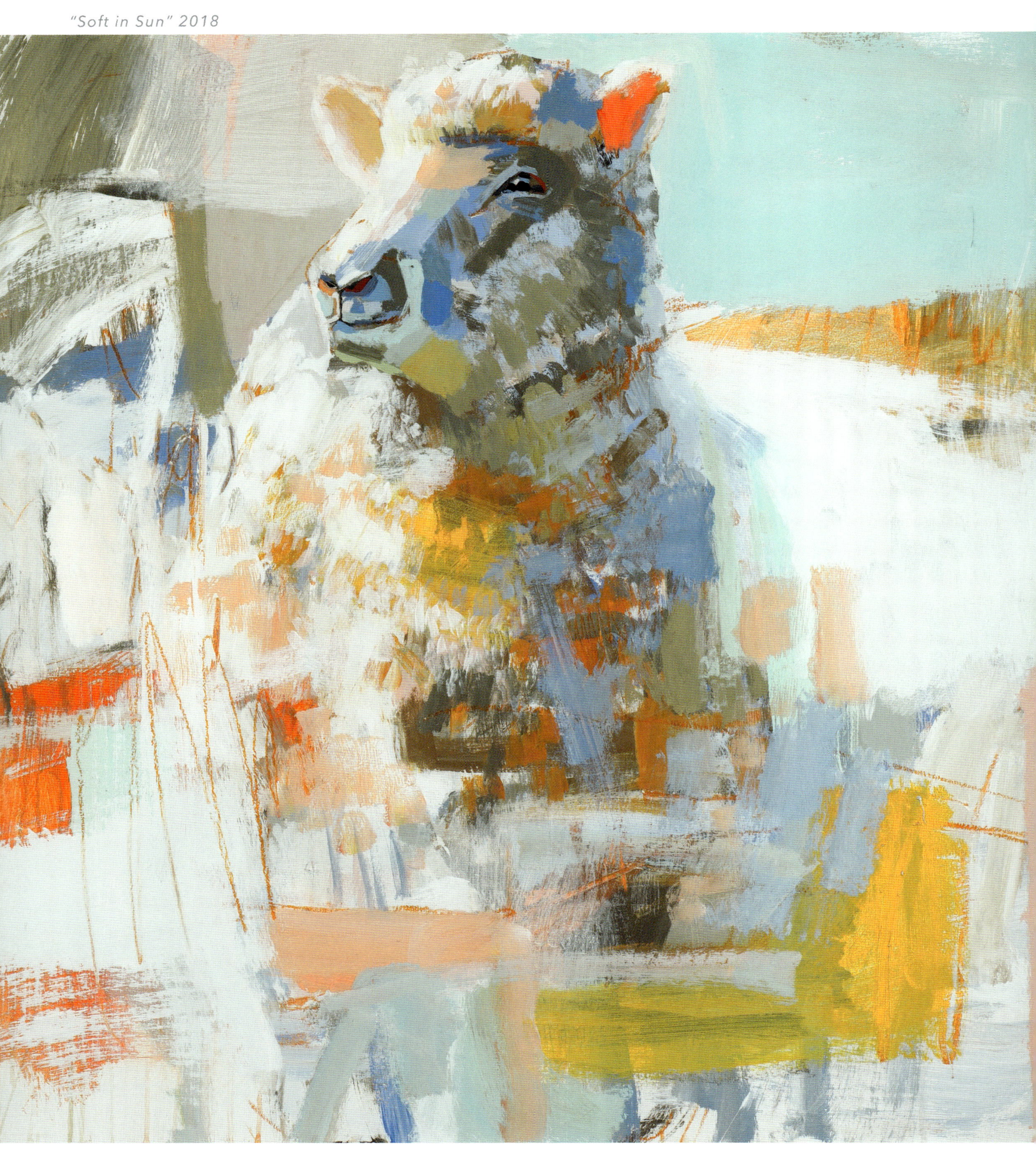

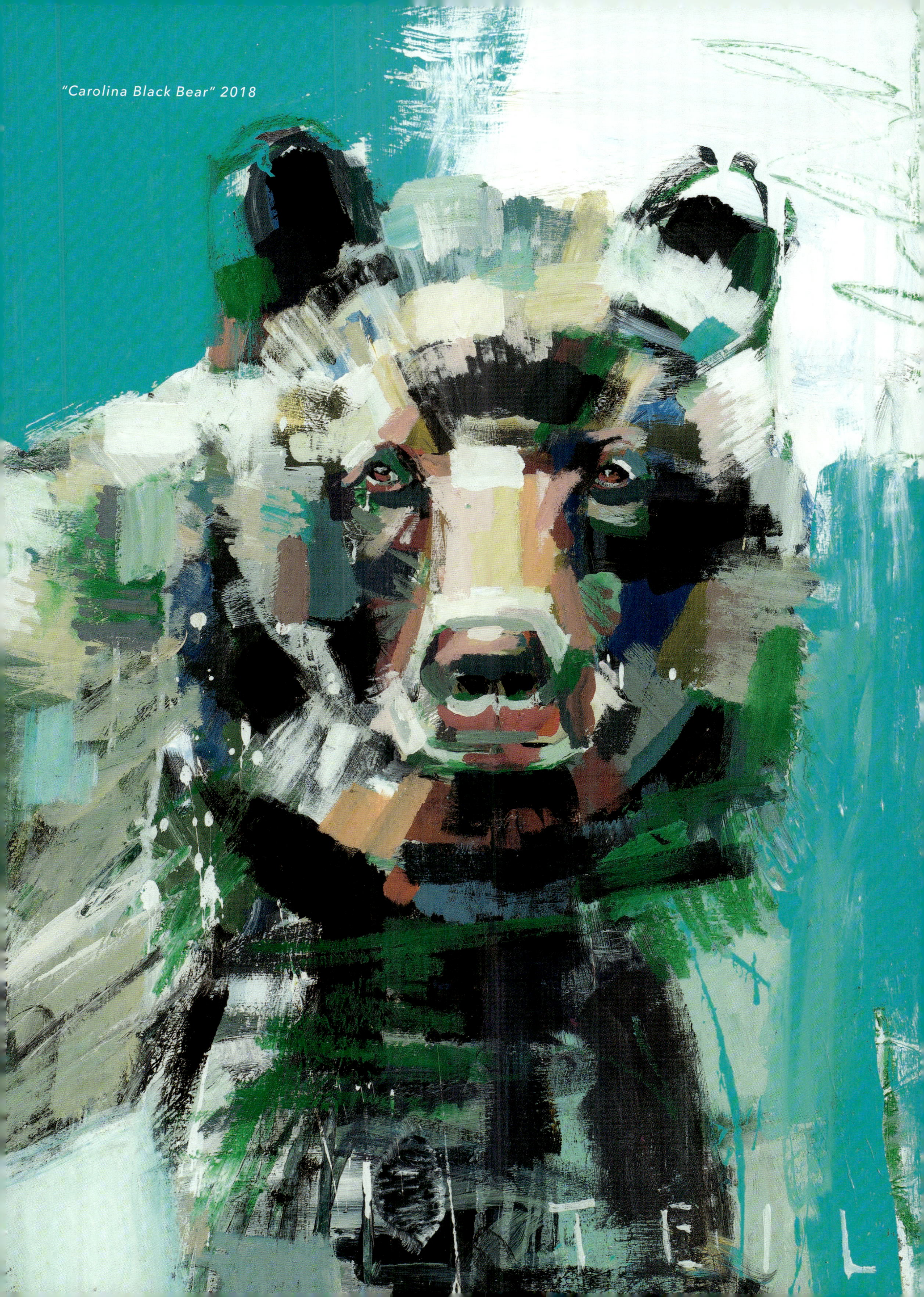

"Carolina Black Bear" 2018

"Emerald Stomp" 2016

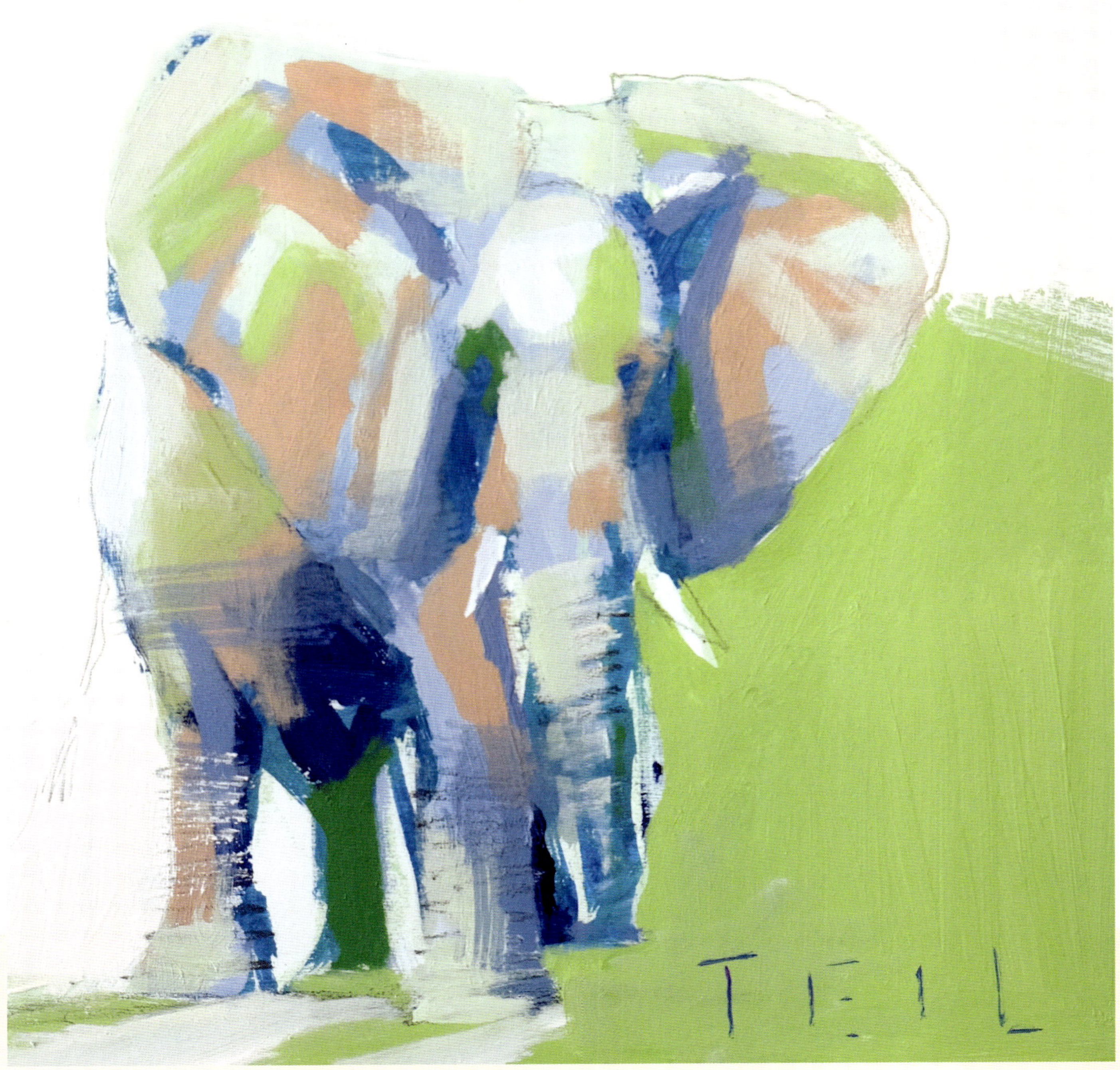

"Luminous Bull" 2016

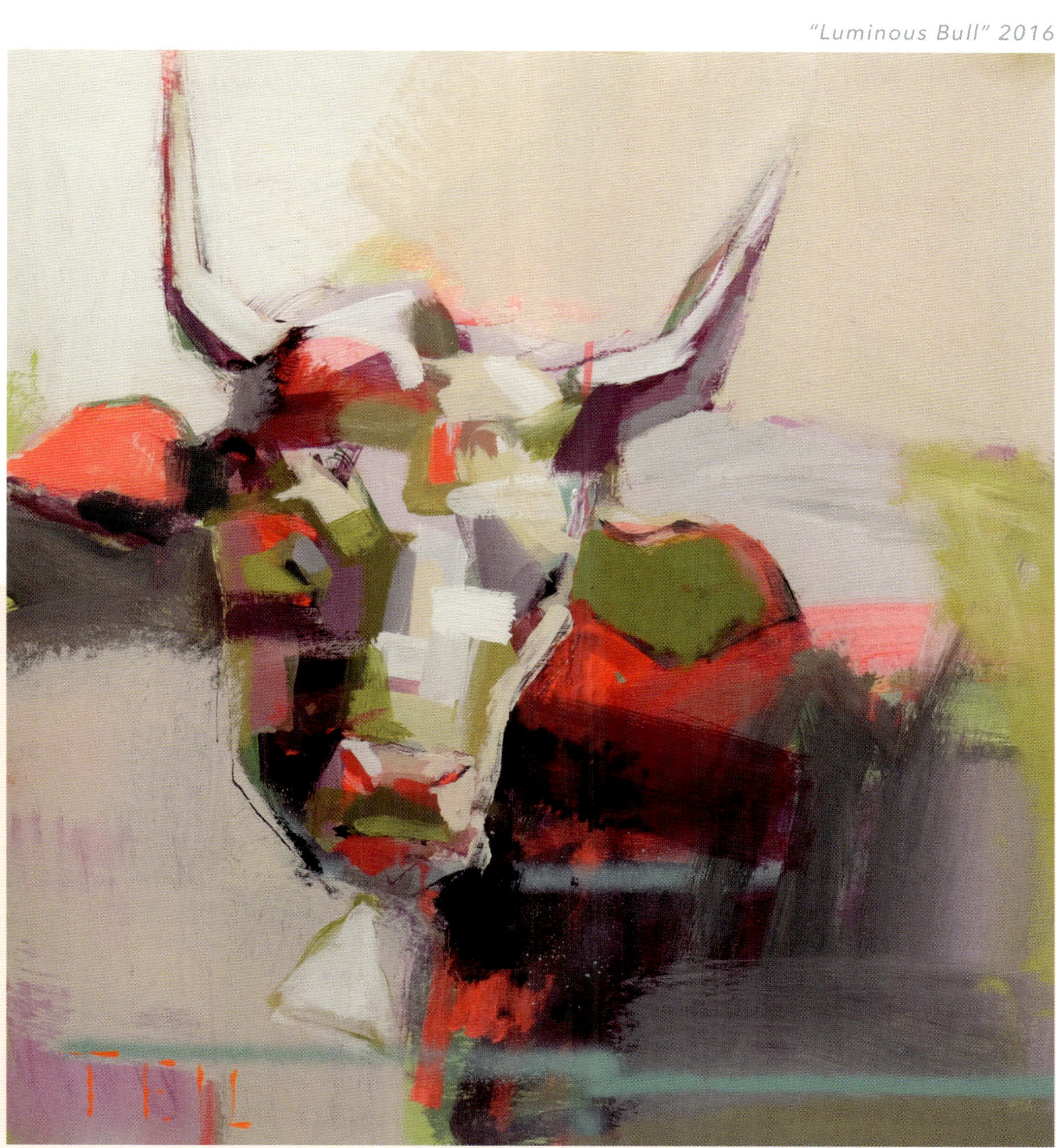

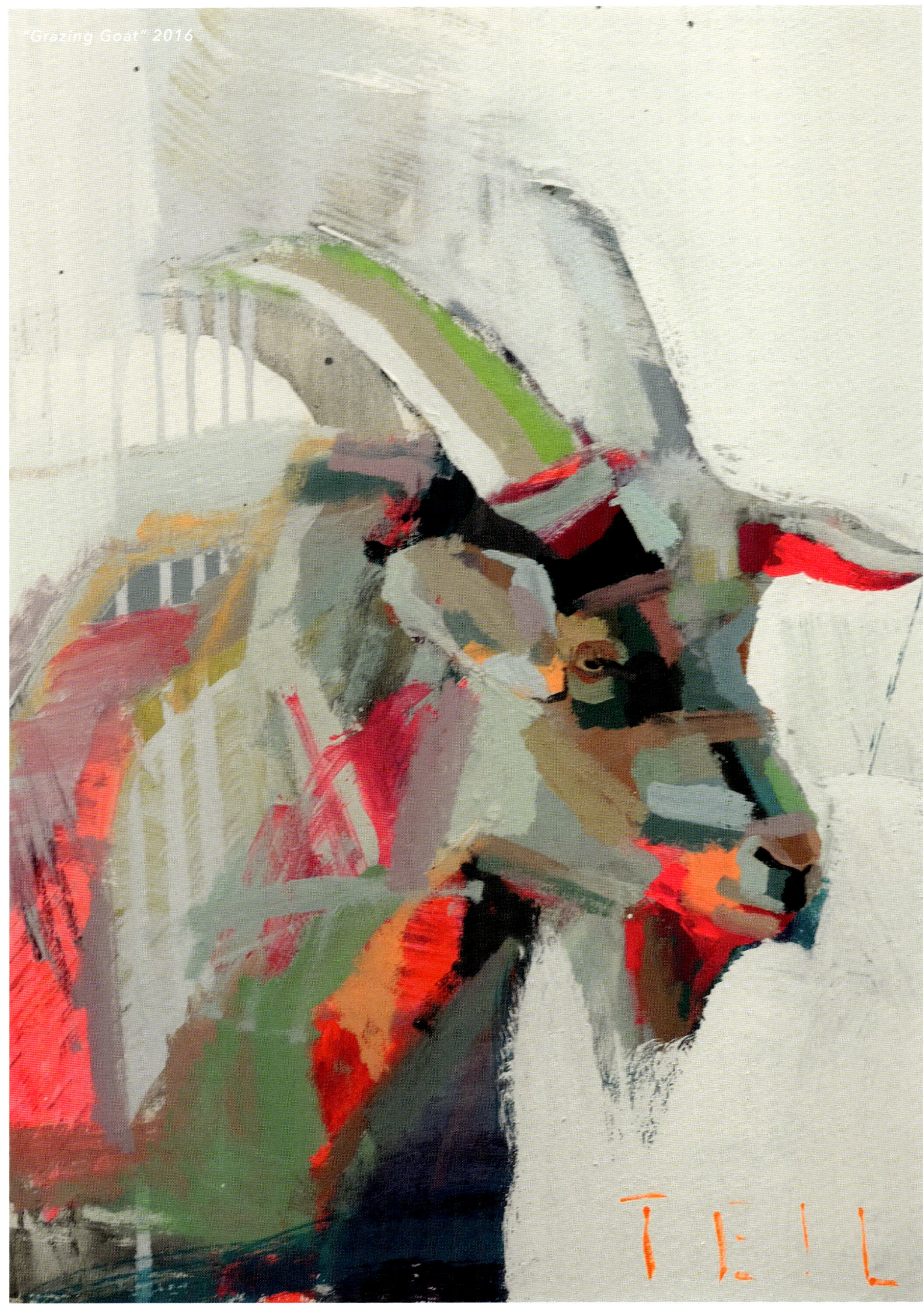

"Grazing Goat" 2016

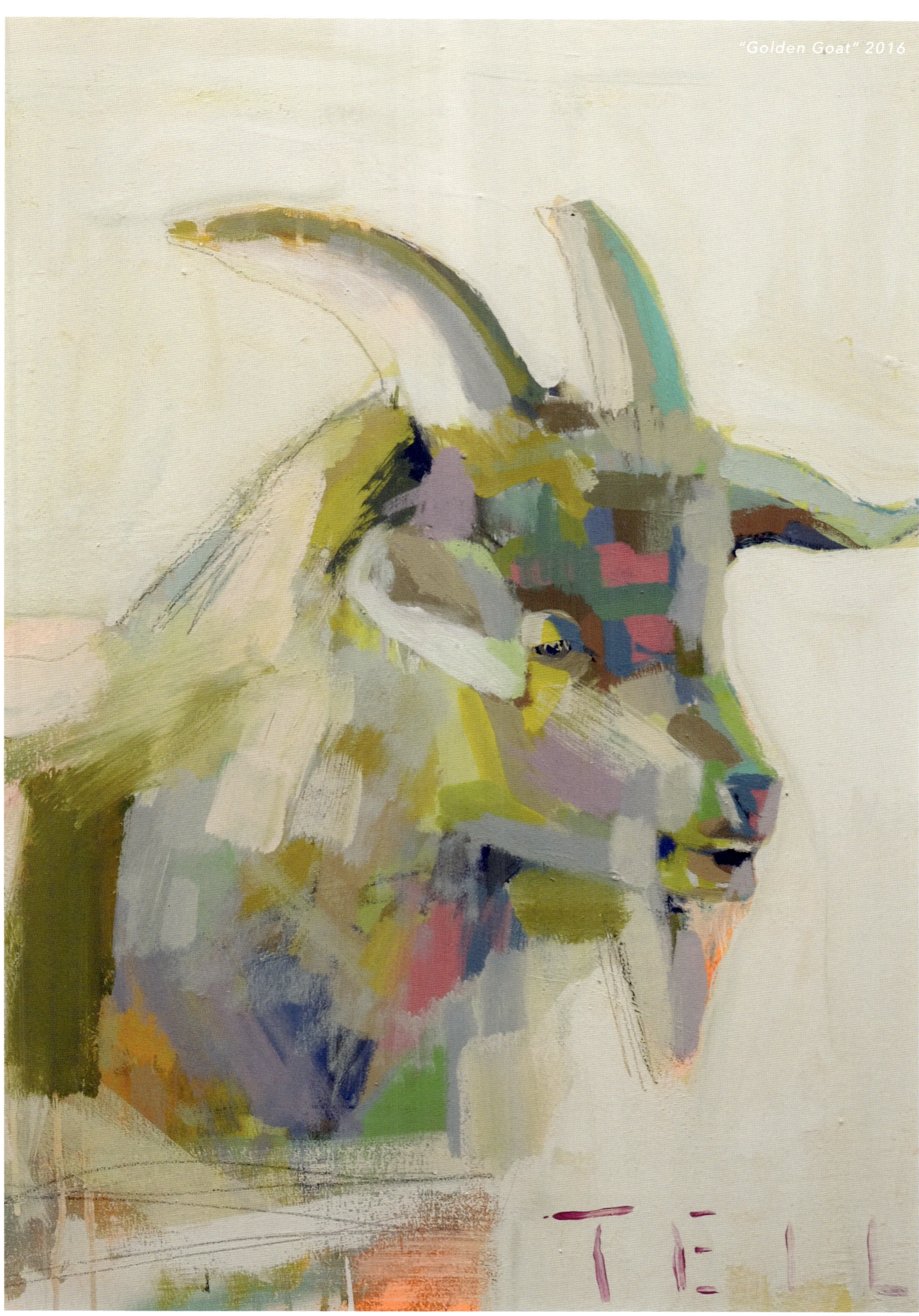

"Golden Goat" 2016

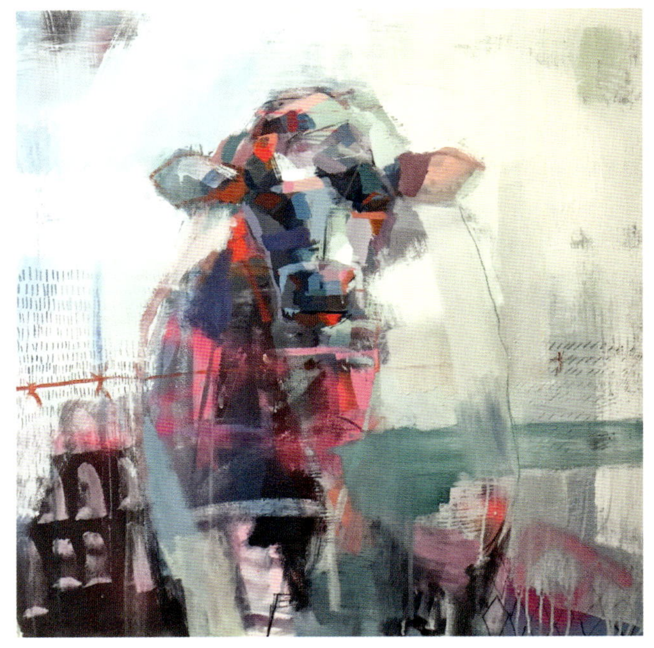
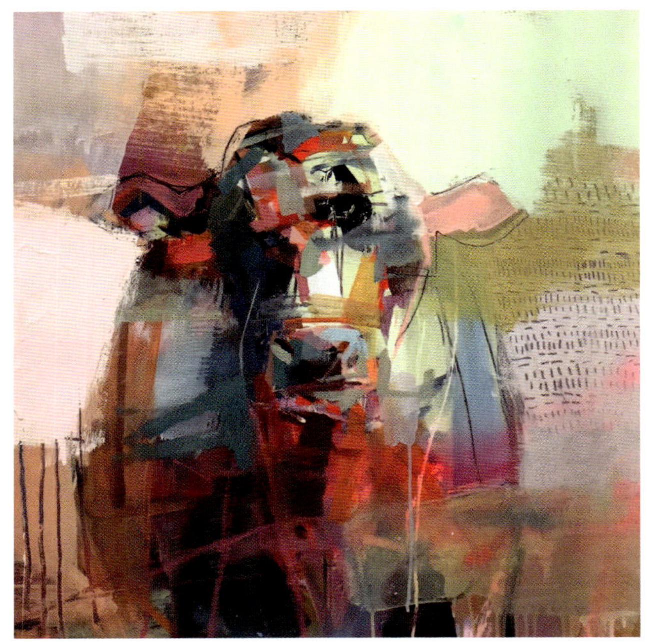
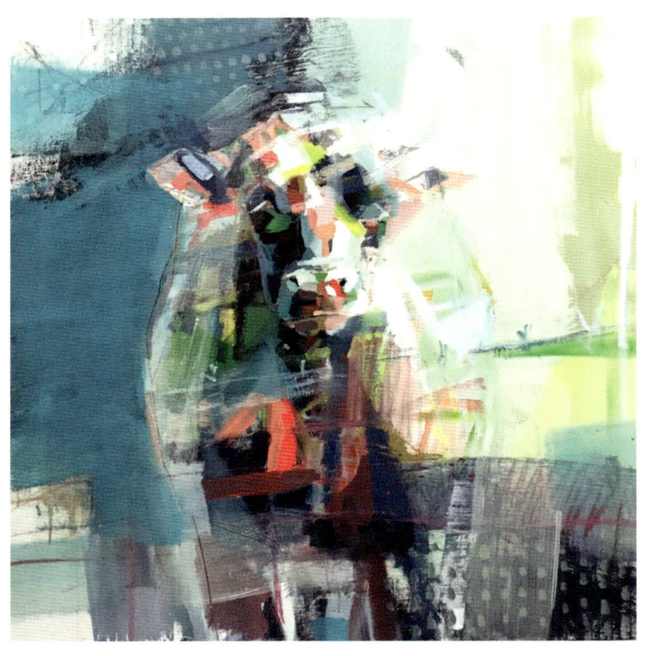
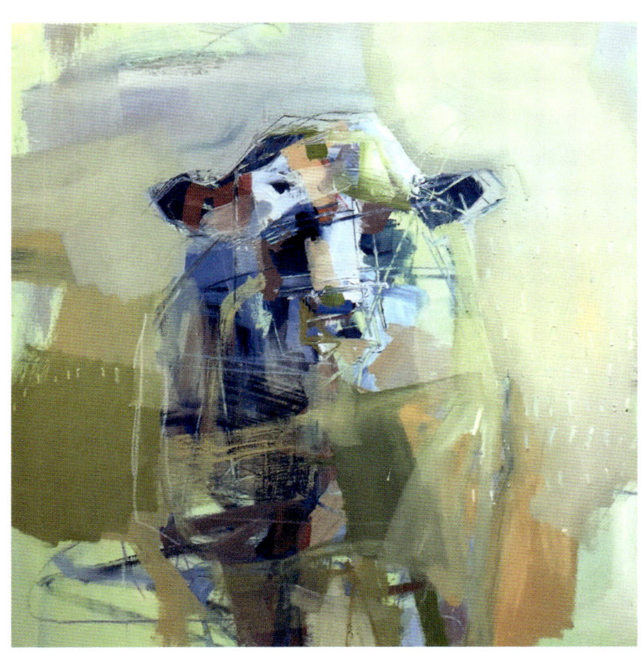
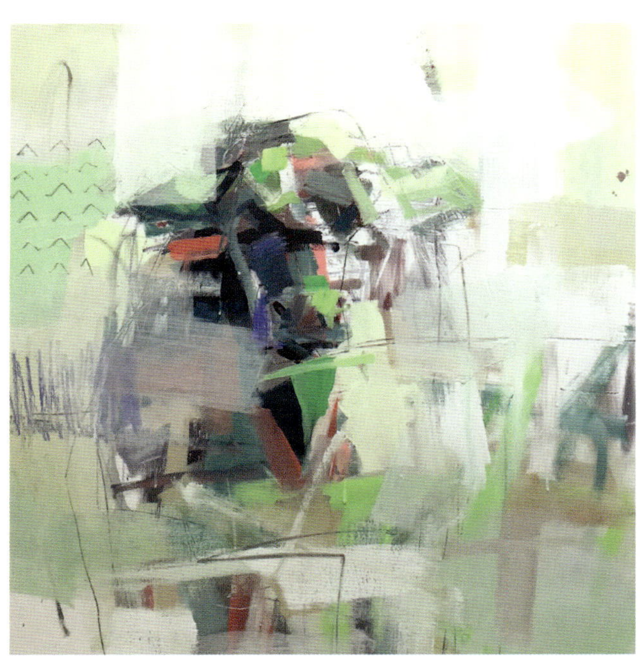
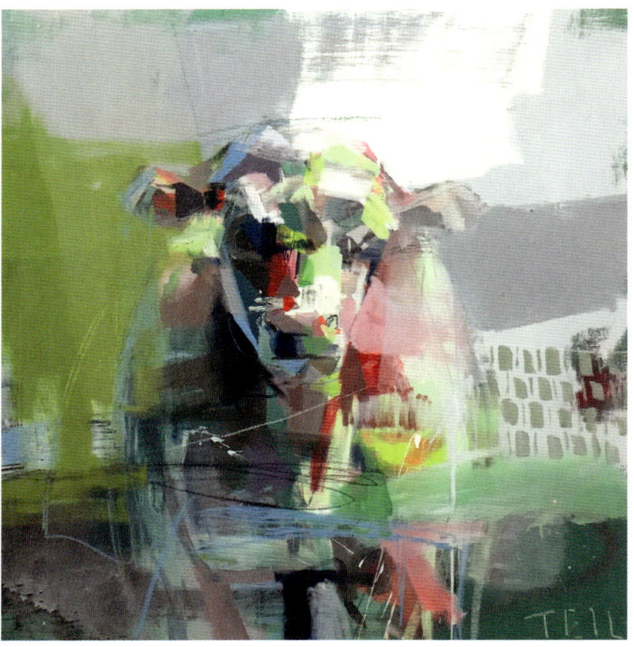

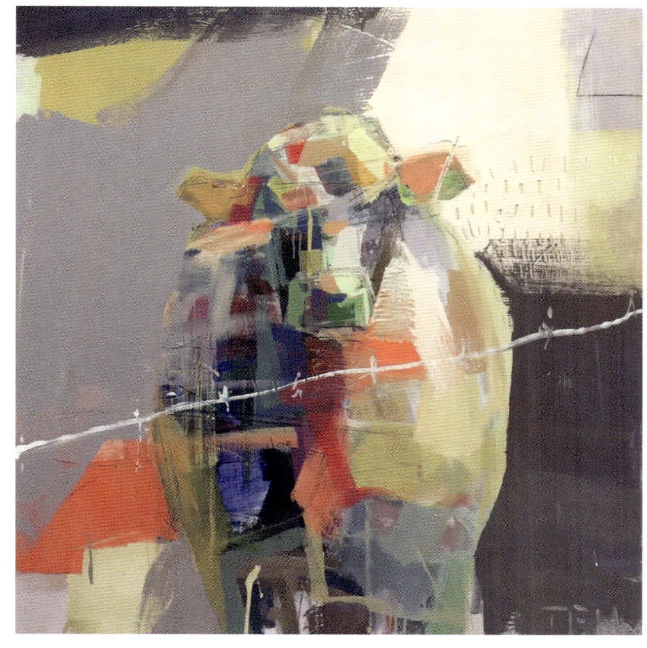
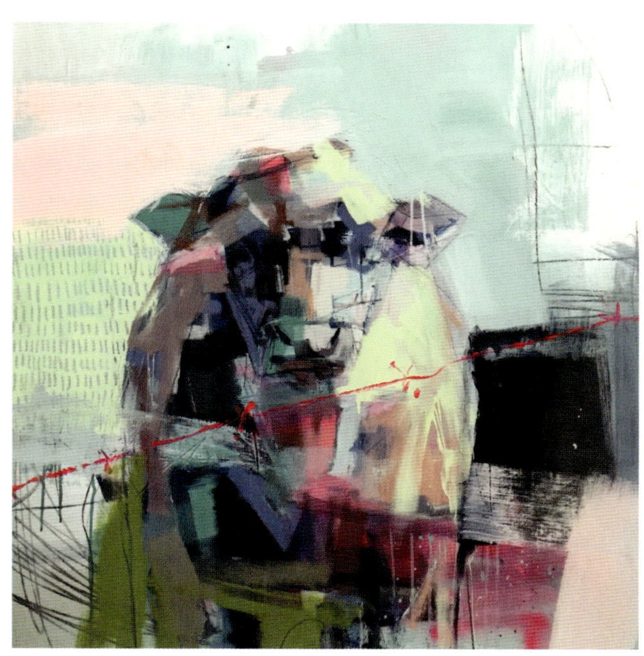
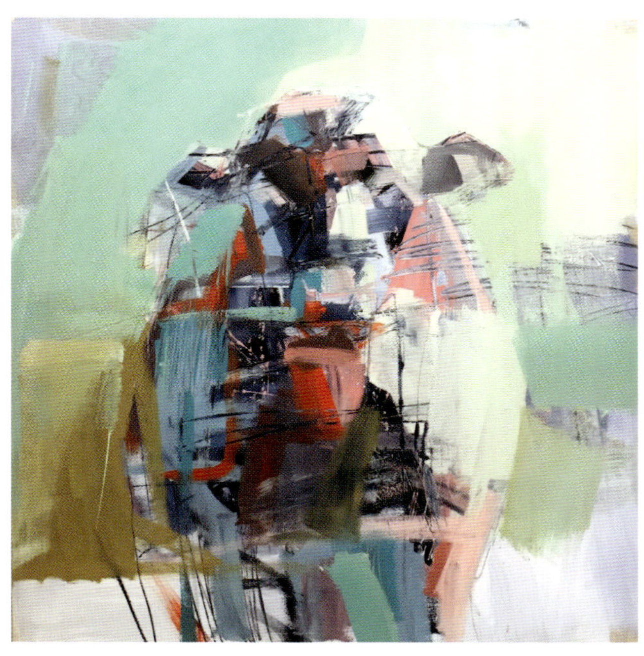
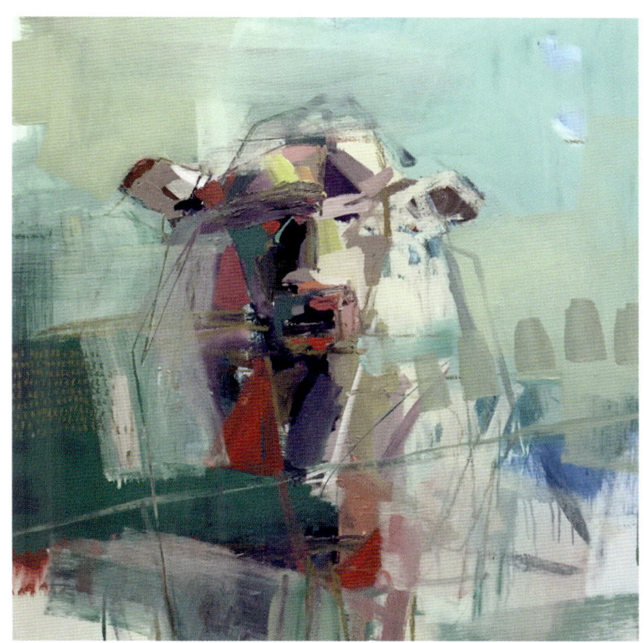
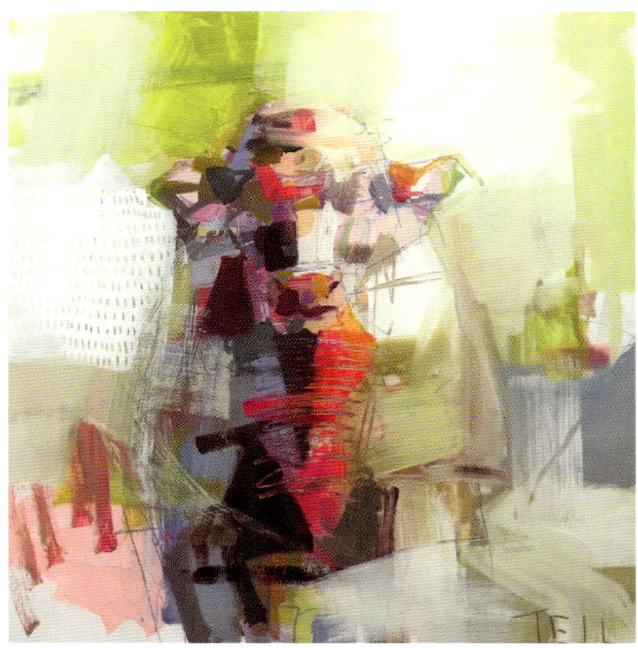
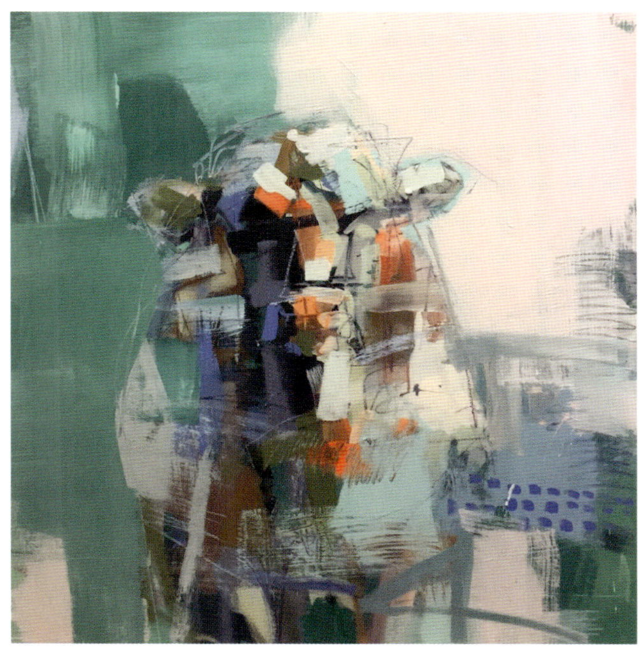

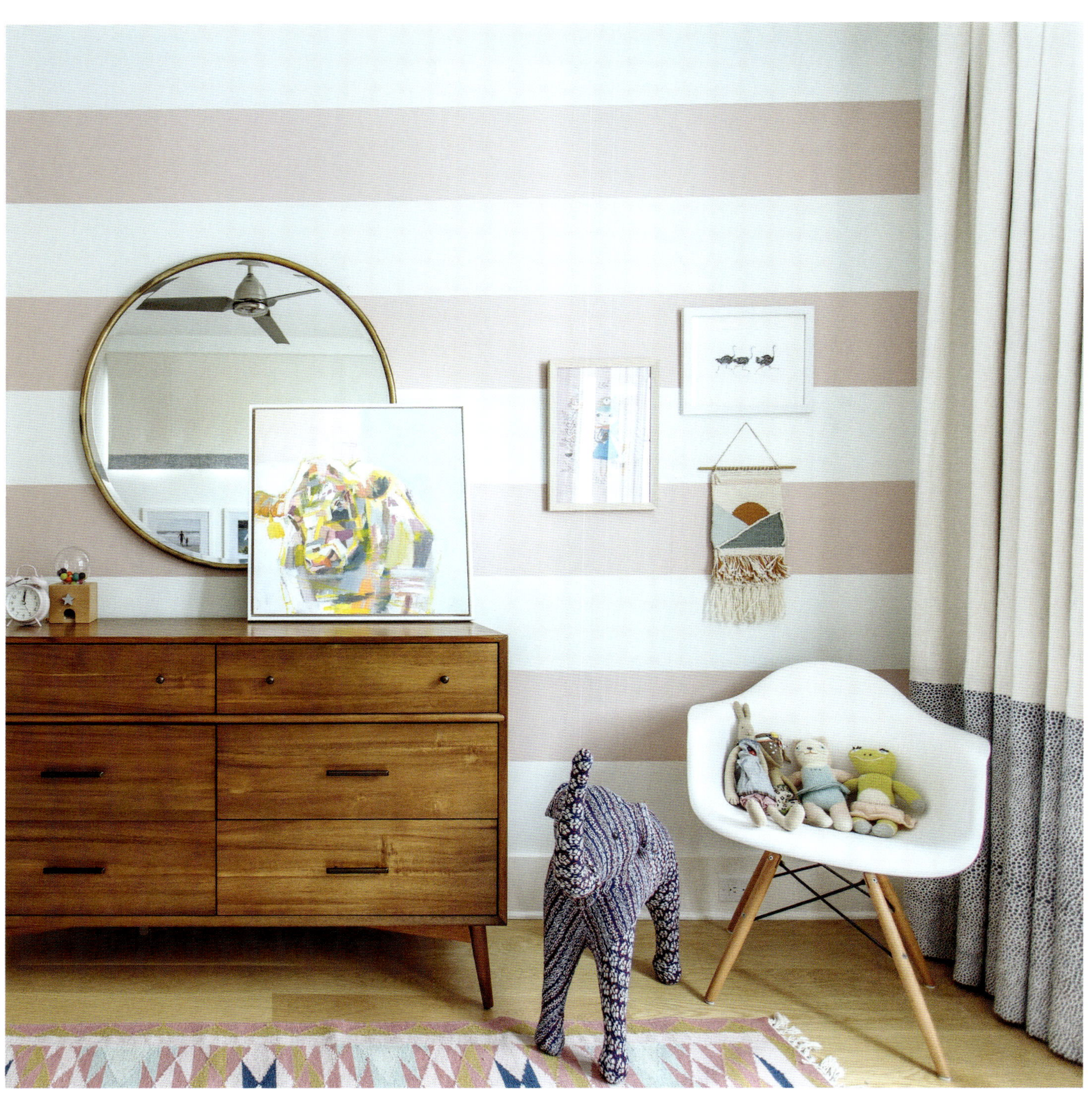

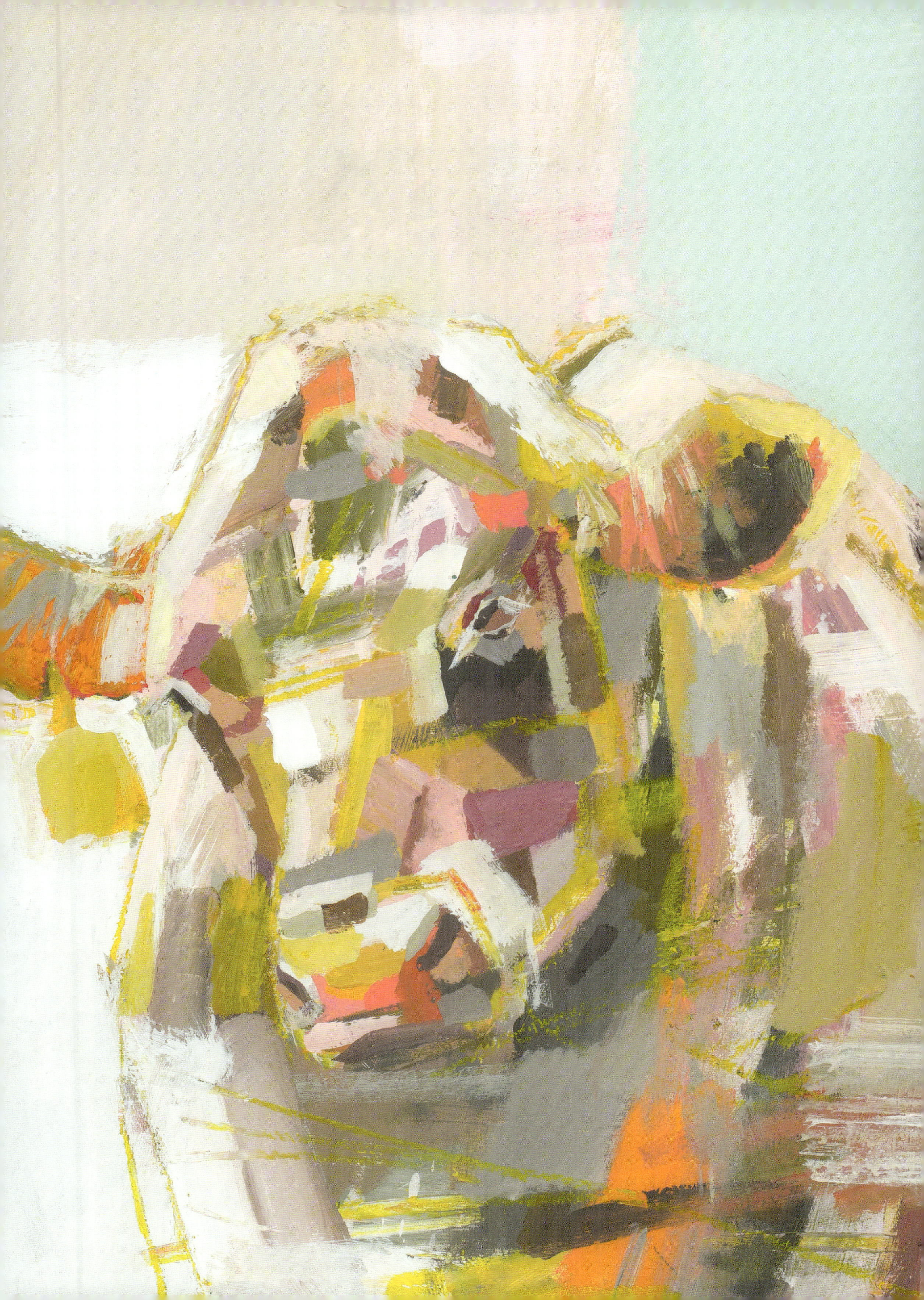

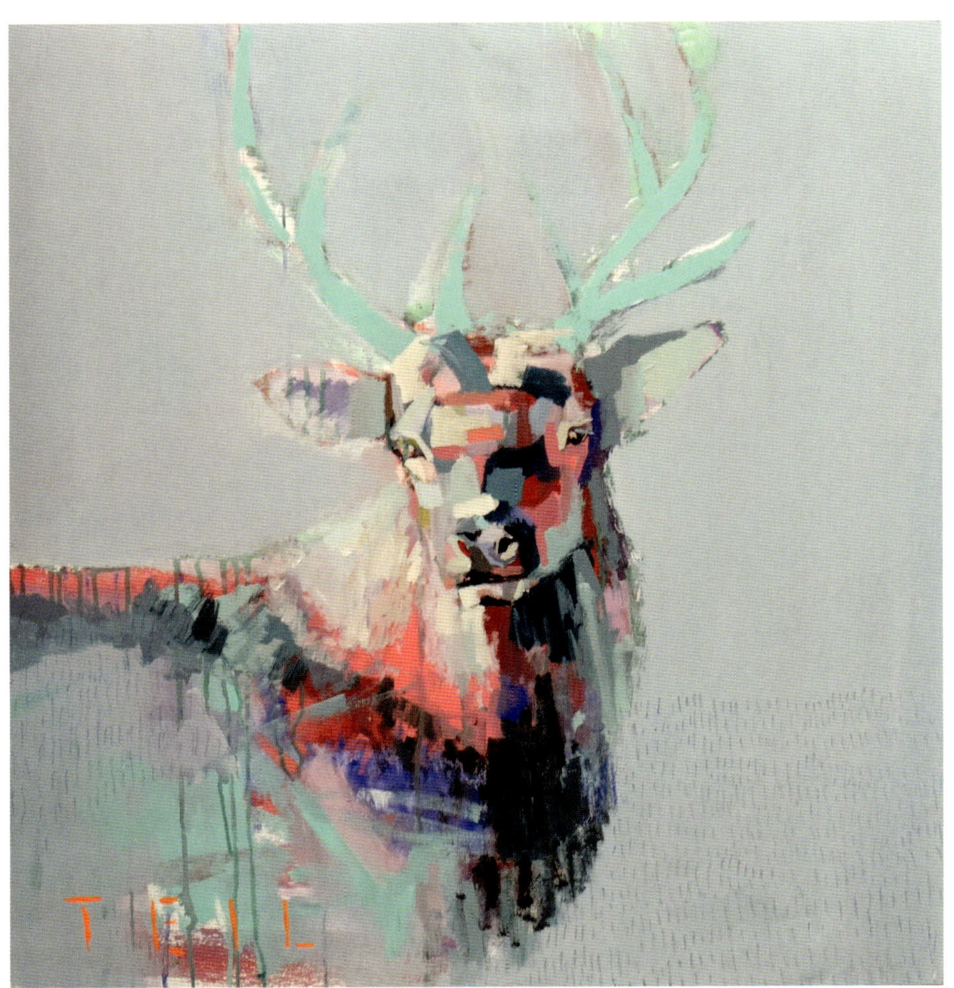

"Spring Buck" 2016

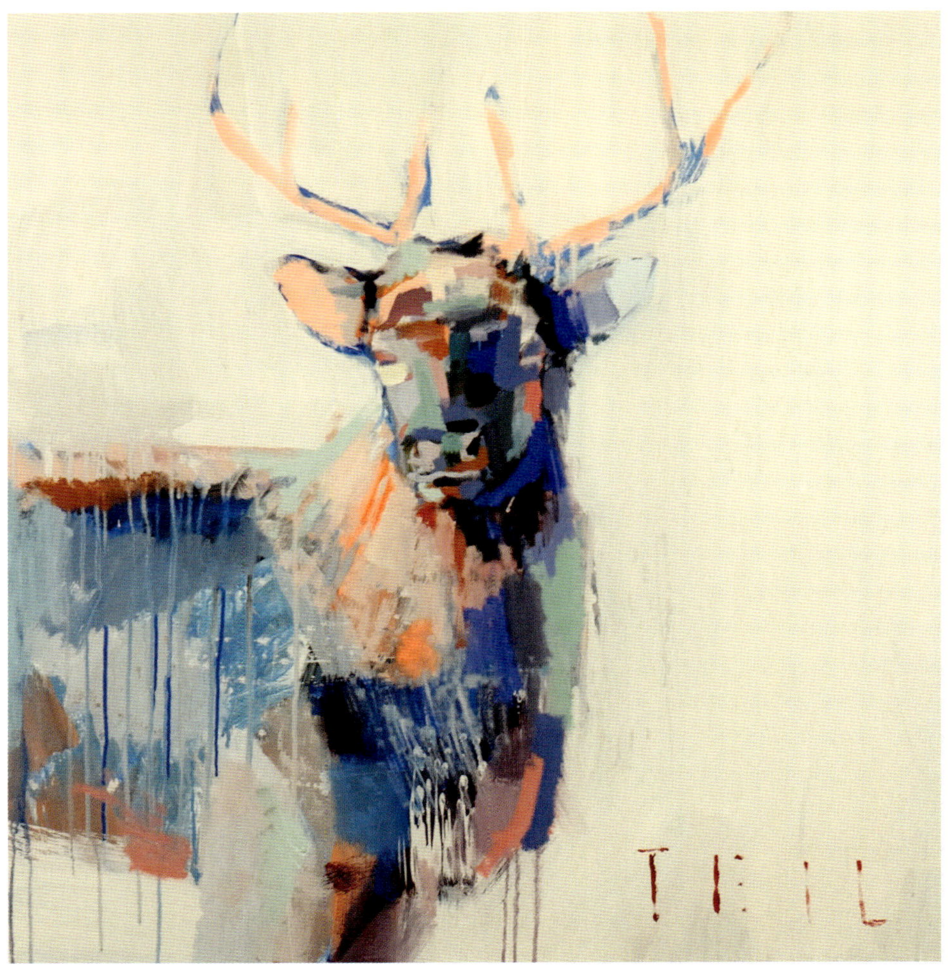

"Autumn Buck" 2016

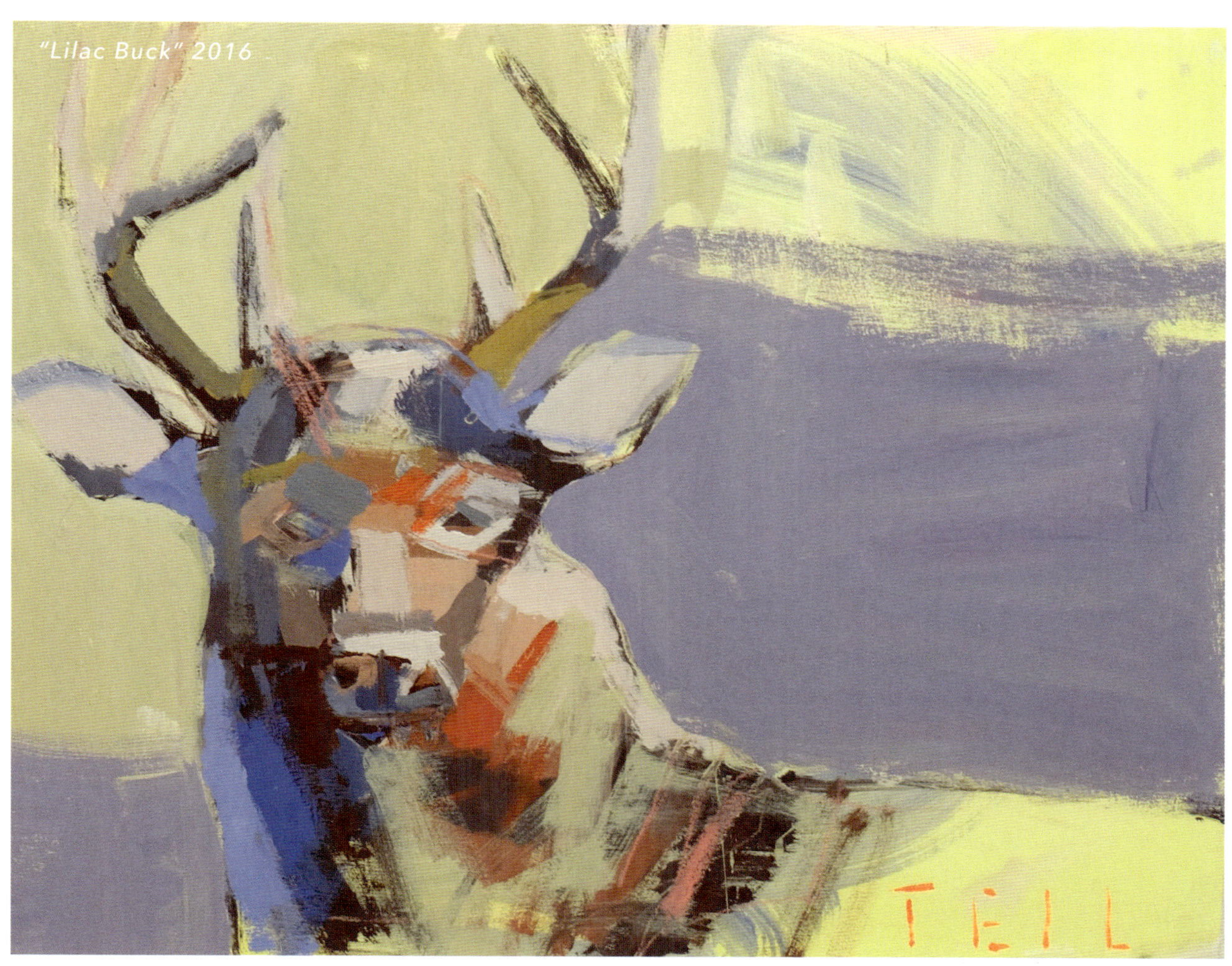
"Lilac Buck" 2016
TEIL

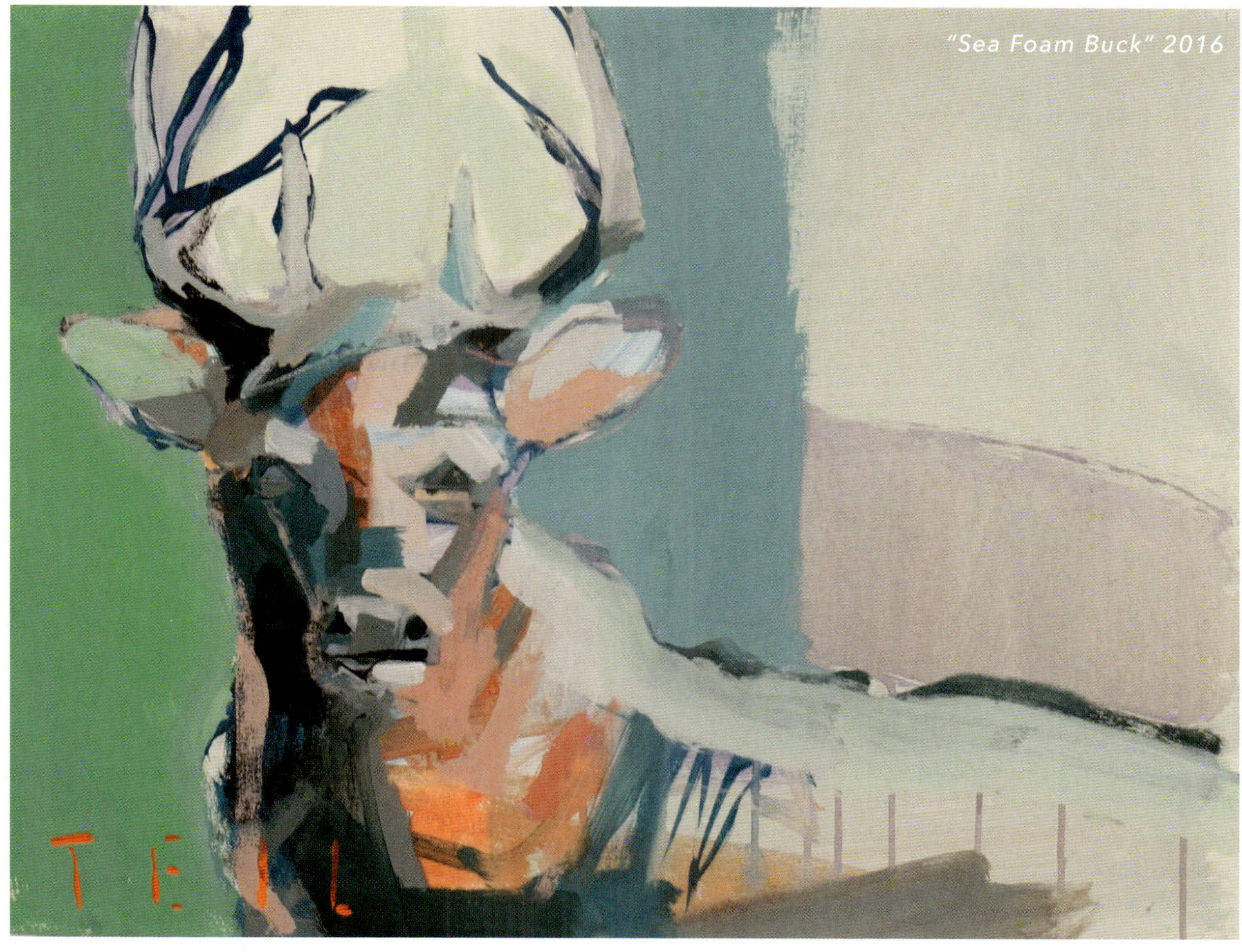
"Sea Foam Buck" 2016
TEIL

"Midday Stare" 2016

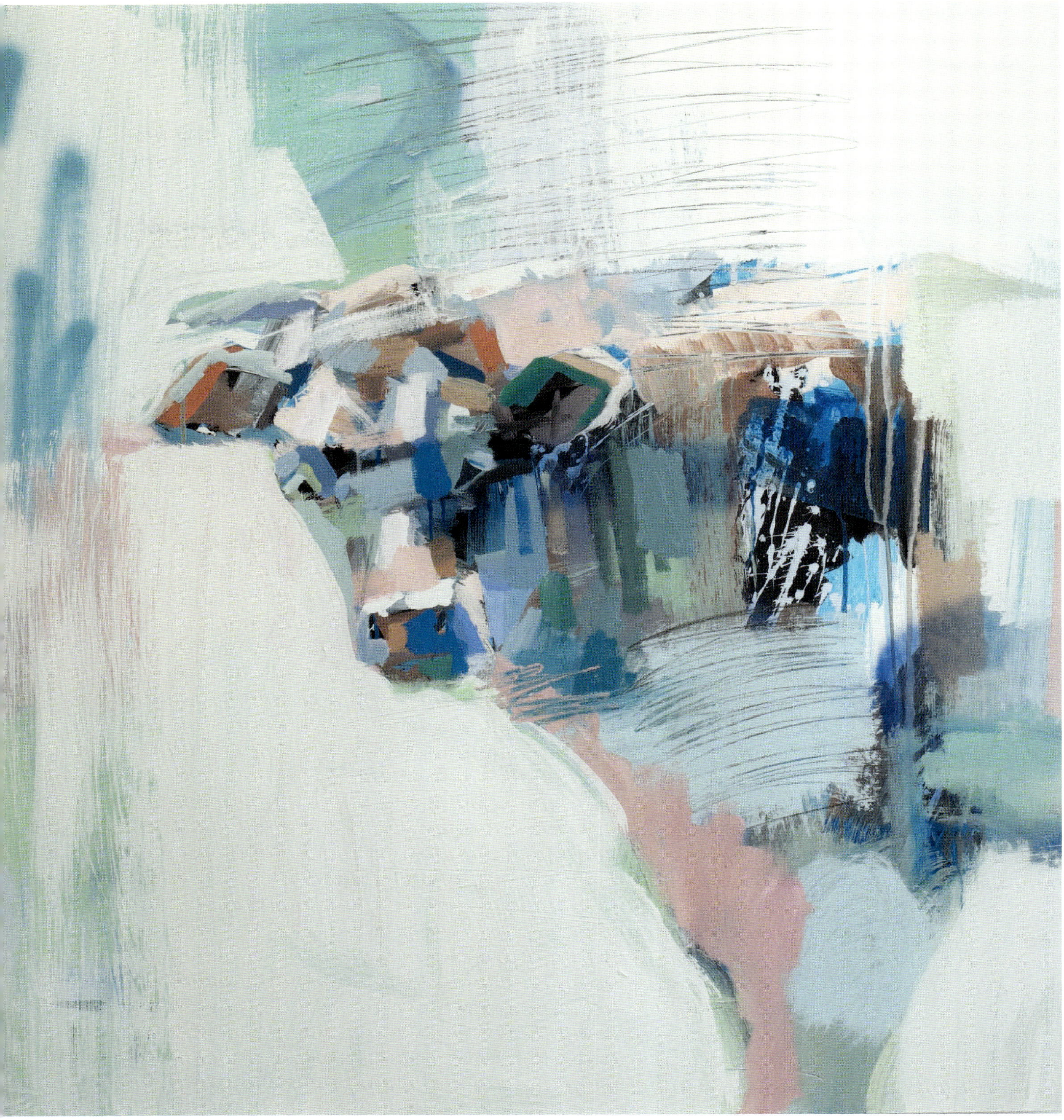

"Grizzly Gaze" 2016

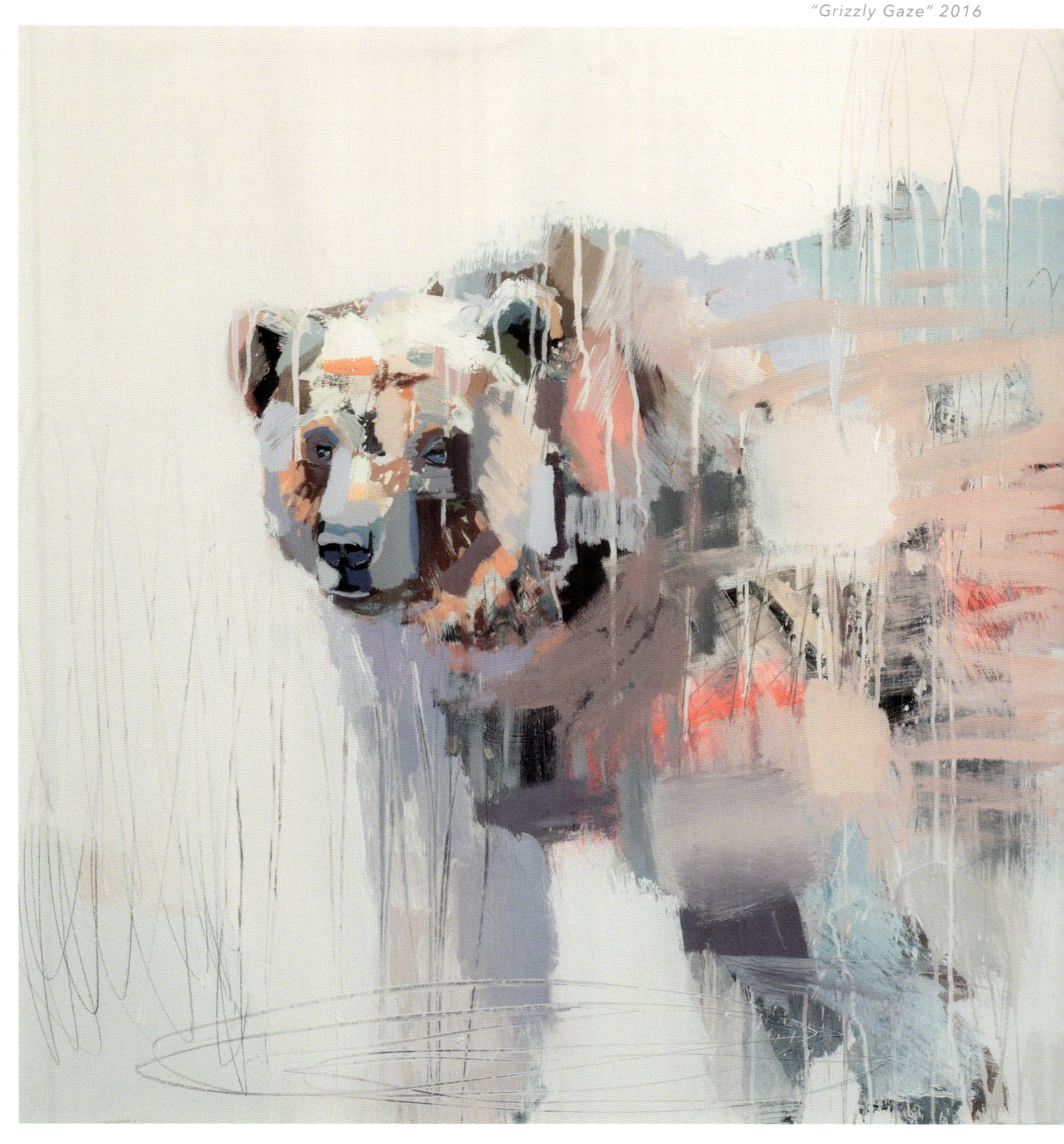

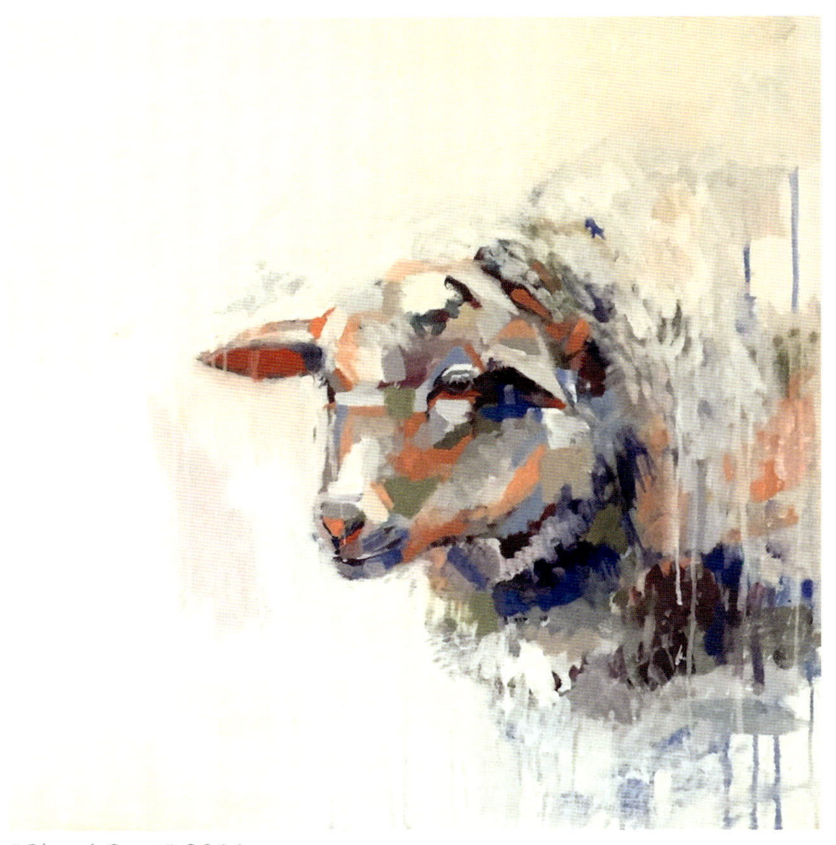

"Cloud Coat" 2016

"Friendly Fluff" 2016

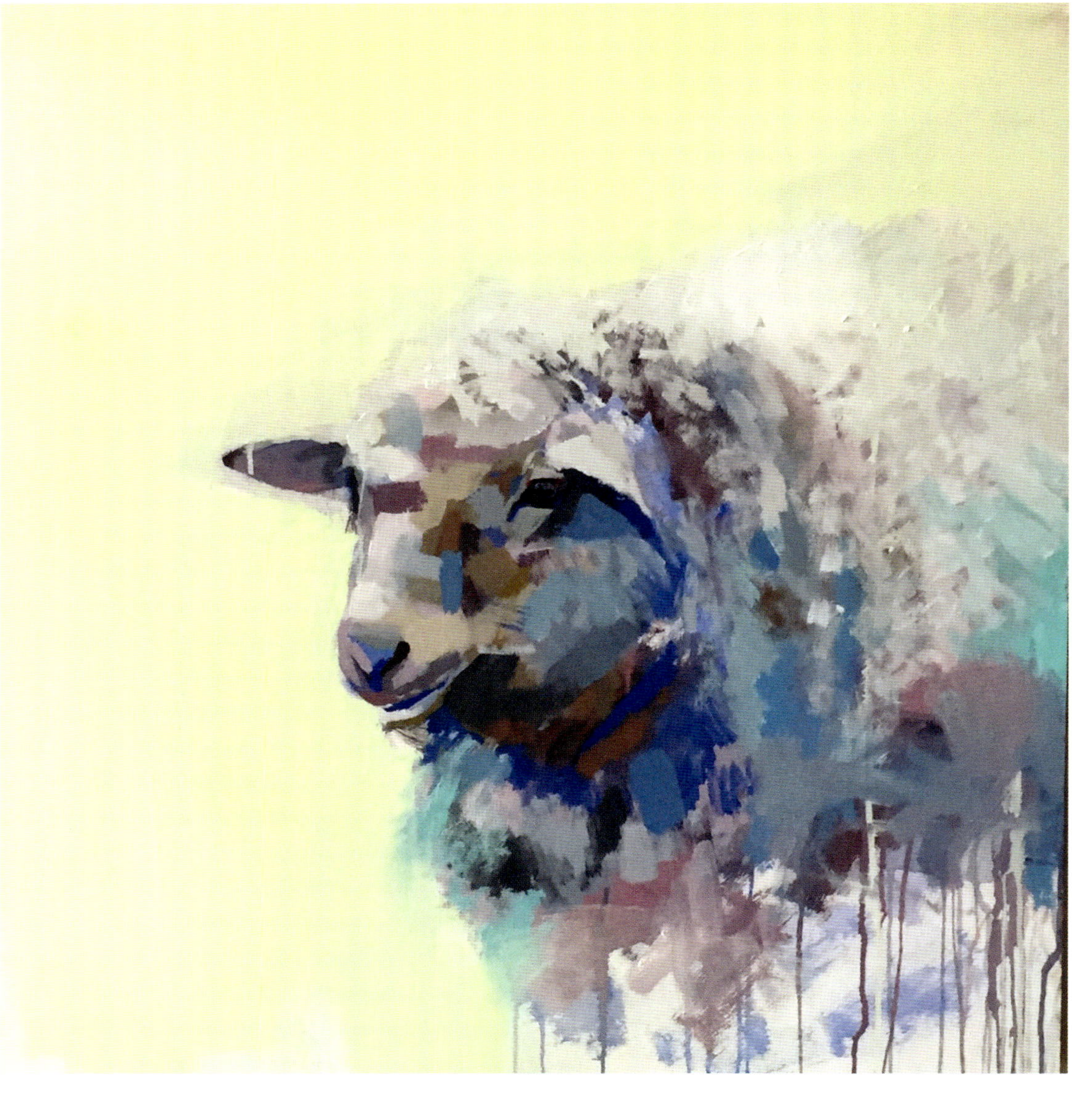

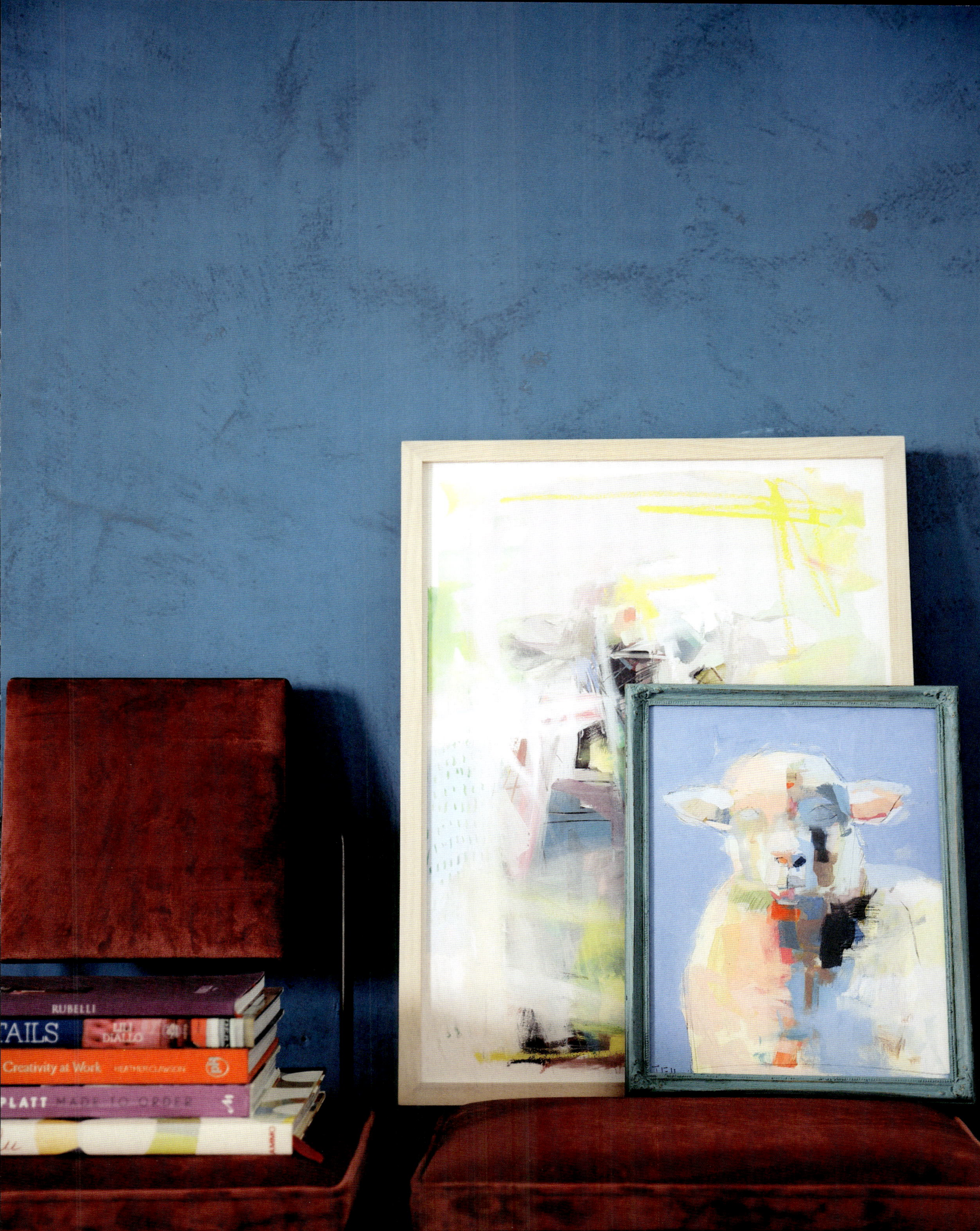
RUBELLI
TAILS
Creativity at Work
PLATT MADE TO ORDER

"Royal Tusks" 2016

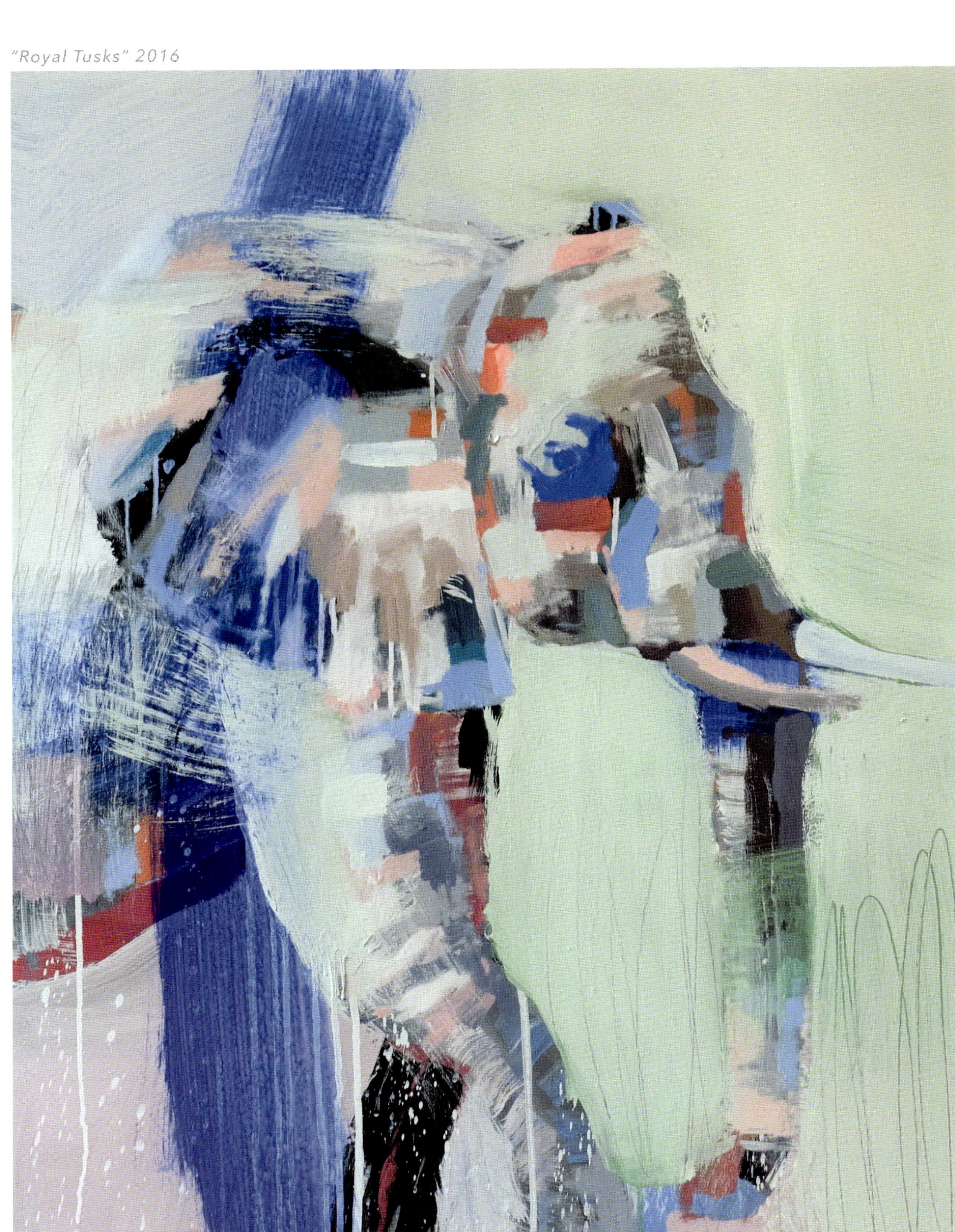

"Spring Roaming" 2016

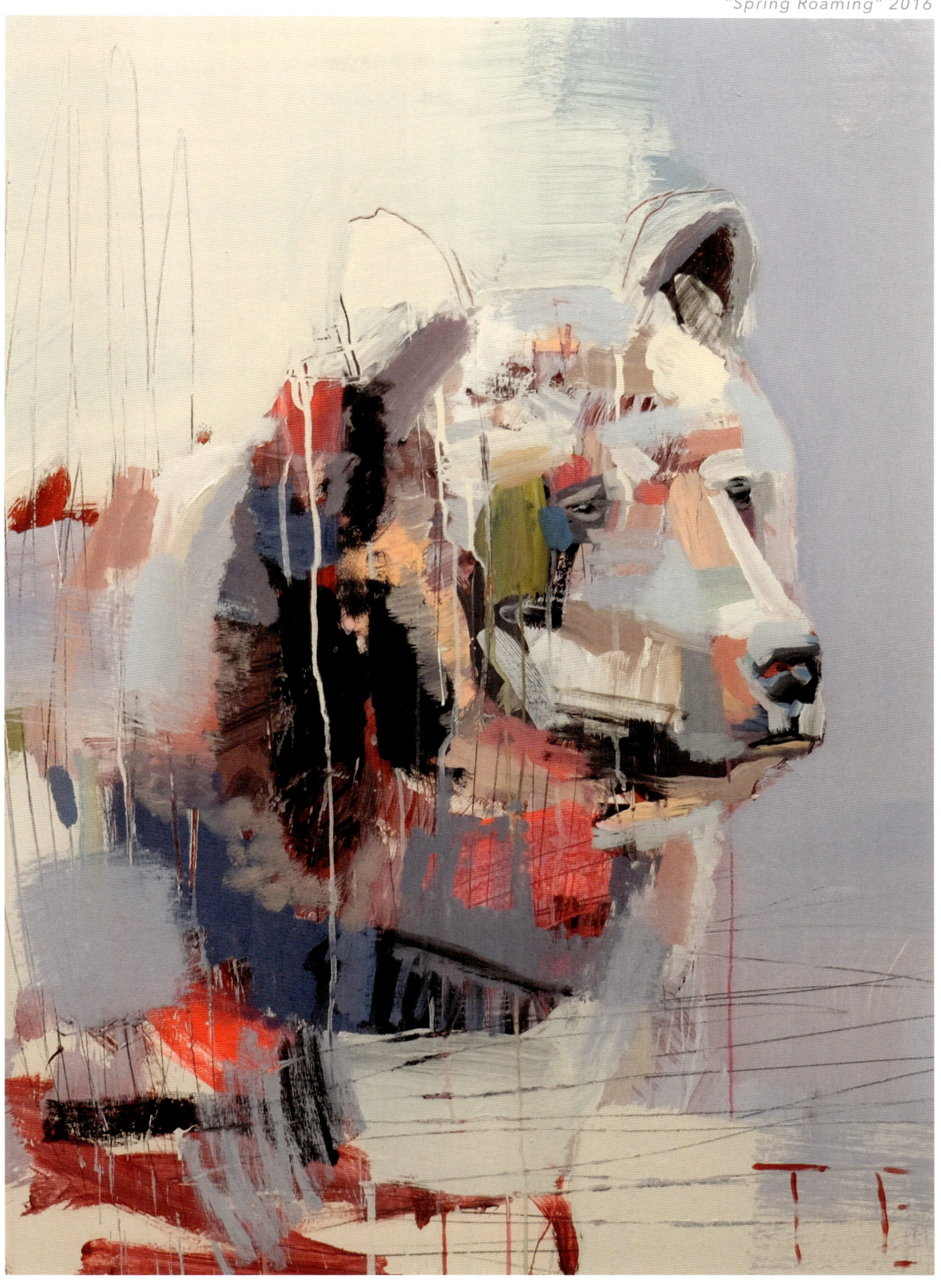

"Ray of Strength"2016

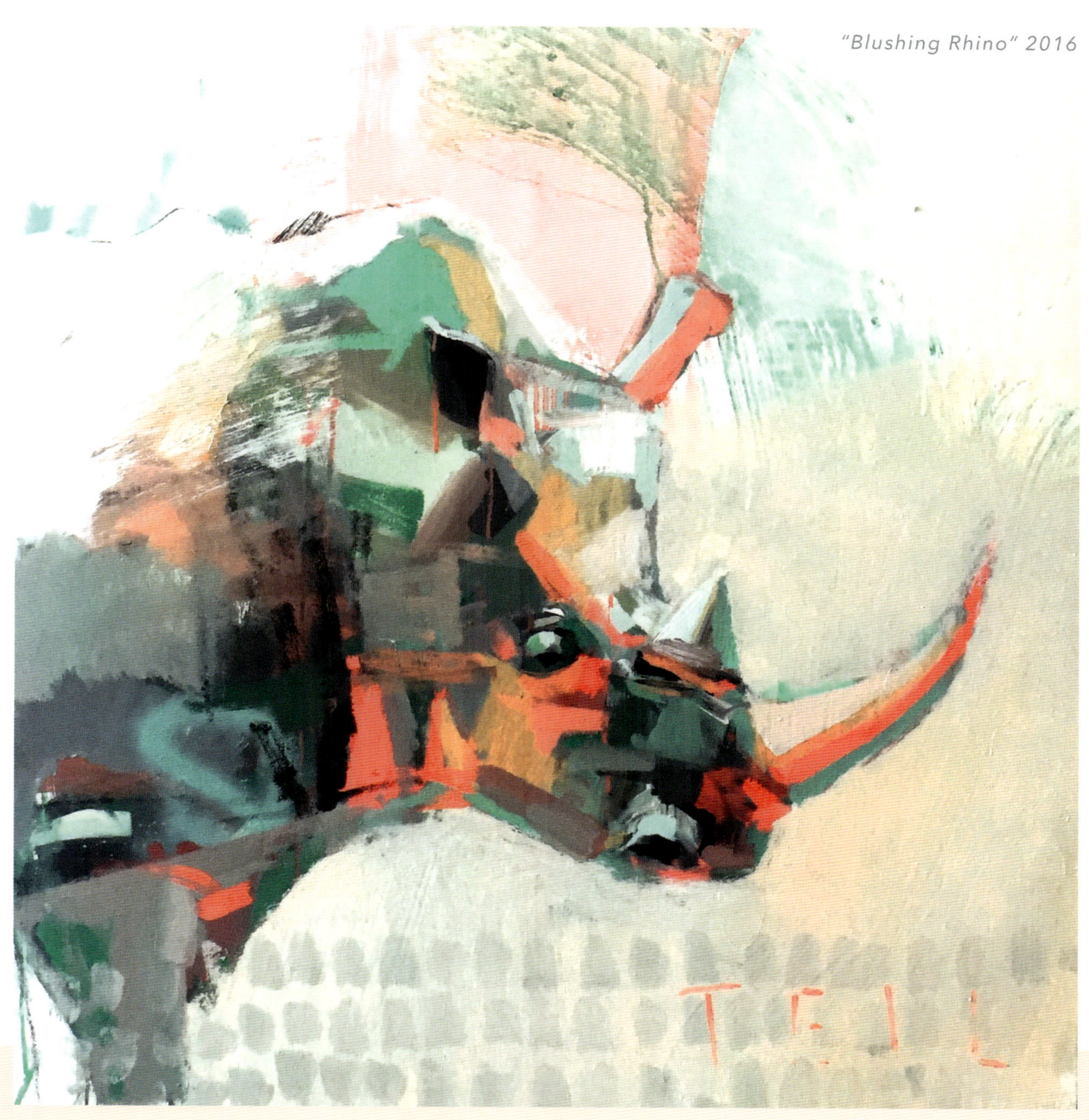

"Blushing Rhino" 2016

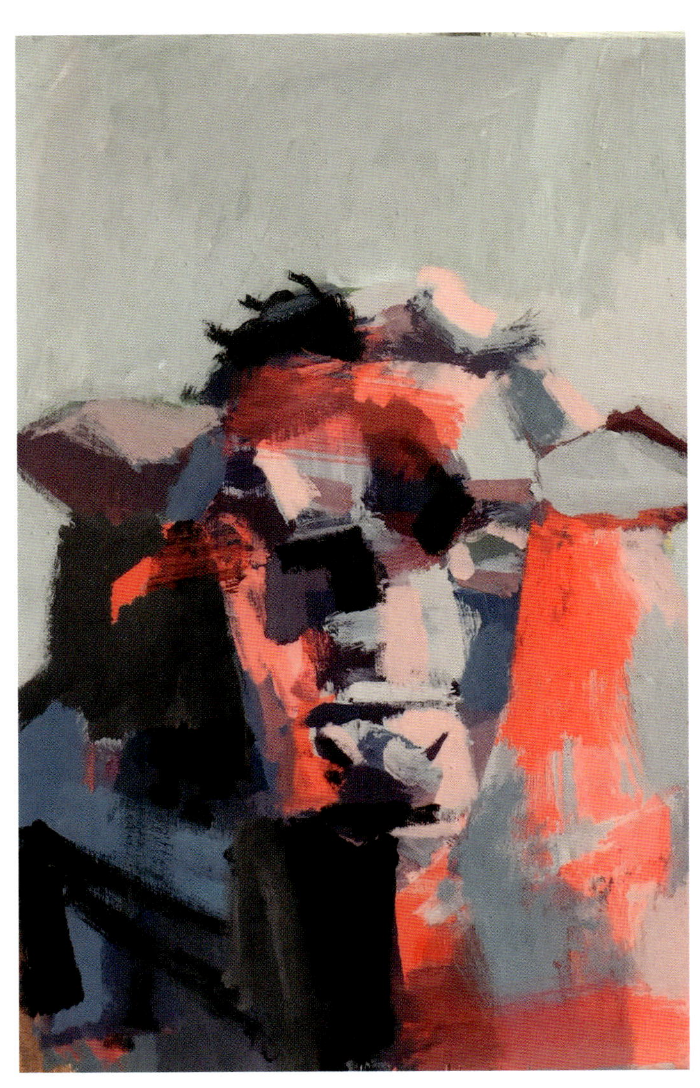

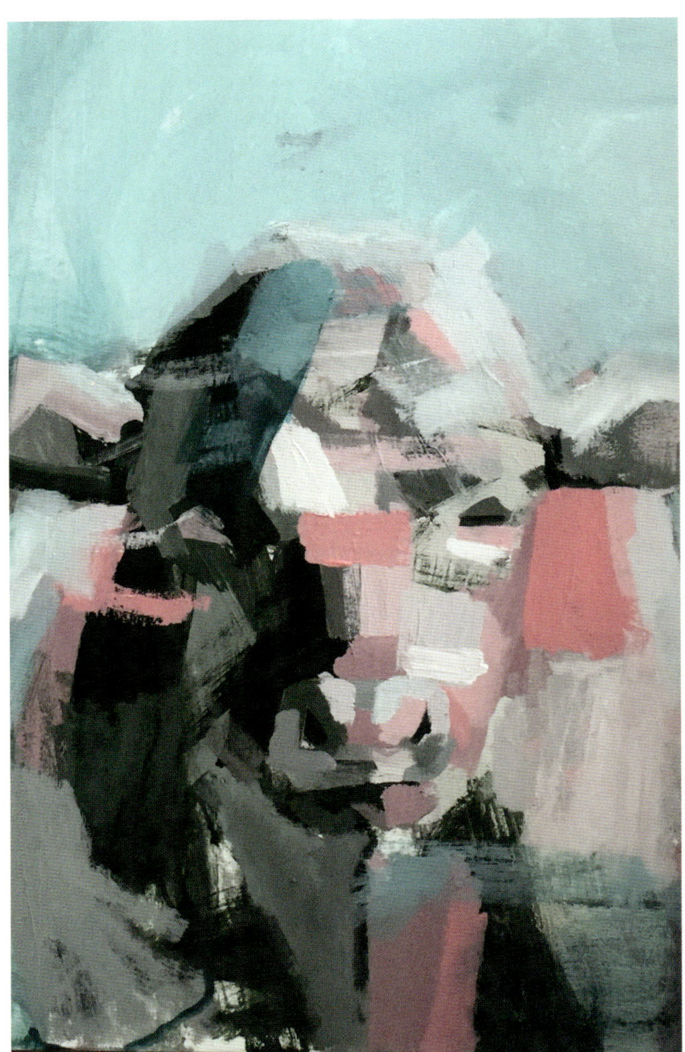

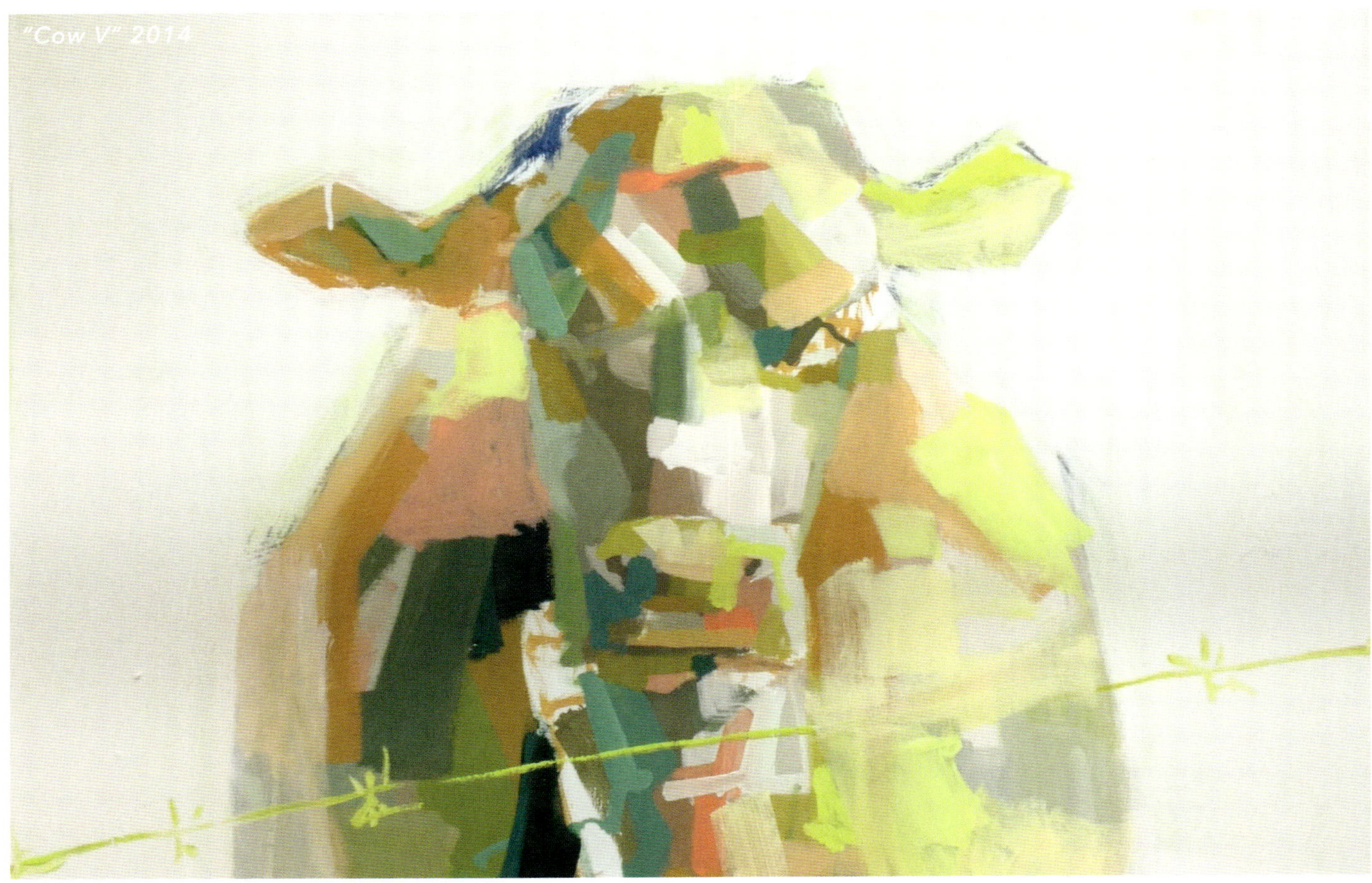

"Cow V" 2014

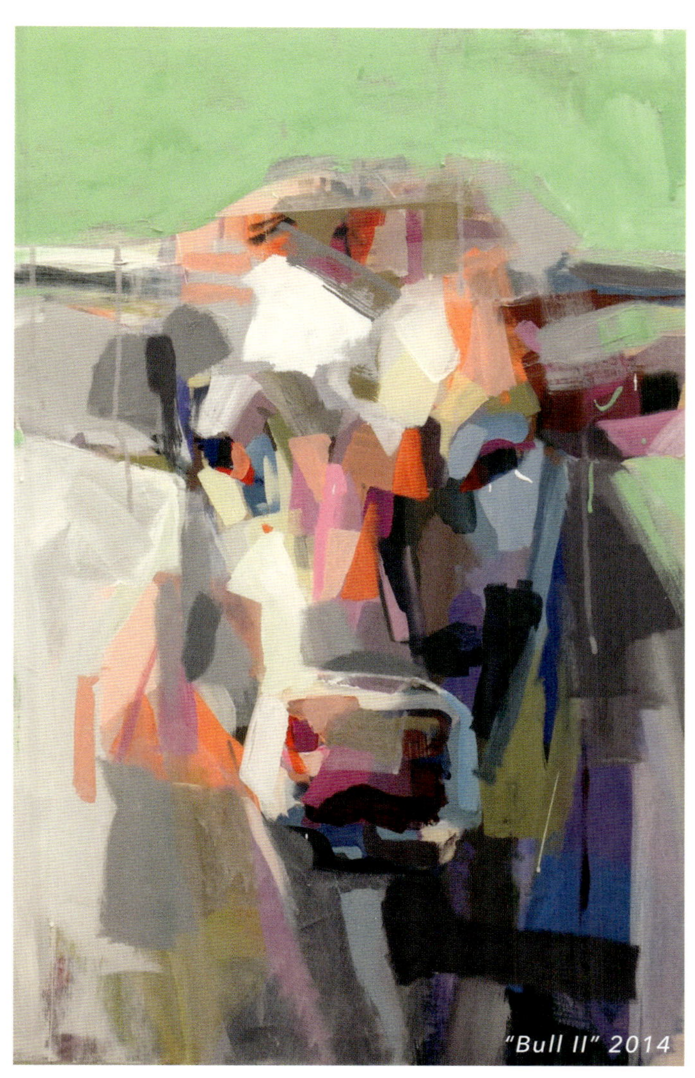

"Bull II" 2014

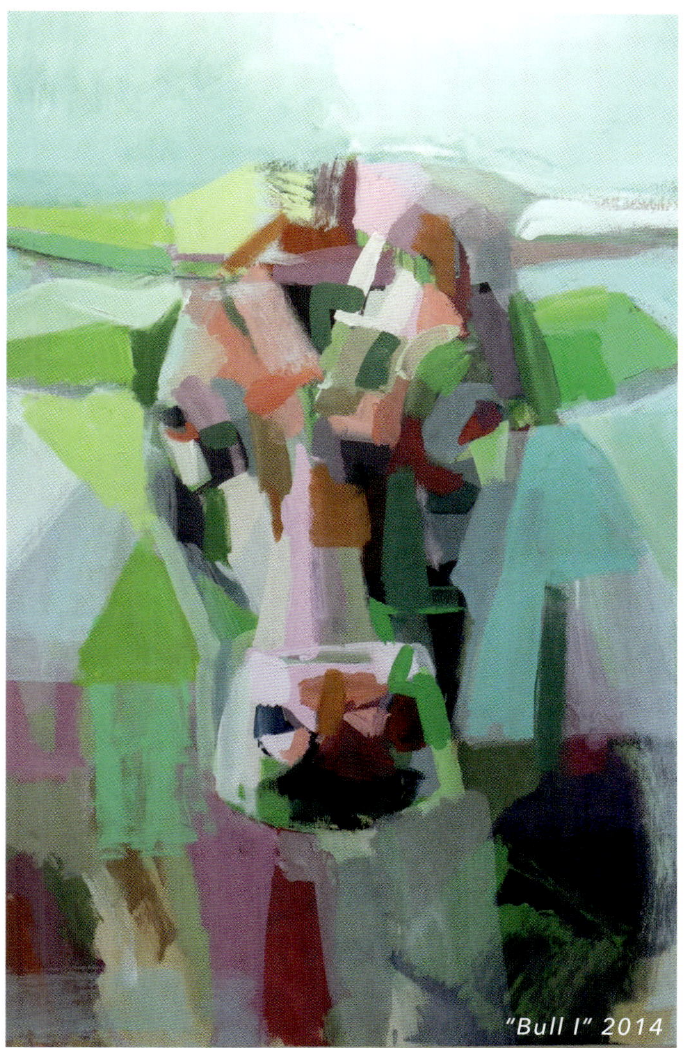

"Bull I" 2014

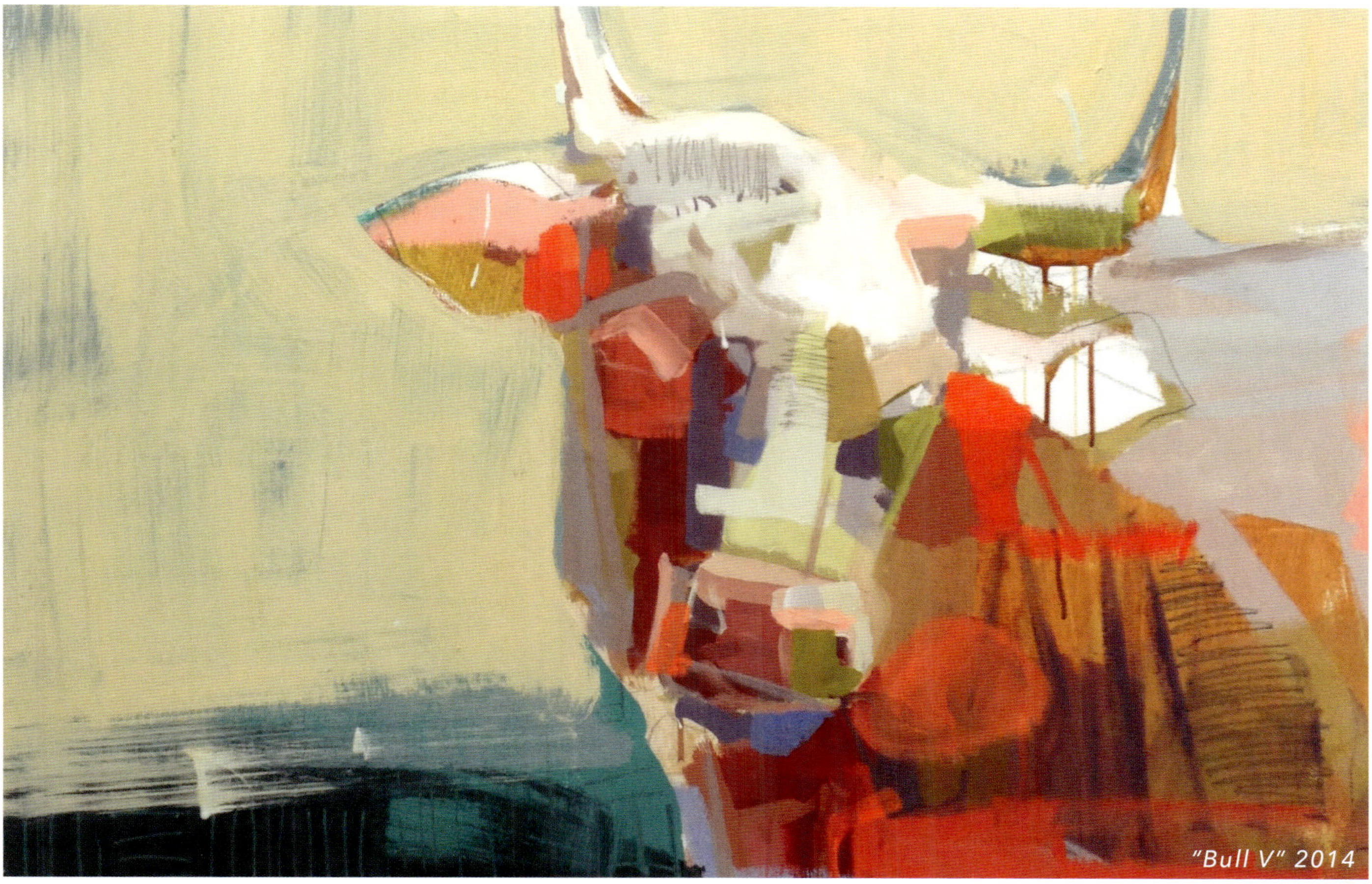

"Bull V" 2014

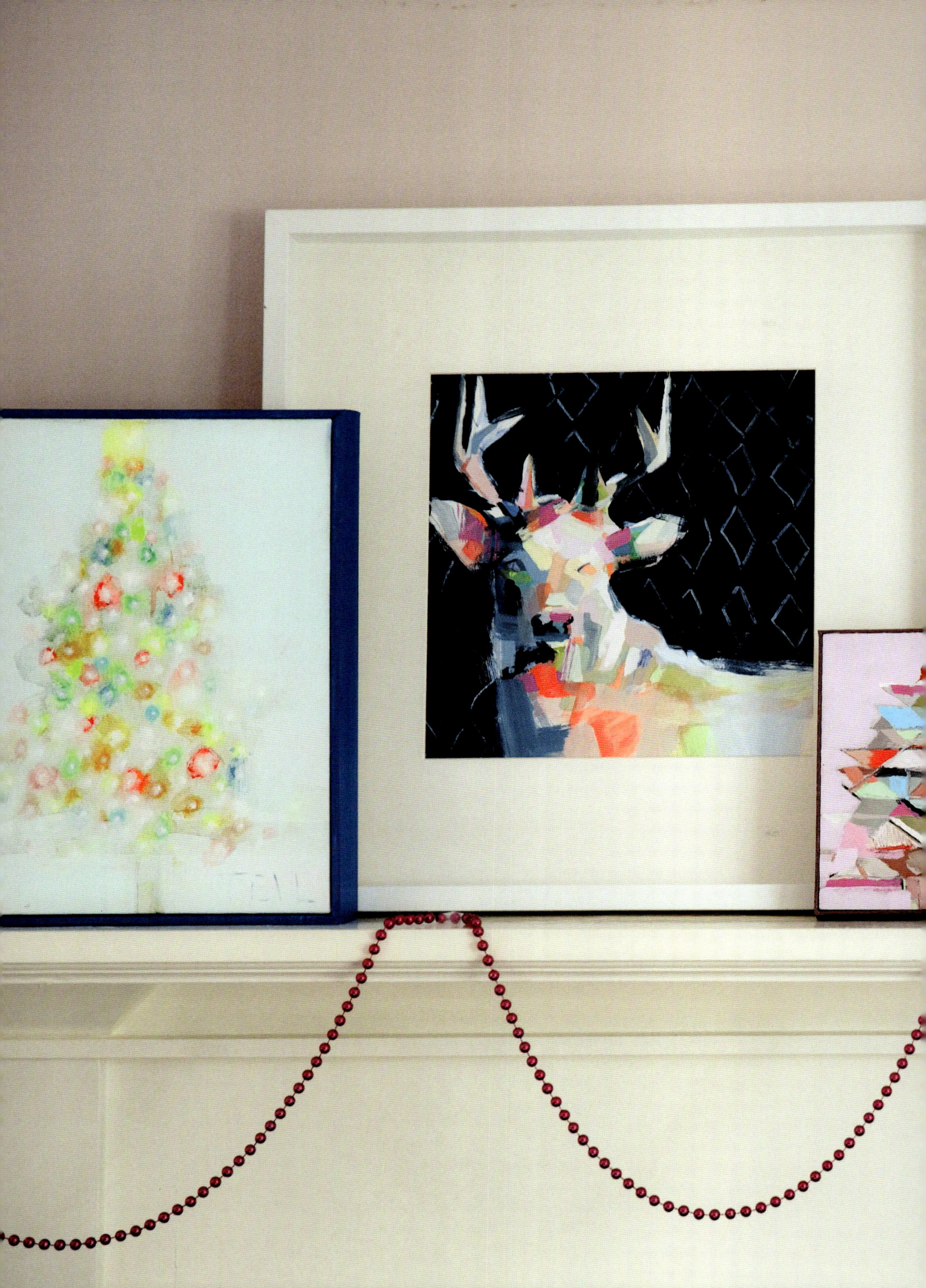

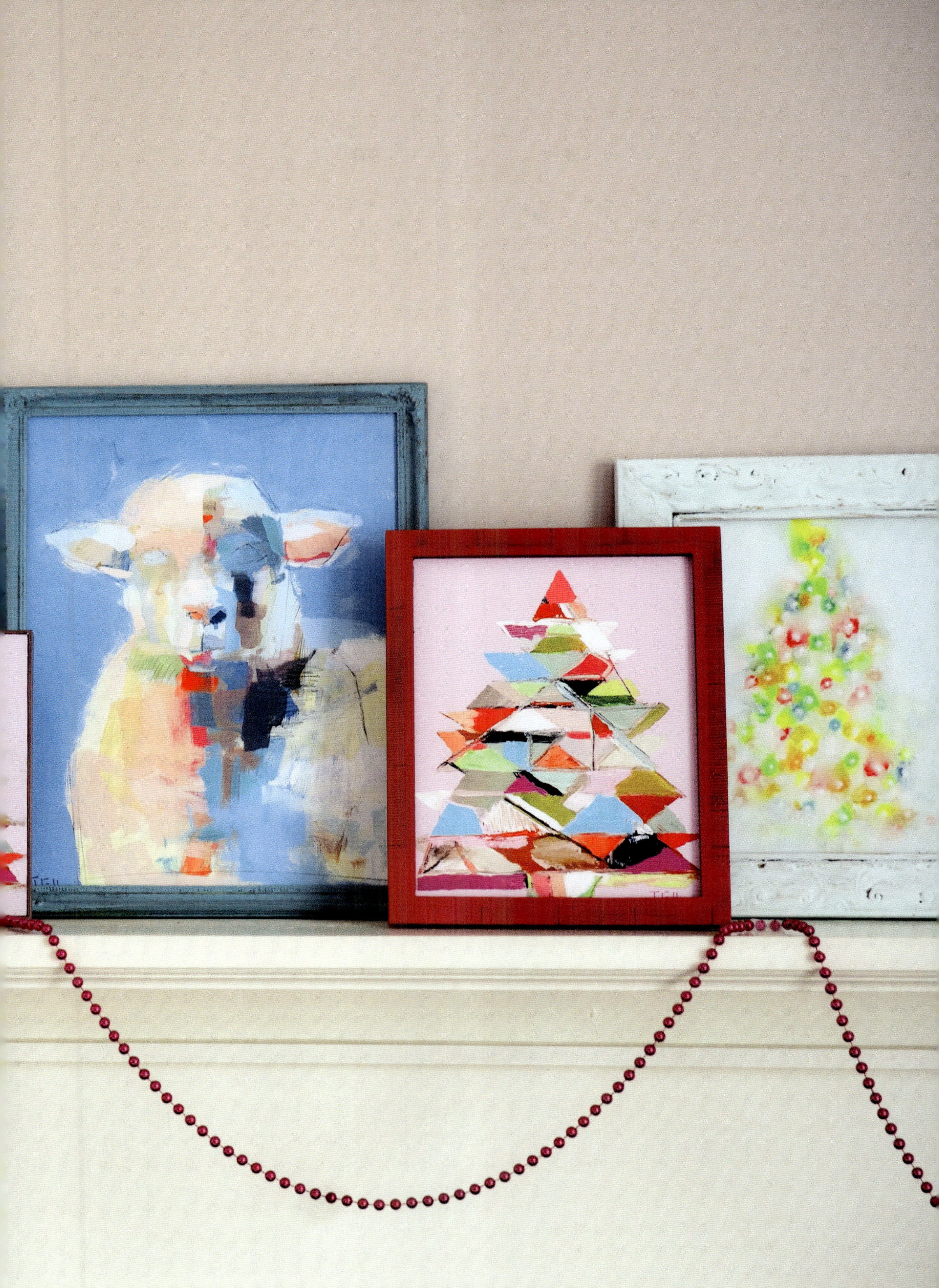

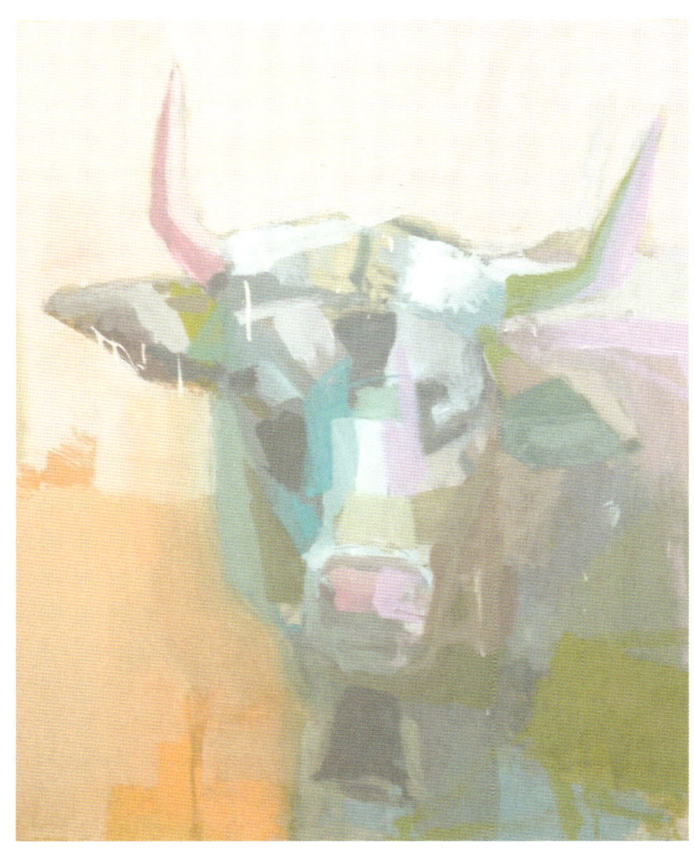

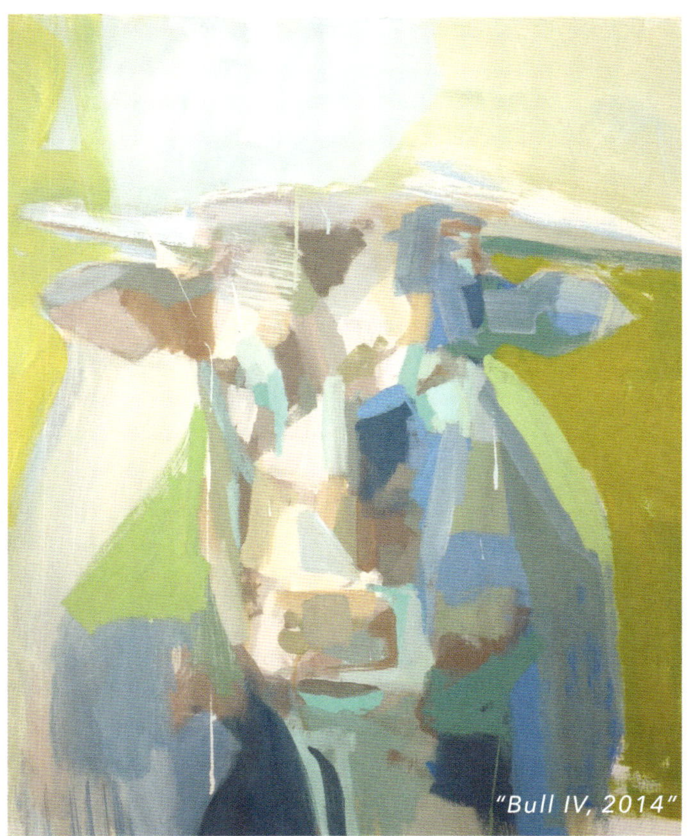

"Bull IV, 2014"

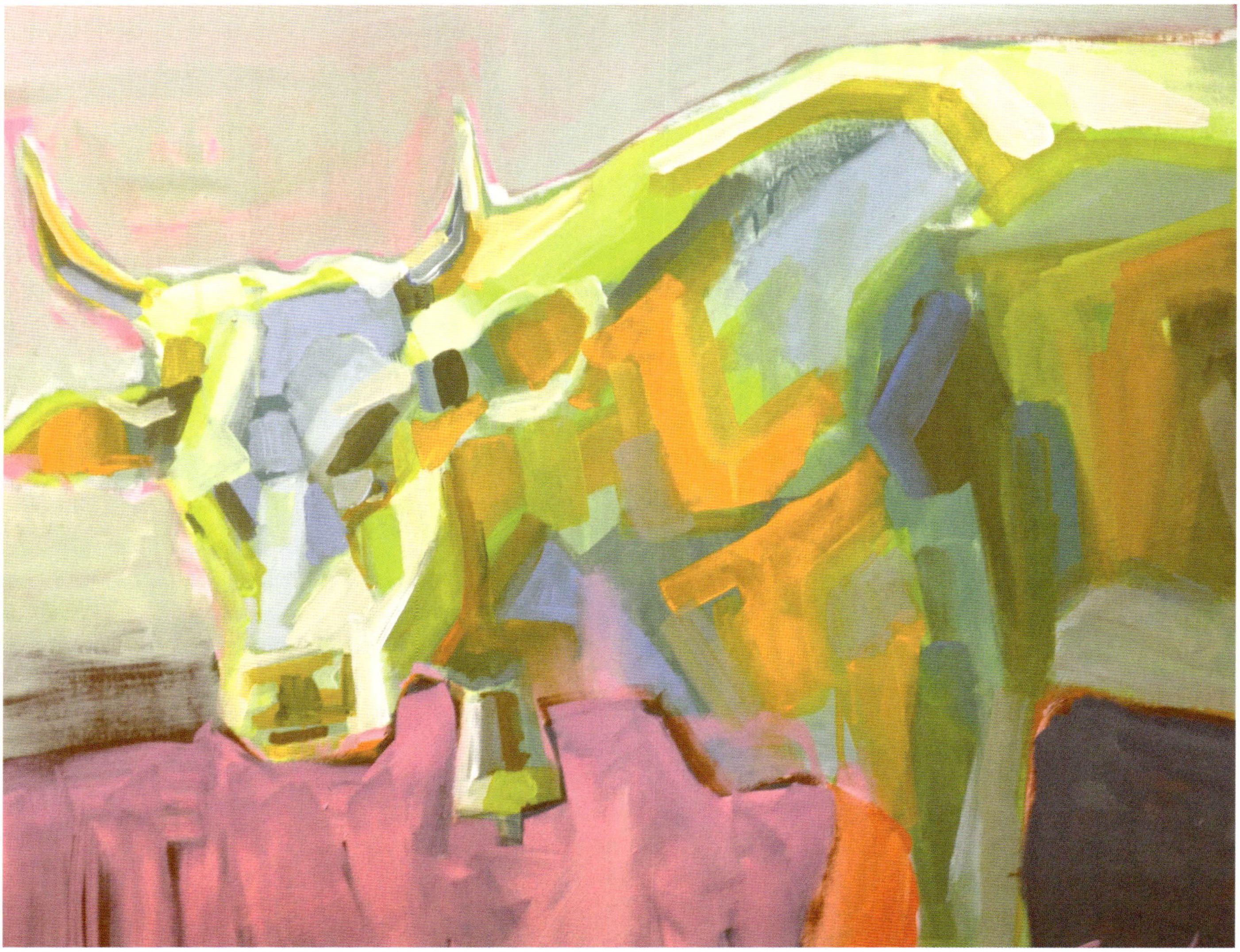

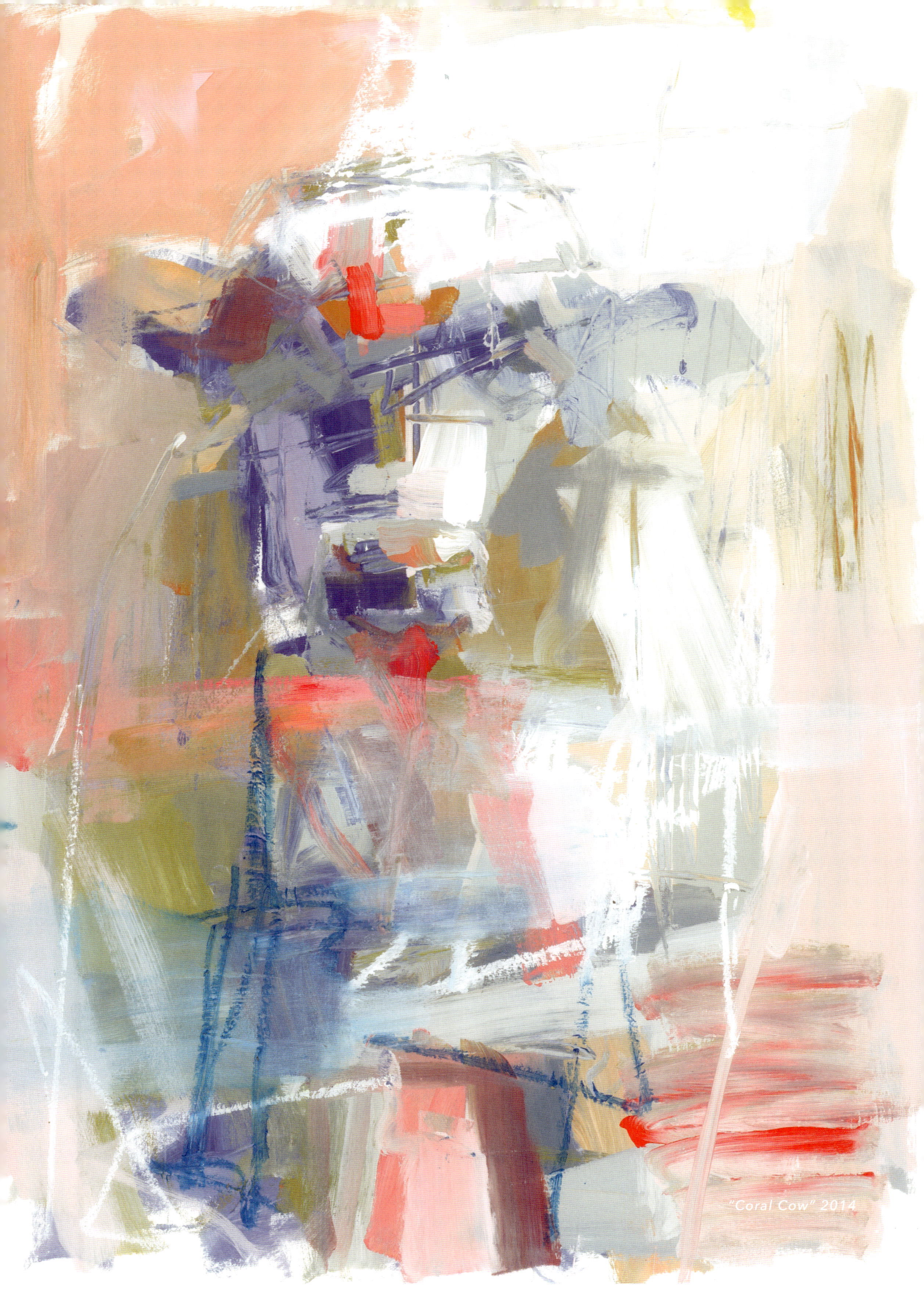

"Coral Cow" 2014

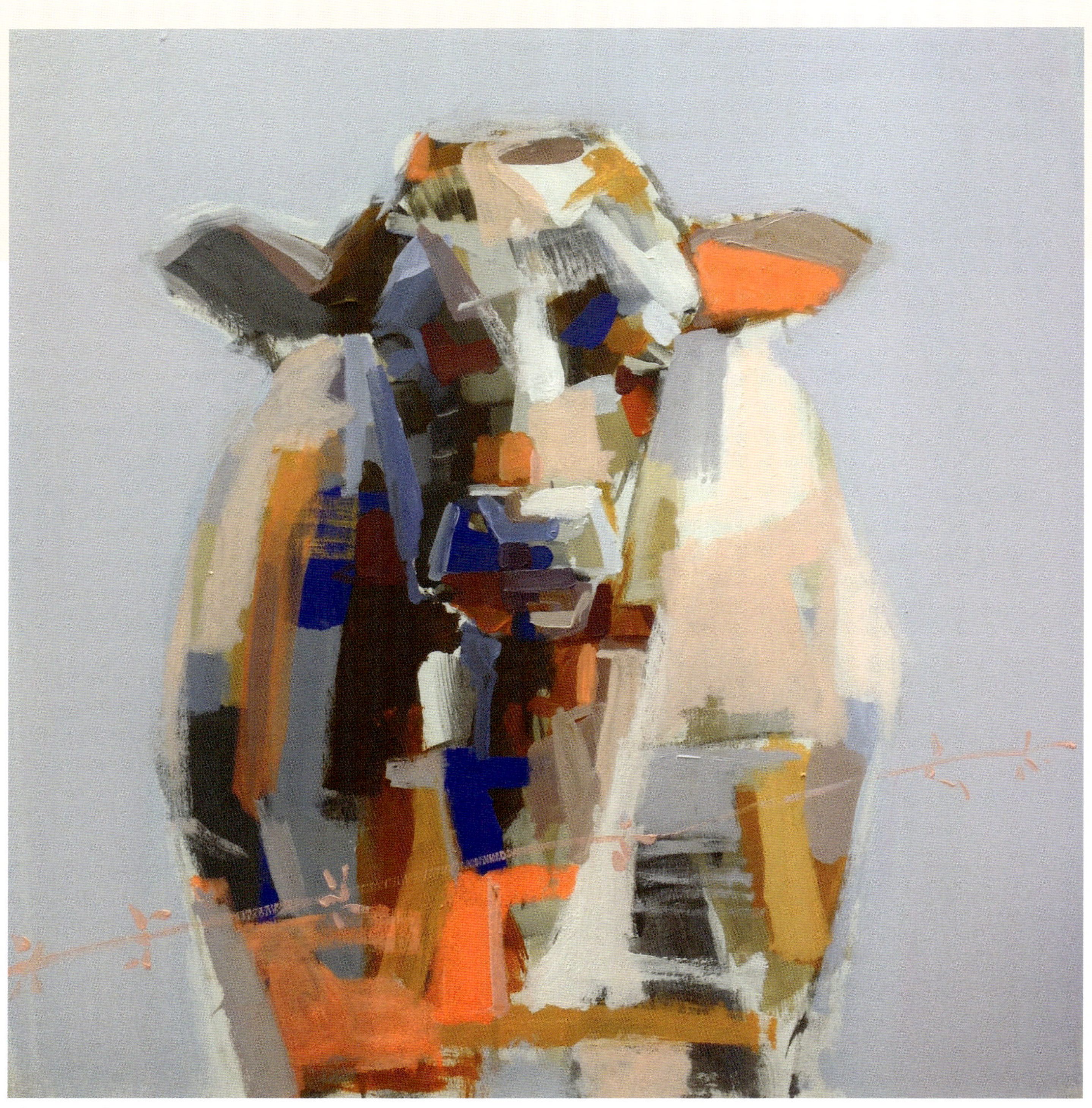

"Cow VII, 2014"

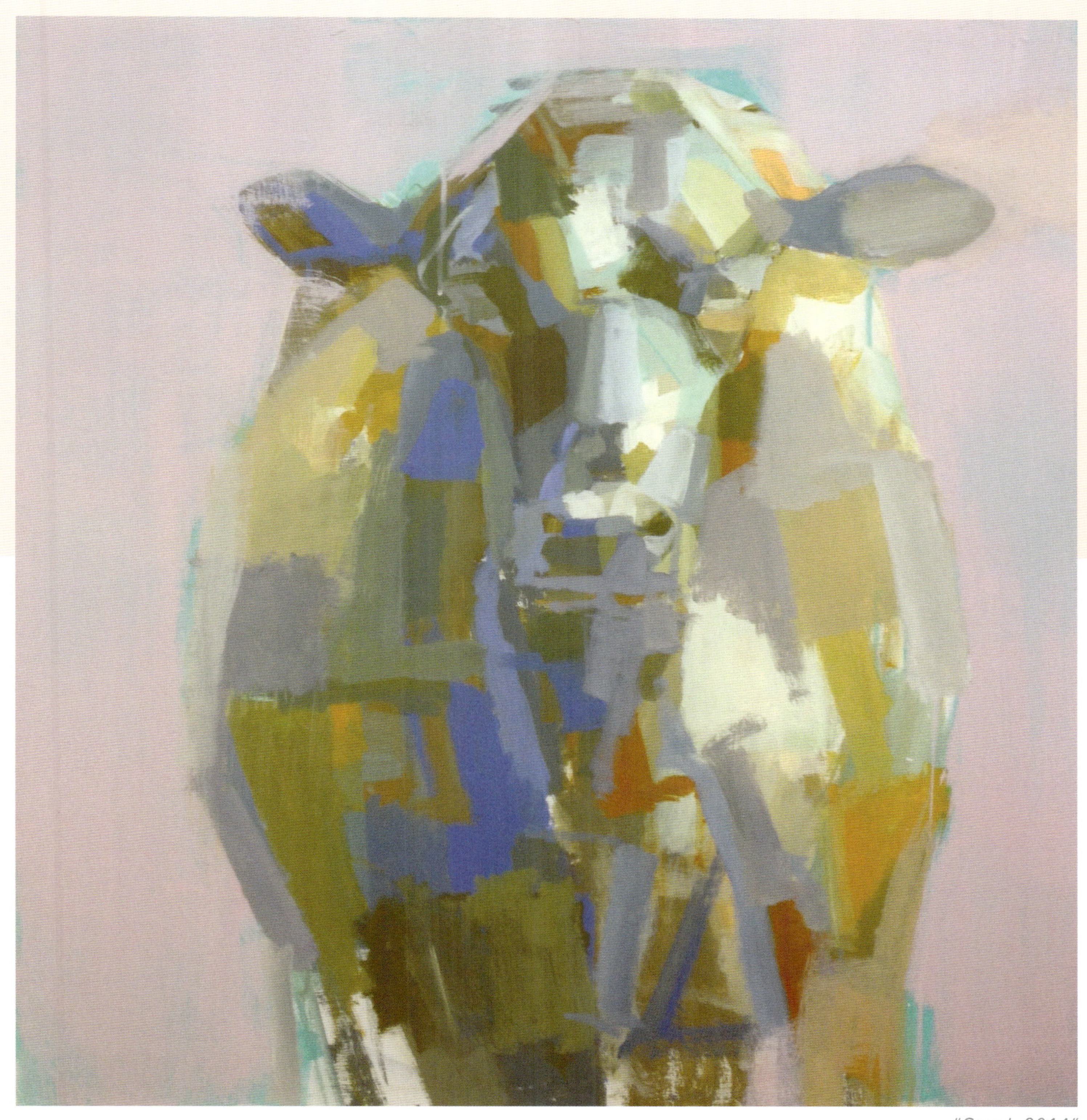

"Cow I, 2014"

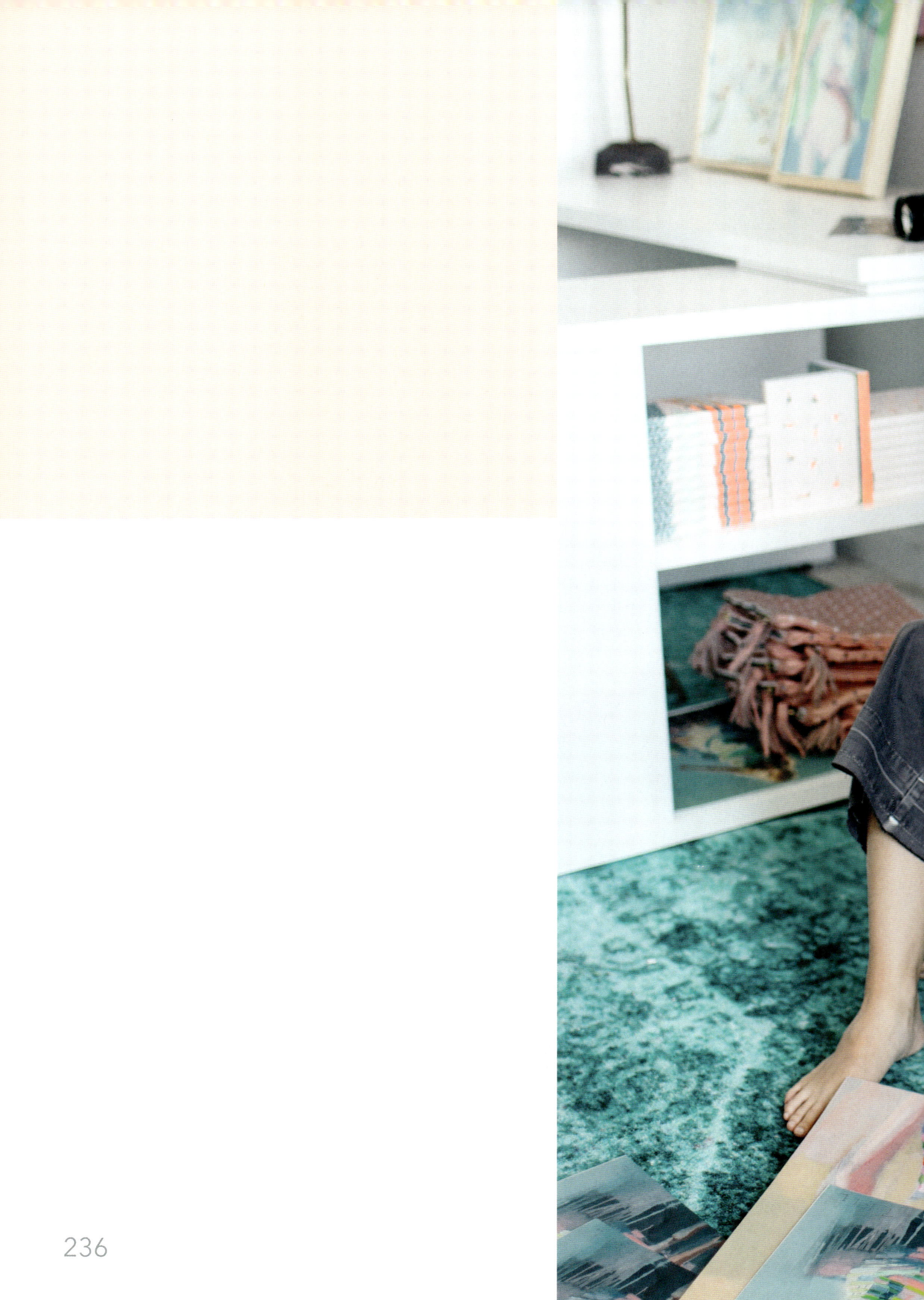

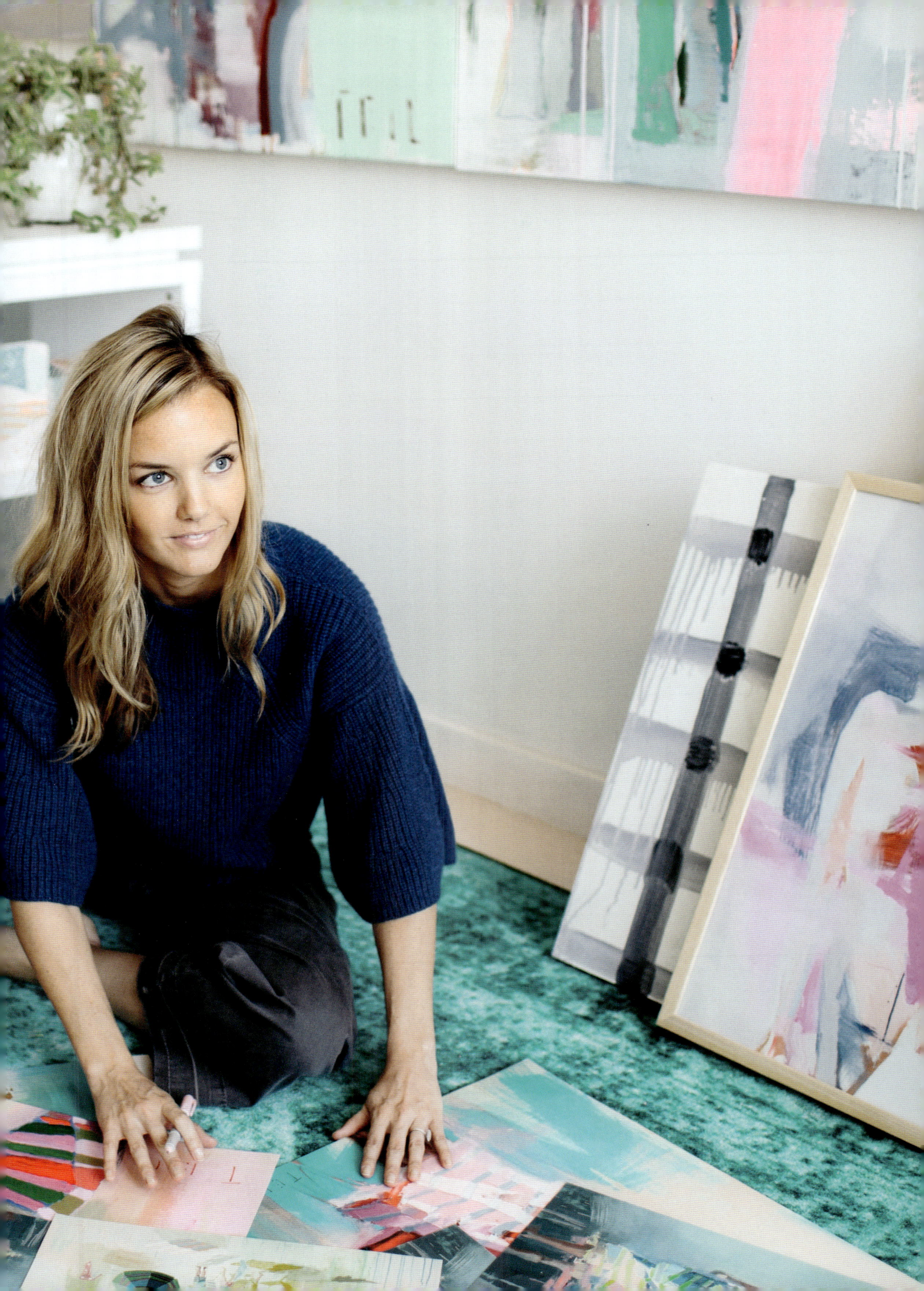

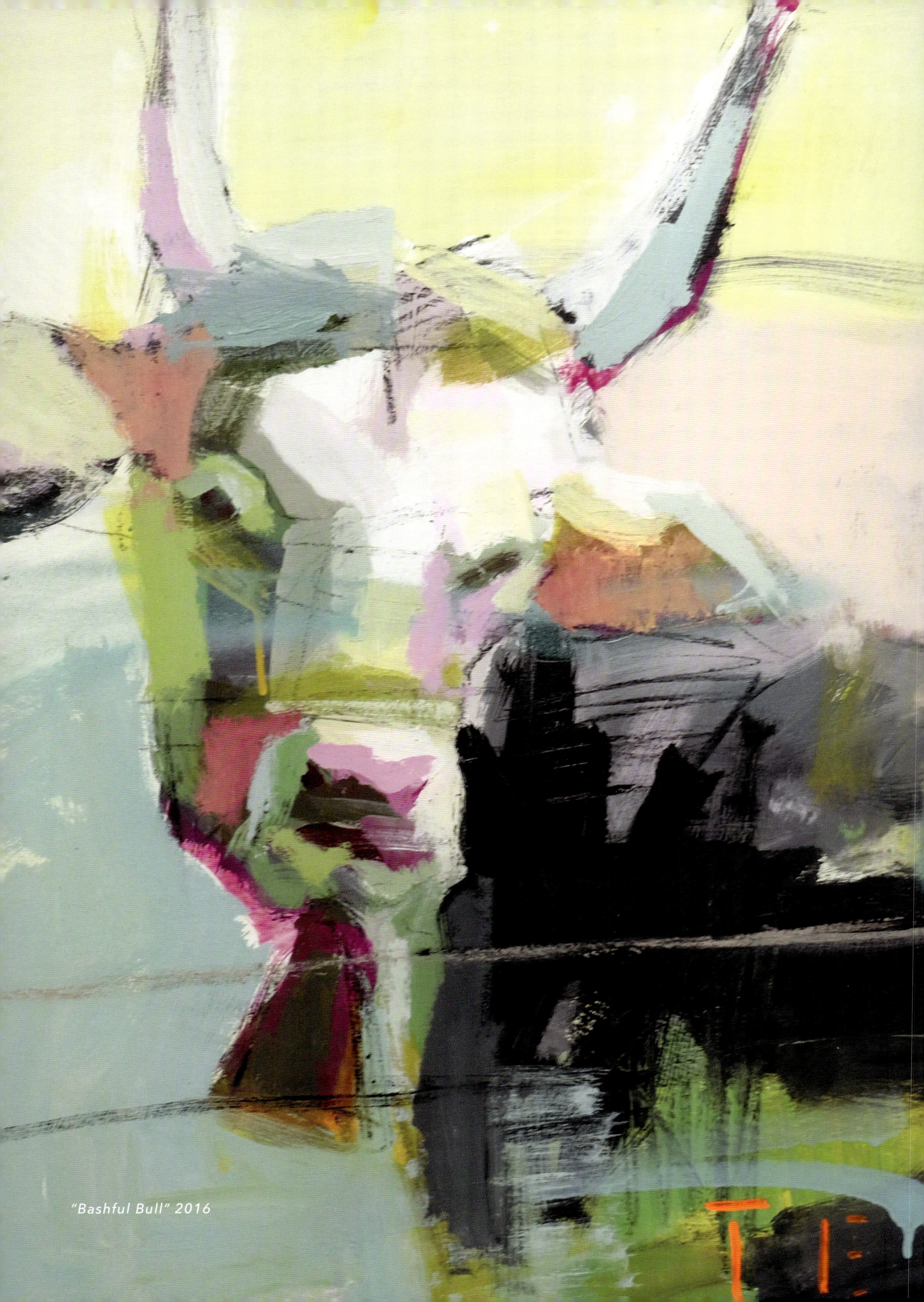
"Bashful Bull" 2016

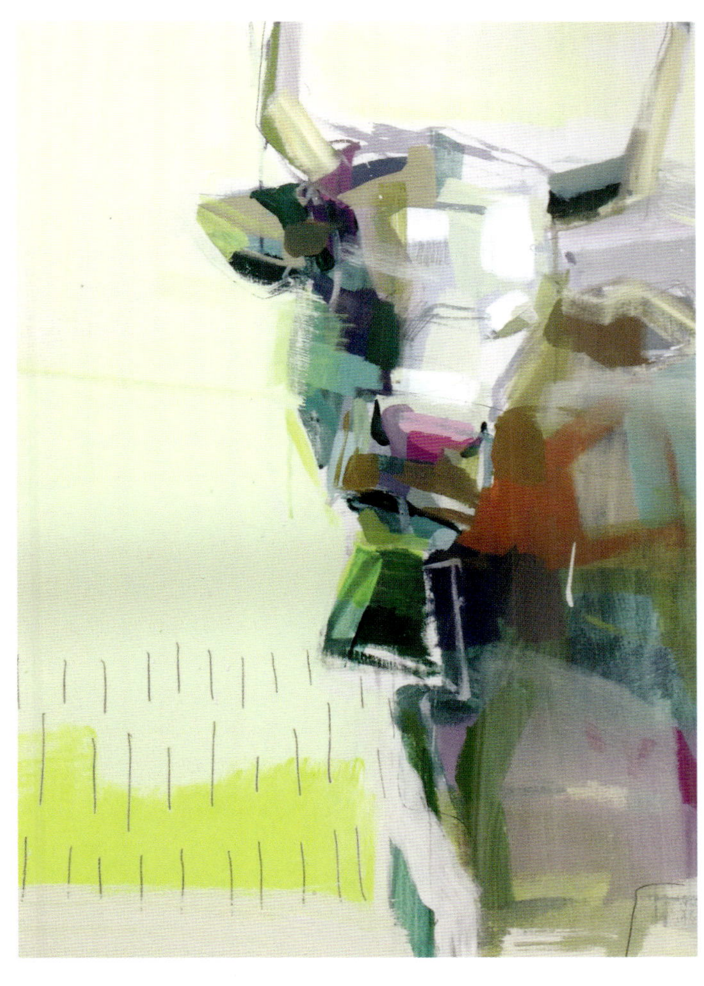

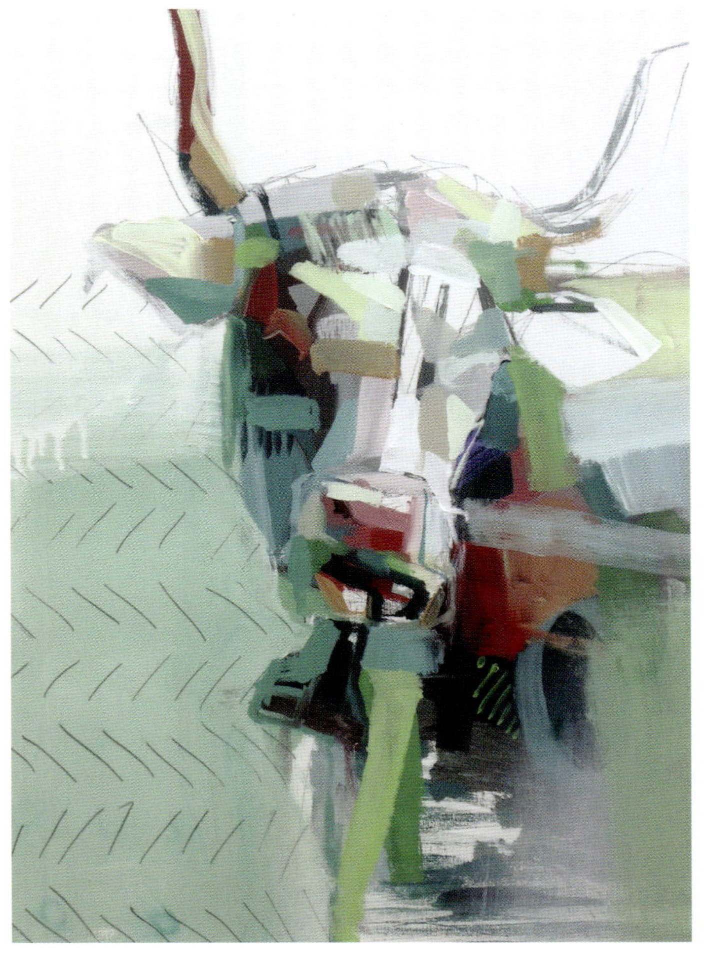

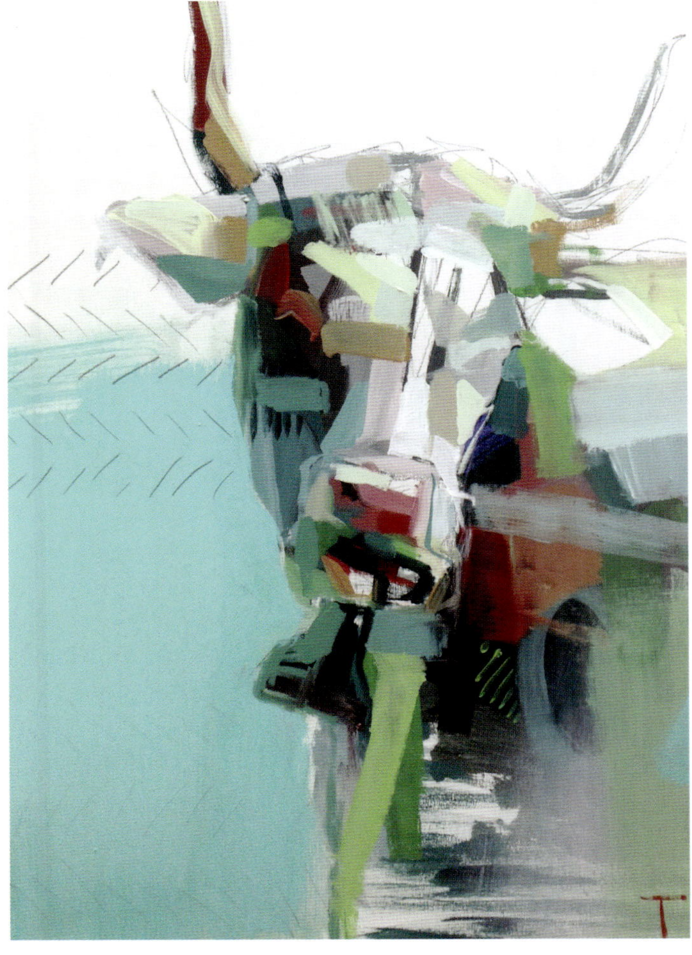

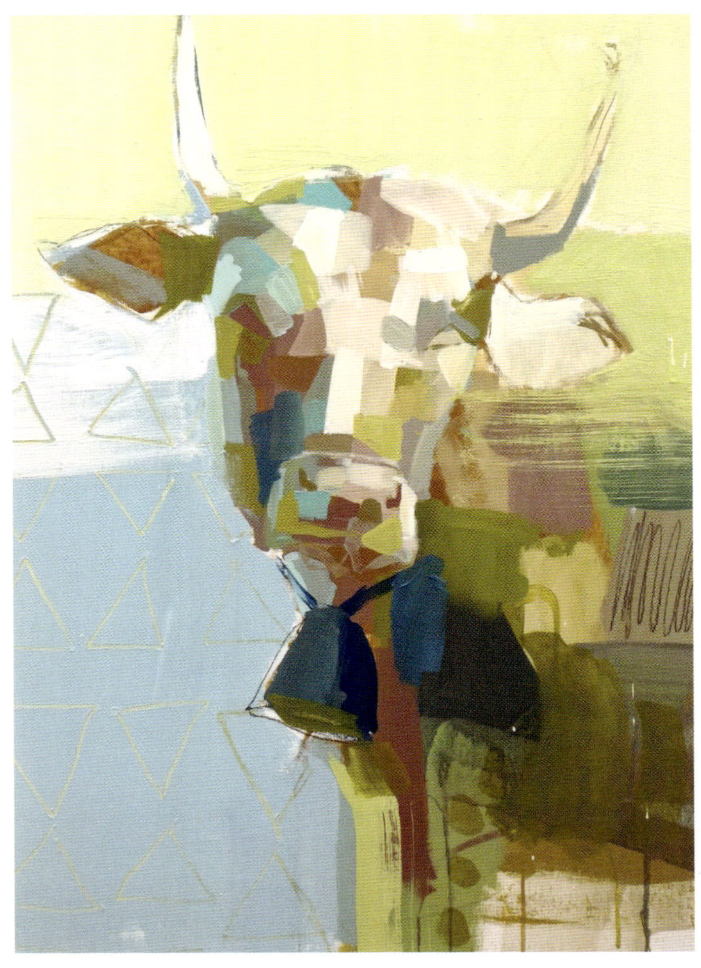

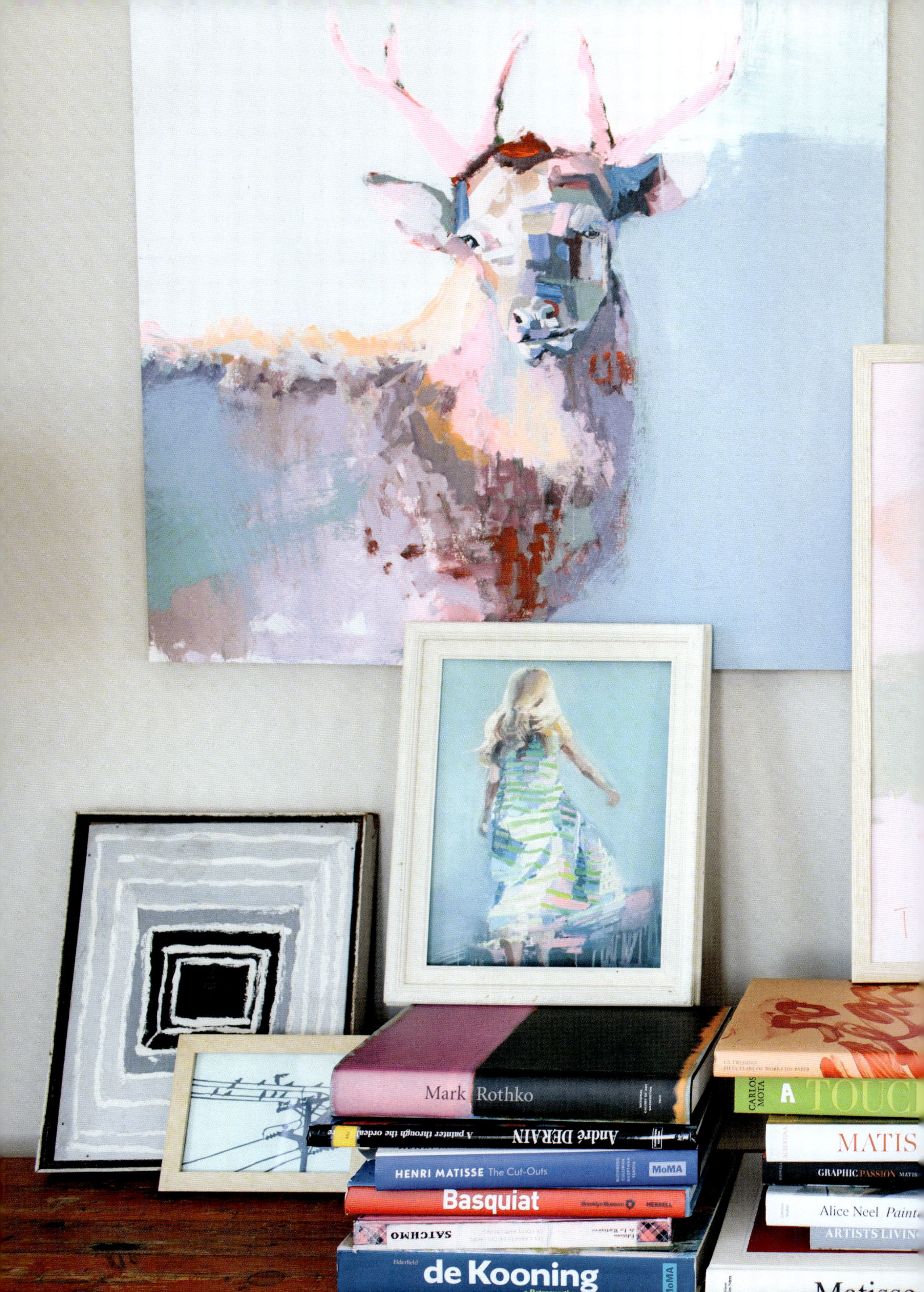
Mark Rothko
HENRI MATISSE The Cut-Outs
MoMA
Basquiat
de Kooning
CARLOS MOTA
A TOUC
MATIS
GRAPHIC PASSION
Alice Neel
ARTISTS LIVIN

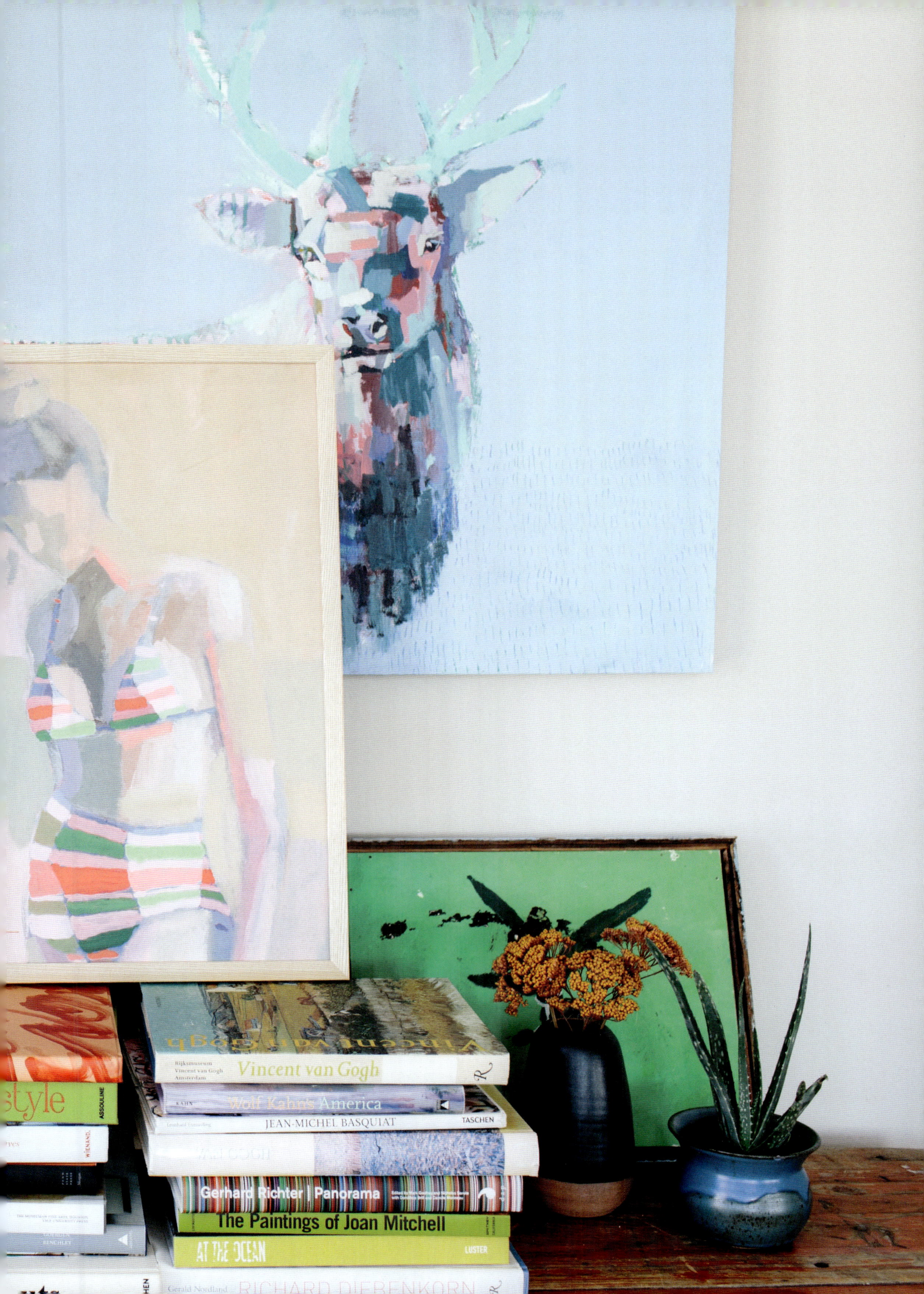

style
ASSOULINE
Rijksmuseum
Vincent van Gogh
Amsterdam
Vincent van Gogh
Wolf Kahn's America
JEAN-MICHEL BASQUIAT
TASCHEN
Gerhard Richter | Panorama
The Paintings of Joan Mitchell
AT THE OCEAN
LUSTER
Gerald Nordland
RICHARD DIEBENKORN

"Pink Point" 2018

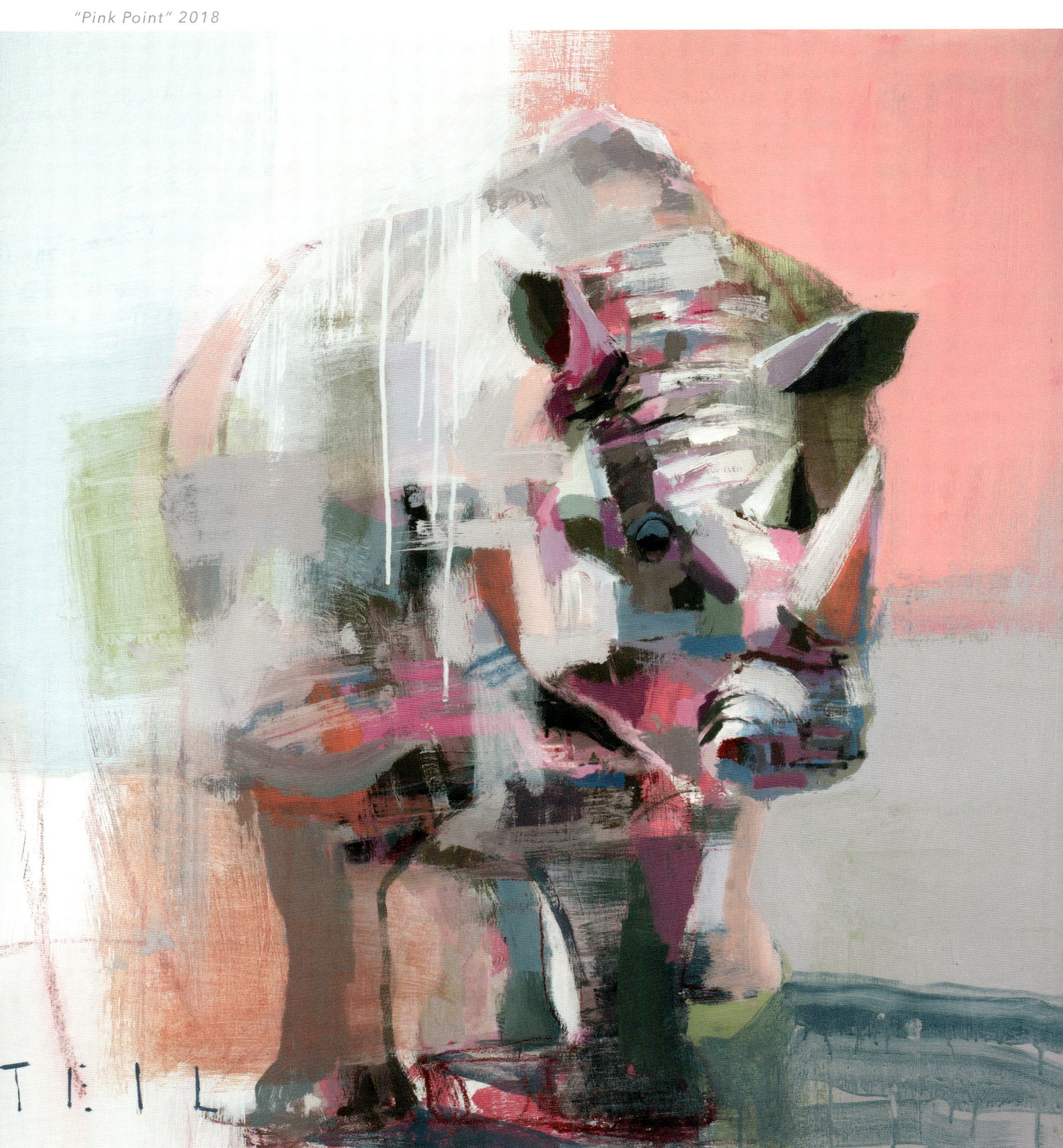

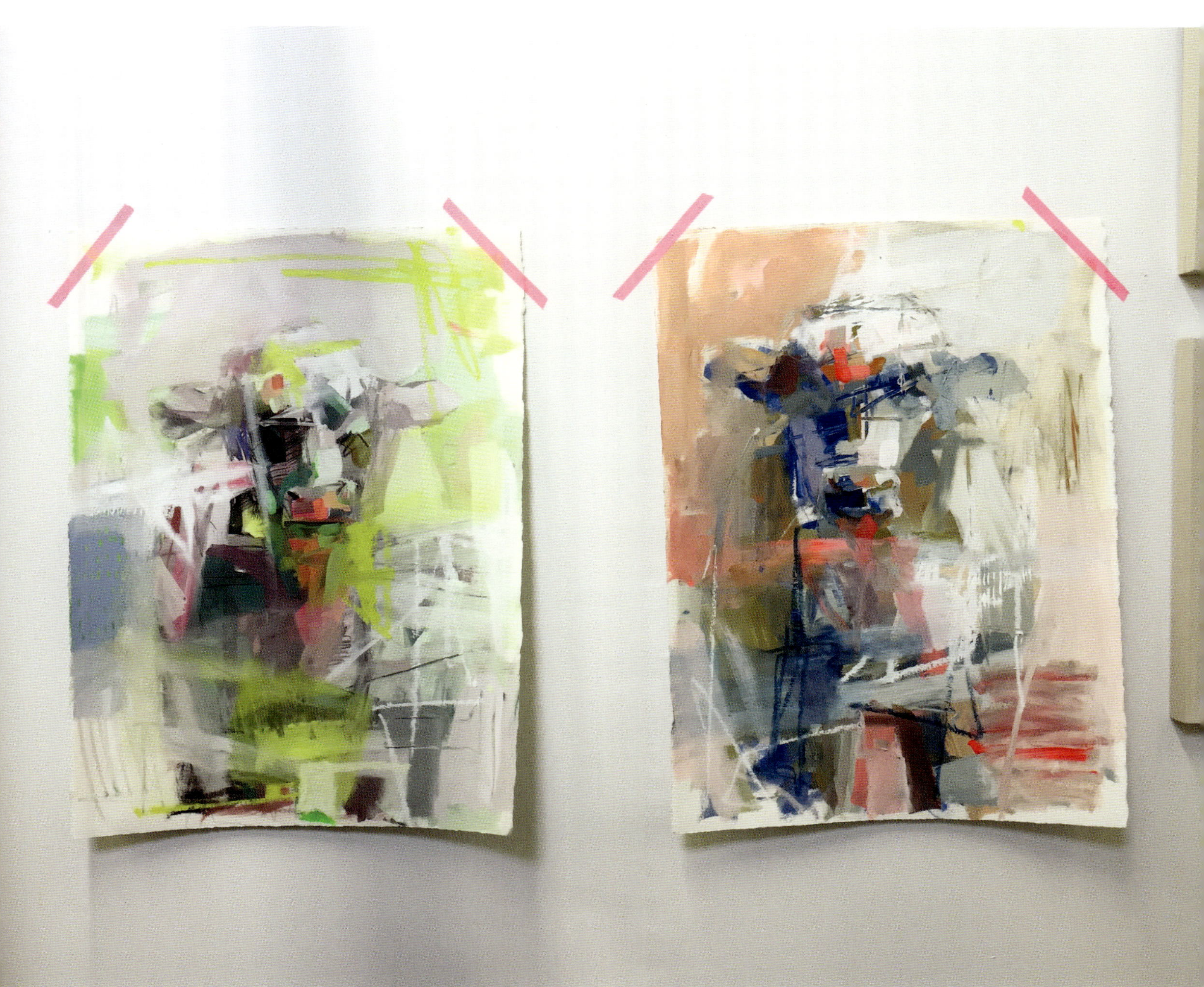

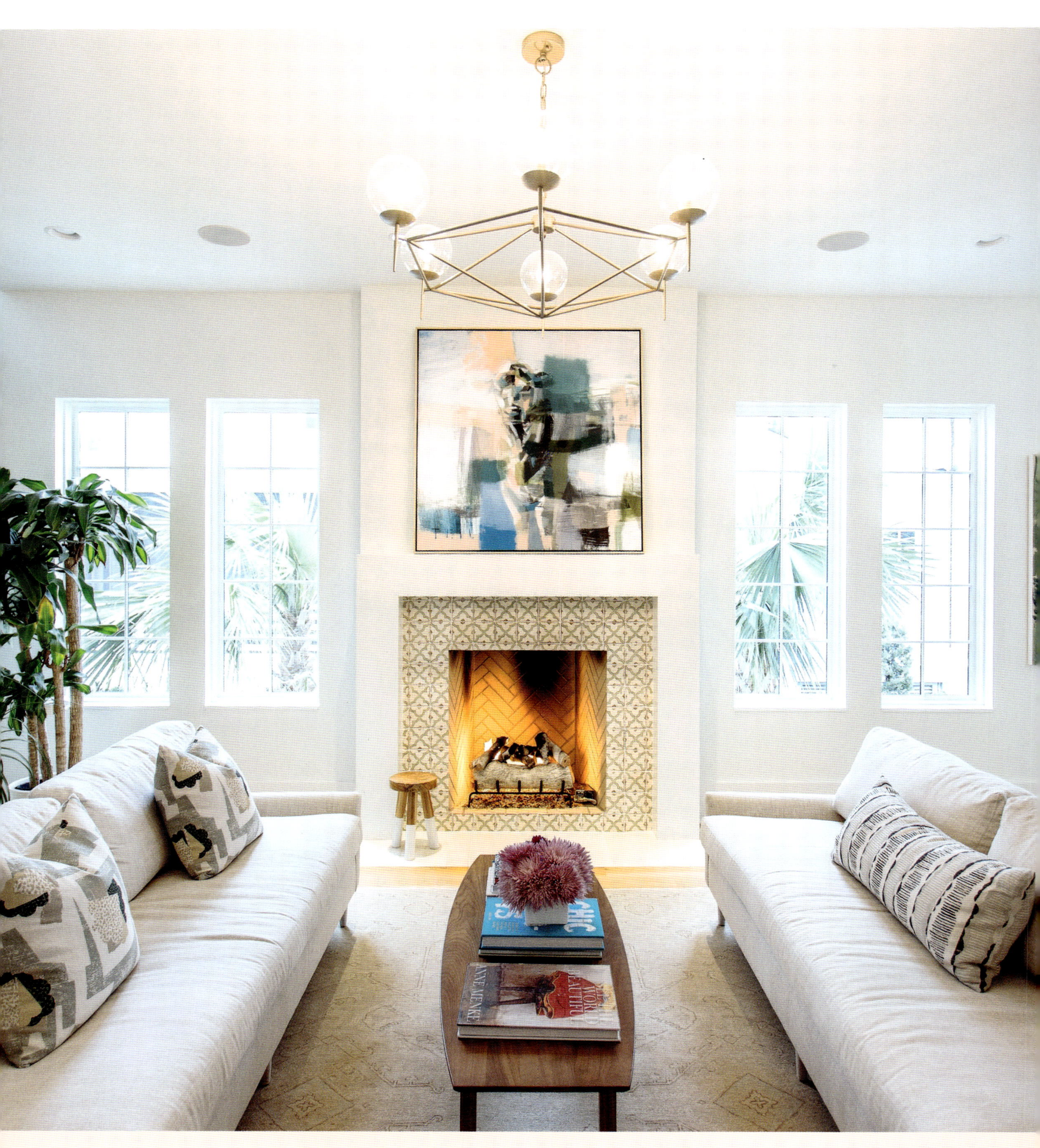

"On the Hunt" 2016

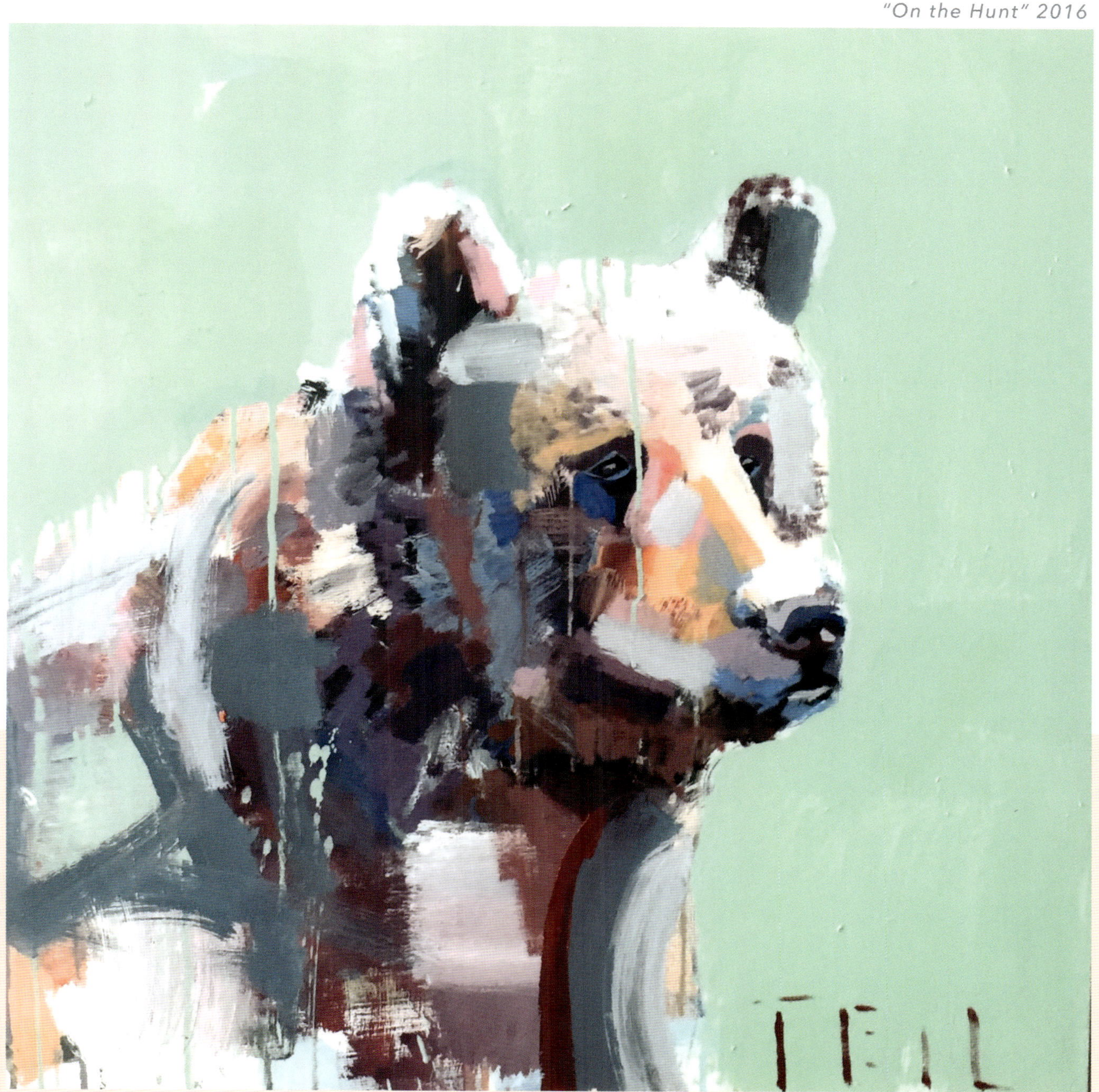

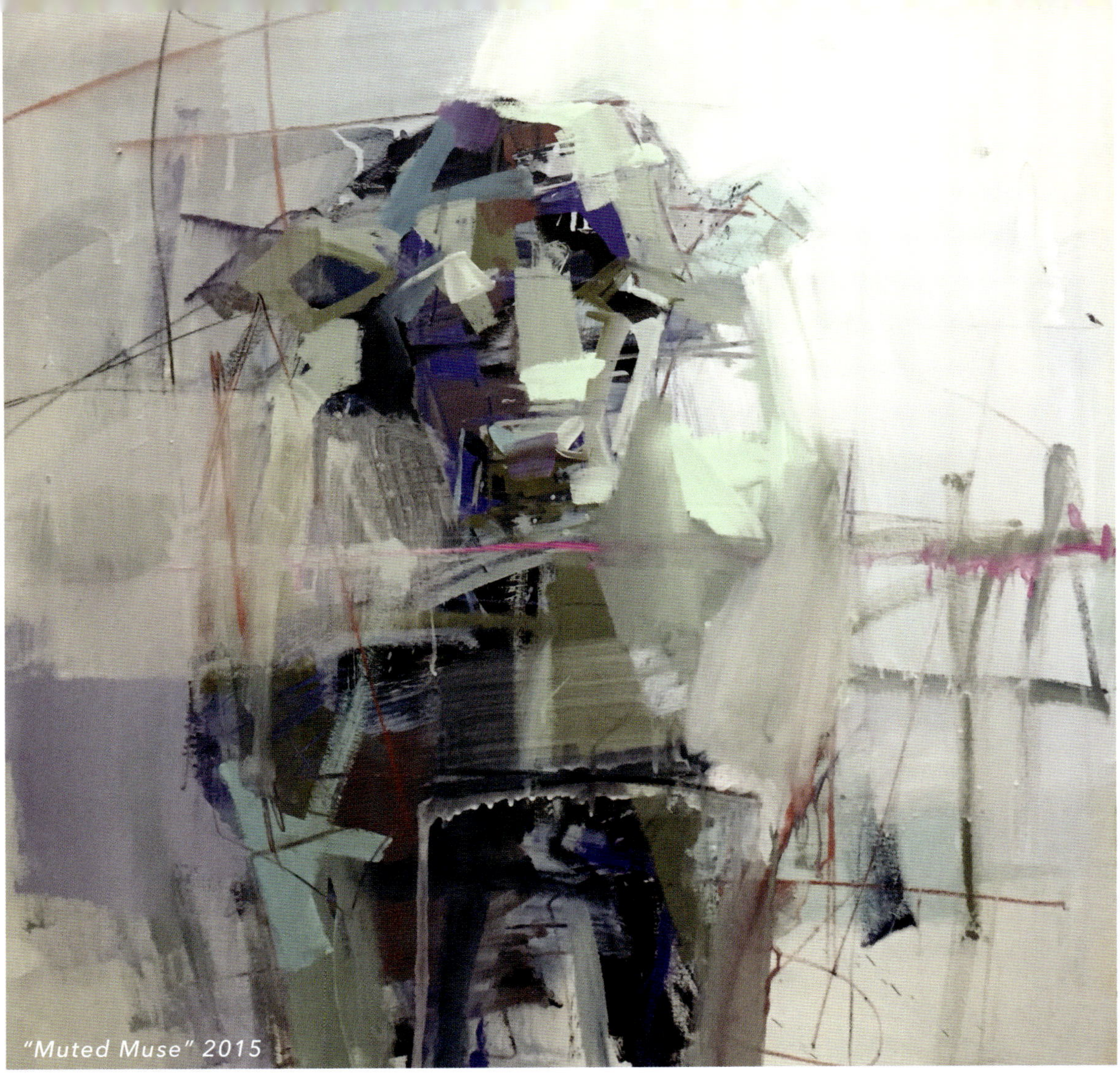

"Muted Muse" 2015

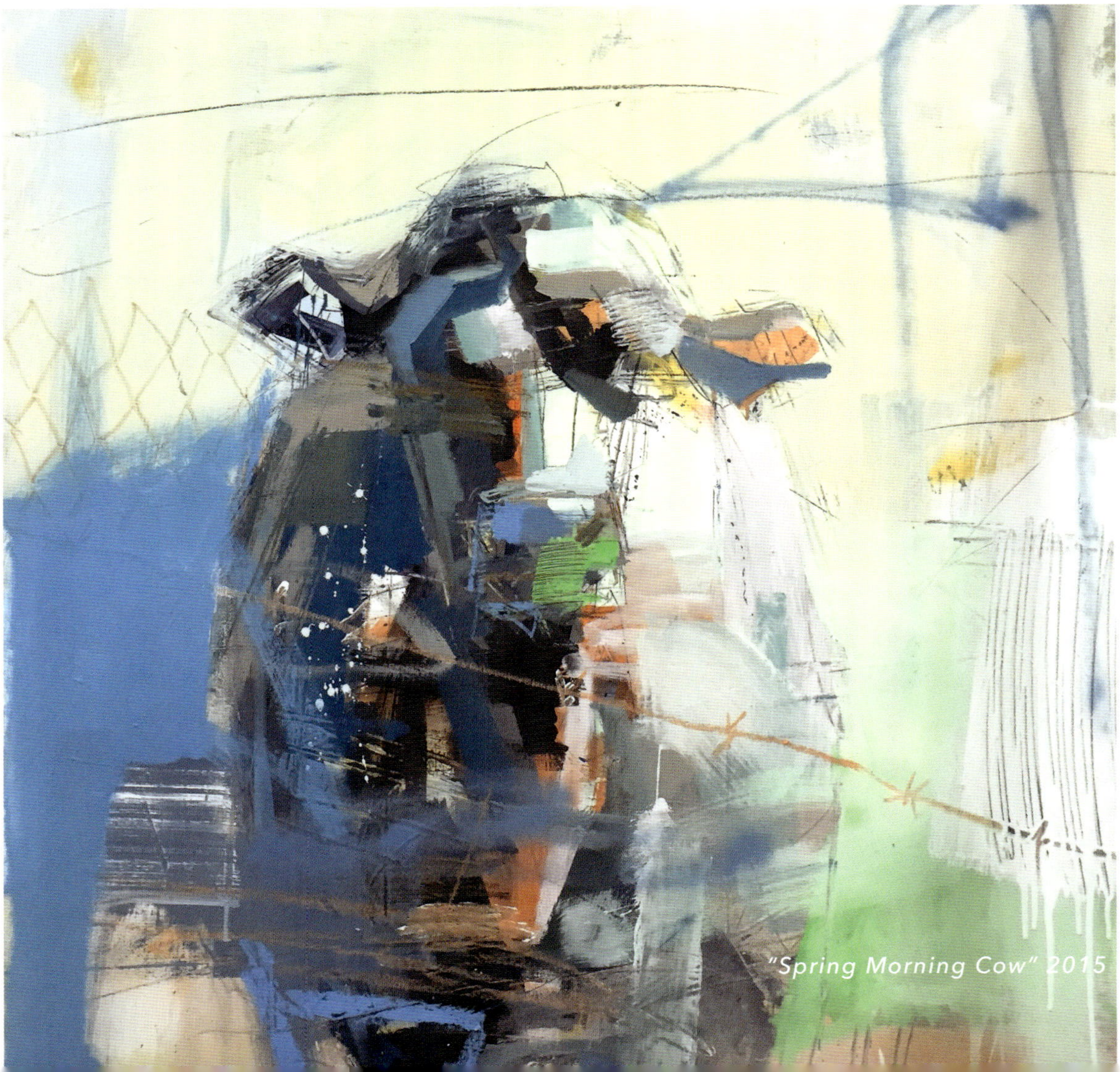

"Spring Morning Cow" 2015

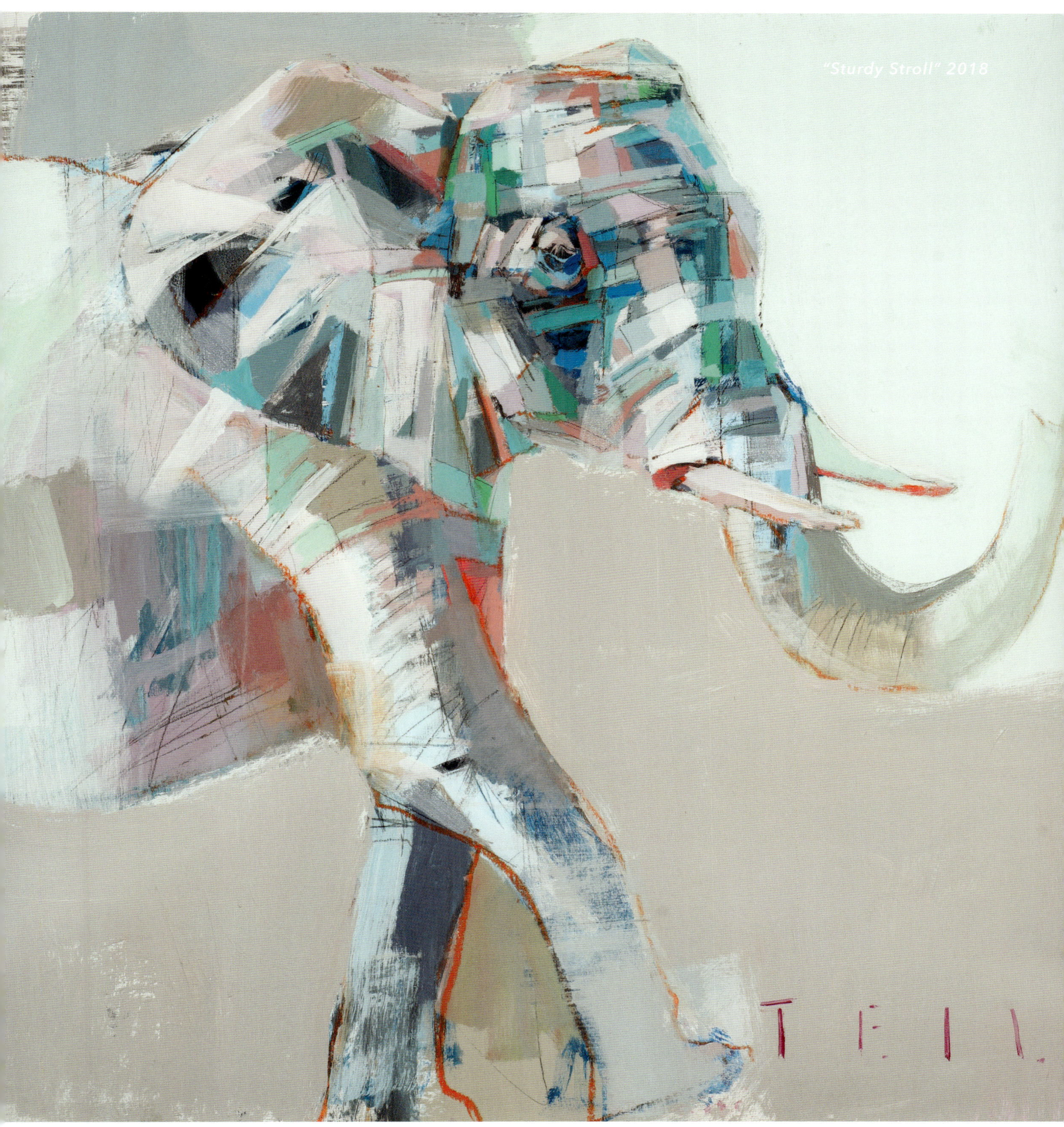

"Sturdy Stroll" 2018

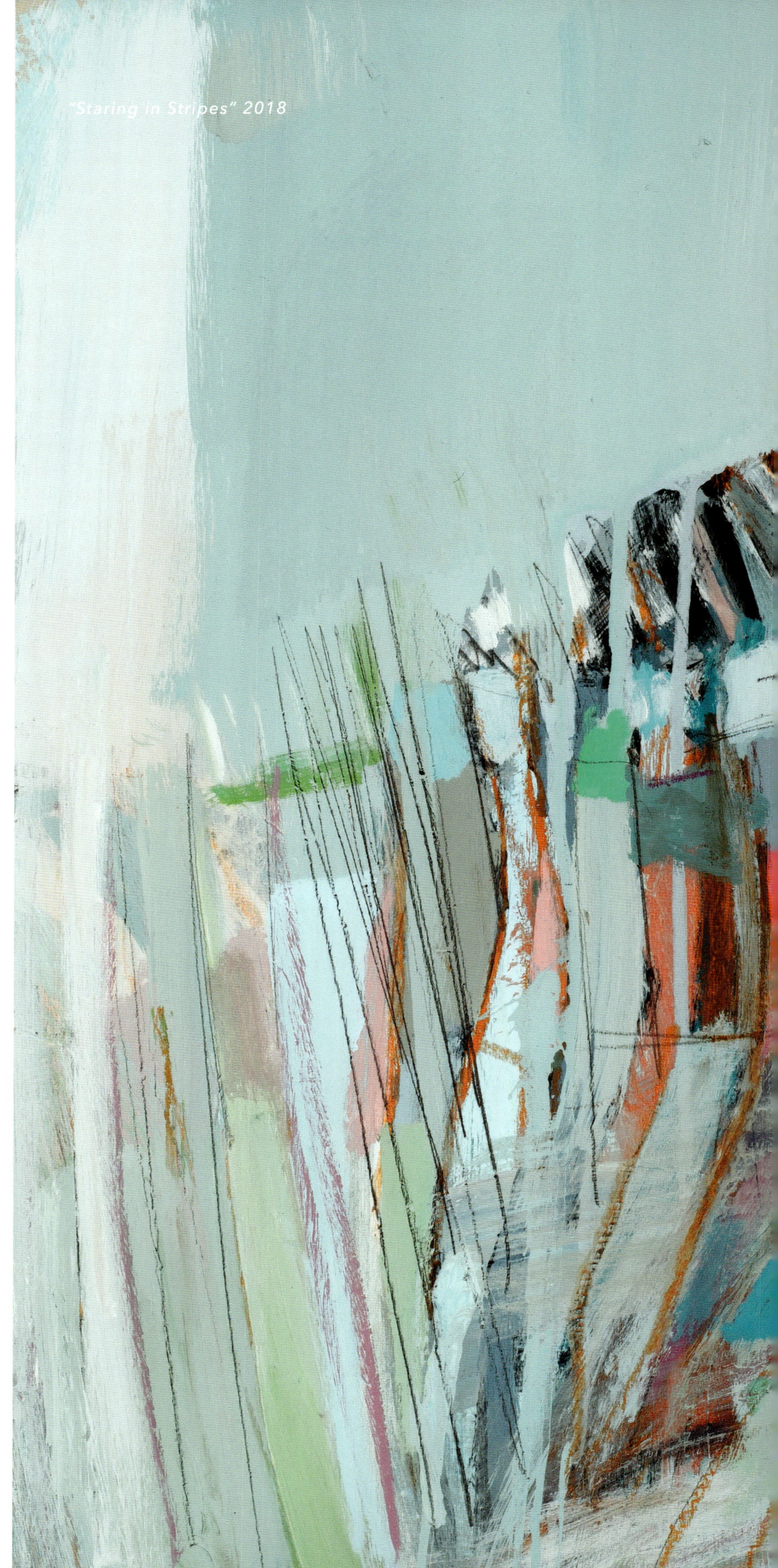

"Staring in Stripes" 2018

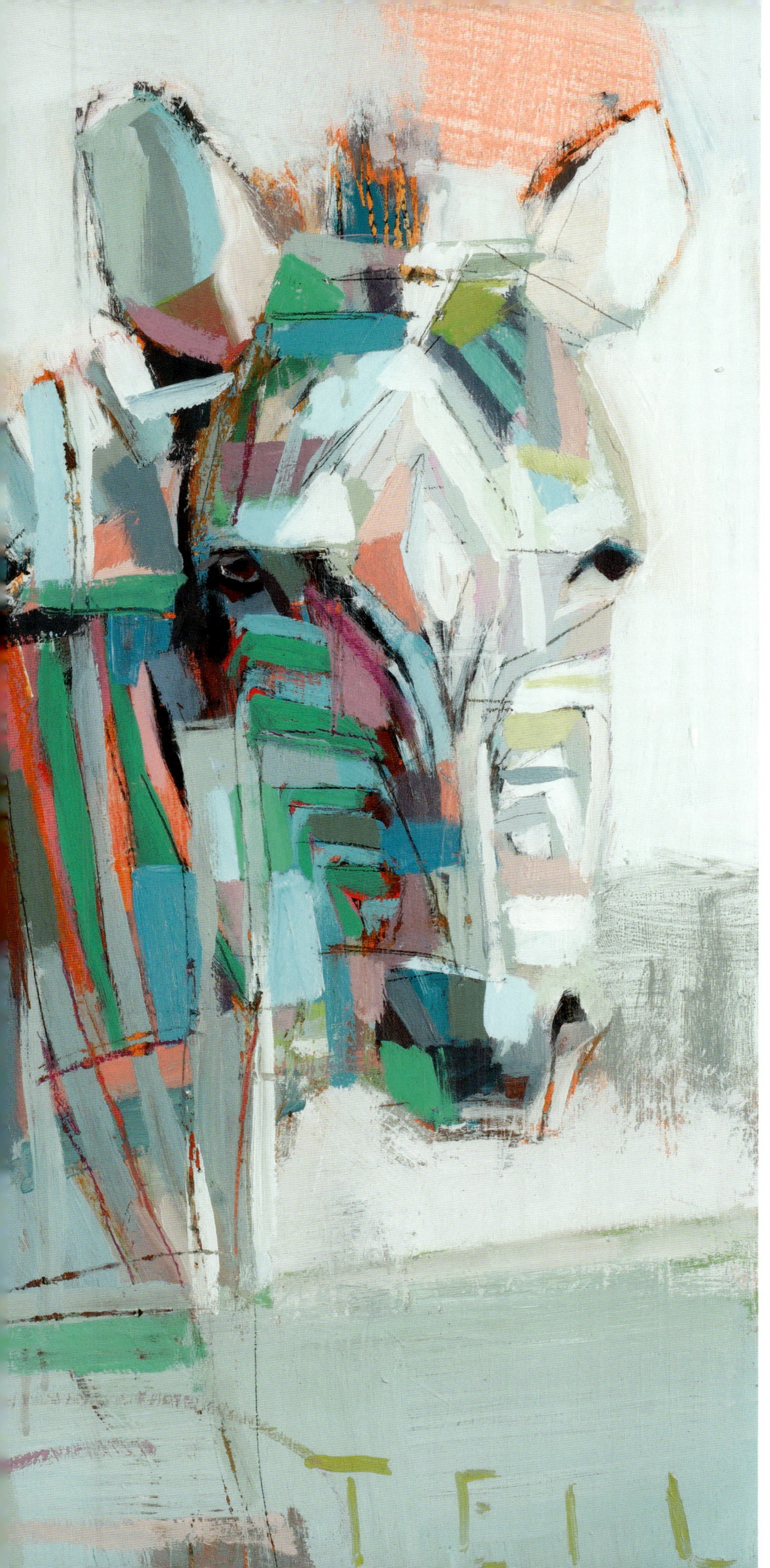

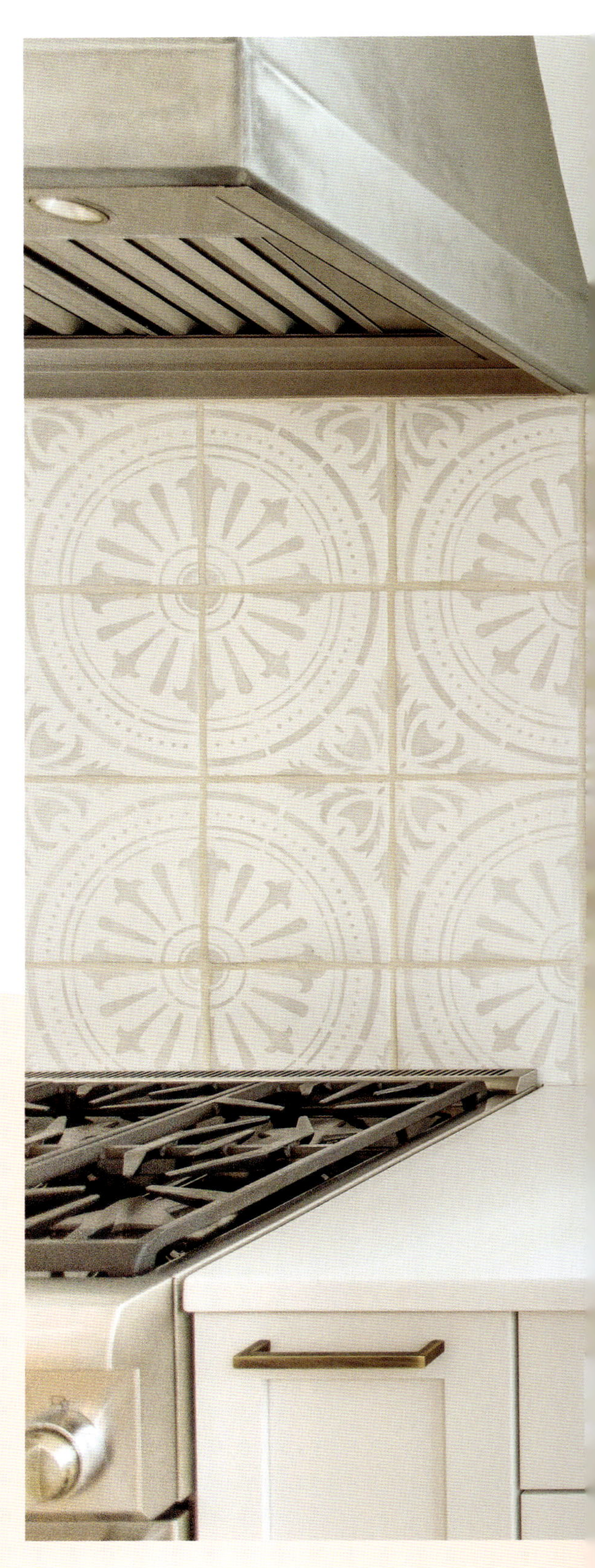

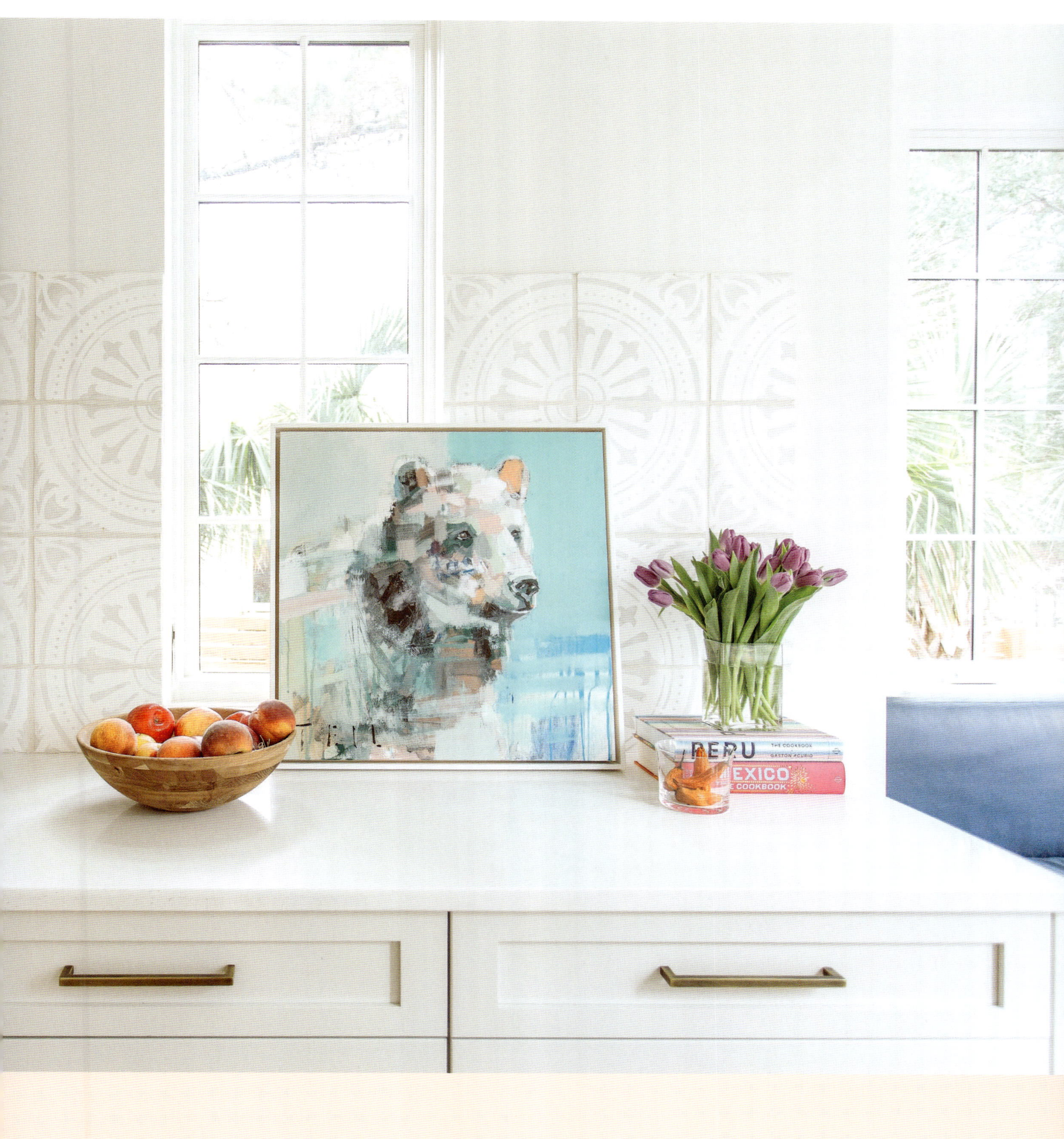
PERU
THE COOKBOOK
GASTON ACURIO
EXICO
COOKBOOK

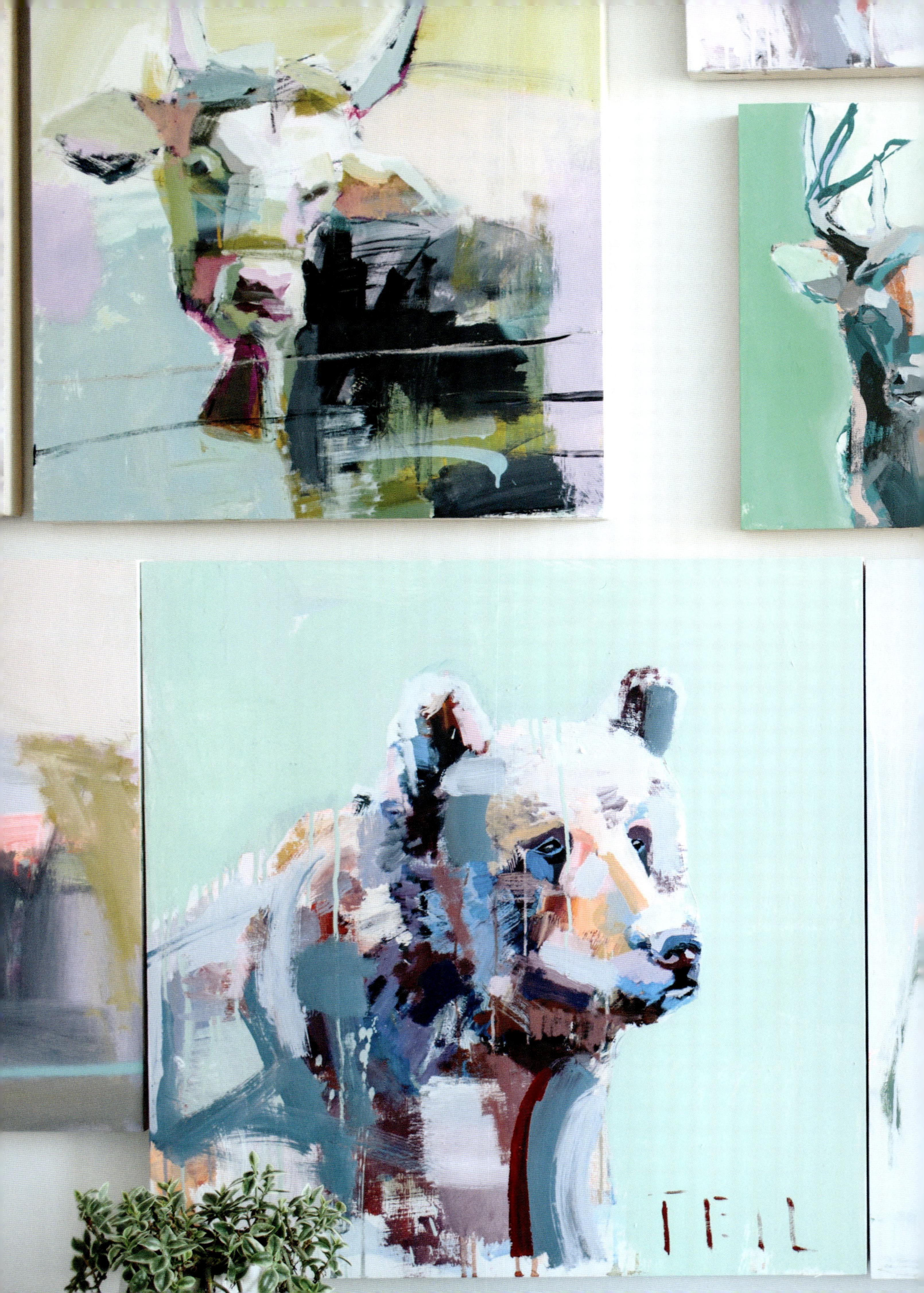
TEIL

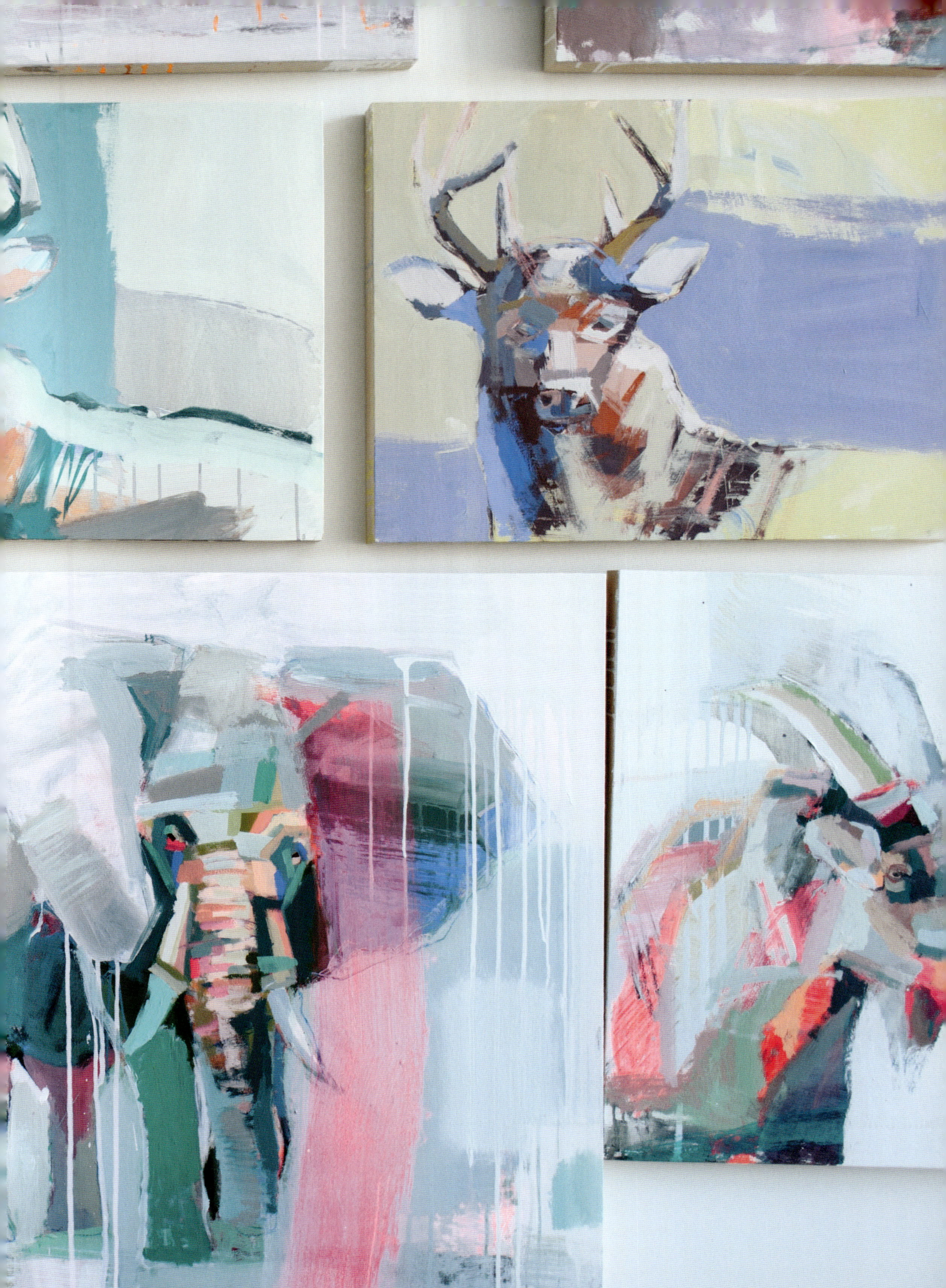

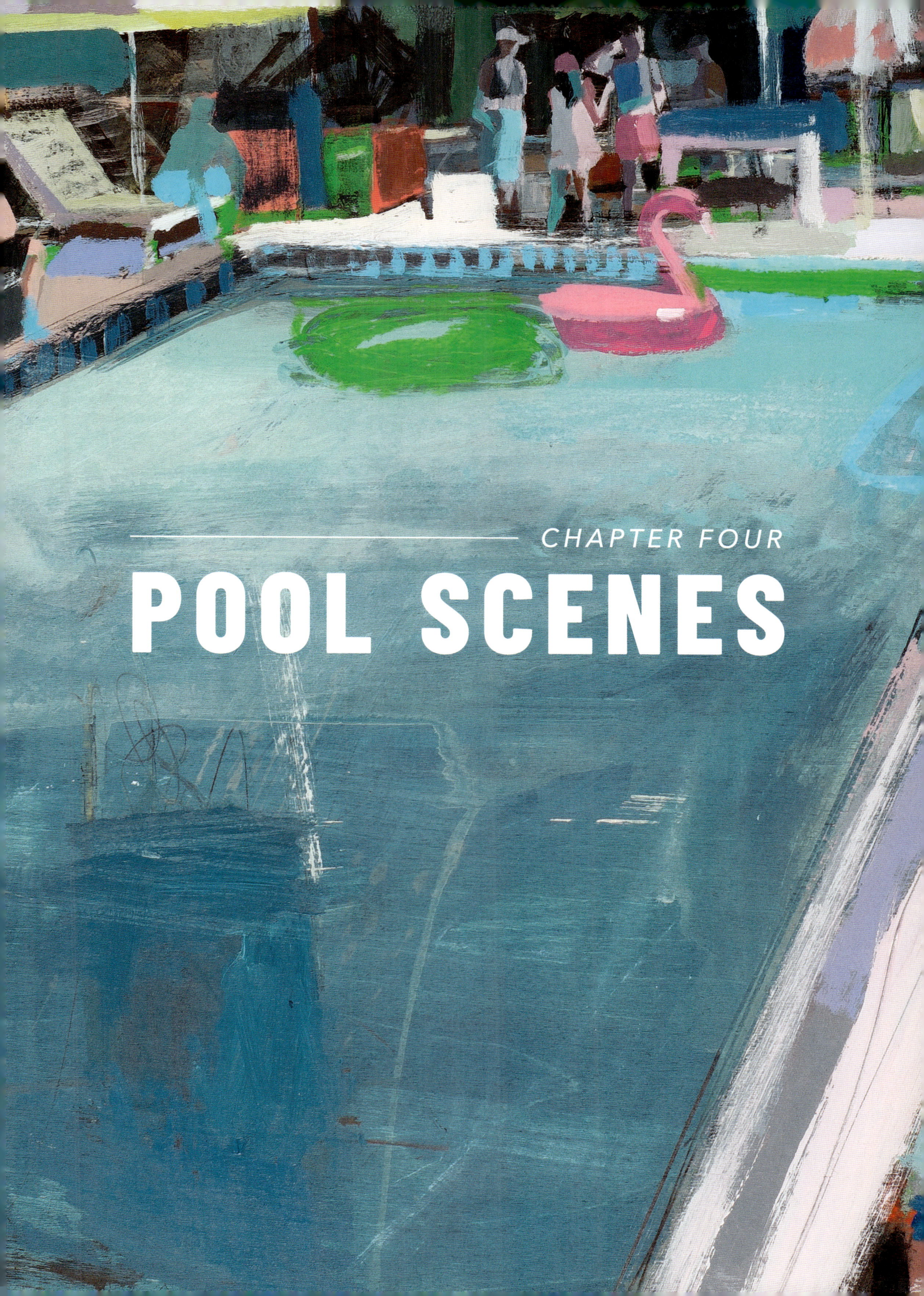

CHAPTER FOUR

POOL SCENES

"Cool Off" 2017

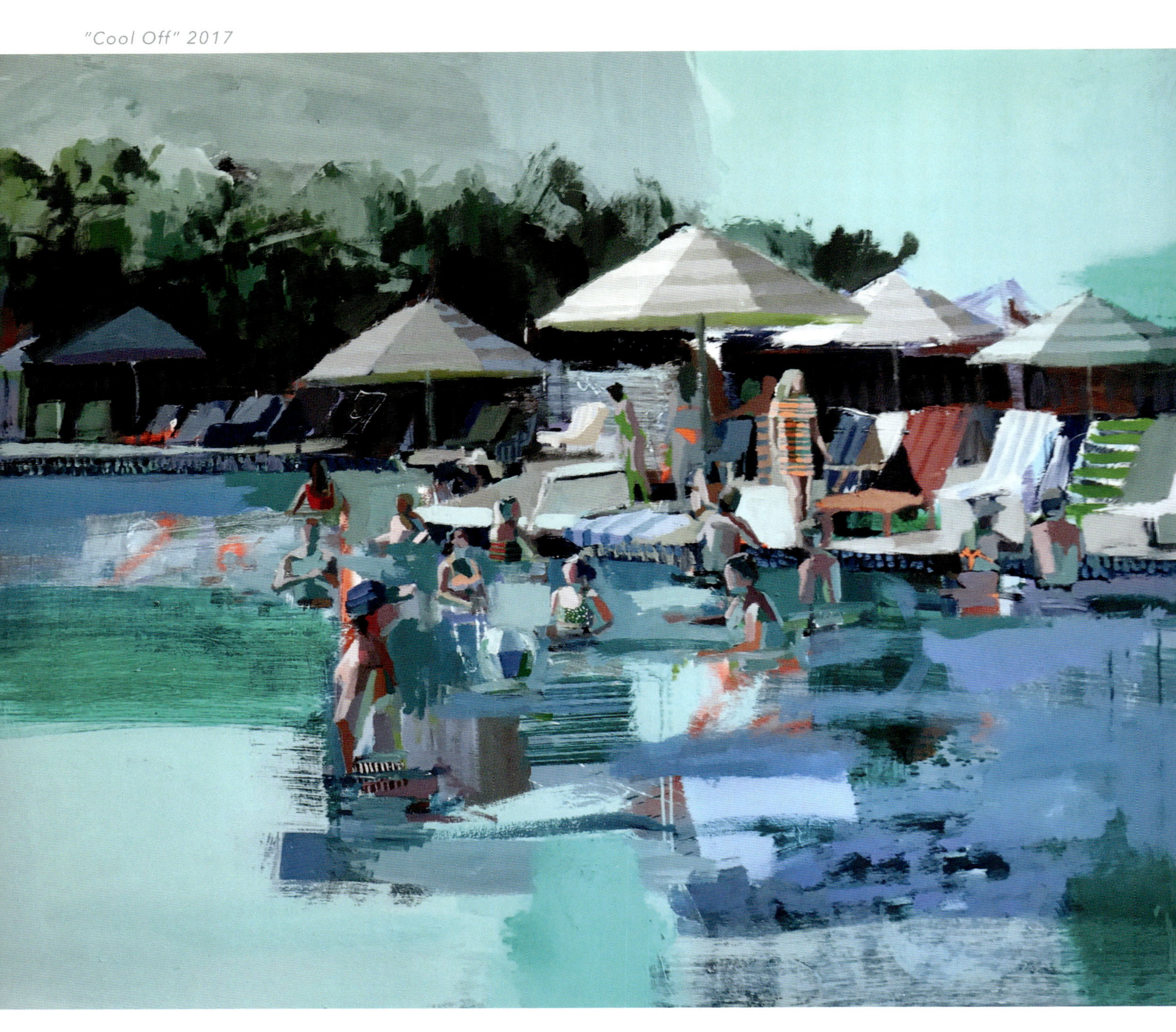

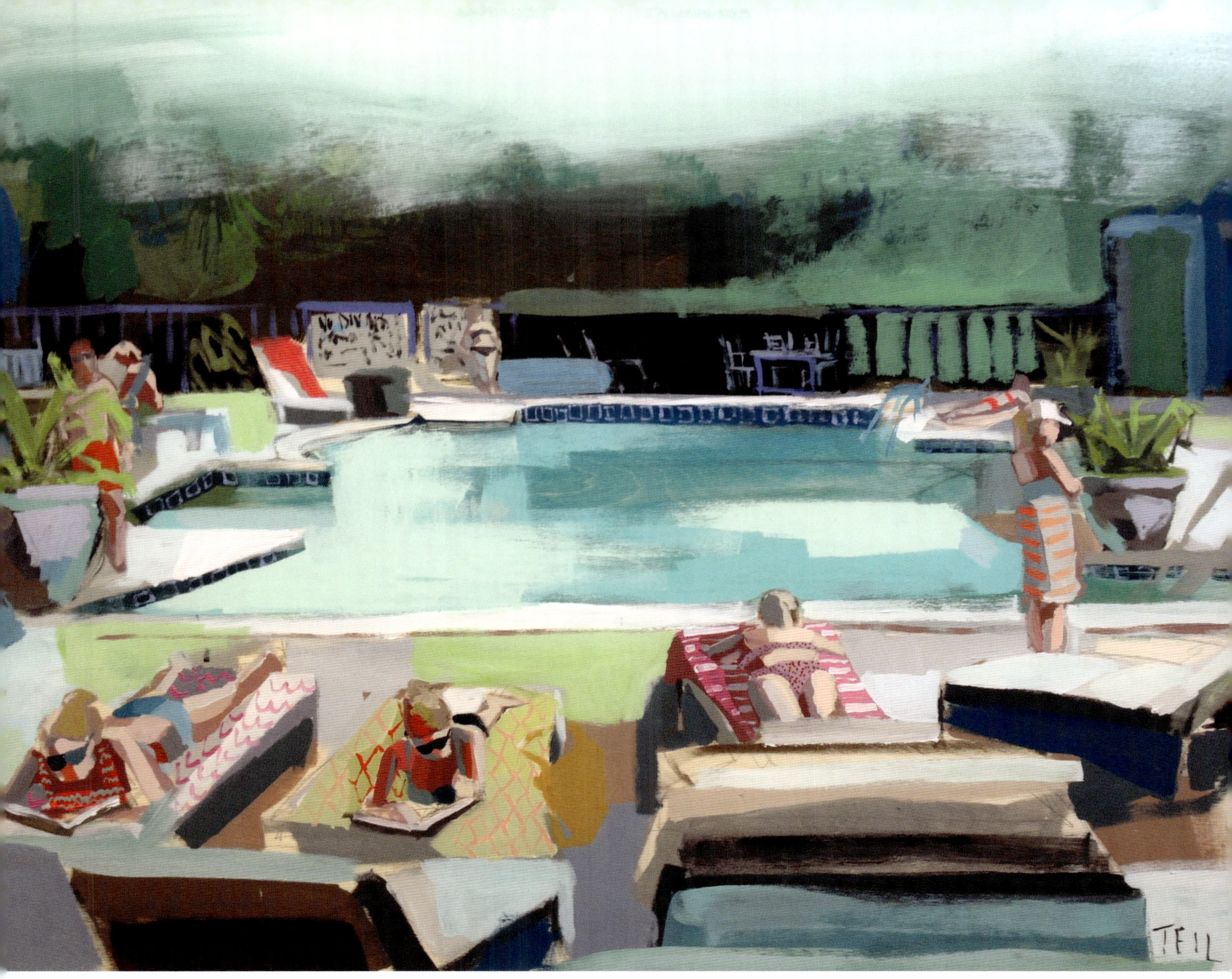

THE POOL SERIES IS

is a continuation of a "summer themed" body of work. They consist of many similar elements, such as the sunbathing figures and umbrellas, but they resonate closer to home with the viewer, depicting something found perhaps in their own backyard.

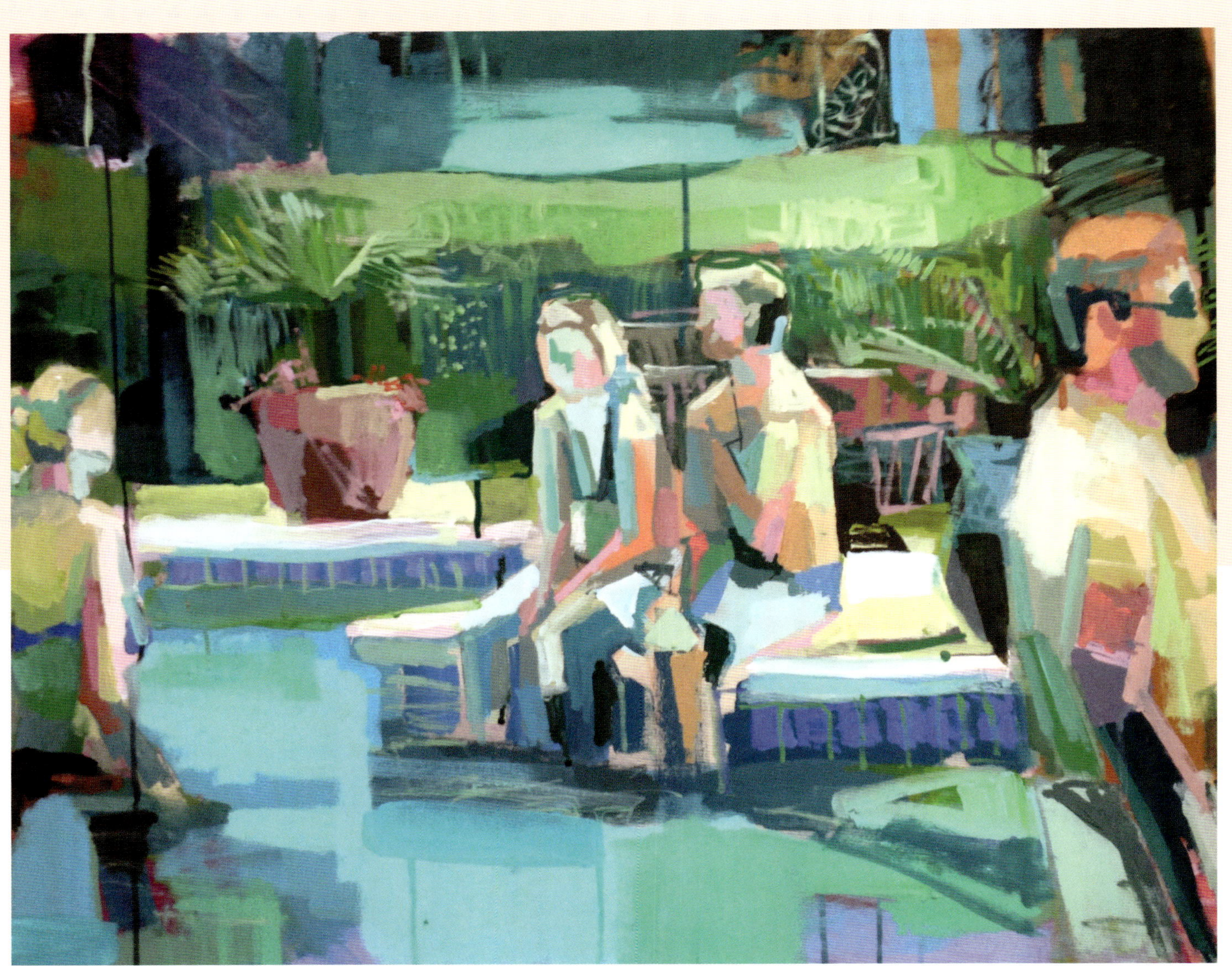

"First Warm Saturday" 2013

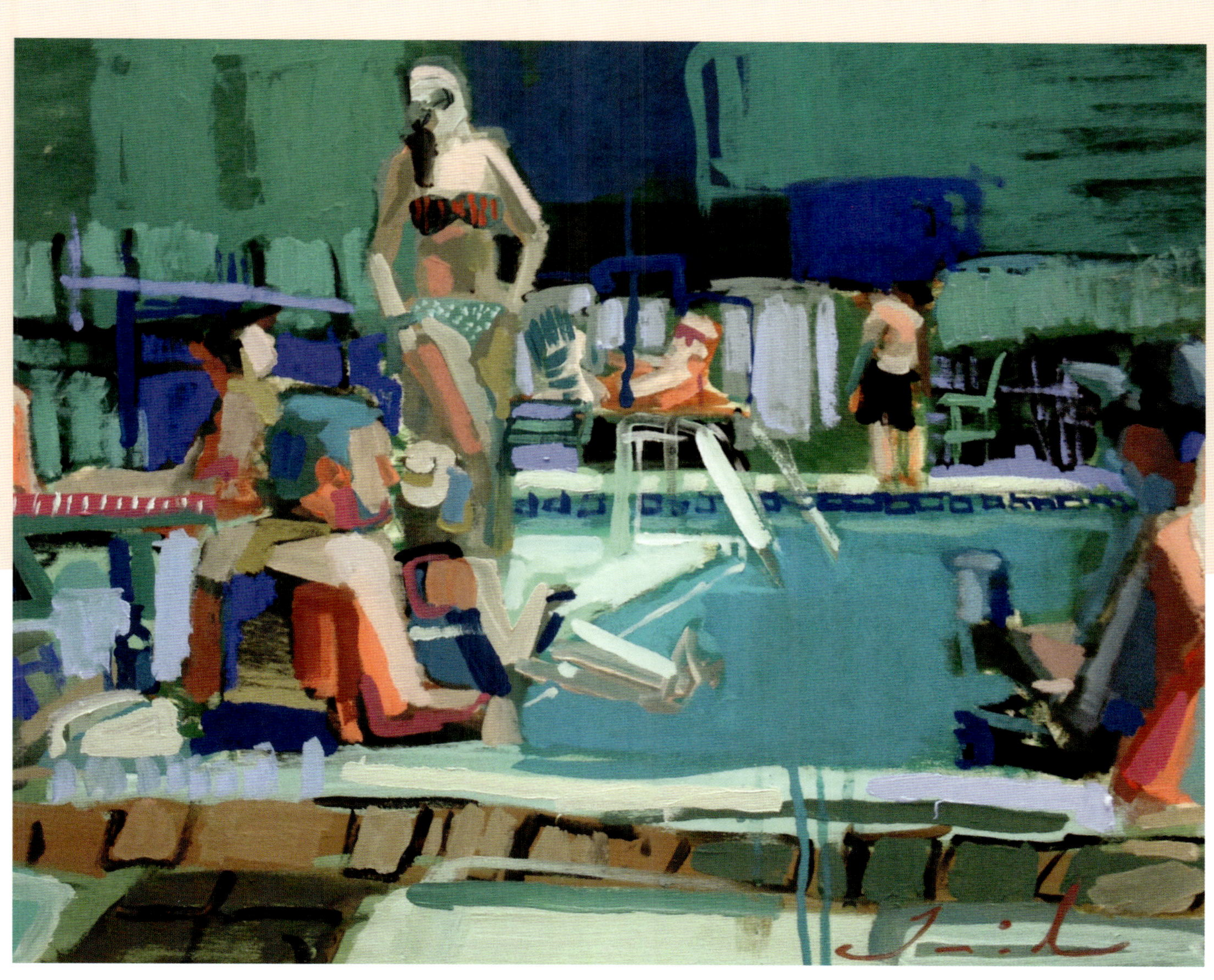

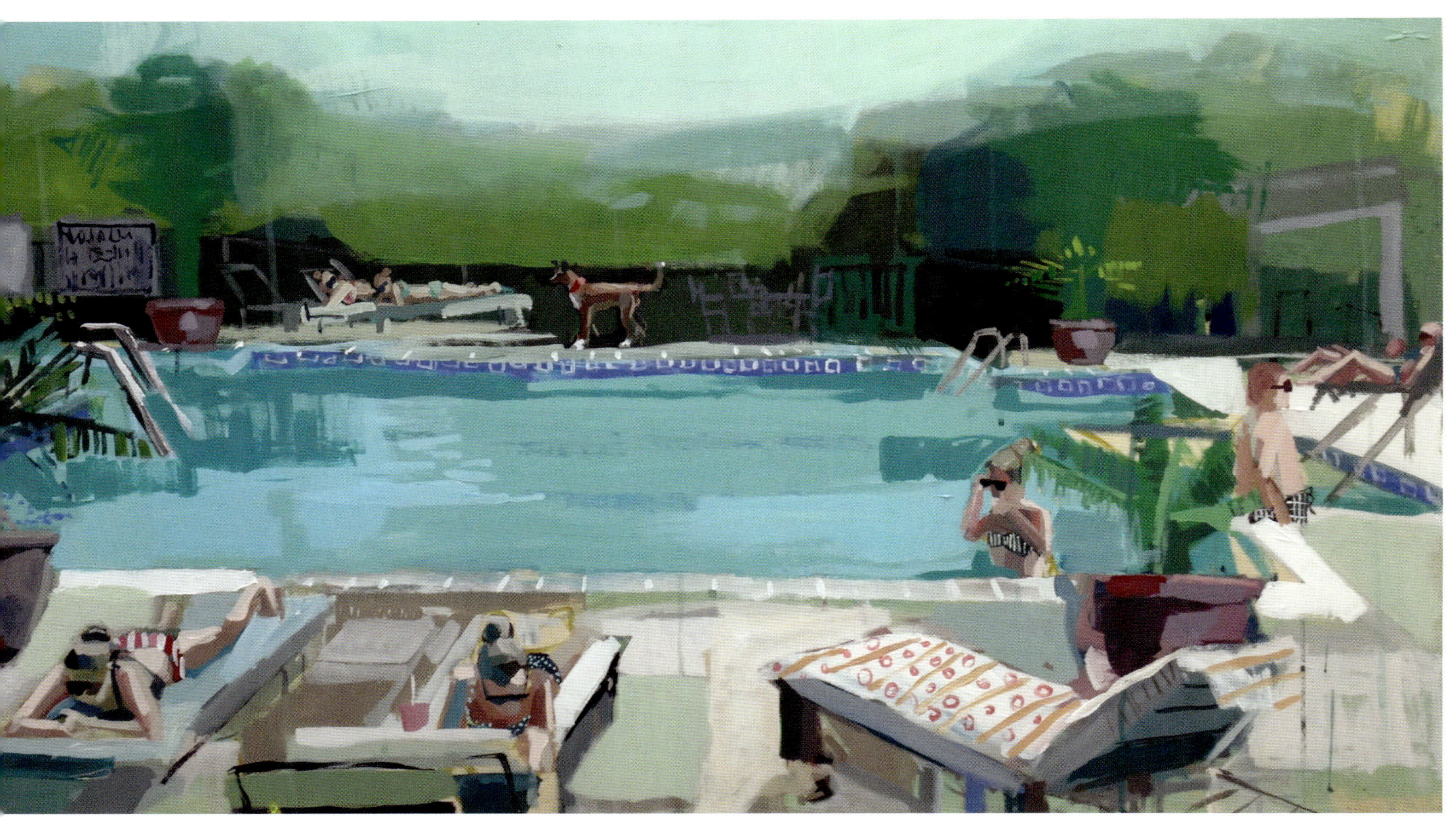

DEEPER TONES EXIST with each pool scene, while still remaining sunny and playful. Each one contains shadowed landscaping and vast fields of "deep-end" blues that portray a subtle moodiness. One aspect of this series I

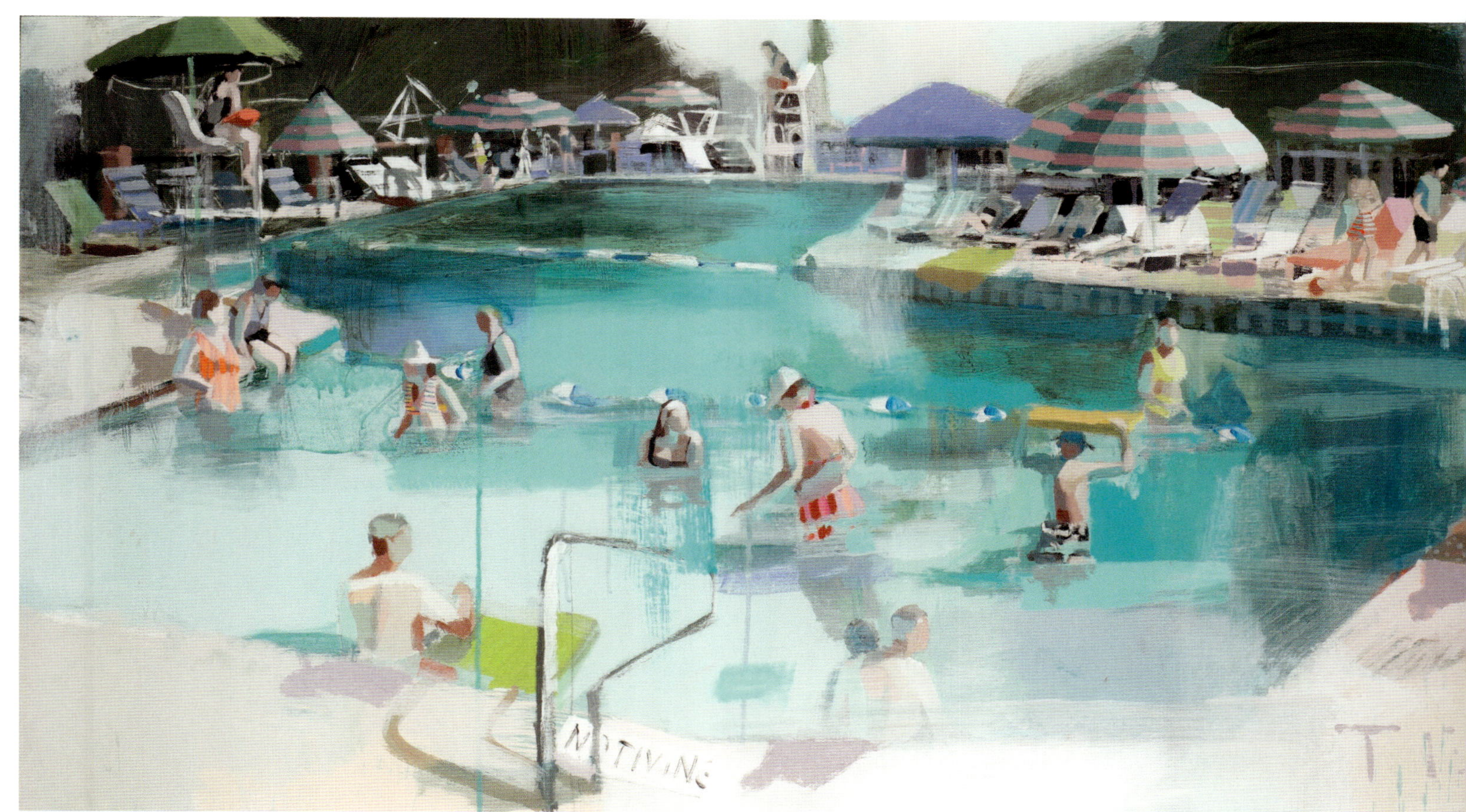

"Pool Chatter" 2018

enjoyed emulating is the reflecting aqua blues bouncing off the swimmer's skin tone. Light and reflection play a leading role throughout this body of work, which is a continuing theme throughout these water-themed series.

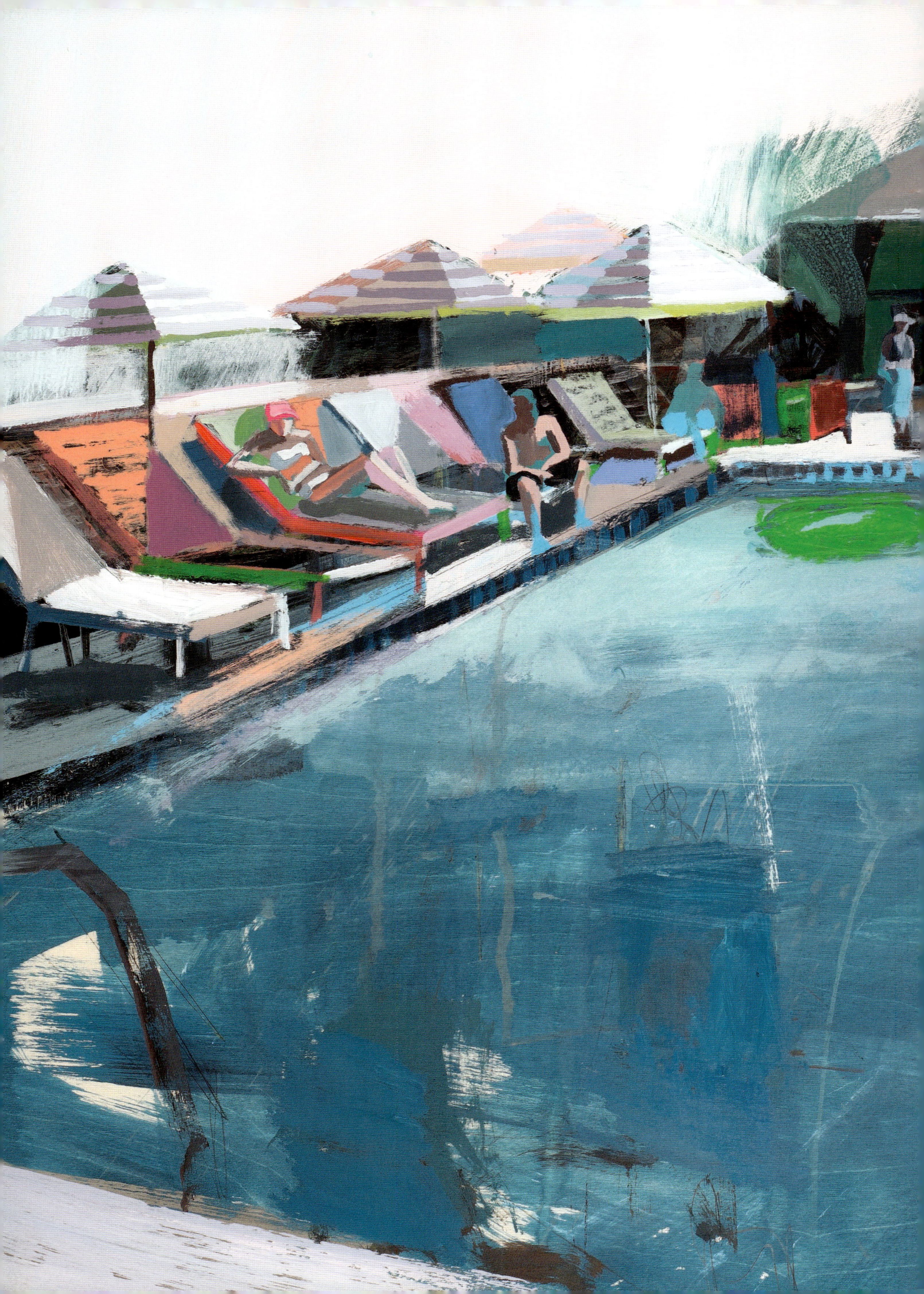

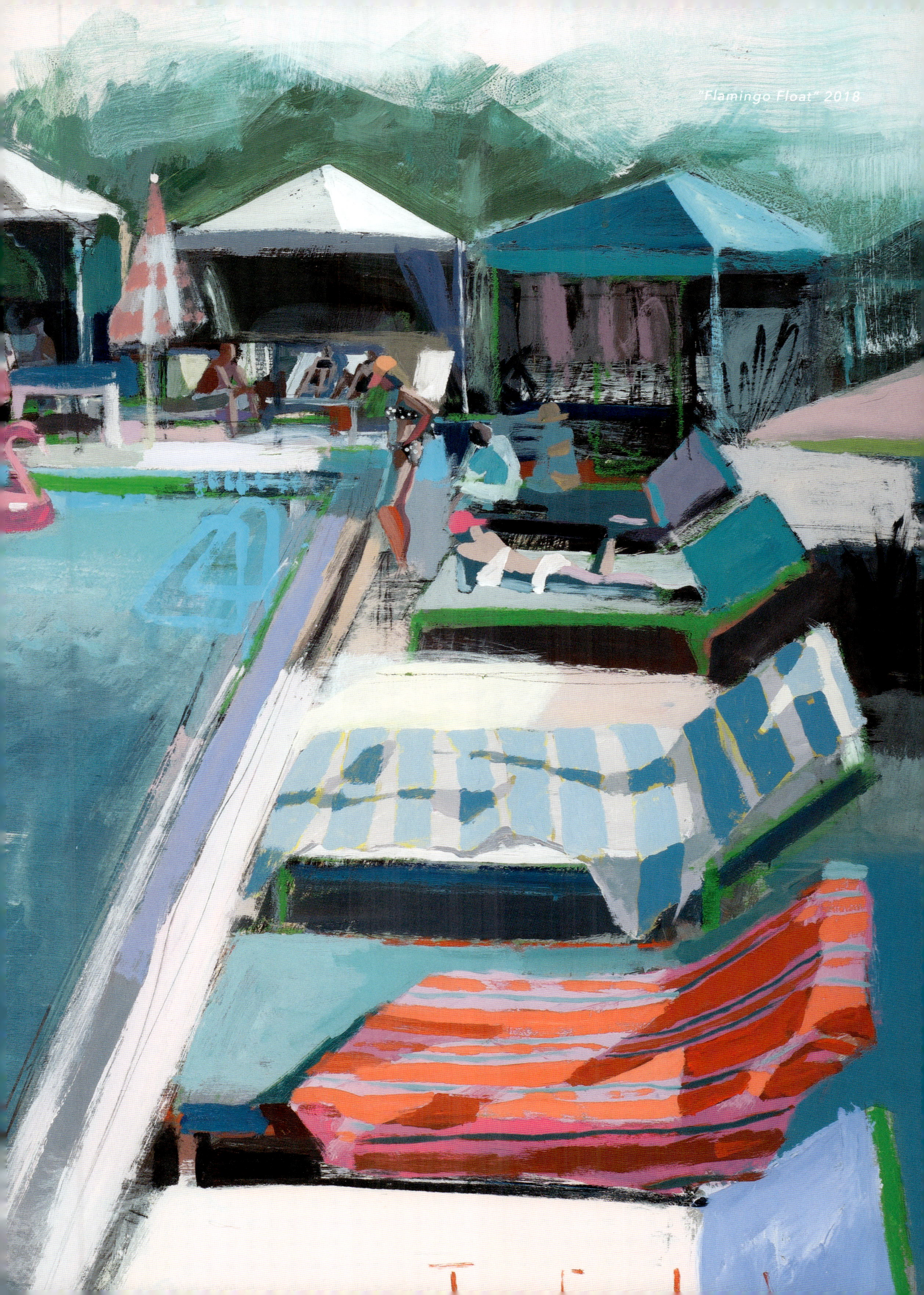

"Flamingo Float" 2018

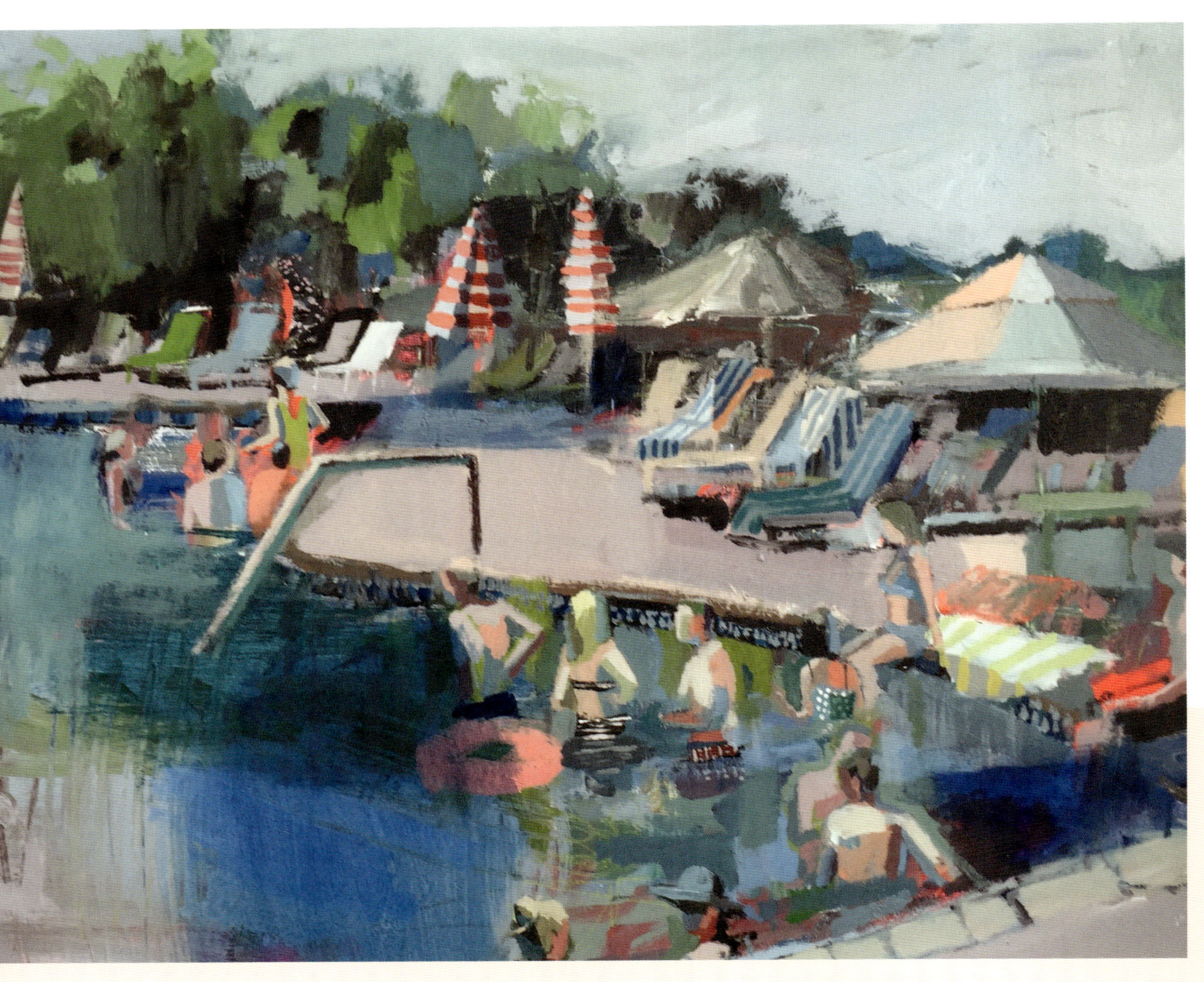

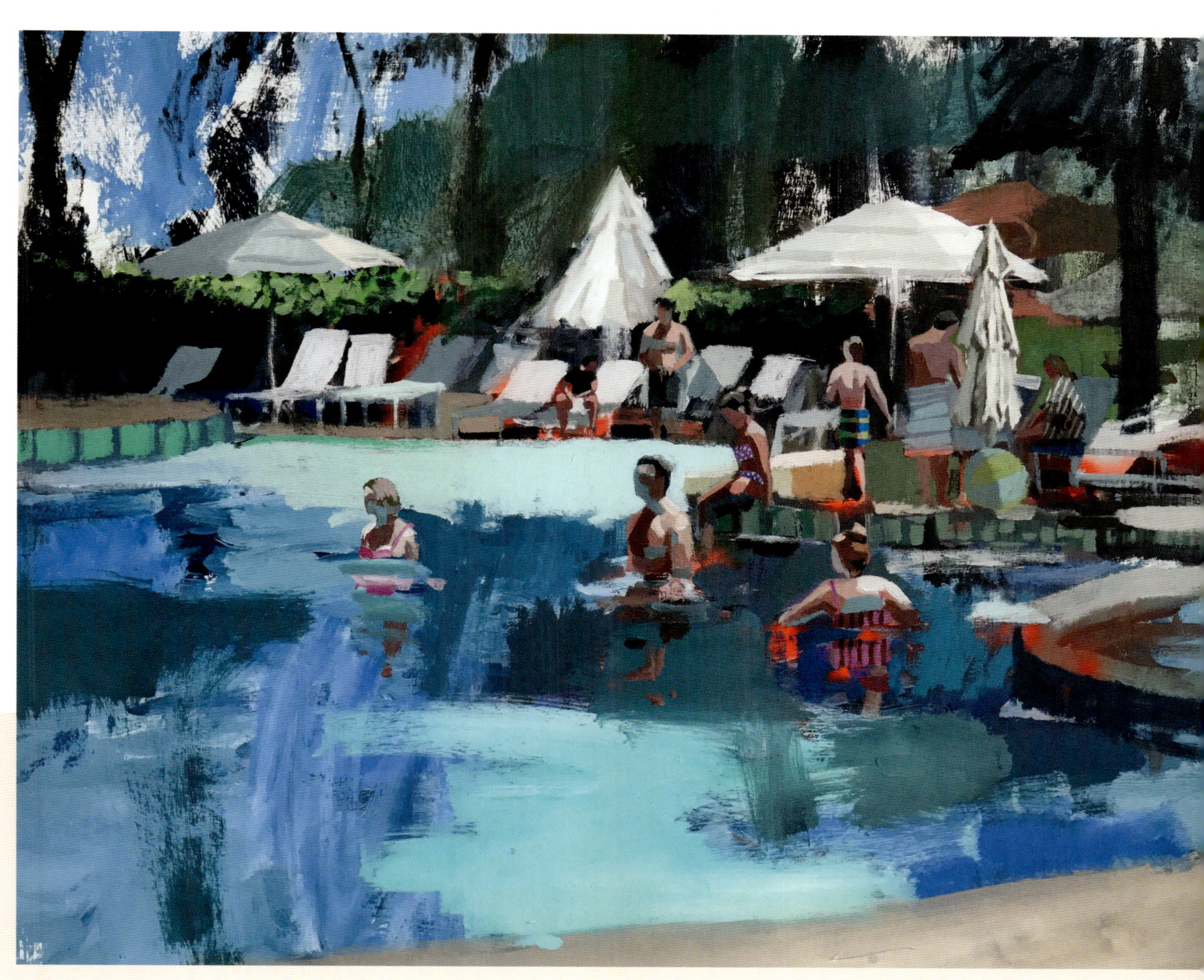

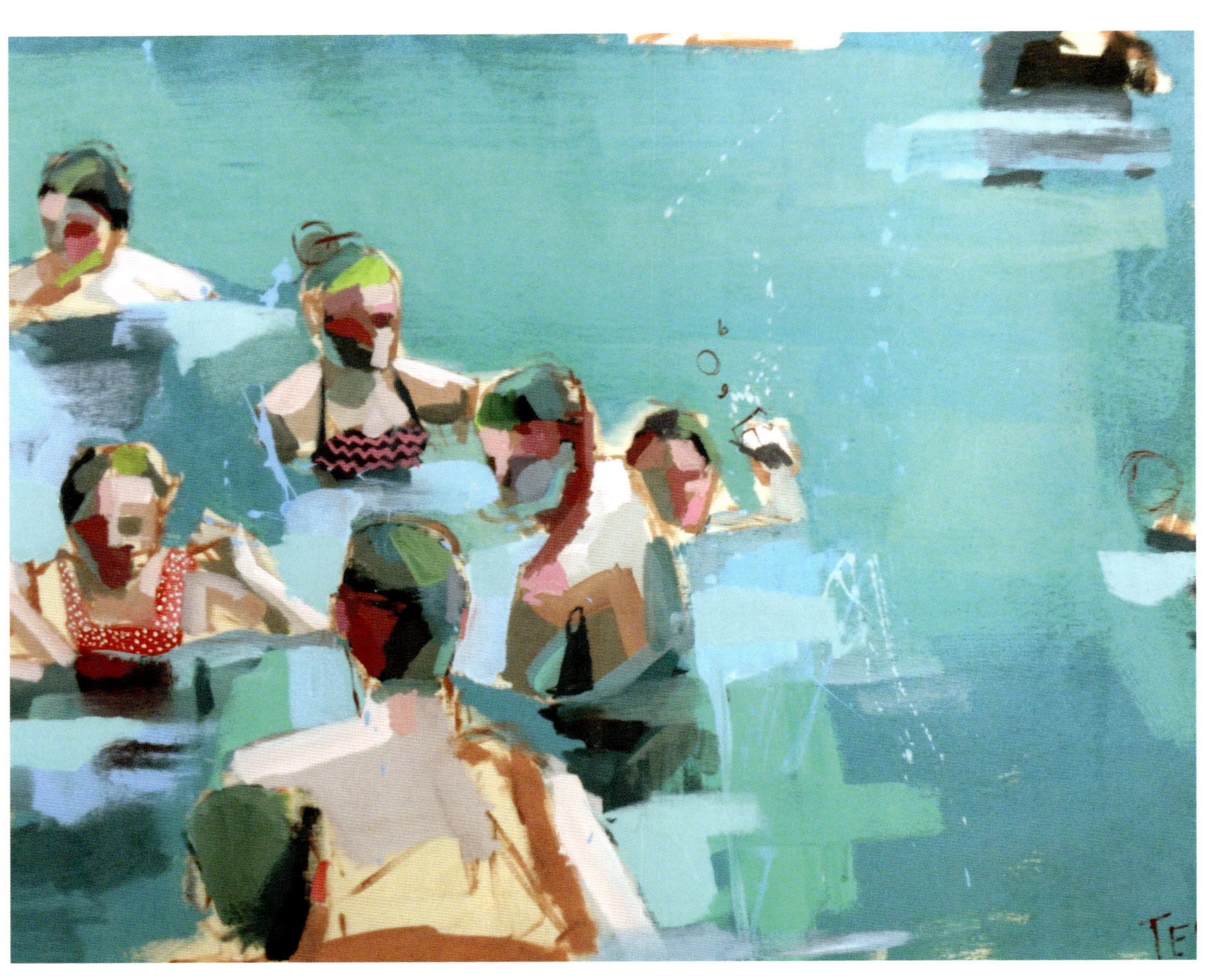

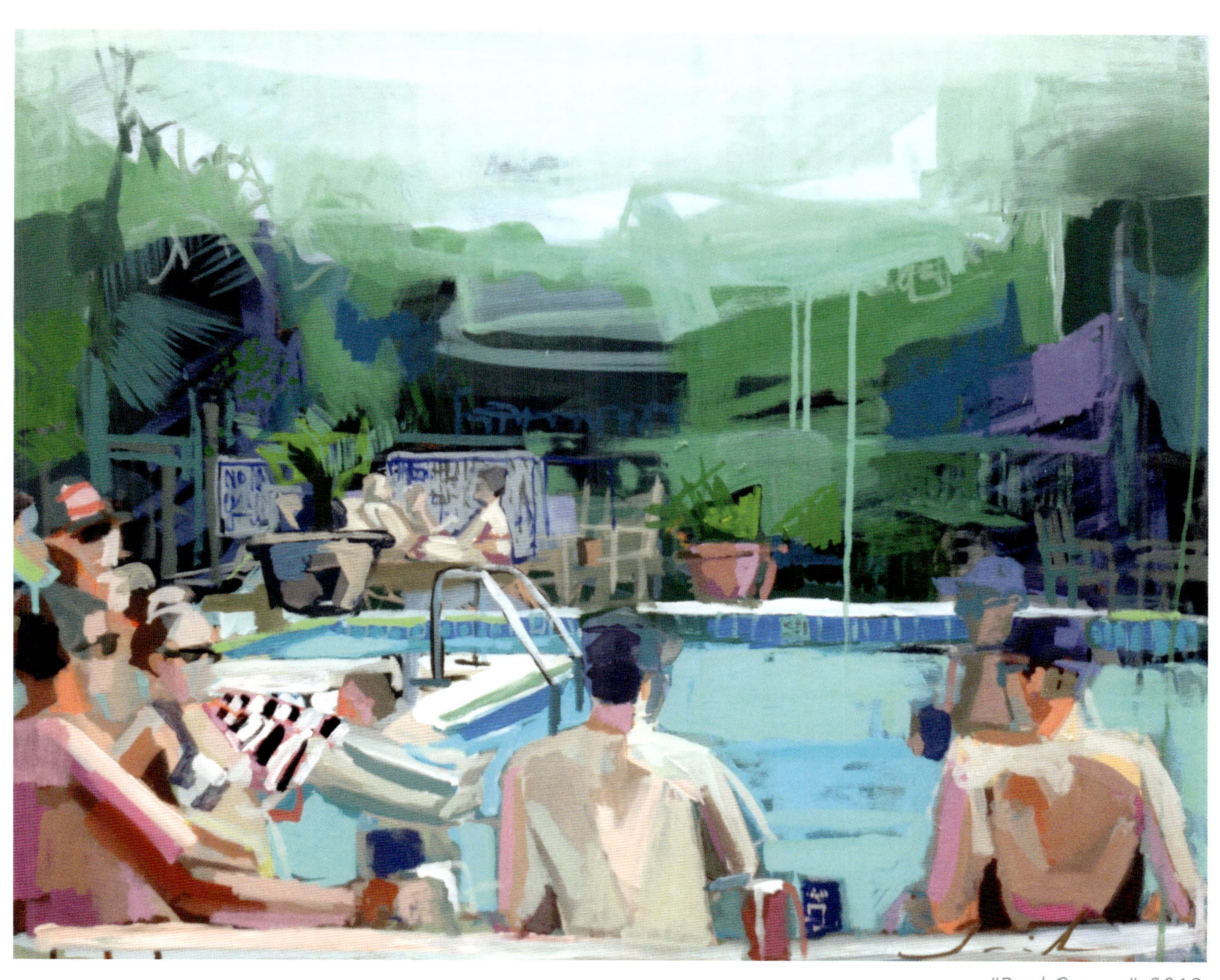

"Pool Corner", 2013

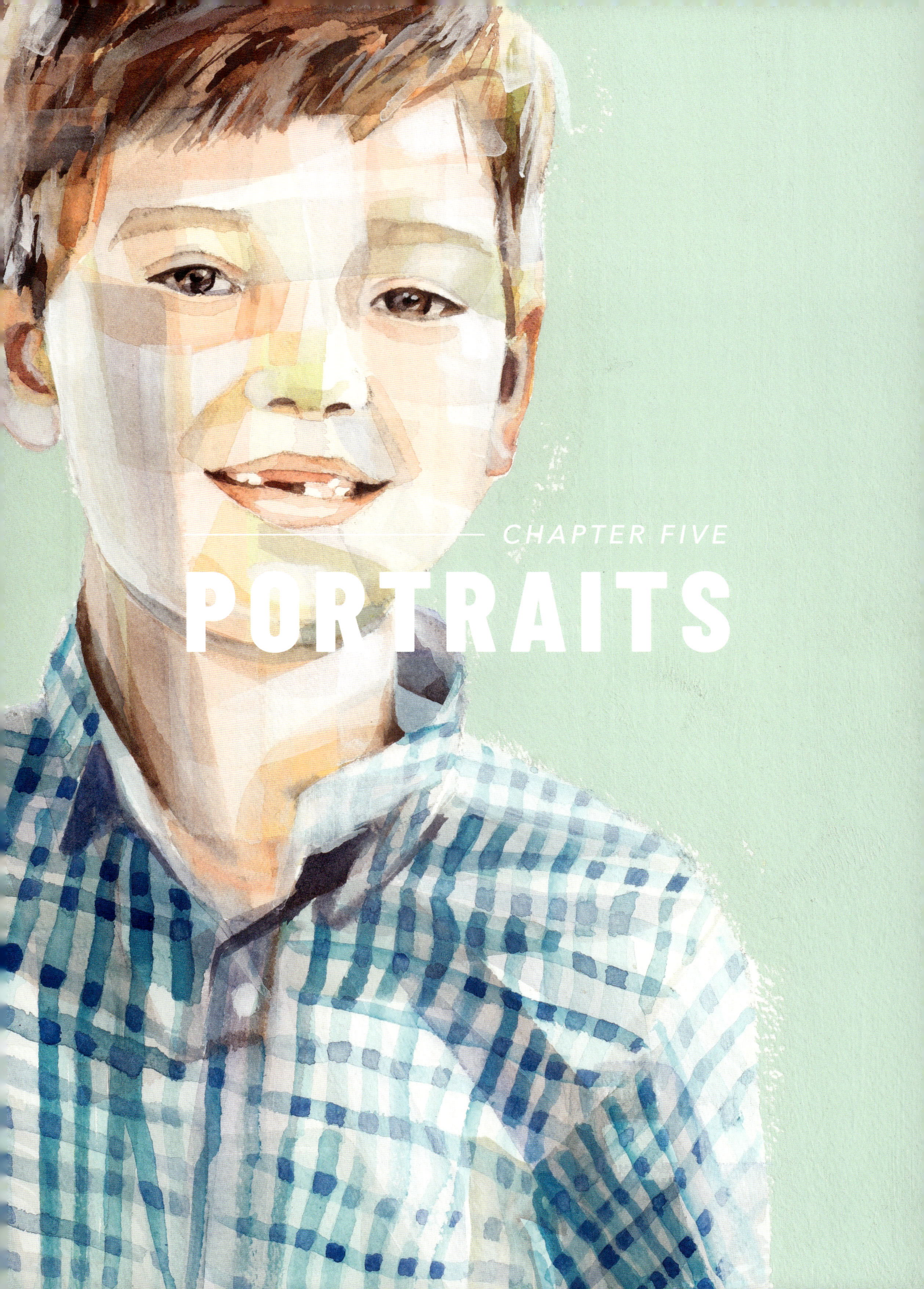

CHAPTER FIVE

PORTRAITS

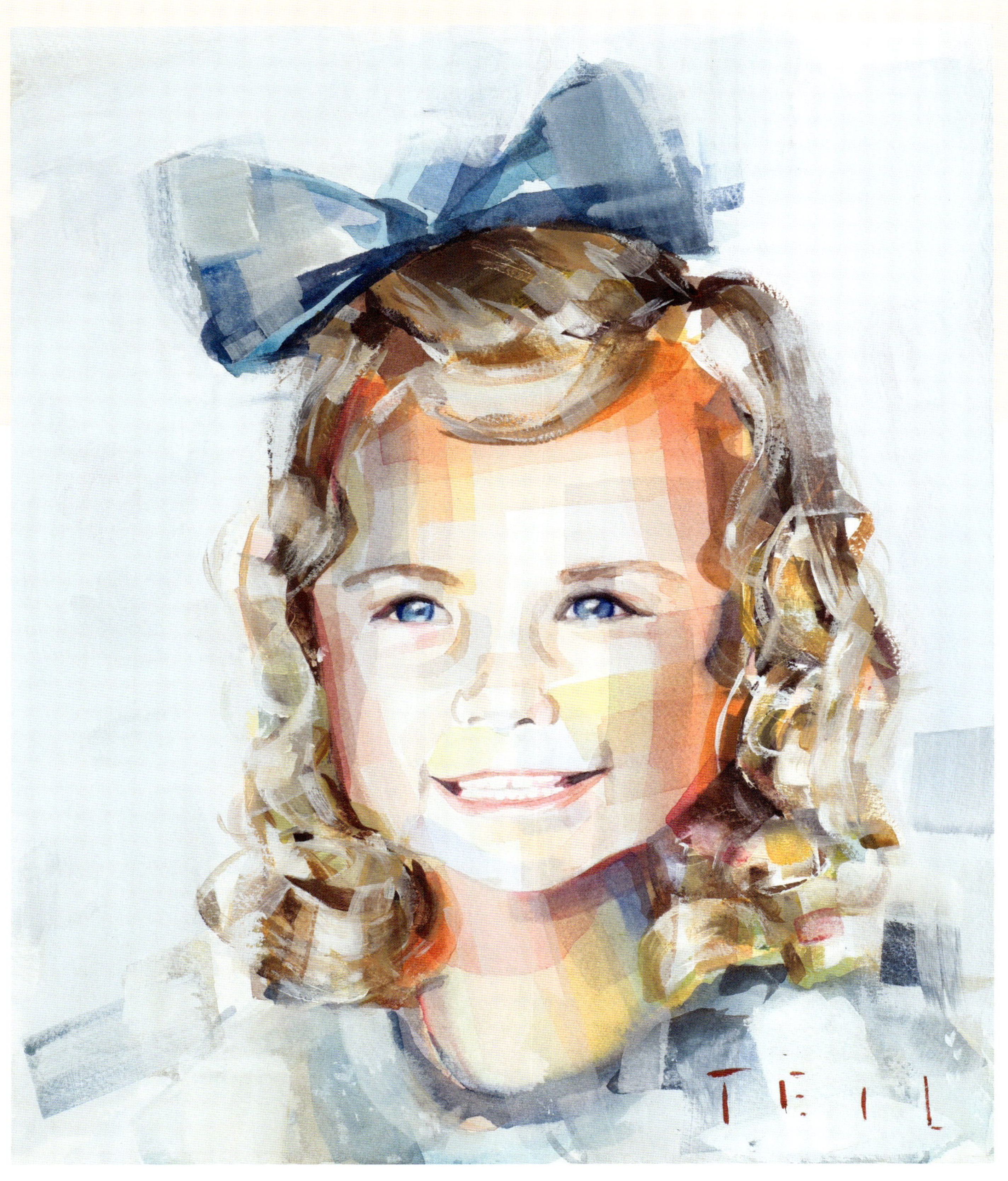
TEIL

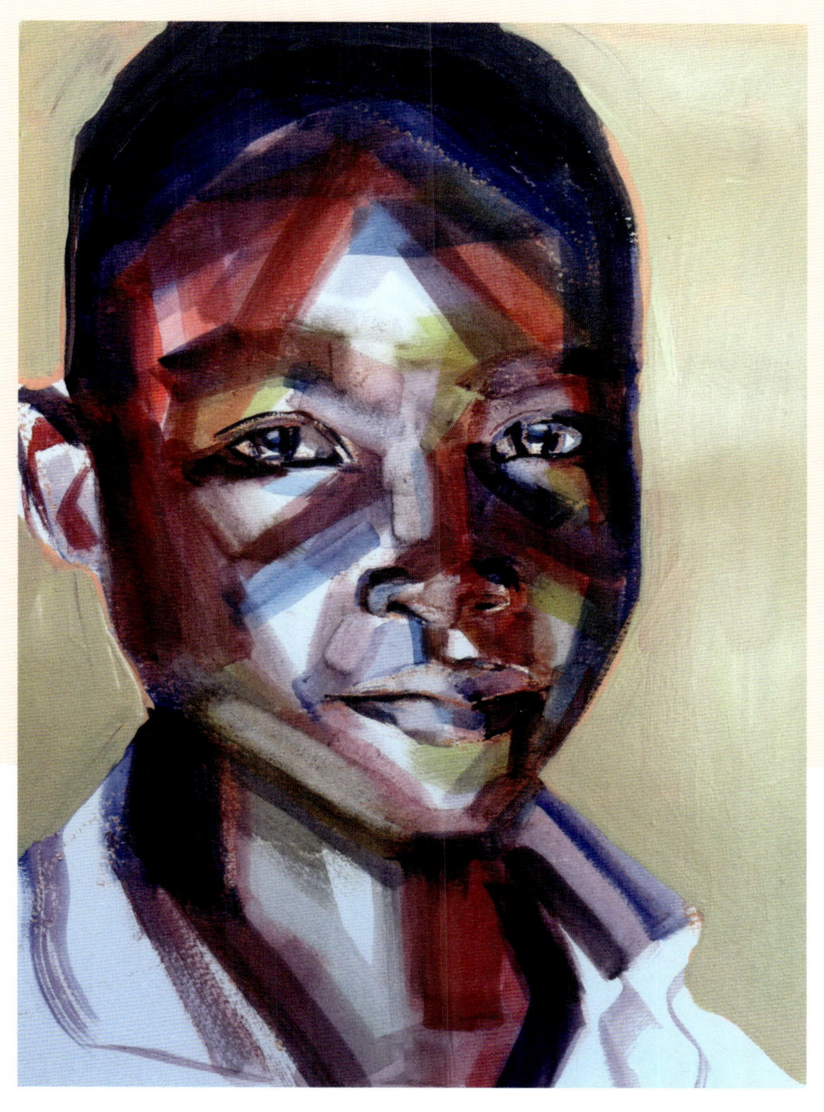

DURING THE SUMMER

of 2012, I was asked to fill in for a watercolor class at the local Charleston studio space, Redux Contemporary Art Center. In order to refresh myself on the medium, I pulled out a few small tubes buried at the bottom of my supply drawer and my cleanest brushes lying nearby. I scrolled through my recent photos of a trip to Uganda and came across a photo of an African woman wearing a subtle smirk. It had been several years since I worked with watercolors, but I picked up my square-shaped brush and began this African portrait with watered-down, bold strokes.

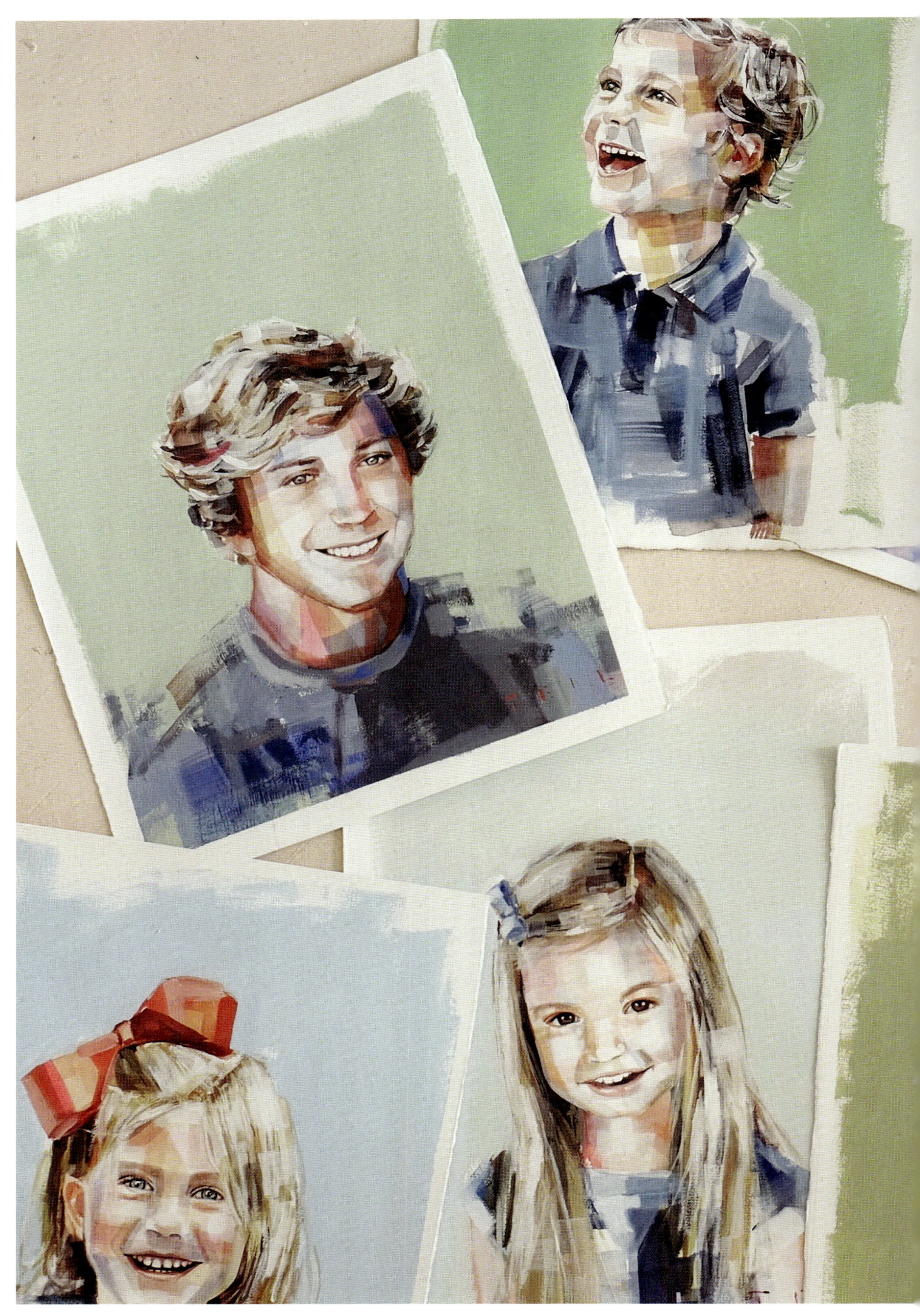

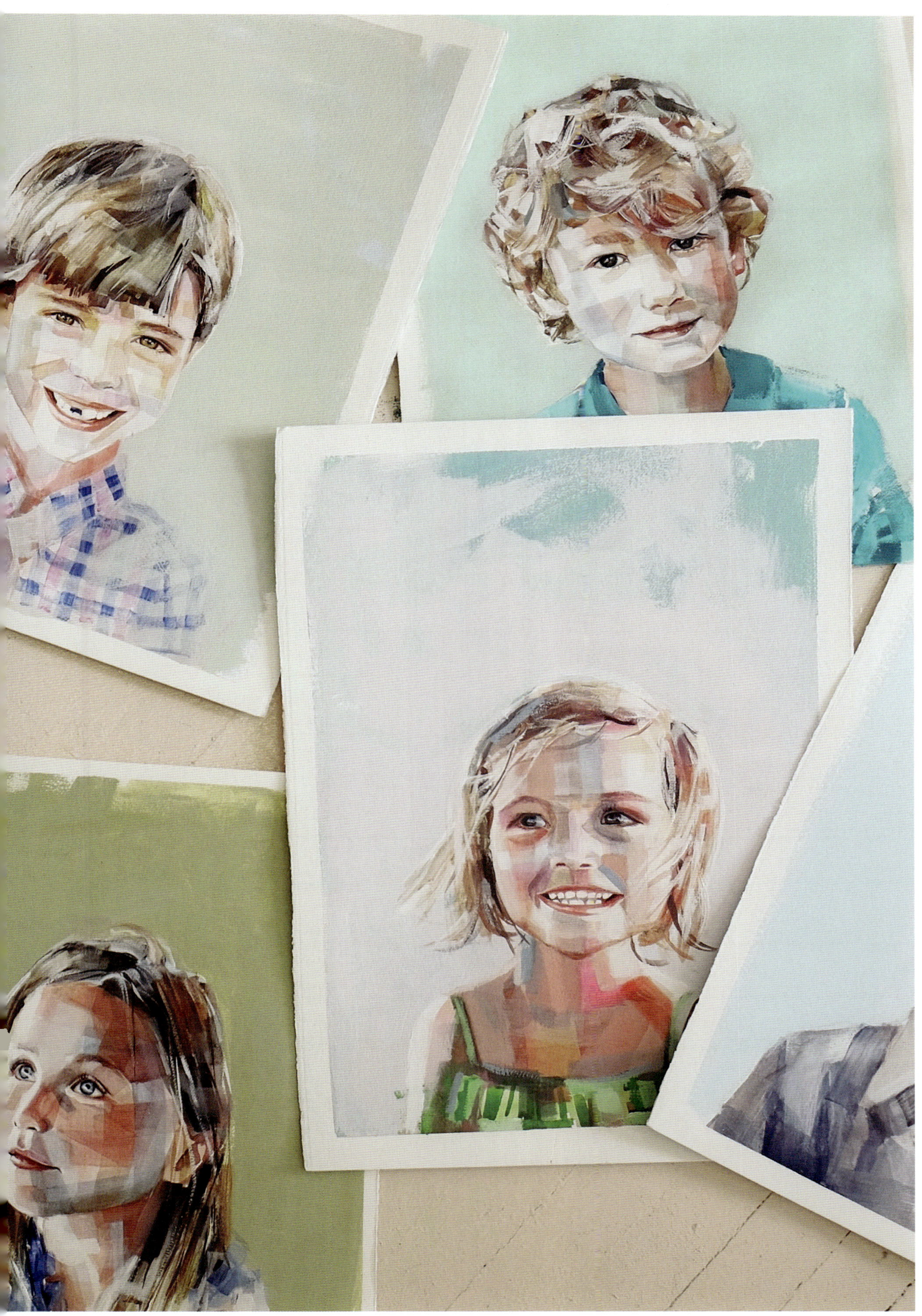

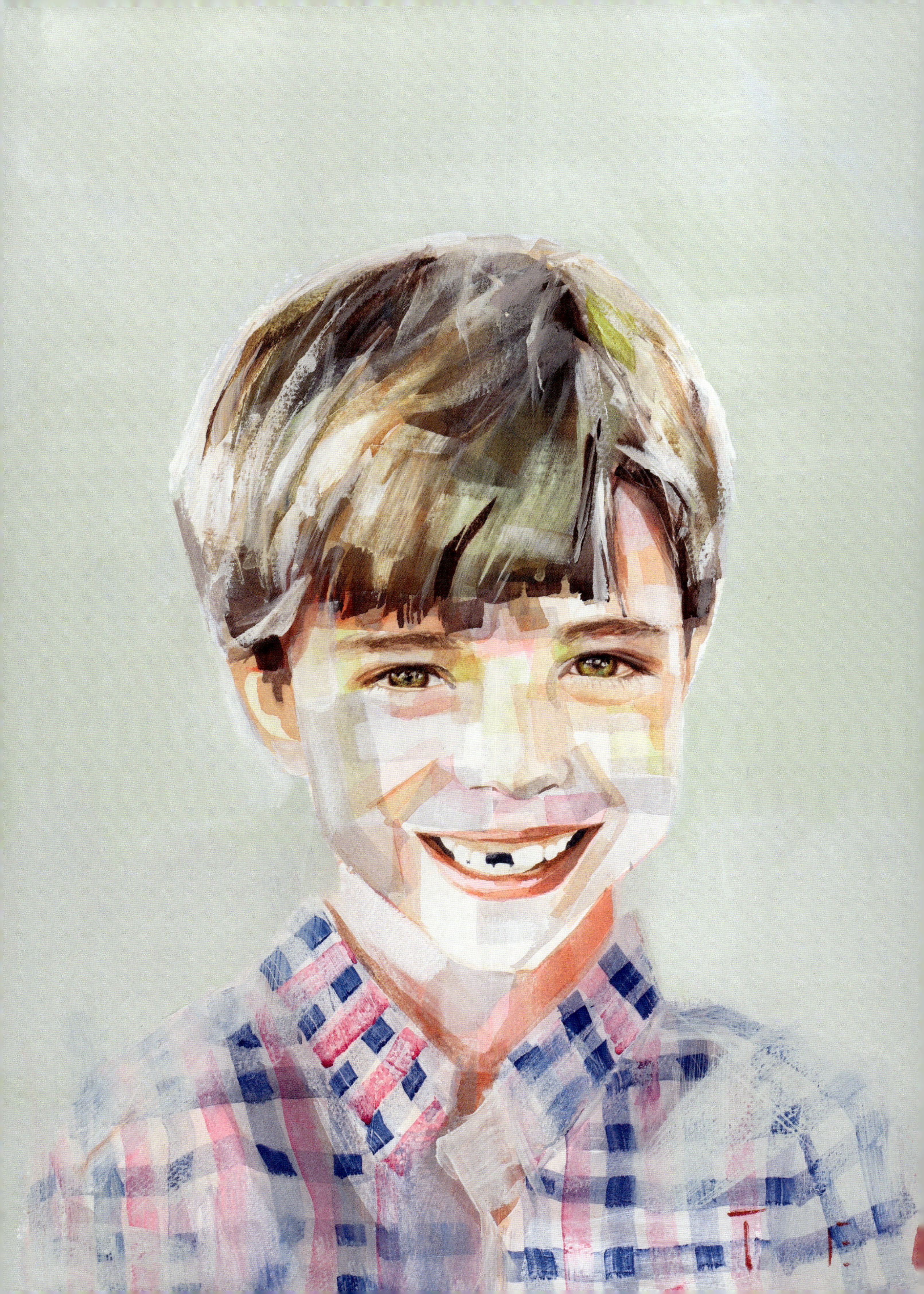

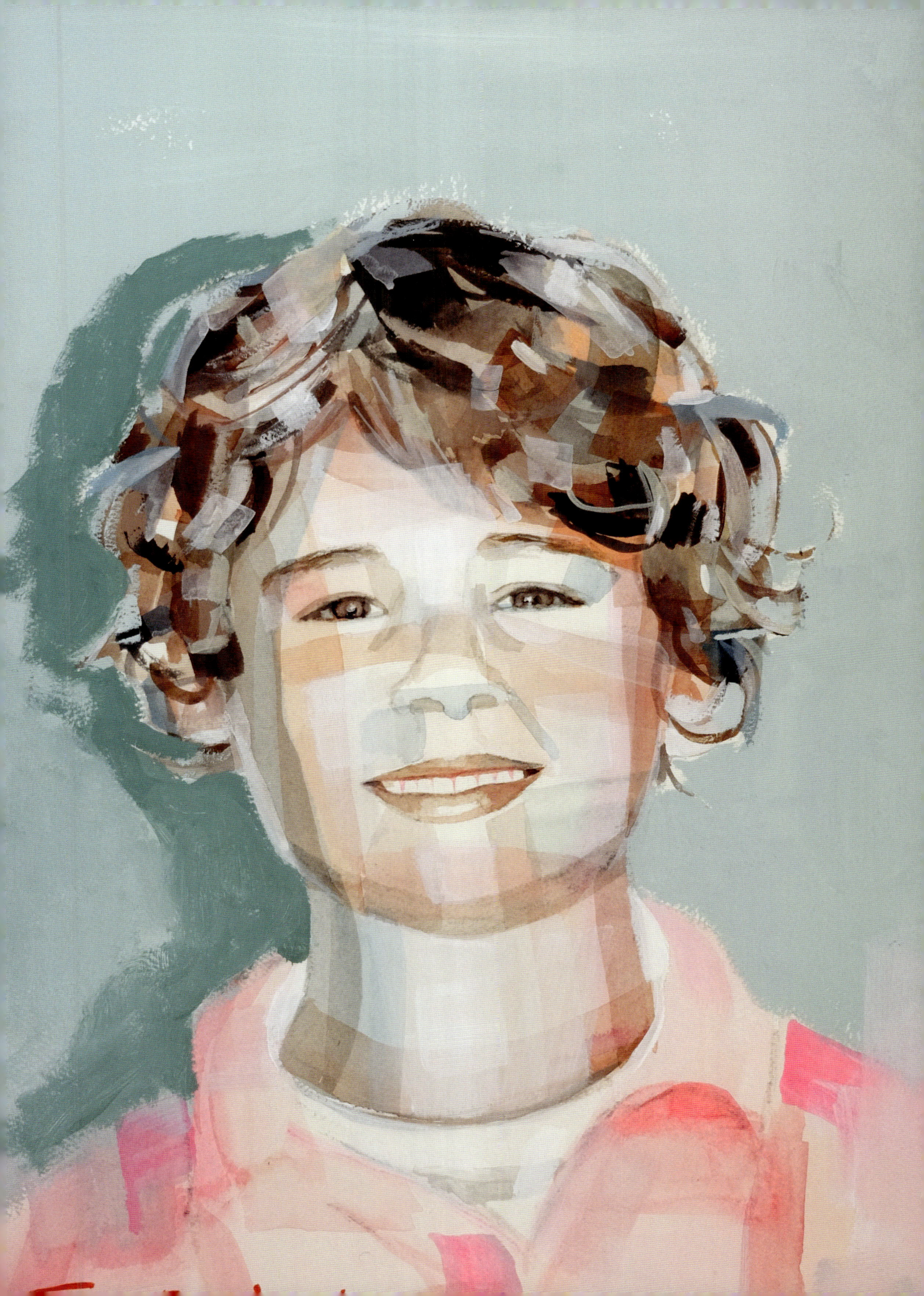

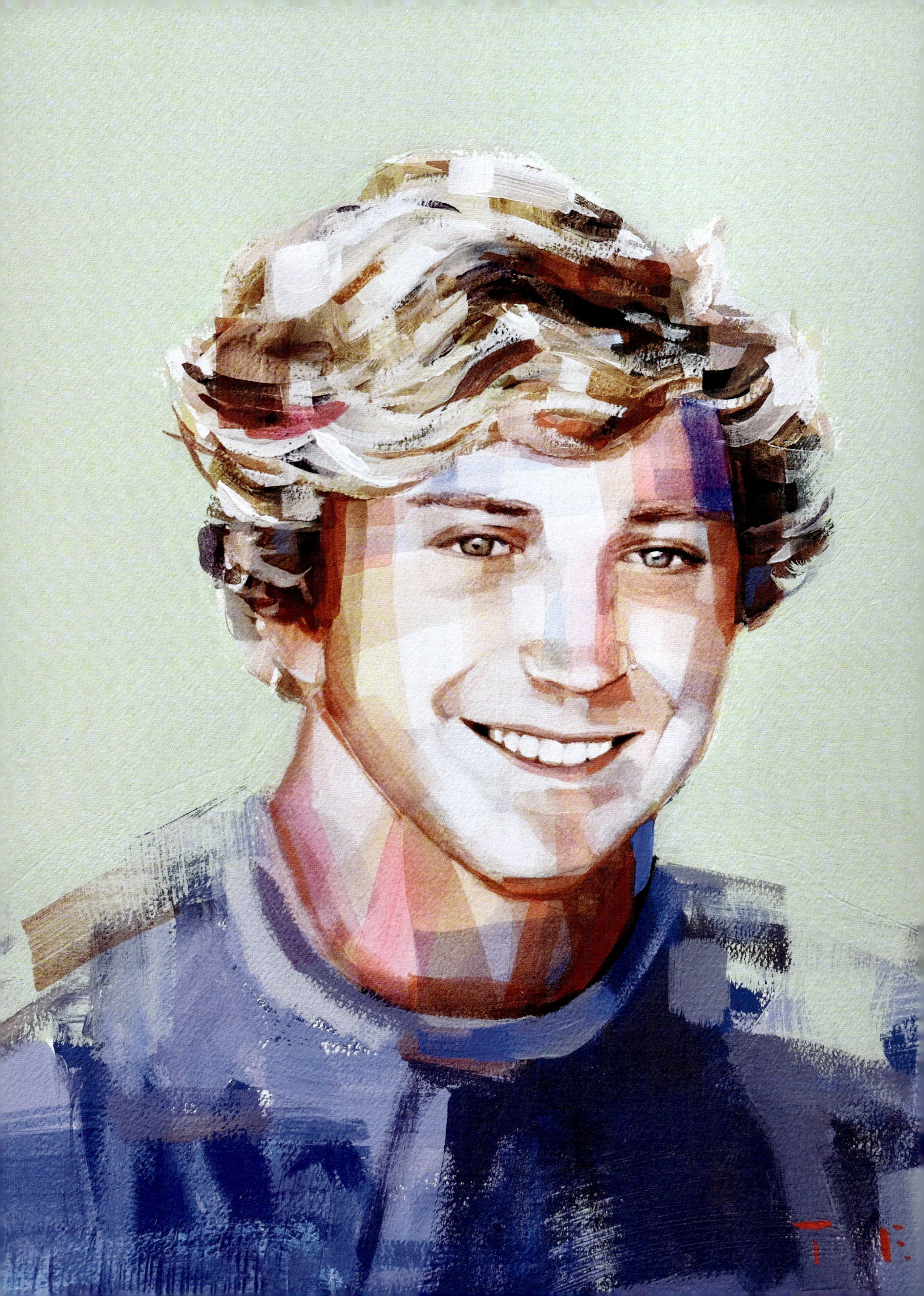

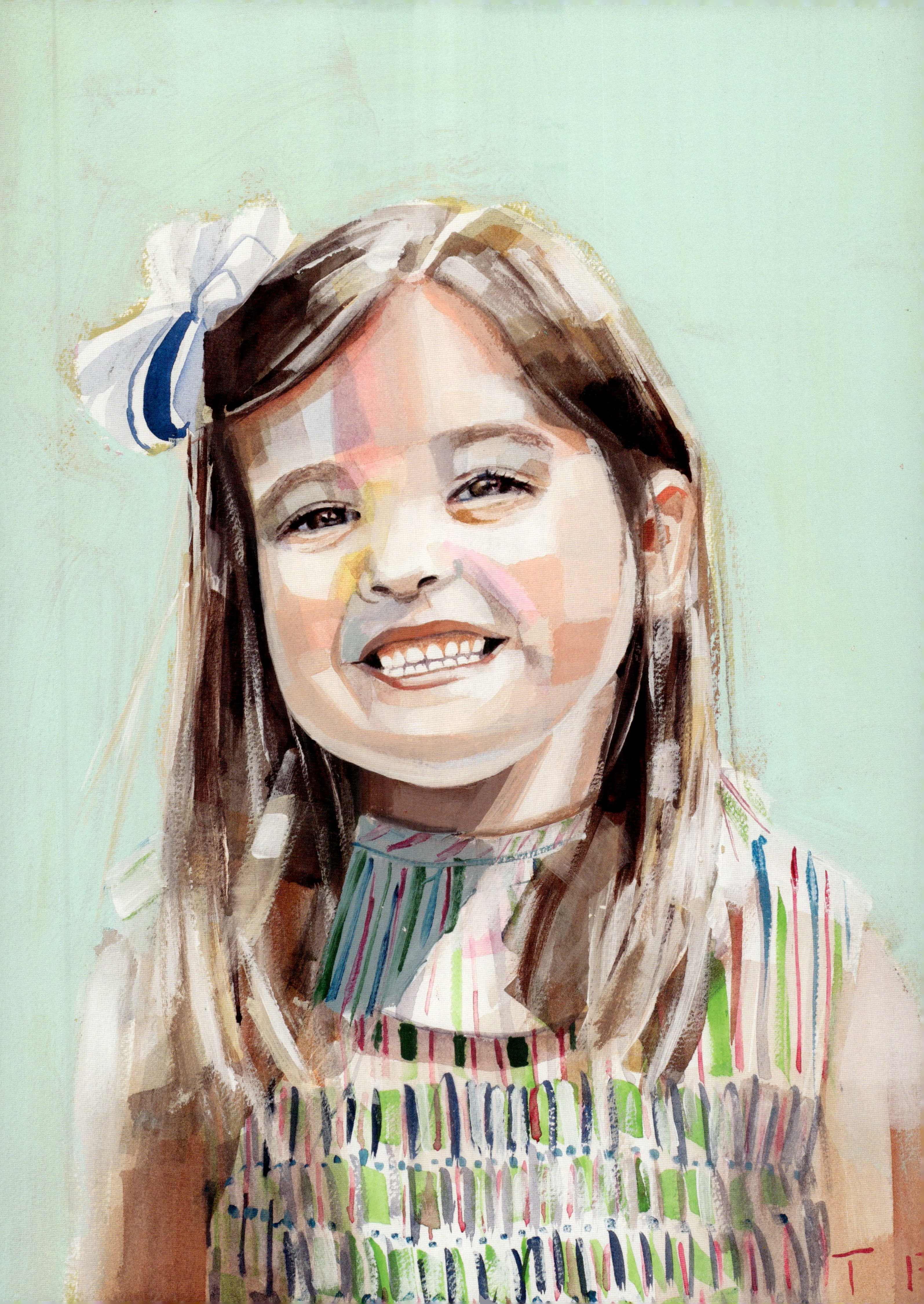

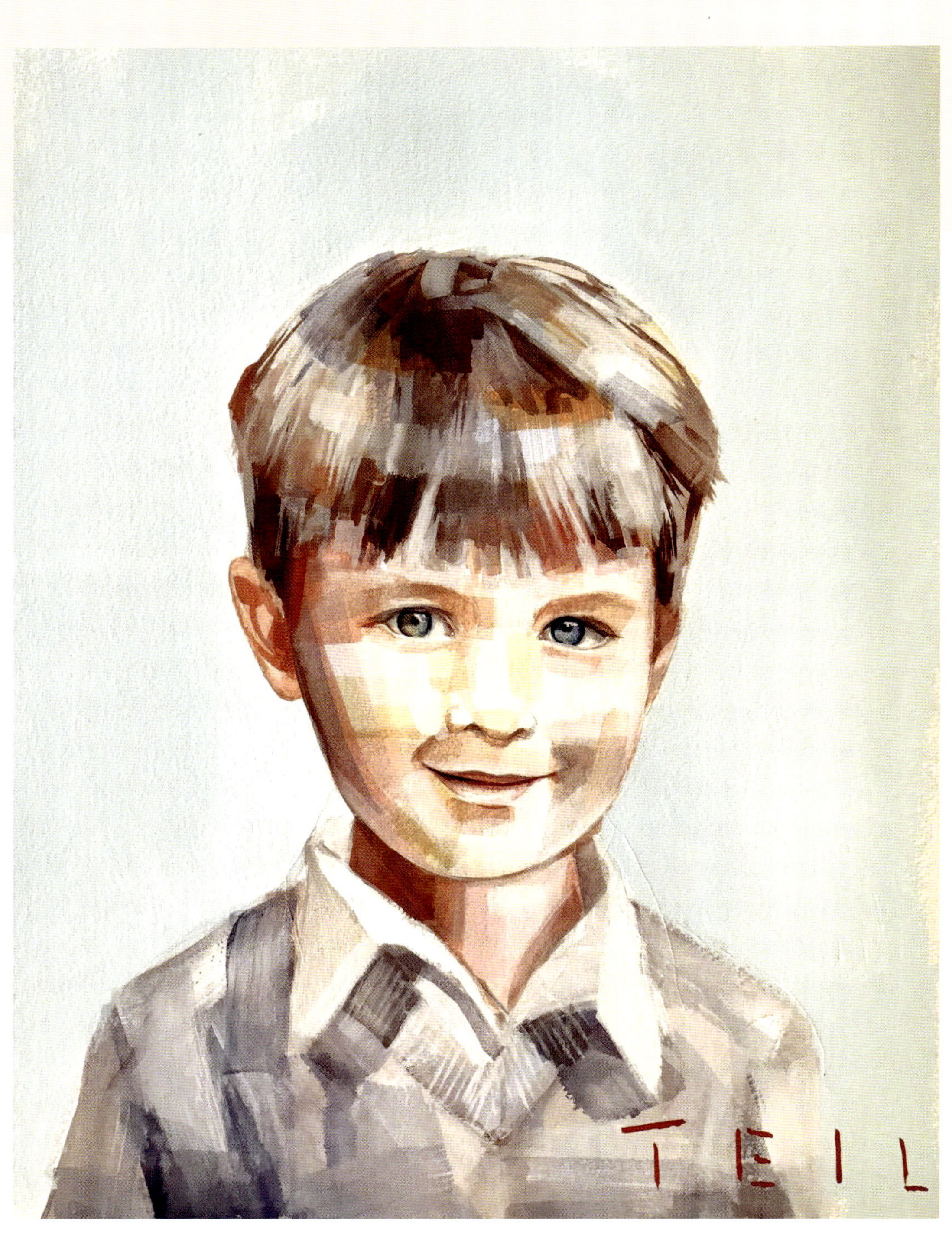
TEIL

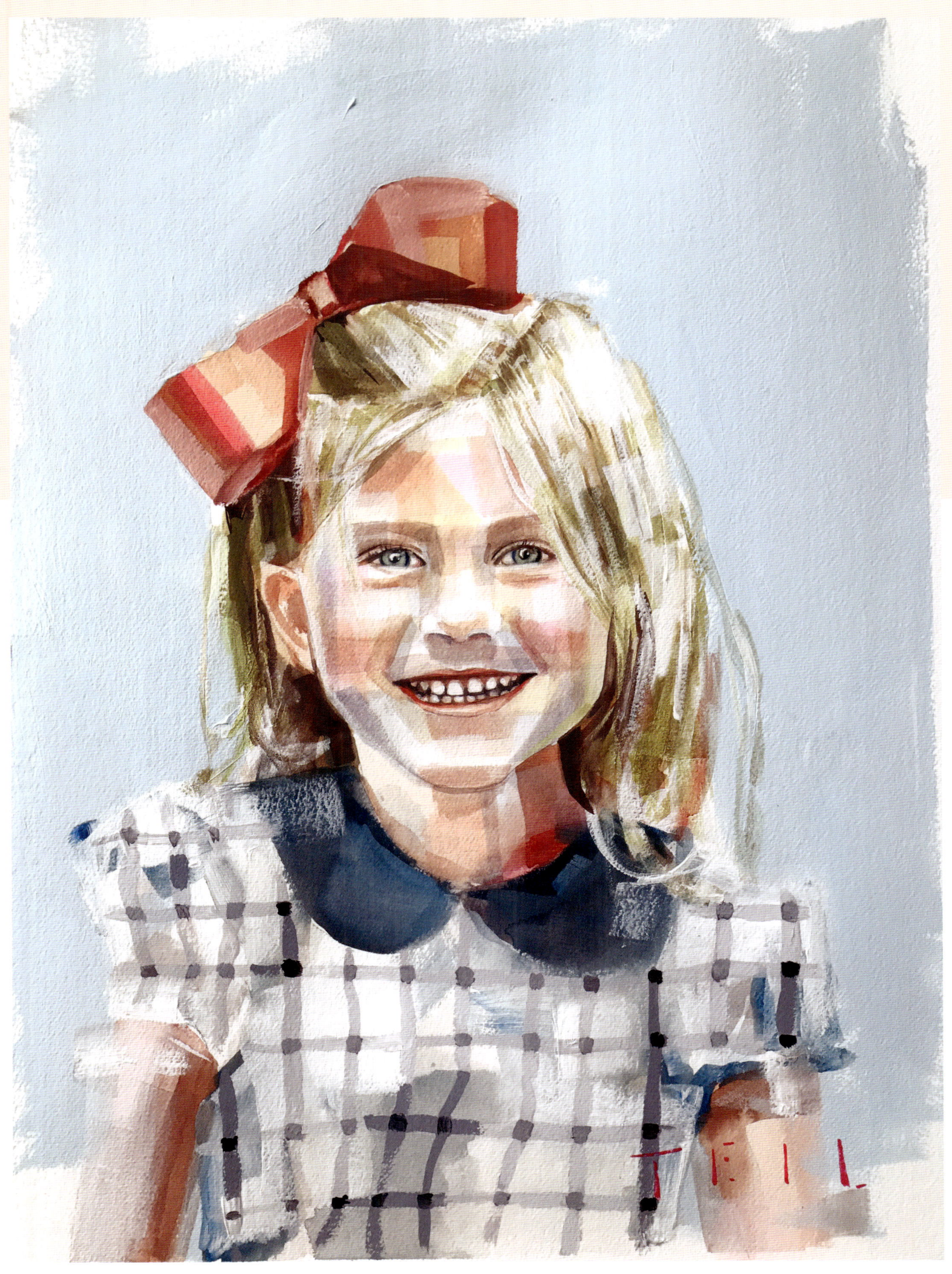
TELL

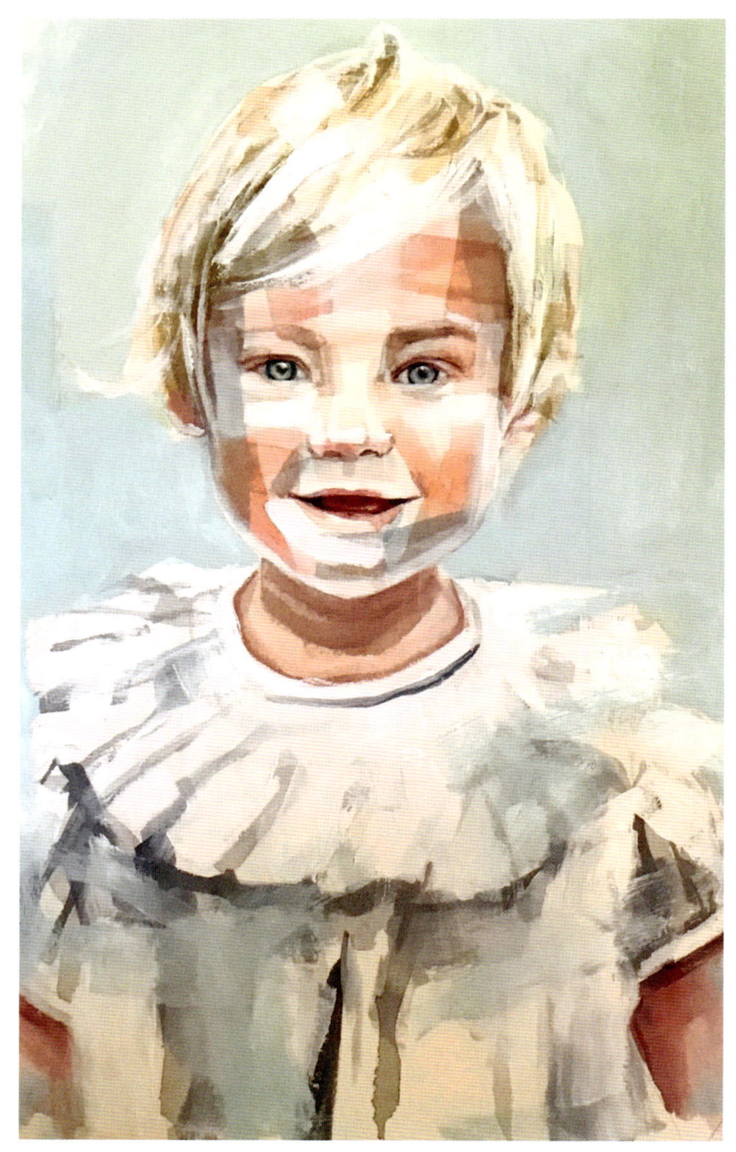

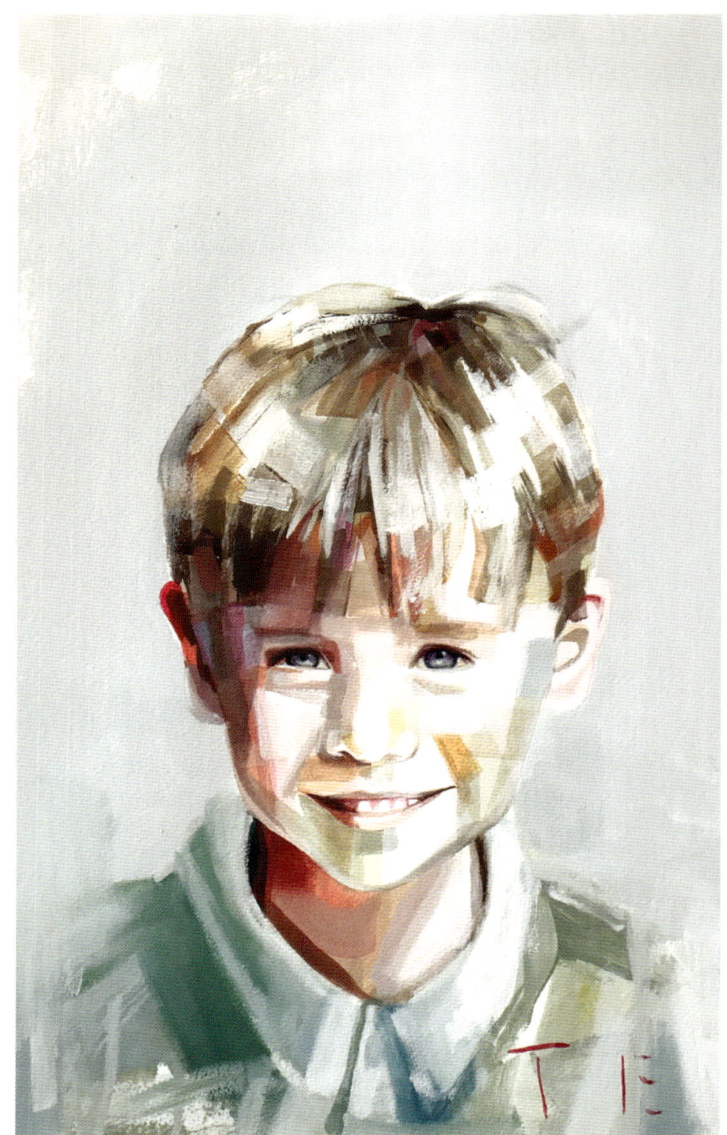

Because I wasn't extremely confident in this approach at a portrait, each wide stroke consisted of a mildly committed thin wash containing minimal pigment. After each layer of strokes dried, I applied another layer of transparent strokes. The more layers I added, the more interesting the painting became as it revealed the

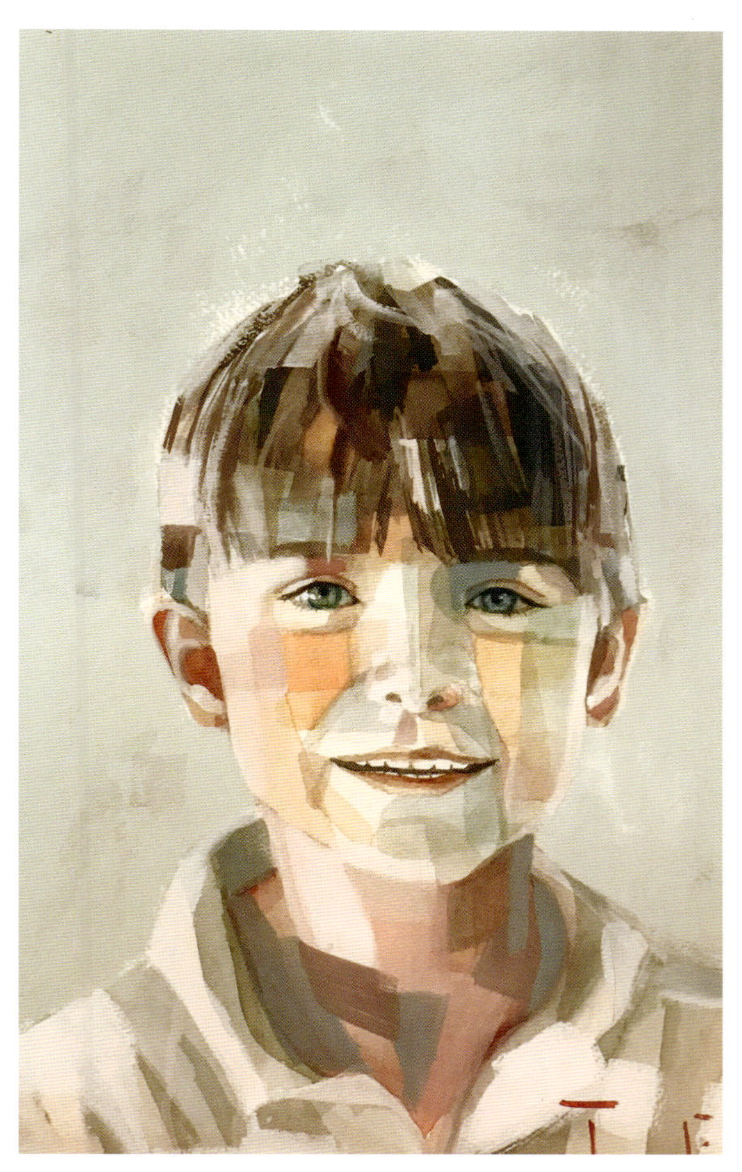
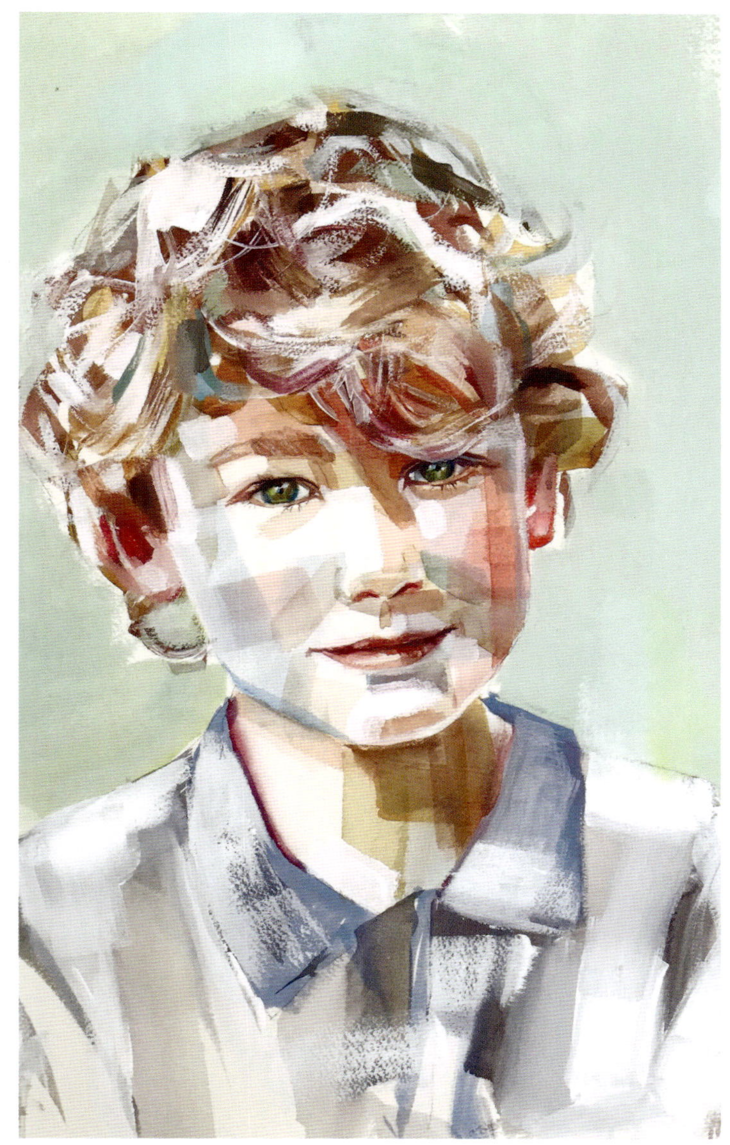

history of each previous translucent layer before. The straight and angular strokes slowly provided enough information to portray a face. After her skin was complete, I desired a touch of realism to debut in this portrait. I switched to my smallest and sharpest brush and went after the eyes.

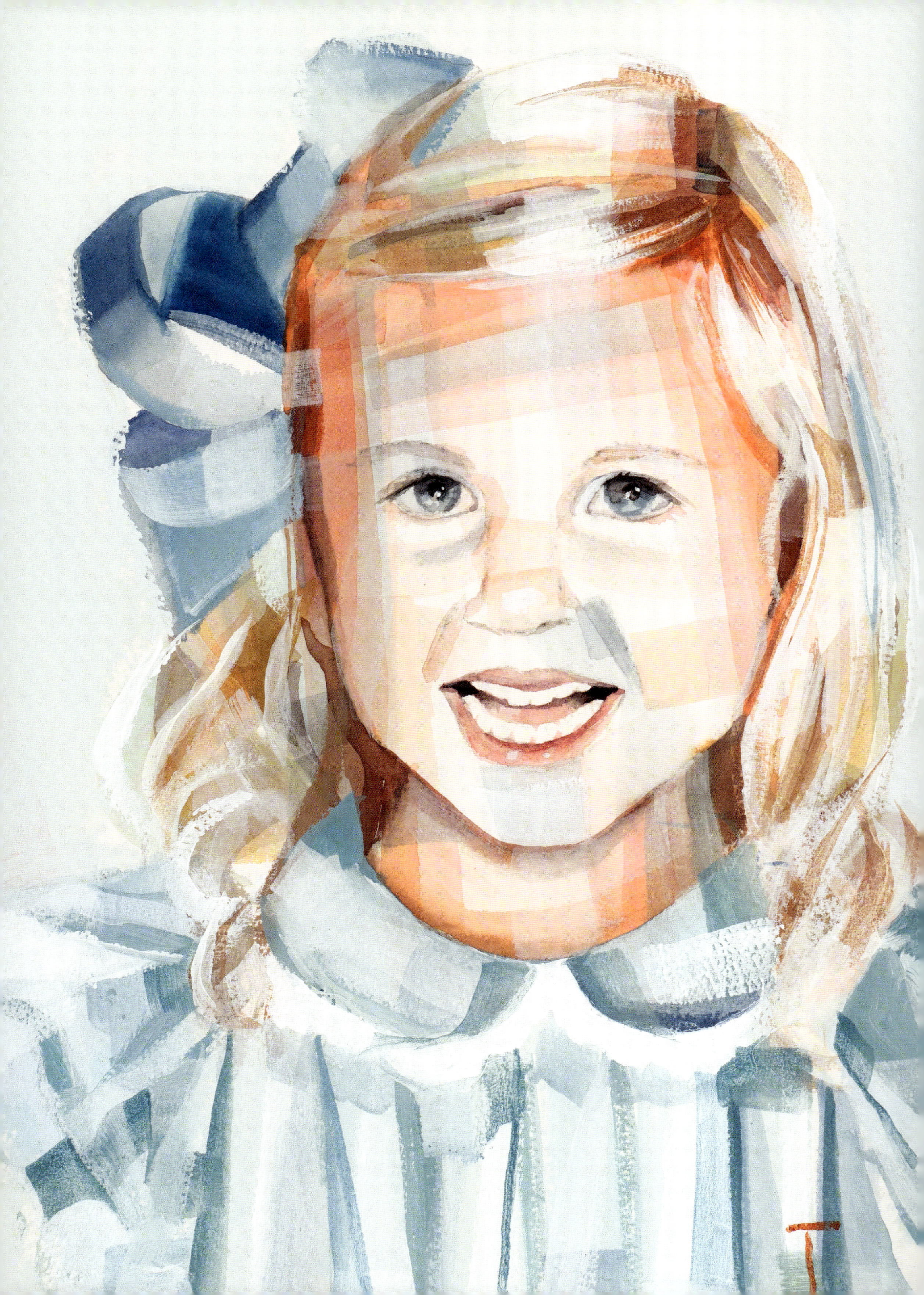

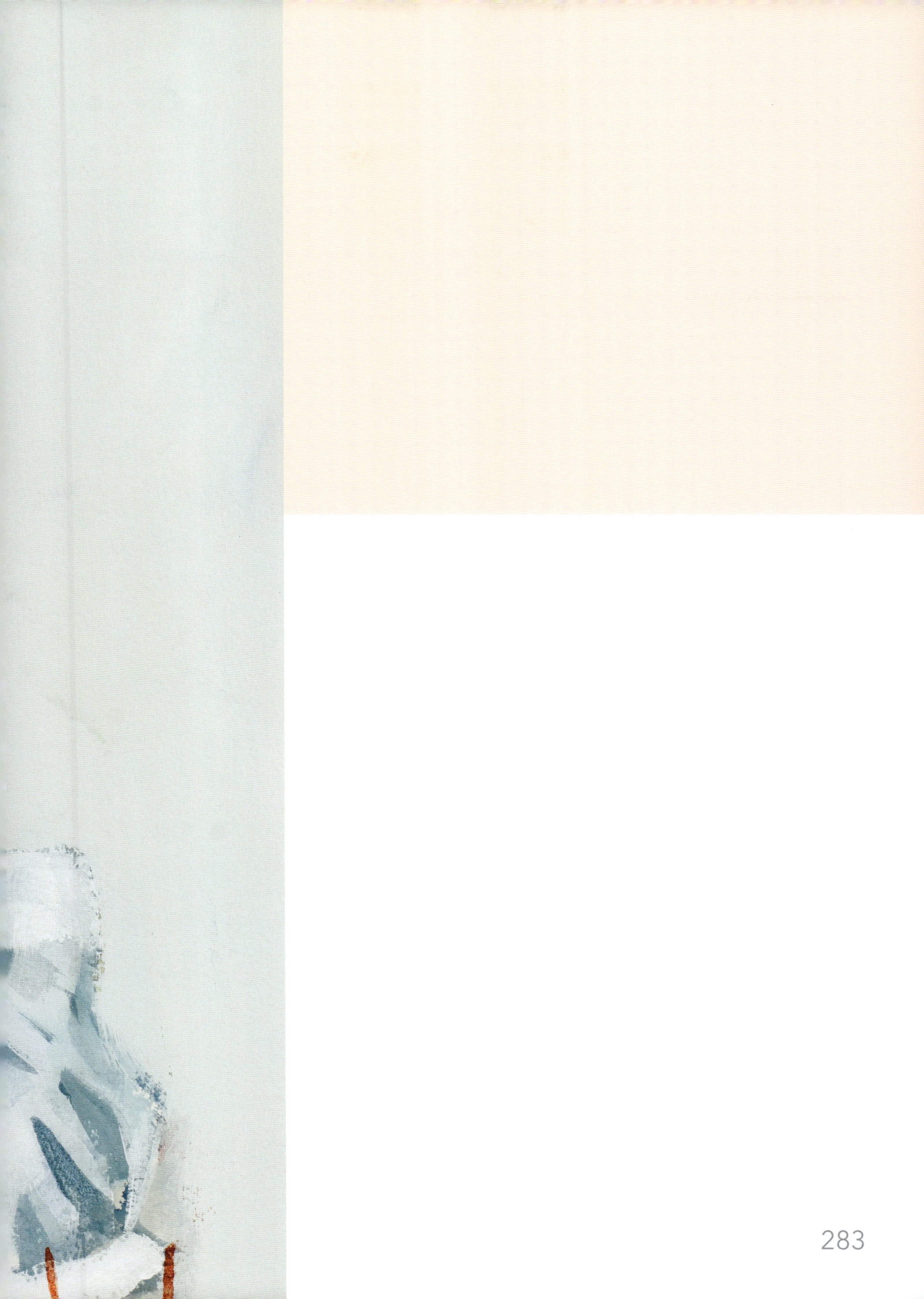

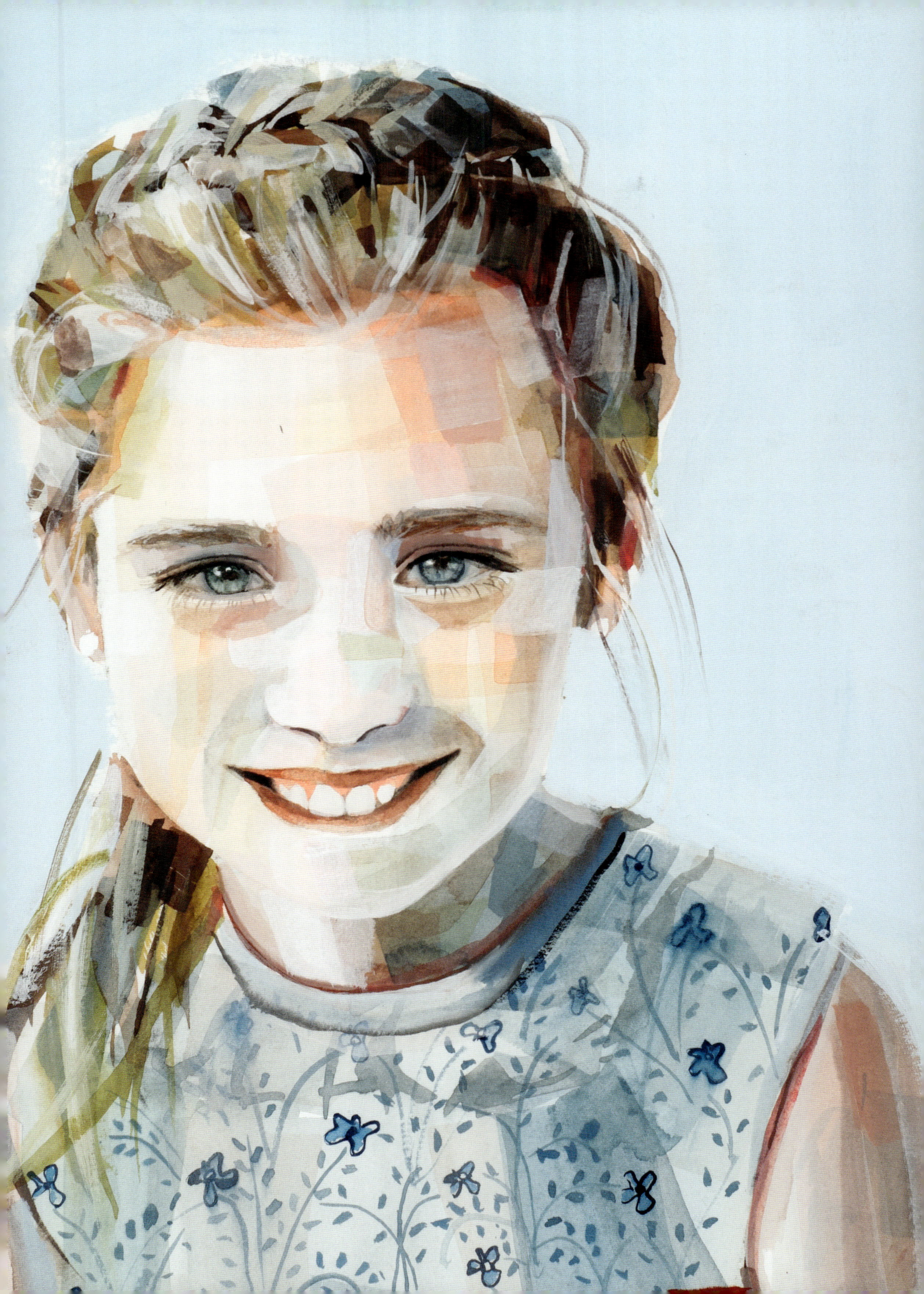

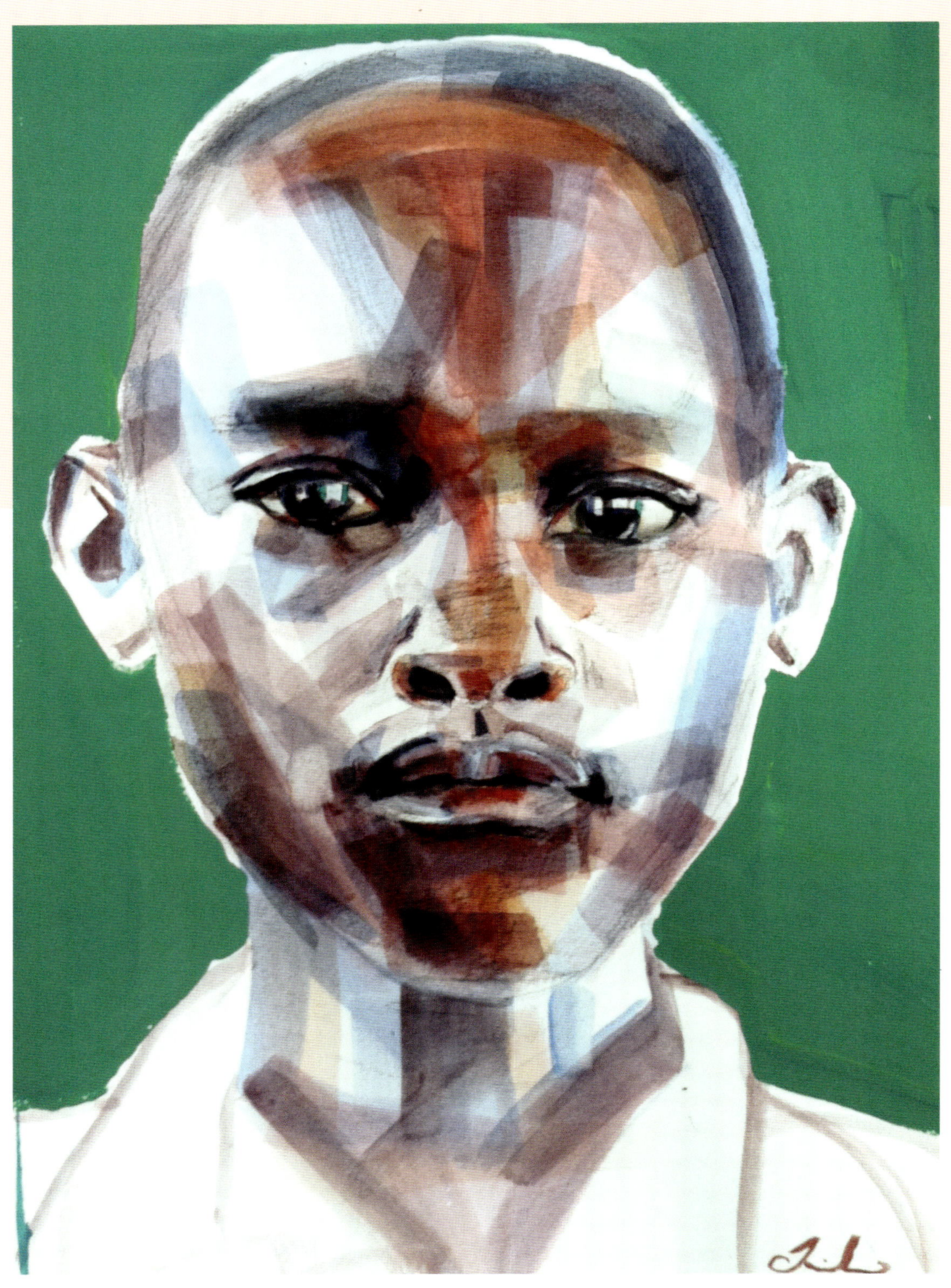

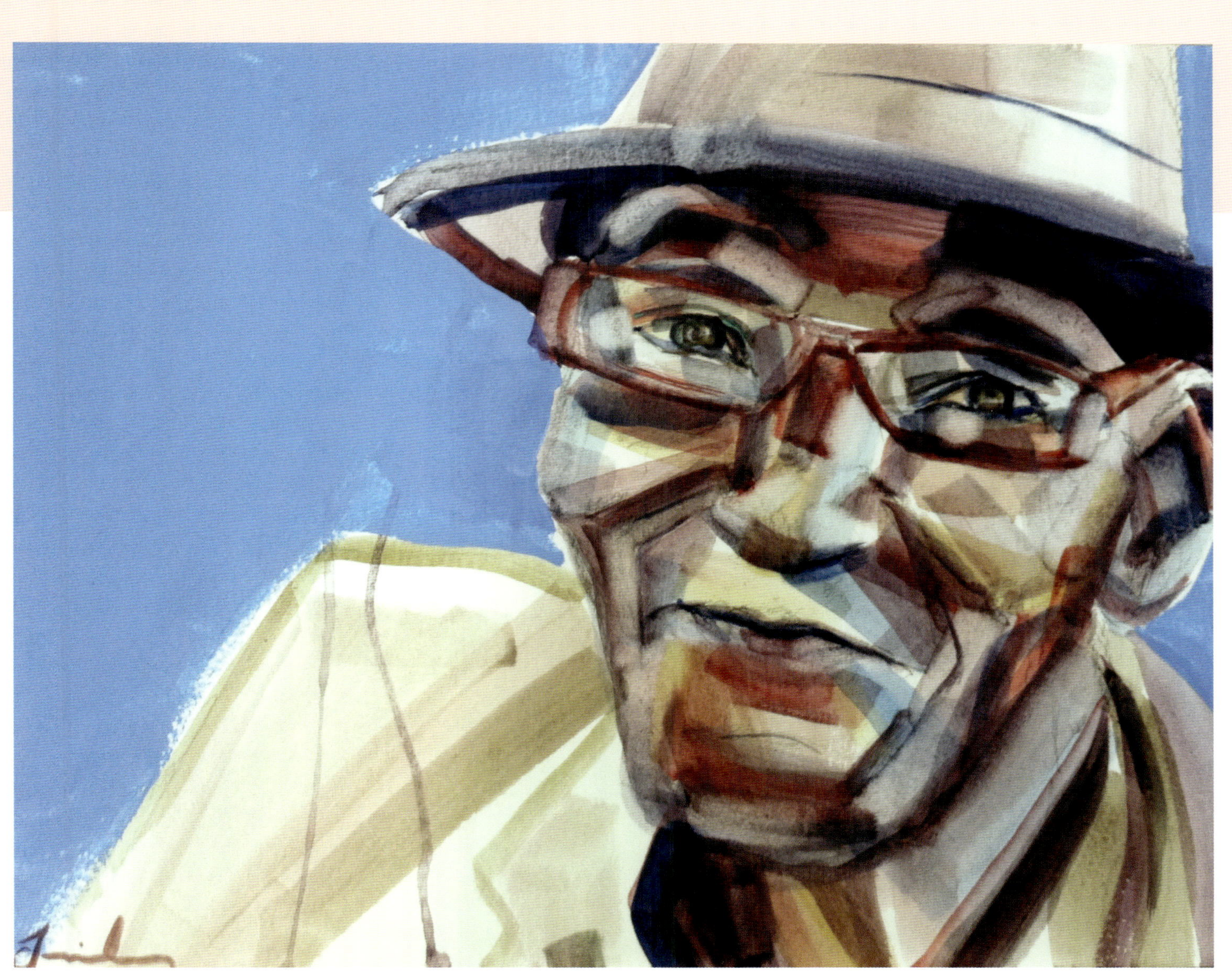

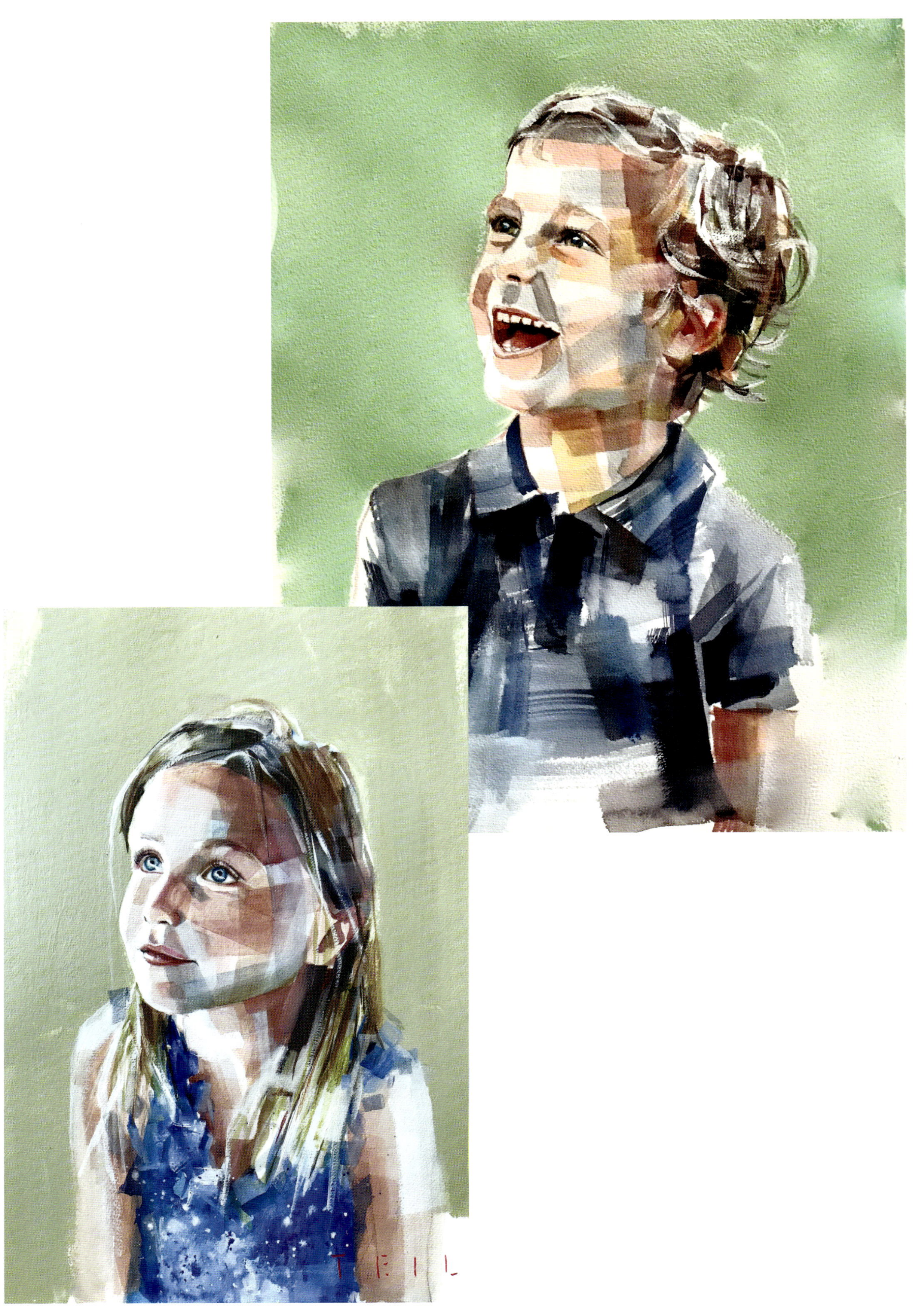
TEIL

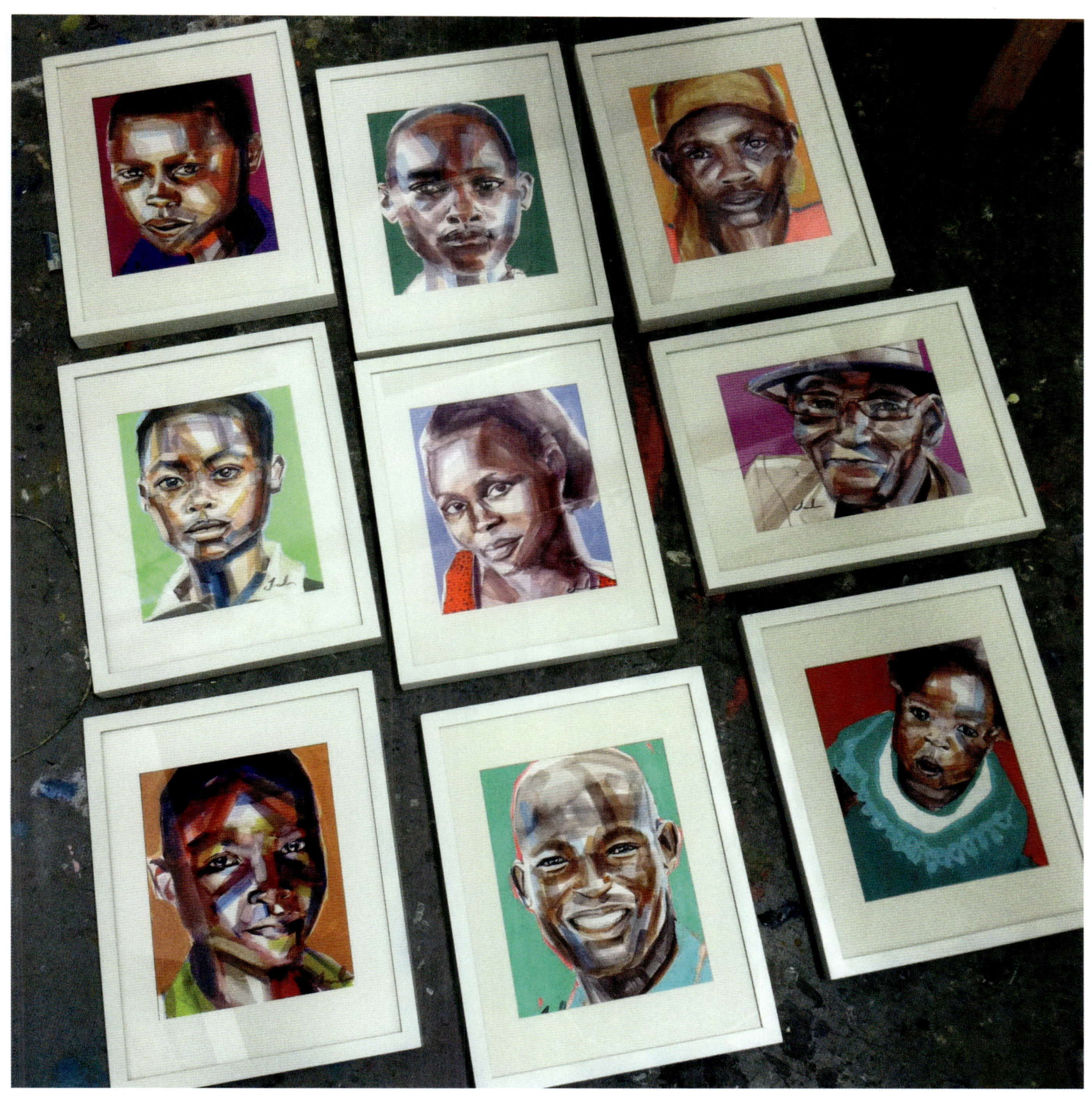

I NOW HAD TWO PAINTING LANGUAGES present: the bold, straight, washy strokes and the tightly rendered realism. It needed one more language. I then added a flat acrylic background. As soon as her portrait was complete I was eager to try more! Though watercolor is quite unforgiving (as each mistake is difficult to conceal), the various marks the medium provides are diverse and rewarding.

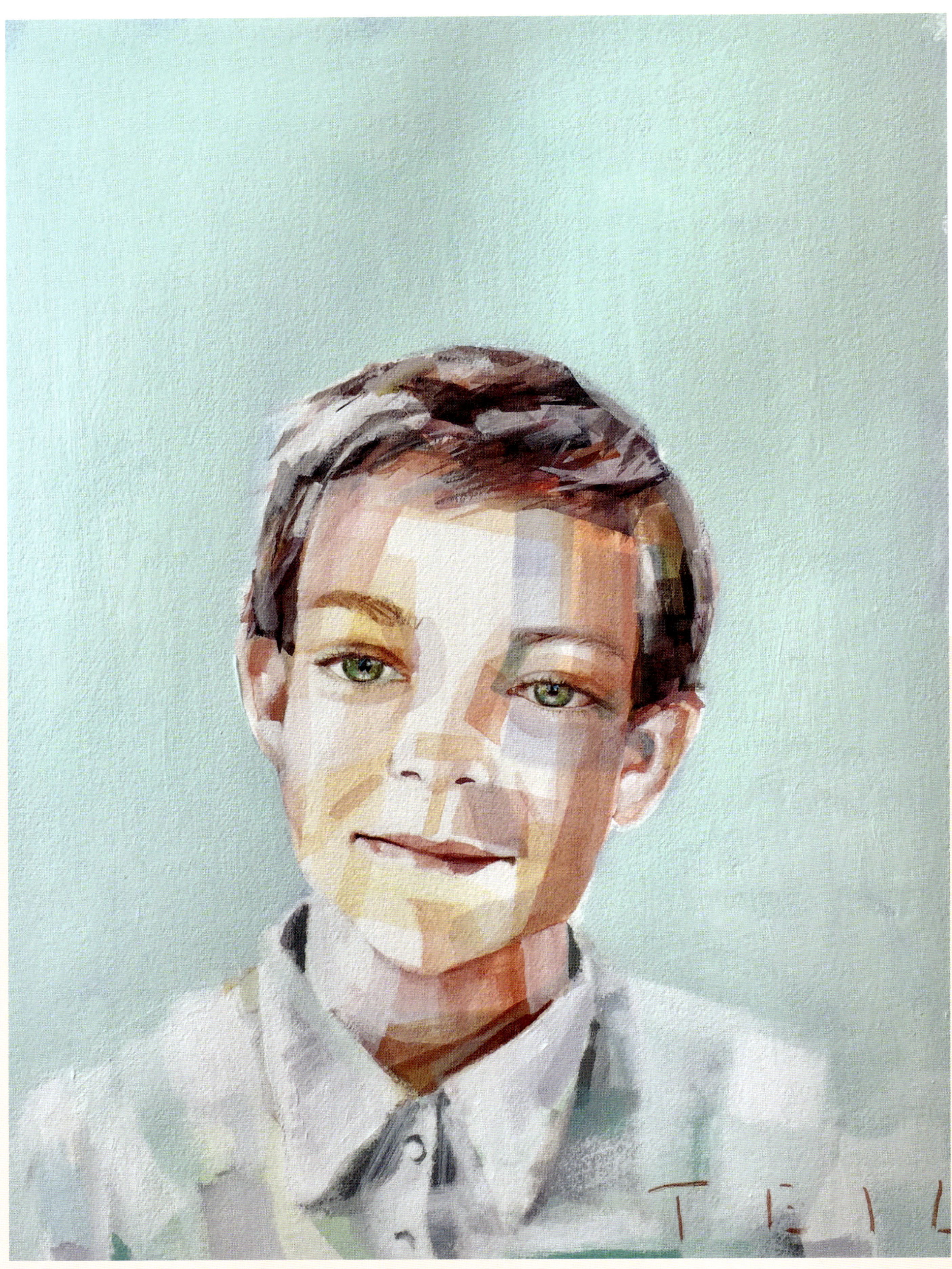

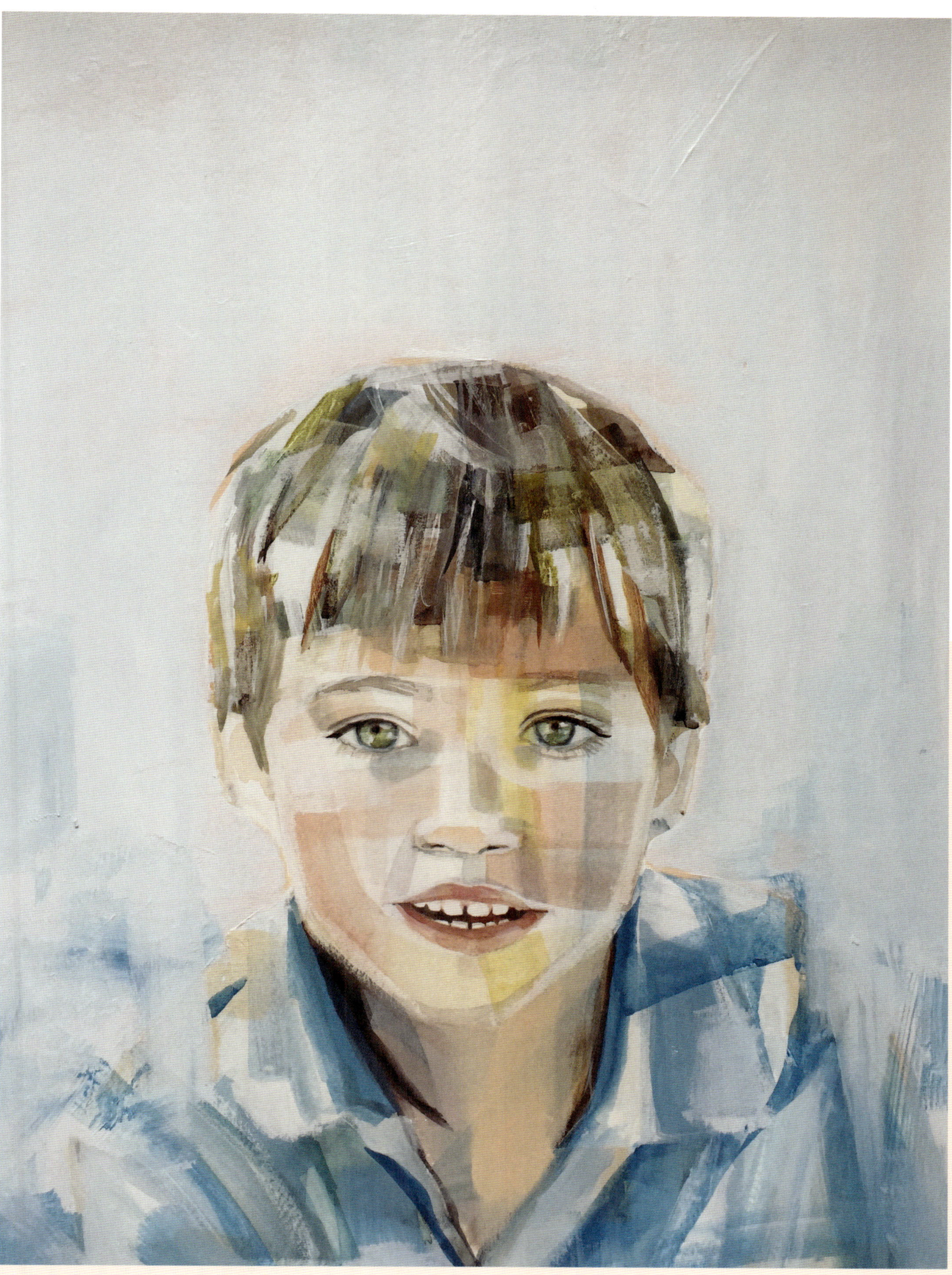

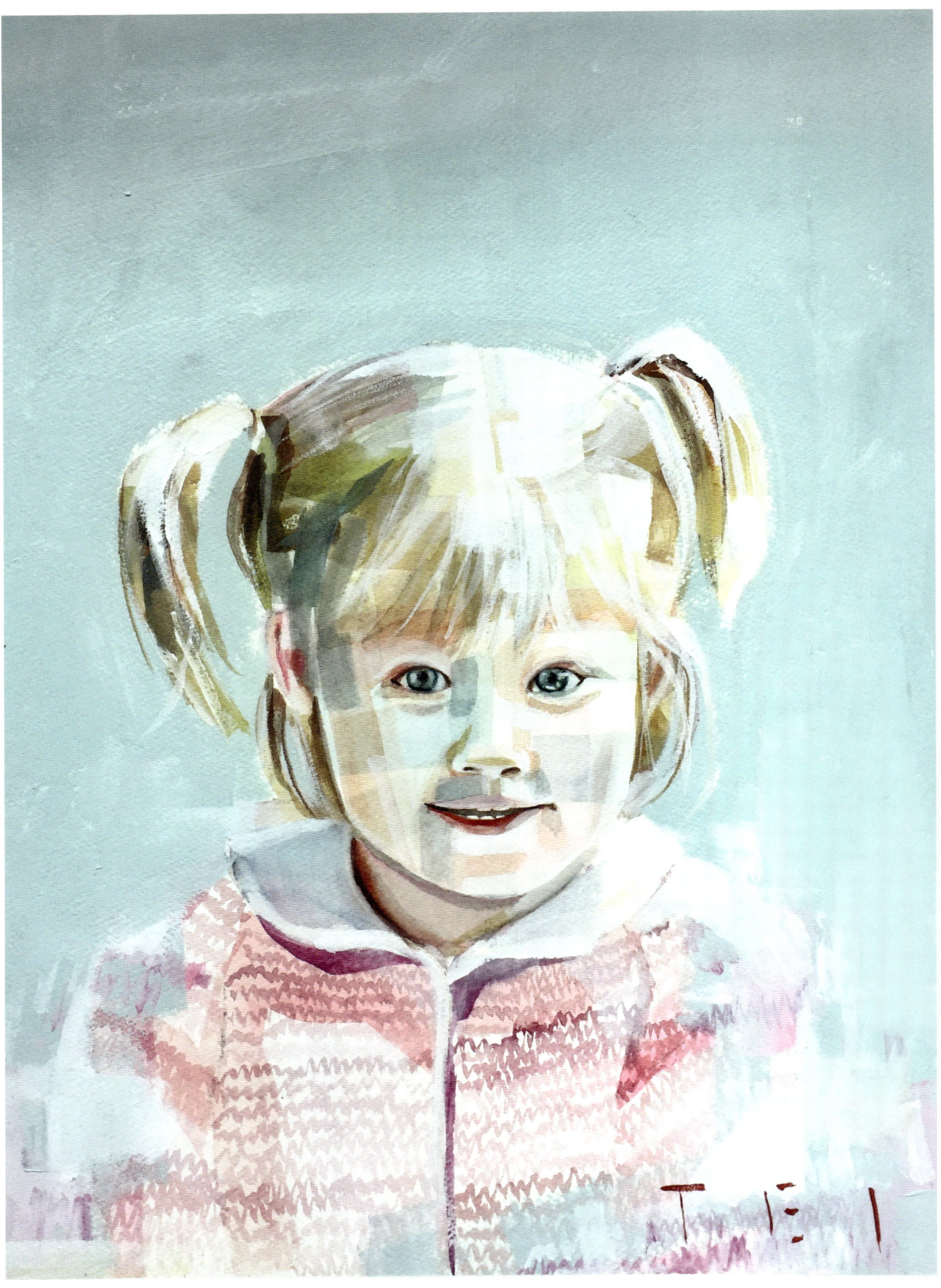

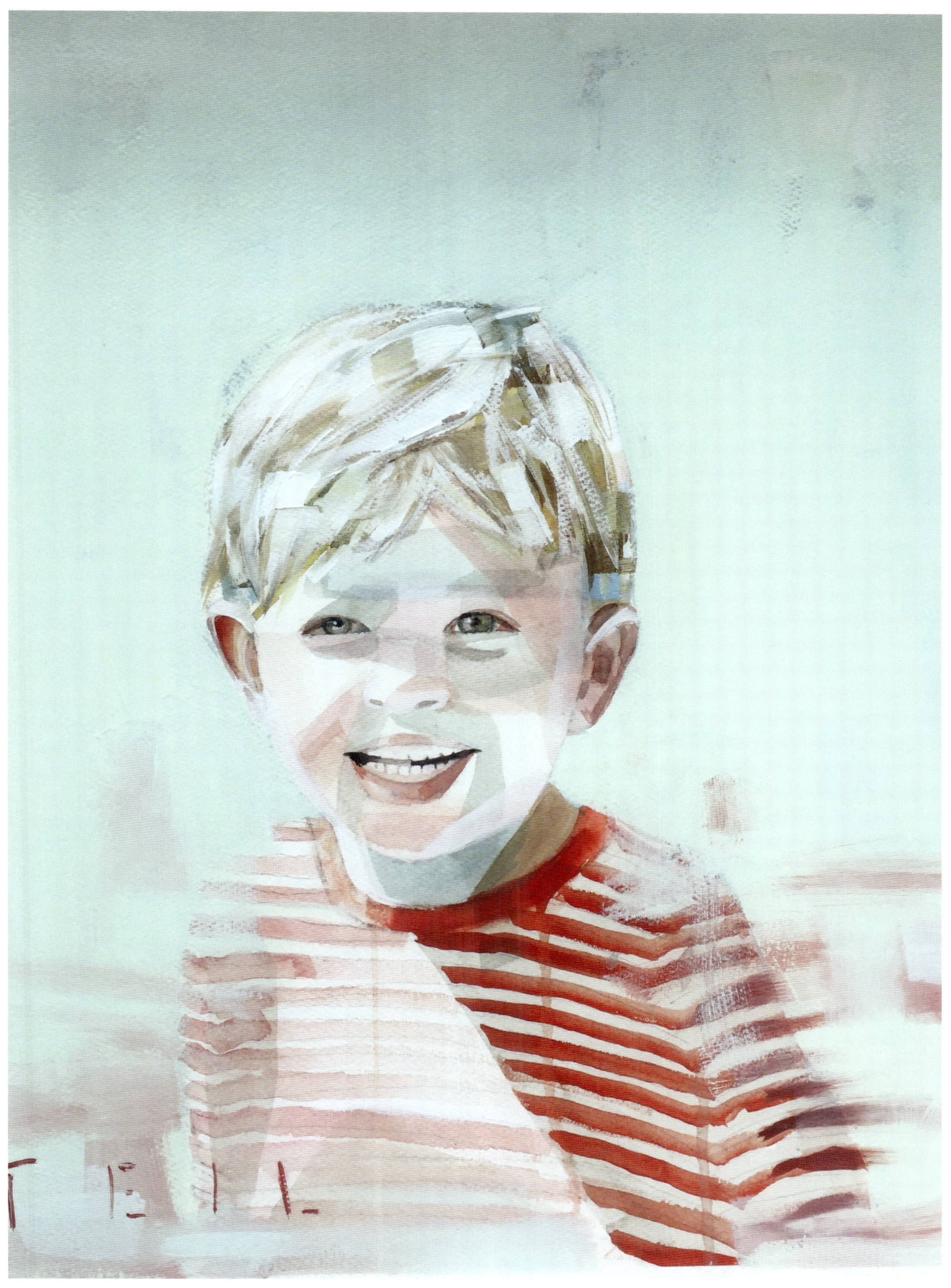

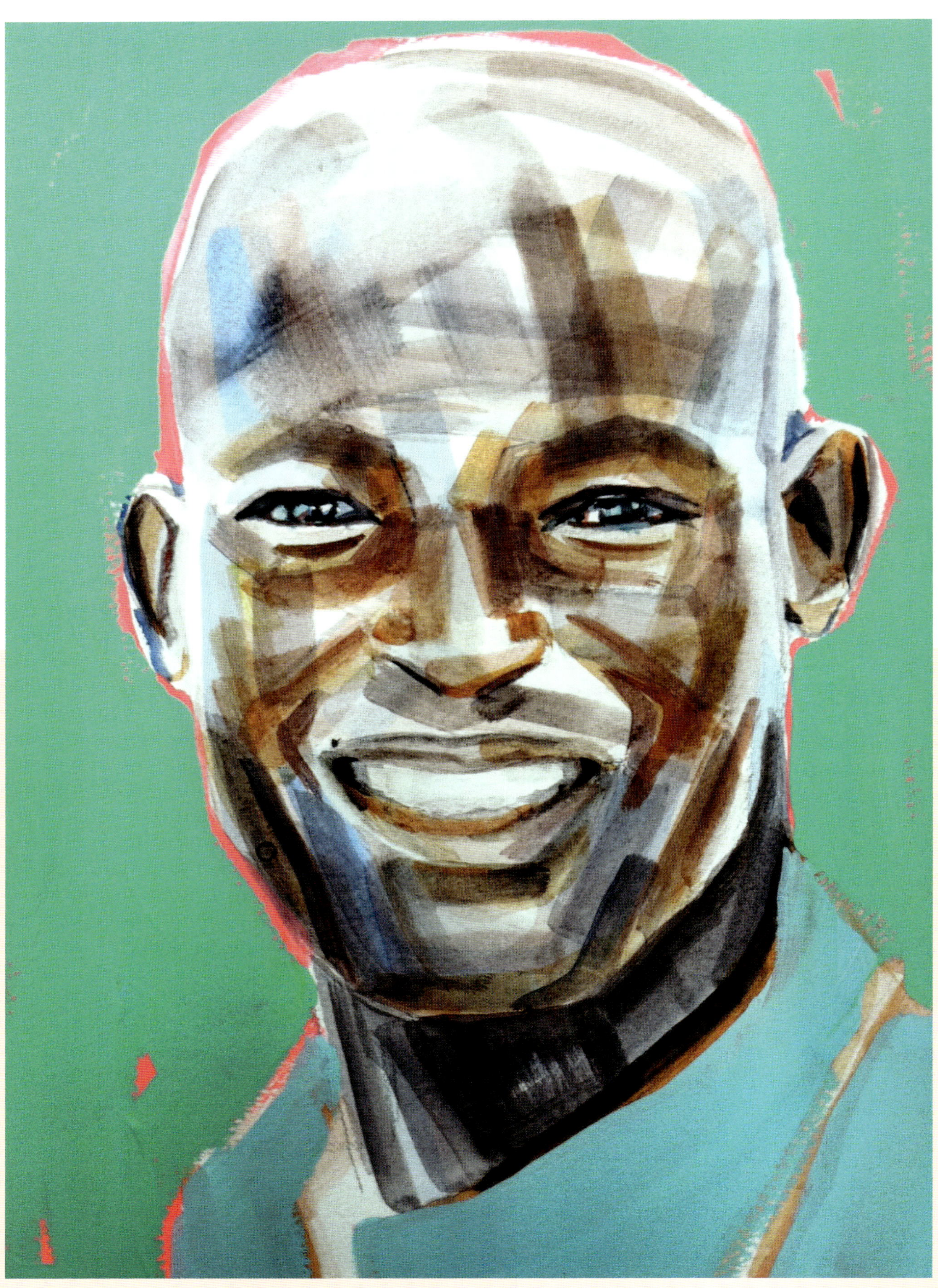

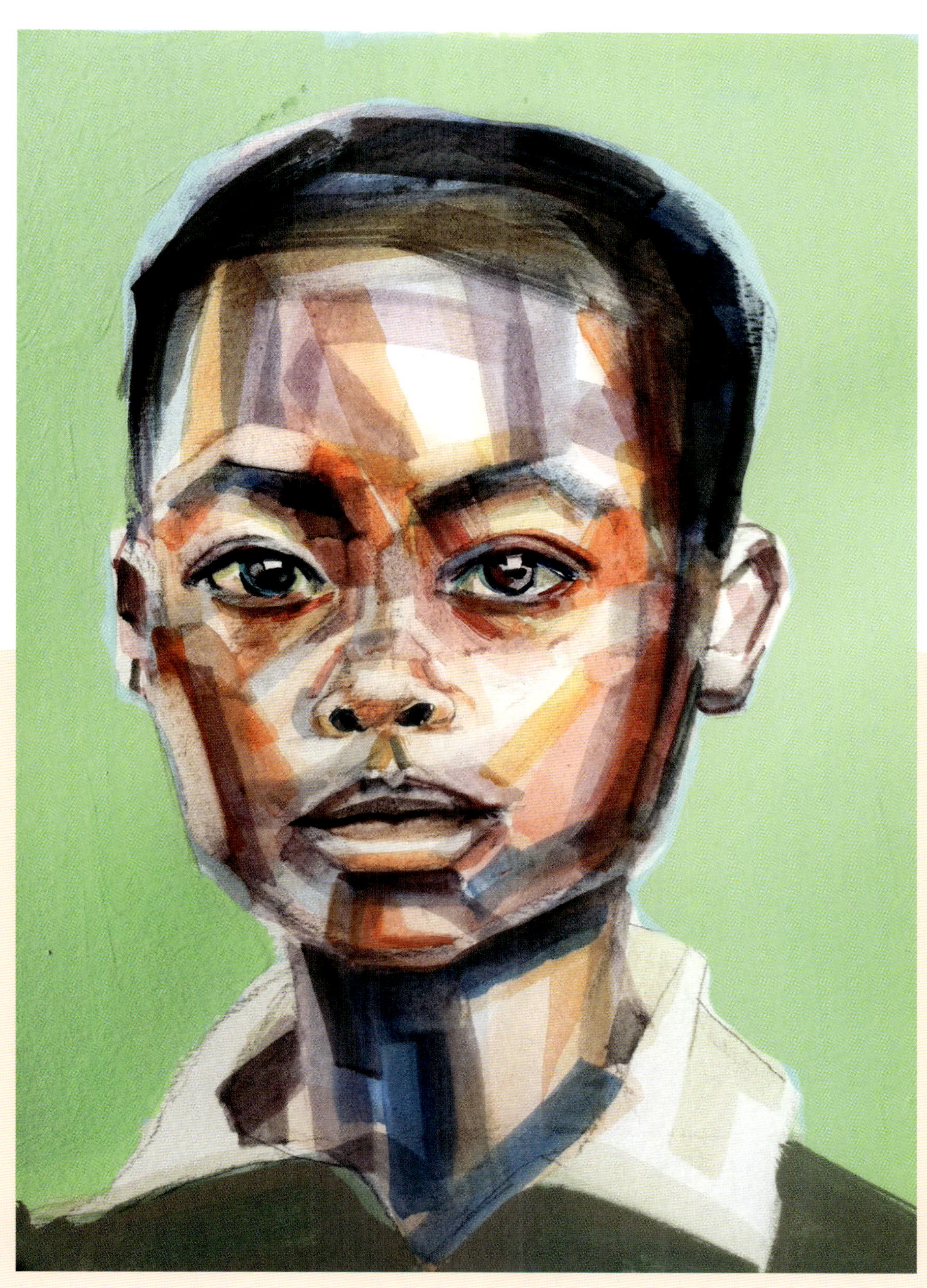

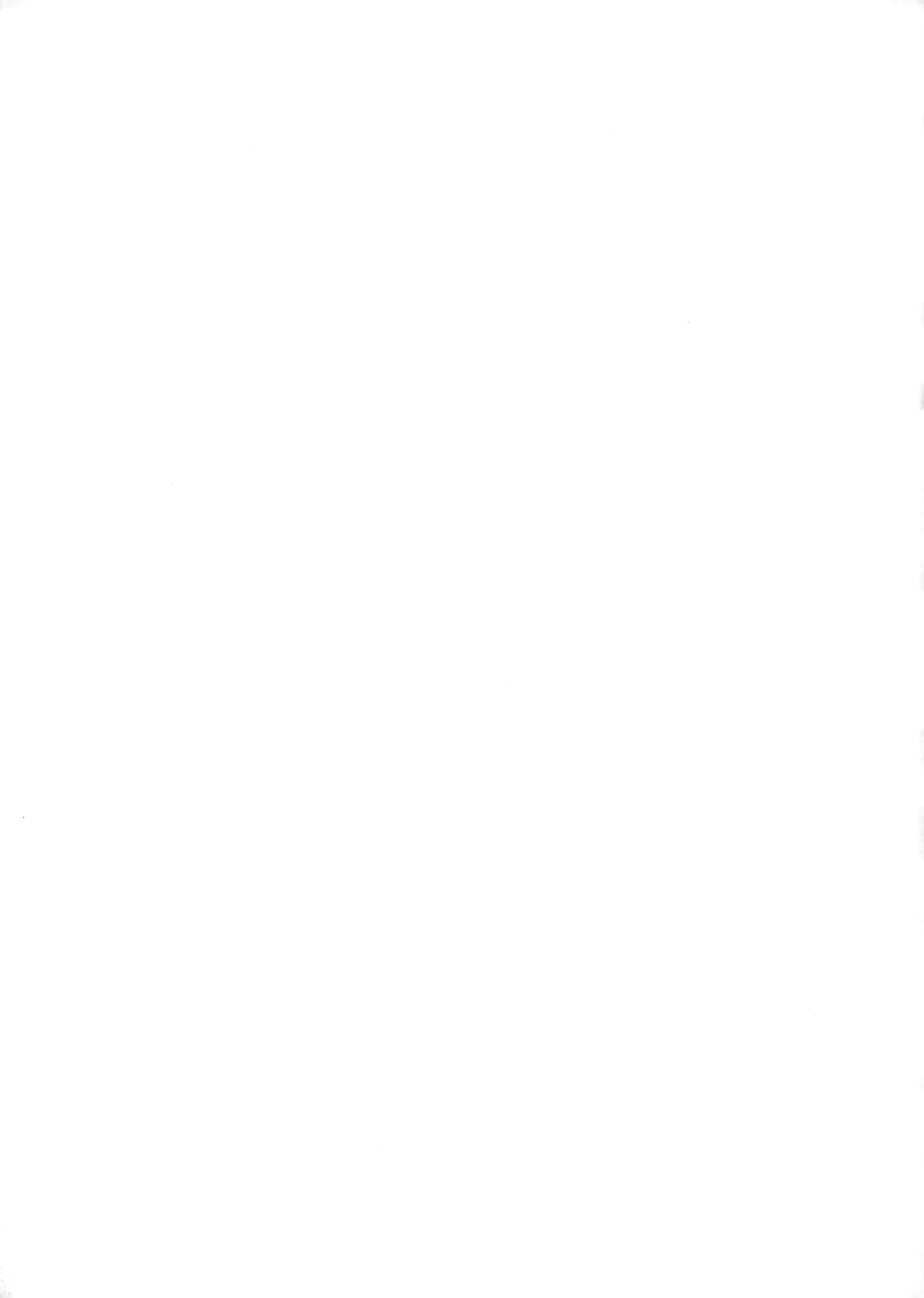

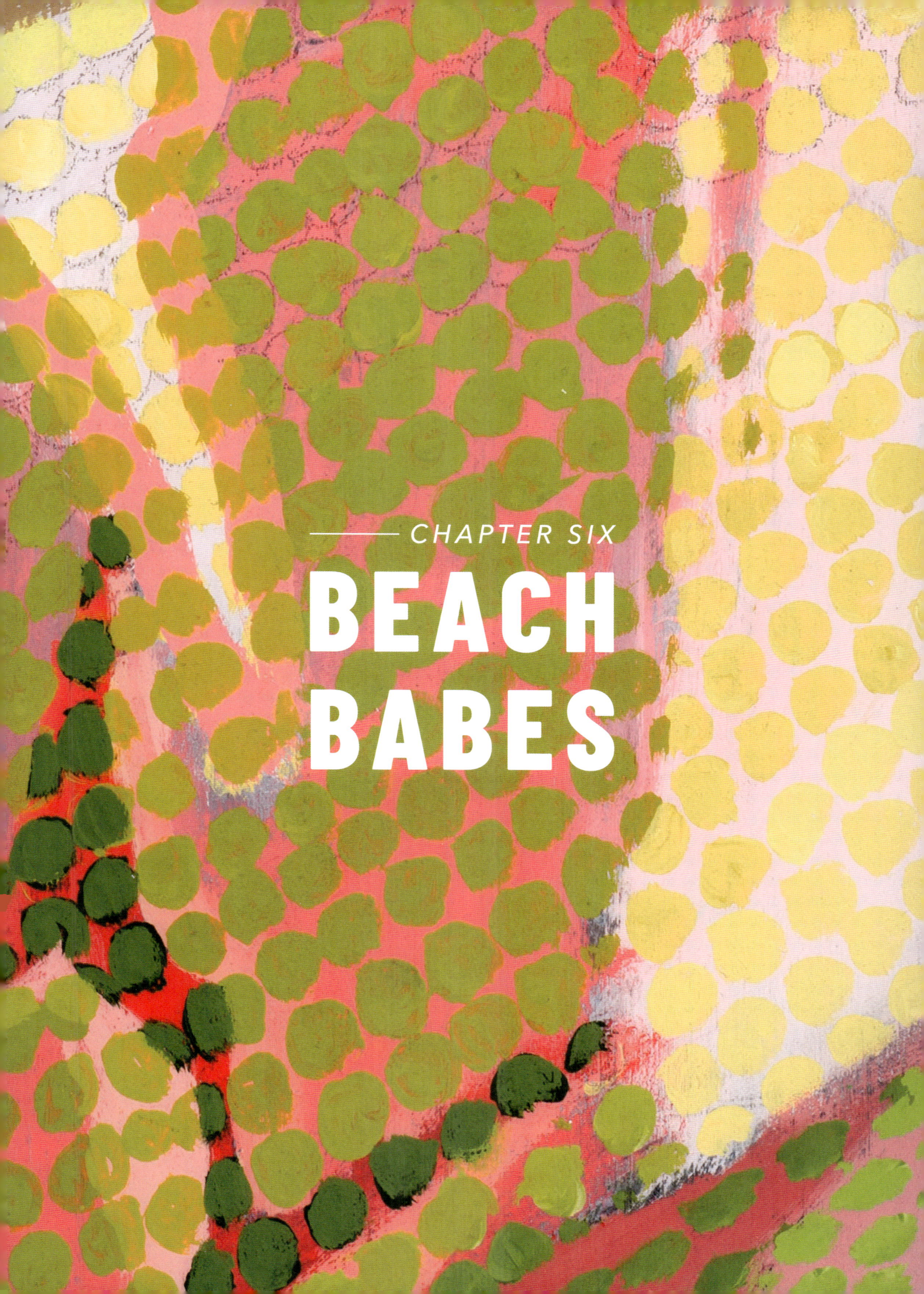

CHAPTER SIX

BEACH BABES

THE BEACH BABES

series is a closer look into the forms within the beach and pool paintings. I love focusing in on one subject and closely rendering the human figure and tightening the pattern in the swimsuit. This subject also offers the opportunity to experiment with an alternative light and shadow palette, which is a concept derived from the early French fauvism movement in the 1900s. The flat fields of color filling the negative space of the beach babes are layered with experimental shades, leaving room for me to find a harmonious color combination in the the final piece. This playful subject is meant to bring the sunsoaked figure to the forefront, but mainly highlighting the playful pattern dancing in the summer rays.

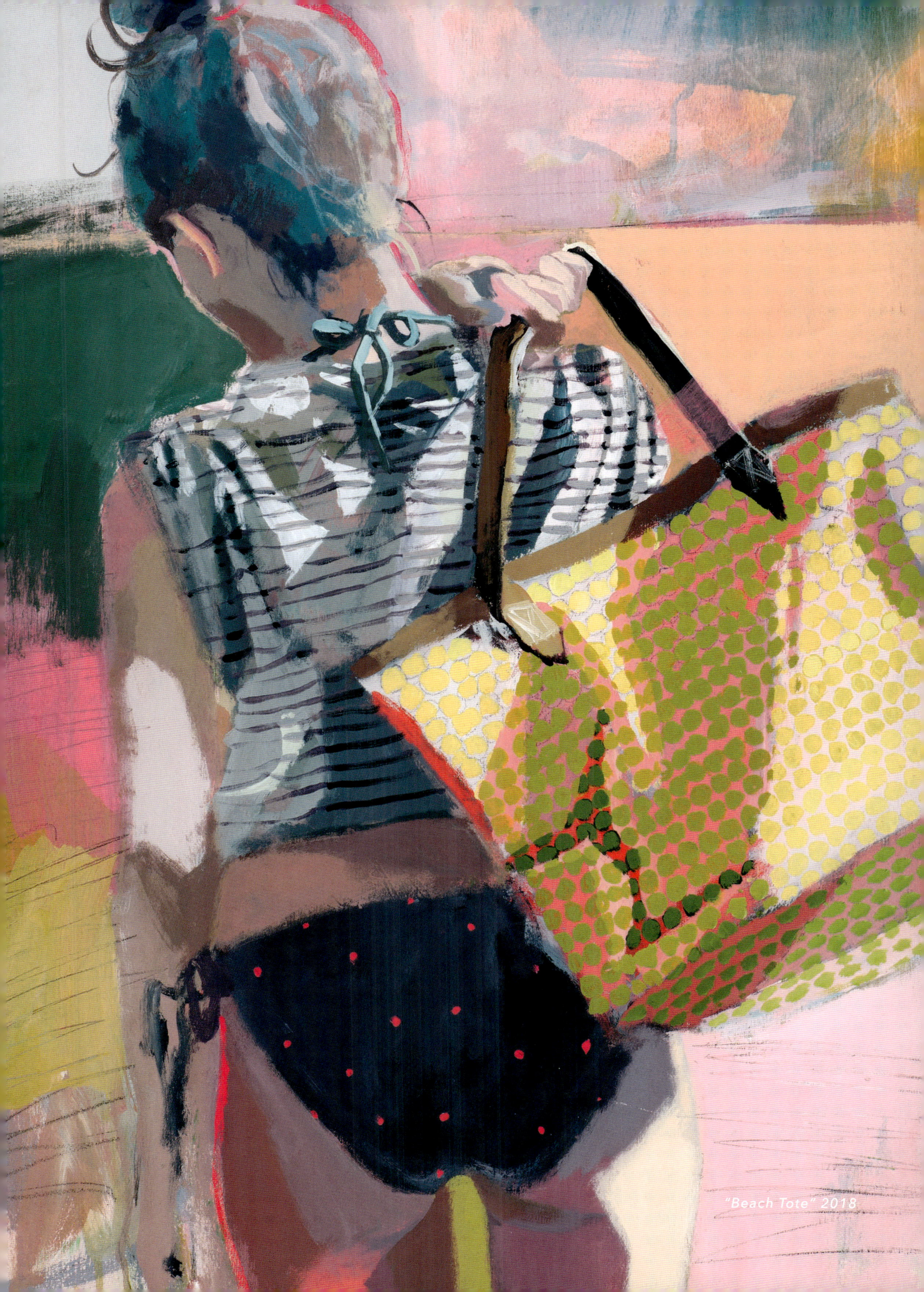

"Beach Tote" 2018

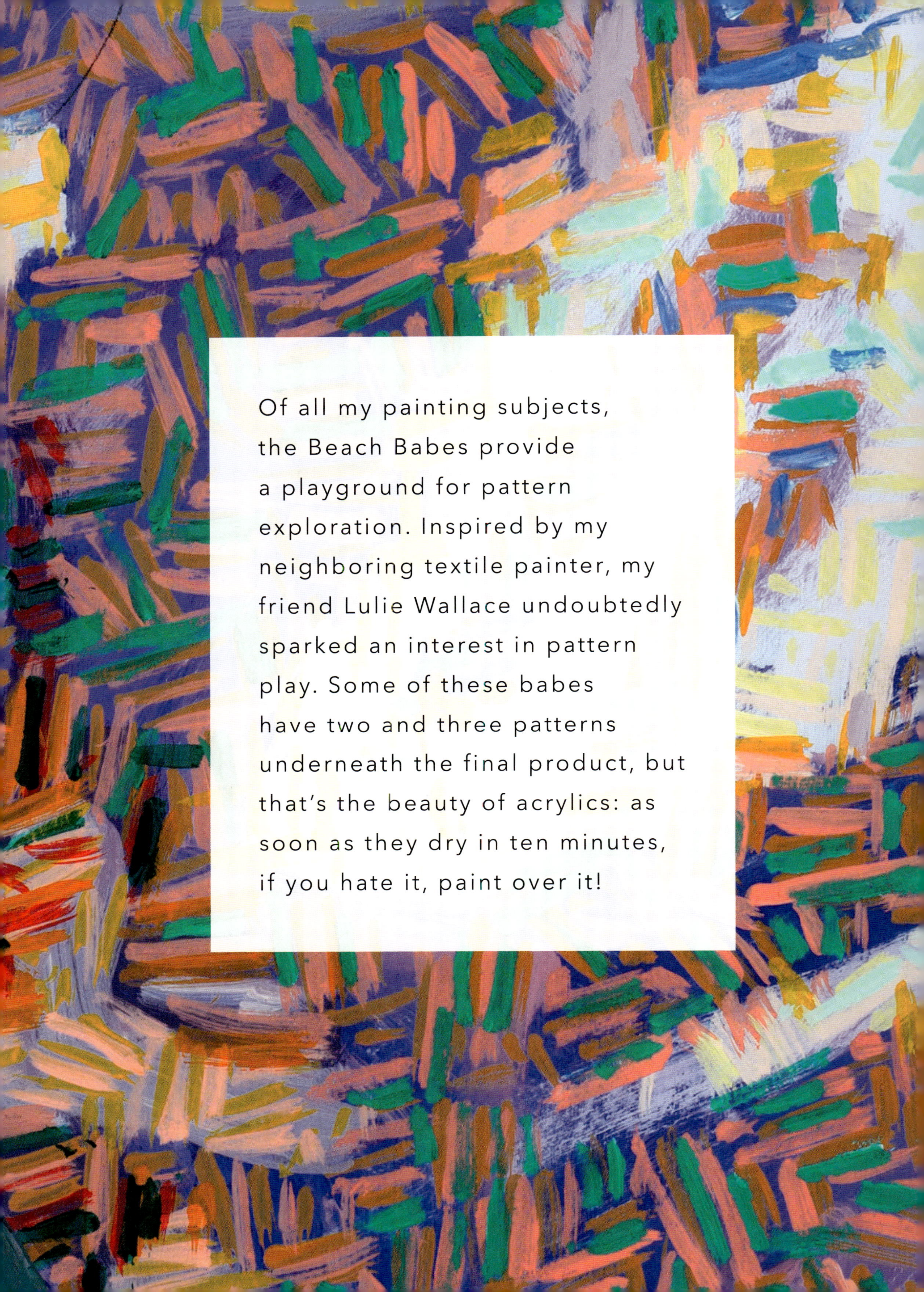

Of all my painting subjects, the Beach Babes provide a playground for pattern exploration. Inspired by my neighboring textile painter, my friend Lulie Wallace undoubtedly sparked an interest in pattern play. Some of these babes have two and three patterns underneath the final product, but that's the beauty of acrylics: as soon as they dry in ten minutes, if you hate it, paint over it!

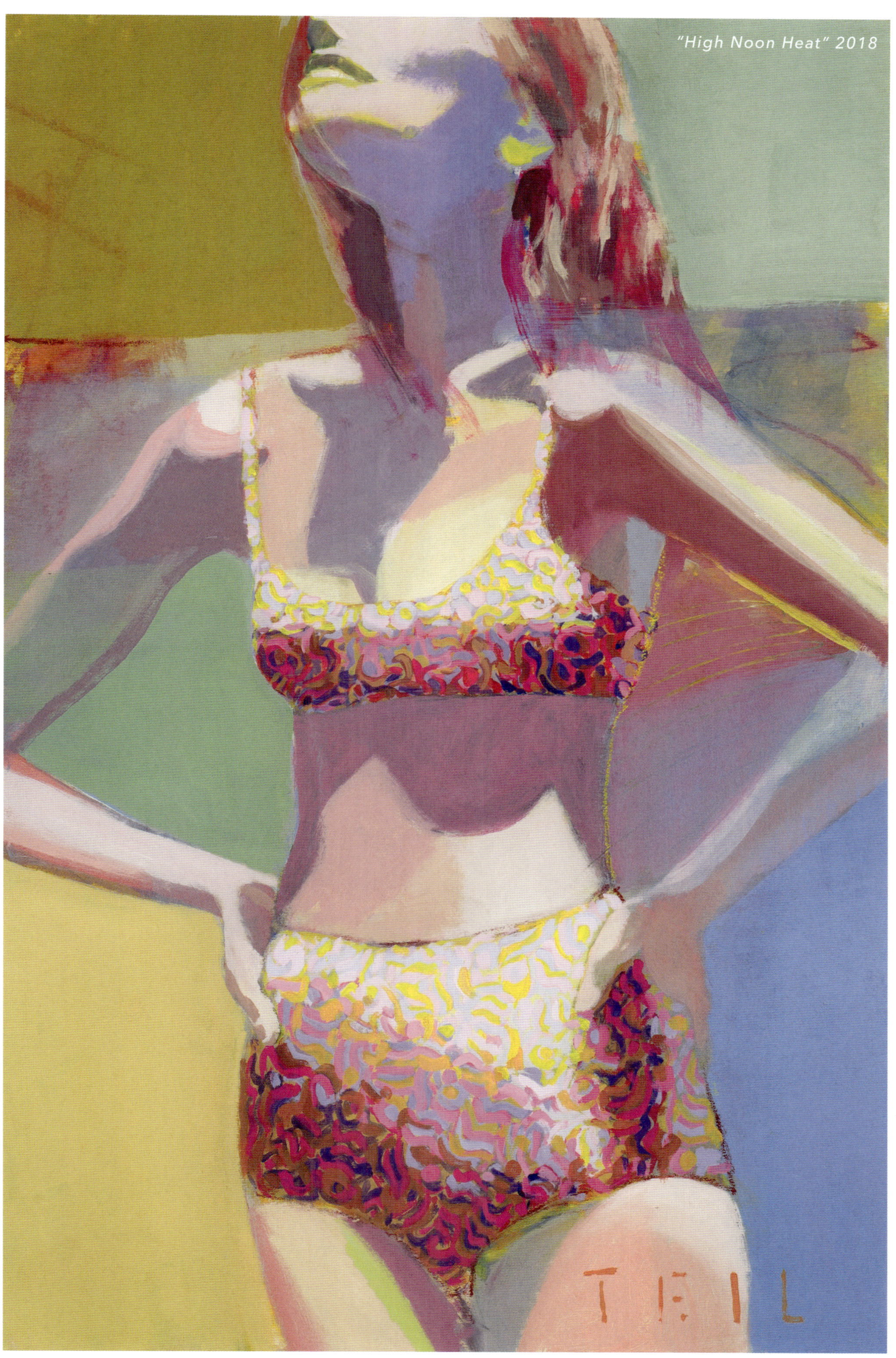

"High Noon Heat" 2018

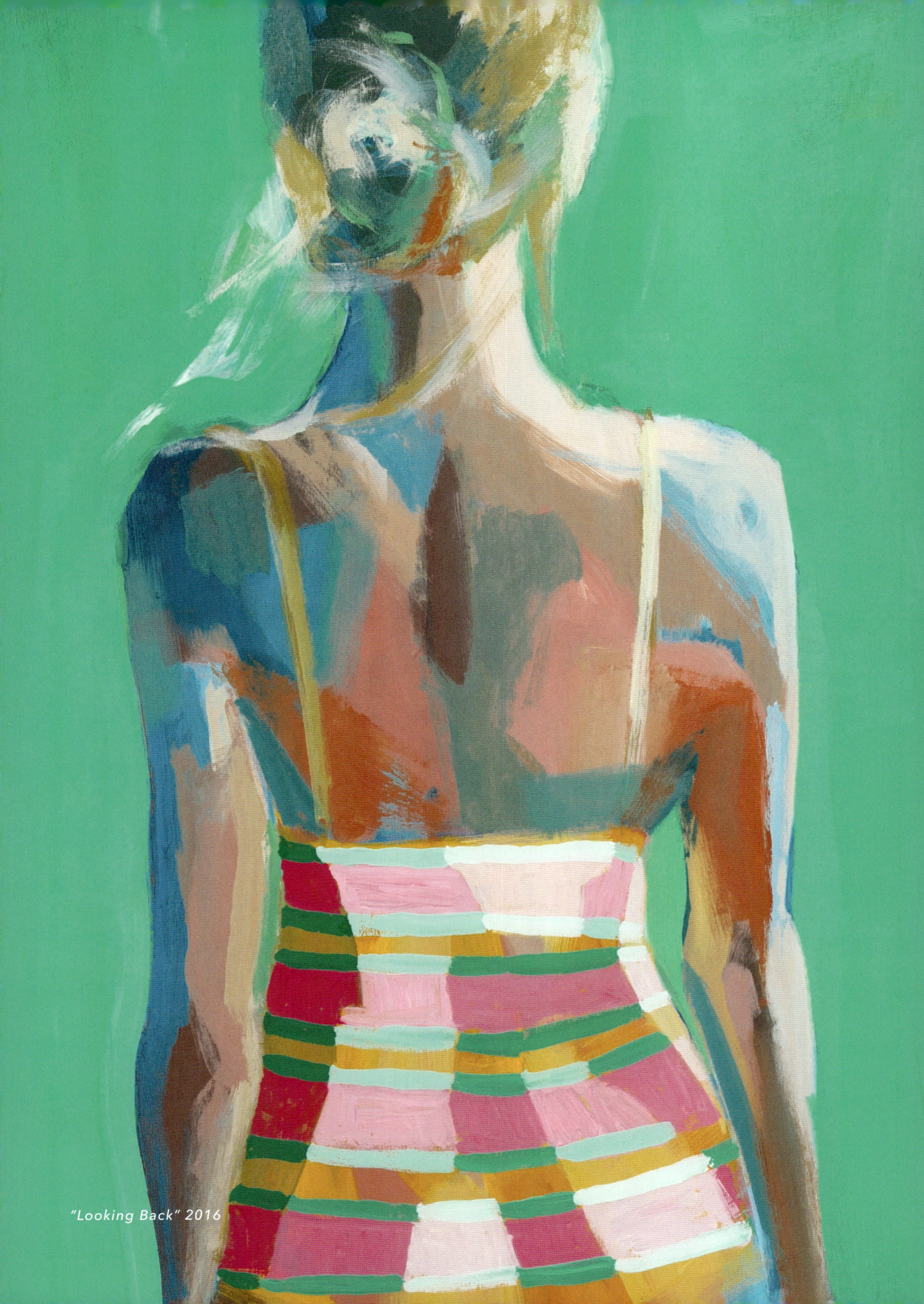

"Looking Back" 2016

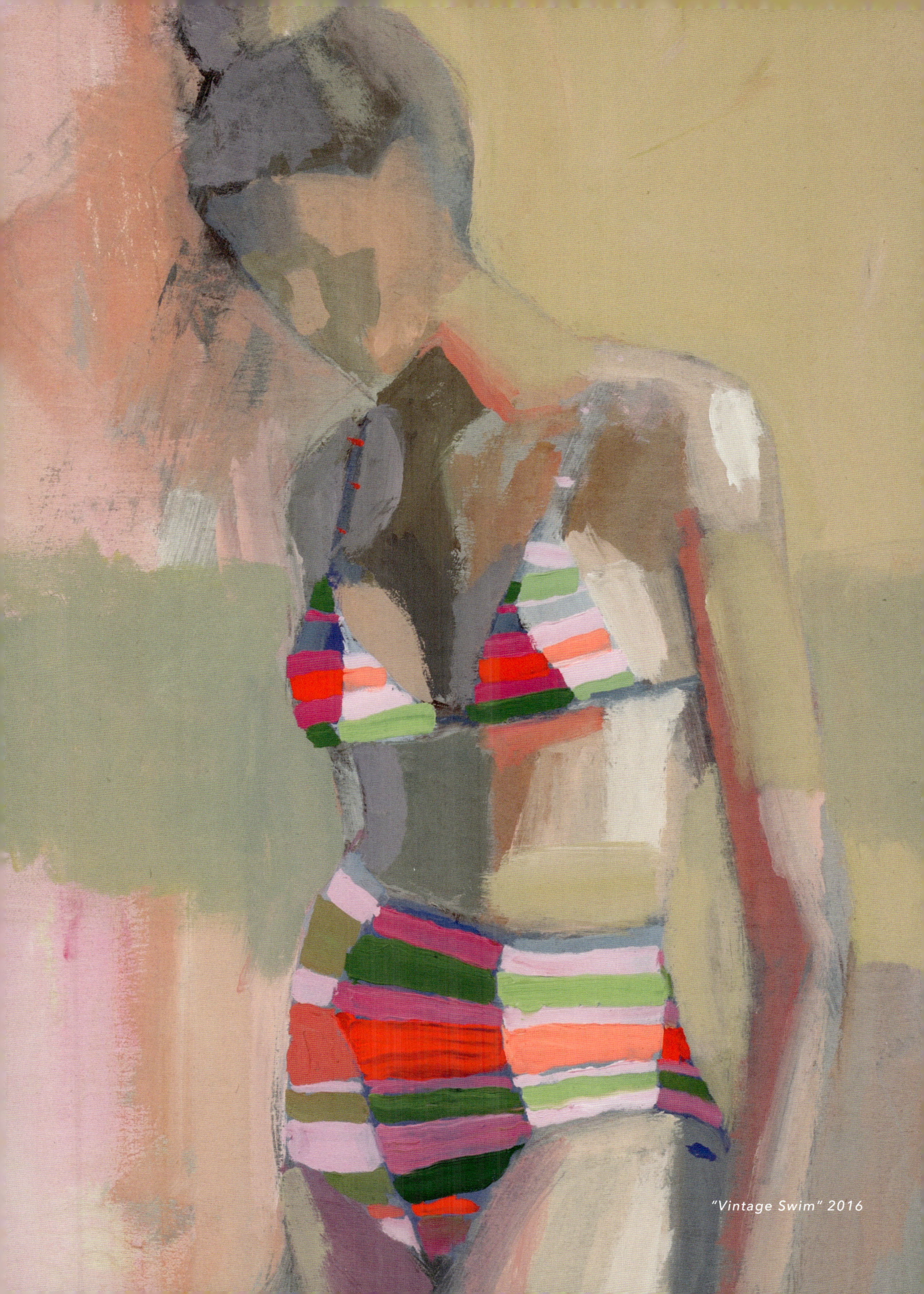

"Vintage Swim" 2016

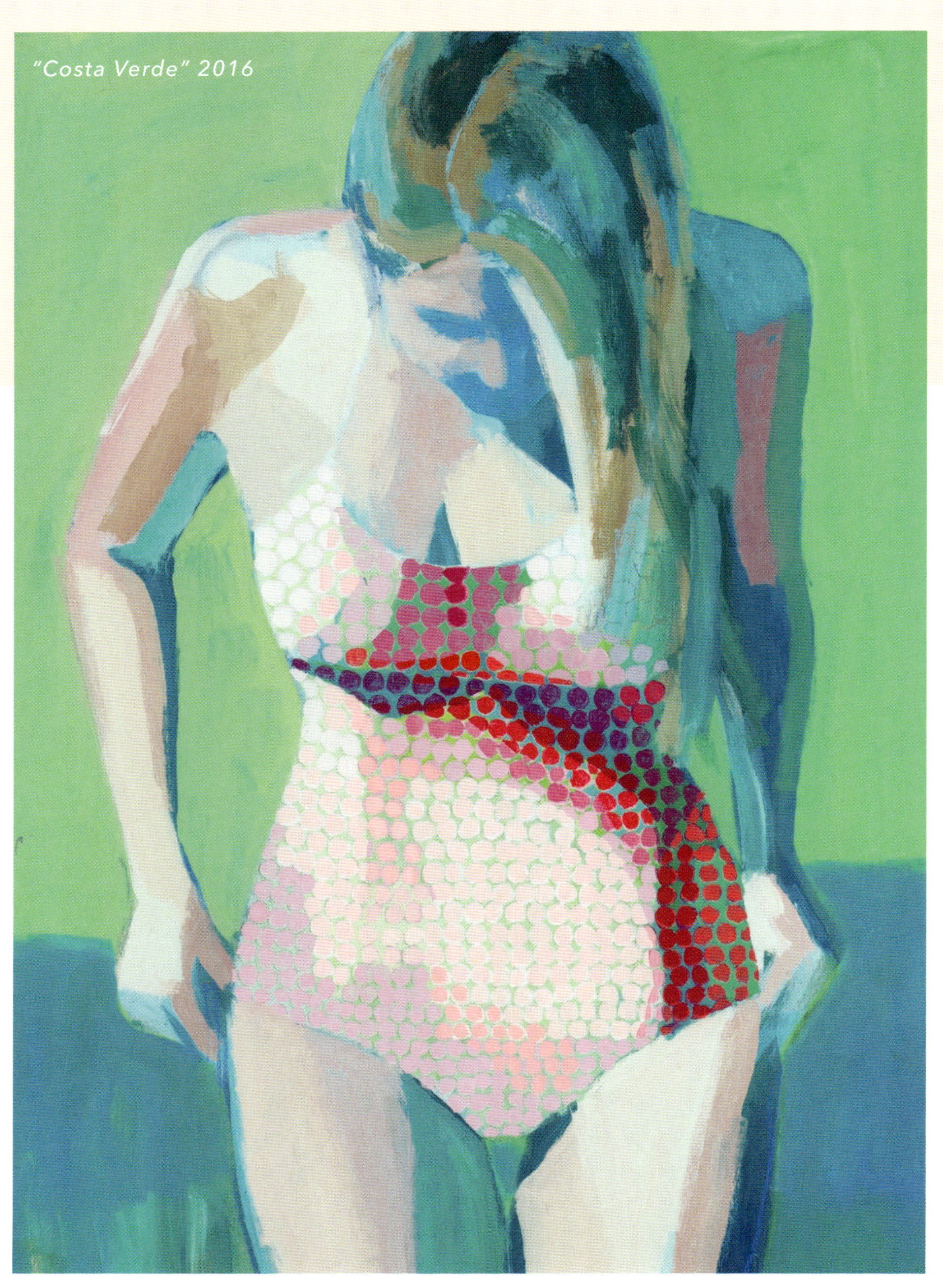

"Costa Verde" 2016

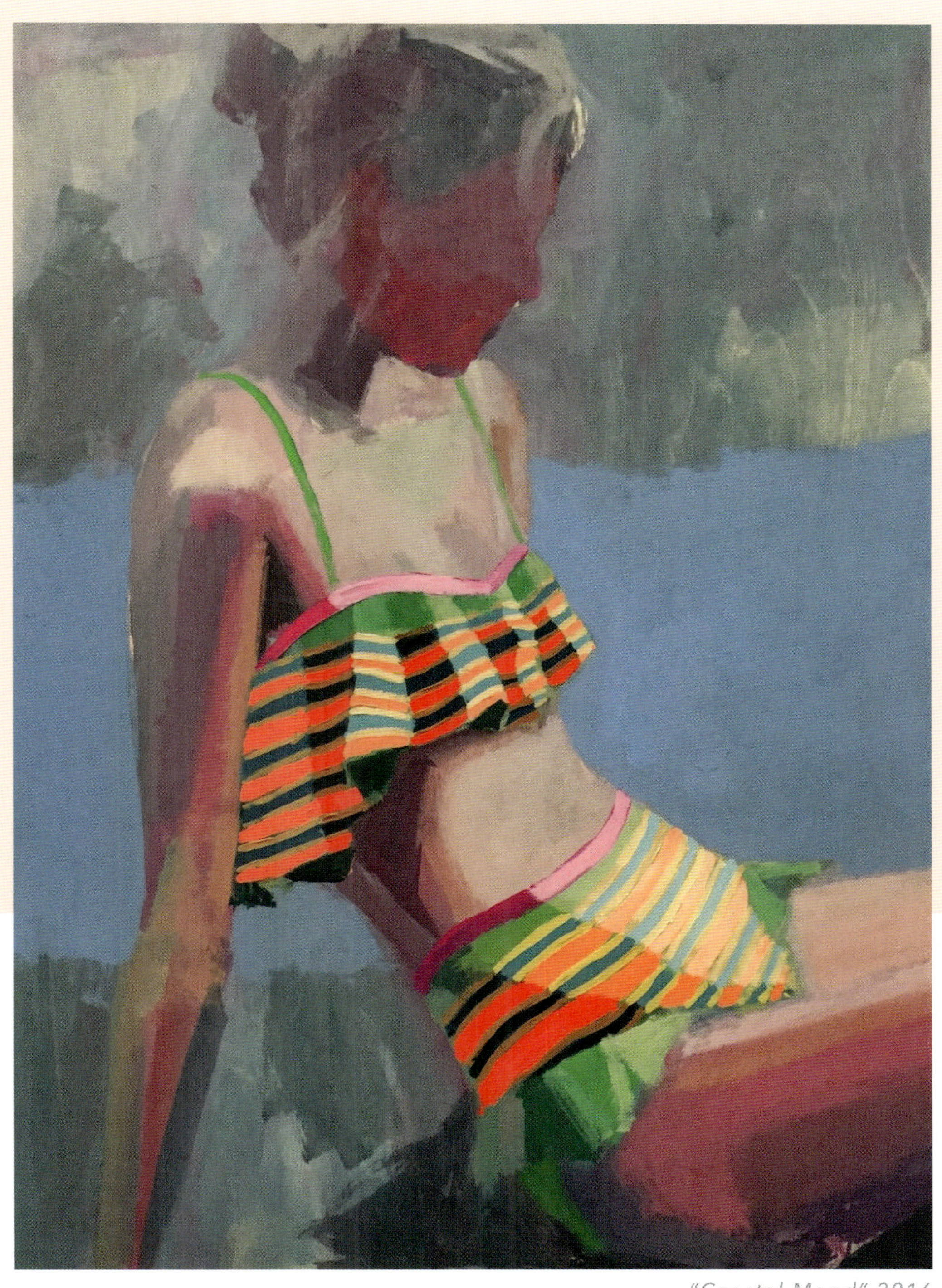

"Coastal Mood" 2016

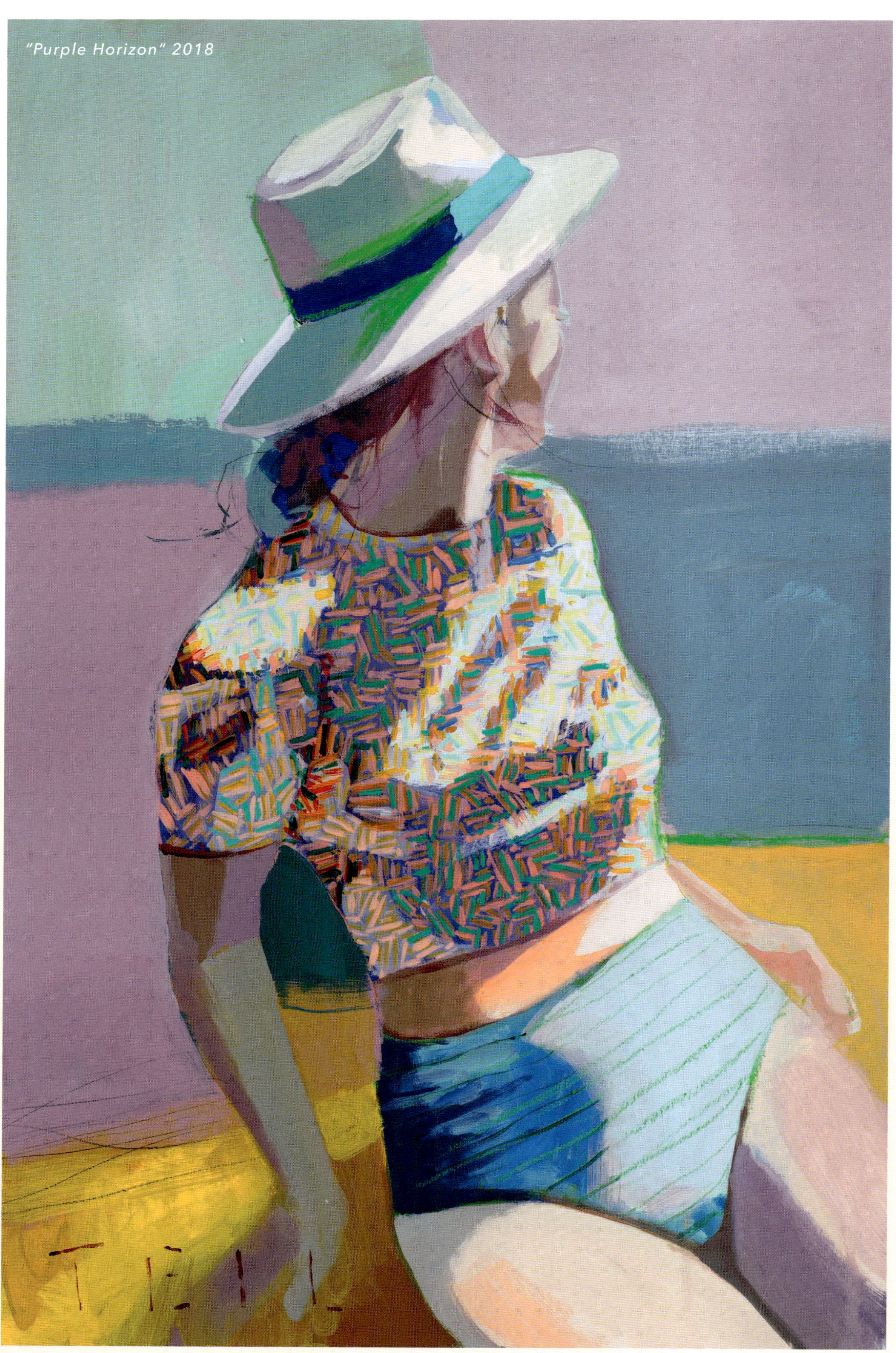
"Purple Horizon" 2018

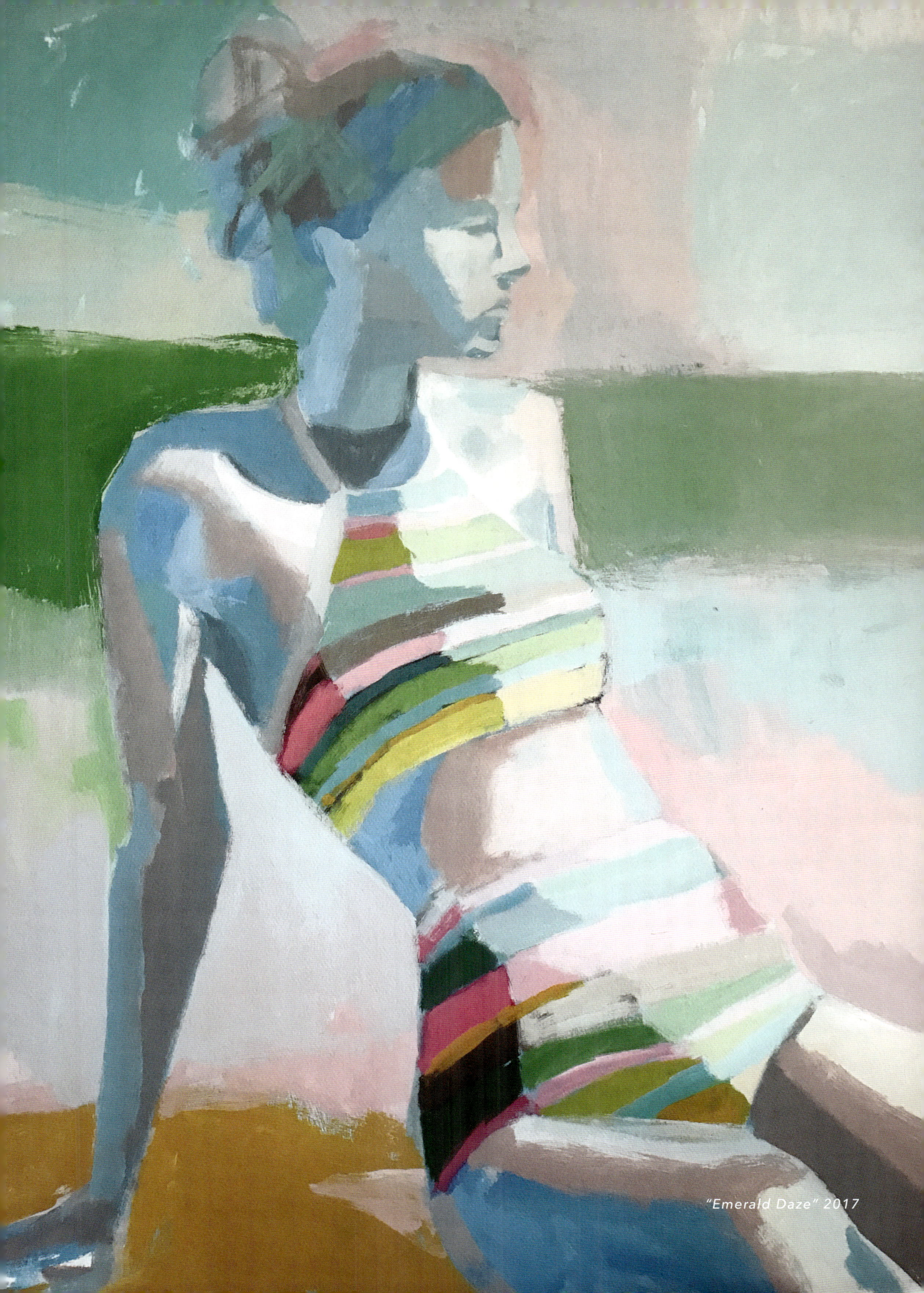

"Emerald Daze" 2017

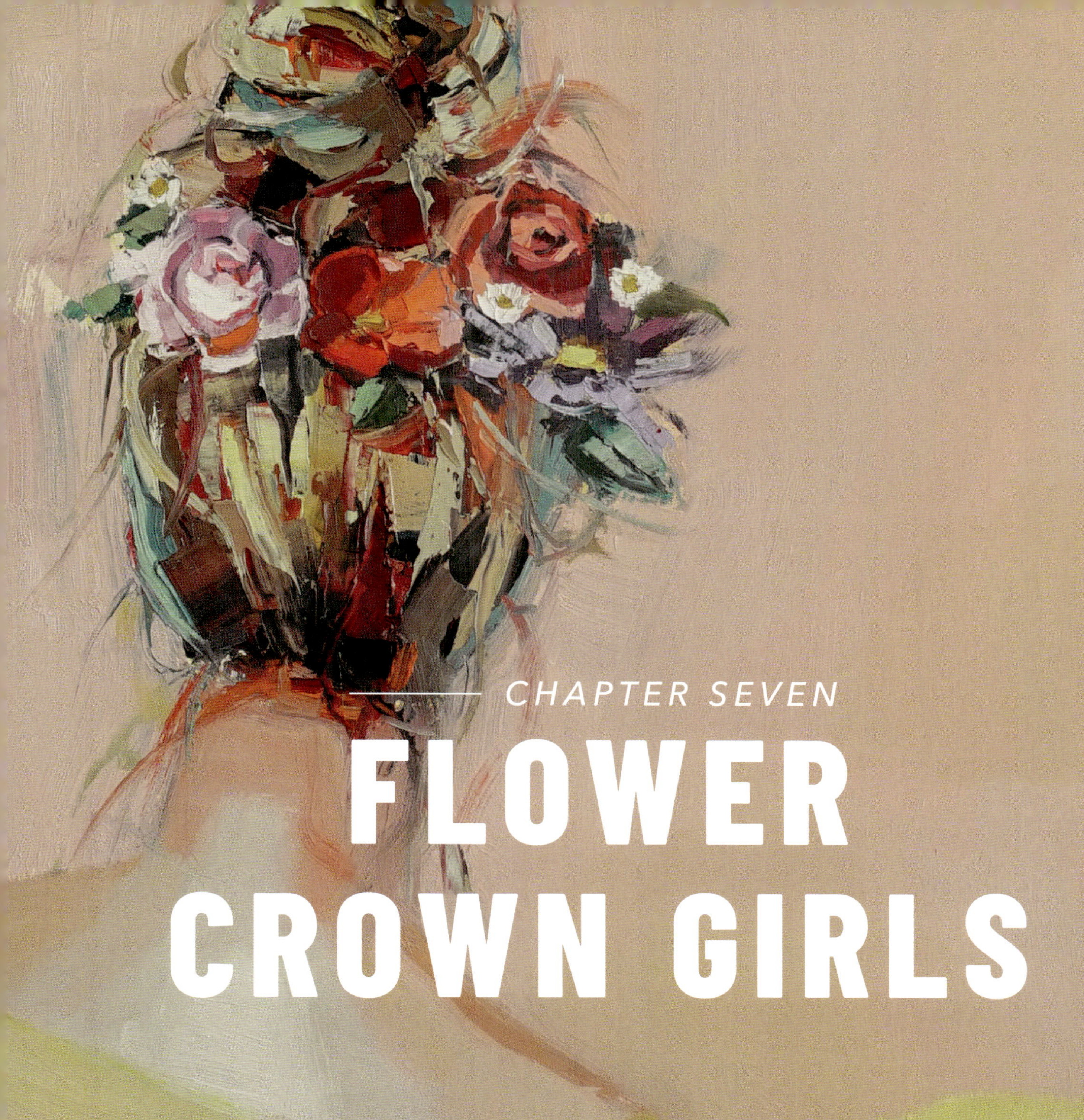

CHAPTER SEVEN

FLOWER CROWN GIRLS

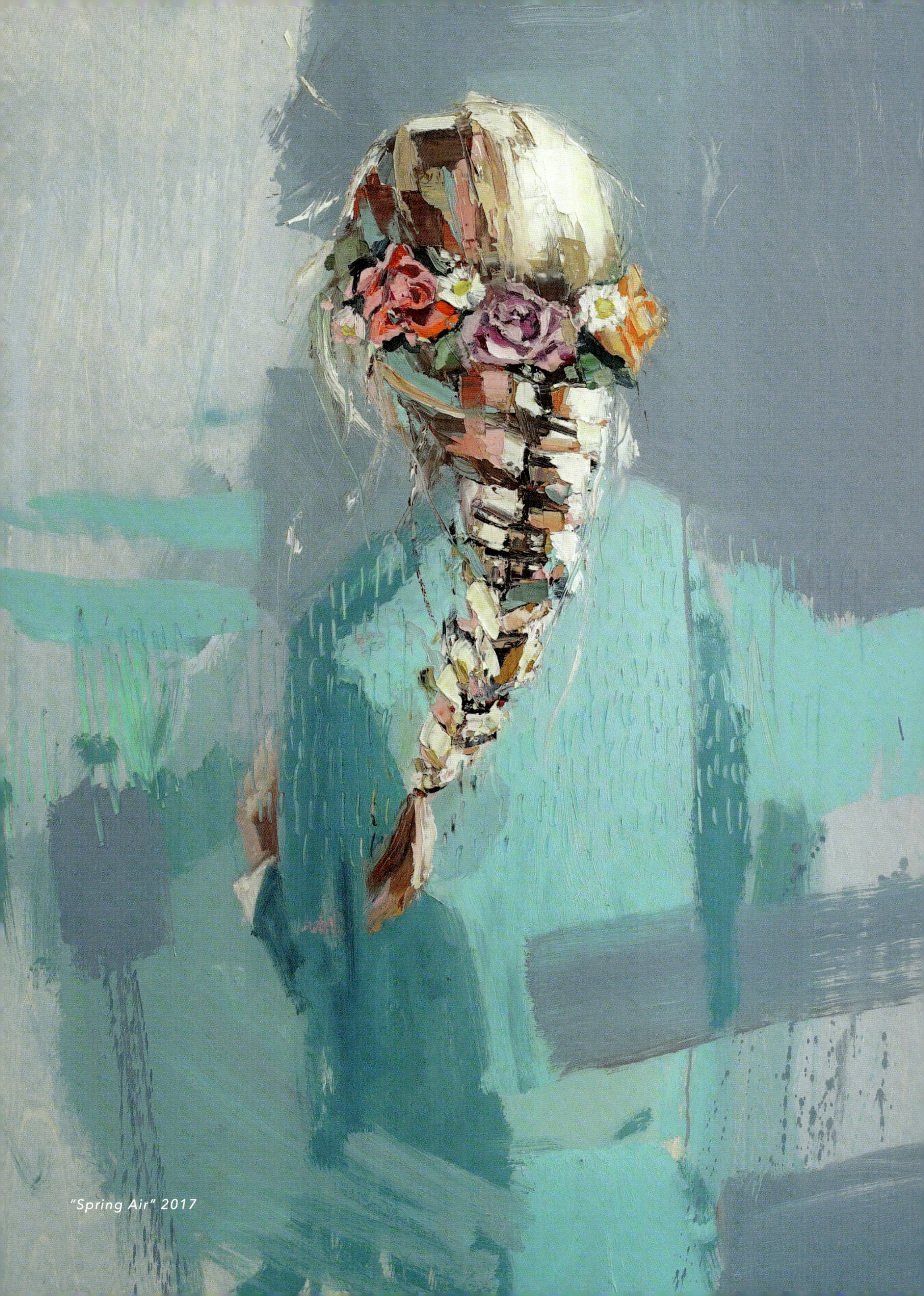

"Spring Air" 2017

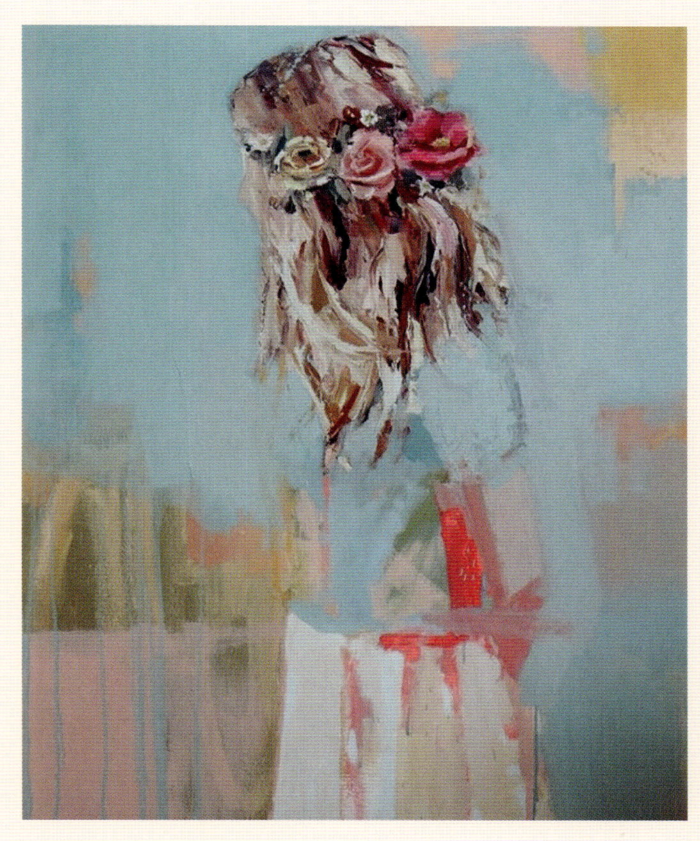

AFTER COMPLETING

a few commissions of impressionistic oil paintings of children's portraits, I particularly enjoyed painting their hair. Using an "impasto" approach, I laid rich and heavy oils on the canvas and transferred them around with a palette knife to render movement through wind-blown hair. I sat on the idea of making "hair" the leading character in an entire series and wondered how I could make it an interesting subject.

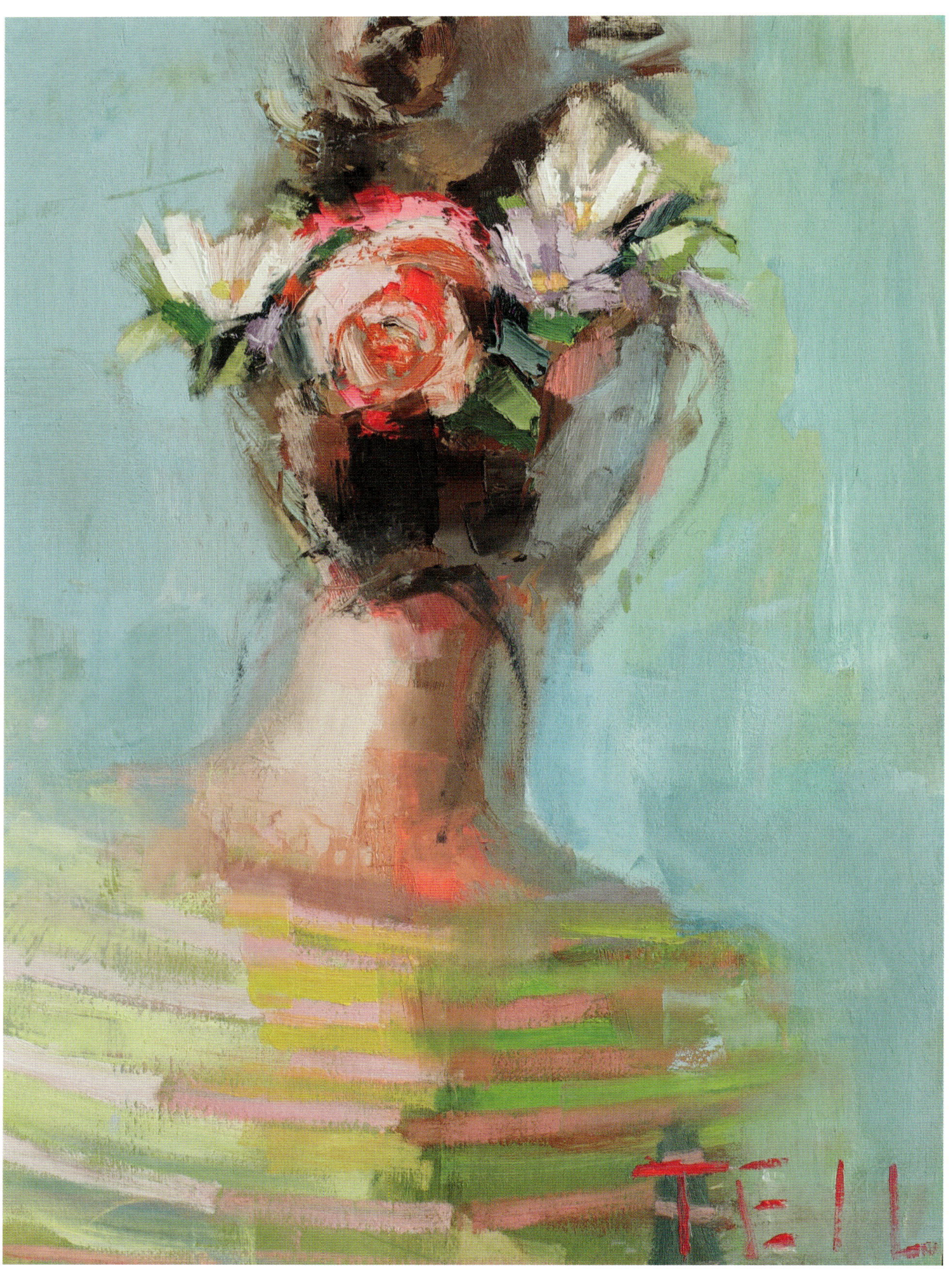

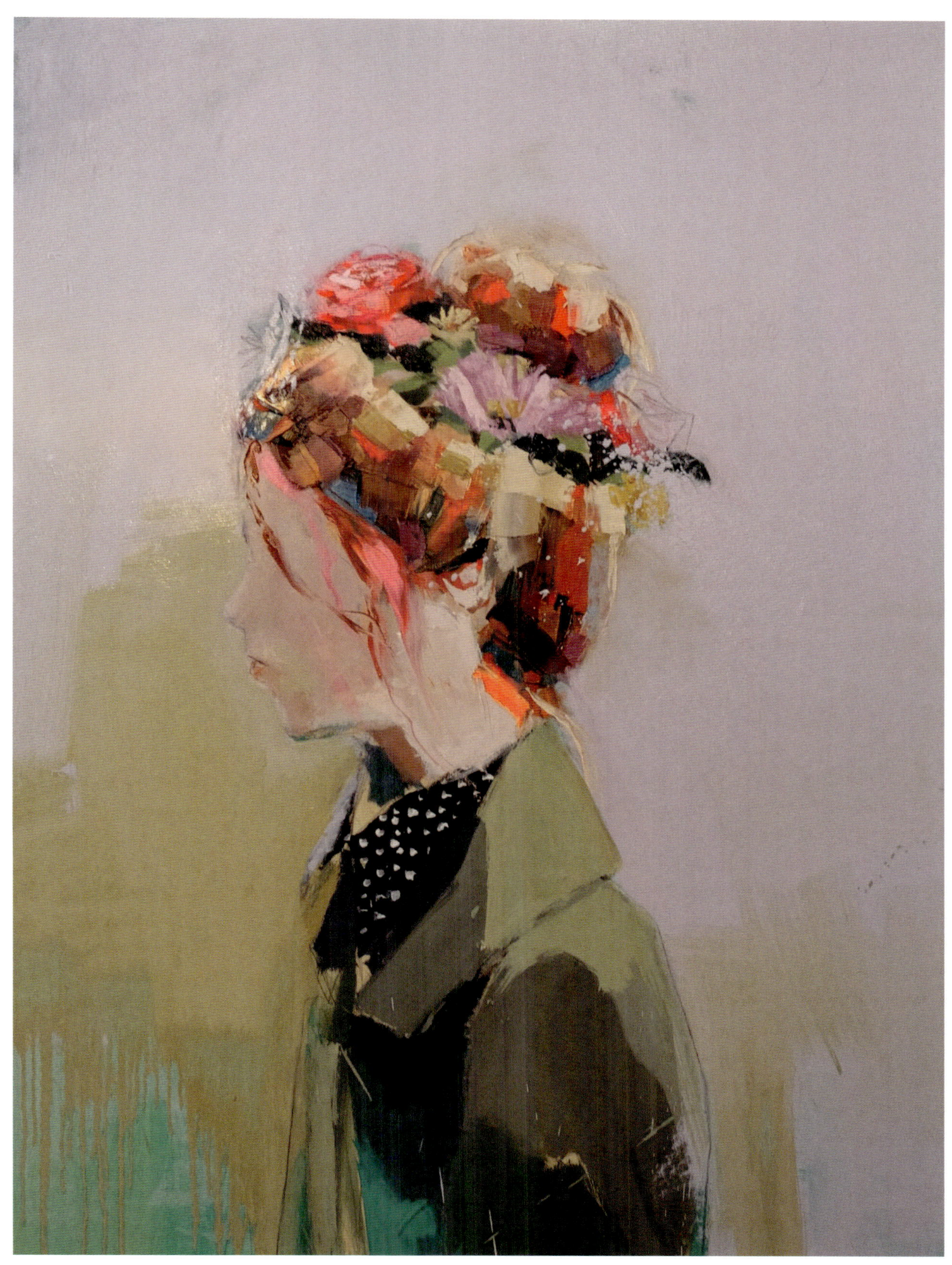

"East Chic" 2016

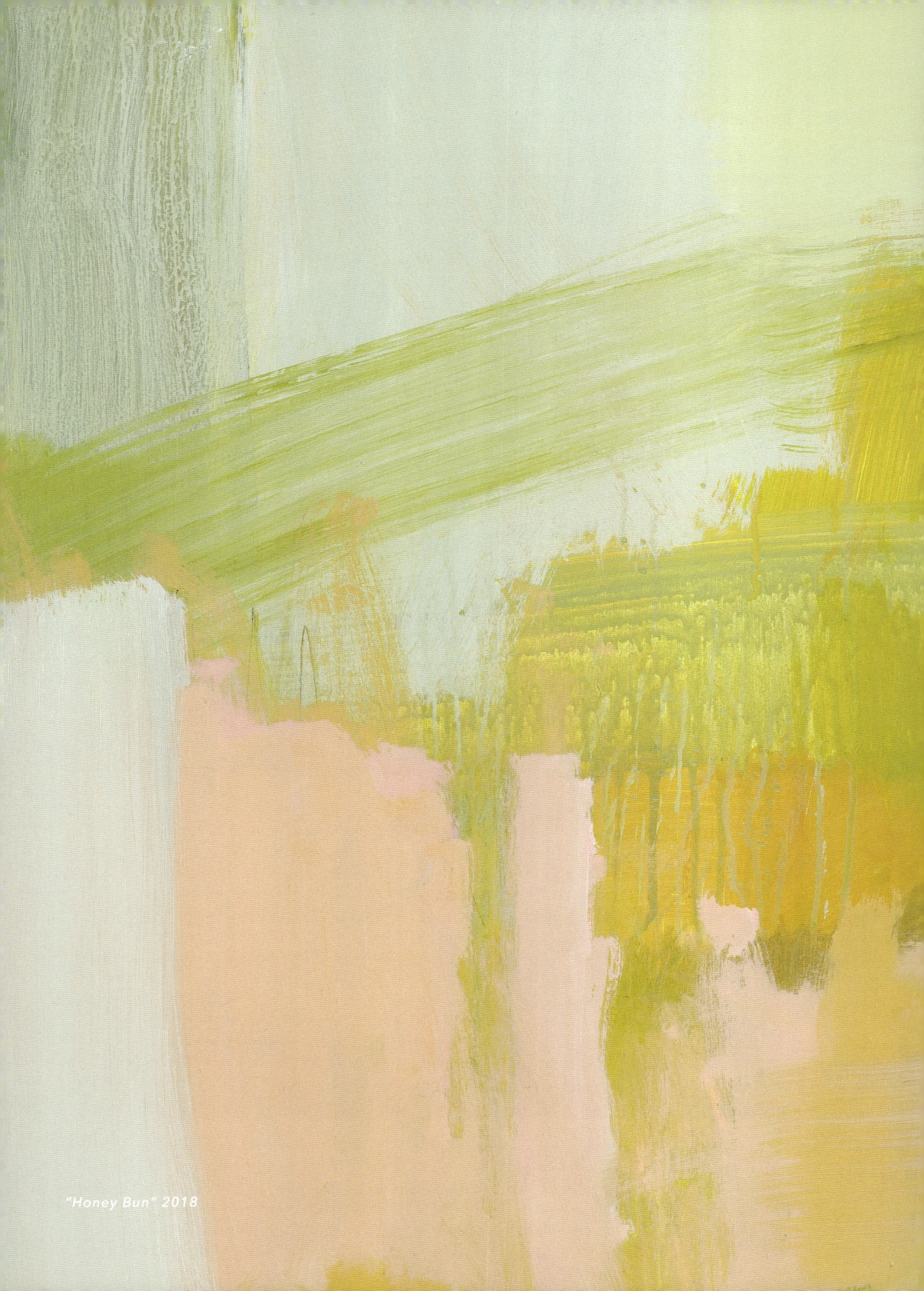

"Honey Bun" 2018

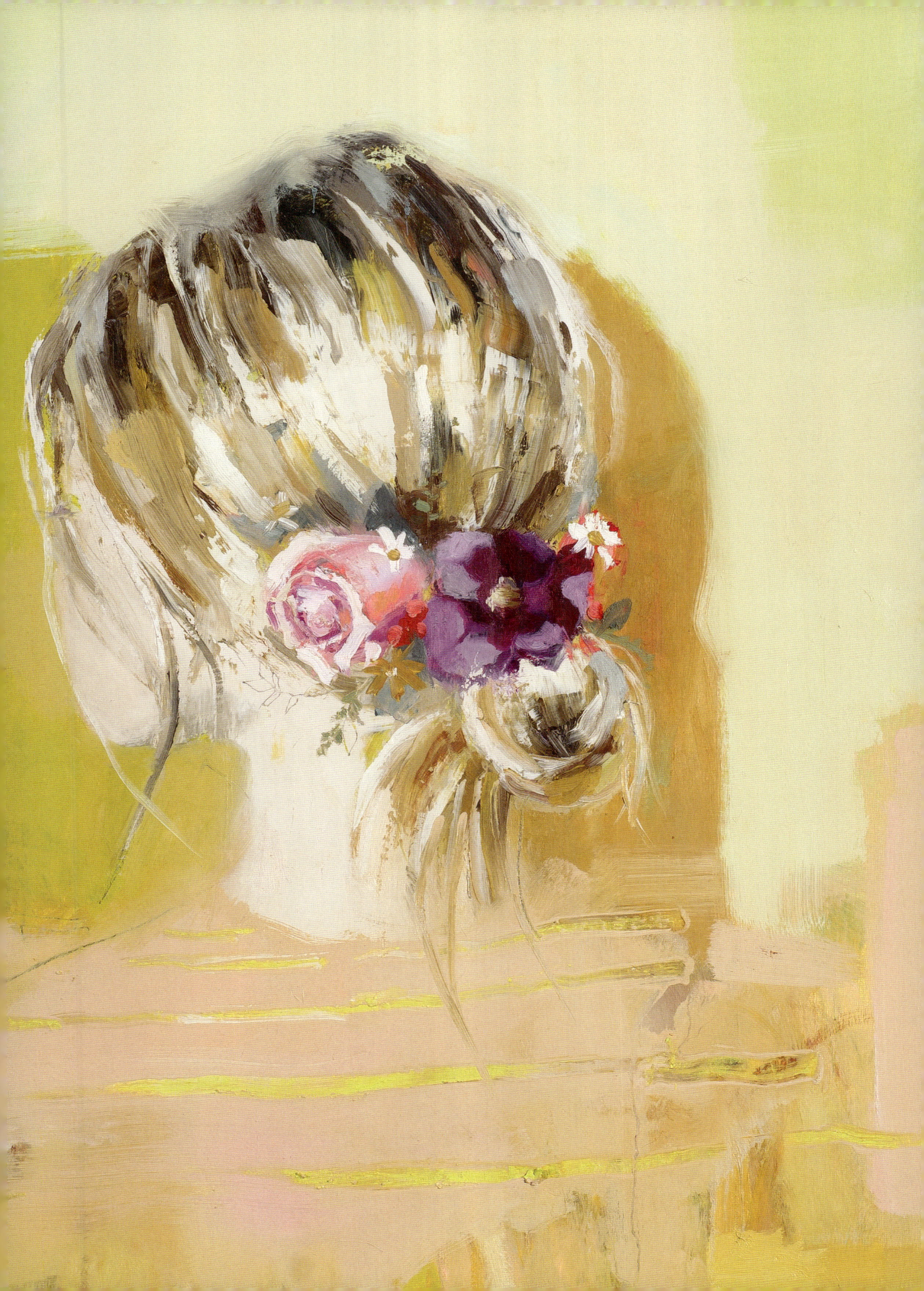

One day, I decided to just go for it and paint a female profile featuring a long blonde braid, adding a crown of florals as an afterthought. The first painting was a success, and the flower crown girls were born. This body of work consists of rich, thick texture, thin painterly washes, tight details, and flat patterns, producing a confident, feminine figure as the final product. Each crowned lady displays her own distinct personality, making the flower crown girls a favorite series among women.

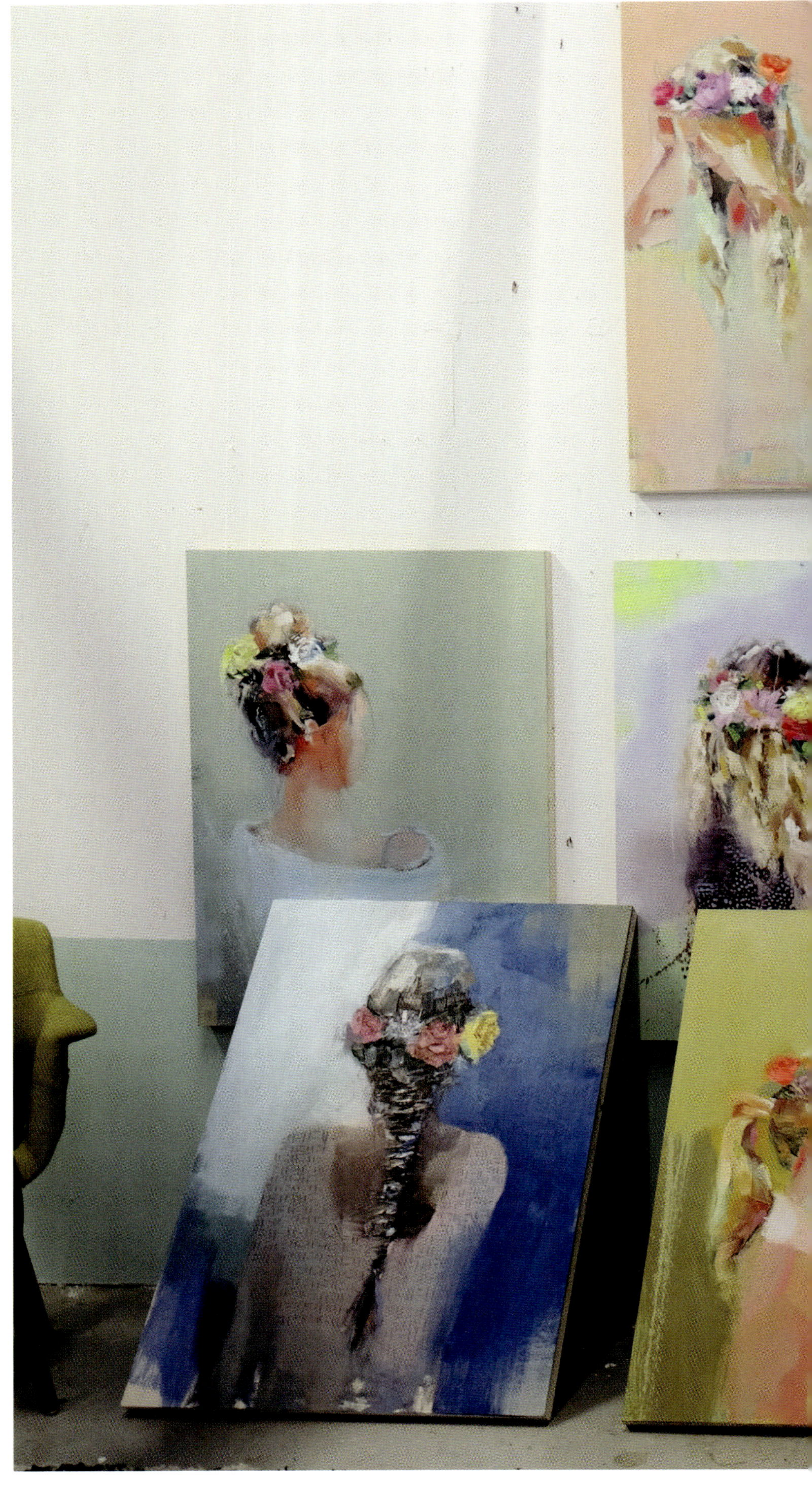

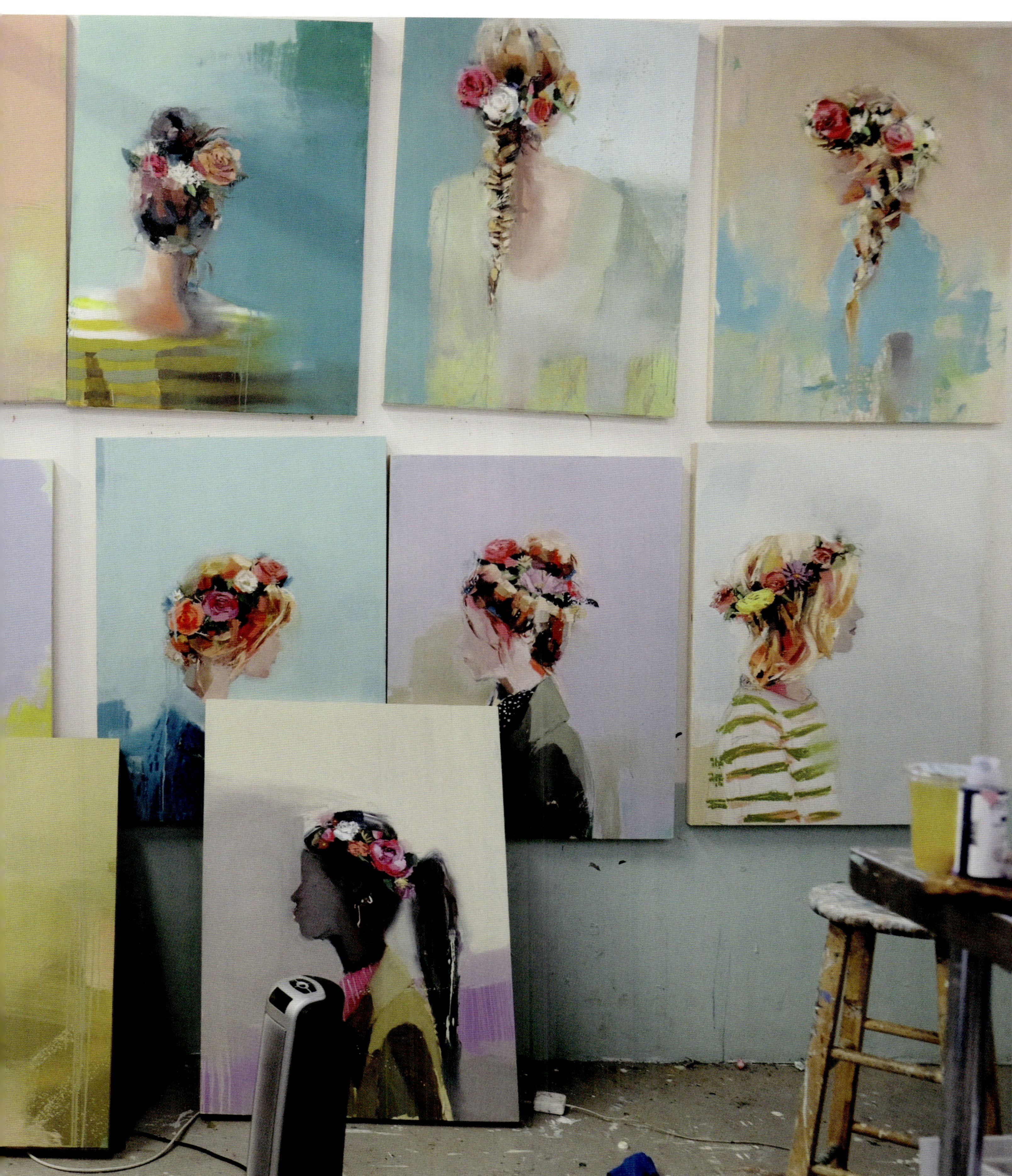

"Wrapped" 2016

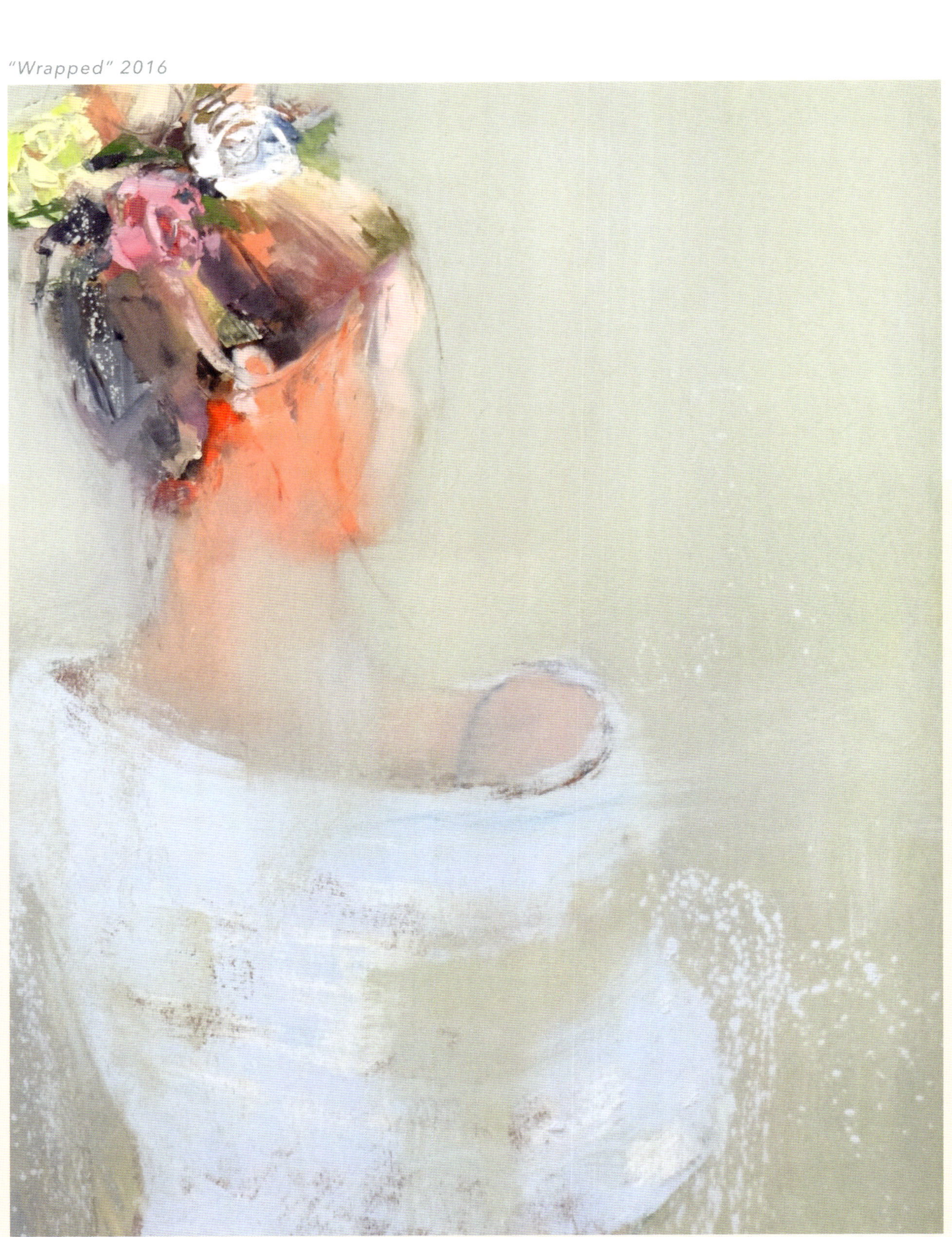

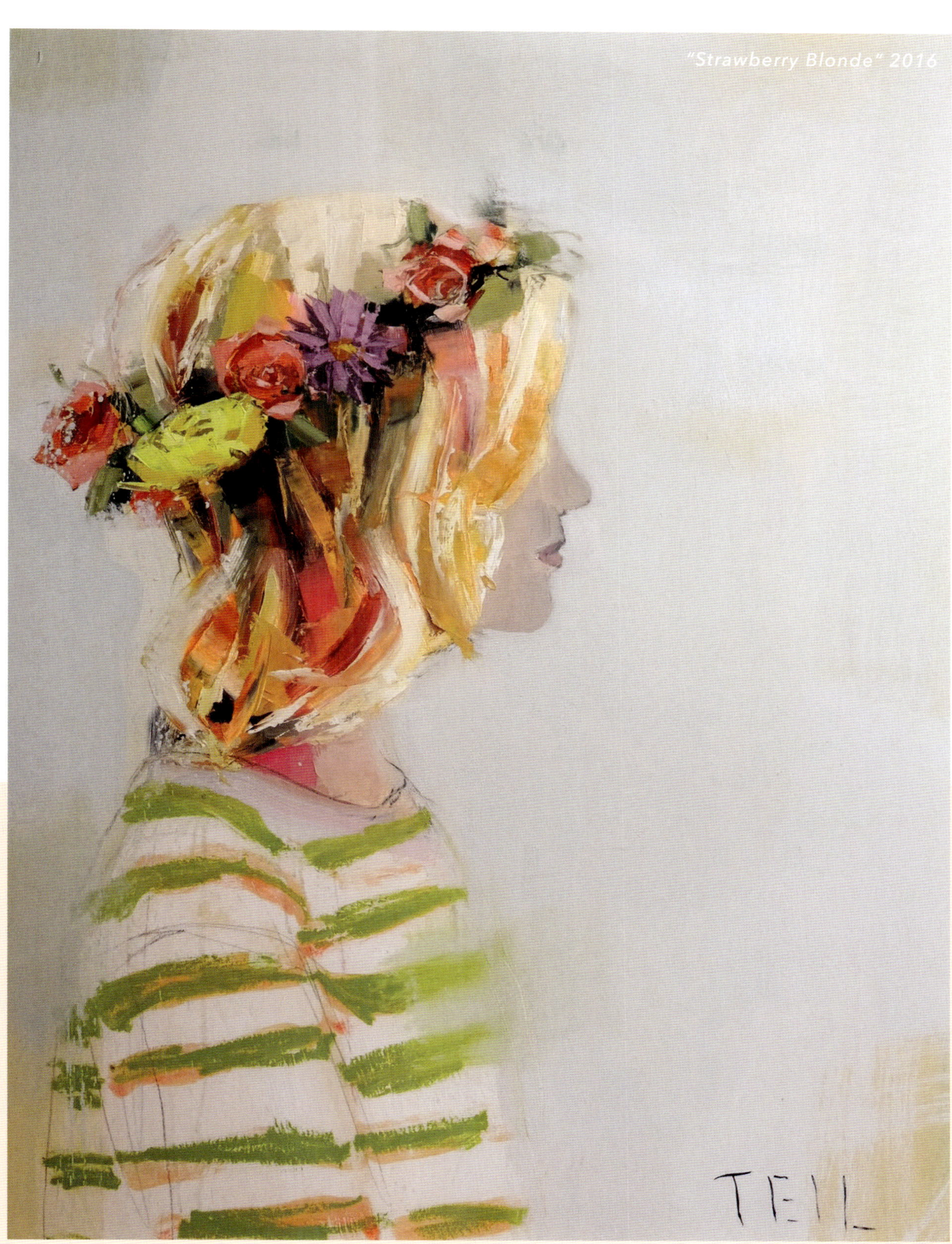

"Strawberry Blonde" 2016

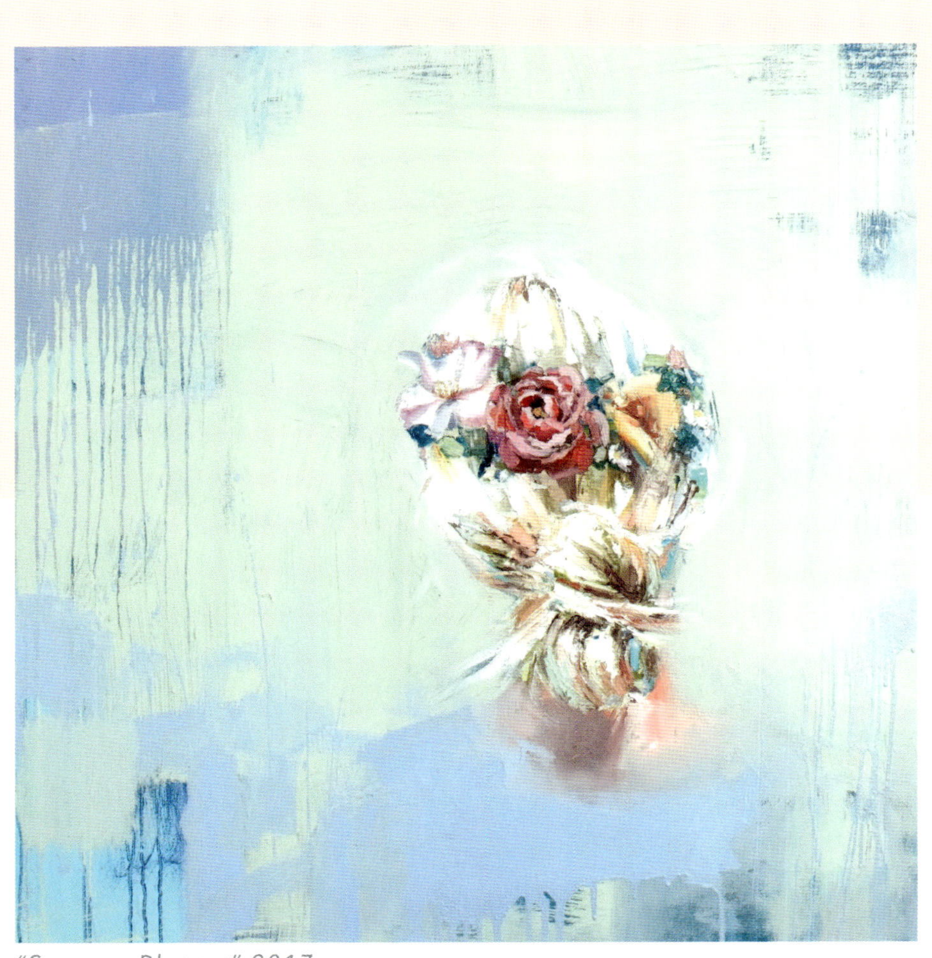

"Summer Blooms" 2017

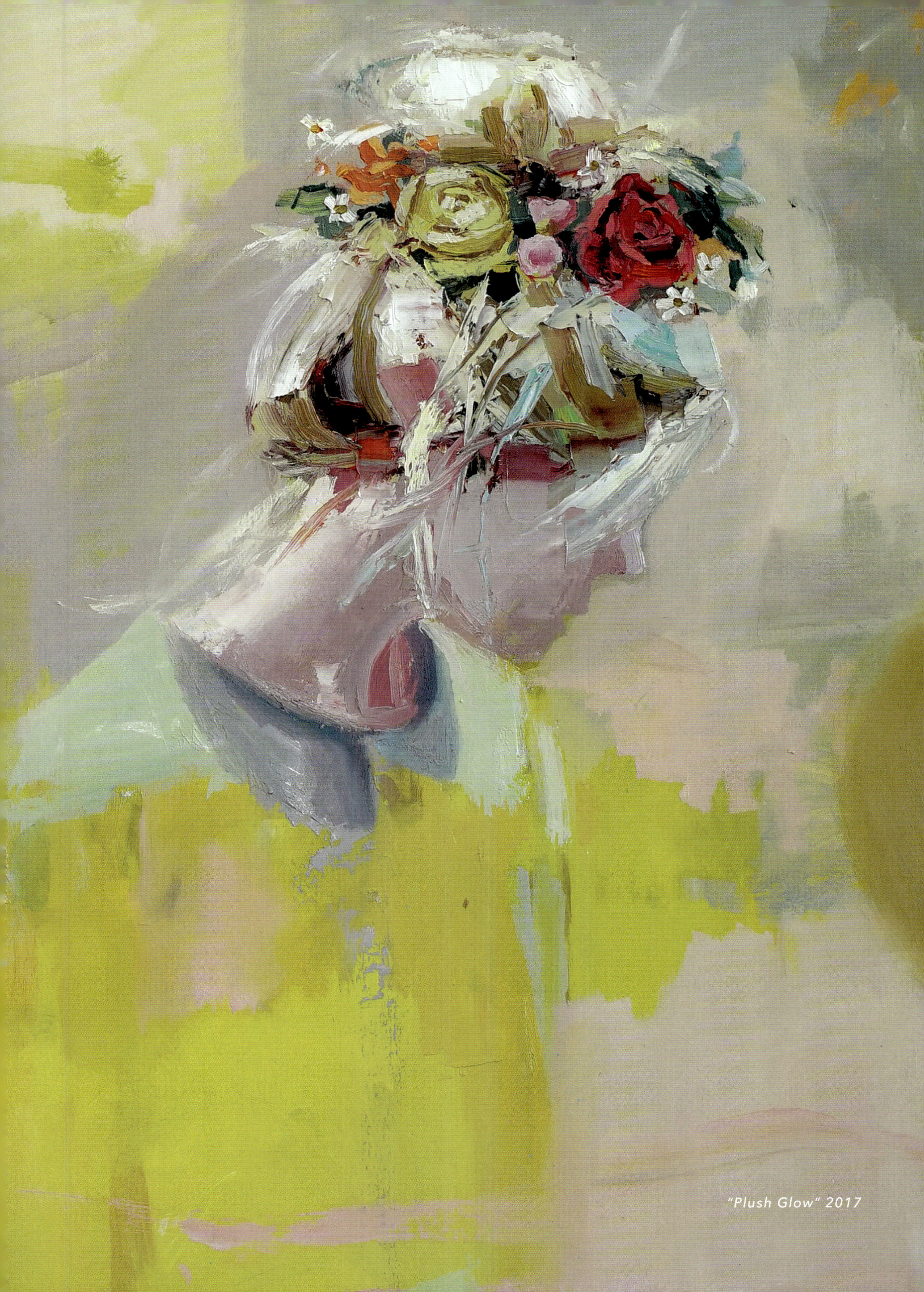

"Plush Glow" 2017

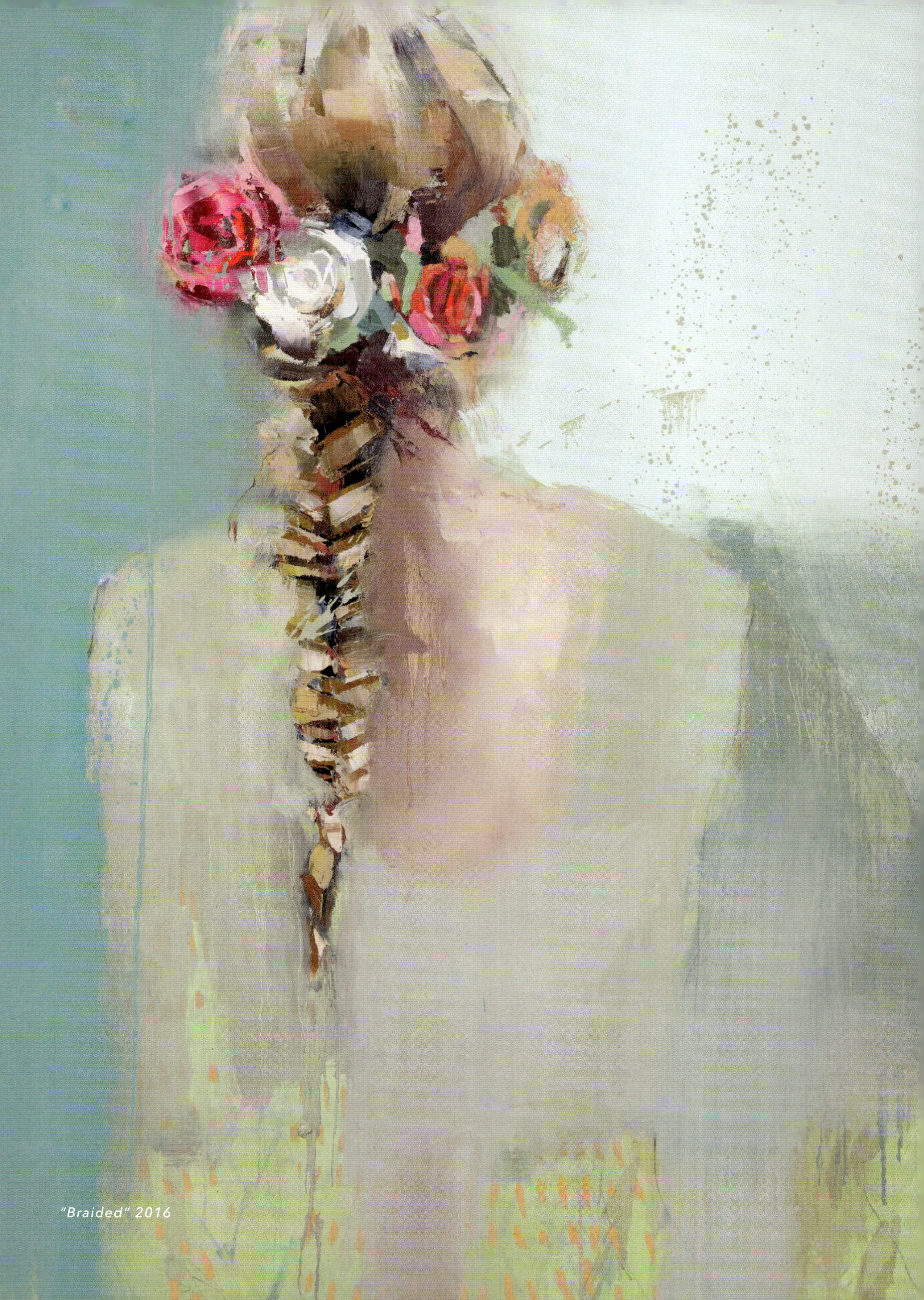

"Braided" 2016

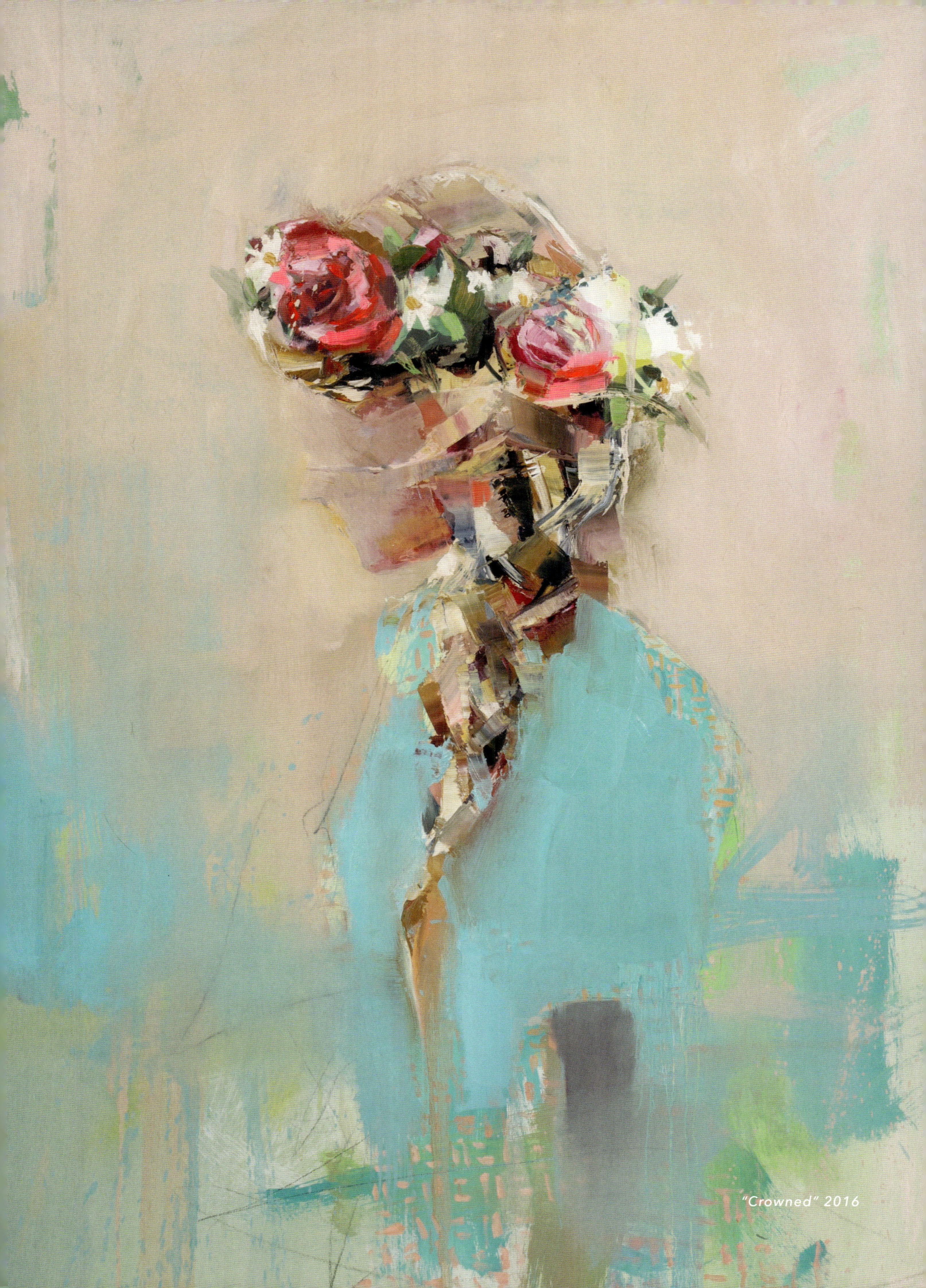

"Crowned" 2016

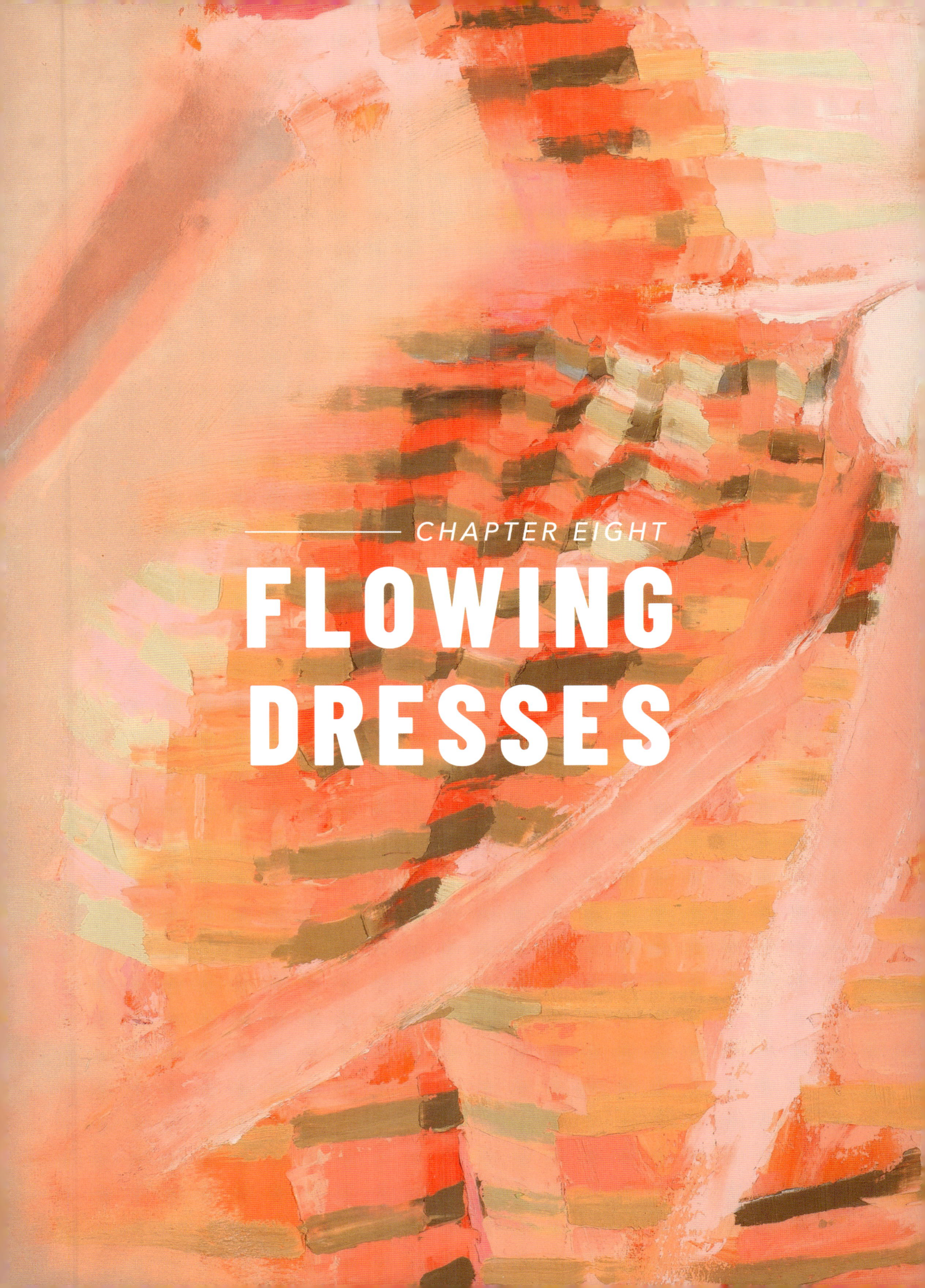

CHAPTER EIGHT

FLOWING DRESSES

I LOVE THE OPPORTUNITY

to give all of my attention to a single standing subject, and that chance arises while painting the flowing dresses. This group of girls is about whimsy, movement, pattern, and light. Each one depicts a carefree posture. The background is a field of color, open and free, with each girl staring off into its depths. The dresses display bends and folds of the material, prompted by playful movement or perhaps a soft breeze. One of the most distinct characteristics of this series is the way the sunlight plays off of the pattern of the dresses. Each dress proudly boasts its bold stripes in various shades of light, creating an array of colors dancing around the figure.

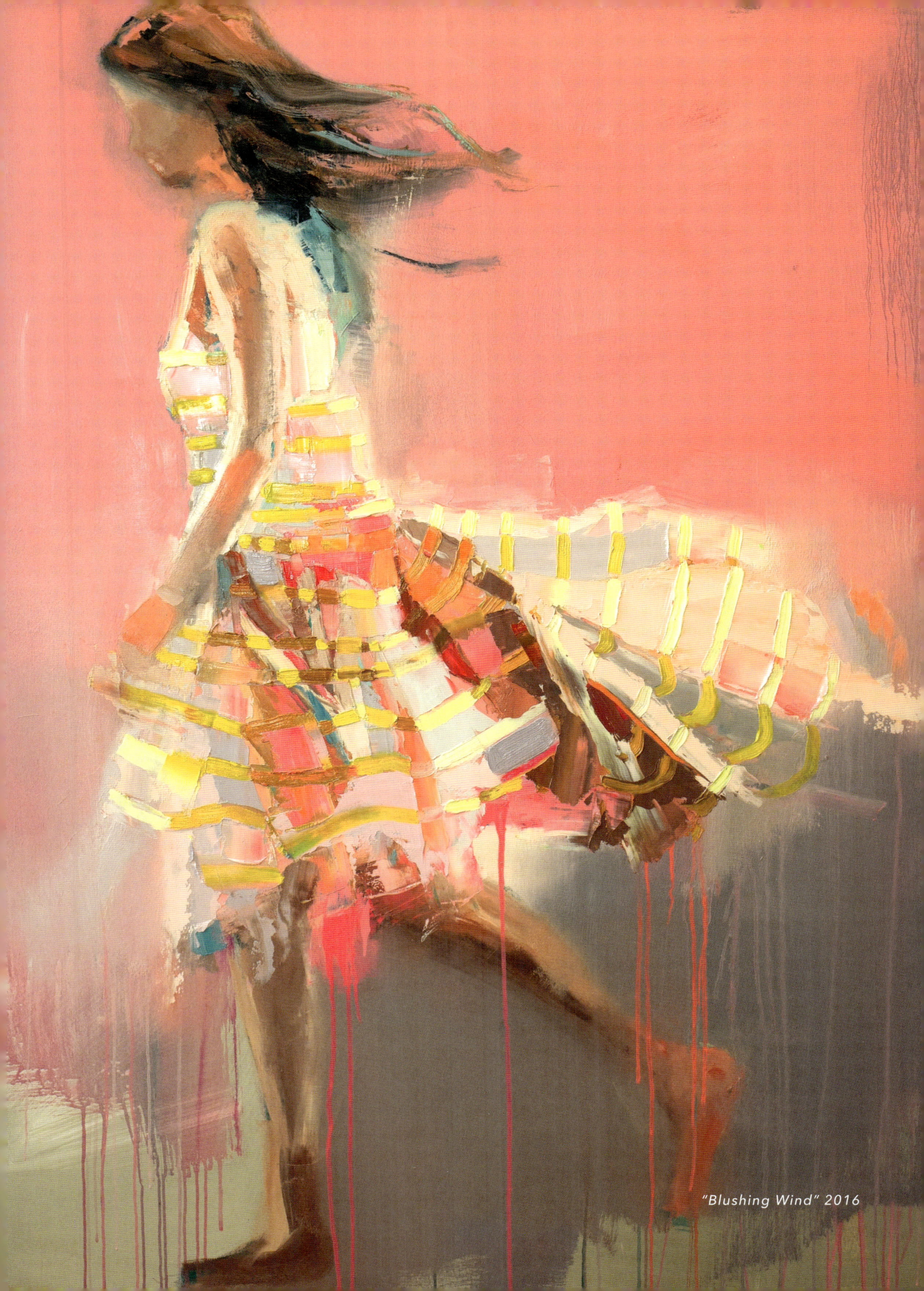

"Blushing Wind" 2016

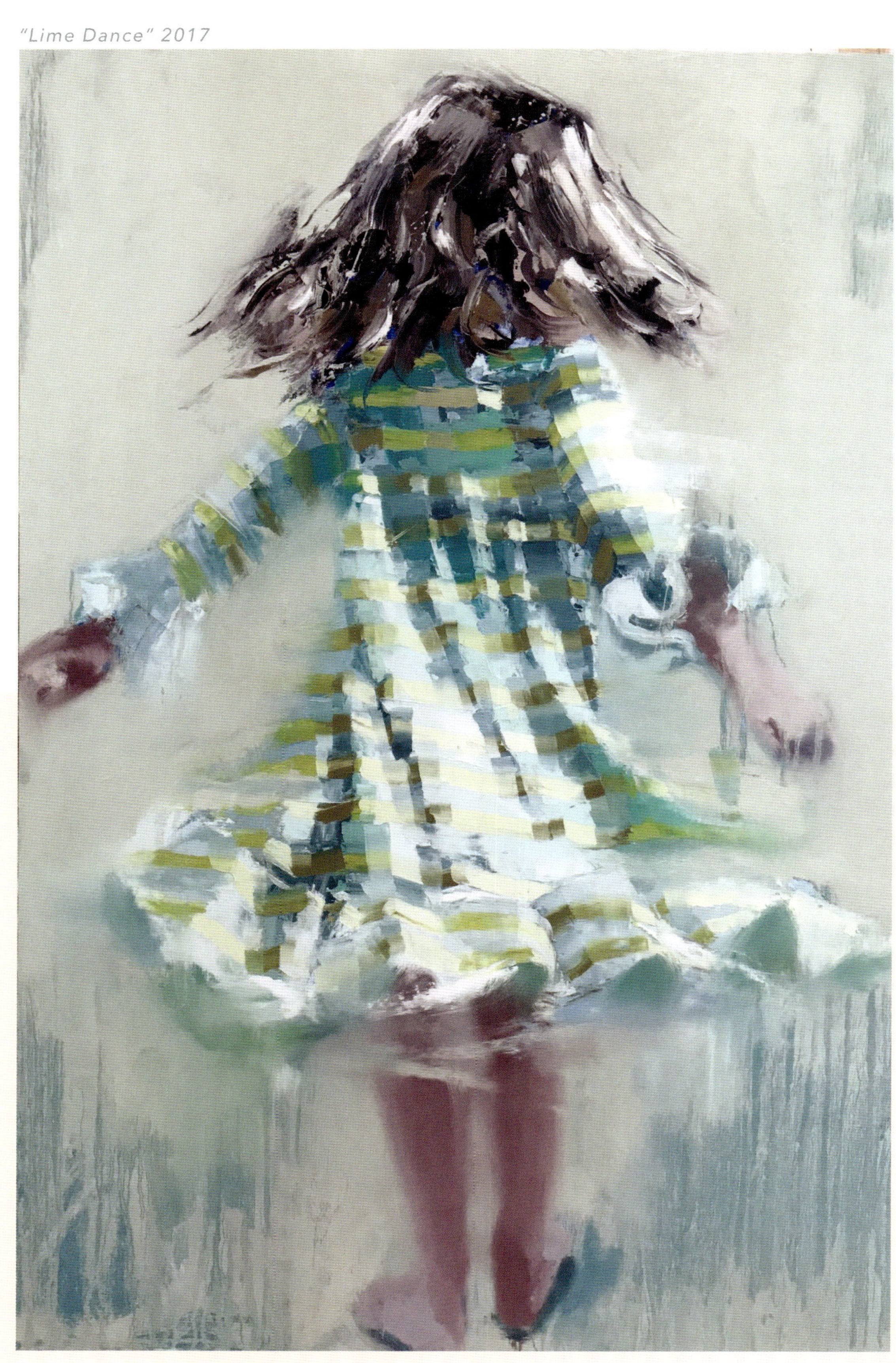

"Lime Dance" 2017

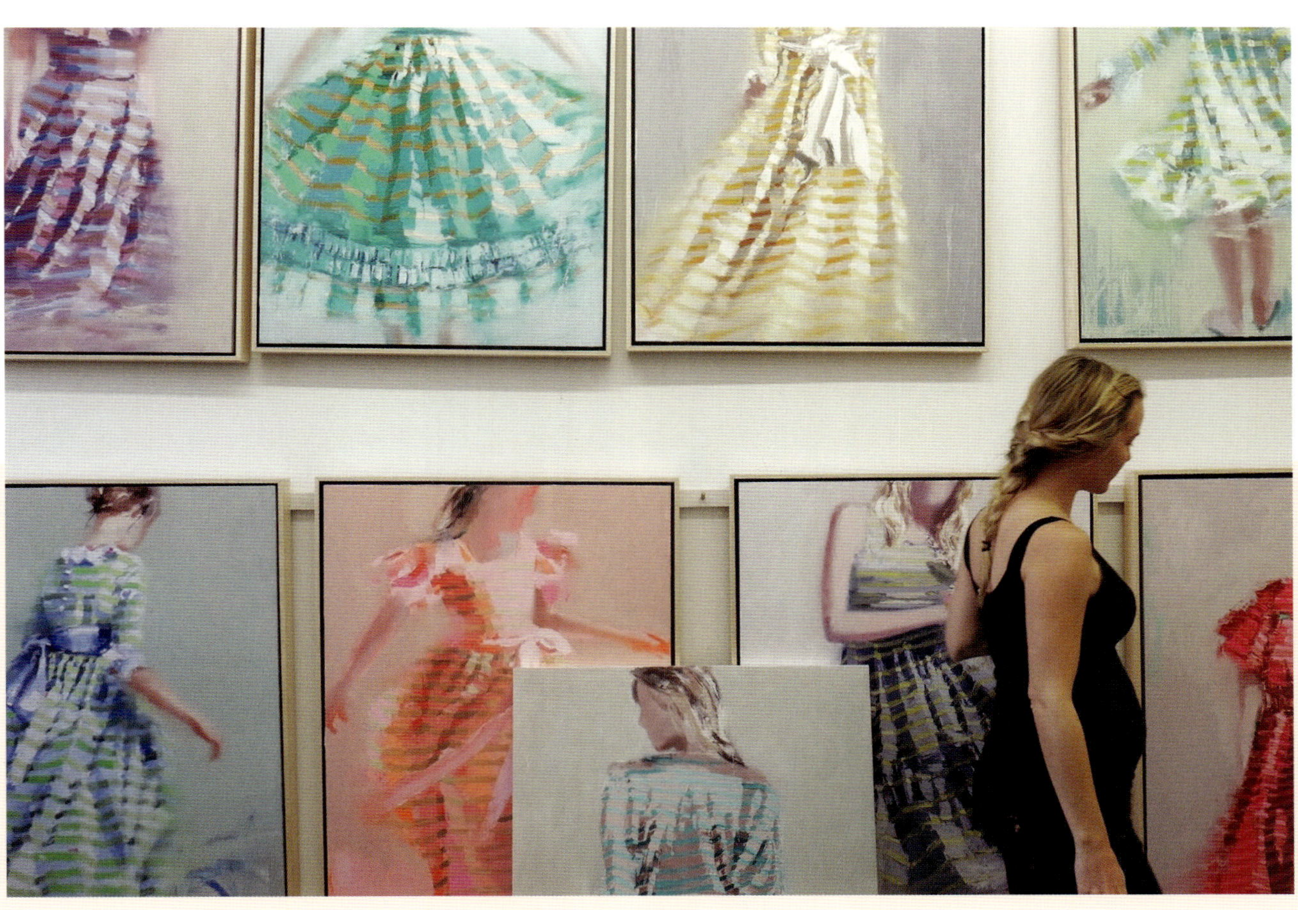

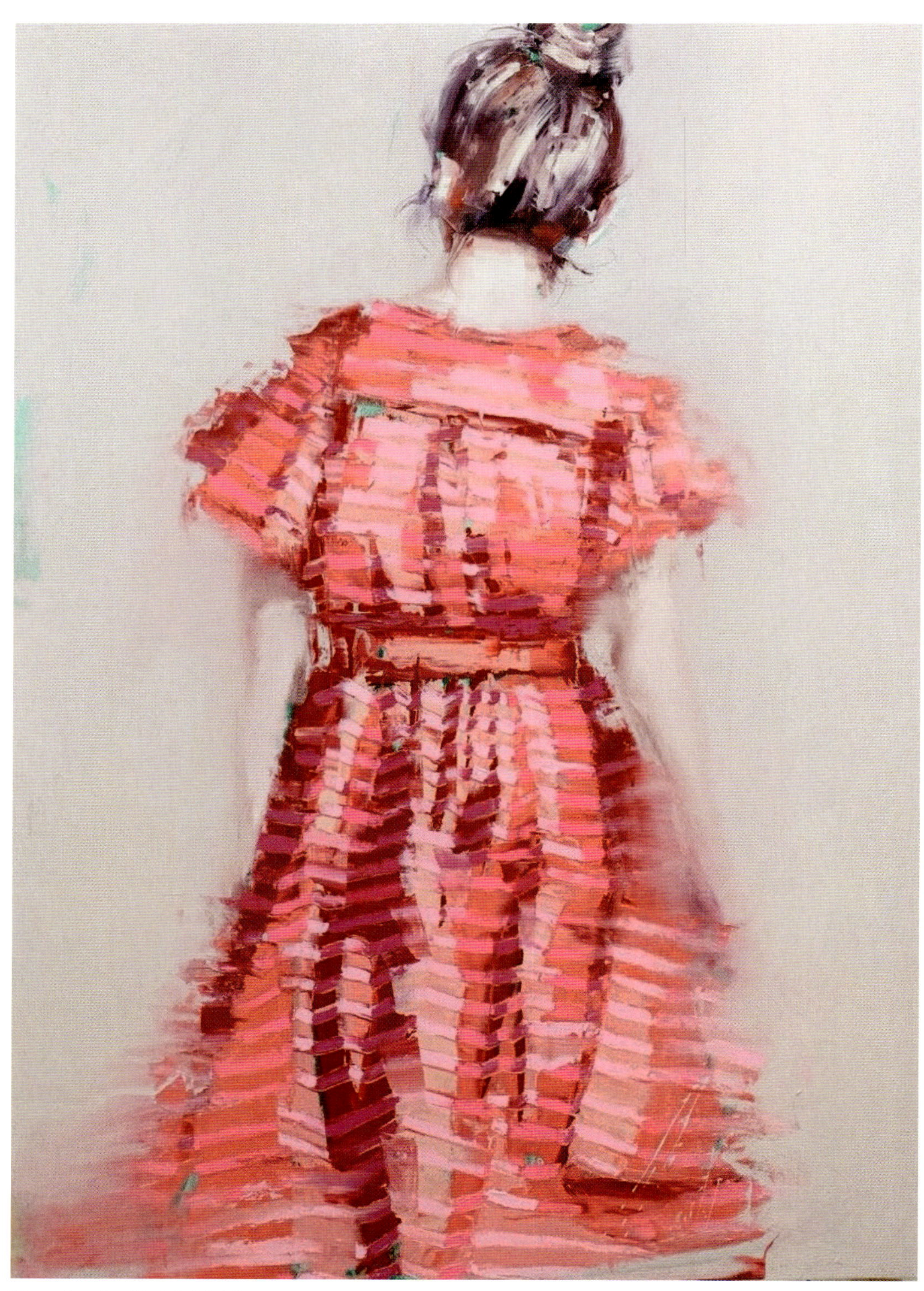

"Ponder in Pink" 2017

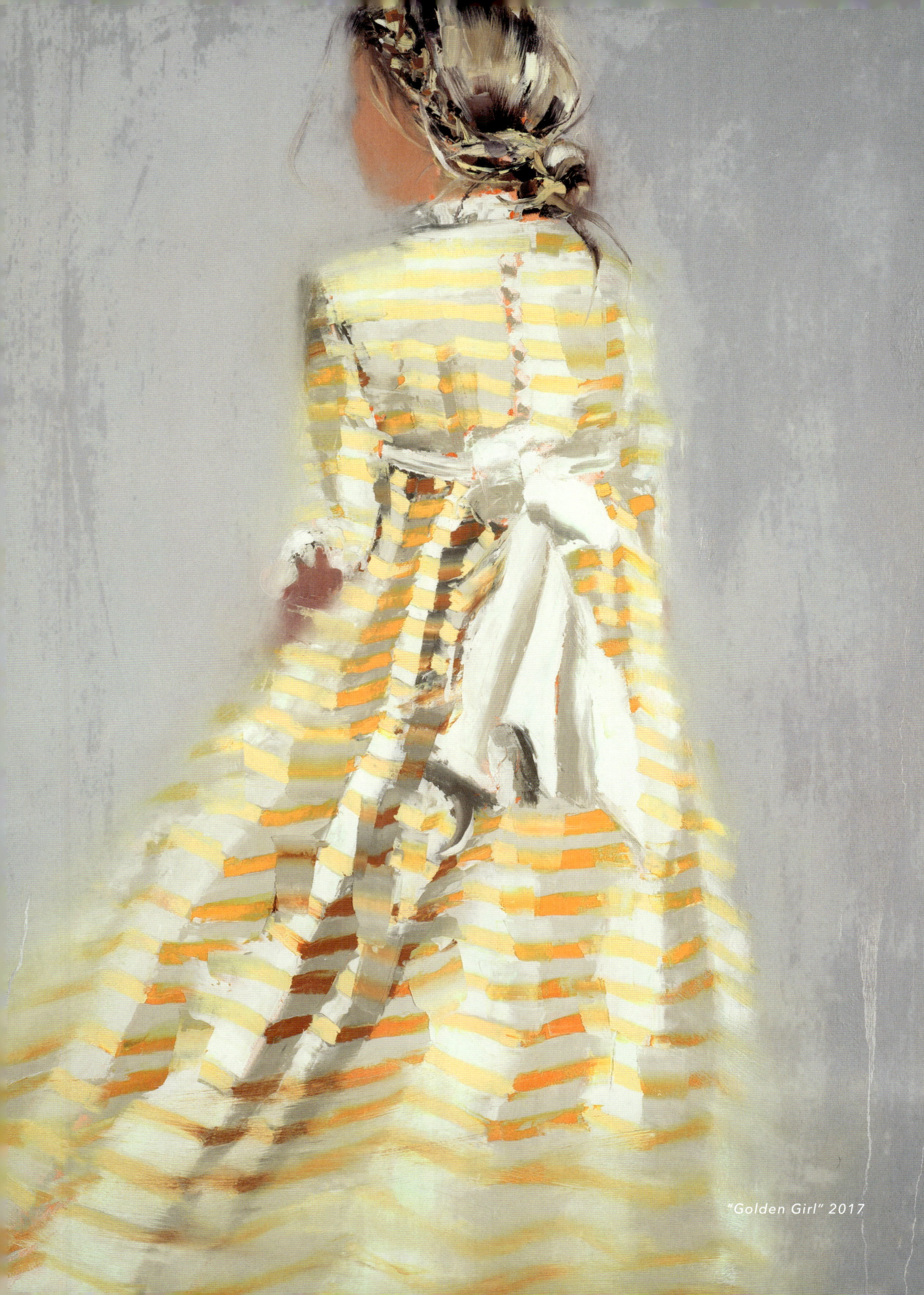
"Golden Girl" 2017

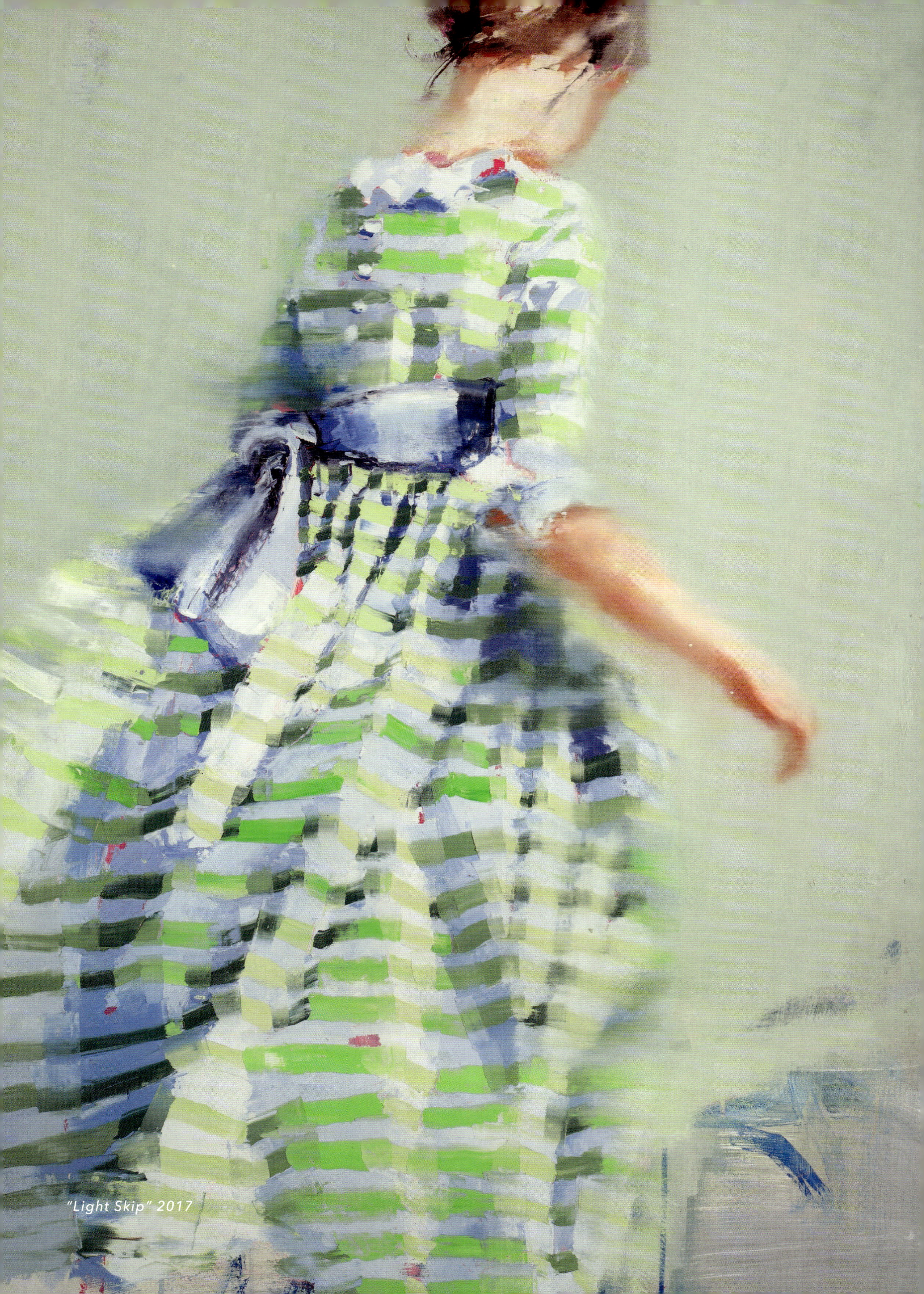

"Light Skip" 2017

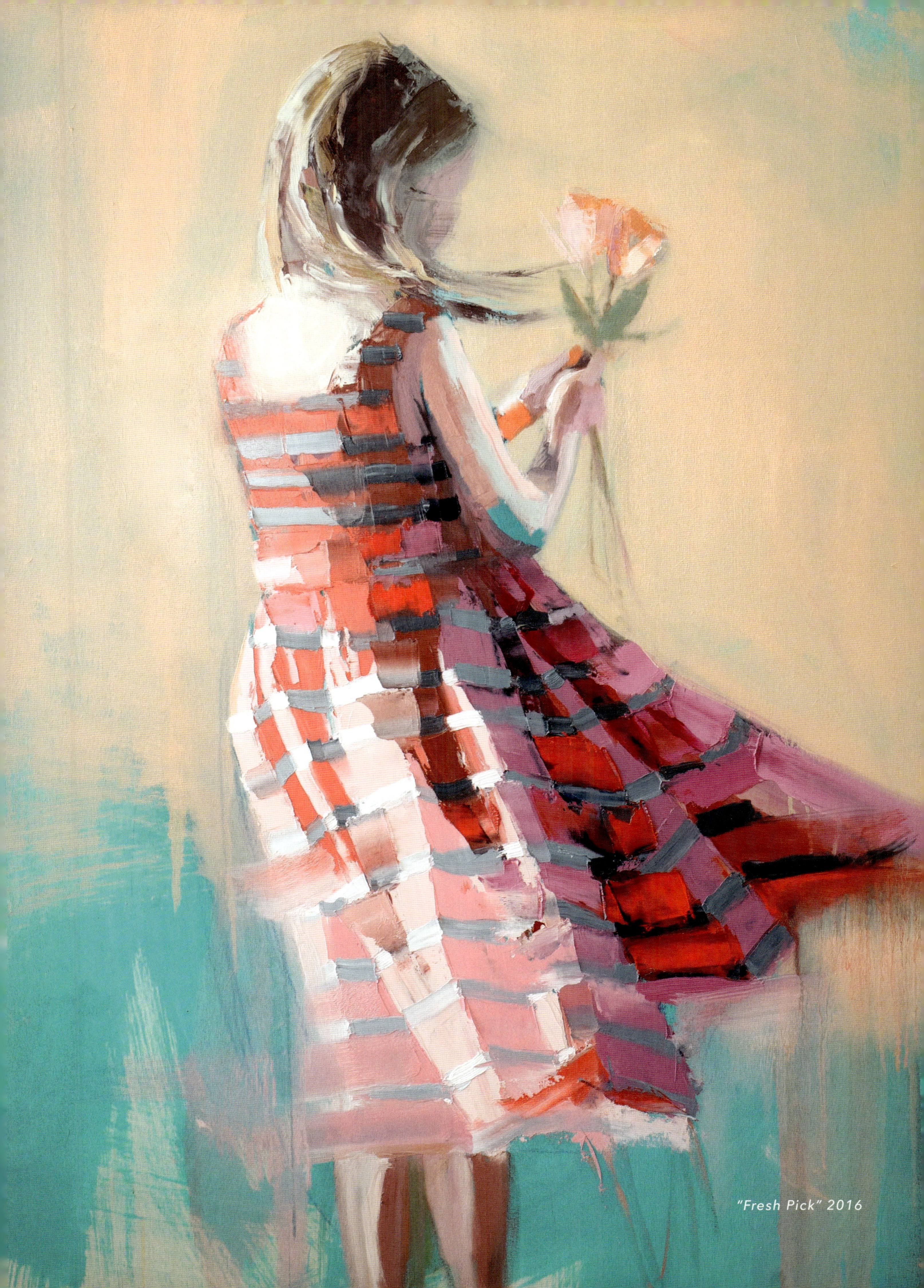

"Fresh Pick" 2016

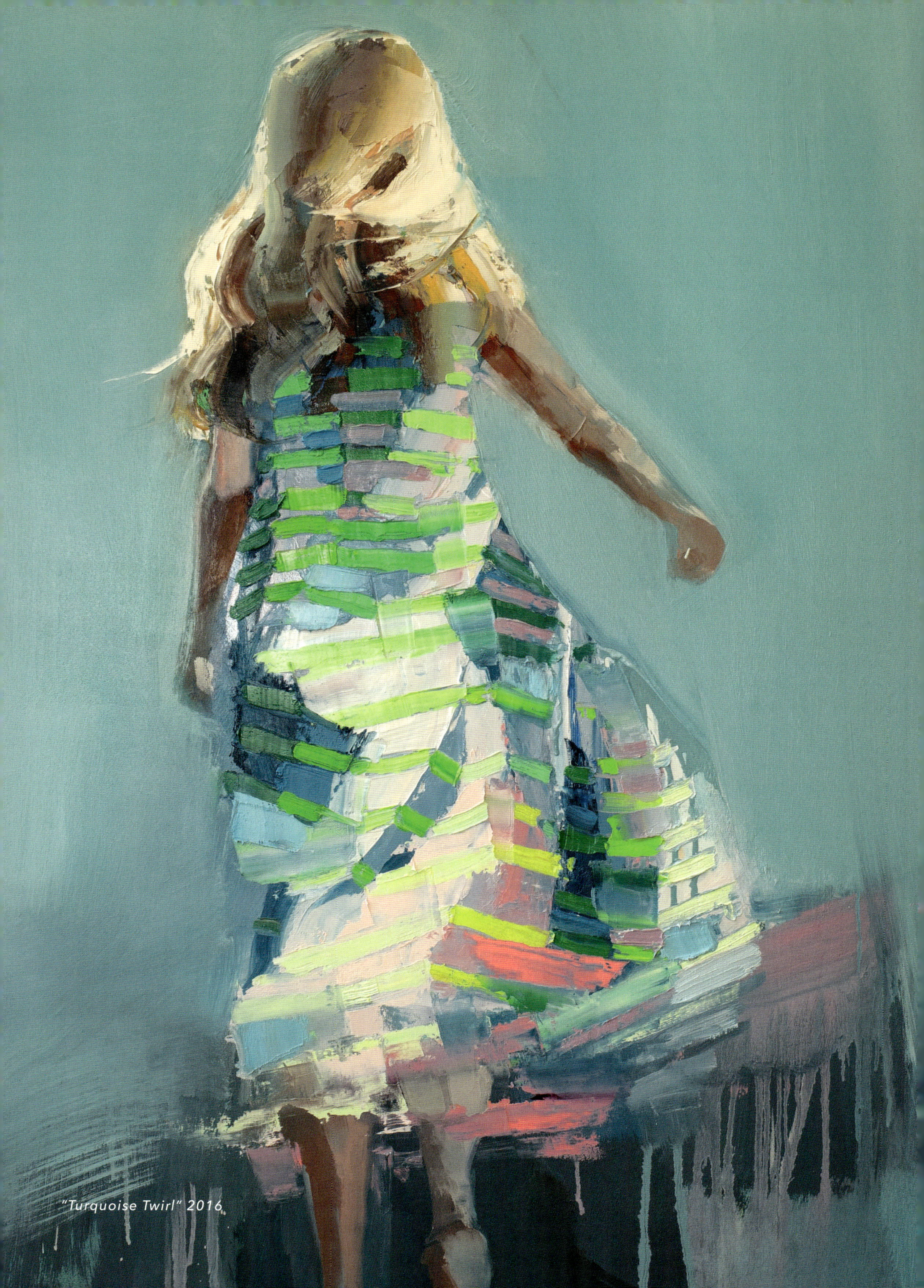

"Turquoise Twirl" 2016

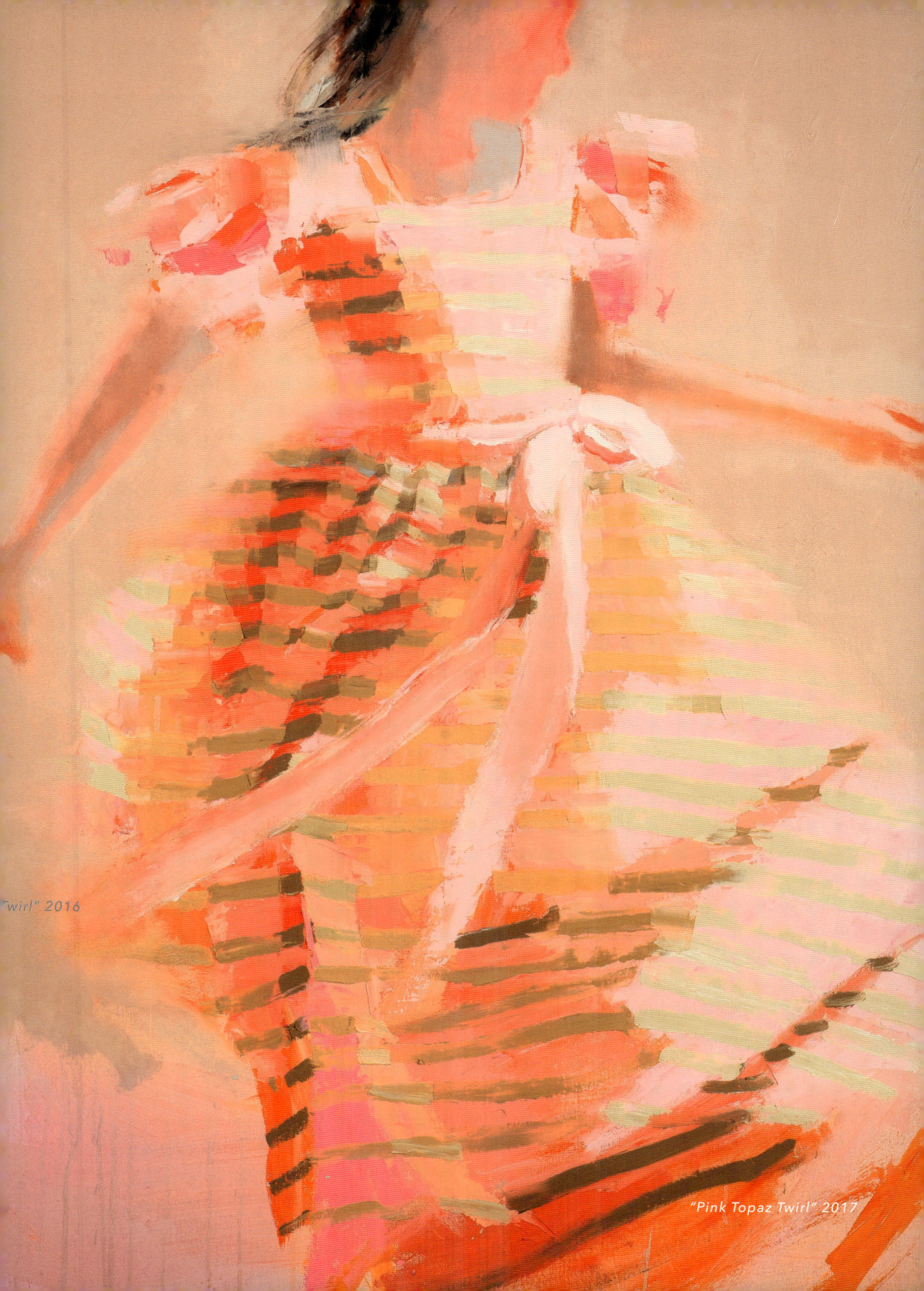
"wirl" 2016

"Pink Topaz Twirl" 2017

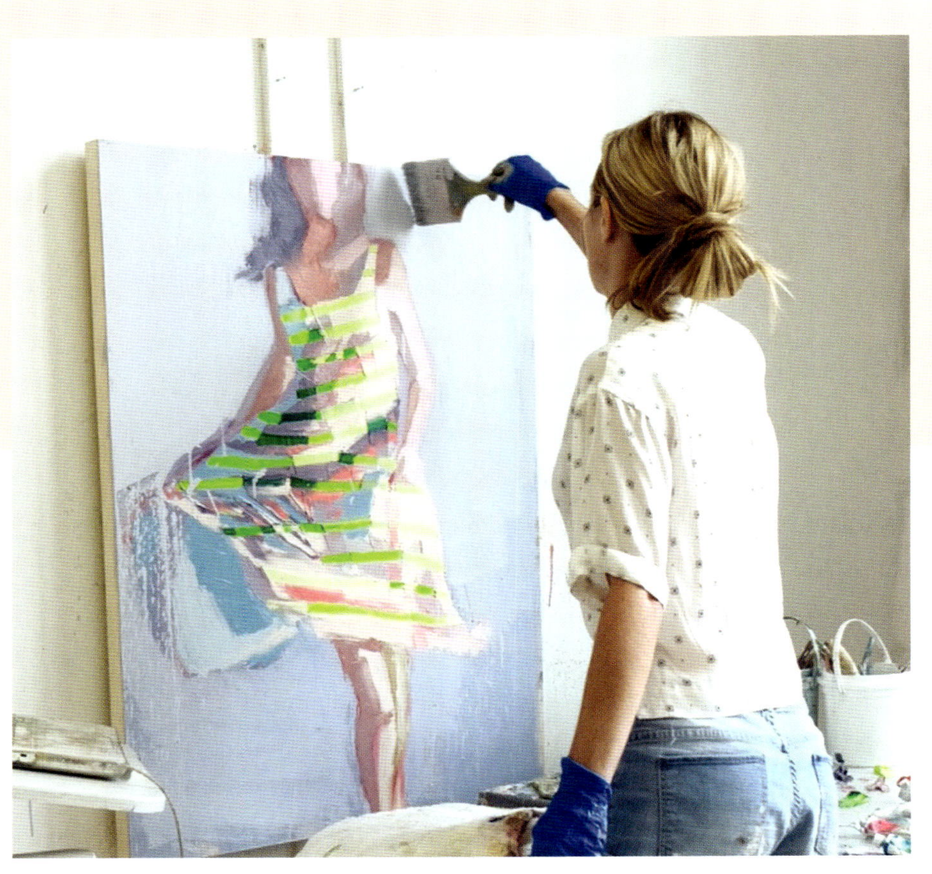

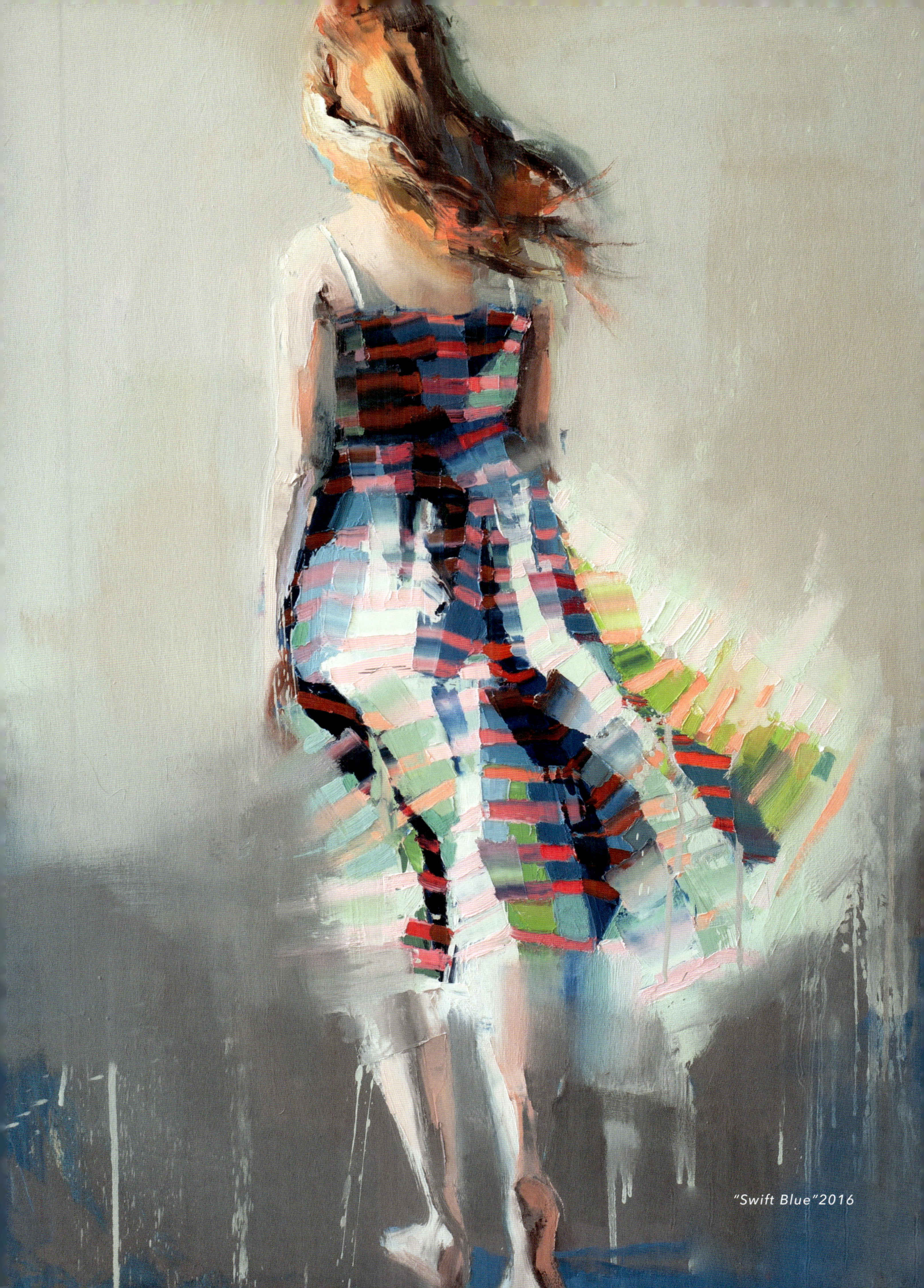

"Swift Blue" 2016

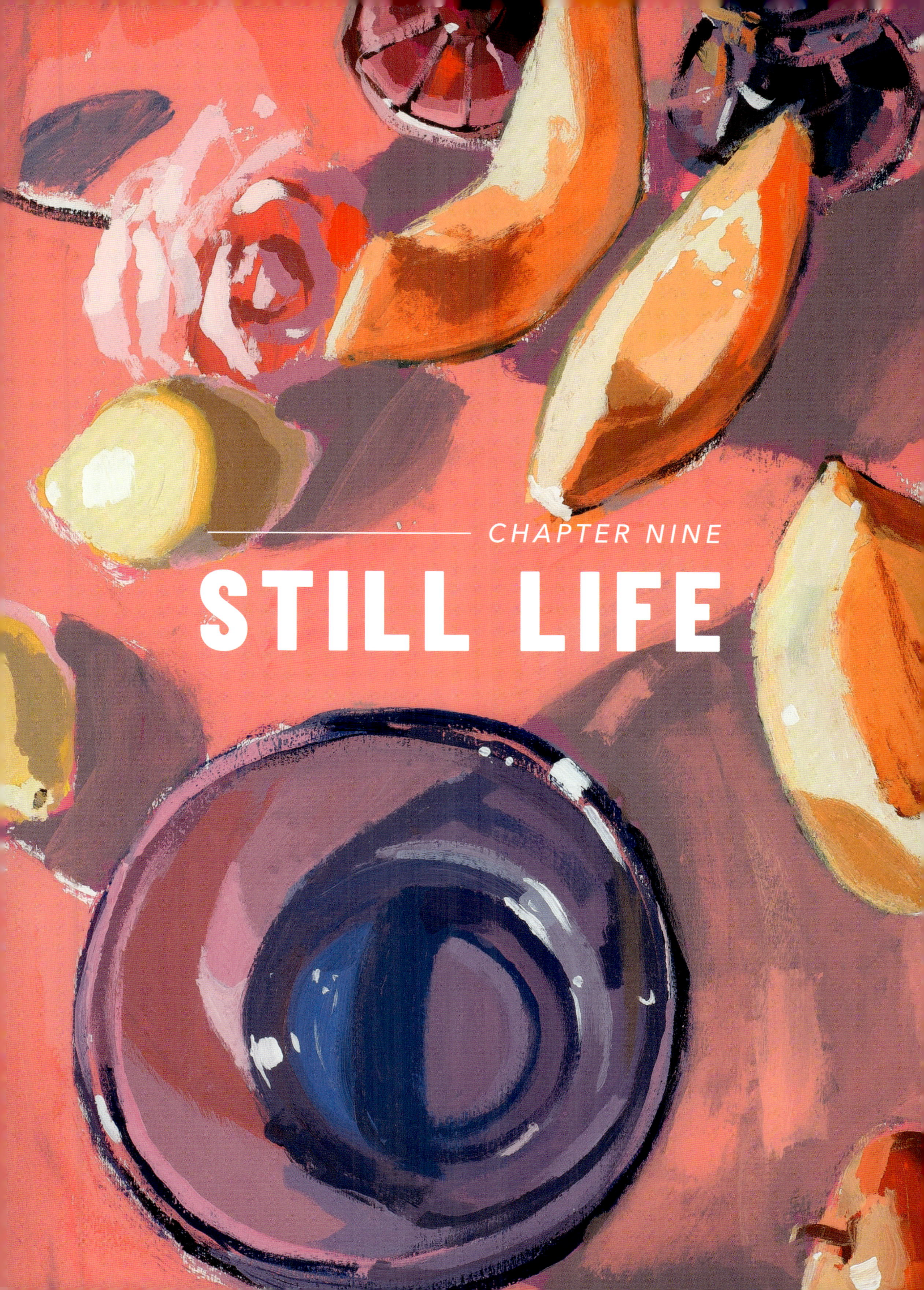

CHAPTER NINE

STILL LIFE

CONTINUING THE THEME

of light and reflection, the still life collection portrays just another avenue in following sunlight travel through ordinary objects. This subject is captured from an aerial viewpoint, providing the most advantageous perspective in seeing light beams radiate through transparent vases, fruit, flowers, and everyday kitchenware.

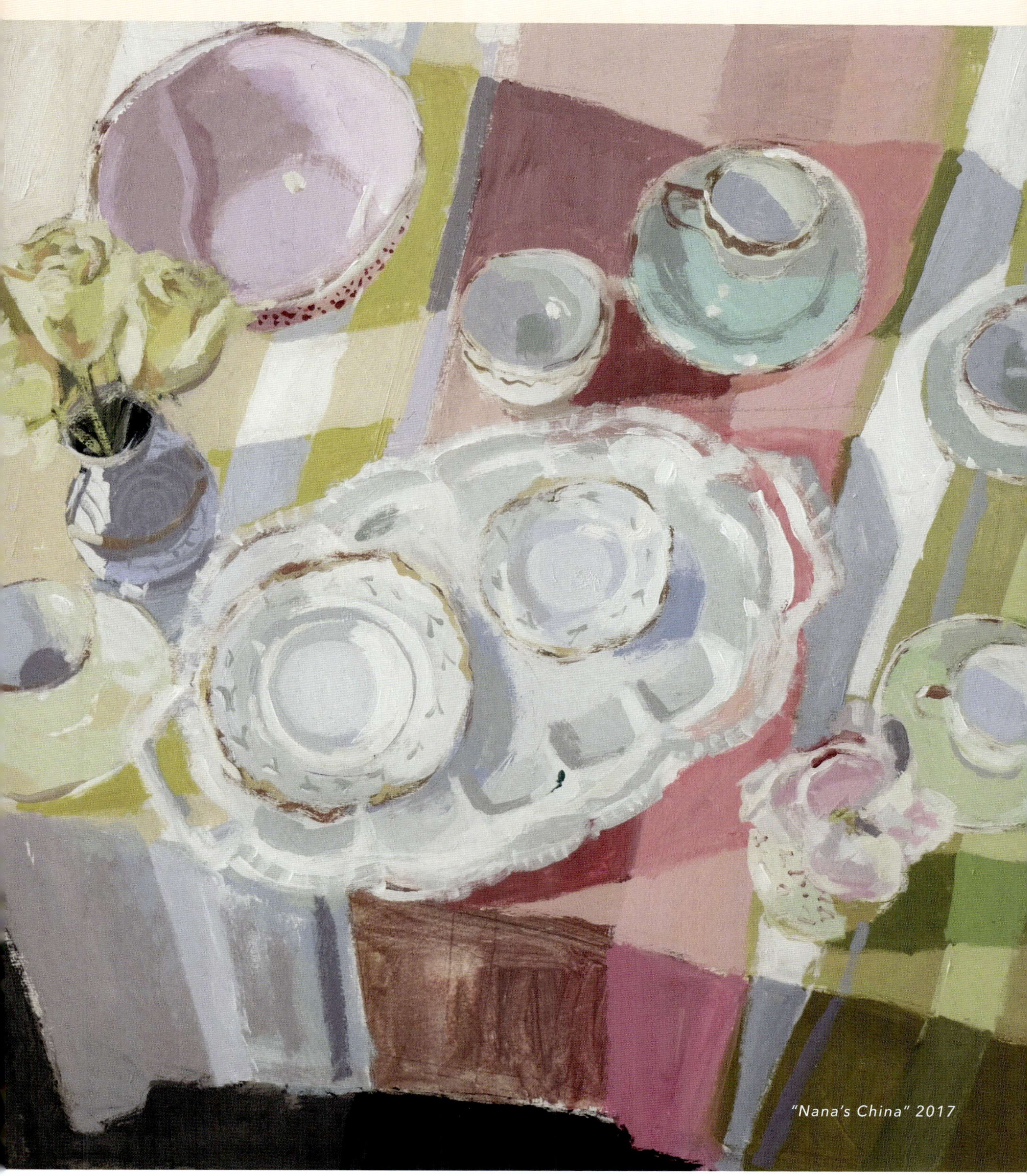
"Nana's China" 2017

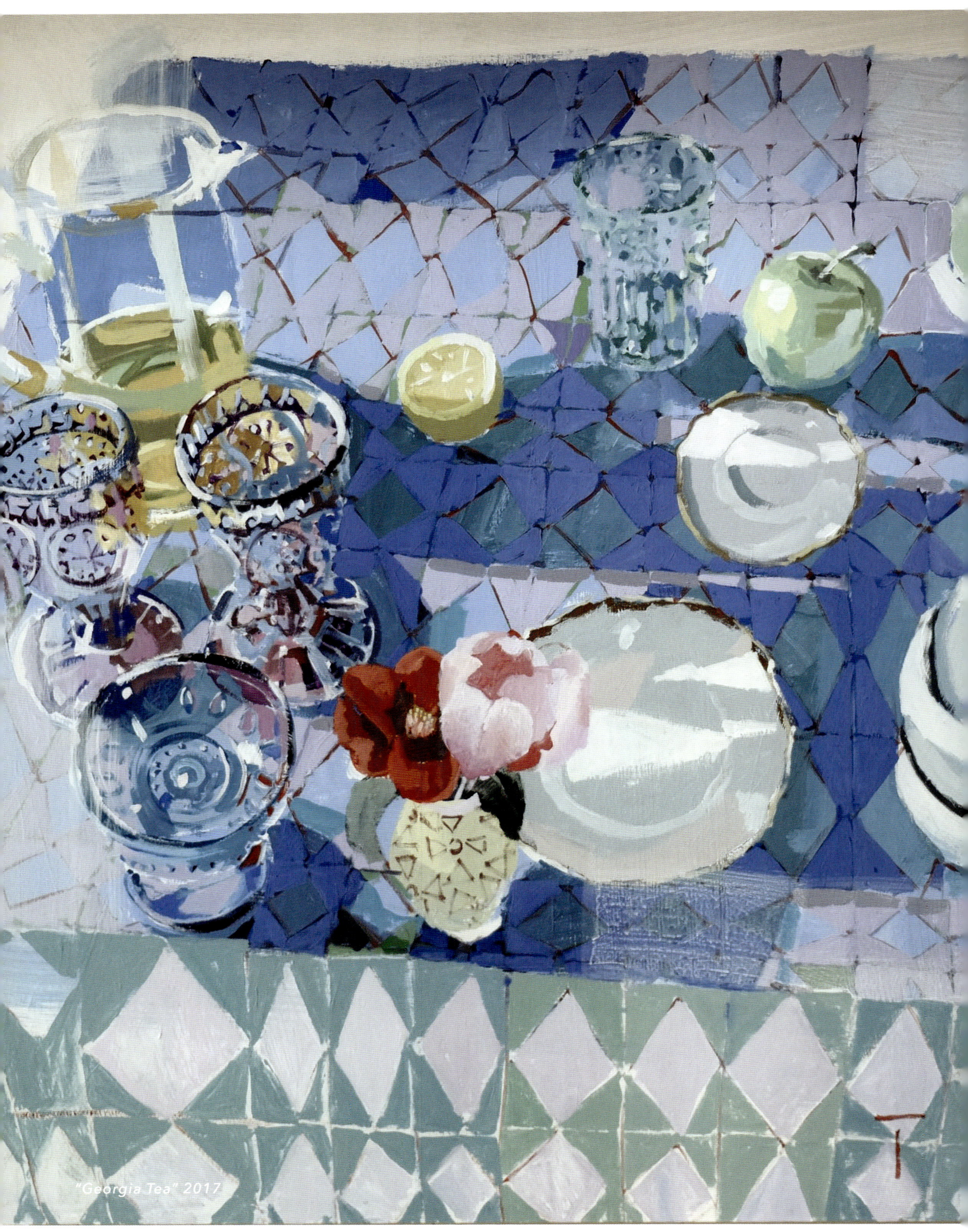

"Georgia Tea" 2017

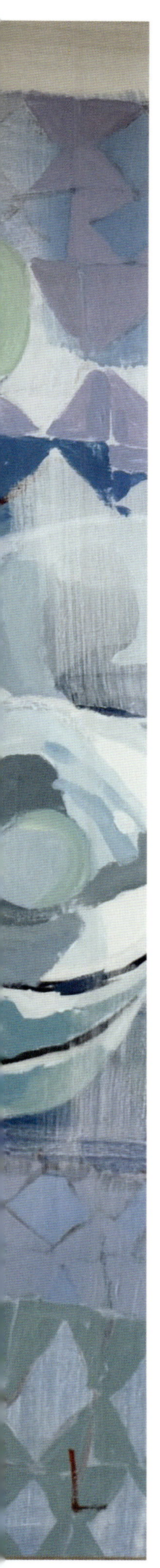

THE GOAL IN THIS SERIES was to attract the viewer to mundane items by accentuating and illuminating them with light manipulation. Each piece holds several objects lying still on a bold color or patterned tablecloth. The flat and graphic pattern play contrasted with dimensional elements is another theme that carries throughout my artwork, and most dominantly in the still life paintings.

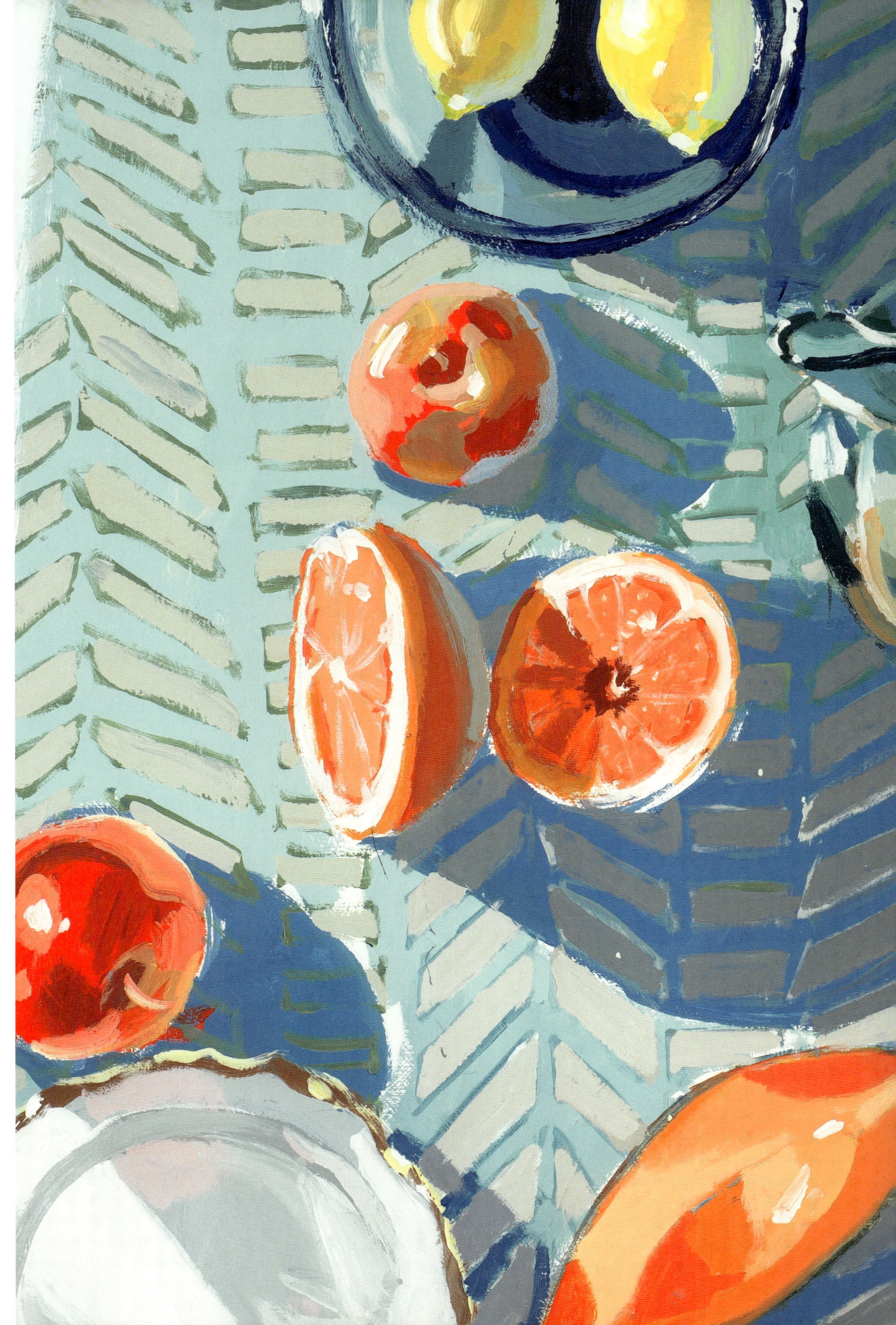

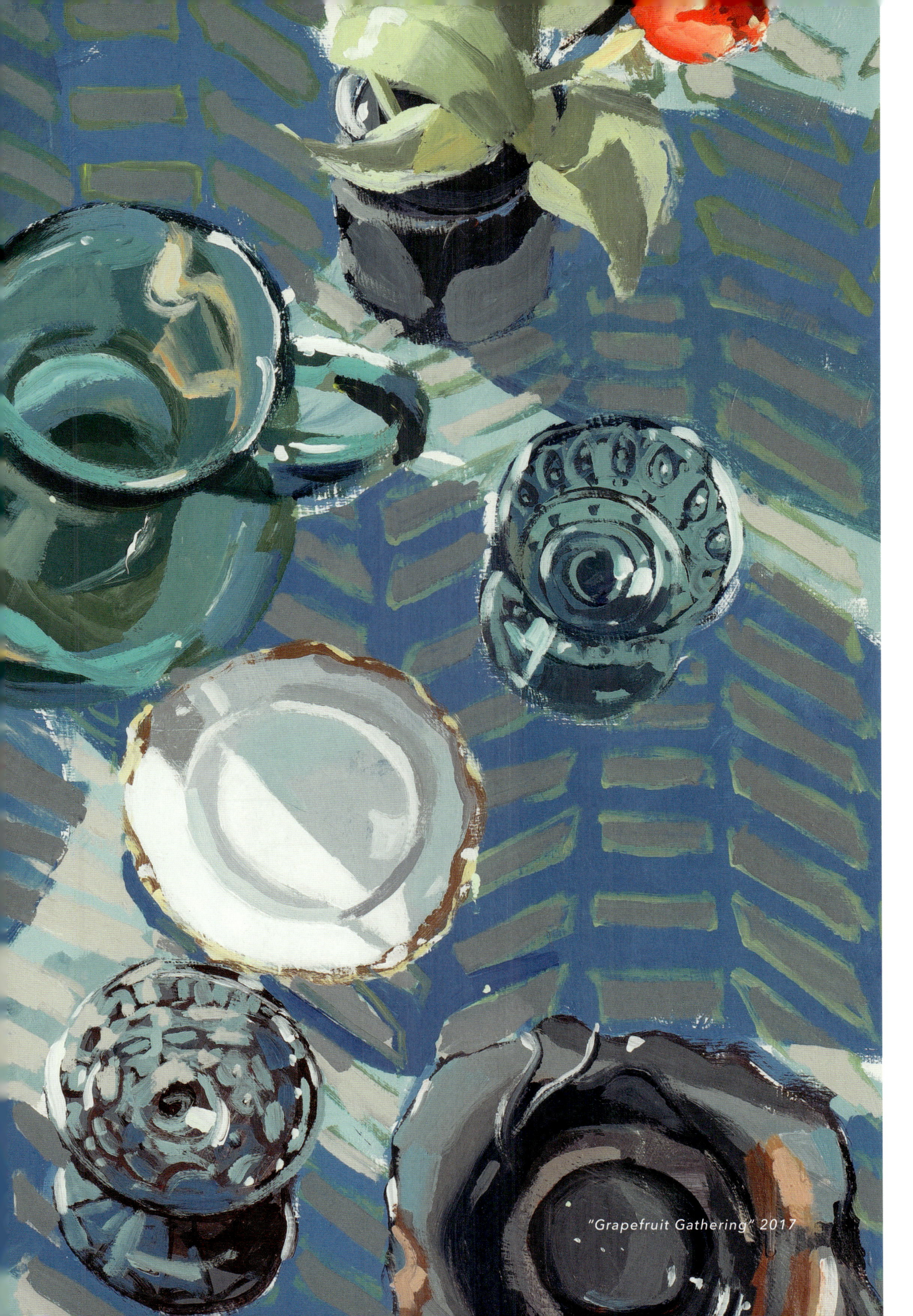
"Grapefruit Gathering" 2017

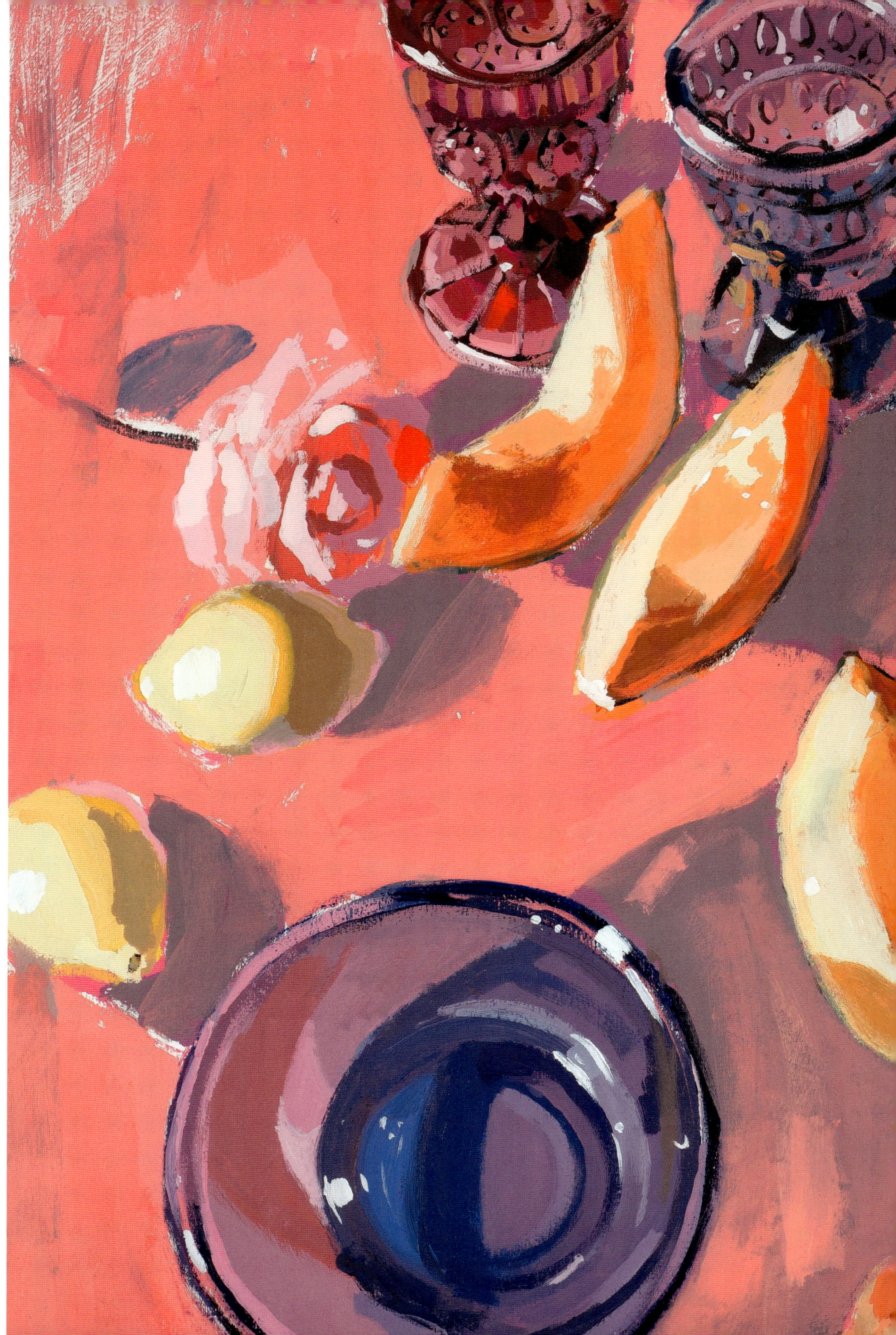

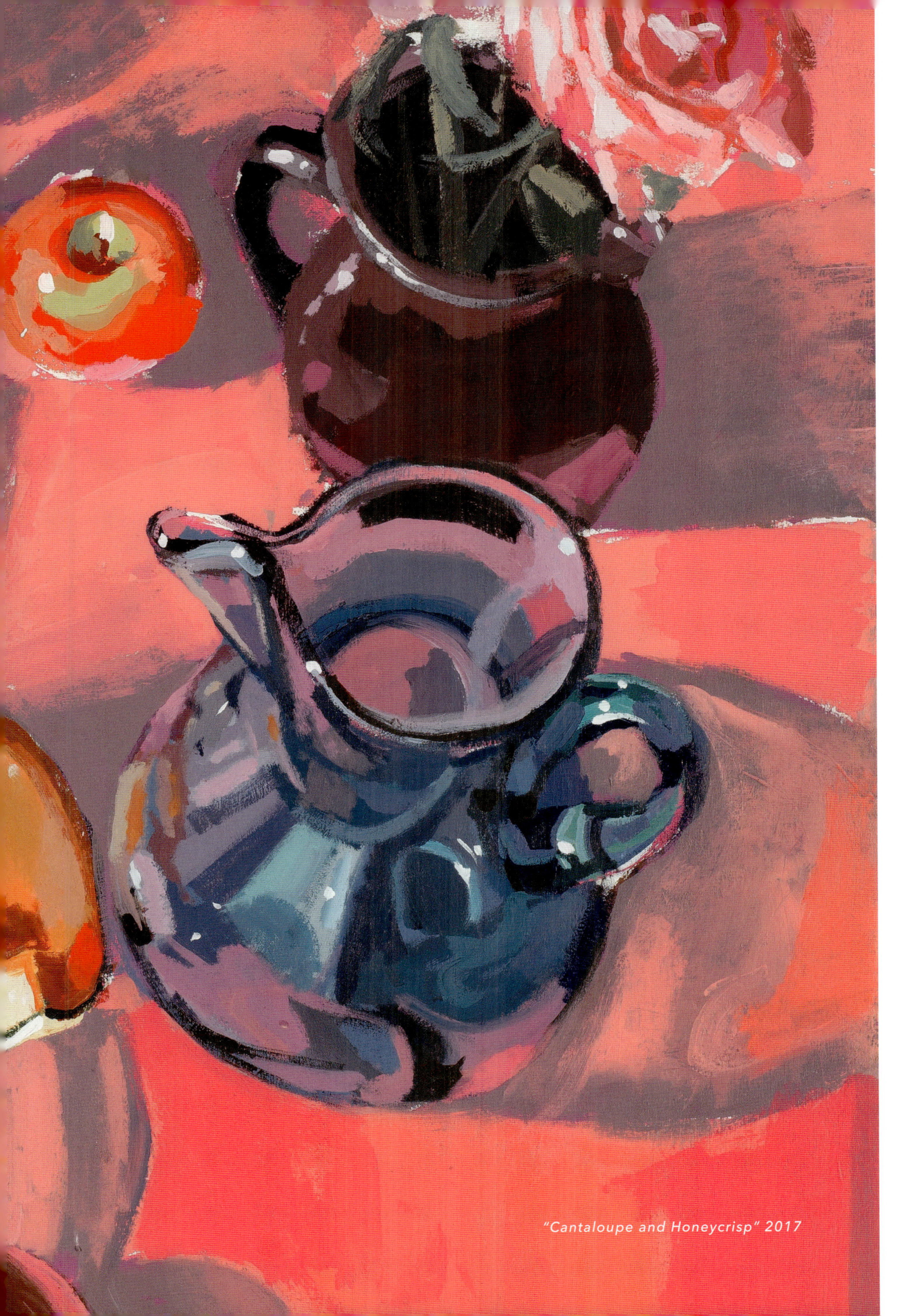

"Cantaloupe and Honeycrisp" 2017

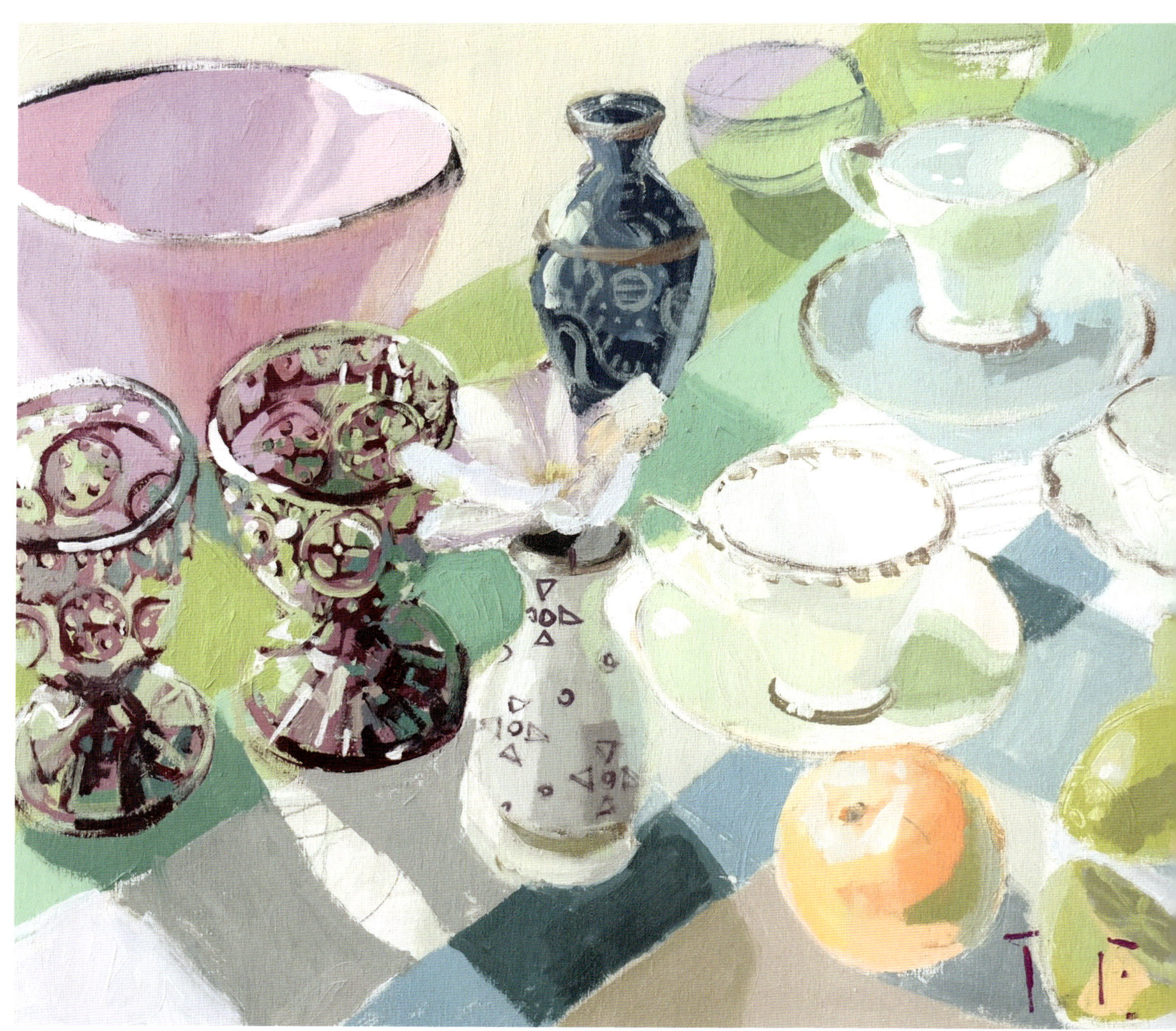
"Morning Company" 2017

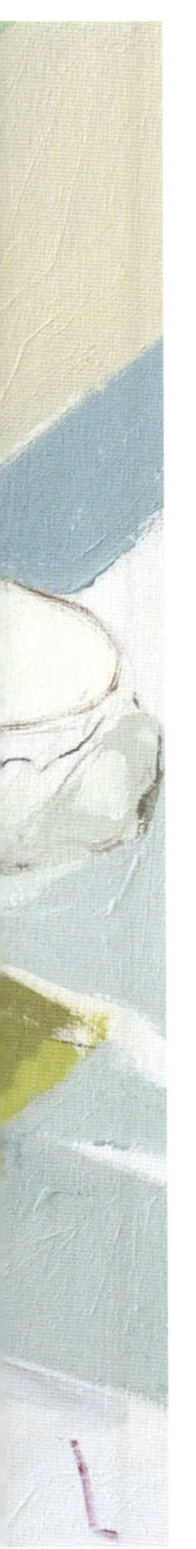

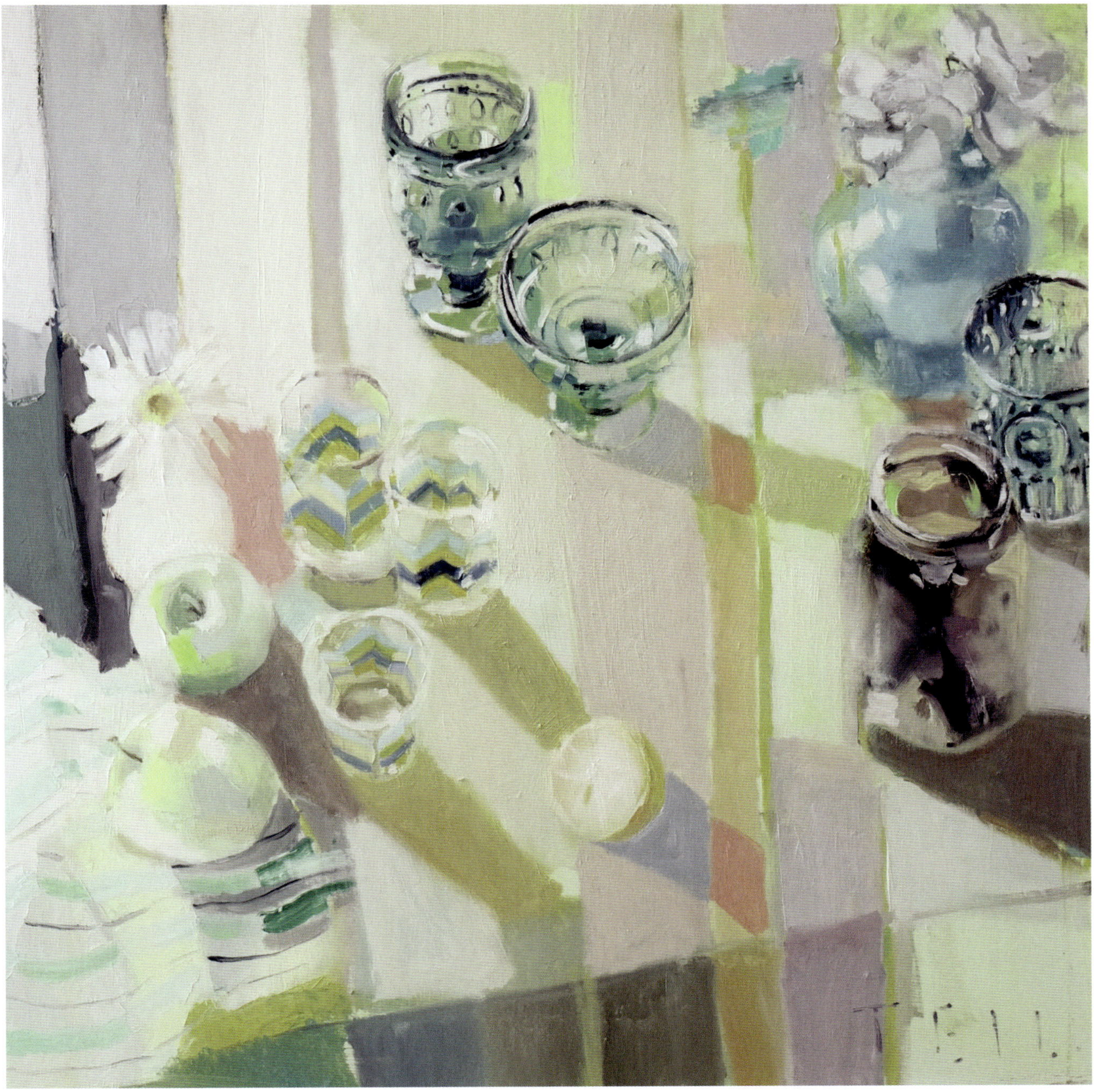

"Summer Set" 2017

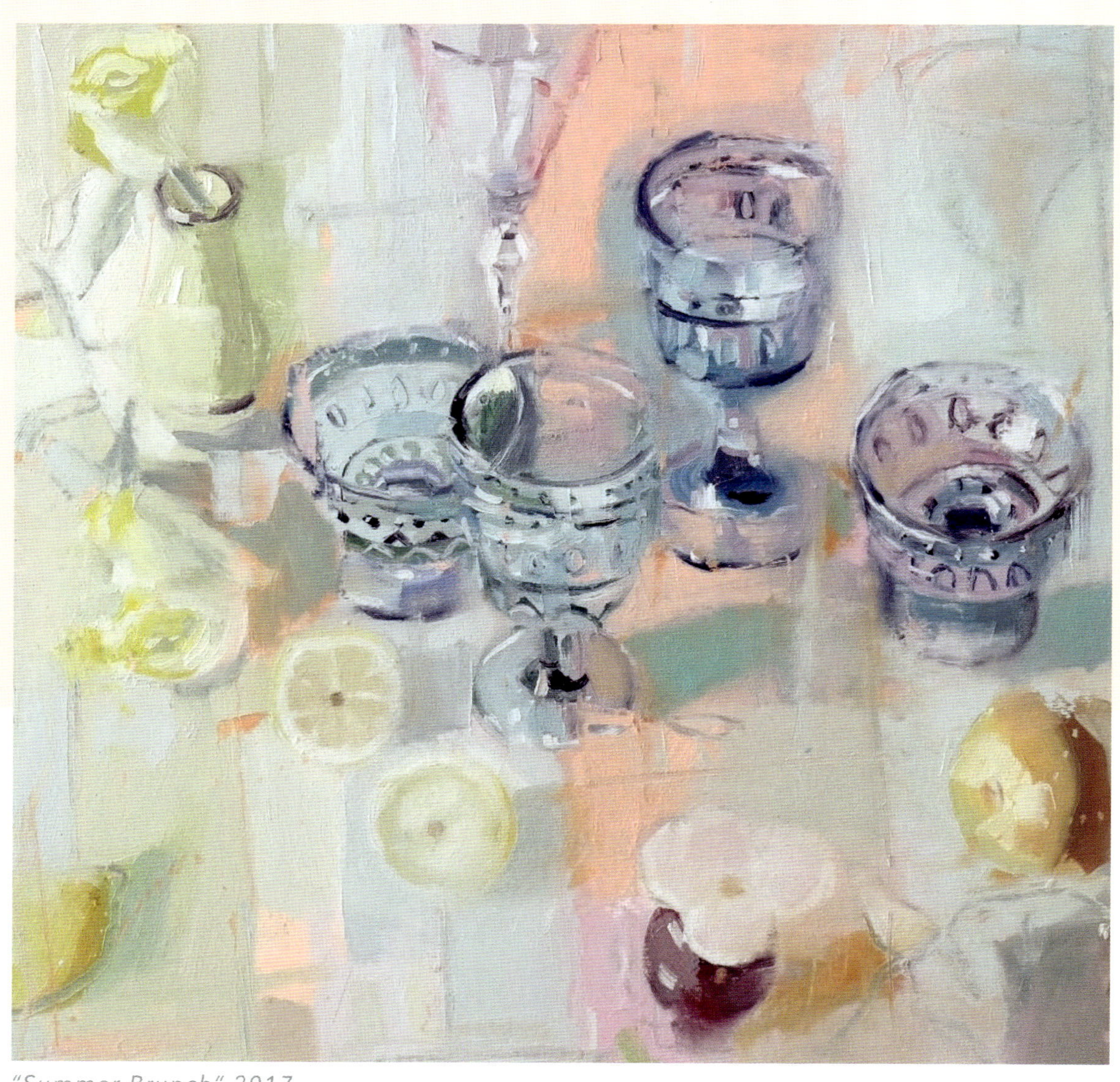

"Summer Brunch" 2017

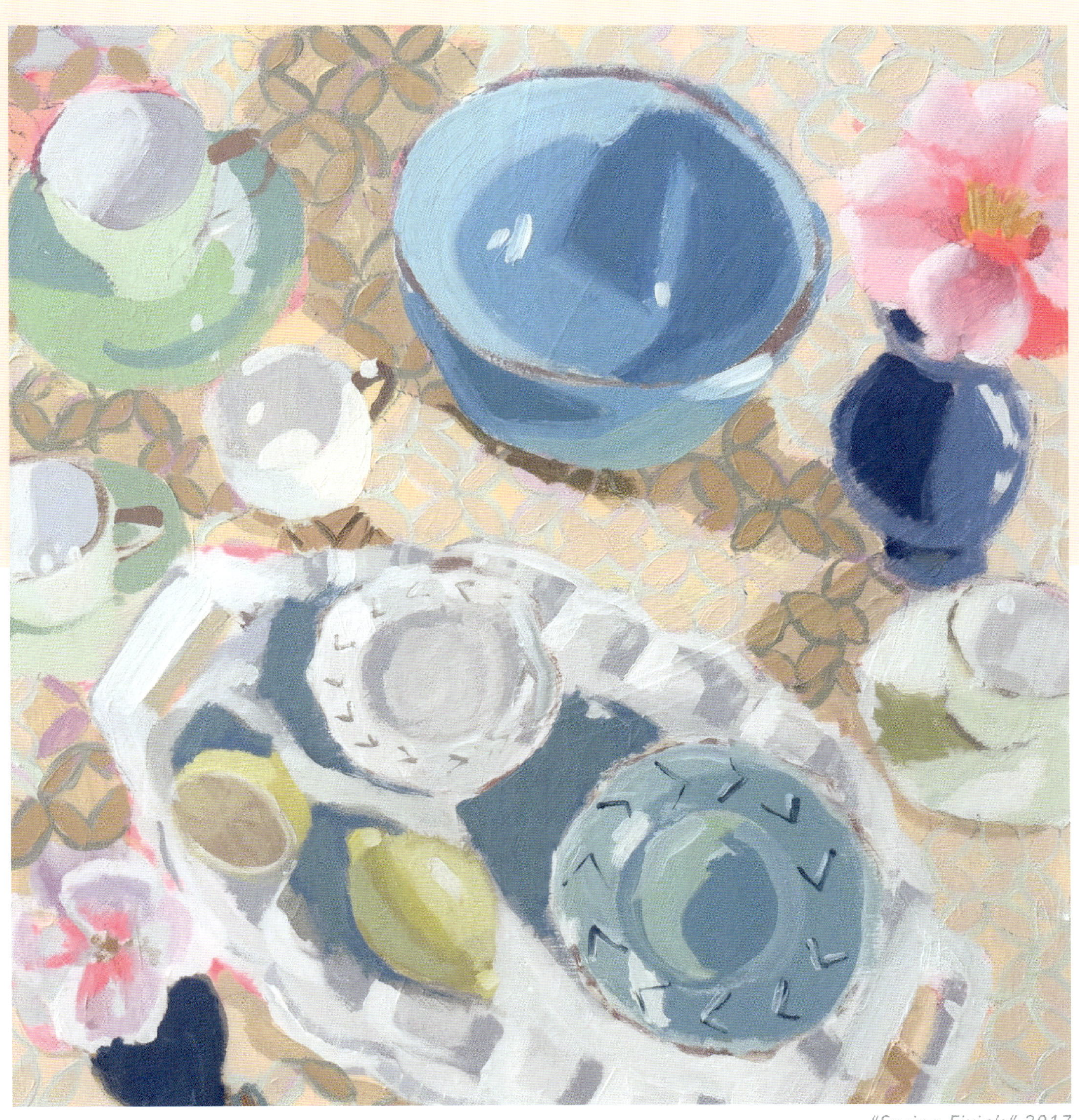

"Spring Fixin's" 2017

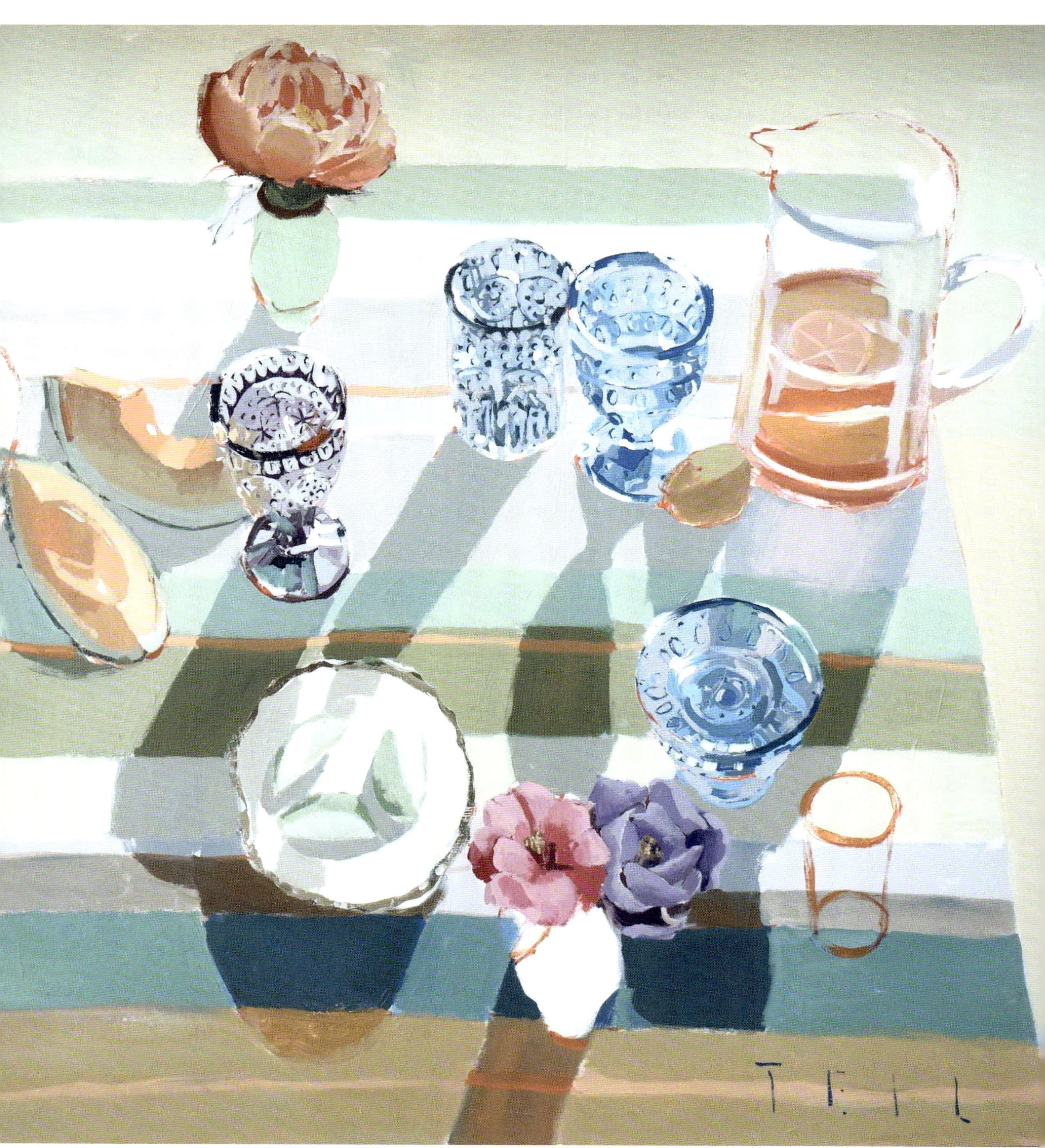

"Sunrise Breakfast" 2017

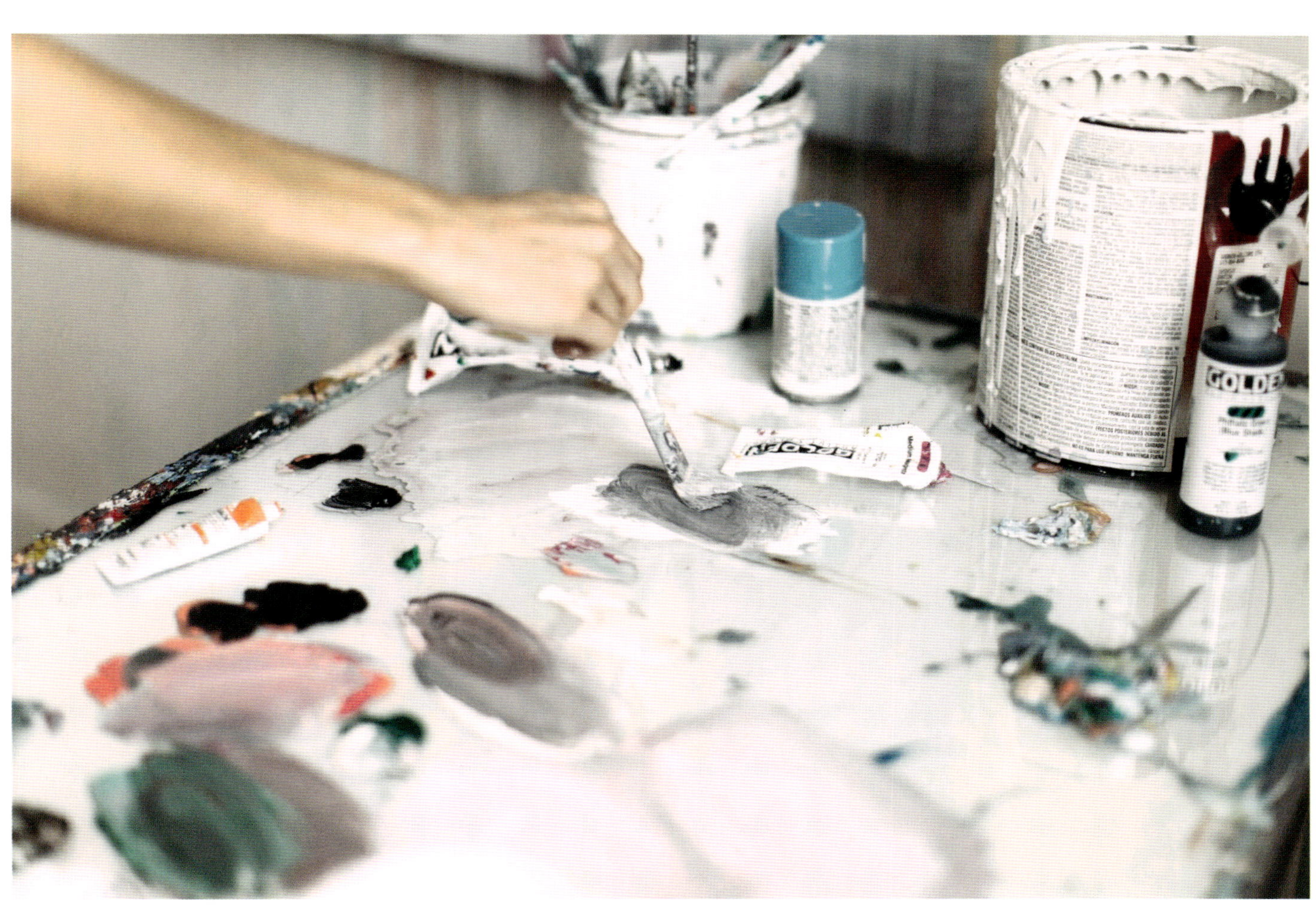

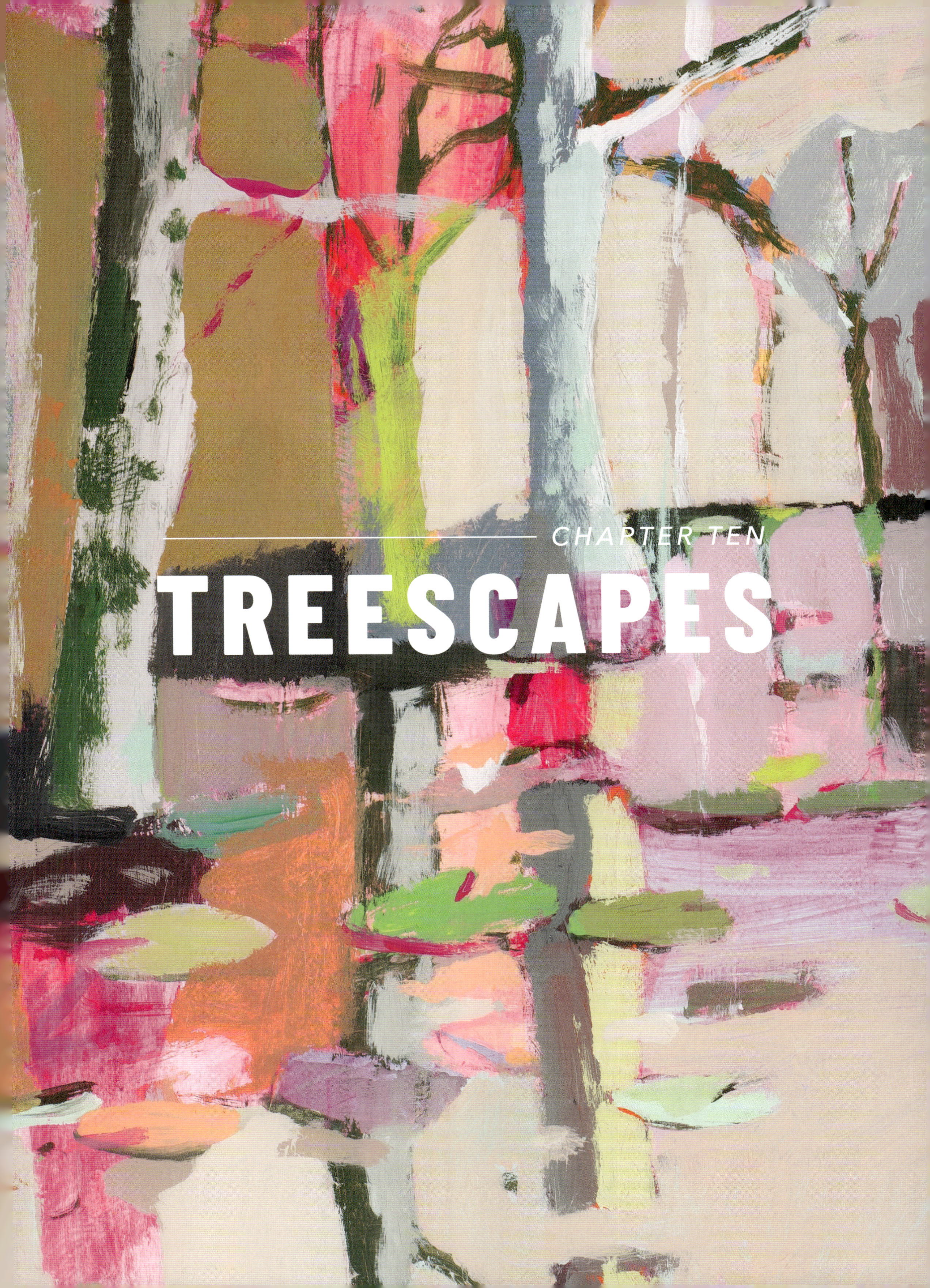

CHAPTER TEN

TREESCAPES

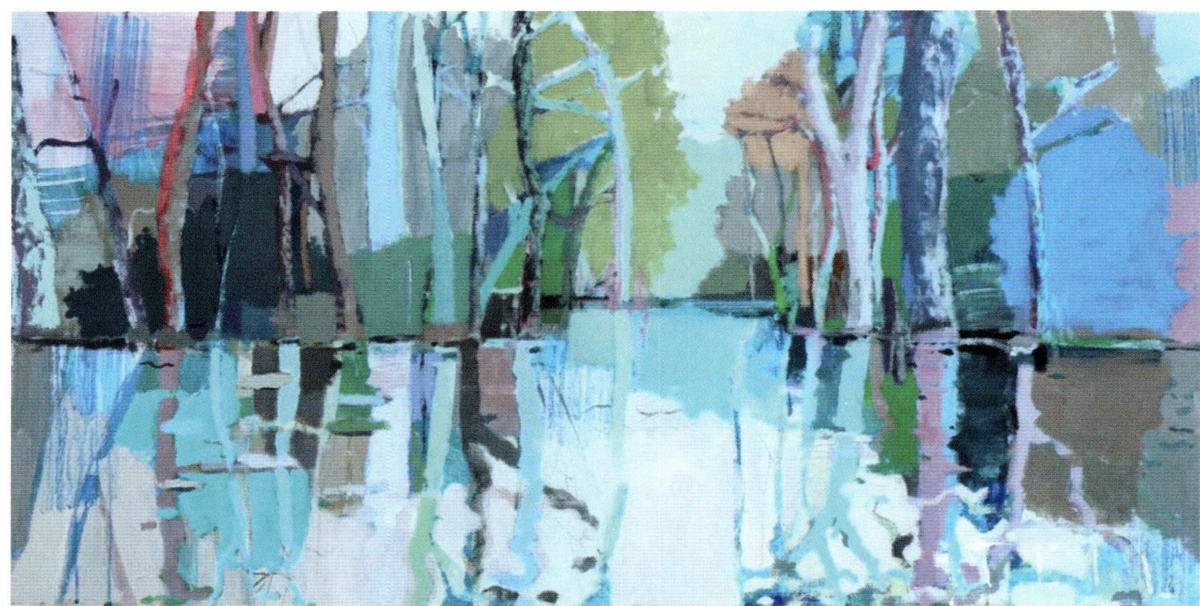

"Dancing Trees" 2018

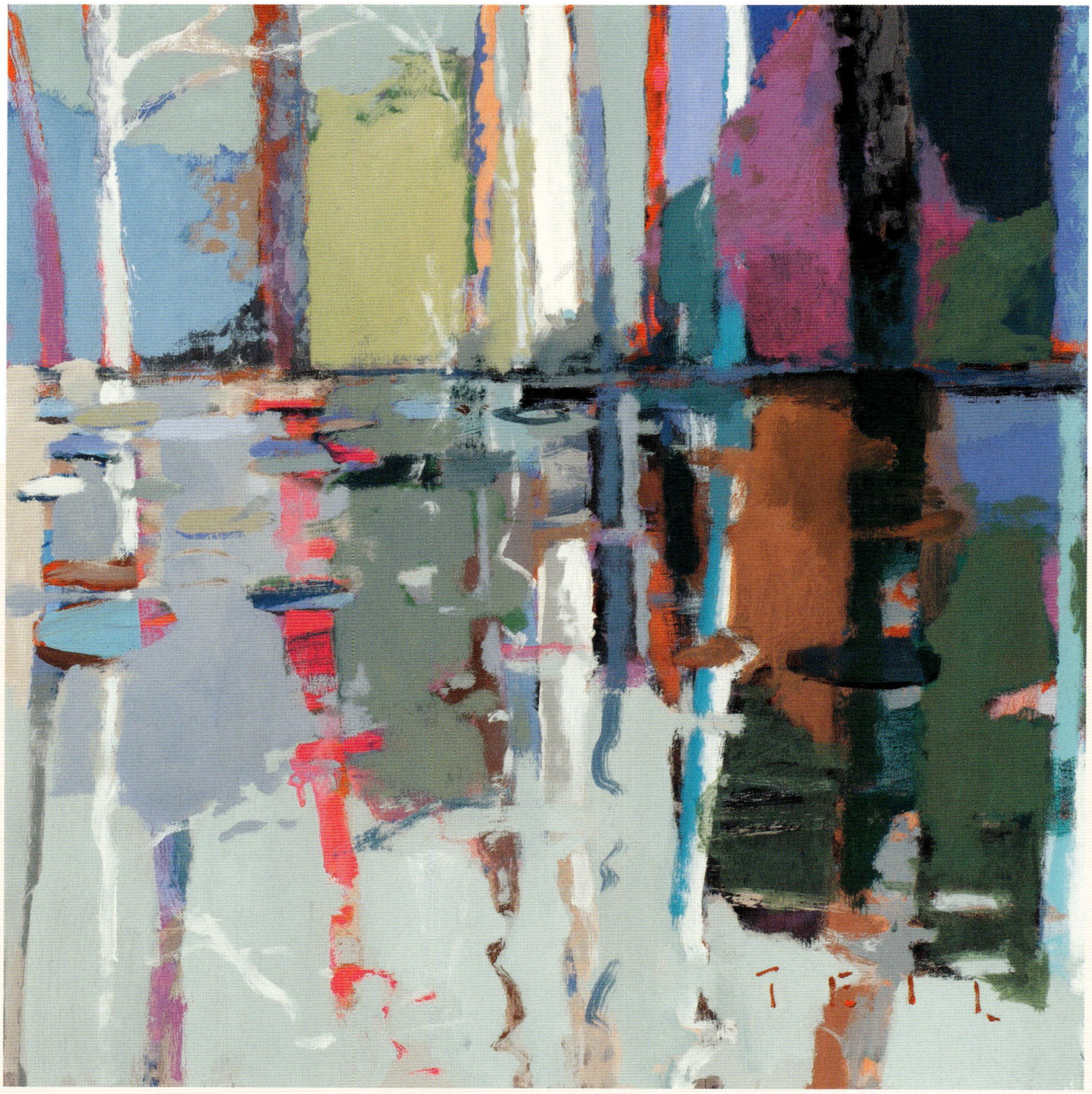

"Bending Birches" 2018

ONE OF MY

earliest commissions was from a friend in Charleston who requested that I paint something representing his faith in God. As I pondered what could depict such a sublime subject, I came across a verse, John 8:12: "I am the light of the world. Whoever follows me will not walk in darkness, but will have light of life." A scene popped into my head that portrays a vast contrast of darkness and light: a forest! I have sporadically revisited this subject ever since and decided to create a small series of treescapes as my first collection postpartum. The color palette in this series is more experimental and taught me not be afraid to mark over a cherished area on the canvas for the sake of a happy accident.

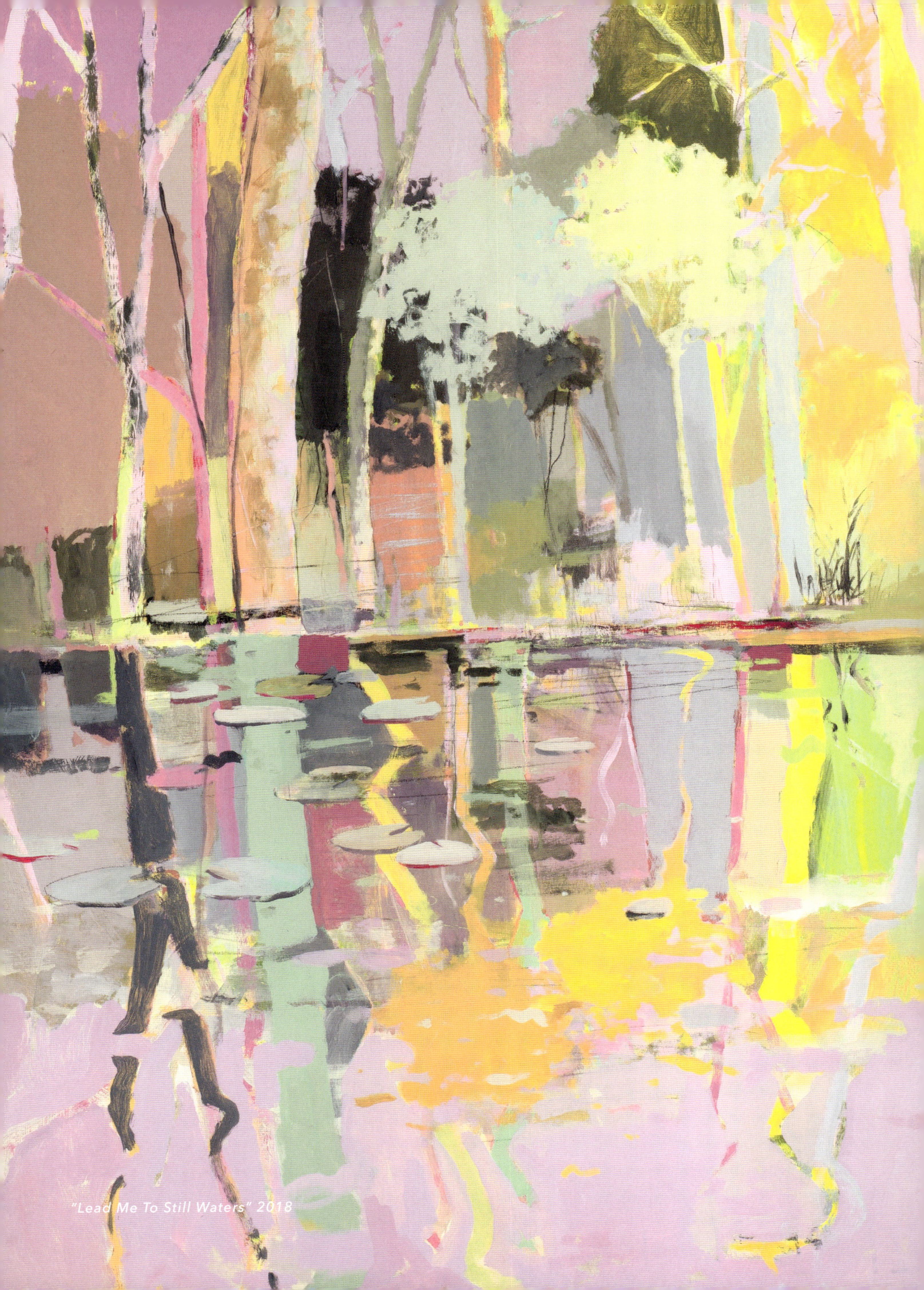
"Lead Me To Still Waters" 2018

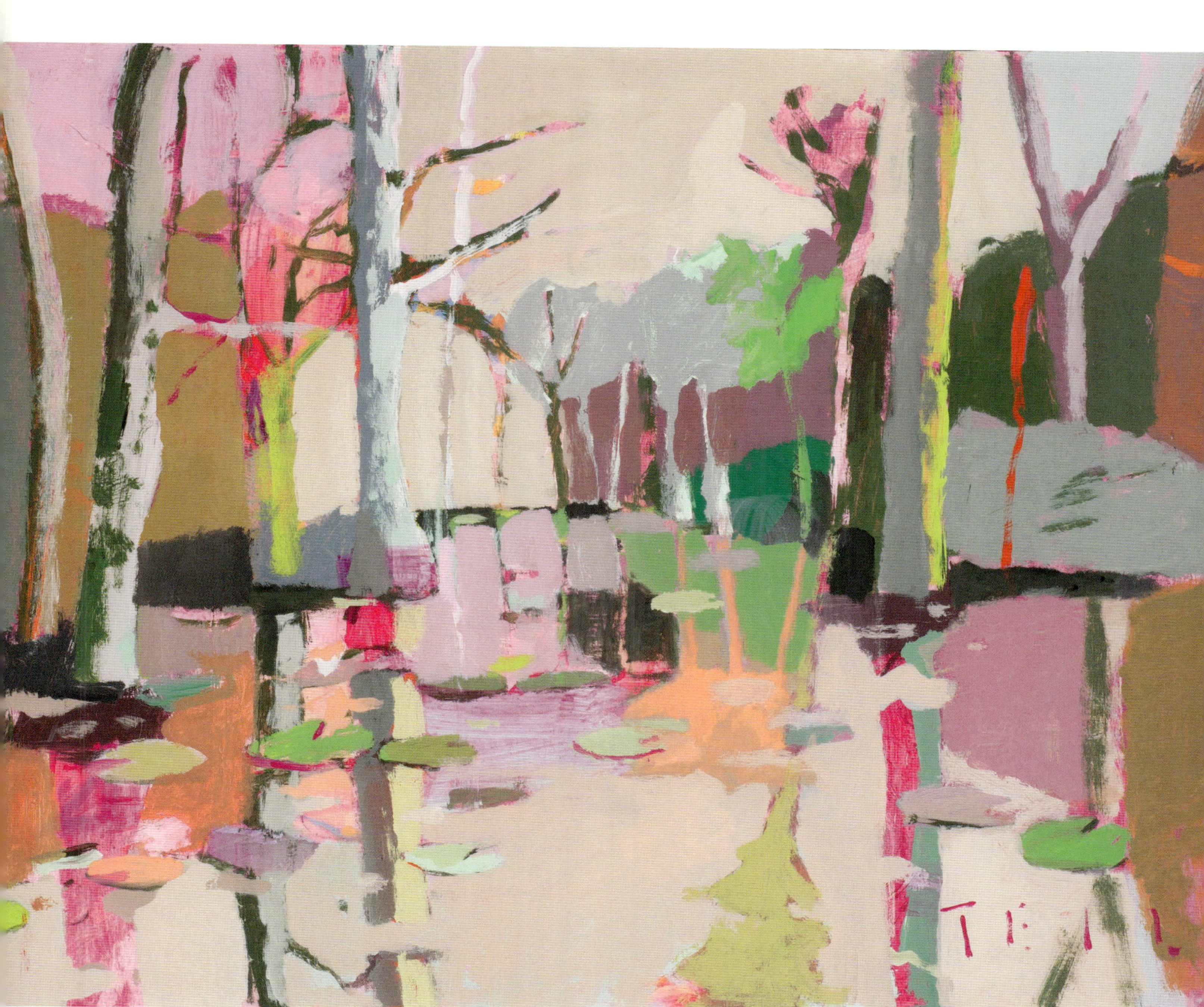

"Pink Cypress" 2018

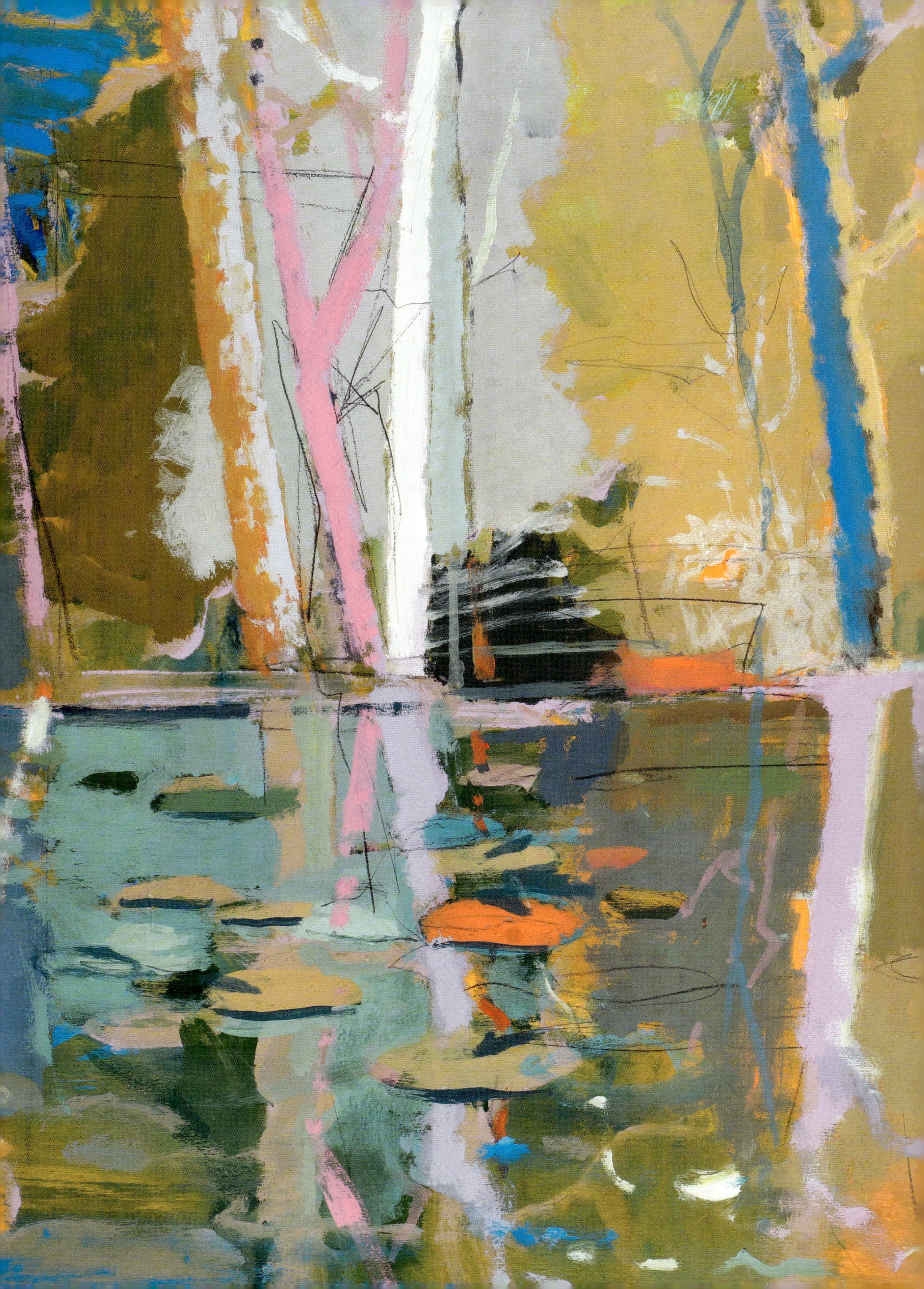

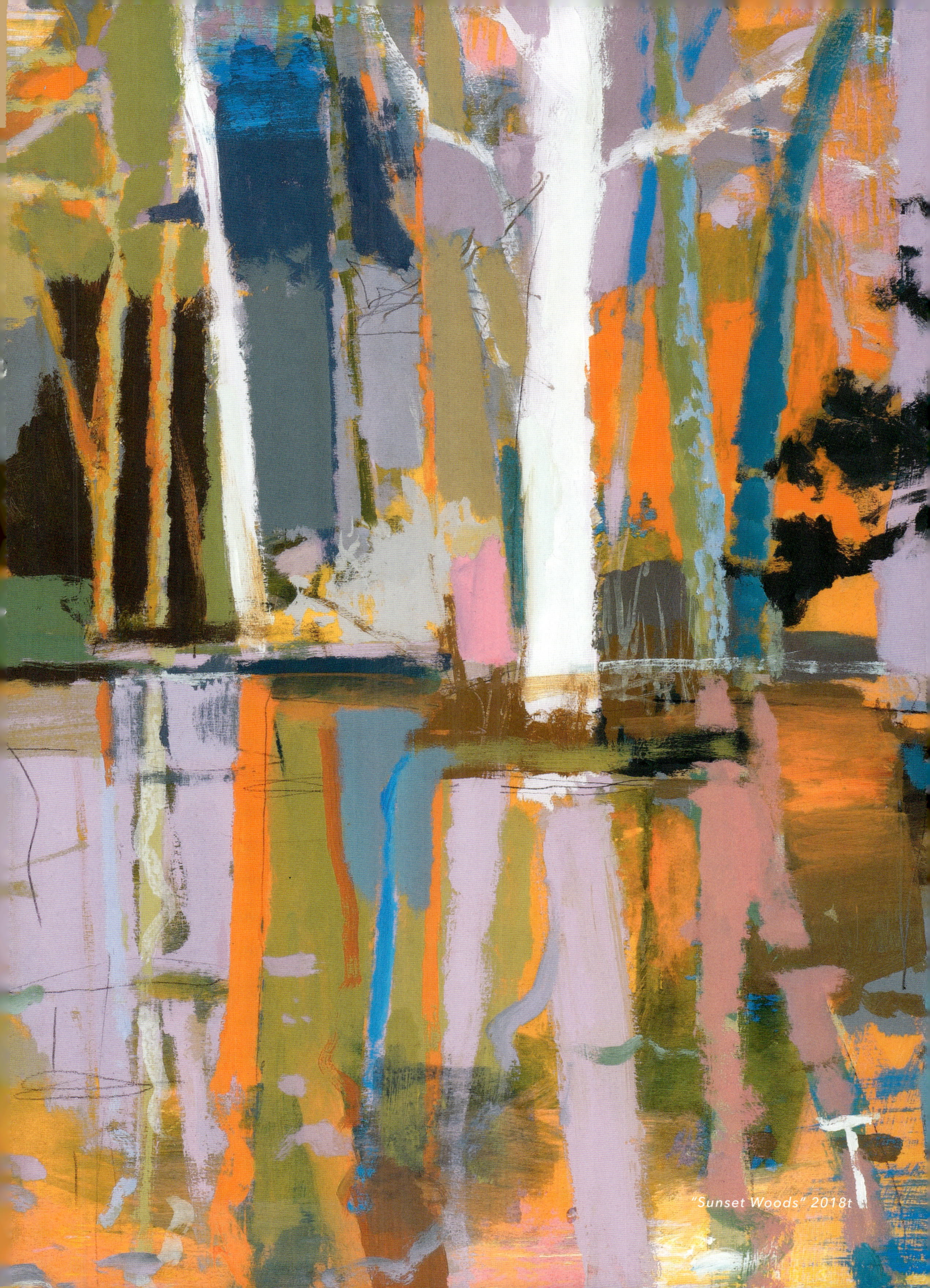

"Sunset Woods" 2018t

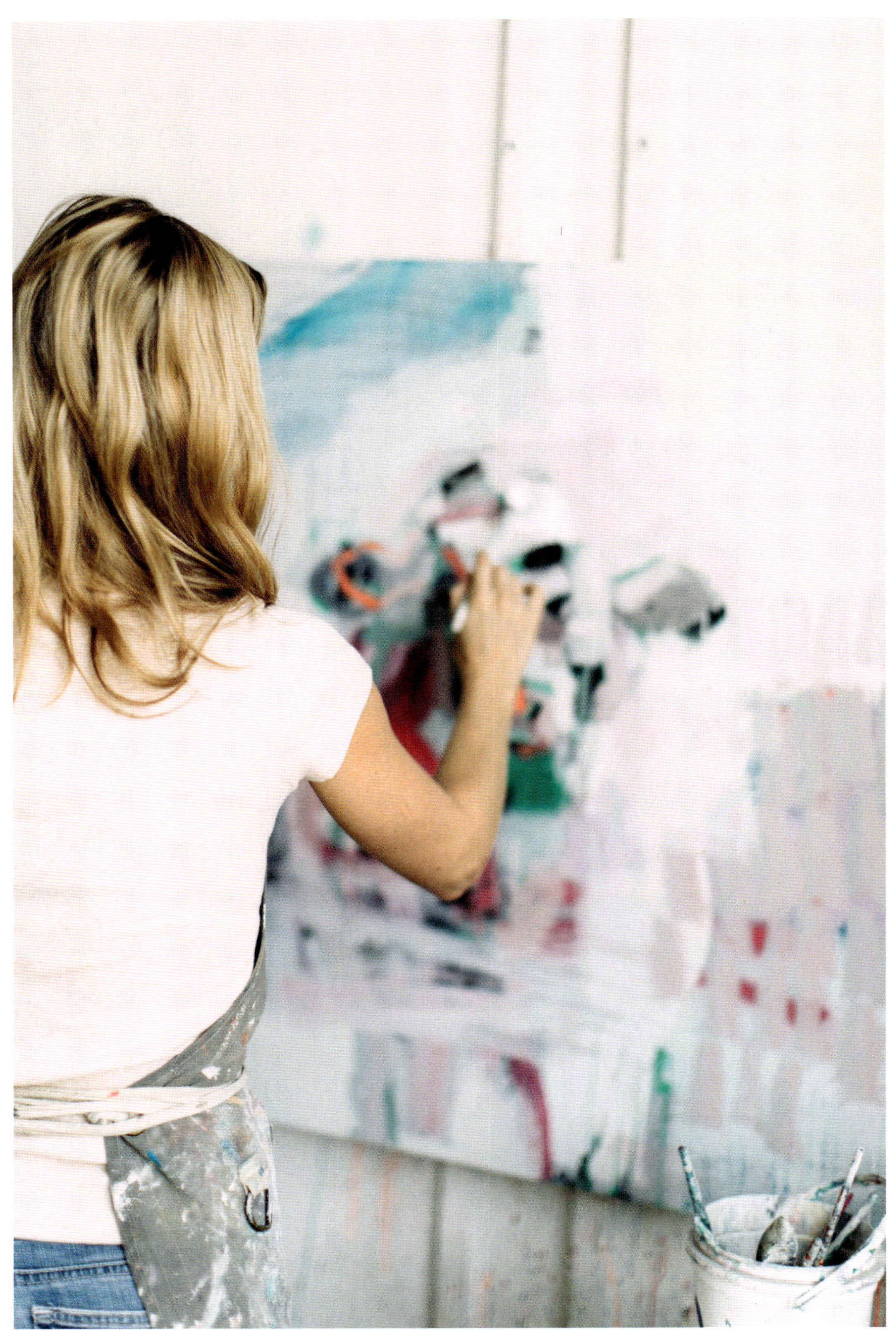